Managing the Windows 2000 Registry

Managing the Windows 2000 Registry

Paul Robichaux

Beijing · Cambridge · Farnham · Köln · Paris · Sebastopol · Taipei · Tokyo

Managing the Windows 2000 Registry
by Paul Robichaux

Copyright © 2000 O'Reilly & Associates, Inc. All rights reserved.
Portions of this book appeared previously under the title *Managing the Windows NT Registry*, Copyright © 1998 O'Reilly & Associates, Inc.
Printed in the United States of America.

Published by O'Reilly & Associates, Inc., 101 Morris Street, Sebastopol, CA 95472.

Editor: Robert Denn

Production Editor: Mary Anne Weeks Mayo

Cover Designer: Edie Freedman

Printing History:

    August 2000:   First Edition.

Nutshell Handbook, the Nutshell Handbook logo, and the O'Reilly logo are registered trademarks of O'Reilly & Associates, Inc. The association between the image of an orangutan and the topic of the Windows 2000 Registry is a trademark of O'Reilly & Associates, Inc.

Many of the designations used by manufacturers and sellers to distinguish their products are claimed as trademarks. Where those designations appear in this book, and O'Reilly & Associates, Inc. was aware of a trademark claim, the designations have been printed in caps or initial caps.

While every precaution has been taken in the preparation of this book, the publisher assumes no responsibility for errors or omissions, or for damages resulting from the use of the information contained herein.

Library of Congress Cataloging-in-Publication Data

Robichaux, Paul E.
   Managing Windows 2000 registry/Paul Robichaux.--1st ed.
     p. cm.
   ISBN 1-56592-943-8
   1. Microsoft Windows (Computer file) I. Title.

QA76.76.O63 R6226 2000
005.4'4769--dc21

ISBN: 1-56592-943-8
[DS]

Table of Contents

Preface .... *ix*

1. *A Gentle Introduction to the Registry* *1*
   A Brief History of the Registry *1*
   What Does the Registry Do? *10*
   Advantages Offered by the Registry *17*
   Registry Zen *20*

2. *Registry Nuts and Bolts* *22*
   How the Registry Is Structured *22*
   What Goes in the Registry *44*
   Getting Data In and Out *54*

3. *In Case of Emergency* *56*
   Don't Panic! *56*
   Safety Strategies *57*
   All About Emergency Repair Disks *61*
   Backing Up the Registry *71*
   Restoring a Backed-up Registry *83*

4. *Using RegEdit* *90*
   Know Your Limitations *90*
   Learning the RegEdit Interface *91*
   "Just Browsing, Thanks" *93*
   Connecting to Other Machines' Registries *95*
   Searching for Keys and Values *96*

	Printing Registry Contents *98*
	Working with Keys and Values *98*
	Exporting and Importing Data *106*
	RegEdit Command-Line Options *112*

5. *Using RegEdt32* *114*
   How RegEdt32 and RegEdit Differ *114*
   Learning the RegEdt32 Interface *115*
   Browsing with RegEdt32 .... *119*
   Remote Registry Editing *121*
   Searching for Keys *123*
   Saving and Loading Registry Keys *124*
   Printing Registry Contents *127*
   Editing Keys and Values *127*
   Registry Security Fundamentals *134*
   Securing Registry Keys in Windows 2000 .... *136*
   Securing Registry Keys in Windows NT *143*

6. *Using the System Policy Editor* *151*
   All About System Policies *151*
   Introducing the System Policy Editor *158*
   Managing Policies with POLEDIT *159*
   Distributing Policies *168*
   What's in the Standard Policy Templates *173*
   Picking the Right Policies *184*

7. *Using Group Policies* *186*
   What Are Group Policies? *186*
   Introducing the Group Policy Snap-in *193*
   Managing Policies *198*
   Distributing Policies *203*
   What's in the Standard Policy Templates? *208*

8. *Programming with the Registry* *210*
   The Registry API *210*
   The Shell Utility API Routines *247*
   Programming with C/C++ *264*
   Programming with Perl *272*
   Programming with Visual Basic *284*

Table of Contents

9. Administering the Registry *296*
    Setting Defaults for New User Accounts *296*
    Using Initialization File Mapping *300*
    Limiting Remote Registry Access *303*
    Fixing Registry Security ACLs
    in Windows NT *307*
    Adding Registry ACLs to Group Policy Objects *311*
    Encrypting HKLM\SAM with SYSKEY *313*
    Miscellaneous Good Stuff *322*
    Using the Resource Kit Registry Utilities *326*
    reg: The One-Size-Fits-All Registry Tool *328*
    Spying on the Registry with RegMon *345*

10. Registry Tweaks *351*
    User Interface Tweaks *352*
    Filesystem Tweaks *356*
    Security Tweaks *358*
    Performance Tweaks *364*
    Network Tweaks *372*
    Printing Tweaks *374*

11. The Registry Documented *377*
    What's Here and What's Not *377*
    HKLM\HARDWARE *378*
    HKLM\SOFTWARE *379*
    HKLM\SYSTEM *388*
    HKU *411*
    HKCR *412*
    HKCU *414*
    HKCC *424*
    HKDD *424*

A. User Configuration Group Policy Objects *425*

B. Computer Configuration Group Policy Objects *471*

Index *505*

Preface

Keys and Values and Classes, Oh My!

The Registry scares people. Practically every Windows NT user or administrator has some horror story of the damage done to a machine by careless Registry editing. Microsoft doesn't try to discourage this perception, either; the articles in their Knowledge Base, as well as documentation in the various resource kits, is liberally peppered with warnings about the dire consequences of screwing up something vital if you make a mistake while editing the Registry.

While making a mistaken Registry edit can indeed send your machine to Blue Screen of Death territory quick as a wink, there's no reason to be afraid of the Registry any more than you'd be afraid of a chainsaw, your car, or a high-speed lathe. If you know how to safely handle any of those inanimate objects, you can do much more work with them than you can manually.

This book teaches you how to safely use the Registry; how to administer, back up, and recover Registry data on computers running Windows 2000, both locally and over the network; and how to use the Registry editing tools Microsoft supplies, and when you should—and should not—do so. Much of the material also applies to Windows NT, since there are more similarities than differences between the two.

Who's This Book For?

This book is for anyone running Windows 2000, particularly people responsible for administering networks of Windows 2000 computers or providing technical or help desk support. It's also for programmers who are familiar with the Win9x Registry and its workings but are making the move to the similar-looking but internally different Windows NT/2000 world.

To get the most out of this book, you should be familiar with the Windows 2000 user interface; you should know how to right-click, run programs, and so on. Some background as a Windows NT or Windows 2000 administrator would be useful, but it's not required.

How This Book Is Organized

The book is organized into 11 chapters:

Chapter 1, *A Gentle Introduction to the Registry*, locates the Registry in the evolution of Windows systems. After a historical discussion of INI files and their traditional role as the repositories of configuration information, the chapter offers an apologia for the Registry, its philosophy, and its advantages.

Chapter 2, *Registry Nuts and Bolts*, discusses the keys, subkeys, values, and hives that comprise the Registry structure.

Chapter 3, *In Case of Emergency*, provides the compendium of caution. The major topics of discussion include the creation of emergency repair disks and strategies for effectively backing up and restoring the Registry.

Chapter 4, *Using RegEdit*, is a complete guide to the original Registry editor.

Chapter 5, *Using RegEdt32*, is a similar guide to Microsoft's 32-bit Registry editor.

Chapter 6, *Using the System Policy Editor*, explains the roles of system policies and the management of them with POLEDIT.

Chapter 7, *Using Group Policies*, describes Windows 2000's group policy object (GPO) mechanism and explains how to use it to apply policy settings.

Chapter 8, *Programming with the Registry*, presents the Registry API and follows up with sections on how to administer the Registry with programs implemented in C++, Perl, and Visual Basic.

Chapter 9, *Administering the Registry*, covers a number of vital topics, including user accounts, INI file mapping, remote access, security, and a number of Resource Kit utilities.

Chapter 10, *Registry Tweaks*, is a collection of tips and tricks you can use to bring your own system's Registry under control.

Chapter 11, *The Registry Documented*, is a snapshot of the Registry keys created by the Windows 2000 and NT systems.

Appendix A, *User Configuration Group Policy Objects*, describes the group policy settings applicable to user accounts. These include desktop lockdown and security policies.

Appendix B, *Computer Configuration Group Policy Objects*, describes the group policy settings that can be applied to computers, including the security and software installation policy components.

Conventions Used in This Book

This book uses the following typographic conventions:

`Constant width`
    Indicates a language construct such as a data type, a data structure, or a code example.

`Constant width italic`
    In syntax statements, indicates placeholder elements for which the user must provide actual parameters.

Italic
    Indicates filenames, URLs, commands, variable names, utilities, and function names. Italic is also used to highlight the first mention of key terms.

Registry pathnames can get long and unwieldy. To save space, they are set in roman text, and the top-level keys are abbreviated as follows:

HKCR	HKEY_CLASSES_ROOT
HKCU	HKEY_CURRENT_USER
HKLM	HKEY_LOCAL_MACHINE
HKU	HKEY_USERS
HKCC	HKEY_CURRENT_CONFIG
HKDD	HKEY_DYN_DATA

 This icon marks text describing NT4-specific features that still have relevance in a a Windows 2000 context

 The owl icon designates a note, which is an important aside to the nearby text.

The turkey icon designates a warning relating to the nearby text.

Comments and Questions

The information in this book has been tested and verified, but you may find that features have changed (or you may even find mistakes!). You can send any errors you find, as well as suggestions for future editions, to:

O'Reilly & Associates, Inc.
101 Morris Street
Sebastopol, CA 95472
(800) 998-9938 (in the United States or Canada)
(707) 829-0515 (international/local)
(707) 829-0104 (fax)

There is a web page for this book, where examples, errata, and any plans for future editions are listed. The page also includes a link to a forum where you can discuss the book with the author and other readers. You can access this page at:

http://www.oreilly.com/catalog/mwin2reg/

To ask technical questions or comment on the book, send email to:

bookquestions@oreilly.com

For more information about our books, conferences, software, Resource Centers, and the O'Reilly Network, see our web site at:

http://www.oreilly.com

Acknowledgments

When I first approached Robert Denn at O'Reilly & Associates about revising *Managing the Windows NT Registry* to cover Windows 2000, neither of us realized what we were getting into. The devil is always in the details, and Windows NT and Windows 2000 are superficially similar in lots of ways—but then the details rear their ugly heads.

As with my other O'Reilly books, I was fortunate to work with a team of true professionals at O'Reilly's Cambridge office, led by the tireless (and very patient) Robert Denn. Steven Abrams was the editorial assistant for this book.

This book benefited from the technical knowledge and writing skill of two other writers. Tom Fronckowiak, cryptographer to the stars, wrote Chapter 7 and revised Chapters 10 and 11 when my schedule began to oppress me. Likewise, Greg Bacon applied his considerable Perl talents to revising the Perl coverage in Chapter 8 so that it was more in keeping with an O'Reilly book; something my own meager Perl skills would have prevented. Tye McQueen, author of the Win32::TieRegistry module, generously allowed me to use his documentation as a base for the Perl discussion.

The technical review process for this book took longer than usual, in large part because of the volume, and quality, of technical review comments I got back. I'd like to thank my friend Glenn Fincher for taking time out of his busy schedule to review the book; in addition, my thanks go to the other reviewers, Jon Forrest, Cory L. Scott, David White, and Adam Wood.

I would be remiss if I didn't mention that this book was entirely written on a variety of Apple Power Macintosh and PowerBook computers. In fact, I even wrote the code in Chapter 8 on the Mac using Metrowerks CodeWarrior, then tested and debugged it on a "real" PC running Windows 2000. I use and manage Windows NT and 2000 every day, but I'm a more productive writer with the Mac—go figure.

I am indebted to David Rogelberg and the staff of StudioB Productions, the literary agency that represents me. David makes the easy tasks happen invisibly and handles the hard tasks without ever breaking a sweat, raising his voice, or appearing rattled in the least. I appreciate his negotiating skills, his extensive web of industry contacts, and his role as the voice of reason.

Lastly, I could not have even considered this project without the love, support, and help of my wife Arlene and my two sons, David and Thomas. I am truly blessed to have such a loving and supportive family.

1

A Gentle Introduction to the Registry

The Windows 2000 Registry plays a key role in making Windows 2000 work. It serves as a central data repository, and it's involved in everything you do with Windows 2000 computers, from the initial boot sequence to logging in and running applications and services. For such an important component, though, there is surprisingly little documentation that explains how the Registry works, what's in it, and what it's good for. Even seasoned Windows NT administrators who are making the leap to Windows 2000 admit to being a little unsure of the Registry's inner workings.

Part of the Registry's mystery comes from the fact that its data is stored in a special format that can be read only with the tools and programming interfaces routines Microsoft provides; part comes from the strict warnings against Registry tampering plastered on page after page of Microsoft (and third-party) documentation, books, and web pages. However, since the Registry's an integral part of Windows 2000, you should be comfortable using, repairing, and modifying it if you want to administer Windows 2000 systems. The overall goal of this book is to demystify the Registry's workings and help you understand when, how, and why Windows 2000 services, applications, and operating-system components use it so you'll be better able to administer the machines under your care.

A Brief History of the Registry

Before I plunge into the nuts and bolts of working with the Registry, let me set the stage by explaining how the Registry gained its starring role in Windows 2000. Besides being good preparation for amazing your friends with computer-industry trivia, the Registry's path to fame illustrates some of its strengths and weaknesses.

In the beginning, of course, there was no Registry. MS-DOS applications were responsible for storing their own persistent settings in configuration files. The operating system had its own set of configuration files; the most famous of these files are *config.sys* and *autoexec.bat*, which control hardware and operating system settings.

At first blush, this approach may seem reasonable. After all, applications' settings are generally private, and they don't usually affect other programs. Most components of MS-DOS itself weren't configurable anyway, so there was little need (or demand) for a better configuration mechanism. If the configuration data for a single application was lost or corrupted, restoring it was reasonably simple and could be done without affecting anything else on the computer.

Windows 3.0

Windows 3.0 improved on the MS-DOS approach by introducing the idea of a single, systemwide set of operating-system preference and settings data. In addition to DOS' configuration files, Windows 3.0 itself added four *initialization files* (*progman.ini, control.ini, win.ini,* and *system.ini*) that contained information about the system's hardware configuration, device drivers, and application settings. These files quickly became known as *INI files*, after their extension.

Microsoft chose a simple, human-readable ASCII format for INI files; not only did this ease the task of writing programs to use these files, but it also made it possible for end users to inspect and change their contents. One of the important features Microsoft wanted to deliver in Windows 3.0 was Macintosh-like customization; users wanted to be able to set their own color schemes, fonts, desktop backgrounds, and so on. By default, the Windows File Manager included a file mapping so that double-clicking an INI file would open it in the Notepad text editor, as shown in Figure 1-1.

In addition to storing Windows' settings in INI files, Microsoft provided a set of API routines (often called the *private profile API*) that gave programmers a way to create their own initialization files. The theory was that application programmers could use INI files to store private settings that were specific to their applications. Settings that could be useful to several applications—for example, lists of which fonts were installed on a computer—lived in the system's INI files, while application-specific settings were in the application's private INI files. Application programmers enthusiastically embraced this idea, and before long most applications used INI files for their private settings.

However, INI files weren't perfect; in fact, they suffered from some fairly serious weaknesses:

```
[Encryption]
Card=LJL_ENT
Card=LJL_FORT
;Card=LJL_DES
EntrustEncryptionAlgorithm=CAST
BypassProfileSelection=1
;DontIncludePlainTextFileIfSigning=0
Default Per=0
Receipt=0
Crypt Mode=SIGN
Card=LJL_Fort
OverWrite=1
SaveOpenMessagesInTheClear=No
Update=1
Timeout=0
SendAsSingleAttachment=1
DontIncludePlainTextIfSigning=0
DontUUencodeAttachments=0

[Directories]
ADDRESSBOOK=C:\MS-ARMOR\ENTRUST.DIR
;ADDRESSBOOK=C:\MS-ARMOR\KEYCACHE.DIR
;Tracer=DebugLog.txt
MultiCryptoPrefs=C:\MS-ARMOR\mprefs.txt
PLUGINS=C:\MS-ARMOR\plugins\
FORTCACH=C:\MS-ARMOR\FORTCACH\
```

Figure 1-1. Simple INI file

They were easily editable

An old quote from the Unix *fortune* program says that you can make software foolproof, but you can't make it damn-fool proof. INI files quickly provided a concrete example of this old saw; because INI files were editable, users felt free to edit them. This flexibility did make it easy for users to customize their environments or make necessary changes; it also made it much easier for a user to break a single application, an entire service (such as printing or file sharing), or Windows itself by making an accidental or ill-informed change to an INI file.

They were easy to break

INI files provided a one-time link between a program and its settings; they weren't dynamic enough to reflect changes in the machine's configuration or environment. For example, many presentation graphics programs built a list of available fonts during their installation process. If you later added—or, worse, removed—fonts, the presentation package might or might not notice the changes, meaning either that you couldn't use newly installed fonts or the package could crash while trying to use fonts the application thought were still available. This lack of flexibility was partly due to the fact that Windows didn't have any way to be notified when something on the computer was changed; without these alerts, there was no way to tell when INI file data needed to be updated.

They led to Balkanization
   Microsoft didn't provide any explicit guidelines as to where INI files should be stored or what should go in them; in the absence of these rules, application programmers felt free to put INI files in various locations. Some used the Windows directory itself, while others stored their INI files in the same directory as the application or in some other seemingly logical location. To compound the problem, some applications put their private data directly into *win.ini*, while others kept their own private copies of such things as font lists and printer settings that were explicitly supposed to be shared between applications.

They had implementation limits
   INI files had to be smaller than 64 KB in length; in addition, the Windows profile API calls blissfully ignores all but the first instance of settings with the same name within one section of the file. An even more serious limit was that INI files were inseparably bound to the original PC concept of "one user, one machine"; there was no way to easily move settings around so that users who needed to use different computers could keep their preferred settings.

The First Registry: Windows 3.1

Windows 3.1 added several new features that improved interapplication integration and ease of use. Chief among them were two new technologies, Object Linking and Embedding (OLE) and drag and drop. Both features required an up-to-date, correct database of program locations and capabilities. For example, object embedding could only work if the source and destination applications had some way to communicate exactly what type of data was being embedded, and the File Manager required access to a database of mappings to associate files with the applications that created them.

To provide this information, Windows 3.1 included the first Windows *registration database,* which quickly became known as the Registry. This Registry offered solutions to several of the problems posed by INI files:

The Registry provided a single place to store data
   Instead of segregating data into separate INI files, both system and application-specific configuration data could be stored in the Registry. In the original Windows 3.1 implementation, all Registry data was stored in a single file named *reg.dat*. Keeping system and application settings in one place reduced both the number and complexity of INI files; in addition, having a one-stop system for storing preferences and setting data made it possible to better share information such as font lists between different applications.

The Registry wasn't as easy to edit
> INI files were plain text, so it was easy to edit them. This was both a blessing and a curse; users could make changes when necessary, but they were often prone to making unnecessary or instability-causing changes. The data in *reg.dat* was stored using an undocumented binary format, and the only way users could edit it was with the Windows 3.1 Registry editor. Windows 3.1 also introduced the first version of the Registry access API, thus making it possible for programmers to read and write Registry data directly from their programs.

The Registry had a clearly defined hierarchical structure
> The structure of INI files was haphazard at best: sections could appear in any order within the file, and values could appear anywhere in the section. There was no good way to group related settings, especially when they might appear in different files!

However, the Windows 3.1 Registry still wasn't perfect. It supported only a single hierarchy for storing all system and application settings, and the *reg.dat* file was still subject to the 64-KB size limitation that hampered INI files. In addition, Windows 3.1 itself didn't improve on the problem of synchronizing the Registry's contents with the state of software, fonts, and other items actually loaded on the computer, so there was no guarantee that the Registry, the INI files, and the actual software loaded on the computer would stay in synch. Finally, the Windows 3.1 Registry didn't offer any solution to the problem of allowing users' settings to move with them to different computers on a network, or even allowing more than one user to keep settings on a single machine.

Despite these shortcomings, the Windows 3.1 Registry introduced several features that carried over to its successors. First and foremost is the concept of the Registry's hierarchy, which looks much like the structure of a Windows directory tree. In a filesystem, the topmost item is a root directory, which can contain any number of files and folders. Each folder can in turn contain nested subfolders or files, and you can uniquely identify any object on the disk by constructing a full pathname that points to it; for example, *c:\users\paul\proposal.doc* and *c:\program files\eudora\attach\proposal.doc* are different files, even though they share the same name. The topmost item in the Registry's structure (corresponding to a root directory in a filesystem) is a *root key*. All other keys in the Registry are children of one of the root keys (although Windows 3.1 supported only one root key, named HKEY_CLASSES_ROOT). Each key can contain either *values* (the Registry equivalent of a data file) or nested *subkeys*, equivalent to nested folders. Just as with files and folders, you can uniquely identify a Registry key by building a full path to it.

In addition to providing a hierarchy for keys, the Windows 3.1 Registry introduced the idea that keys have names and values. The key's name (for example, DisableServerThread) can be combined with the full path to the key to identify it (as in HKEY_LOCAL_MACHINE\System\CurrentControlSet\Control\Print\DisableServerThread). The value of the key holds whatever data belongs to the key; the actual contents vary from key to key.

Windows NT 3.1, 3.5, and 3.51

Windows NT was introduced in 1993 as Microsoft's industrial-strength operating system. It was expressly designed to compete with Unix workstations and servers; since these machines easily supported multiple users who could take turns using a single computer, shared workspaces, and networkwide configuration sharing, Microsoft decided that NT needed to do all these as well. To accomplish these goals, NT required a more flexible and capable Registry than that in Windows 3.1, so they kept the basic concepts but changed both the implementation and capabilities to match NT's requirements.

As noted before, the NT Registry is key to everything NT does: from the time the machine boots until you shut it down, applications, drivers, and services depend on the data they get from the Registry to do their jobs. Since the Registry was going to be ubiquitous, some implementation changes were needed. First to go was the old 64-KB limit; NT Registry files can grow as large as needed. Instead of using a single file, NT's Registry data is split into a number of files, but they all appear as a single set of keys. To handle the wider variety of data required to support the new system components and features, Microsoft split the single hierarchy of the Windows 3.1 Registry into several root keys (see Chapter 2, *Registry Nuts and Bolts*, for details on these keys). In addition, a great deal of effort went into optimizing the Registry-handling code to keep Registry performance from being a systemwide bottleneck.

The operating system's underlying security model could easily take up a book on its own, but I'll boil it down to its bare essence: every object in a Windows 2000 machine has a unique security ID, is owned by someone, and can have its own access control list (ACL) that determines who can read, modify, and remove the object. Most system resources—files, devices, the Win32 subsystem, and Registry keys, for example—are objects that have unique identifiers; this identifier may have a security identifier attached to it or not, depending on the type of object. The Registry itself is an object, as are all its keys; this means that each root key or subkey can have an ACL associated with it, so it's possible to grant very fine-grained control over which users and system components can read and modify keys. This security model continues in Windows 2000, by the way.

Another key feature of Windows NT was its ability to allow multiple users to share a single computer, with complete security partitioning between files and objects belonging to different users. The Security Reference Monitor, which is charged with enforcing that partitioning, depends on the presence of object-specific security access tokens bound to these objects.

NT also provided tools that could remotely access the Registry on one computer from another; for example, a system administrator could use his machine to view and modify the Registry on any machine to which he had administrator access. This made it easier for administrators to troubleshoot and fix Registry-related problems, since they could often make an initial diagnosis without leaving their desks.

Microsoft encouraged developers writing NT software to use the Registry instead of INI files. They set a fairly good example by making most NT system components and applications use the Registry themselves; as an added incentive, they provided a special facility that lets older Windows 3.x programs use the Registry instead of an INI file automatically by creating a copy of the INI file in the Registry.

To top off these changes, the original version of NT included a brand-new, 32-bit Registry editor, *RegEdt32* (see Figure 1-2). Each root key appears in its own child window; in addition to showing keys in a familiar tree format, *RegEdt32* adds commands for connecting to remote computers' registries, viewing and changing access controls on keys, and exporting and importing Registry entries. (All these commands are explained in Chapter 5, *Using RegEdt32*.)

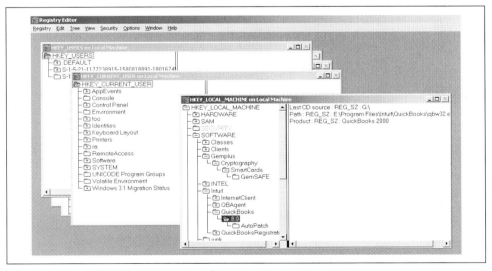

Figure 1-2. *RegEdt32, the NT Registry editor*

NT 3.5 and 3.51 didn't make any fundamental changes to the Registry's implementation or behavior; they did, however, add new keys to the Registry to support new features. Different versions of NT have different sets of Registry keys; for example, some keys that were part of the 3.51 Registry aren't in 4.0; conversely, 4.0 adds a number of new keys that weren't present (and won't be recognized by) NT 3.51.

Windows 95 and 98

Windows 95 introduced a new interface to the Windows world; as it turns out, many of these interface changes, and the underlying Registry keys, made it into Windows NT 4.0. There are a number of architectural similarities between the Windows NT 3.51 and Windows 95/98 Registries. Both support multiple root keys, and both store their data in several different files instead of Windows 3.1's single file. The Win9x Registry is also tightly integrated with—and heavily used by—all components of the OS. However, the underlying implementation is very different between the two; in fact, there's no Microsoft-supported way to migrate data between the two operating systems' Registries or share data between them. The basic ideas remain the same, though. Win95 has the same set of root keys from NT 3.51, plus two new ones: HKEY_CURRENT_CONFIG and HKEY_DYN_DATA. The overall organization of the two Registries is similar. The Win95 Registry doesn't support NT-style security (though you can enable remote access), but it does support hardware and user profiles in much the same way. See *Inside the Windows 95 Registry*, by Ron Petrusha (O'Reilly & Associates) for a complete dissertation on the guts of Win95's Registry implementation.

Windows NT 4.0

NT 4.0 combined the underpinnings of NT 3.51 with the Win95 user interface; given this heritage, it's not surprising that NT 4.0 has a large number of Registry keys with names identical to Win95 keys. The primary Registry-related change between NT 4.0 and its predecessors was the addition of two new root Registry keys. In NT 4.0, a single machine may have several hardware profiles that reflect different configurations; for example, a laptop computer running NT might have one profile that includes drivers for devices in a docking station (for use when it's docked) and another, with different drivers, for when it's on the road. HKEY_CURRENT_CONFIG provides access to the current hardware and driver configuration, but what's in that configuration depends on which hardware profile the user chooses during the boot process. HKEY_CURRENT_CONFIG was included in NT 4.0 so that Win95 applications that use it would be able to run under NT 4.0. HKEY_PERFORMANCE_DATA provides a root key for information that's generated on demand, such as Performance Monitor counter data. This dynamic data isn't stored in the Registry, but applications can access it locally or remotely by using the standard Registry API calls.

In addition to these changes, NT 4.0 fully integrated the Win95 concept of *system policies*. These policies control what users may and may not do on their machines; for example, a policy can specify that users can't use the Run command in the Start menu and that they can't move icons around on the desktop. These policies can apply to individual users or computers, members of defined groups, or all machines or users in an NT domain, and they can be applied against the user's settings or against the machine's settings in HKEY_LOCAL_MACHINE. In Windows NT, policies are actually implemented as Registry settings; the System Policy Editor (shown in Figure 1-3) provides a friendlier (and safer!) alternative to the Registry editor for building and distributing system policies to one or many computers in a domain or workgroup.

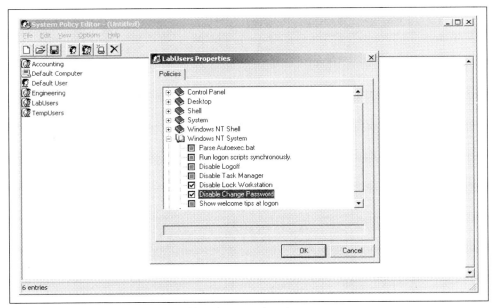

Figure 1-3. SPE for managing small- or large-scale policies

Windows 2000

Windows 2000 was originally called Windows NT 5.0. Given that fact (which Microsoft is trying hard to obscure), perhaps it's not surprising that not much in the Registry is different between NT 4.0 and Windows 2000. Early rumors said that the metabase, used by the Internet Information Server (IIS) product family, would supplant the Registry in Windows 2000, but neither the metabase nor the Active Directory have completely replaced the Registry. The Windows NT Registry editors survive virtually unchanged, as do the application programming interfaces programs use to read and write Registry data (though there are some new additions and extensions). There are a number of internal changes to the HKEY_LOCAL_MACHINE and HKEY_CLASSES_ROOT hives, and a number of Windows NT 4.0 keys have been moved or superseded.

The system facilities that use the Registry, however, are another matter. The NT 4.0 System Policy Editor is still present, but it's been largely replaced by Windows 2000's support for group policy objects (GPOs; discussed in more detail in Chapter 7, *Using Group Policies*). GPOs store their settings in the Active Directory, though settings in a policy may actually be applied to the user or computer portions of the target computer's Registry.

What Does the Registry Do?

The concept of a central repository that holds all the system's configuration data may strike you as a boon (since it keeps applications and services from scattering their settings in hundreds of small files buried in odd locations) or a danger (since it provides a single point of failure). The truth is somewhere in between these extremes. The Registry provides a neat, tidy way for applications, device drivers, and kernel services to record configuration data. That data can be used by, and easily shared between, the original owner or by other system components. At the same time, if the Registry is damaged, the effects can range from not being able to use a single application to not being able to boot Windows 2000 at all. (Chapter 3, *In Case of Emergency*, details the backup and recovery tools you can use to keep this single point of failure from causing trouble.)

It Holds Lots of Important Stuff

The chief role of the Registry in Windows 2000 is as a repository for configuration data. In this role, it acts as a sort of super-librarian; system components can look for their own configuration information in the Registry, then use what they find to control how they interact with other system components. The "important stuff" stored in the Registry falls into six separate categories; each category's data is gathered during a particular stage of the boot process, as shown in Figure 1-4.

Hardware configuration data

As part of the Windows 2000 boot loader's normal execution, it runs a program called *ntdetect*; as its name implies, *ntdetect* figures out what hardware exists on the computer. This configuration data is basically an inventory of five things:

What Does the Registry Do?

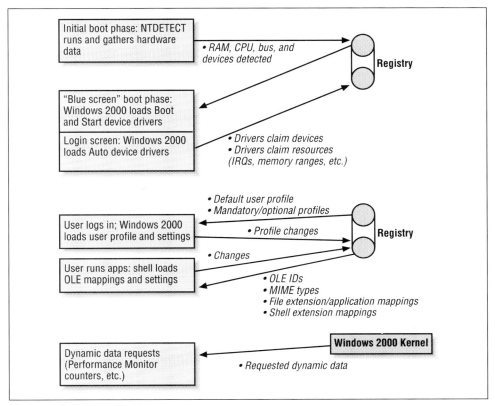

Figure 1-4. Registry data exchange

- The number, kind, and type of system processors
- The amount of system physical RAM
- The types of I/O ports available
- The bus types (PCI, EISA, ISA, VLBus, etc.) the system contains
- The kinds of plug-and-play devices present
- The devices found on those system's buses

Once all this information has been gathered, *ntdetect* stores it in memory and maps it to the Registry's HKEY_LOCAL_MACHINE\HARDWARE subtree so that the Windows 2000 kernel and device drivers have access to it. No hardware configuration information is written to disk, because at the time the kernel loads, it the needed drivers won't have been loaded yet! (However, hardware profiles' configuration information can be stored on disk; the profile tells the device loader what devices to configure after it's finished detecting hardware.) Because knowing the low-level details of the hardware is critical to the kernel, this detection phase has to happen first. Unlike the Windows NT 4.0 version, the Windows 2000 HKEY_LOCAL_MACHINE\HARDWARE subtree can be dynamically modified after the machine is booting; this facility supports the dynamic loading and unloading of device drivers, which is required for proper support of Universal Serial Bus (USB) and FireWire/IEEE-1394 devices.

Driver parameters and settings

After the hardware detection phase, the boot loader loads the Windows 2000 kernel, which handles the difficult work of finding the right driver for each device installed in the computer. The kernel can load device drivers in three different places. Drivers that are set to load during the boot phase load immediately after the kernel. These drivers are typically low-level drivers that provide basic services to other drivers, such as the drivers required to support PCMCIA cards and SCSI disk drives. Once those drivers have loaded, the spiffy new Windows 2000 loading screen (complete with a progress bar at the bottom) appears; in addition to the other things happening during this boot phase, the kernel also loads any drivers whose load state is set to "system." These drivers, which are usually mid-level components such as the CD-ROM driver, normally require the presence of one or more boot drivers such as the IDE, SCSI, or ATAPI drivers. Once Windows 2000 has started its GUI, the logon dialog appears, and the kernel begins loading all drivers marked as "automatic." Automatic drivers can be loaded as a result of some system action or automatically as part of the GUI startup. If the system has previously detected a new USB or IEEE-1394 device, it can attempt to load the matching driver at this point. If no matching driver is found, the Add New Hardware wizard can be run after a user logs on.

No matter where it loads in the boot process, each driver makes heavy use of the Registry during its initialization. As each driver loads, the kernel uses the Registry for three things. First, the kernel's driver loader walks through the hardware configuration inventory to figure out which driver to load for each device. Second, once Windows 2000 identifies the right driver for a device, the driver starts; as part of its startup, the driver claims the device it "owns" by marking it as owned in the Registry. Finally, the driver reserves whatever machine resources it needs; for example, the generic SoundBlaster16 driver provided as part of Windows 2000 attempts to reserve an IRQ, port address, and DMA block to talk to the sound card. Which values it requests depends on the hardware configuration information gathered by *ntdetect*. Once the driver has staked out the device and resources it needs, the Registry reflects the driver's reservations so other drivers that load later in the boot sequence won't try to seize them. Each of these steps uses a separate subtree under HKEY_LOCAL_MACHINE\HARDWARE; see the specific subkey mappings in Chapter 2 for complete details on which subkeys correspond to each phase.

Dynamic data

Actually, no dynamic data is stored in the Registry at all! Instead, the kernel intercepts requests for subkeys of the HKEY_PERFORMANCE_DATA key and returns the requested data directly. Because the data for this key is assembled on demand and not written to disk, HKEY_PERFORMANCE_DATA doesn't show up in the Registry editor. This is less of a problem than it might seem, since that data isn't directly of use to you anyway. The Windows 2000 performance monitoring tools (and, of course, kernel components) can get to it when needed.

User profiles and user-specific settings

From its inception, Windows NT supported the idea that more than one person could use a single computer. Each user on a Windows 2000 or NT machine (whether it's a workstation or a server) has her own *profile* that controls when, how, and whether she can log on; what scripts or programs are executed at logon time; and what she can do once logged on. In addition, the user's profile stores the contents of her Start menu, the appearance of the desktop, and other look-and-feel settings. The profile's actually a composite of the data from several different subkeys in the Registry, including security account manager (SAM) data for the user, plus a number of settings scattered around in different places in the Registry. To users, however, it looks like it's all one seamless collection of data; your workspace magically reappears when you log onto any computer in your domain.

In earlier versions of NT, these profiles were only usable on one machine—you and your officemate could share a PC in your office, but if you had to go down the hall to use another machine, your profile wasn't available, and you'd be stuck with an unfamiliar workspace. To solve this problem, NT 4.0 included support for two new types of profiles: *roaming* and *mandatory*. In many environments (such as college computing labs or workstation clusters in an engineering office), it makes sense for a user's settings to be kept on a central server and downloaded to whatever machine the user actually logs onto. This makes it possible for a user to sit down at any machine, not just the one at her desk, and go right to work. Roaming profiles make this possible; when you log onto a machine in a domain that uses roaming profiles, your profile is fetched from the server and cached in the local machine's Registry. Mandatory profiles work the same way, but with a twist: by renaming an ordinary profile with a *.man* extension, the system applies the policy automatically and restricts the end user's ability to change its settings. In practice, this means that administrators can build profiles that configure users' workspaces a certain way and don't allow users to change them—a great help for environments where lots of people need to share machines.

System and group policies

Besides the user's profile, other Windows 2000 settings can find their way into the Registry. For computers that are part of an Active Directory domain, GPOs largely supersede the system policy mechanism that defines and distributes policies for Windows NT 4.0 clients. You still use the native Windows NT 4.0 System Policy Editor (SPE) to set policies for Windows NT 4.0 and 9x machines in your Windows 2000 domains; you also use it to create policies for Windows 2000 machines that aren't part of an Active Directory domain.

GPOs are set using the group policy object editors (discussed more in Chapter 7) instead of SPE. That's not the only difference: while system policy settings are "sticky" (persistent and hard to remove, not unlike an old piece of bubble gum), GPO settings are applied in special areas of the Registry dedicated for that use. This makes them easy to reverse or remove, since reversing a setting in the policy automatically applies that setting to whatever machines or user accounts it's targeted to. It's possible to attach an SPE template file to a GPO, offering the best of both worlds by allowing you to use the same template files (such as the ones included with Office 2000) for Windows 9x/NT and Windows 2000 clients.

OLE, ActiveX, and COM

Windows 3.0 introduced the concept that a file's extension can be used to automatically figure out which program created it. Adding these *file associations* to the Windows File Manager meant that Windows users could double-click on a data file to launch the application that created it and open the file.[*] In Windows 3.0, these associations were kept in the *win.ini* file, but in Windows 3.1 and later, they're stored in the Registry instead. Windows 95 and NT 4.0 extend the concept of associations to include information about the kind of data stored in the file, too; this is especially useful for figuring out what to do with data downloaded by a web browser.

Windows 3.1 also marked the debut of Object Linking and Embedding, or OLE. OLE was designed to allow users to build compound documents that contained several different types of data. For example, you could create a Word document and embed an Excel chart and an Imagineer Technical[†] mechanical drawing in it, then edit either of the embedded objects without leaving Word using what

---

[*] This is, of course, only one of the many Macintosh features Microsoft "adopted" as part of the Windows GUI. While reading the rest of this book, see how many others you can spot.

[†] Imagineer Technical is a little-known but very cool 2D drafting and technical illustration package from Intergraph. I used to work on its OLE support code, so I still have a soft spot for it.

Microsoft called *in-place activation* (IPA). IPA required a large amount of new information to work; to start with, there had to be a list of all the types of data that could be embedded in a document, plus some way to figure out which program to run when the user wanted to create a particular kind of data object. The original Windows 3.1 Registry had only one root key, HKEY_CLASSES_ROOT; its purpose in life was to store the data OLE needed to function.

In 1993, Microsoft started touting the Component Object Model, or COM, as the wave of the future. (The combination of COM and OLE has since been retitled ActiveX; you've probably heard of *that* by now.) The basic idea behind COM is that developers can break their software down into lots of little, independent objects that communicate with each other via COM interfaces.* As with OLE, though, COM requires still more new data to make it work. Each type of object has to have its own unique ID so the system can tell them apart; in addition, the system has to somehow keep track of which interface methods a particular object supports (especially since COM objects can pass commands back and forth). ActiveX controls, which can be embedded in web pages, Office documents, and other kinds of documents, have the same requirements; the system has to be able to turn the unique class ID into the name of the program it should run to create, draw, or edit the object. All this data (and more besides) lives under the HKEY_CLASSES_ROOT subtree.

The primary change in Windows 2000 is that the settings in HKEY_CLASSES_ROOT are now split into two categories. In the old-style scheme, both file associations and MIME type mappings are stored in a single Registry file. The default permission settings for HKEY_CLASSES_ROOT allow any user on a machine to change these settings. This is a bad idea for two reasons. First, users may want their own MIME type mappings. For example, two users who share a workstation might disagree on whether Internet Explorer or Netscape is the best browser; under NT 4.0 the MIME type settings for HTML would continually be pingponging back and forth as the two browsers reset the default MIME types. The second reason is more serious: permitting any user on the machine to change file associations allowed any user to change those associations so that untrusted, or even malicious, applications could potentially be run without the user's knowledge. Windows 2000 solves this problem by putting MIME type mappings into the user-specific section of HKEY_CURRENT_USER and moving the file associations and OLE/COM mappings into a system subkey that has tighter permissions than the Windows NT equivalent.

---

* If you really want more details, try *Inside OLE*, by Kraig Brockschmidt (Microsoft Press) or *ActiveX Controls Inside and Out*, by Adam Denning (Microsoft Press). Neither are recommended for the faint of heart.

Application settings

So far, I've only talked about how the operating system uses the Registry. Applications can use it too, and most well-written Win32 applications do. The proliferation of INI files in Windows 3.x was bad for users, but it was every bit as bad for most software vendors—imagine trying to troubleshoot a customer's problem when your product's settings are intertwined with settings for every other program on that user's computer! The Registry offered a neat solution to this problem, with the twin benefits of better performance and some tamper-resistance thrown in as *lagniappe*.*

Microsoft's guidelines (which may be, and frequently are, freely ignored by Microsoft and third parties) say that third-party programs should install program-specific settings in the HKEY_LOCAL_MACHINE\SOFTWARE\<*VendorName*> subtree. For example, Netscape's products keep their settings under HKEY_LOCAL_MACHINE\SOFTWARE\Netscape. This key is for settings that pertain to the program itself, not the user's configuration settings for that program. User-specific settings go under the user's key in HKEY_USERS. This is a subtle but important distinction. As you can see in Figure 1-5, the settings under the Netscape Navigator key in each of the Registry root keys are quite different. HKEY_LOCAL_MACHINE\SOFTWARE\Netscape\Netscape Navigator\4.04 (en) stores information about where different components of Navigator are installed, while the corresponding entry under HKEY_CURRENT_USER\SOFTWARE\Netscape has settings that apply only to your configuration, such as where your personal bookmark file is stored.

Applications and system components can store any kind of data in the Registry: configuration settings for hardware or software, user preferences, paths to shared components, licensing information, and so on. Most "modern" Win32 applications tend to keep all their settings in Registry values. For example, the Office 97 and 2000 suites use the Registry to store information about each user's preferences for which toolbars are displayed, whether the Office Assistant appears, and so on. Netscape and Microsoft's web browsers both keep their user profile data in the Registry.

Of course, applications can freely use any of the other types of data stored in the Registry. For example, an image-retouching program can use the Registry to get the I/O address of the port to which the user has connected his digital camera, or a web page editor might use it to fetch a list of all the ActiveX objects a user can

---

* *Lagniappe* (lan' yap) is a Cajun French word meaning "something thrown in for free as part of a deal." For example, "Mais, I bought dat houn dog from Pierre, and he t'rew in 10 pound of shrimp for lagniappe."

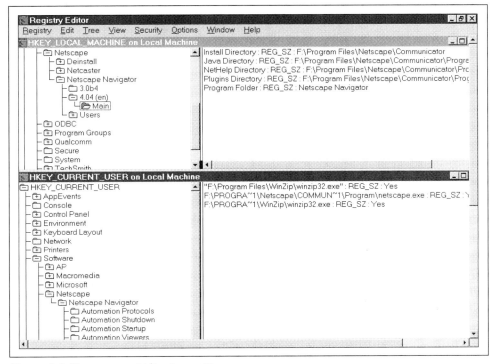

Figure 1-5. User versus application settings

embed in a page he's designing. For the most part, though, well-behaved applications will read, but not modify, keys that aren't theirs.

Advantages Offered by the Registry

The Registry offers a number of significant benefits to programmers, users, and administrators. These benefits stem from the characteristics just described.

It Keeps Everything Tidy

Instead of the dozens (or even hundreds) of separate INI files typically found on a Windows 3.1 machine, Windows NT/2000 machines usually only have a few, and those typically belong to 16-bit legacy applications that can't use the Registry. Windows 2000 itself uses the Registry for its configuration data, as do almost all 32-bit applications written for Windows 9x and NT/2000. There's more to tidiness than just the reduction in clutter that comes from eliminating INI files, though. Centralizing where configuration information is stored makes it easier for administrators to back up, restore, and secure the data.

It Provides Security

Access control for the Registry comes in two sizes. First, you can set individual workstations or servers to disallow any remote Registry connections. While this is secure, it also makes it impossible to use the System Policy Editor to set and inspect policies on that machine. A better and more fine-grained solution is to use the built-in ACL features. As I mentioned earlier, each Registry key, from the root keys on down, can have its own set of access permissions in the form of ACLs that apply to the keys.

Each access control entry (ACE) in an ACL actually has two parts: a permission (as shown in Table 1-1) and the account or group name that holds the permission. You'll learn more about these permissions in Chapter 5. ACL permissions are usually written like this, with the holder first and the permission following:

```
Everyone:Read
paul:Full Control
Engineering:Full Control
```

Table 1-1. Registry Access Permissions

Permission	What It Allows
Read	Read-only access to a specific key, its subkeys, and their values (includes Query Value and Enumerate Subkeys)
Full Control	All of the above rights; Full Control allows the holder to do literally anything to the keys with that permission
Query Value	Getting the data or contents of a specific key's value
Set Value	Changing the value of a specific key
Create Subkey	Creating a new subkey under the key that holds this permission; the new subkey inherits the parent's permissions unless they're explicitly changed
Enumerate Subkeys	Traversing all subkeys of a specific key and getting their full pathnames
Notify	Getting or setting auditing notifications
Create Link	Creating a symbolic link (such as a shortcut or a Unix symlink) that points to another key in the Registry
Delete	Removing the specified key, its subkeys, and all associated values
Write DAC	Changing the Discretionary Access Control (DAC), or permissions, on the specified key
Write Owner	Changing the owner associated with the specified key
Read Control	Reading the ACL for the key

Any account or group that is listed in the ACL has the matching permission; any group or account that's *not* in the ACL can't get access. This gives precise control over Registry access, since anyone you don't explicitly include in an ACL can't get access.

In addition to whatever accounts you've defined on your workstation or domain, you can use the operating system's built-in accounts and groups. In particular, you'll see the Authenticated Users pseudo-account* that grants read access to most keys in the Registry, while the Administrators groups usually have Full Control access to all keys. Since many NT software installers require write access to the HKEY_LOCAL_MACHINE\Software and HKEY_CURRENT_USER\SOFTWARE subkeys, you'll often see them tagged with Everyone:Full Control. Applications that use the Windows Installer—which includes any application written exclusively for Windows 2000—are smart enough not to require this access, but many administrators will want or need to run software designed for NT on their Windows 2000 machines.

It's also worth mentioning the SYSTEM account name; SYSTEM refers to processes and services owned by the kernel, so it's usually used to grant Full Control access to many of the keys in HKEY_LOCAL_MACHINE.

Besides their access controls, Registry keys also have owners; for example, the Administrators group owns the HKEY_LOCAL_MACHINE\HARDWARE subkey. You can restrict access to parts of the Registry by changing their ownership to a single account to which you control access; since any account that's not in an ACL won't have any access, everyone except the owner is locked out.

As an additional security feature, NT allows you to create an audit trail of access to, and operations on, the Registry. When you enable auditing for a key, you specify two things:

What actions you want audited
    You can create an audit trail of the success or failure (or both) of all of the permissions in Table 1-1 except Read, Full Control, and Write Owner.

Which accounts are audited
    The accounts you specify will generate audit trail entries when they attempt one of the actions you specify.

The auditing data is written to the Windows 2000 event log, where you can view it with the Event Viewer MMC snap-in or parse it with programs or scripts you've written.

It Allows Remote Management

Every computer running Windows 2000 has a Registry. If you're supporting more than one of these machines on a network, you'll be happy to know that the

---

* Authenticated Users isn't really an account; it's a special token that matches any authenticated user. NT 4.0 SP3 introduced Authenticated Users, which is similar to the older (and deprecated) "Everyone" pseudo-account.

Registry supports network inspection *and* modification. This capability, which is built into *RegEdit* and *RegEdt32*, allows you to troubleshoot and fix some types of Registry problems on network machines from your desktop. In addition, network Registry access makes it possible to automatically inspect the Registry of every machine on your network—a valuable way to gather statistical ("how many of our machines are still running Netscape Navigator 2.x?") or configuration ("what machines have *impala.oreilly.com* as one of their DNS servers?") data.

The old-style system policy mechanism requires network access to the Registry; there are also a number of useful administrative tools and utilities that build on network Registry access. For example, the *ERDisk* product from Aelita (*http://www.aelita.net*) allows you to build an emergency repair disk (ERD) for a machine across the network; in fact, you can automatically build updated ERDs for all the machines on your network every night if you like. Microsoft's System Management Server (SMS) product makes heavy use of network Registry access.

Registry Zen

Even if you're accustomed to using Windows, the Registry may sometimes seem like a New Orleans graveyard at midnight, full of strange shadows, half-glimpsed terrors, and legendary tales of misfortune. In this vein, I want to digress a little to talk about the philosophy behind the Registry, as well as the Zen of editing and using it.

First of all comes the obligatory scare tactic. Microsoft's documentation contains many warnings about the dire consequences that can result from editing the Registry if you aren't careful and knowledgeable. Instead of repeating these warnings, I'll offer one of my own, but just once, so you won't have to keep seeing it over and over.

The Registry is a key component of Windows 2000. If you remove a necessary key or change a key's value to an out-of-range value, some programs repair the damage automatically, but others fail spectacularly. Microsoft's Registry editors immediately make changes, so there's no backing out if you make a mistake. Please don't edit the Registry on your production machines until you've read Chapter 3, which explains how to recover from a damaged Registry.

You can think of the Registry like one of those self-service storage warehouses that have popped up across North America like sheet-metal mushrooms. If you've never seen one, let me briefly digress: these warehouses, which usually have catchy names such as "Public Storage" or "U-Store-It," are fenced compounds filled with long, low metal buildings. These buildings are segmented into individual garages. When you rent a space, you get the magic code that opens the outer gate, and you use your own lock to secure the unit you've rented. Once you've rented it, the space is yours to use as you wish (though you're not supposed to live in them or keep anything illegal or dangerous there).

Just like the local U-Store-It, every tenant of the Registry has its own individual space, where it can store anything under the sun. Access to that space is controlled both by the operating system and the tenant who created the keys. Also like the real-world equivalent, the landlord takes no responsibility for protecting what's in individual spaces; that's up to the renter (or application). That's where the analogy stops, though. In Windows 2000, Registry keys fall into three groups:

Keys you don't need to edit directly
> Keys in this group have some other way to set their value; most control panels are nothing more than pretty interfaces that make it easy for you to change settings in the Registry without using a Registry editor. The Explorer's file types dialog box is another good example; all it does is display, and allows you to change, data in the HKEY_CLASSES_ROOT tree.

Keys you must edit directly
> In the grand Microsoft tradition, the Registry is chock-full of keys whose values can't be edited anywhere else. Windows 2000 is pretty good about exposing formerly hidden features as settings in various GPOs, but since many Windows 2000 components are thinly disguised reissues of Windows NT 4.0 pieces and parts, hidden settings live on. In addition, some settings (such as the setting that controls whether Caller ID is used to identify incoming remote access calls) are available only by editing the Registry directly.

Keys you should leave alone altogether
> Just because you *can* edit a key in the Registry doesn't mean you *should*. Many of Windows 2000's subsystems, particularly device drivers, are intended to be self-tuning; they continually adjust their settings based on the system's workload. If you directly adjust a setting behind its owner's back, your reward can be anything from reduced performance to an unbootable machine.

2
Registry Nuts and Bolts

Chapter 1, *A Gentle Introduction to the Registry*, was just that: it was an introduction, and it was gentle. Now it's time to get down to business and focus on how the Registry actually works. In this chapter, you'll learn how the Registry is organized, both logically and physically, and how data gets into and out of it.

How the Registry Is Structured

Since the Registry is such an important part of Windows 2000, understanding how it's put together is crucial to learning how to use, modify, and protect its data. Let's start by examining the basic structures and concepts that underlie the Registry. Once you understand how these pieces fit together, we can move on to the data that actually lives in the Registry.

The Basics

You may find it helpful to think of the Registry as a filesystem; their organizations are similar in many respects. Both have a well-defined hierarchical structure, and they both support the concept of nesting items within other items. Files are identified by names and paths. Likewise, every key in the Registry is identified by a full path that identifies exactly where to find it. Since the Registry can be shared and accessed over a network, this full path can optionally include a computer name, which works as it would for a file share. The data within a file can be interpreted by applications that understand that file type. So it is with Registry keys, whose values can be understood and used by applications, kernel services, and other Registry clients.

Root keys

Root keys are like disk volumes: they sit at the root of a hierarchy and aren't contained or "owned" by any other item in the hierarchy. Windows Explorer groups all local disks together under "My Computer," and the Win95 *RegEdit* app does the same for Registry keys, but these groupings are fake, since the disks and root keys are actually logically separate entities. The groupings just provide a convenience for users. The six root keys that make up the Registry (see the section "The Big Six" later in this chapter) are logically independent of one another; to reinforce this idea, the Windows 2000-specific Registry editor, *RegEdt32*, shows each root key in an individual window.

In Windows 2000 and Windows NT 4.0, there are six root keys:

    HKEY_CURRENT_USER
    HKEY_LOCAL_MACHINE
    HKEY_CURRENT_CONFIG
    HKEY_PERFORMANCE_DATA
    HKEY_USERS
    HKEY_CLASSES_ROOT

Earlier versions of NT don't have HKEY_CURRENT_CONFIG or HKEY_PERFORMANCE_DATA.

Subkeys

Think of a subkey as a subdirectory somewhere on disk. Any key in the Registry may have subkeys. Just as folders are contained inside other folders, these subkeys can in turn hold other subkeys, and so on down the line. (Throughout the rest of the book, I'll call a subkey's parent a *parent* key.) Naturally, the root keys all have subkeys, but no parent keys; any other key, though, can have both parents and subkeys.

A subkey can have values of its own, or it can be a placeholder for subkeys that contain values themselves. For example, HKEY_CURRENT_USER\Software has subkeys, but it doesn't have any values attached to it. By contrast, HKEY_CURRENT_USER\Software\Netscape\Netscape Navigator is a subkey too, but it has several values of its own in addition to those of its subkeys. For example, the Netscape Navigator key has subkeys named Bookmark List, Mail, and Security, among others. The Bookmark List key in turn has a value named File Location. If you talk about the value named HKEY_CURRENT_USER\Software\Netscape\Netscape Navigator\Bookmark List\File Location, then you've completely described the path to a particular value. Leave off File Location, and you're talking about a subkey.

Values

Speaking of values, now would be a good time to mention that any Registry key may have zero or more values attached to it. These values normally have three components:

- A *name*, which identifies them both to Windows 2000 and you. Just like files, there can be many Registry values with the same name, but each key can only have one value with a particular name. The combination of the value's name and the path used to reach it must be unique. This means that it's okay to have values named Stuff under both HKEY_CURRENT_USER\Software\SomeVendor\AProduct and HKEY_CURRENT_USER\Software\BigCompetitor\AnotherProduct, but neither of those keys may have more than one value named Stuff.

- A *datatype*, which tells the Registry and its clients what kind of data the value represents. The "Major Datatypes" and "Minor Datatypes" sections later in this chapter elaborate on the available types for Registry data.

- Some *contents*,[*] which are subject to any limitations imposed by the value's type. In Windows 2000, the contents must be smaller than 64K of data. As a practical matter, 2 KB is about the point beyond which performance starts to suffer. In reality, most keys are much smaller—a few dozen bytes at most.

As with most other statements that include the word "normally," there's an exception to this three-part rule: Registry keys can have a single value with no name. The Microsoft editing tools show this value with a name of (Default) or <No Name>; applications can still reach it by querying the key it's attached to. This behavior is an artifact from Windows 3.x, but many modern applications still use this unnamed value.

The combination of these components makes it possible for Registry clients (including editors, applications, and the OS itself) to locate specific values, figure out what kind of data they contain, and get that data.

Hives

Hives aren't just for beekeepers any more.[†] In the Registry world, a hive is a portion of the Registry tree structure from any subkey under a root key on down. For example, the SOFTWARE hive contains HKEY_LOCAL_MACHINE\Software and all

---

[*] The contents are just the value's value. This is confusing at best.

[†] In *Managing the Windows NT Registry*, I admitted to not knowing where the term "hives" came from. It turns out that the Registry stores its data using a type of database called a b-tree. Where do bees live? In hives, of course.

its subkeys, and their subkeys, and *their* subkeys, on down to the values attached to the "deepest" subkey.

Hives are significant because each hive corresponds to a disk file that contains the hive's data. Instead of INI files, these hive files are the actual on-disk location for the system's crucial configuration data. Consequently, they're what you need to back up and restore (you'll learn how to do this in Chapter 3, *In Case of Emergency*). Windows 2000 normally uses eight hives: HARDWARE, SAM, SECURITY, SOFTWARE, SYSTEM, .DEFAULT, and two for the currently logged-in console user (one contains the user's profile, while the other contains the user-specific portion of HKEY_CLASSES_ROOT).

|NT4| Windows NT has only one hive for the logged-on user instead of two; it contains all the user's profile data.

You'll learn what each hive is for and where its corresponding file is stored in the section titled "Hives and Files" later in this chapter. In the mean time, if you look at HKEY_LOCAL_MACHINE\SYSTEM\Control\CurrentControlSet\Control\hivelist, you can get a sneak preview of the list of supported hives.

Links

The Windows 2000 shell and filesystem support shortcuts. (You might be familiar with aliases or symbolic links, the Mac and Unix equivalents.) All a shortcut does is point to something else. For example, the Internet Explorer icon on your desktop is actually a shortcut to the real installation of whatever version of IE you have installed, if any. When you double-click it, the shell can resolve the shortcut to find the thing it points to and run that instead.

The Registry equivalent of a shortcut is called a link. These links provide alternate paths and names for Registry subkeys. For example, the entire HKEY_CURRENT_USER root key is a link to the current user's subkey under the HKEY_USERS root. Since links can be built dynamically, it's easy to construct a link whose destination varies depending on some condition or other. Windows 2000 uses these links internally in a number of places; HKEY_LOCAL_MACHINE\System\Controls\CurrentControlSet is a link whose origin depends on which set of device drivers, hardware components, and system software is currently active.

Registry road map

Figure 2-1 shows a road map of the root keys and their major hives. As you can see, several keys and subkeys are actually links to areas in different root keys. You may find it helpful to refer back to this figure as we plunge forward into discussing the six root keys themselves.

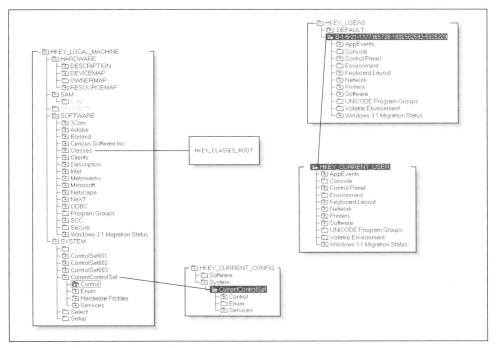

Figure 2-1. The Registry's overall organization

The Big Six

The root keys are, well, the root of the Registry's hierarchy. In the Windows 3.1 Registry, there was only one root key; in Windows NT 3.1 there were four, but Windows 95, NT 4.0, and Windows 2000 all have six. These keys form the foundation upon which all the Registry's capabilities rest. They provide a logical structure for grouping related items, and each of them plays a role in providing configuration data to clients and kernel components.

> You'll notice that all the names start with odd nonwords like HKEY and REG. Microsoft uses a system called Hungarian notation for naming variables. In this scheme, the name of every variable, datatype, or constant starts with a short code that identifies the type of data it is. This notation carried over into the Registry's design. HKEY is actually a handle to a key, which seems reasonable for the root keys.

HKEY_LOCAL_MACHINE

HKEY_LOCAL_MACHINE (abbreviated HKLM) is the king of the Registry. Its job is to consolidate and store all the systemwide configuration data for a particular computer. HKLM includes the hardware configuration data without which Windows 2000 couldn't even boot. Besides that, it also holds settings for the computer's network connections, security configuration, device driver settings, and more.

There are five major subkeys under HKLM, each of which plays a critical role in keeping Windows 2000 running. They're enumerated in the section "Major Subkeys of HKLM" later in the chapter. As you may have noticed in Figure 2-1, some of the other root keys and their subkeys are actually links to subkeys of HKLM; that's another reason why this root key is so important. For example, HKEY_CLASSES_ROOT is actually a link to HKLM\SOFTWARE\Classes.

HKEY_USERS

Under Windows 2000 and NT 4.0, HKEY_USERS (also known as just plain old HKU) contains all the profile and environment settings for users on the local machine. These settings comprise all the per-user controls controllable by the System Policy Editor (see Chapter 6, *Using the System Policy Editor*, for more on SPE), plus user-specific environment variables, as well as user-specific software settings. In Windows 2000, many of these profile settings are actually applied by group policy objects, using the rules discussed later in this section. The GPO provides the settings, and those settings are applied to HKU when the policy is downloaded. Changes to the user's settings are stored in her profile, but the GPO-specified settings can always override it. However, HKU still contains much of the user-specific data, since in Windows 2000 it is mapped to the hive file that contains the user's profile.

Each subkey of HKU is named by its security ID, or SID, a long string of digits that uniquely distinguishes every system object, process, user, and computer on an Windows NT/2000 network. Once an object is created, its SID never changes, but, its name can, so Windows 2000 uses the SID to keep track of user account profiles to keep them working when you change your account name from FredSmith to "The Administrator Formerly Known As FredSmith."[*] For a more concrete example, the SID for my account on my desktop machine is S-1-5-21-220523388-1214440339-682003330-1001,[†] so when I log on locally to that desktop machine, I see subkeys with that name under HKU.

---

[*] I wanted to include that odd-looking symbol used by the Artist Formerly Known as Prince but, strangely, it's not anywhere on my keyboard.

[†] And you thought it was hard to spell "Robichaux!"

In Windows NT 4.0, there are at least two subkeys of HKU. The first, .Default, contains a default group of settings (surprise!) named .DEFAULT that are applied when someone whose profile isn't already in HKU logs in. This facility provides a default profile that any profile-less user gets if there's no default profile in the NETLOGON share. The second group of settings are for the built-in Administrator account.

Windows 2000 is a little different; at any time when a user is logged on to the machine's console, there will be three subkeys under HKU. The first is .DEFAULT, which serves the same function it does in NT 4.0. The other two contain the settings of the logged-on user: one (named with the SID) contains the profile data, and the other (named with the SID with the string "_Classes" appended) contains the user-specific setting stored in HKCR. Windows 2000 users also get settings automatically from a special profile that's available to all users; it's stored in the *Documents and Settings\All Users\NTUSER.DAT*. Settings in the user's profile override the contents of the All Users profile, so the all-users default for a particular setting applies only if the user hasn't created a conflicting setting.

When you create local accounts on a machine running Windows 2000 (whether Professional or Server), their profiles are stored under HKU when they first log on from that machine's console. When that logon takes place, Windows 2000 copies the standard profile from HKU\.Default and creates a new subkey under HKU, named with the account's SID. Until an account logs on interactively, no profile exists for that account. At this point, you might be wondering what's under the individual subkeys of HKU, since each user on an Windows 2000 machine has her own subkey, which stores her settings independently of everyone else's. Instead of answering that directly, let's see what lives in HKEY_CURRENT_USER.

HKEY_CURRENT_USER

Surprise! HKEY_CURRENT_USER (better known as HKCU) is actually a link to the currently logged-in user's subkey in HKU. (On machines running Terminal Server, each user has his own HKCU, and Windows 2000 uses the correct one for each user—one of the benefits of HKCU being a link to a subkey of HKU!) Using a link was a smart decision on Microsoft's part; the link allows applications to look up things they need without needing to obtain the current user's SID first. When faced with the choice of finding data in HKCU\Software\KoolStuff\AnApplication or the mysterious-looking HKU\S-1-5-21-1944135612-1199777195-24521265-500\Software\KoolStuff\AnApplication, the choice is pretty clear. More importantly, since the Windows 9x family lacks the API routines needed to get SIDs, code written to use HKCU can run without modification on Windows 95/98, NT, 2000, and even CE.

Microsoft's guidelines require that applications should put *their* settings into HKLM and users' settings into HKCU. The idea is that settings that apply to all users on a machine go in that machine's key, while settings that users may—and probably will—change should be stored somewhere else. HKCU provides this mechanism; as an added bonus, a collection of subkeys under HKCU can be used as an individual user profile, and it's easy to store, load, or remove settings on a per-user basis. In fact, when Windows 2000 loads a profile, it actually copies data from the stored profile into HKCU.

HKEY_CLASSES_ROOT

HKEY_CLASSES_ROOT (better known as HKCR) made its debut in Windows 3.1 and has been around ever since. It serves as a giant lookup table that maps file extensions to the applications that own them. The Windows 2000 shell components (the desktop interface, Windows Explorer, the File Manager, and Internet Explorer 5.x) all make heavy use of HKCR, as do OLE container and server applications and ActiveX-capable software.

HKCR works because each registered file type or OLE class has two subkeys associated with it. File extensions are registered under their own name; for example, Microsoft registers HKCR\.doc, HKCR\.xls, and HKCR\.ppt (among others) as keys for Office 2000 document types. The file extension key's value specifies the default file type to associate with the extension. For example, the default value of HKCR\.doc is WordPad.Document.1, since WordPad comes with the standard Windows 2000 installation.

Besides the associated name, the file extension's key can contain a subkey called ShellNew. The Windows 2000 shell uses this subkey's value to figure out how to create a new instance of that file type when the user requests it. In addition to ShellNew, the file extension key can contain one or more document type keys that tie the extension to particular document types. This allows a single extension such as *.doc* or *.bmp* to be shared by several applications on the same machine. Each of these document type keys contain a ShellNew key.

The file extension key tells the shell what type corresponds to a document, but so what? The Windows 3.1 File Manager could do that too. In order to support OLE embedding and linking, HKCR has some additional tricks that center on the file type key. This key's name matches the default value of an extension key: when you install WordPad, you'll get a new key named HKCR\WordPad.Document.1, which matches the file type specified in HKCR\.doc. Its structure looks like this:

- The CLSID key specifies the globally unique class ID of this particular OLE object type. Windows 2000, and thus OLE and ActiveX clients and servers, use these class IDs to figure out what type of object to create when you create a new embedded or linked object.

- The DefaultIcon key's value tells the Windows 2000 shell where to find the icon for the file type. This is usually the name of the program or DLL that created the file; the value must also include the integer ID of the icon to use, since the executable can contain many different icons.

- The Insertable key specifies that this particular type of OLE object may be inserted and embedded in other OLE document types. For example, WordPad documents are insertable, but XML documents aren't because HKCR\xmlfile doesn't have an Insertable key.

- The BrowseInPlace key is almost the opposite of Insertable; its presence indicates that the specified object type can be browsed using in-place activation instead of inserting.

- Protocol stores information OLE needs to support embedding, linking, and in-place editing, including which OLE verbs (open, in-place activate, deactivate, etc.) the object supports. OLE containers use this data to decide which commands to pass on to embedded or linked objects.

- Shell holds subkeys that list the types of operations that can be done on the file type from the shell. In the case of WordPad, there are three: Shell\Open, Shell\Print, and Shell\PrintTo. Each of these has a Command subkey that contains the actual command line the shell can use to carry out the associated action. When you select a file in Explorer and open, print, or right-click on it, Explorer look up the file's type in the Registry, then looks for a subkey of Shell for that file and the requested command. For example, if you double-click a Microsoft Word 2000 document, Explorer looks for HKCR\Word.Document\Shell\Open\Command and executes the command it finds there.

HKEY_PERFORMANCE_DATA

HKEY_PERFORMANCE_DATA, or HKPD for short, was originally introduced as HKEY_DYN_DATA in Windows 95. It provides a central clearinghouse for dynamic data that is rebuilt anew each time the OS starts. In Win95, it stores performance data plus some other useful information; under Windows 2000 and NT 4.0 (it's not present in NT 3.x), HKPD stores performance data only. "Stores" is perhaps a misnomer; none of the data in HKPD is ever written to disk. Instead, when an application requests a subkey value for any of HKPD's subkeys, the kernel gathers the appropriate dynamic data, makes a fake subkey under HKPD, and passes it back to the requester. Since the data doesn't exist until it's requested, you could even argue that it's not stored in memory.

There's another catch, too: alone among the Big Six, HKPD doesn't appear in the Windows 2000 Registry editors. (It does appear in the Windows NT version of *RegEdit*, though it's labeled as HKEY_DYN_DATA.) You can't directly enumerate or expand HKPD, either, as you can in Win95; only kernel clients can get or set values for keys under HKPD, making it pretty worthless to most of us.

HKEY_CURRENT_CONFIG

HKEY_CURRENT_CONFIG, abbreviated HKCC, is the one-stop shopping center for data about the computer's current hardware configuration. If you've defined hardware profiles using the Hardware tab of the System control panel, when Windows 2000 boots you can choose whatever hardware profile reflects your current hardware setup. The profile is actually a subset of HKLM; when you choose a profile, it's stored in the key HKCC actually links to, HKLM\SYSTEM\CurrentControlSet\Hardware Profiles\Current. Like HKDD, HKCC is new in NT 4.0 and later; it's not present on NT 3.51 machines.

Now that you've made it through one and a half chapters, it's time to start using the conventional abbreviations for the root keys. From now on, I'll refer to root keys with the abbreviations given above, even when they're in paths. Get used to reading HKCU\Software\Microsoft... instead of the fully spelled-out version.

Hives and Files

The Registry appears to be a single monolithic blob of data, but it's not. Instead, it's made up of several hives. Each hive is a separate file or memory block that contains a Registry subtree. The kernel knits these individual hives together into a single seamless block. When your application (or any other) queries the Registry, it doesn't have to be concerned with which physical hive the desired key lives in.

Windows 2000 maintains a list of which hives exist on a particular machine in HKLM\SYSTEM\CurrentControlSet\Control\hivelist. This key normally contains seven entries, as shown in Table 2-1. Each entry's value contains the full disk path to the corresponding hive file. Interestingly, these paths aren't specified with drive letters; instead, they use paths based on the hierarchy of loaded device drivers. At the time the kernel loads, the driver hierarchy can be set up, but drive letters can't. The entry for the SOFTWARE hive on a machine that boots off the first partition on a SCSI disk with ID 0 looks like this:

    \Device\Harddisk0\Partition1\WINNT\System32\Config\Software

The first half of the path, *\Device\Harddisk0\Partition1*, tells the kernel where to find the disk volume itself (it can either be FAT16, FAT32, or NTFS); the second part, *WINNT\System32\Config\Software*, points to the hive file itself. By default, hives live in the *System32\Config* subdirectory of the system's install directory.

Table 2-1. Hives and Files

Hive Name	Hive File	Corresponding Registry Key
.DEFAULT	DEFAULT	HKU\.DEFAULT
HARDWARE	None; this data is dynamically generated and isn't written to disk	HKLM\HARDWARE
SOFTWARE	Software	HKLM\SOFTWARE
SAM	SAM	HKLM\SECURITY\SAM
SYSTEM	System	HKLM\SYSTEM
SECURITY	Security	HKLM\SECURITY
SID	Defaults to *Documents And Settings\userName\NTUSER.DAT*[a]	HKU*SID*
*SID*_Classes	Same base path as SID key, plus *Local Settings\Application Data\Microsoft\Windows\UsrClass.dat*	Some data under HKEY_CLASSES_ROOT

[a] For a clean installation of Windows 2000, this is the default location. For an upgrade from Windows NT, the profiles end up in *%systemroot%\profiles\userName\NTUSER.DAT*. Microsoft is trying to keep user data out of the system folder.

This table contains a few surprises. First, let's start with the HARDWARE key. It doesn't have a permanent hive because its data is never stored on disk—but there's an entry for it in the hive list anyway. There's undoubtedly a good reason for this, but no one outside Microsoft knows what it is.

Next are the *SID* and SID_Classes hives. Those aren't their real names; *SID* is just a placeholder for the SID of the user currently logged into the console. This hive actually points to the user's profile, which can be stored anywhere on the machine but is usually in the *Profiles* subdirectory of the system directory. For example, when I'm logged into my desktop PC, the hivelist entry for my SID points to ...*Profiles\Paul\ntuser.dat*. The exact value of this hive's entry depends on whether the user has an existing profile, whether it can roam, and whether it's mandatory. The *ntuser.dat* file for an individual user (along with some other files and folders in the same directory) makes up that user's profile, more on which in a bit.

By now, you might be wondering why these files exist as separate entities at all. The answer is twofold. The first reason is that splitting the Registry data into the groupings shown in Table 2-1 provides a clean separation between different types of data. The user's profile data (for example) should go in its own hive, since it doesn't have anything to do with the hardware, software, or security configuration of the machine. Likewise, the SAM database goes in its own hive because its data may not belong just to the local machine; for Windows NT servers that are domain controllers, the SAM hive holds the domain SAM, too. As a bonus, dividing the Registry into several components makes it possible to restore whole sections of the

Registry without affecting others. The hive organization was chosen with this in mind. As you'll see in the section "All About Emergency Repair Disks" in Chapter 3, the ability to restore only part of the Registry can be invaluable.

Access Controls and Security

Windows 2000 implements access control and security for the Registry in four overlapping levels. The specifics of how you actually use these settings are discussed in other parts of the book, but it's helpful to understand them at a high level before you begin implementing them.

Control via Registry APIs

The simplest and least effective control method is via a key that Microsoft provided, first in Win95 and then in NT 4.0 and Windows 2000, which administrators can use to disallow Registry editing on a machine. The good news is that this key, HKCU\Software\Microsoft\Windows\CurrentVersion\Policies\System\DisableRegistryTools, exists. The bad news is that this key doesn't actually do anything! Microsoft's Registry editors check the key and refuse to run if it exists; however, there's no enforcement of this method, so third-party Registry editors can, and do, ignore this value with no penalty.

Worse still, users can clear this flag themselves if they have access (and permission) to use the System Policy Editor or group policy objects on their local machines. Don't depend on this flag to keep any but the least sophisticated users out of your Registry; even though it's not much help, it's still worth setting.

Remote-access control

The next step up the security ladder is to restrict who can attach to, and modify, your Registry remotely. By default, Windows NT machines grant remote read access to their Registries. This stands in sharp contrast to Win95, where you have to manually install the Remote Registry Access service on clients whose Registries you want to edit remotely. Windows 2000 is somewhere in the middle. It also has a remote Registry access service, but it's started by default, and it allows read-only access to ordinary users. Depending on the account permissions you have, you may even be able to make changes to other systems' Registries; however, you may disallow it manually as described in the section "Fixing Registry Security ACLs in Windows NT" in Chapter 9, *Administering the Registry*.

OS-level security controls

In Windows NT and Windows 2000, Registry keys all have access controls and permissions attached to them. Unfortunately, by default, in NT 4.0 prior to Service Pack 3, most keys in the Registry had Everyone:Full Control as their permissions.

User Profiles Demystified

Windows 2000 and NT support three types of profiles: *normal*, *mandatory*, and *roaming*. Normal profiles are just that: plain, unadorned, ordinary groups of settings that live on a single machine in a user's *ntuser.dat* file. If you have a normal profile on one machine, it won't follow you to another machine, and you may change or modify it as you wish. Roaming profiles follow users from machine to machine: they live on the network and are downloaded to a machine when a user logs in. That makes it possible for a user's settings to follow her from machine to machine. For example, if you turn on roaming profiles, a new user who logs on for the first time gets a new profile based on the default profile settings in your domain. When she logs out, her profile is copied back to the profile directory you associated with her account, from which it can be downloaded on the next machine she logs into. A mandatory profile is one that can't be changed by the end user. As an administrator, you'll find it useful occasionally to specify unchangeable profile settings for your users and computers. You can combine these types, too: you can have normal or mandatory roaming profiles.

For domain accounts, the workings are a little different. Each account can have a profile location specified. Let's say you're administering Windows 2000 domain named *ADMIN* that has a few dozen workstations in it. You add a new account for Catbert, your new VP of human resources.[a] There are three possible scenarios:

Catbert doesn't have a mandatory or roaming profile
> The first time he logs onto any machine in the *ADMIN* domain, that machine creates a new profile for him, using the SID of his domain account. The new profile is based on the contents of that machine's default user profile (taken from *All Users\ntuser.dat*). Changes made to his profile on one machine won't be visible on any other machine.

Catbert has a roaming profile
> The first time he logs onto a domain machine, that machine attempts to fetch Catbert's roaming profile from the storage location defined in his account. In a Windows 2000 domain, the location of the profile is part of the Active Directory data that defines Catbert's account, but the profile itself is just a file stored on some server. If he is ever logged on to any other machine in the domain, and if the profile server is available, the logon machine makes a local copy of Catbert's profile under HKU; if not, it makes a new profile based on the domain default profile and uses it instead. On subsequent logons, Windows 2000 compares the

—Continued—

> locally cached profile with that stored on the server; if they're different, Catbert gets to choose which profile he wants the machine to honor. Any changes he makes to his profile on one machine is copied back to the stored profile on the server, and the changes appear on other machines when he logs into them.
>
> *Catbert has a mandatory profile*
> Mandatory profiles must be used. When setting up an account, the domain admin specifies which mandatory profile Catbert's account will use. When Catbert logs onto a domain machine for the first time, Windows 2000 gets that profile from the profile server and uses it. If the server can't deliver the profile for some reason, Catbert's logon attempt will fail. If Catbert makes changes to the profile, they aren't mirrored back to the server.
>
> When you create a user account, you assign it using the Profile button of the User Properties dialog in the User Manager or User Manager for Domains (for NT) or the Active Directory Users and Computers or Local Users and Groups snap-ins in Windows 2000. Once you specify the UNC path to the profile, Windows will automatically download—and upload—the profile so the user has a consistent environment. If you don't explicitly provide a profile for a user account, that account will use the local or domain default profile. This, then, is the profile you should edit if you want to change what profile-free users end up seeing.
>
> The best way to build a default profile for your users is to create a special account for profile editing. Log on as that account and modify the profile to your liking, then log off and back on as Administrator. Once you do that, you can use the Copy To… button on the User Profiles tab of the System control panel to copy the profile account's profile to whatever share you specified in the User Manager. The next time a user with a profile logs in, her workstation gets an updated copy of the profile.
>
> To specify that a profile should be mandatory, name it *ntuser.man*. You still have to modify each user's account so that it points to the mandatory profile, but once you do Windows 2000 faithfully downloads and applies it when a user logs in. Changes made on the local workstation, however, aren't propagated back to the original profile as they are with regular profiles.
>
> ---
> a. If you don't read the *Dilbert* comic strip: a) you should, and b) you won't get this joke.

This led to a security exploit popularly known as the "RedButton" or "MWC" exploit, where an untrusted program could attach to and modify Registries on machines where the exploiter had no Administrator access. SP3 fixes this problem;

in addition, the section "Fixing Registry Security ACLs in Windows NT" in Chapter 9 explains how to set adequate access controls on your Registry keys.

Windows 2000 doesn't suffer from this problem nearly as much, because it has a much less permissive set of default permissions. With appropriate application of security templates (discussed in more detail in Chapter 9) you can tighten things down even further.

As an additional safety measure, you can—and should—set up auditing events to log changes to the Registry on critical machines. There's a fine line between doing this too much and not enough; there are guidelines in Chapter 9 as well.

System Key Security (SYSKEY)

Microsoft has frequently (and not always fairly) been criticized for leaving security holes in its products. In particular, an exploit was reported in mid-1997 that took advantage of the fact that NT 4.0 and earlier stored some account passwords—those for services—in the Registry. Even though the passwords were obfuscated, having them there represented a security risk, since an attacker could, in theory, grab the hive files and figure out the passwords.

To fix this, Microsoft introduced a new feature called System Key Security, or *SYSKEY*, in Service Pack 3 for NT 4.0. SKS encrypts a portion of the Registry (mainly the SAM and SECURITY subkeys of HKLM) using the CryptoAPI cryptographic services. As a practical matter, this makes it statistically very unlikely that someone can get useful information out of your Registry unless the attacker knows or steal the key used to encrypt it. You can choose your own password (which then must be entered when you boot the machine), or you can have the system generate and store a password. Either way, without that password, the SAM data stored in the Registry is useless. It's important to note that *SYSKEY* doesn't keep people from browsing the Registry or opening keys with the programming interfaces, and it doesn't prevent them from actually making a copy of the SAM hive itself; it just encrypts the SAM data so it's no longer directly useful for password crackers such as *l0phtcrack*.* (However, a tool such as Todd Sabin's *pwdump2*, or future versions of *l0phtcrack*, make it harder to extract these hashes.)

Windows 2000 turns on *SYSKEY* by default, and there's no way to turn it off. This might seem like an odd thing to do; after all, Windows 2000 uses the Active Directory to store user account information, so why would there be a SAM hive present in the first place? Not every Windows 2000 machine is an AD domain controller; for example, member servers or Windows 2000 Professional machines may still have local accounts on them. So can domain controllers, for that matter. In

---

* *l0phtcrack* is a very fast, robust, and full-featured password cracker for Windows NT and Windows 2000. Check it out at *http://www.l0pht.com/l0phtcrack*.

Service Packs Versus Hotfixes

Microsoft often issues bug fixes and enhancements for its operating system products. These changes come in two flavors. *Service packs* include a large number of fixes, plus occasional enhancements. While there's no fixed schedule, they usually appear at least every six months, and sometimes more often. As I write this, it's been a little over three years since NT 4.0 shipped, and there have been six service packs released for it. These updates are usually referred to as SPs, and when used with a number (i.e., SP3) you can tell what SP is being discussed.

As of the time of this writing, Windows NT 4.0's current service pack is SP6a. There aren't any service packs available for Windows 2000 yet, even though Microsoft started working on SP1 as soon as they'd released the gold master version of Windows 2000. One important change to Windows 2000 is the new "slipstream" update model, in which each service pack can be incorporated with the base distribution. This makes it possible to create a sharepoint for distributing Windows 2000, then add service packs directly to the sharepoint so that they're installed as part of the normal install instead of adding them after installation.

The service-pack mechanism is the same for Windows 2000 and NT. First, remember that SPs are cumulative. If you install NT 4.0 SP6, it includes all the patches and fixes included in SP1 through SP5. You can use the system utility *hotfix.exe* to get a quick indication of which SPs are installed on a particular machine; you can also find the same data yourself in HKLM\Software\Microsoft\Windows NT\CurrentVersion\CSDVersion.

Unlike SPs, hotfixes are intended to fix one or two critical problems. For example, the IIS 3.0 denial-of-service attacks that brought down Microsoft's web site several times in 1997 quickly led to the release of a hotfix that repaired that specific problem. In their hurry to get hotfixes out the door, Microsoft can't always do complete tests on them before release; if you install a hotfix that fixes a problem you don't have, you may end up with new problems caused by the hotfix itself!

Regrettably, some SPs have been released without adequate testing as well. My best advice is this: install a new SP on one or two machines to see how it does before rolling it out across your network. If Microsoft releases a hotfix for a problem you're experiencing, get it and install it. If it's a security-related hotfix, get it and install it even if you're not having the problem. Otherwise, leave it alone.

addition, machines that don't run the AD services have a local SAM hive; domain controllers have one too, with AD information mirrored into it.

NT4 Once you turn on SKSKEY, it can't be turned off. If you want to turn on SKSKEY on your Windows NT machines, complete instructions are given in the section titled "Encrypting HKLM\SAM with SYSKEY" in Chapter 9.

Major Datatypes

The Registry can directly store and manipulate 11 different types of data: seven major and four minor. This doesn't seem like very many at first, but remember that applications can use the seven fundamental types to store whatever kind of data they want. Only the application knows what the data actually means, and Windows 2000 doesn't care; it happily stores and retrieves whatever data you pass it as long as you specify one of the following types for it.

REG_DWORD

REG_DWORD is a double word (the DWORD is Hungarian notation for a double word). Since a word is a 16-bit number representing the range 0–65535, a double word is just two 16-bit words, so it's a 32-bit value, probably the most common datatype in the Registry. A REG_DWORD value can hold any integer up to 2^{32}. Even though this provides a range of more than four billion possible values, many Registry keys use REG_DWORD to stand in for Boolean[*] values: you'll see a lot of keys whose values can either be 1 or 0. In other cases, the value represents a quantity of something, like the percentage of time a replication request can echo on the network or the number of seconds allowed between replication attempts. The hard part is knowing what the value represents, since without that there's no way to intelligently decide whether it needs to be changed. Chapter 10, *Registry Tweaks*, points out some of the most significant or interesting Registry keys, and others are documented in Microsoft's knowledge base (*http://support.microsoft. com*) and in the Windows 2000 and NT Server resource kits.

There is one other stumbling block: the Registry editors default to showing REG_DWORD values in hexadecimal, not decimal, and you have to use hex values when you're setting them unless you tell the editor you're entering decimal or binary values. This isn't too surprising, since the Registry stores values internally as raw bytes, not in decimal. It can be annoying to have to set Registry values for things such as replication timers: "Start with the time, which is 2 days, 4 hours, 30 minutes—that's 189,000 seconds, which is, ah, 0x2d620 hex."[†]

---

[*] "Boolean" comes from George Boole, the mathematician who first described formal systems for working with problems whose solutions could only be expressed in terms of truth or falsehood. This makes a good trivia question for springing on coworkers.

[†] Yes, I *did* do that by hand—proof of a misspent youth.

REG_SZ

In Hungarian notation, *S* means "string," and *Z* means "terminated with a zero byte at the end." Put them together, and you get the REG_SZ datatype, which stores fixed-length strings by tacking on a zero at the end of the string. This extra zero is usually called the string's *terminator*. The simple string "W2K" actually takes up four bytes when stored as a REG_SZ: three bytes for its contents, and one for the terminator. The terminator is mostly invisible to you (unless you write programs to manipulate Registry values in C or C++); the Registry editing tools add, remove, and store the terminator as appropriate, and they don't display it.

After REG_DWORD, REG_SZ is probably the second most-common Registry datatype. Strings are pretty versatile; they can store human-readable names, file paths, version numbers, and lots of other useful tidbits. These strings can contain Unicode characters, which means they're not limited to the ASCII character set. If you have occasion to edit the Registry on a machine running the Japanese, Korean, or Chinese versions of Windows NT/2000, be prepared to see non-ASCII characters aplenty.

REG_MULTI_SZ

Sometimes it's useful to store a group of related strings as a single block. For example, since a single PC can have more than one video BIOS, NT stores the identification strings for each video BIOS it finds in HKLM\HARDWARE\DESCRIPTION\SYSTEM\VideoBiosVersion. To support this aggregation, Windows 2000 supports a special datatype called REG_MULTI_SZ—a fancy name for what is essentially a collection of several Unicode strings. Programs that use REG_MULTI_SZ values get the strings as a block and can add to or remove from the block at will. Of course, you can edit the strings too, using the editor provided as part of *RegEdt32*; see Figure 2-2.

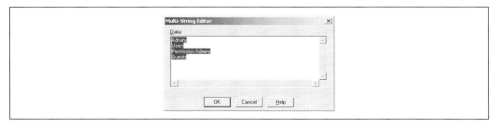

Figure 2-2. The multiple-string editor in RegEdt32

REG_EXPAND_SZ

As part of what passes for its system scripting language, Windows 2000 provides a number of system-defined variables. You may already know that these variables can be used in *.BAT* files, the Environment Variables button on the System control panel's Advanced tab, and directly from Windows 2000's command line, but they can also be used within Registry values of type REG_EXPAND_SZ. For example, the *%SystemRoot%* environment variable points to the root directory of the OS installation (it's usually *C:\WINNT* or something similar). If a Registry key has type REG_EXPAND_SZ and a value of %SystemRoot%\Media, any caller who retrieves the value can expand the embedded variable to its true value. You might think, based on the name, that the Registry would expand the embedded variable itself; sadly, this isn't the case. You have to do it yourself, as you'll see in Chapter 8, *Programming with the Registry*. In all other respects, this type is identical to REG_SZ.

REG_BINARY

Programmers often use binary representations directly. For example, using a mask of binary digits is a convenient way to represent features or flags that may or may not be set; each bit in the mask can represent a separate on-off flag, making it possible to pack 32 independent flags into a single DWORD. Of course, it's often useful to store arbitrary binary data—pictures, cryptographic keys, encrypted passwords, and so on—in a binary format. *RegEdt32* supports storing and editing binary values with the REG_BINARY type. Binary data is totally raw; there are no terminators, string expansion, or anything else. What you put in is what comes back out. Figure 2-3 shows the binary value editor; you'll learn more about how to use it in Chapter 5, *Using RegEdt32*.

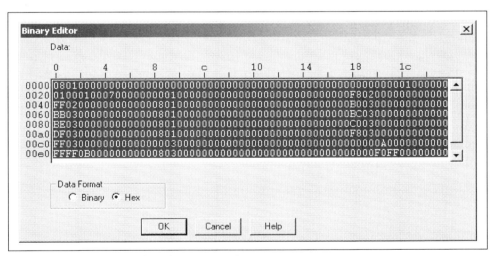

Figure 2-3. The binary value editor in RegEdt32

REG_LINK

In the section "Links" earlier in this chapter, you learned that the Registry supports links that tie one subtree to another, much the same way you figure out that

"Charles Windsor" and "Prince Charles" are actually the same person. These links have their own datatype, REG_LINK, which actually looks just like a REG_SZ. Let's say you have an intranet application that stores its configuration information in HKLM\Software\BigCorp\NiftyApp*version*, where *version* is the application's version number. If you want to read the application's settings without regard to what version was installed, you can create a new key named HKLM\Software\BigCorp\NiftyApp\CurrentVersion and make it a REG_LINK; its link value would be HKLM\Software\BigCorp\NiftyApp*version*. To reach the application's communications settings, you can always refer to HKLM\Software\BigCorp\NiftyApp\CurrentVersion\CommSettings, no matter what the actual value of *version* is; the Registry API routines automatically resolves the link and takes you to the correct destination of HKLM\Software\BigCorp\NiftyApp*version*\CommSettings.

As a more immediate example, consider HKCU. Software written for Windows 2000 must be aware that there can be several different user accounts on a single machine, each with its own unique SID. Win9x applications may be aware that multiple users sometimes share a computer, but the Win9x Registry doesn't have SIDs—making it impossible for a Win9x app to find the current user's settings when run under Windows 2000. Enter HKCU, which is a link that Windows 2000 builds at logon time. Instead of having to know what the current user's security ID is and how to resolve that to a name, the application can just look for settings under HKCU.

You can't create a new REG_LINK value from within *RegEdit* or *RegEdt32*. You can use the Registry API calls described in Chapter 8 to create these types if you need to; most often, though, you won't.

REG_QWORD

If a DWORD is a double word, it stands to reason that a QWORD would be a quad word, right? In fact, that's exactly what it is: four 16-bit words, providing a way to store a 64-bit quantity in a single Registry value. You'll probably see these values only in applications running on Windows 2000 Advanced Server or Datacenter Server, and then only on 64-bit hardware. You can create and manipulate QWORD values with the Registry APIs discussed in Chapter 8, but you can't edit them with *RegEdt32* or *RegEdit*.

Minor Datatypes

In addition to the datatypes presented above, Windows 2000 supports four additional types that are less frequently used but still worth discussing. The first two,

REG_NONE and REG_DWORD_BIG_ENDIAN, aren't used very often, but they're available if you need them. The remaining two are reserved for use by Windows 2000; *RegEdt32* can display them but won't let you change any of their values.

> The Windows 2000 Registry editors won't let you create new values using any of the types described in this section, though you can use the Registry programming APIs to create REG_NONE and REG_DWORD_*_ENDIAN values. If you try creating new values or keys using the resource types, however, the default ACLs won't let you put them in HKLM\HARDWARE, where they belong. You can create them elsewhere, but NT ignores them.

REG_NONE

REG_NONE is a nice antidote to the more complicated datatypes featured in this chapter; it's just a big zero. It's used to indicate the presence of a value only; since REG_NONE doesn't store any values, you can't use it to retrieve or store data in a key, but you can see whether the key is there or not. This is useful in some limited situations where the existence or absence of a key indicates something important, but it's a much better idea to use actual value types, and REG_NONE is rare.

REG_DWORD_BIG_ENDIAN

It's an often-forgotten fact that Windows NT was designed to work well on other types of CPUs besides the ubiquitous Intel x86. At one point, NT actually ran on five different CPU families: Intergraph's Clipper, the MIPS CPU family, DEC (now Compaq) Alphas, the Apple/IBM/Motorola PowerPC chip, and the x86. Windows 2000 is now available only for x86 CPUs, but its multiplatform heritage lives on.

Not all these platforms order their bytes in the same way, though. "Big-endian" platforms put the most significant byte of a quantity in the lowest address, while "little-endian" platforms put the least significant byte at the low address. Figure 2-4 shows how the hex number 12345678 is represented with both kinds of "endianness."

To mix data between little- and big-endian machines, one end or the other has to swap the byte ordering. Even though NT was originally designed for little-endian machines (the x86 and MIPS), Microsoft realized that it might be desirable to run it on big-endian platforms someday. In aid of that goal, they gave us REG_DWORD_BIG_ENDIAN, which is rarely if ever seen on little-endian machines. It stores DWORD values in big-endian order, without translating them back to little-endian order on little-endian machines. Unless you're running Windows NT on a PowerPC or Alpha (or an early beta of Windows 2000 on an Alpha), you probably won't ever

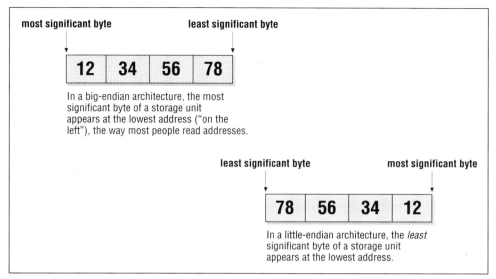

Figure 2-4. The hex number "12345678" in big- and little-endian form

see any values of this type in your Registry. In Windows 2000, there's also a corresponding REG_QWORD_LITTLE_ENDIAN type.

 There's also a REG_DWORD_LITTLE_ENDIAN type, but you won't ever see it on little-endian machines; it's only there so big-endian machines have a way to store little-endian data. NT automatically converts big- or little-endian data to the correct representation when you query a key's value and tell the Registry you're storing it as an ordinary DWORD.

REG_FULL_RESOURCE_DESCRIPTOR

Computers have finite resources; in particular, Intel-based PCs suffer from a limited number of IRQs and direct-memory access (DMA) address ranges. Someone has to be in charge of allocating this finite supply of goodies to requesters; in Windows 2000, it's the hardware abstraction layer (HAL), which loads as part of the boot process, that provides this necessary service. The resource arbitration's goal is (if at all possible) to keep two or more devices from fighting over the same resource.

To make this work, the Windows 2000 kernel stores information about what resources are available in HKLM\HARDWARE; this information's gathered at boot time and stored in RAM, which is then mapped to Registry keys. Completely describing a resource requires quite a bit of data, and the operating system aggregates all the data for a resource into a resource descriptor. The REG_FULL_RESOURCE_DESCRIPTOR datatype consolidates this data, as shown in Figure 2-5. (These fields may look familiar to you, since Microsoft's old-school *WinMSD* diagnostic tool for Windows NT used a similar format.)

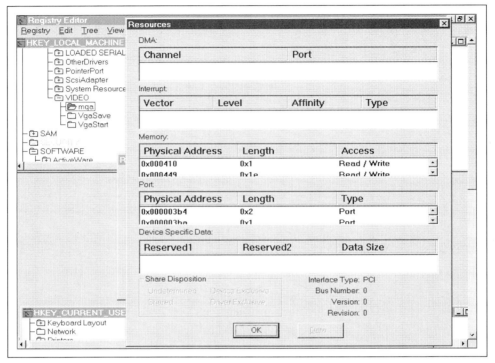

Figure 2-5. The resource descriptor display in RegEdt32

REG_RESOURCE_LIST

Even though the number of resources on a particular computer is finite, it can still be large. Instead of scattering many values of type REG_FULL_RESOURCE_DESCRIPTOR around, the Registry offers REG_RESOURCE_LIST, a type designed to group related resource descriptors into a single unit. Figure 2-6 shows a sample of *RegEdt32*'s display for this datatype.

What Goes in the Registry

No two snowflakes are alike. It's not quite true to say that no two Registries are alike, but they can vary significantly from machine to machine. There's a standard set of keys Windows 2000 uses, but even this standard set varies somewhat, depending on whether the computer's running Windows 2000 Professional or a

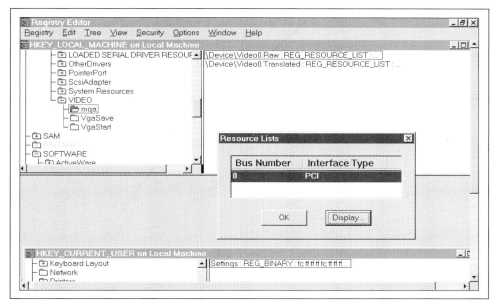

Figure 2-6. The resource list viewer in RegEdt32

member of the Windows 2000 Server family, what optional components are installed, and how the machine's network connection is configured.

The Registry help files included with the Windows 2000 Resource Kit (as well as the material in Chapter 11, *The Registry Documented*) explain what individual keys are for, but using that data to grasp what's important is like trying to build a watch out of a bag full of parts; it's much more instructive to examine a working watch and see how its parts relate. To provide a working watch for your entertainment, this section examines the most important subkeys of the root keys described earlier in this chapter.

Major Subkeys of HKLM

HKLM's purpose is to store all the important configuration data for the local machine. It doesn't contain any information about other machines on the network or about user-specific configuration data; instead, it's nothing but settings for the machine where it's stored. HKLM has four important subkeys.

HARDWARE

All the keys and subkeys of HKLM\HARDWARE are generated by Windows 2000 at boot time and exist only in memory; they aren't stored on disk. This may seem odd, but when you consider the Windows 2000 boot process, it makes more sense. The boot loader (*NTLDR.COM*) is loaded by the standard DOS boot mechanism. When it executes, it loads and starts the Windows 2000 kernel. The kernel in turn must first start up the hardware abstraction layer; the HAL provides a buffer between the gory details of hardware resources and the neatly structured system of device drivers the operating system uses to talk to hardware. For this approach to work, the HAL must register the hardware it finds, but at the time it finds those devices, it may not have found any disks to register the data on! Keeping the hardware keys in memory nicely solves this problem.

There are four subkeys of HKLM\HARDWARE. For the most part, your interaction with them will be very limited, especially since you can't change them. All the information you might gain by manually inspecting these subkeys is more easily available through the System Properties dialog box. Having said that, though, here they are:

DESCRIPTION

This subkey keeps track of which hardware devices are present. During the boot phase, the hardware-detection software creates entries under this key for every hardware device it can find. Note that it keeps track of ports, not devices on those ports; it will find a parallel printer port, but doesn't check to see what's attached to it. Disk controllers are an exception to this rule.

DEVICEMAP

DEVICEMAP links the list of which devices are present and the drivers that make them available to the system. Each driver starts up and attempts to take control of whatever device it controls. If the driver succeeds, it registers its ownership of the device in DEVICEMAP. This isn't much different from the human process of registering car titles at the county courthouse.

|NT4| *OWNERMAP*

This subkey ties bus devices to particular system buses. Many machines support multiple buses; e.g., PCI, ISA, EISA, or VLBus controllers can all coexist on a single machine. OWNERMAP registers which installed cards are attached to which buses.

RESOURCEMAP

As its name strongly suggests, RESOURCEMAP provides a map of what resources are available. To be more specific, it lists the IRQs, DMA port addresses, and bus controller slots supported by the hardware. Drivers choose from this list to reserve the resources they need; as they successfully claim hardware, they register which resources they're using here so other drivers won't try to use them too. The actual contents of this key are much different in Windows 2000 than in Windows NT; the 2000-specific version includes a new subkey for the Plug and Play manager.

SECURITY

The SECURITY subkey holds two important collections of data. First off, it caches the local copy of the Security Account Manager database in HKLM\SECURITY\SAM. This database is the foundation of all the system's access controls. Besides ACLs for every object that has permissions assigned to it, this subkey contains a roster of local or domain accounts and groups, since the ACLs grant permissions to groups and users. This subkey actually maps to a separate hive, and its data is normally readable only by kernel services that have the appropriate "need to know." The SAM data has been kept here since Windows NT 3.1 first shipped, although in Windows 2000 it's kept here only for backward compatibility and to support machines that aren't part of an Active Directory domain.

As you learned in the previous sidebar "User Profiles Demystified," NT 4.0 adds the capability to use user and group policies. These policies also live in subkeys of HKLM\SECURITY. These policies control what users can and can't do on the machine, ranging from small things like changing the desktop wallpaper to big things like rebooting servers or editing the Registry. The data in the SAM is encrypted, so you can't directly access or modify it. Instead, you need to use the System Policy Editor (as described in Chapter 6) to set profiles, which NT then loads automatically into this subkey when they're needed.

Not even the Administrator account has permission to open these subkeys. Even if you change the ownership rights on SECURITY or its hive so that your account can open it, you'll find that the data there is encrypted. Even if you manage to decrypt it, the data is in an undocumented format that probably won't do you any good. Don't despair, though: there are functions in the Win32 API you can use to create, read, and change security descriptors, permissions, and policies.

The HKLM\SAM subkey just points to HKLM\SECURITY\SAM; it's provided as a convenience for parts of the kernel that need access to the SAM data.

SOFTWARE

Applications and system components store their settings under subkeys of SOFTWARE. By convention, programs that keep things here are supposed to create subkeys using the program and/or vendor name, then put their settings underneath. HKLM\SOFTWARE\TechSmith\Snagit32 thus contains settings for TechSmith's SnagIt/32 screen-capture utility. Most of the operating-system components keep their systemwide settings under HKLM\SOFTWARE\Microsoft*ComponentName*. Settings that belong only to a single user are stored elsewhere. The exact contents of this subkey vary from machine to machine, depending on what software's installed. My best estimate is that about 80% of the time you spend viewing or editing the Registry will be spent in various subkeys of HKLM\SOFTWARE.

In particular, HKLM\Software\Microsoft\Windows NT holds most of the specific software configuration settings. In addition, there's a counterpart key named HKLM\Software\Microsoft\Windows that provides an equivalent to the Win95 key with the same name. The Windows 2000 shell (which, of course, is largely based on the Windows NT 4 shell's code) makes heavy use of this key for tracking where applications are installed and how they can be uninstalled when needed.

SOFTWARE\Policies. Group policy objects can store their settings in four distinct keys, three of which are under HKLM. Policy settings that are new for Windows 2000 (say, for instance, the setting that controls whether the user is forcibly logged off or not when her smartcard is removed) generally live under HKLM\Software\Policies. User-specific settings live in HKCU\Software\Policies.

What about the things you could set with the SPE from NT 4.0? Most of these settings were moved to the GPOs, which means you modify them through the Group Policy snap-in. In Windows NT they were stored under HKLM\Software\Microsoft\Windows\CurrentVersion or HKLM\Software\Microsoft\Windows NT\CurrentVersion; in Windows 2000, they're stored in a new subkey called Policies under one of those two keys. As you'll see later in the chapter, settings in the GPO can still be applied to the Registry, just as they are with the SPE.

SYSTEM

The SYSTEM subkey contains a potpourri of critical data. If HKLM is the most important part of the Registry, SYSTEM is its most important subkey. It has four subkeys that merit further discussion:

|NT4|
- The Disk subkey contains information stored by NT's Disk Administrator application: which drives have which drive letters, whether any drives are part of stripe or mirror sets, and so on. This information can later be used to help regenerate damaged disks or rebuild stripe and mirror sets if something goes *boom*. If you haven't run Disk Administrator on a machine, this subkey won't exist, and it doesn't exist on Windows 2000 machines.

- Subkeys exist for each *control set*. A control set is nothing more than a group of driver settings, hardware profile settings, and Registry entries; one control set is loaded every time the system boots. Since you can change drivers, hardware profiles, and other control-set elements, the kernel creates one control set subkey under HKLM\SYSTEM for each control set it sees. At a minimum, there will be two sets: one that you last used to boot, and the last one that successfully booted. This "last known good" set can be a lifesaver when things go wrong, as you'll see in Chapter 3. When you change control-set settings, Windows 2000 creates a new control set. The sets are named with a sequence number; ControlSet001 is first, followed by ControlSet002, ControlSet003, etc.

- The Select subkey remembers which control sets exist on the machine, which was the last known good set, and which was the last to cause a failed boot.

- The MountedDevices subkey is new for Windows 2000. It's used by the Logical Disk Manager, a new system component that gives Windows 2000 the ability to mount, unmount, format, and repartition disks on the fly, without rebooting. There are two kinds of values here: the first kind (of the form \??\Volume{*volID*}) lists all the known volumes, while the second kind (of the form \DosDevices*driveLetter*) ties known volumes to particular drive letters.

- The Setup subkey is Windows 2000's way of detecting whether it's in the middle of installation. When you install Windows 2000, it goes through a multi-step installation process; once the first step completes, the machine actually boots into a "light" version of the OS so *ntdetect* can do its work and map the hardware. If this phase fails, the machine is in limbo: Windows 2000 isn't completely installed, but its boot loader is. The boot loader checks the value of HKLM\Setup to see whether Setup was running when the machine was last booted; if so, it restarts the setup process.

SYSTEM\CurrentControlSet. CurrentControlSet is almost, but not quite, a link to whatever control set was used to boot the machine. The kernel copies the current control set (as pointed to by the SYSTEM\Select key) to the CurrentControlSet and Clone keys early in the boot process. System services, control panels, and well-behaved applications use CurrentControlSet instead of using a particular ControlSetXXX key, since it may move or even be deleted without the application's knowledge. The structure of CurrentControlSet is thus identical to any of the ControlSetXXX keys; for convenience, I'll describe it since that's the actual subtree NT uses while running:

- Control holds much of the system's configuration information. Among other things, subkeys of Control contain information about the time zone the machine's in (TimeZoneInformation), what directories contain Windows 2000 and its system files (Windows), and what the computer's network name is (ComputerName). These data are all static; the system loads them at startup. Though they can be changed, the changes don't normally take effect until the next time Windows 2000 boots. In Windows 2000, the Control subkey also contains a great deal of dynamically generated information. For example, the Control\PnP subkey lists the PCI cards and devices detected at the last boot.

- Enum contains information about the hardware devices found in the system during the boot phase. It has two subkeys: HTREE and ROOT. HTREE contains subkeys for those devices that were actually found, while ROOT contains subkeys for all devices that have installed drivers.

- In contrast to Control, Services holds configuration parameters for all of Windows 2000's services and kernel drivers. Some of these settings are new (such as the RemoteRegistry service and the smart-card server and client drivers), while others are left over from NT 4.0. When you add services, they typically add their own keys here as well.

- Hardware Profiles holds the hardware profile settings that appear in HKCC. At a minimum, there are two entries under this key: Current holds the current profile, and 0001 holds the default profile. If you define multiple profiles, the profits get new sequence numbers: 0002 is the second profile you define, 0003 the third, and so on. Each profile's key in turn contains its own copy of the CurrentControlSet key that matches the profile.

Major Subkeys of HKCU

The user profiles stored under HKCU are actually made up of data from ten major subkeys. Since the values under these keys control most of the environment and desktop settings that NT lets you customize, it's worth examining each of these subkeys.

AppEvents

The AppEvents subkey stores the mappings between system events (new mail arrived, window maximized, Windows logout, and so on) and sounds. You set these mappings with the Sound control panel; in addition to the system events, applications can define their own events (Visual C++ defines "compilation done"). When a listed event occurs, NT can look in HKCU\AppEvents and play the appropriate sound.

Console

Console stores the console window properties you set with the Console control panel or the "Command Line" Properties dialog available from the console window itself. When you change the default command-line window's size, position, buffer size, or font, those changes are stored here.

Control Panel

Control Panel doesn't directly store anything; instead, it's a placeholder for the system's control panels. Each control panel that wants to store persistent settings on a per-user basis can create its own subkey under HKU\Control Panel and use it however it wants. Control panels that manage systemwide settings, such as the Network and System panels, store their settings in subkeys of HKLM.

Environment

Environment holds the user-defined environment variables set in the Environment Variables dialog (triggered by the button of the same name on the System control panel's Advanced tab). Systemwide environment variables are kept in HKLM\System\CurrentControlSet\Control\Session Manager\Environment.* Interestingly, when you make changes to the user-environment variables, the changes don't take effect until you log off and back on, but changes to the system's environment variables take effect immediately (though applications that use environment settings may need to be restarted to pick up the changes).

Identities

If you're using Outlook Express or MSN Messenger, the Identities subkey contains subkeys for each mailbox or message recipient identity. This allows multiple users to share an Outlook Express installation, keeping each individual "personality" separate from the others.

Keyboard Layout

Keyboard Layout retains the user's preferred keyboard layout. If you're used to the standard U.S. English layout you may not know that, like the Mac, Windows 2000 supports international keyboards whose layouts are different from the standard QWERTY layout. For example, the standard French keyboard's upper row starts with AZERTY. Windows 2000 needs to know the physical layout of the keyboard so it can map keystrokes to the appropriate character codes, especially since you can switch between input locales on the fly.

Printers

The Printers key has two subkeys. Settings stores the user's default print settings, including the name of the default printer and whatever page-setup parameters the user has set. Connections contains one subkey for each installed printer to which the current user can print. If no printers have been defined, this key is either empty or missing, since Windows 2000 creates it the first time a printer's created. Once a printer's been defined, a new subkey named after the print server and printer (for example, ARMORY,HP5M Postscript) appears under Connections. The new subkey's values store the name of the printer driver DLL used with the printer and the name of the print server (if any) that shares the printer to other users.

Remote Access

This subkey holds settings used by the Dial-Up Networking system.

---

* Okay, you caught me; they're *really kept* in HKLM\System\ControlSetXXX.

Software

Software, like Control Panel, is a placeholder for a set of subkeys. The exact list of subkeys varies, since any software vendor can create program-specific keys. Applications are supposed to use HKCU\Software for user-specific settings (such as the location of private mail folders) and keep their systemwide settings in HKLM\Software; however, many applications don't have any systemwide settings, so they keep everything under HKCU\Software.

SYSTEM

It might seem that HKCU and HKLM\SYSTEM would mix about as well as motor oil and Perrier. Normally, that's true; however, Windows 2000 allows users to set some per-user options that override settings that usually live in HKLM. For example, the spiffy new Windows 2000 Backup utility lets you specify which files *not* to back up; if you override the default settings for a particular user, HKCU\SYSTEM\CurrentControlSet\Control\BackupRestore\FilesNotToBackup contains that user's list of files to be excluded. Likewise, other applications and components can store settings in HKCU\SYSTEM if they override corresponding settings somewhere in HKLM.

It turns out that this subkey exists only when an application (such as Windows 2000 Backup) creates it. A brand-new 2000 installation doesn't have this key.

Other

UNICODE Program Groups holds program group settings from previous versions of NT installed on the machine. This key is always present, but on machines that have never had a pre-4.0 version of NT, it is empty. On machines that have been upgraded from NT 3.x to NT 4.0, it contains information about the defined user and system Program Manager groups, but the key's main purpose under NT 4.0 is as a placeholder for backward compatibility.

The Volatile Environment key stores per-user environment settings that change between logon sessions. The only key NT 4.0 routinely creates here is LogonServer, which points to the computer that validated the user's logon.

On Windows NT systems that were upgraded from Windows 3.x, there is a Windows 3.1 Migration Status subkey under HKCU. This subkey, which is also present on NT machines upgraded from Windows 3.x to NT to Windows 2000, stores the contents of the original *REG.INI* file, as well as assorted settings from other INI files. NT can automatically map INI files to sections in the Registry, making it possible for 16-bit applications to automatically use the Registry without being rewritten. (For more information on building your own mappings, see the section "Using Initialization File Mapping" in Chapter 9.)

Major Subkeys of HKCC

HKCC was originally introduced in Windows 95, and it appeared in NT 4.0 strictly to allow Win95 applications that use HKCC to run under NT. Windows NT and 2000 both support the concept of multiple hardware profiles; a profile is just a small set of Registry keys that define the hardware available to the computer. The most often-cited example for which hardware profiles are useful is that of a laptop. Let's say you buy a fancy laptop and a docking station, then install Windows 2000 on it. You can use the laptop in three configurations:

- At your office, plugged into the docking station. You can use your docking station's display adapter and Ethernet card, and you have access to DNS, DHCP, and WINS servers for your intranet.
- On the road, with a PC Card modem to give you dial-up access to your intranet. In this mode, you need drivers for the modem and Dial-Up Networking, and you need different settings for all your network software. You also don't want the drivers for your docking station loaded.
- In the field, where you have no net access (well, you could use a satellite phone, but at $6/minute let's just stick with the "no access" plan).

Each configuration can be stored as a unique hardware profile. When you boot Windows 2000, you can tell it which one to use, and Windows 2000 loads the appropriate drivers and settings. All the machine's hardware profiles are stored in the Hardware Profiles subkey of control sets under the HKLM\System tree. More importantly, system components and applications that are savvy enough to know about HKCC can query it to see what kind of hardware is currently installed.

HKCC contains two subkeys: Software and System\CurrentControlSet. These are sufficient to store the individual profile settings; as you learned earlier in the chapter, CurrentControlSet actually stores driver settings. In addition, HKCC stores the settings that are different from the default. If you use a profile that adds devices not present in the default profile, they are added in HKCC and merged with the default set.

What About the Other Root Keys?

At this point, you might be wondering why this chapter doesn't discuss the major subkeys of HKCR, HKPD, and HKU. The real reason is that none of these root keys has any particularly interesting subkeys under them! HKPD is opaque and can't be browsed. HKCR has many subkeys, each of which has the same format and similar contents, and it's only a link to portions of HKLM\Software\Classes anyway. Finally, HKU's structure and contents are described earlier in this chapter in the section titled "Major Subkeys of HKCU." The subkeys discussed in that section are the real meat of the Registry; for more details on individual subkeys not covered here, see Chapter 11.

One interesting difference in Windows 2000 is that class data is split between HKCR and HKCU\Classes, at least from the OS' point of view. Users and applications, though, see a single seamless set of class registrations because Windows 2000 merges HKCR and HKCU\Classes so that a query under HKCR actually queries both of them.

Getting Data In and Out

There are several ways to move data into and out of the Registry; which one you use depends on what you're trying to accomplish and the amount of time you're willing to spend. Each of them is covered in more detail in later chapters.

First of all, you can make direct calls to the Win32 Registry API routines. At bottom, this is what all the other methods eventually do; the OS' security components and the undocumented internal format of the hive files ensure that the only way to load data is to use these routines. The basic process is fairly simple: you start by opening a key or subkey by its name. Once you've done so, you can do things to that key or its subkeys: you can query its value, create new subkeys beneath it, or even ask about its security settings. You can continue to use that particular key until you're done it, at which time you must close it again. Here's a small sample that shows these steps in action; it gets the computer's network name and uses it to print a welcome message. You'll learn more about programming for the Registry in C (as in this example) in the section titled "Programming with C/C++" in Chapter 8.

```c
// Hello, World! for the Registry: gets this machine's name and prints
// it out.
#include <windows.h>
#include <winreg.h>
#include <stdio.h>

void main(void)
{
   unsigned char lpName[MAX_PATH] = "";
   DWORD nNameLen = MAX_PATH;
   HKEY hkResult, hStartKey = HKEY_LOCAL_MACHINE;
   LONG nResult = ERROR_SUCCESS;

    nResult = RegOpenKeyEx(hStartKey,
            "SYSTEM\\CurrentControlSet\\Control\\ComputerName",
            0L, KEY_READ, &hkResult);
   if (ERROR_SUCCESS == nResult)
   {
         nResult = RegQueryValueEx(hkResult, "ActiveComputerName", 0, 0,
                                   lpName, &nNameLen);
```

```
            if (ERROR_SUCCESS == nResult)
                printf("Hello, world, from %s!", lpName);
    }
    RegCloseKey(hkResult);
}
```

The next step up the evolutionary ladder of Registry access is to use a library or language that removes you from direct contact with the Registry API routines. Depending on your needs and inclinations, there are several ways to accomplish this:

- If you're using Visual Basic or Delphi, you can use a third-party library such as Desaware's Registry Control for Visual Basic (*http://www.desaware.com*). These libraries typically wrap several API calls into one, so you can more easily perform the typical find-query-close cycle by making a single call. The Desaware control is covered at length in Chapter 7 of *Inside the Windows 95 Registry*.

    In addition, Microsoft makes available another package that simplifies Registry handling from Delphi and VB: see *http://www.microsoft.com/vbasic/downloads/download.asp?ID=026*.

- The Win32 version of the Perl programming language includes a number of features that ease access to Registry data from Perl programs. Besides wrapping the find-query-close cycle for you, they make it easy to enumerate and search keys and quickly put the results into associative arrays. You'll see how to harness these features in the section titled "Programming with Perl" in Chapter 8. For a complete treatment of Win32 Perl, see *Learning Perl on Win32 Systems* by Randal L. Schwartz, Erik Olson, and Tom Christiansen (O'Reilly & Associates).

- The Windows Scripting Host (WSH) provides a module called the Windows Management Instrumentation (WMI); WMI provides a rash of Registry calls you can use from within your WSH scripts.

- The Windows 2000 Resource Kit includes a tool called *REGINI.EXE* that allows you to load text files of settings into the Registry. This is a handy and fast way to take a predefined set of data and jam it into the Registry; best of all, you can easily use *REGINI* to automate the process of loading Registry data into many different machines. Note that this tool works fine under Windows 2000, even though it's not included in the resource kit.

The final layer of Registry editing and spelunking revolves around using Registry editors. In addition to *RegEdt32* and *RegEdit*, there are a number of freeware and shareware alternatives floating around.

3

In Case of Emergency

By now, you've probably gotten the impression that working with the Registry is serious business. *How* serious it can be may not become apparent until the first time one of your Windows 2000 machines stops working because of a problem with the Registry. This stoppage may be slight—say, Office 2000 stops working—or it may be profound, resulting in the Blue Screen of Death or a lockup before the logon dialog appears.

Either way, this chapter will teach you two things: how to prepare for that eventuality, and how to recover from it smoothly when it does happen. If you're wondering why this chapter is here instead of further back in the book, the reason is simple. It's a very good idea for you to know how to restore your Registry *before* you learn how to edit it.

Don't Panic!

Scaring people is often a good way to get their attention. For example, you may have had to suffer through intentionally vivid films of auto accidents in drivers' education class; the rationale behind this kind of shock treatment is to blast the viewer out of his comfortable "it won't happen to me" mindset. This tactic is often effective, but, when exaggerated, it can backfire.

Instead, ask yourself a question. "Self, what would happen if my Windows 2000 machines were abducted by aliens?" Just think: all your hardware, and the data it contains, gone in a heartbeat. Sure, it's easy to disregard the risk of hardware failure, fire, theft, or Registry corruption—that won't happen to *you*—but aliens? Look what happened to Elvis.[*]

---

[*] He's still alive, you know, although thankfully no one's sent me any recent sighting reports.

Instead of panicking and running out into the streets like people do in alien-invasion movies, wouldn't it be nice if you could lean back in your chair and smile, knowing that your Registry data could easily be restored without breaking a sweat? There's nothing like that state of calmness that comes from having a known good backup of your critical data, and that's why I encourage you to read, and heed, the material in the rest of the chapter. Don't panic, but don't fall asleep, either.

Safety Strategies

The first step towards effectively preparing yourself to handle Registry problems is to adopt some strategies to safeguard your data. There are a number of fascinating books about the minutiae of planning for disaster recovery, but this isn't one of them, so I'll leave it to you to find out about off-site backups, fire suppression, and the other facets of preparing to deal with catastrophic failures. If you want to read more on this subject, check out the free (and very scary) Disaster Recovery Journal (*http://www.drj.com*). Instead, I'll present two simple concepts that will save your bacon if you implement them. While they're targeted at helping you recover from Registry failures, you can also apply them to other situations that might render your Windows 2000 machines (or any others, really) unusable or unavailable.

Make Backups

The cardinal rule of data protection is *don't depend on a single copy of your data!* Of course, this rule is usually observed in the breach. You'd probably be surprised at the number of experienced administrators who make sure to back up data on all machines on the network, then forget to back up their own personal workstation! As you'll see in the later section, "Backing Up the Registry," there are several ways to duplicate the Registry's contents. Whichever you choose, though, the following four principles will make sure your backup strategy works for you, instead of leading you into a false sense of security:

Make regular backups

If you back up data only at irregular intervals, you run the risk of losing an indeterminate amount of data. Ask yourself this: if you had to reload your Registry tomorrow from the most recent backup, how recent would it be? Would it reflect all the configuration and user account changes you've made since that last backup? (Hint: as often as the Registry's contents change, the most likely answer is probably a rueful "no.")

Only you know how frequently your Registry data changes, so only you know how often to back it up. Remember that every change to the domain or local SAM database—including adding or removing accounts, changing the default profile, changing account policies in the User Manager, or modifying any local or global groups in a Windows NT domain—is actually a change to the Registry. On top of these changes, installing or removing any Windows 2000 component can cause changes, as can installing or removing applications.

However often things change, establish a consistent schedule and stick to it. Since Windows 2000 includes an easy-to-use frontend for scheduling tasks, you no longer have an excuse not to be making regular backups. You can probably schedule Registry backups in parallel with other scheduled maintenance actions. I know of several sites that schedule software installations and major account changes twice weekly; that night, they back up the new changes. At worst, they lose no more than the previous update's changes.

Make sure your backup software is working

There aren't many feelings that compare to the despair of trying to reload data from a backup and finding that the data is missing or unusable. Oops. To prevent this, you should make a regular habit of inspecting the data that is actually sitting on your backup media. Make sure that the backups contain everything that should have been backed up, and that the modification and update times are reasonable.

If you're using conventional backup software, you can check to make sure the files named in the section "But What Needs Backing Up?" later in this chapter are actually making it onto the backup media. If you're building an emergency repair disk (ERD), you can check the timestamps on the files to make sure they correspond to your expectations.

As a practice measure, one day when you're feeling brave, go out and find a scratch machine somewhere on your network. Back up its Registry using your preferred method, then intentionally damage it and see whether you can restore it. *Be sure not to do this on a production machine*, but be sure to do it. Experience is the best reassurance, and if you're comfortable with the process of restoring a damaged Registry you'll be much less stressed when the time comes to do it for real.

Don't leave anyone out

Your backup plan needs to include every machine that's important. At a minimum, make sure you're backing up all your Windows 2000 servers, especially domain controllers and any other machine whose presence and function are critical to your network. If you have special-purpose servers running software such as Microsoft Exchange Server, Lotus Notes or Domino servers, or Netscape's server products, make sure you include them as well, since server products like these often make exceptionally heavy use of the Registry for their own settings.

User workstations present a slightly different kettle of fish. If every user has her own workstation, you probably need to back them all up. If all users share a pool of workstations, and your network is set up to use roaming profiles, you may be able to slip by without backing up the Registry data of pool machines. If one crashes, you have to reload whatever software was on the machine to restore its installation entries in the Registry, but the user account and profile data are transparently restored by Windows 2000 as users log in.

Make sure your backups reflect recent changes
Even if you make regular backups, you still need to keep your ERD up to date. In Windows NT 4.0, the ERD contains the local machine's SAM database and portions of HKLM and HKU. In Windows 2000, the ERD contains information the operating system can use to repair a damaged Windows 2000 installation, but no Registry data. That means that you have to unlearn the old NT 4.0 habit of relying on the ERD as a Registry backup.

The *RDISK* utility (which you'll learn how to use later in this chapter) displays a message telling you not to depend on ERDs as a backup tool. This is good advice; an ERD should be part of your backup plan, not a substitute for one.

This leads me to another general principle: make backups when things change. For example, one network administrator I know instituted a strict policy of updating ERDs and Registry backups before installing prerelease or beta versions of any web browser. To her delight, this strategy saved her a significant amount of trouble when the browser's installers misbehaved and damaged the Registry.

Be Prudent

"Fools rush in where angels fear to tread." When Alexander Pope said so in 1711, he wasn't talking about Windows 2000, but his words apply, in spades, to working with the Windows 2000 Registry, since it represents a potential single point of failure that can render your whole machine unusable if you make a mistake while editing it.

The best defense against this sort of mistake is simple: abstinence! However, it's not always possible to avoid editing the Registry yourself; some settings and parameters aren't editable anywhere else. Here's how you can exercise maximum prudence to guard yourself against Registry mishaps:

Practice random acts of self-restraint
A wise man named Mitch Ratliffe once opined that computers allow people to make mistakes faster than any invention other than handguns and tequila. You

should keep that thought in mind whenever the temptation to edit the Registry enters your mind. *Don't* change a value just to see what it will do when changed; if you want to know what a particular key does, look it up in Chapter 11, *The Registry Documented*, instead of tweaking it to see what breaks.

In the same vein, don't remove keys or their values unless you've previously uninstalled the software that uses those values. You may be certain that no one needs the data in HKLM\Software\SomeVendor\SurfWriter, but it's generally not wise to test your certainty by arbitrarily whacking the whole subkey to see what happens. Instead, you can use the *REGCLEAN* utility (provided with Microsoft's Developer Studio, Visual Basic, and Visual C++ products, or at *ftp://ftp.microsoft.com/softlib/mslfiles/regcln41.exe*) to automatically clear out any superfluous entries in HKCR. You're on your own for clearing out other keys and values in other root keys.

Many people still have REGCLEAN Version 4.1. This version is dangerous under Windows NT and Windows 2000; make sure you get Version 4.1a or later if you want to use it.

Practice safe security

Of course, self-restraint is a virtue, but so is good security. You can think of it as a way to help others have self-restraint when it comes to your data. Make sure you follow the suggestions for choosing appropriate Registry permissions and auditing settings in Chapter 9, *Administering the Registry*.

[NT4] In particular, if you choose to enable *SYSKEY* protection on a Windows NT 4.0 computer (as described in "Adding Registry ACLs to Group Policy Objects" in Chapter 9), make sure you pay careful attention to the description of what you must do to restore a *SYSKEY*-protected Registry. Remember that *SYSKEY* is always on for Windows 2000 machines!

Use the scientific method

Sometimes there actually are good reasons for editing Registry values. Microsoft's Knowledge Base (*http://support.microsoft.com*) is chock-full of articles that explain how to tweak normally invisible Windows 2000 and NT parameters. These settings are often worth changing for security, performance, or bandwidth-related reasons; however, it can be hard to tell whether making the changes will work well for you or not.

If possible, set aside a machine or two on your network for experimenting with these sorts of seemingly necessary changes. Doing so gives you a safe area to make changes, then study their effects, without compromising any of your production machines. If the changes have the desired effect, you can always add them to more machines when it's convenient; if, by chance, they turn out to be detrimental, you don't have a long list of user or server machines to fix.

Consider buying better tools

Neither of the Registry editors provided with Windows 2000 support an "undo" function, and neither of them log what changes were made during an editing session. While word processor, CAD, spreadsheet, and other "productivity" applications have had both of these features for years, they haven't made the leap into Microsoft's OS development group. There's good news and bad news to report. First the good news: there are other third-party editors that allow you to undo changes at any time, even if you've already applied them. The bad news: they cost money. Consider Symantec's Norton Utilities for NT (available from *http://www.symantec.com/*). For its US$100 or so purchase cost, you get a Registry editor that combines many of the features included in *RegEdit* and *RegEdt32* with a robust undo capability. As it turns out, you can use the Norton Registry Editor under Windows 2000, too, by installing it on Windows 9x or Windows NT, then copying the needed files to your Windows 2000 machine. If $100 is too rich for your blood, you can instead use the shareware *RegView* and *RegView Pro* applications (available from *http://www.xnet.com/~vchiu/regview.shtml*), which runs fine under NT and Windows 2000 and offers its own undo facility.

Jerry Honeycutt created an *.INF* file that allows you to install and use the Windows NT version of Norton Registry Editor with Windows 2000. It's available from *http://www.robichaux.net/files/nre-install.inf*.

All About Emergency Repair Disks

The very phrase "emergency repair disk" sounds ominous, like something the crew aboard the ill-fated *Mir* space station might keep close at hand. In fact, the ERD (as it's usually called) is a terrific insurance policy that can protect you from a number of potential Registry mishaps, up to and including losing the password to your Administrator account. However, ERDs won't do you any good unless you keep them up to date; you must also be careful to keep close physical control over them, since they contain a good bit of sensitive data that could potentially make it easier to compromise a machine.

Remember, ERDs can be used only to repair the Registry under Windows NT, not Windows 2000. If you've migrated to Windows 2000, you can (and should) still make ERDs using Windows 2000 Backup, but you don't use them to repair the Registry.

What Is an ERD?

An ERD is nothing more than a FAT-formatted* floppy containing a subset of data needed to recover some of the system's configuration. A Windows NT ERD includes data from several Registry hives; when you create an ERD, you're actually making a backup copy of the Registry's most essential data in a form that Windows NT can directly use to replace damaged or missing keys. Windows 2000 ERDs don't include this Registry data, but you get the same functionality by backing up Windows 2000 Registry data using the Windows 2000 Backup application and storing it on a floppy or other backup media.

Both the Windows 2000 and NT ERDs keep copies of additional useful data:

- The configuration files used to run DOS and Win16 programs (*autoexec.nt* and *config.nt*).

- A copy of the current setup log file, *setup.log*. This file tracks the list of files installed during Windows 2000's setup phase, including a checksum; this log file enables setup, repair, service pack, and hotfix installers to know whether they're replacing the right files or not.

[NT4]
- The default user profile for the machine, normally stored in *ntuser.dat*.

ERDs created under Windows NT contain copies of the SAM, SECURITY, DEFAULT, SOFTWARE, and SYSTEM hives. This data comes from the *%systemroot%\repair* directory, which is usually updated as part of the process of generating an ERD. To get the same functionality under Windows 2000, you can copy these files yourself, use a batch file or script to do it, or use Windows 2000 Backup, as described later in the chapter.

From now on, when I talk about ERDs I'll assume you're building them with the *rdisk* tool under Windows NT or using one of the methods described above under Windows 2000. The important thing is that you have one at all.

---

* Because the ERD is a FAT filesystem, it doesn't have access controls. Be sure to safeguard your Windows NT 4.0 ERDs as sensitive material, since they can contain SAM data.

Wherever this data is, it's specific to a particular machine, so you can generally use it to repair only the machine it originally came from. To be more exact, if you take the emergency repair data from one machine on another, portions of the target machine's Registry will be summarily replaced with the repair data's contents. In the case of the SAM database and large chunks of HKLM, this can render the machine unusable.

When you back up Registry data under Windows 2000, what format the hives end up in depends on how you do it. If you just copy the files from the *repair* directory, you can load them with *RegEdt32*. If you use Windows 2000 Backup, you'll probably have a *.bkf* file that can be read only with the backup tool. Registry files on a Windows NT ERD are compressed, so you can't directly modify or view them; in all other respects, they're ordinary files, so you can back them up, archive them, or copy them to other media without uncompressing them.

 When you build an ERD under NT 4.0, you're making a snapshot of the Registry's contents at that point in time. Any changes you make after building the ERD won't be preserved, which is why it's so important to keep your ERDs up to date. For example, if you make an ERD for a machine, then change its Administrator account password, the ERD will contain the old password. If you ever use the ERD, you'll find the password set back to its old value—which you may no longer remember!

 By default, the ERD you build while installing Windows NT contains the original SAM created when NT is installed. You must use the /s switch (see the section "Using NT's RDISK utility" later in this chapter) to force RDISK to back up the current SAM data instead.

What ERDs Can and Can't Do

Windows 2000 ERDs can't restore any Registry data, but you can use them to restore system configuration settings. On the other hand, a Windows NT ERD can restore data for any of the hives it has backed up: *S*AM, SECURITY, DEFAULT, SOFTWARE, and SYSTEM. When you reapply ERD data to a system, you are generally restoring data on a wholesale basis, so the entire contents of a hive are replaced with the ERD's copy.

When you restore a Windows 2000 Registry by using the system's recovery console, you can copy only entire hive files, so you can replace any or all of the individual hives. When running Windows NT setup, its repair application allows you to choose which hives to replace, but not which individual values to update.

In either case, applying ERD data requires you be able to boot your machine. To use the Microsoft-provided repair utilities for 2000 or NT, you need your original bootable installation CD. If you prefer, you can install the Windows 2000 recovery console so that it is available when you need it, but you have to do this before you need it.*

Applying a Windows NT ERD takes all the data in that section of the Registry back to *status quo ante*: all changes you've made since the ERD was created will be lost. As long as you keep your ERDs reasonably up to date, this shouldn't be a problem, especially since many applications and components are now smart enough to recognize when their Registry entries are missing and will recreate them when needed.

As useful as the ERD is, it's not magical. First of all, it can't restore what's not on it; you must keep your ERDs up to date if you want them to be available to you at crunch time. Secondly, the Windows NT ERD doesn't store anything in HKU (or HKCU, for that matter) except *ntuser.dat*, so it doesn't preserve user-specific settings. It also doesn't restore all of HKLM\SOFTWARE, so be alert to the fact that application installations and user preferences in your Registry won't be preserved by the ERD. If you copy all the hive files when you're making your Windows 2000 ERD, you won't have this problem.

How to Make an ERD

Making an ERD is pretty simple. Both Windows 2000 and NT include utilities that do most of the work for you. However, if you want to create a repair disk that contains Registry information under Windows 2000, you have some additional work to do.

Using Windows 2000 Backup

The Windows 2000 Backup utility was completely rewritten, so it looks a lot different from its NT predecessor. It does the same things as Windows NT Backup, but it has a ton of new functionality, including the ability to back up files to disk or CD-R/CD-RW. It incorporates the function of the *RDISK* tool, too (as described in the next section), so you can use one tool to back up the Registry and create an ERD. The Windows 2000 Backup utility is discussed more fully in the section "Using Windows 2000 Backup" later in the chapter, so for now I'll confine my discussion to the process of creating an ERD.

---

* You install the recovery console by running *winnt32.exe* with the /cmdcons switch. That instructs the setup program to modify the boot loader and add the recovery console as a choice during the boot process.

When you launch Windows 2000 Backup, you see the Welcome screen, shown in Figure 3-1. To create an ERD, you can either click the Emergency Repair Disk button on this screen or use the Tools → Create an Emergency Repair Disk command.

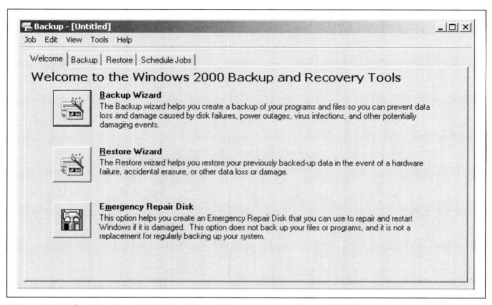

Figure 3-1. The Windows 2000 backup welcome screen, from which you can create an ERD

When you tell Windows 2000 Backup to create an ERD by either method, you see a very simple dialog, as shown in Figure 3-2. Note that this dialog doesn't say anything about putting Registry data onto the repair floppy; that's because it does no such thing. You can, however, use the "Also backup the registry in the repair directory" checkbox to force Windows 2000 Backup to copy the hive files to the *%systemroot%\repair* directory, as I mentioned earlier. What do you do with the files once they're in that directory? For starters, you can use Windows 2000 Backup itself to make a backup copy; you can also copy the files to another computer via the network, onto a removable disk, or onto a CD-R or CD-RW.

NT4 *Using NT's RDISK utility*

RDISK.EXE is a fairly simple application to use; its main window is shown in Figure 3-3. As you can see, there are only two useful things you can do with *RDISK*; each of the four buttons in the window controls a single function of the utility. The Help and Exit buttons do what you'd expect, so I won't discuss them here.

The Update Repair Info button does just that: it makes a private copy of the data described earlier and stores it on your hard disk. NT's setup utility can use this

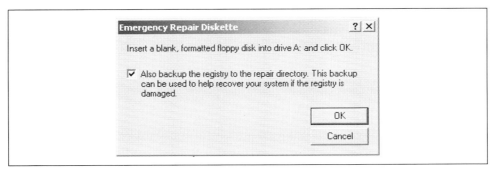

Figure 3-2. The ERD dialog

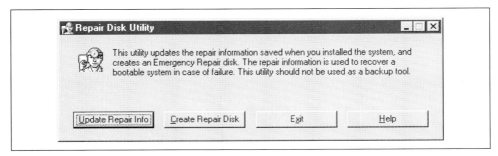

Figure 3-3. The RDISK utility

data to try to repair some parts of a damaged installation without having an ERD available. When the update is complete, you see the dialog shown in Figure 3-4, which allows you to create an ERD immediately or defer it until later.

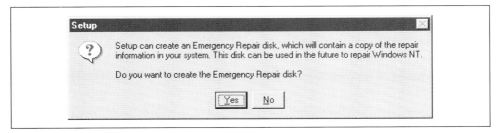

Figure 3-4. Generating an ERD with RDISK

 While you might be tempted to copy *RDISK* from an NT machine onto a Windows 2000 machine, don't give in to temptation: it won't work.

Clicking Yes in this dialog generates an ERD, while clicking No (as you'd expect) does nothing. You may notice that the dialog shown in Figure 3-4 is titled Setup; there's a good reason for it, namely that NT's setup executable uses the same dialog to ask if you want to build an ERD during installation. It's a good idea to build an ERD when you install NT on a machine, then file it away in a safe place so you can use it if the Administrator account password for the machine is ever lost or forgotten. This works because the original ERD contains whatever Administrator password you chose during the NT install process. However, remember that applying that ERD resets all the Registry data to the state it was in when you made the ERD, not just the administrator password.

You can also kick off *RDISK* with two switches. `/s` has exactly the same effect as starting *RDISK* and clicking "Update Repair Info"; it copies the contents of the security and SAM hives to the floppy. If you instead use the `/s-` switch, that starts *RDISK* and copies the repair files into the *REPAIR* subdirectory without prompting you to insert a floppy disk. This latter switch is extremely useful for automating or scheduling Registry backups.

You actually create an ERD with the Create Repair Disk command, or by choosing Yes in the dialog presented after you use the Update Repair Info button. *RDISK* asks you to insert a formatted floppy (but not without warning you that its contents will be erased). Once you've inserted the floppy and clicked OK, *RDISK* creates an ERD by copying the system's copy of the repair files to the floppy. When the ERD's done building, you can pop out the floppy and put it in a safe place.

If you use the `/s` switch, the ERD will contain a complete copy of the source machine's SAM and security data. This data is much sought after, since it can be run through a password cracker like *l0phtcrack* and used to find weak passwords that can then be used to enter your system. Treat ERDs as sensitive material and keep them away from public scrutiny.

How to Repair Your Registry with an ERD

An ERD won't do you any good unless you can apply its data to a machine when needed. Depending on what's wrong with the machine you're trying to repair, you may be able to boot it or not. Which repair tack you take depends on whether or not you can boot the machine and log on with an account that has Administrator privileges.

|NT4| There's one caveat I need to share before we start talking turkey: NT ERD floppies are compressed using Microsoft's standard compression tool. You've

undoubtedly seen files whose extension ended with an underscore, like those on the NT distribution CD. These files are compressed with Microsoft's tool, as are the ERD files. To manually restore data from these files, you need a copy of *EXPAND.EXE*, Microsoft's utility for expanding these compressed files. You probably have a copy sitting around somewhere on your disk, or perhaps on one of your Microsoft product CDs. Make sure you have it handy before starting a manual ERD restore. In fact, make sure you have a recent copy of *EXPAND.EXE*; older versions can't handle NT 4.0's compression format.

Using the Windows 2000 setup utility

I've mentioned several times that a Windows 2000 ERD doesn't contain any Registry data, but the *repair* directory does, and (in conjunction with the ERD) you can use the Windows 2000 setup utility to repair a damaged Registry. To do this, boot with the Windows 2000 CD (or boot floppies, if you've made a set). When the setup program asks whether you want to install Windows 2000 or repair an existing installation, select the repair option and provide the ERD when prompted. Setup then asks you to choose a repair mode: fast or manual.

In fast mode, the setup program uses the files in the *repair* directory to repair the Registry. It also fixes the boot sector, the boot loader, the startup environment, and any system files that need repair. In manual mode, you get to choose which items the system attempts to repair, but repairing the Registry is not one of your choices! That means you can't rely on manual mode to save your bacon if you have a Registry problem; it's either fast mode or one of the other repair methods described in the rest of this section.

Using the Windows 2000 recovery console

One of the best new features in Windows 2000 is its recovery console. The console offers you a limited command shell you can boot into; all told, it offers about 25 commands to do things such as repair the partition table, copy files hither and yon, or enable or disable system services. One of the things you can do is copy files. Assuming you have someplace to copy them from, you can quickly repair any individual hive file using this method. Figure 3-5 shows a sample of what this might look like.

Of course, for this approach to work you have to have the console available. There are two ways to start the console at boot time. One is to use the Windows 2000 setup CD (or boot floppies). When you boot using either of these media, you have to let the initial part of the boot sequence complete. Eventually, the setup program will ask whether you want to repair an existing installation or start a new one. Choose the repair option, then specify that you want to use the recovery console instead of the ERD. Why? Because the Windows 2000 ERD enables setup to

All About Emergency Repair Disks

```
Microsoft Windows 2000(TM) Recovery Console.

The Recovery Console provides system repair and recovery functionality.

Type EXIT to quit the Recovery Console and restart the computer.

1: C:\WINNT

Which Windows 2000 installation would you like to log onto
(To cancel, press ENTER)? 1
Type the Administrator password: ********
C:\WINNT>dir temp
 The volume in drive C has no label
 The volume Serial Number is 94b6-0a13

 Directory of C:\WINNT\temp

11/11/99  07:16a   d--------            0 .
11/11/99  07:16a   d--------            0 ..
11/11/99  12:54p   -a-------      5840896 software
        3 file(s)      5840896 bytes
                     210993152 bytes free

C:\WINNT>copy temp\software system32\software
Overwrite software? (Yes/No/All): y
        1 file(s) copied.

C:\WINNT>
```

Figure 3-5. A recovery console session

scan for missing or downlevel files; it doesn't do anything to the Registry. Once the console comes up, you can use the *copy* command to copy any hive file to the *system32* directory, then reboot the machine. (The second way to start the console is to use the boot-selection menu, but this only works if you've already installed the recovery console.)

The recovery console is a pretty blunt implement. There's no way to selectively reload individual keys or values, and (as of this writing) there's no way to extend the recovery console by adding arbitrary executables. However, when something drastic is wrong, you can often fix it using the provided tools.

Unlike Windows NT, Windows 2000 doesn't come with its own set of bootable installation floppies; you need to make a set with the *makebt32.exe* utility, found in the *bootdisk* directory on the distribution CD.

Using RegEdt32

If you can successfully boot the operating system and log into a privileged account, restoring data from an ERD is easy to do with *RegEdt32*. First, you have to find the ERD hive file you want to restore from.

NT4 You then have to uncompress the hive file if it originally came from an NT 4.0 ERD. *EXPAND.EXE* takes two arguments: the source filename and its destination name. Since hive files don't have extensions, you shouldn't specify one for the output name. Here's an example:

```
expand default._ default-save.
```

Next, launch *RegEdt32*. Depending on what you're trying to restore, now is when you'll have to make some choices. If you want to reload data that was accidentally deleted, or that you need to refer to, without overwriting an existing hive, you can load the hive from your ERD into a new subkey of HKLM or HKU by using the Registry → Load Hive... command. If you want to load the ERD data and replace the existing hive, you need to use the Registry → Restore... command. Both commands are documented more fully in the "Using RegEdt32 and RegEdit" section later in this chapter.

Using NT's setup application

Sometimes your only hope of restoring a downed NT machine is to restore all or part of the Registry from an ERD by using NT's setup program. This last-chance restoration is the original reason for the ERD, and there are times when nothing else will do the trick.

This scheme works because of the way NT's setup process works. NT's installer proceeds in three separate phases. In the first phase, NT copies just enough of the NT kernel and its support drivers and infrastructure to your hard disk. It then reboots into NT, using the newly made skeleton copy of NT and proceeds with the "blue screen" portion of the setup process. It's at this point that you can tell Setup you're repairing an existing NT installation. If you're not doing a repair, the third phase begins after another reboot; that's the familiar Windows GUI portion of the installation.

To get the ball rolling, you need to get NT setup started. If you have the original boot floppies and CD, you can use them; otherwise, if you have Windows 3.1, DOS, or Windows 95 installed (with appropriate CD drivers), you can boot it and run the setup program from the CD. Once you've done so, the first install phase completes, then your machine reboots. When it does, you can tell Setup whether you want to repair an existing installation (you do) or perform a complete installation. When you select the repair option, the setup installer asks you which hives you want to restore (SYSTEM, SECURITY, SOFTWARE, DEFAULT, and USERS are your choices). Once you've chosen, you are prompted to provide the ERD and the saved hives are restored. After the restoration's complete, you can reboot.

Backing Up the Registry

You probably remember from the "Hives and Files" section of Chapter 2, *Registry Nuts and Bolts*, that each hive of the Registry is stored in a separate file. While it might seem reasonable to assume that you can just back up these files as though they were Word documents or some other innocuous file, the harsh reality is that you can't. The NT kernel always keeps the Registry data files open, so ordinary backup software won't be able to back them up. However, there are ways to successfully duplicate the files for safekeeping; we explore three ways in the remainder of this section.

But What Needs Backing Up?

In Chapter 2 you learned that the Registry's made up of several hives, which are actually files that live on your disk. They're normally stored in the *System32\Config* subdirectory of your system volume; you can always find the correct location by examining the value of HKLM\SYSTEM\Control\CurrentControlSet\hivelist.

If you change to *System32\Config* (or wherever your files are) and get a directory listing, you'll see five files whose names match the hives listed in Table 2-1: DEFAULT, SAM, SECURITY, SOFTWARE, and SYSTEM. (The other hives, SID and HARDWARE, aren't stored here.) The hive files themselves don't have extensions on them, but there are other files with the same names that do have extensions. Files whose names end in *.LOG* contain log and auditing information for the corresponding hive, while files with the *.SAV* extension keep backup copies of Registry transactions so a hive can be automatically restored if the system crashes. Finally, there's one file with its own unique extension: *SYSTEM.ALT* contains a transaction log of the *S*YSTEM hive. If the computer crashes, the boot loader can automatically replace the SYSTEM hive with *SYSTEM.ALT* if the latter has more current data.

You can back up any or all of them; however, as long as you're going to the trouble of backing them up at all you should back them all up. Special note to the curious: you can't rename, move, or delete these files while the operating system is running, since the kernel owns them and is holding them open for exclusive access; other applications that try to modify the files cause a sharing violation when they try.

The Old-Fashioned Way

In the days before Windows NT and Windows 2000, backing up Windows' configuration files was simple. You could just boot into DOS without starting Windows, then do whatever you needed to do. In fact, the "boot-edit system files-reboot-run Windows" routine is familiar to most Windows users, not just heavy-duty administrators. Windows 95 and 98 modified this tactic a bit; not only could you boot directly into DOS, you could use the built-in "safe mode" to tweak configuration files before rebooting. Windows 2000 offers a safe mode, but in safe mode the OS still has a firm grip on the hive files, so you can't use it to back up or restore your files. (Of course, NT itself has no safe mode at all.) By booting into another operating system (DOS, Windows, Linux, OS/2, or whatever else you have installed) or the Windows 2000 recovery console, you can still copy your files. There are four basic things you need to do a manual backup of your Registry files; which ones you use depends on your system configuration:

- If you want to back up your Registry to a backup device, you need appropriate drivers for it (whether you're using a tape drive of some sort or a removable-media drive like a Zip, Jaz, Orb, or similar). If you're using the recovery console, note that you can't load any extra drivers in it.

- If you can't (or don't want to) use the recovery console, and you don't already have another bootable operating system installed on your machine, you'll need a DOS, Linux, or OS/2 boot disk that includes a command shell.

- If your system partition uses the NTFS filesystem, you need a driver to allow your alternate OS to read it.

- You may need some kind of compression utility (unless you're booting into a Win32 OS to do your backup, don't depend on *WinZip32*, which won't run under DOS or Windows 3.x). You need this because the uncompressed hive files can be several megabytes in size, so you won't be able to store them on a floppy without compressing them.

You can't use a system boot floppy to accomplish this task if your boot partition is NTFS; even though the floppy contains its own copy of the boot loader and kernel, it will use the configuration settings in the Registry on your "normal" system volume. You can use a separate boot disk if it contains a complete 2000/NT installation, as it would if you installed the OS onto a Zip or Jaz removable disk and booted from it.

Once you've gathered all these things, you're ready to proceed. The first step in making a backup is to determine whether you can boot from another OS on your disk. If you can't, you need an alternative way to boot your machine from a floppy or removable disk. Once you've arranged a bootable configuration, you must also identify what type of filesystem your boot and system partitions are using; that determines whether your boot disk or OS needs additional drivers.

> ### Boot Versus System Partitions
>
> Windows 2000 allows you to separate boot and system partitions. However, Microsoft's terminology is backwards: they define the system partition as the place where the boot loader is installed and the boot partition as the place where the system files live! While this is undoubtedly confusing, just remember that each term means the opposite of what you'd think, and you'll be fine.
>
> If your system partition is FAT, that means that you can boot DOS, Windows, or another OS that requires a FAT boot partition, but your Windows 2000 system files can still be on an NTFS partition. This is a good solution if you need to dual-boot another OS and Windows 2000. If you just want extra recoverability, install Windows 2000 again so you have a parallel installation you can boot into when needed.
>
> If you don't ever need to boot from another OS, or if you're willing to use a floppy for those times when you do, you can use NTFS for your boot *and* system partitions. This setup offers maximum security; it may offer better performance and disk-space usage, depending on the size of your drive.

If your boot and system partitions are both using FAT, you don't need any special drivers (other than those you need for whatever backup device you're using). However, if your boot partition uses the NTFS filesystem, you'll need an additional driver to allow whatever OS you boot to read it. For Windows 3.1, 95/98, or DOS, you can use the excellent (and free!) *NTFSDOS* driver. NTFSDOS comes in several versions, including a read-only free version and versions that run under MS-DOS and Windows 9x. They're all available from *http://www.sysinternals.com/*. If you're using Linux, a similar read-only driver is available from *http://www.informatik.hu-berlin.de/~loewis/ntfs/*.

Once you've accomplished these two steps, you're ready to back up the files themselves. Here's what to do:

1. Boot your computer, using whatever OS you've chosen. Get to a command prompt and change to the *System32\Config* subdirectory of your installation directory. Make sure you can see the hive files you want to back up.

2. If you're using a backup program, start it, point it at the hive subdirectory, and tell it which hive files to back up. It should do the rest.

3. If you're not using a backup program, use your preferred compression utility to create a new archive containing the files from the *System32\Config* directory you want to back up.

4. Safeguard your backup archive, tape, or disk; it contains a complete and readable copy of your entire Registry.

You might wonder whether this approach is worth the hassle. The answer is "it depends." Windows 2000 does a great job; as a bonus, it allows you to back up files even without a tape drive. On the other hand, if you don't have a tape drive, you can't use Windows NT Backup. Many third-party backup utilities can back up to floppies or removable disks, but not all of them can back up the Registry. You can always use *REGBACK* and *REGREST*, but they may not always be available when you need them. The ERD mechanism works well and is easy to use, but it has a critical defect: it doesn't back up the entire Registry, just what Microsoft thought were the most important parts.

Using Windows 2000 Backup

As part of the overall Windows 2000 facelift, Microsoft threw out the old NT backup utility and replaced it with a new tool they licensed from Veritas. The resulting tool is still called *NTBACKUP.EXE*, but other than that it's quite different in most respects. In particular, its user interface is completely revamped, and it takes advantage of Windows 2000's media services toolkit to let you do backups using tape autoloaders, optical jukeboxes, hierarchical storage management (HSM) packages, and other exotica.

Windows 2000 Backup takes an all-or-nothing approach to backing up the system's configuration data. When you select what data you want to back up, you'll see a category called System State; when you back that up, there are actually five separate pieces of data that get backed up. The bulk of the Registry constitutes one piece, the Active Directory database is another, as are the system's boot files, the COM+ class registry (drawn from HKCR) is the fourth, and the system volume (or SYSVO; the Windows 2000 equivalent to the NETLOGON share in NT) is the final item.

Earlier in the chapter (Figure 3-1), you saw the Welcome screen that appears when you start Windows 2000 Backup. In keeping with the overall wizard-ization of Windows 2000, the first two buttons on that screen will take you directly to the Backup and Restore wizards respectively. The corresponding Backup and Restore tabs offer similar functionality, and since the wizards are easy to understand once you grasp the manual process, I'll start there.

Here's how to do a manual backup of the Registry using Windows 2000 Backup:

1. Launch Windows 2000 Backup (Start → Programs → Accessories → System Tools → Backup). Click the Backup tab. (If you prefer the wizard interface, either use the Tools → Backup Wizard command or click the Backup Wizard button on the Welcome tab.)

2. Use the tree control on the left side of the Backup tab to select the items you want backed up. In particular, make sure the System State item is checked.

(Note that you can't select or deselect individual subparts of the System State item.) Of course, you should feel free to include any other files or folders you want backed up.

3. Use the Backup destination control to select where you want the backup file to go. On systems without a tape drive, the default is to store the data to a backup file (with a *.bkf* extension) in a directory you specify. If you have a tape drive, you can select it instead of the default setting of "File."

4. Select the file or tape you want the backed-up information to be stored on with the "Backup media or file name" field and its associated Browse... button.

5. Click the Start Backup button. The backup will run; by default, you'll get a summary log file. If you use the Tools → Options command, you can use the Log tab to change the level of logging detail. Don't turn it off altogether.

Make sure to turn on backup logging *and* check the log files to be sure your backups are capturing the data you expect. Not much is worse than being lulled into a false sense of security by your backup scheme only to find it didn't back up the data you really needed!

Using Windows NT Backup [NT4]

Microsoft provides a backup utility, *NTBACKUP.EXE*, as part of the standard NT Workstation and Server installations. As with many other bundled utilities, it's not the be-all of backup tools, but it works tolerably well and it's included for free. It can back up local or network volumes (as long as they're already mounted), and it does a good job of logging errors and exceptions.

Lots of tools can do the same things as *NTBACKUP*, but unlike some other backup tools (particularly those designed for Windows 95), *NTBACKUP* has one important feature: it can back up the Registry to any supported tape device.* This Registry backup captures an up-to-date copy of the Registry files from the local machine; if you're backing up network drives and include the Registry, you get the Registry of the machine that's running *NTBACKUP* along with data from whatever drives you've mapped. *NTBACKUP* doesn't back up Registry data from any remote machine, so don't depend on it to do so, or you'll be seriously disappointed.

---

* This is only a skeleton description of *NTBACKUP*. For more details, see O'Reilly's *Windows NT in a Nutshell* by Eric Pearce, and *Windows NT Backup and Restore* by Jody Leber.

Figure 3-6 shows the main interface of *NTBACKUP*. The main window contains two child windows at startup. The Drives window shows a list of all mounted volumes on the current machine (including shares connected over the network), while the Tapes window shows a list of all the available tape devices.

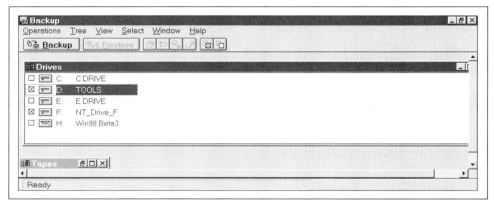

Figure 3-6. NTBACKUP

A basic backup with *NTBACKUP* requires just three simple steps:

1. Use the Drives window to select the drives and files you want backed up. Double-clicking a drive expands it into a File Manager-like window with two panes. The left pane contains a tree view of the folders on the disk, while the right pane contains a list of the files in the selected folder. Each item in either pane has a checkbox next to its file or folder name. If the checkbox is marked, the file or folder is backed up; if it's cleared, it won't be. Figure 3-7 shows a sample window with some files marked.

2. Click the Backup button or use the File menu's Backup command. You see the dialog shown in Figure 3-8. Make sure the Backup Local Registry checkbox has an X in it, then click OK. The backup will start.

3. Go do something else while the backup runs. When it's done, put the tapes in a safe, secure place.

For best performance, you may want to run *NTBACKUP* only after stopping other applications on your computer. The Registry files will be backed up even if system components are using them; however, other files (like SQL Server databases, Office documents, or any other file) are backed up only if they're closed. To ensure a complete backup of all of your machine's data, I recommend closing all other applications and stopping any shared services (IIS, SQL Server, Netscape FastTrack or Enterprise, and so on) whose files you want to back up.

Backing Up the Registry

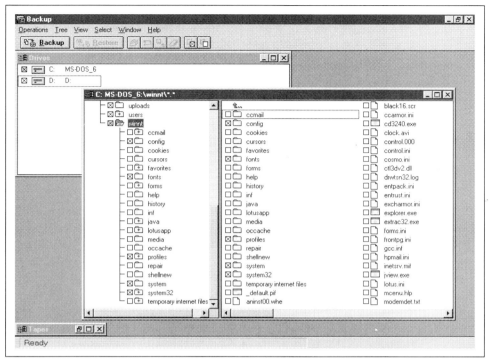

Figure 3-7. The NTBACKUP file selection window

 Use the Log File field in the Backup Information dialog (see Figure 3-8) to specify where you want the log to go. If you want to make sure you see it, put it in the Administrator's desktop folder (try *%systemroot%\PROFILES\Administrator\Desktop*).

Using REGBACK

The *REGBACK* utility does pretty much what its name implies: it allows you to back up all or part of the Registry. Microsoft recommends that you use *NTBACKUP* for making Registry backups if you can, but *REGBACK* is still a useful tool in its own right, since you can use it to export parts of the Registry for storage onto media that the Windows NT backup utility doesn't support, namely floppies and removable-media drives. You can also execute *REGBACK* from the command line, so you can schedule Registry backups or perform them as part of a batch file. For example, you can schedule a nightly Registry backup of some, or all, of your machines and put the backup files on a central server. In addition, *REGBACK* stores its output as uncompressed files, so you don't have to worry about having the correct decompression tool handy.

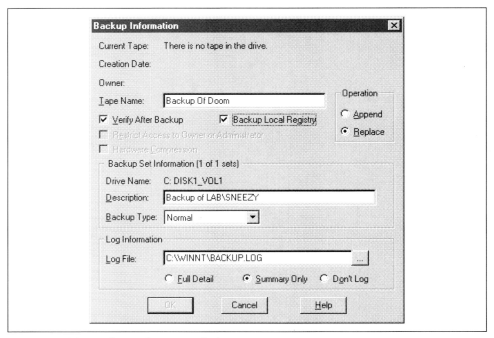

Figure 3-8. The Backup Information dialog

There are some caveats to using *REGBACK*, though; let's examine them before I tell you how to use it:

- The account that you use to run *REGBACK* must have the "Back up files and directories" right. Windows 2000 uses this right internally to let certain accounts copy files without giving them read access; this allows a backup-only account to copy files owned by other users without being able to open them. The Administrator account has this right by default, as do any accounts that you've placed in the Backup Operators group.

- *REGBACK* backs up only the hives in the *System32\Config* directory, not any of the other files stored there. In addition, it won't back up inactive hives that you've unloaded with *RegEdt32*. However, it warns you with an error message indicating what files it found that need to be copied manually.

- *REGBACK* isn't very flexible. If you try to back up files to a device that doesn't have enough space, it will silently fail. If the destination for your backup already has hive files in it, the backup will silently fail. *NTBACKUP* doesn't have either of these limitations.

You can run *REGBACK* in two modes. In the first mode, every active hive in your Registry is backed up to a directory you specify, like this:

```
regback directory
```

Backing Up the Registry

The specified *directory* has to be on a mounted volume; you can't use UNC paths. *REGBACK* cheerfully back ups all the Registry hives it finds on your machine and warns you of any files it didn't back up, like this:

```
C:\>regback \regsave
saving SECURITY to \regsave\SECURITY
saving SOFTWARE to \regsave\SOFTWARE
saving SYSTEM to \regsave\SYSTEM
saving .DEFAULT to \regsave\DEFAULT
saving SAM to \regsave\SAM

***Hive = \REGISTRY\USER\S-1-5-21-1944135612-1199777195-24521265-500
Stored in file \Device\Harddisk0\Partition1\WINNT\Profiles\Administrator\
            ntuser.dat
Must be backed up manually
regback <filename you choose> users S-1-5-21-1944135612-1199777195-24521265-500
```

Notice that *REGBACK* warned that it didn't copy my user account hive, but it gave me a command line that would do so—the last line of its output. This command line uses the second mode that *REGBACK* supports, one that allows you to back up a specified hive instead of the entire Registry:

```
regback  output hivetype  hivename
```

output

Specifies where you want the saved hive to go; can be a full or partial pathname, but cannot be a UNC path.

hivetype

Accepts only two hive types: **machine** represents HKLM, while **users** represents HKU. If you supply any other hive type, *REGBACK* fails with an error message.

hivename

Specifies a subkey immediately beneath either HKU (either .DEFAULT or one of the SID-identified subkeys) or HKLM (SOFTWARE, SYSTEM, and so on). If you specify a key that's not immediately beneath either HKLM or HKU, *REGBACK* will fail.

This form of *REGBACK* saves the entire contents of the specified hive to the file you specify; there's no way to save individual values within a hive. If you want to back up an entire Registry, you may still prefer to use this form of the command, since you can specify the filename for each hive's output file—a valuable feature when you want to back up several machines on a network to the same directory on a server. This snippet shows the output from me telling *REGBACK* to preserve my main subkey under HKU:

```
C:\>regback d:\regsave\paul users S-1-5-21-1944135612-1199777195-24521265-500
saving S-1-5-21-1944135612-1199777195-24521265-500 to d:\regsave\paul
```

REGBACK returns standard DOS-style error codes: 0 for success, 1 if there were files that need to be manually backed up, and 2 if something else went wrong (disk full, bad hive type, and so forth). You can use the ERRORLEVEL construct in a batch file to branch when errors occur. For example, this small batch file attempts to back up HKLM\SOFTWARE to a central directory:

```
regback j:\save-me\enigma-software machine SOFTWARE
if ERRORLEVEL 1 echo "Some files weren't backed up"
if ERRORLEVEL 2 echo "An error occurred."
```

The Windows 2000 Resource Kit costs about $300, and the NT Resource Kit is around $150. You might wonder whether it's a necessary expense. The answer is a resounding "yes." The *REGBACK* and *REGREST* utilities alone can literally save you days of effort when rebuilding a trashed machine. In that light, the cost of the Resource Kit seems more reasonable, and I recommend it highly.

Using RegEdt32

You can do some rudimentary backup and restore tasks with nothing more than *RegEdt32*. It allows you to load previously stored hives into your Registry, then unload them later (though you can only unload hives you loaded yourself). In addition, you can export keys and hives in a format that *RegEdt32* can reload at a later time.

You can't actually save any of the predefined hives (i.e., the hives stored in *System32\Config*) from *RegEdt32*, but there's a good reason for this limitation: those hives are already saved as disk files! Remember, a hive is a disk file that contains Registry keys. You can load a hive that you've saved in *RegEdt32* (or gotten from somewhere else); see the section "Using RegEdt32 and RegEdit" later in this chapter for more details.

RegEdt32 does allow you to do something else, though; you can save any key that's not a root key into a hive file. To keep from confusing the "big" hives (which store the root keys' contents) from the files you can create, I'll call them "honeycombs" (after all, what's a hive full of? Well, besides bees). When you create a honeycomb file, *RegEdt32* takes the specified key and its subkeys and stores them in a file that uses the hive format. You can then move the file to any other Windows 2000 machine and load it into that machine's Registry (with some caveats that I'll discuss later).

The mechanics of doing this are simple: select the key or subkey that you want to save, then use *RegEdt32*'s Registry → Save Key command. When the standard Save

Backing Up the Registry 81

dialog appears, specify a filename; the editor happily saves your key's contents to the file (assuming you have adequate permission to read all the keys and their values). Once the save is finished, you can copy, compress, fold, spindle, and mutilate your new honeycomb file just like any other, plus you can load it into the Registry on any Windows 2000 machine—either in place of or in addition to existing keys.

Using Text Files

You might think that using a plain-text file to represent the Registry is crazy. While it's not the best way to make a complete copy, and it's not a very good way to make copies for restoration use, there are some sensible reasons to use this method. For example, if you periodically dump the contents of a Registry key (whether a root key or any subkey) to a text file, you can use a file comparison tool such as *WinDiff* to highlight changes between the two files. This is an invaluable strategy when you're trying to figure out what Registry keys and values have changed due to software installation or user tinkering. It's also a winning plan for tracking what your own home-grown software does to the Registry and how that matches up with what you wanted it to do.

There are a number of tools for dumping Registry contents to text files. Which one you use is largely a matter of personal preference; they're all free, and they all work well.

Using RegEdt32

RegEdt32 can save any Registry key (and its subtrees) as text. The output is pretty verbose, as shown in this sample from HKLM\SOFTWARE\Netscape:

```
Key Name:          SOFTWARE\Netscape\Netscape Navigator\4.0 (en)\Main
Class Name:        <NO CLASS>
Last Write Time:   6/24/97 - 11:26 PM
Value 0
  Name:            Install Directory
  Type:            REG_SZ
  Data:            C:\Program Files\Netscape\Communicator

Value 1
  Name:            Java Directory
  Type:            REG_SZ
  Data:            C:\Program Files\Netscape\Communicator\Program\Java

Value 2
  Name:            NetHelp Directory
  Type:            REG_SZ
  Data:            C:\Program Files\Netscape\Communicator\Program\NetHelp
```

To save a subtree, all you need to do is select the subtree (or root key) you want to save, then use *RegEdt32*'s Registry → Save Subtree As... menu command. You are prompted for a file to save the data in, then *RegEdt32* spits out the data you selected. However, it's worth noting that there's no way to import this data back into the Registry again! You can use a file-comparison utility such as *WinDiff* to compare two file dumps generated by *RegEdt32*, but you can't restore the Registry's contents based on a *RegEdt32* file.

Using REGDUMP

Andrew Schulman's *REGDUMP*[*] produces similar output to that generated by *RegEdt32*, but it's more nicely formatted, as you can see from this sample:

```
Netscape Navigator
  CurrentVersion="4.0 (en)" -> ""
  4.0 (en) -> ""
    Main
      Install Directory="C:\Program Files\Netscape\Communicator"
      Java Directory="C:\Program Files\Netscape\Communicator\Program\Java
      NetHelp Directory="C:\Program Files\Netscape\Communicator\Program\NetHelp"
```

Like the output from *RegEdt32*, *REGDUMP* output is primarily useful for your reading pleasure; there's no way to take a dumped file and import it back into the Registry. However, because *REGDUMP*'s output is compact and neatly formatted, it lends itself well to use with *WinDiff*.

Using RegEdit

Alone among the utilities in this chapter, *RegEdit* can generate text dumps of the Registry that it can actually import and restore again. When you run *RegEdit*, you can use its Registry → Export Registry File... command to produce output that looks like this:

```
[HKEY_USERS\S-1-5-21-1944135612-1199777195-24521265-500\Software\inetstp\
    Netscape Navigator\Bookmark List]
"File Location"="C:\\Program Files\\Netscape\\Navigator\\Program\\bookmark.htm"
"Start Menu With"="Entire Listing"
"Add URLs Under"="Top Level of Listing"

[HKEY_USERS\S-1-5-21-1944135612-1199777195-24521265-500\Software\inetstp\
    Netscape Navigator\Cache]
"Cache Dir"="C:\\Program Files\\Netscape\\Users\\cache"
"Disk Cache SSL"="no"
"Disk Cache Size"=dword:00001388
"Memory Cache Size"=dword:00000400
```

---

[*] *REGDUMP* made its debut in Chapter 5 of *Inside the Windows 95 Registry*.

Note that each key is enumerated with its full path; this makes it possible for *RegEdit* to tell exactly where a key and its values belong when it reimports the exported file. Choosing the command produces the dialog shown in Figure 3-9. The controls in the "Export range" group let you export the entire Registry or just the currently selected branch. In addition, you can edit the branch shown in the "Selected branch" field to further tighten the output's scope.

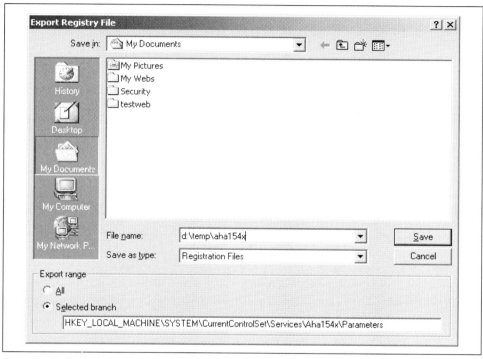

Figure 3-9. Exporting a Registry key

 At this point, you might be wondering why the Resource Kit's *REGINI* utility isn't discussed here. Although it can change the contents of the Registry based on the contents of a text file, there's no way to automatically generate that text file from an existing Registry; you have to build the *.REG* file yourself.

Restoring a Backed-up Registry

Now that you know how to back up your Registry, the next logical step is to learn how to restore it. You need to be comfortable enough doing this that the prospect doesn't scare you; no one looks forward to repairing a damaged Registry, but it shouldn't be frightening either. Practice until you're comfortable with the approaches described in the rest of the section.

The Old-Fashioned Way

Restoring the Registry from a manual backup isn't useful in all circumstances, since to restore the hive files you must be able to boot your machine and gain access to Windows 2000's boot partition, as described earlier in the chapter. Once you've booted your machine into DOS, Linux, or some other OS that gives you access to the partition where your hive files are stored, all you need to do is copy the backup copies over to the original hive directory. (Of course, you have to uncompress them first if they're compressed!) Reboot into Windows 2000, and you're done.

While this approach is appealingly simple, it has its disadvantages. Apart from requiring that you be able to boot into another OS, it has the drawback of being indiscriminate. When you restore a hive, you'll be restoring everything in the hive. This can have the unwanted consequence of removing changes you wanted to keep while fixing whatever problem originally required you to use a backup.

Using Windows 2000 Backup

Restoring a Registry backup with Windows 2000's backup utility is fairly painless. It's not smart enough to check whether you're restoring to the same machine you backed up from, so you must be careful to avoid installing the wrong Registry (including the SAM database and HKLM\SECURITY subtree) on the wrong machine.

Earlier in the chapter, you saw Figure 3-6, which shows *NTBACKUP*'s user interface. To make a backup, you had to select a drive (and its subfolders and files) to back up. Guess what? To restore from a backup, you do the opposite and select a tape to use for the restoration. Here's how the process works:

1. Use the Tapes window to select the tape that contains the files you want backed up. The selection interface works just like the one shown earlier in Figure 3-7; you mark the items you want restored. You have to restore at least one item to restore the Registry. Though you can restore files to any drive, you can only restore the Registry to the drive where it normally lives.

2. Click the Restore button or use the File menu's Restore command. You'll see the dialog shown in Figure 3-10. Make sure the Restore Local Registry checkbox has an X in it, then click OK. The restore will start.

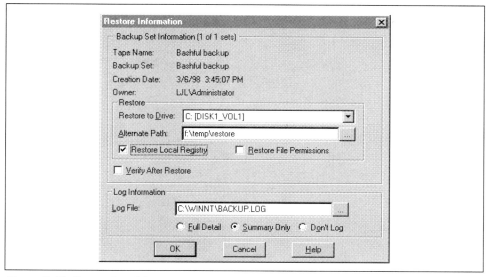

Figure 3-10. Restore Local Registry

Using REGREST

If you back up your Registry with *REGBACK*, naturally you'll use its companion, *REGREST*, to restore it. *REGREST* can use only the files created by *REGBACK*, but since they come as a pair, that shouldn't be an impediment. However (like its partner), *REGREST* has some limitations you should be aware of.

First, and most seriously, it runs only under Windows NT and Windows 2000. *REGREST* actually works by repeatedly calling the RegReplaceKey API routine, meaning that it has to have access to the Windows 2000 registry to do its work. Even though this routine exists in Win95, the Win95 version operates only on the Win95 Registry. If you can't boot your machine into Windows 2000, you'll need to use an ERD to fix it, not a *REGREST* backup.

 Of course, you should plan on keeping a copy of *REGREST* on any boot disks you might use to effect a Registry repair.

Second, you can run *REGREST* only from accounts that have "Restore files and directories" privilege. In most cases, that means your local Administrator account, plus any accounts you've added to the Backup Operators group. (Of course, you can grant this right to any user.)

Next, *REGREST* works only with *REGBACK* files that are on the same volume as the hive files themselves. If your backup files are stored elsewhere, you have to move them to your Windows 2000 boot volume before running *REGREST.*

Finally, you have to reboot your machine before *REGBACK*'s changes will take effect. This is sometimes an annoyance, but it's actually a safety feature: you can undo or redo restores as much as necessary, and the changes won't be permanent until you reboot.

If you can live with these four restrictions, *REGREST* is fairly easy to use. It actually operates in three steps:

1. It copies the original hive file to a backup directory that you specify; this allows a graceful fallback position if Steps 2 or 3 fail.
2. It moves the new hive file to the hive directory; this movement requires the "Restore files and directories" privilege mentioned earlier.
3. It repeatedly calls RegReplaceKey to put the new hive file's contents into the Registry. (That's why it can work when the hive files are open, and it's also why you must reboot before the changes take effect.)

Like *REGBACK, REGREST* comes in two flavors. The first restores as many hives as it can find; it looks for files in the backup directory whose names match hive files in the hive directory. When it finds a match, it copies the matching file according to the previous three steps. You use it like this:

    regrest backupDir saveFilesDir

backupDir

Specifies where the files generated by *REGBACK* are stored; must be on the same volume as your Windows 2000 system files.

saveFilesDir

Tells *REGREST* where to put the secondary backup files it creates. If necessary, you can copy these files back to the hive directory before rebooting to undo a restore.

REGREST warns you if there are hives it can't restore automatically, or if errors occurred. Here's a sample transcript:

    C:\>regrest \regsave \backsave
    replacing SECURITY with \regsave\SECURITY
    replacing SOFTWARE with \regsave\SOFTWARE
    replacing SYSTEM with \regsave\SYSTEM
    replacing .DEFAULT with \regsave\DEFAULT
    replacing SAM with \regsave\SAM

    ***Hive = \REGISTRY\USER\S-1-5-21-1944135612-1199777195-24521265-500
    Stored in file \Device\Harddisk0\Partition1\WINNT\Profiles\Administrator
    \ntuser.dat

Restoring a Backed-up Registry

```
Must be replaced manually
regrest <newpath> <savepath> users S-1-5-21-1944135612-1199777195-24521265-500
```

You must reboot for changes to take effect.

The second form of the command allows you to manually restore one hive at a time:

`regrest` *backupFileName saveFileName hiveType hiveName*

backupFileName

> Specifies which hive file (including its full path, if desired) *REGREST* should restore.

saveFileName

> Tells *REGREST* what name and directory to use for the copy it makes of the existing hive file.

hiveType

> Just like *REGBACK*, *REGREST* accepts only two hive types. Specify machine for HKLM or users for HKU. If you provide any other hive type, *REGREST* will fail.

hiveName

> Specifies a subkey immediately beneath either HKU or HKLM. If you specify any other key, *REGREST* will fail.

Using RegEdt32 and RegEdit

As you've seen in earlier sections, the two stock Registry editors shipped with Windows 2000 are useful when it comes time to back up your Registry data. Fortunately, they can also help you restore it should you need to.

Loading hives

You can load hive files created with *RDISK*, *ERDisk*, or *RegEdt32* into your Registry. When you do, however, it's important to note that *RegEdt32* creates a new key that contains your hive or honeycomb contents. That key and the hive or honeycomb it contains remain loaded until you explicitly unload them.

There's another wrinkle, too: *RegEdt32* allow you to load hives only under HKU and HKLM. As a practical matter, this isn't a big deal; it just means that the hives you load are subkeys of one of those two roots, not subkeys of their subkeys. If you have anything other than HKLM or HKU selected when you give the command, you get an error dialog telling you that you don't have permission to load the hive.

When you use the Registry → Load Hive command, *RegEdt32* asks you for a hive file to load. Once you've identified a file, it asks for the name of the key you want the loaded hive to be under. For example, if you load the .DEFAULT hive to a new key named "MyDefaults" under HKU, you see that HKU\MyDefaults is now equal with HKU\.DEFAULT and HKU\sid, and it contains whatever the original hive or honeycomb file contained.

Once a hive's loaded, you can add, remove, or change keys and values in it like any other part of the Registry; the changes are reflected in the associated hive file.

Reloading saved keys

You can reload a previously saved key at any time using *RegEdt32*'s Registry → Restore Key... menu command. However, this command is an accident waiting to happen. Why? Well, when you save a key, the saved key doesn't contain any path data. For example, if you save HKLM\SOFTWARE\Qualcomm\Eudora, its values and all its subkeys are saved—but not the fact that it originally came from HKLM\SOFTWARE\Qualcomm\Eudora. This in and of itself isn't so bad, but the real danger comes when you get ready to reload the key.

When you tell *RegEdt32* to reload a key, you see a warning dialog (shown in Figure 3-11) telling you what's about to happen. It's not an idle warning, either; if you click Yes, the currently selected key in the Registry will have all its subkeys and values replaced by whatever's in your saved file. Not only does the saved key not go where you wanted it, it also destroys whatever happened to be underneath the key you selected! If you accidentally load HKLM\SOFTWARE\Qualcomm\Eudora while you happen to have HKCU\SOFTWARE\AppEvents selected (to pick a fairly innocuous victim), you'll find that *RegEdt32* happily blasts your Eudora settings into the middle of Windows 2000's sound-to-event mapping list. The results are, at best, unpredictable.

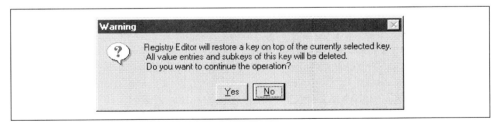

Figure 3-11. RegEdt32 overwrite warning

Of course, this problem can be worked around with a little caution: make sure you have the correct key selected when using this command. Failing that, make sure you have a reliable, up-to-date backup.

Using RegEdit files

Since the *.REG* files produced by *RegEdit* contain the full path for each exported key, they're extremely simple to use. To reimport a *.REG* file, all you need to do is

Restoring a Backed-up Registry

run *RegEdit* and use its Registry → Import Registry File… command. When you do, *RegEdit* imports the file's contents without any further intervention on your part;* it automatically replaces existing keys and their values with whatever's in the file, as well as adding back any keys that are in the file but not in the Registry. It doesn't, however, delete keys in the Registry that have been added since the *.REG* file was created; you have to do that yourself if necessary.

---

* This actually poses somewhat of a security risk, since any *.REG* file that a user can be tricked into double-clicking may make malicious changes. To fix this, change the default action for *RegEdit* to open *.REG* files with *notepad.exe* instead.

4

Using RegEdit

In the first three chapters, you learned what the Registry is, how it functions, and how to safeguard it against accidental damage or loss. Now that you've absorbed this basic knowledge, the real fun starts: now you learn how to modify the Registry's contents. In later chapters, you'll learn how to use the powerful *RegEdt32* application, as well as how to write your own programs that find, store, and modify Registry data. As a departure point, though, let's start with *RegEdit*, a simple, easy-to-use tool that will help you get familiar with the mechanics of navigating and editing the Registry.

Know Your Limitations

The *RegEdit* included with Windows 2000 is a direct descendant of the first version, which shipped with Windows 3.1. That first *RegEdit* couldn't do much because there was so little in the Registry. In the intervening years, Microsoft has added a great deal of data to the Registry, but *RegEdit* itself hasn't progressed too much beyond its original capabilities. Sure, it uses the Win32 common controls, so it looks like a modern application, and it's been rewritten as a 32-bit application for Win9x and NT/2000—but overall, it's still the flat-blade screwdriver of Registry editing tools: ubiquitous but of limited capability.

Let me start by pointing out the useful and desirable things *RegEdit* doesn't do:

- It has no undo or journaling capability, so there's no easy way to back out of an unwanted change or keep an auditable record of changes made.
- It is completely innocent of any understanding of Windows 2000's security features, so you can't view or change permissions or ownership settings for keys.

- You can only create and edit binary, string, and DWORD values. When you view other data types, they're displayed as binary data.

While this list may seem like a harsh assessment, remember how valuable a flat-blade screwdriver can be. It can be a punch, a prybar, a chisel, a spacer, a mallet (albeit a small one), plus it can drive screws. Likewise, *RegEdit* can do some very valuable things: it allows you to search the Registry for a value or key, and these searches can be local or remote. It provides a nicely unified display of all the root keys, allowing you to quickly browse and compare values in different roots. Finally, its limited functionality makes it easy to understand and use.

Learning the RegEdit Interface

I have a weakness for power tools—the more powerful, the better! One thing I've learned is that it's a good idea to spend some time getting accustomed to a new tool before starting a real project with it. This break-in period helps me get familiar with how the tool works, teaches me how it feels as I use it to saw, drill, or whatever, and gives me some confidence that I won't screw up whatever I'm working on.

In the same vein, allow me to present the user interface for *RegEdit*. As you read through this section and its successors, you'll gain an understanding of how *RegEdit* looks, feels, and works, but the best way to cement that knowledge is to launch it and experiment: practice moving around, searching for things, and exploring the Registry. Even after you've mastered the skills needed to administer the Registry, you'll still find *RegEdit*'s search abilities to be quite useful in your everyday administration.

Don't I Know You from Somewhere?

If you've ever used Windows Explorer (or even the old-style Windows File Manager), you'll feel instantly comfortable with *RegEdit*'s interface (shown in Figure 4-1). The application's window is divided vertically. The left pane (which I'll call the *key pane* from now on) shows a tree representing the Registry's hierarchy, while the right side (the *value pane*) shows the values associated with whatever key is selected in the key pane. You can adjust the relative widths of the two panes by dragging the gray bar that divides them.

The value pane is further subdivided into two columns. The first, known as the name column, shows the value's name, while the second (the data column) shows the value's actual contents. You can change the width of these columns by clicking and dragging the divider bar in the header at the top of the value pane.

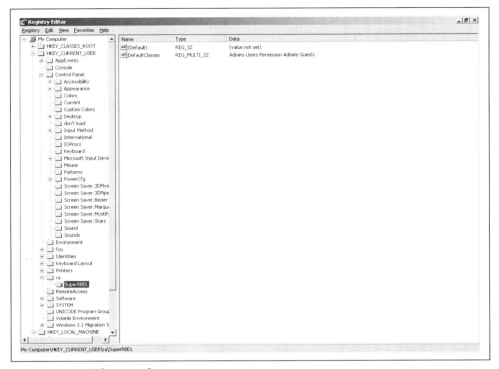

Figure 4-1. RegEdit's interface

By default, *RegEdit*'s main window includes a status bar across its bottom margin; when the status bar is visible, the full path of the currently selected key appears there. This provides a quick reference if you need to make a note of a particular key.

When you first start *RegEdit*, the root keys (HKLM, HKCU, HKU, HKDD, HKCR, and HKCC) appear directly under the My Computer icon. As with Explorer, you can expand or collapse individual keys by clicking the small icon next to the key in the key pane. As you move around, clicking at will, the tree grows and shrinks to reveal the keys you're interested in.

Interface Trivia

As with most other system-administration tools provided with Windows 2000, *RegEdit* provides a View menu. For the most part, the commands here are of little use and seem to have been added for parity with the old-school NT 4.0 tools such as User Manager, WINS Manager, and so on. Nevertheless, in the spirit of completeness, let me briefly describe the commands that live there:

Status Bar
> Controls *RegEdit*'s bottom-of-the-window status bar. When checked, you see the status bar. By default, this option is turned on, and it's useful, so I recommend leaving it that way.

Split
> Activates the vertical bar that segments *RegEdit*'s window. Once you use the Split command, moving your mouse left or right (or using the left and right arrow keys) moves the bar with it. Why this is included is beyond me (though it *does* let you repartition the window when you don't have a mouse).

Refresh
> The only worthwhile command in this menu. *RegEdit* updates its display to reflect any changes you make in the Registry from within *RegEdit*, but it won't notice updates that occur because of other programs. For example, if you're testing a Perl script you've written to do something to the Registry, it would be nice to see the changes immediately. To force an update, you can use the Refresh command (or F5, its key equivalent). You can also use the Refresh command to quickly update the display when you're browsing the Registry of a remote computer.

"Just Browsing, Thanks"

The first thing you should learn to do with *RegEdit* is to browse around the Registry and see what's there. The Explorer-style interface makes the Registry's data very "discoverable"; that's a fancy way of saying you can start off with a high-level view, then see as much or as little detail as you like as you become more comfortable with the Registry's structure.

Navigating with the Keyboard

RegEdit follows the standard Windows conventions for keyboard navigation—not surprising when you consider that the key pane itself is built with the standard tree-list control. When an item is selected, it is highlighted using the standard system highlight color, and you can maneuver about by using the keys shown in Table 4-1.

Table 4-1. Navigational Keys for RegEdit

Key	When Used in…	Action
Tab	Key or value panes	Switches focus between the key and value panes
Return	Value pane	Opens selected item for editing

Table 4-1. Navigational Keys for RegEdit (continued)

Key	When Used in…	Action
Up/down arrows	Key or value panes	Moves focus to the next or previous item in the current pane
Left/right arrows	Key pane	If selected item has subkeys, expands (left arrow) or collapses (right arrow) it; if not, moves to next or previous item
Left/right arrows	Value pane	Scrolls the value pane left or right
PgUp/PgDn	Key or value panes	Moves the focus up or down one pane's worth of data
Home and End	Key or value panes	Moves to top or bottom of pane's contents
Backspace	Key pane	Moves the focus to the current key's parent
Keypad *	Key pane	Expands all subkeys of the currently selected key
Keypad +	Key pane	Expands the immediate subkeys of the currently selected key
Keypad -	Key pane	Collapses the selected subkey

Using the Context Menu

Windows 95 brought the concept of a "context menu" to the Windows world. The basic idea is that by clicking the right mouse button* you can get a pop-up menu of commands or actions that are specific to the object you clicked on. For example, the context menu in Borland C++ has choices such as "Toggle breakpoint" and "Browse symbol," while the corresponding menu for Netscape's Communicator features items such as "Open link in new window" and "Save image to disk."

RegEdit has these context menus, too. There are three context menus you can summon; the commands in each menu duplicate commands that are already present in the application's menu bar:

- Right-clicking a key in the key pane pops up a menu with six commands:
  — *Expand/Collapse* (which one appears depends on whether the key's already expanded or collapsed) opens or closes the selected key. This command is dimmed if the key has no subkeys.
  — *New* allows you to create a new key or value.
  — *Find* opens the find dialog.
  — *Delete* deletes the selected key and all its subkeys.

---

* Or the left one, if you're using a left-handed mouse setup.

- *Rename* allows you to change the key's name without removing and reinserting it.
- *Copy Key Name* copies the current key's full path to the Clipboard.

• Right-clicking a value name in the name column of the value pane displays a smaller menu with three commands. The *Modify* command opens a dialog box that allows you to edit the value; the *Delete* and *Rename* commands are the same as those in the key pane's context menu.

• Right-clicking anywhere else in the value pane displays a single command, *New*.

Connecting to Other Machines' Registries

RegEdit allows you to connect to the Registry of any Windows NT or 2000 machine on your network. Of course, there are two caveats: you must have permission to do so, and the remote machine must be configured to allow remote Registry access. In particular, Windows 2000 machines must have the Remote Registry Access service installed and running (the same is true for Windows 9x machines, by the way).

From within *RegEdit*, you connect to other machines with the Registry → Connect Network Registry... command. You then see a small dialog box that prompts you for a computer name to attach to. This dialog box also contains a Browse button; clicking it displays a network browser window (similar to the one in Windows Explorer) that allows you to poke around your LAN to find the machine you want to connect to. Once you've identified the machine you want to reach, *RegEdit* opens its Registry and displays its root keys in the key pane. Your local machine's root keys are under the My Computer icon; other machines' keys appear under folder icons with their names, as shown in Figure 4-2.

While you're connected to a remote computer's Registry, you can browse keys subject to whatever permission the remote Registry's owner has imposed. Depending on those same permissions, you may be able to modify, create, or remove keys; before doing so, of course, you should make sure that you have both a good backup of the target machine and permission from its owner.

Because *RegEdit* doesn't dynamically update the Registry, you'll quickly become practiced at the skill of using the View → Refresh command (or the F5 key, its accelerator) to force *RegEdit* to update the portion of the Registry you're viewing.

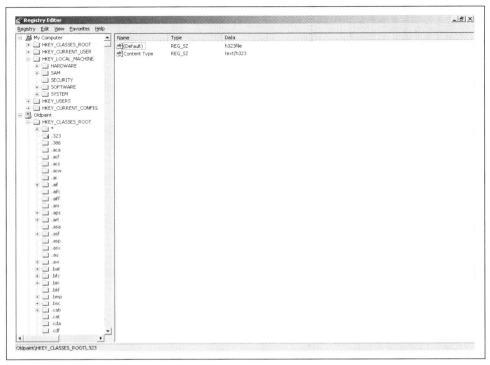

Figure 4-2. Remote Registries and local Registries

RegEdit often fails to allow access to the various root keys of remote Registries even when they are displayed (whereas *RegEdt32* works flawlessly and consistently well). There doesn't seem to be any pattern to the failures. If you have trouble connecting with *RegEdit,* try *RegEdt32* instead.

Finally, when you're done with your Registry connection, you should close it. Knowing how to put away toys is a prerequisite skill for kindergartners and system administrators! The Registry → Disconnect Network Registry command does the job, allowing you to choose from a list of machines you're connected to.

Searching for Keys and Values

One of *RegEdit*'s best features is its ability to search the Registry for a particular key or value. For example, let's say that you want to find where the Dial-Up Networking (DUN) service stores its list of phonebook entries. You could go to Microsoft's Knowledge Base and look it up, but the fastest way to find your

Searching for Keys and Values

answer is to use *RegEdit*'s search function to look for entries whose contents match the name of one of your phonebook entries.

There are a few things you need to know about how searches work. Searches are case-insensitive, so you don't have to pay attention to proper capitalization. By default, searches are substring searches, not literal searches. Searching always starts with the "first" root key, which in *RegEdit*'s case means that all searches have to plow through HKCR first. Finally, the search process accepts only ASCII text and looks only in string values. That makes it impossible to find all the values whose DWORD value is 0x220 or to find data stored in values of type REG_BINARY.

You activate the Find command with the Edit → Find menu command. You then see the dialog box shown in Figure 4-3.

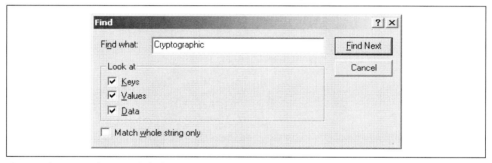

Figure 4-3. RegEdit's Find dialog

Finding values is pretty straightforward: if you want to search the entire Registry, just type your search string into the "Find what" field and click the Find Next button. Of course, you can be more selective by using the four checkboxes in the Find dialog:

- The "Look at Keys" checkbox (on by default) tells *RegEdit* to look for the specified string in the names of keys. Searching for "software" would thus find HKLM\SOFTWARE, HKCU\Software, HKU\.DEFAULT\Software, and perhaps other keys whose names contain "software" in some form or other.

- The "Look at Values" checkbox (on by default) instructs *RegEdit* to search for your string in the names of values, too; searching for "User" with this checkbox set might find HKCR\DAO.User, HKLM\Software\SMIME\Users, and HKCU.

- The "Look at Data" checkbox (on by default) enables *RegEdit* to actually look within values' data for the specified string. Searching for "System" turns up a treasure trove of string values that contain the search string.

- The "Match whole string only" checkbox (off by default) constrains *RegEdit* to reporting only those items that match exactly. Searching for "User" with this option off finds both HKCR\DAO.User and HKLM\Software\SMIME\Users; turning the option on doesn't find either, but does match HKLM\Software\LJL\CurrentVersion\User.

While the search is proceeding, you see a progress dialog. That's perhaps a misnomer, since it doesn't actually indicate the search's progress; it gives you a Cancel button, though. *RegEdit*'s searching performance is poor, so don't be alarmed if searches seem to take a long time.

As with many other programs that include search capability, *RegEdit* provides a convenient shortcut for finding the next item that matches your search target. To find the next match, use the Edit → Find Next command or its accelerator key, F3. When you do, *RegEdit* finds the next match; if it can't find any more matches, it displays a dialog box telling you that no more matches exist.

Printing Registry Contents

If you want to print all or part of the Registry, you're in luck: *RegEdit* can produce a printout that contains the full path, subkeys, and values of the key you select. The Registry → Print... command allows you to print the entire Registry or any subset of it, using the dialog box shown in Figure 4-4.

The "Print range" group gives you a convenient way to filter the keys you print. Selecting the All radio button will (as you'd expect) print the entire Registry. I don't recommend doing this unless you have a very fast printer with a very large paper tray. The "Selected branch" button is a better alternative; with it, you can choose a single subkey to be printed.

RegEdit's printed output is pretty rudimentary. It doesn't have any way to print page headers or footers, and its output isn't indented or otherwise formatted to make it more readable. For quick reference, you may find it more useful to export a portion of the Registry (as described in the section "Exporting Registry Data" later in this chapter), then print it using your favorite text editor.

Working with Keys and Values

By now, you probably have a good feel for the Registry's structure. Once you're comfortable navigating the Registry with *RegEdit*, it's time to move on to the mechanics of working with keys and values in the Registry. *RegEdit* has a complete suite of commands for creating, modifying, deleting, and renaming keys and values. However, it doesn't have a safety net, so be sure to limit your initial

Working with Keys and Values

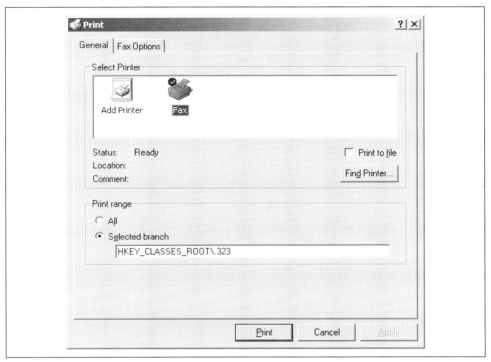

Figure 4-4. RegEdit's Print dialog box

experimentation with editing to changes you can back out if necessary—and don't forget the backup strategies you learned in Chapter 3, *In Case of Emergency*.

 Even though it was mentioned before, it bears repeating: there's no convenient way to undo changes you make when editing the Registry with *RegEdit*. Make sure you've developed and are executing a Registry backup strategy. If you're not, please go back and read Chapter 3 before you start editing anything.

Now is also a good time to mention a few things that *RegEdit* can't do. Chief among them is the fact that it can't directly edit or create values that aren't of one of the three types it supports: DWORD, binary, and string. You can edit values of these other types, but you have to do so by viewing and editing the hex bytes that make up the binary version of the data—not a task to undertake lightly! This limitation makes it harder to edit REG_MULTI_SZ or REG_EXPAND_SZ values, which are fairly common; it's also a problem if you try to modify the more obscure data types discussed in the section "Minor Datatypes" in Chapter 2, *Registry Nuts*

and Bolts. As a practical matter, this isn't a huge hindrance, since most Registry values use one of the three types *RegEdit* supports.

In Knowledge Base article Q155267, Microsoft warns against using *RegEdit* to edit Registry data on a Windows NT machine. That's because RegEdit wasn't designed for, and doesn't understand, some of the data types supported by Windows NT and 2000. You'll be OK if you stick to editing DWORD and REG_SZ values.

A Word About the Clipboard

RegEdit would have been a much better application if it had full Clipboard support, allowing you to cut, copy, and paste keys and subkeys, especially when you're viewing more than one machine's Registry from a single instance of *RegEdit*. Though it doesn't explicitly have much Clipboard support, you can still manage to exchange names and values through the Clipboard if you keep in mind the available ways to do it.

Let's start with key names: to copy a key's name to the clipboard, you can use the Edit → Copy Key Name command, *RegEdit*'s only Clipboard command. This command copies the key's full path, including the root key, to the Clipboard as a text string, ready for use elsewhere. When renaming a key, for example, you can paste a name into the Rename dialog box instead of typing it.

Likewise, it's possible (though not through the menu) to copy a *value's* name or value. To accomplish this, open the editing dialog box for the value whose name or value you're interested in, either by double-clicking it or using the Edit → Modify command. When the edit dialog box appears, you can use the mouse to select either the name or the value, then issue the appropriate Windows shortcut or context menu command to copy, cut, or paste the value.

Modifying Values

The most common use for *RegEdit* is to modify existing values. Many of the settings stored in the Registry are accessible through various control panels and snap-ins, but others aren't, and applications often keep private settings that occasionally require adjustment.

You can modify a value by double-clicking its entry in the value pane, by selecting it and using the Edit → Modify command, or by selecting Modify from the right-button context menu. What happens next depends on the value type you're modifying. However, in all cases, once you click OK in the editing dialog, the change is made, and there's no way to undo it other than changing back the value by hand or restoring from a backup. Note that most applications and system components won't notice changes to a Registry value if they're made once the application is running; you'll usually have to quit and restart the application before the changes take effect.

Modifying a string value

The Edit String dialog box (pictured in Figure 4-5) is pretty simple; it displays the selected value's name and data. You can select and copy the value name, but you can't change it. You can change the value's data using the "Value data" field. Like the name field, this field supports the Windows cut, copy, and paste keyboard shortcuts, so you can quickly paste in values from elsewhere. You'll see this dialog box when you select a value whose type is REG_SZ or REG_EXPAND_SZ.

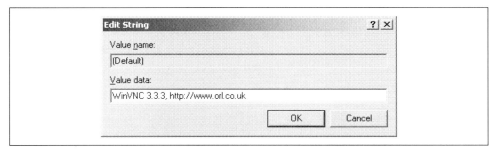

Figure 4-5. The Edit String dialog

Modifying a DWORD value

When you edit a REG_DWORD value, you see the dialog box shown in Figure 4-6. Like the Edit String dialog, you can copy text from the "Value name" field, and you can copy, paste, or cut text in the "Value data" field itself. The two radio buttons in the Base group let you specify a DWORD value in either decimal or hex; if you choose hex, you don't need to add a leading 0x to the value you provide.

 It's a very good idea to always double-check the value you enter to make sure it matches the setting of the Base radio buttons. If you're entering a value in hex, make sure the Hexadecimal button is selected. If the base you select and the data you enter don't match, the change you make may not have the expected effect.

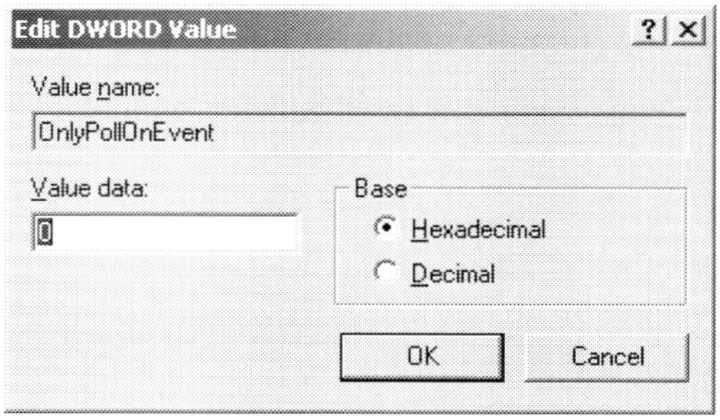

Figure 4-6. DWORD edit dialog

Modifying a binary value

The Edit Binary Value dialog box appears whenever you edit something that's not a DWORD, a REG_SZ, or a REG_EXPAND_SZ. Specifically, when you edit a REG_BINARY, a REG_MULTI_SZ, or either of the resource types described in Chapter 2, you see a dialog box like the one shown in Figure 4-7. Like its predecessors, you can copy text from this dialog's Value name field; however, the Value data field's behavior is a bit different.

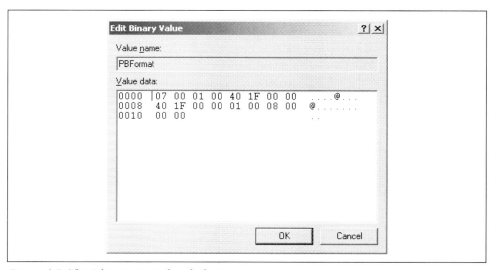

Figure 4-7. The Edit Binary Value dialog

Instead of holding plain text or a single binary value, the Edit Binary Value dialog's Value data field displays as much data as the value holds. Some binary values are a single byte; others, like the one in Figure 4-7, can be hundreds of bytes long. *RegEdit* doesn't care; it displays whatever data is stored for the value. The offset column shows the offset, in hex, at which each block of data starts. The hex display area shows the value's data as blocks of 8 hex bytes per line, and the ASCII display area shows the printable representation (if any) of the corresponding line's hex data.

As with the string and DWORD dialogs, you can cut, copy, and paste text in the Value data field. You can also insert or replace text by highlighting text, just as in a word processor. There's one important difference, though: what you type is interpreted according to where you clicked to select text. If you click on the hex area, whatever you type is taken as hex (only the digits 0–9 and letters A–F are acceptable input, though). If you click in the ASCII display area, what you type is interpreted as ASCII text.

What this means is that you have to be careful. Let's say you want to change part of the value shown in the figure: you want to change the part that says "1705" to say "1999."* If you select the text in the ASCII area and type "1999," you'll get the change you expect. If, instead, you select the corresponding range of bytes in the hex display area and type "1999," *RegEdit* changes the first two bytes, 0x31 and 0x37, to what you typed: 0x19 and 0x99. Not exactly what you had in mind!

You can insert data, too. Just position the insertion point where you want the new data to go and start typing. This is particularly useful for adding strings to a REG_MULTI_SZ value; you still have to make sure to add the hex 0x00 byte that indicates the end of each string. (Better still, use *RegEdt32*, which offers a built-in editor for REG_MULTI_SZ strings.)

Adding New Keys or Values

For the most part, you will probably have little use for the commands that let you add values and keys. This is because of the way applications and components use the Registry; they look for data in predetermined locations, and if you add new data that they don't expect to find, they ignore it. I call this the "hide in plain sight" effect. Think of it like this: if you leave your FedEx delivery person a note taped to your front door asking them to leave your package on the front porch, they will. If, however, you hide the note under your doormat, they won't look for it, won't find it, and won't do what you wanted. So it is with Windows 2000.

However (and you knew this was coming, right?), Microsoft didn't add these commands just to make *RegEdit* look more impressive. There are good reasons to add values and keys; it's just that the circumstances that lead to these reasons are relatively rare. First of all, if you're a software developer, you may need to use *RegEdit* to add keys and values that you use in your own program. The industry trend has

---

* This change makes no sense. Don't do it. It's shown here for instructional purposes only.

been to have installers take care of any Registry changes that need to be made, but before the installer is written sometimes you have to do it by hand.

The second, and probably more common, reason is that Microsoft often adds options or functions to system software that are only accessible by adding new keys to the Registry. These options may be documented in Microsoft's knowledge base (*http://support.microsoft.com*), but they may remain undocumented until Microsoft feels like revealing their presence. Here's an example: let's say you want one Active Directory domain controller to participate in multiple sites. Since a site is a collection of subnets, a server with multiple network interfaces might credibly do so, but you can't configure the server to do so without using the Registry editor. Knowledge Base article Q200498 explains that you must add a new REG_MULTI_SZ value named SiteCoverage to HKLM\System\CurrentControlSet\Services\Netlogon\Parameters, then put the names of all the sites you want the server to join into it. While this capability is documented in the Knowledge Base, it requires you to make a change to the Registry, which brings us to the mechanics of doing so in *RegEdit*.

Third-party manufacturers often take this same approach and put hidden tuning or diagnostic settings into their software or device drivers. These settings can be activated only by adding keys or values with a name known to the software.

The Edit → New command can create new keys or values; it's actually a submenu with four commands in it: New Key, String Value, DWORD Value, and Binary Value. These commands all work in a similar way:

1. Select the key under which you want to create a new key or value.
2. Choose the appropriate command from the menu bar or the context menu.
3. *RegEdit* creates the requested object and gives it a temporary name, which you may edit in place. When you create a new key, it gets an empty value: (Default). Similarly, new string and binary values are empty when created, and new DWORD values have an initial value zero. Figure 4-8 shows the results of some (injudicious) experimentation on my (backup) computer.*
4. If you're creating a value, use the Edit → Modify command to actually assign a real value to the newly created object.

If you're ready to try your newfound powers, look no further than Chapter 10, *Registry Tweaks*; it contains a list of the most frequently sought-after Registry modifications.

---

* Surely you don't think I'd experiment on my *production* machine, do you?

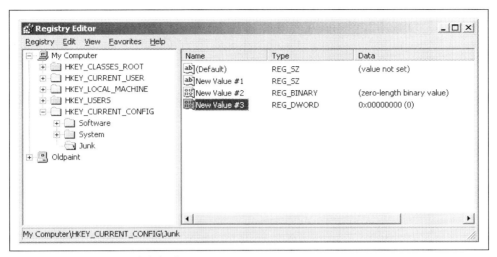

Figure 4-8. New keys and default contents

Deleting Keys or Values

There are times when you may need to remove data from the Registry. For example, even commercial products that include "uninstall" programs may not completely clean up all the Registry entries they've made. However, of all the potential ways to damage your Registry, this is the one I most often see people have problems with. Why? Two reasons: there's no way to undo mistaken deletions from within *RegEdit* or *RegEdt32*, and some deletions don't cause problems until the next reboot. I strongly recommend (again) that you have a current Registry backup on hand before deleting any key you didn't create yourself.

Having said that, on to the instructions. *RegEdit* lets you delete any key except the root keys and any value except the (Default) value some keys have. You can delete keys and values in two ways: by selecting them (using the mouse or keyboard) and using the Edit → Delete command (or its shortcut, the Del key) or by clicking the right mouse button over the target item and using the context menu's Delete command.

When you delete a key, *RegEdit* displays a confirmation dialog box that asks you whether you really want to delete the selected item. However, in a major faux pas, the dialog box doesn't tell you which key you're deleting! Before clicking the "Yes" button in this dialog, closely examine what key or value is selected and confirm that what's selected is what you actually wanted to delete. Once you confirm the deletion, *RegEdit* deletes the selected key, all its subkeys, and all their values. If you accidentally delete a major key such as HKLM\SOFTWARE, you're in for big trouble unless you have that backup handy.

Be very, very careful when deleting keys or values. End of sermon.

Renaming Keys or Values

You can rename keys and values with the Edit → Rename command, which works equally well on keys or values. Select the item you want to rename and give the command, and the item's name changes into an editable text field into which you can type or paste. Hit the Return key when you're done or the ESC key to cancel your changes.

A cautionary note: just because you can rename keys and values doesn't mean that doing so is a good idea. System components and applications always look for values with specific names, and they expect to see them in specific locations. If you change the key or value name for an important parameter, the software that uses it won't be able to find it. Depending on how robust the software is, you may not notice any difference, or your machine may crash. The best heuristic I can recommend is never to rename any keys that belong to the OS itself and to avoid renaming keys whenever possible.

What Were They Thinking, or, the Favorites Menu

About the only noticeable change between the Windows NT 4.0 and 2000 versions of *RegEdit* is the latter's addition of a Favorites menu. It's empty by default, but you can use the Add to Favorites command to add the selected key as a favorite. When you add a new favorite, you can give it whatever name you want; the names of whatever favorites you've defined appear at the bottom of the menu.

To jump to a particular favorite, just select it. *RegEdit* expands the necessary root and subkeys, then highlights your selection. To remove a favorite, use the Remove Favorite command, which displays a small dialog box listing the keys you've defined.

Why did Microsoft add this? I honestly don't know. It couldn't have taken much time, and it might be useful if there are certain keys you edit over and over again, but I confess that, IMHO, they probably could have found a better use for the man-hours invested in building this particular feature.

Exporting and Importing Data

One of *RegEdit*'s unique features is its ability to store Registry data in a human-readable format, then import data in that same format to repair or recreate existing data, or even create new keys and values. Better still, you can create your own files, so you can automate Registry changes needed for your particular network or computing environment. You can also store multiple sets of Registry data and switch between them as needed. This is often useful for system administrators who need to develop their own management tools.

What's in a .REG File?

The *.REG* file format is simple to understand. Fortunately, that makes it simple for programs to parse, too; in Chapter 8, *Programming with the Registry*, you'll see some Perl scripts that manipulate *.REG* files. In the meantime, let's examine the format that *RegEdit* uses so you'll be able to make sense of it when you see it.

Here's a snippet gleaned from my desktop machine's Registry:

```
REGEDIT4

[HKEY_LOCAL_MACHINE\SYSTEM\CurrentControlSet\Services\Browser]
"Type"=dword:00000020
"Start"=dword:00000002
"ErrorControl"=dword:00000001
"ImagePath"=hex(2):25,53,79,73,74,65,6d,52,6f,6f,74,25,5c,53,79,73, \
    74,65,6d,33,32,5c,73,65,72,76,69,63,65,73,2e,65,78,65,00
"DisplayName"="Computer Browser"
"DependOnService"=hex(7):4c,61,6e,6d,61,6e,57,6f,72,6b,73,74,61,74,69, \
    6f,6e,00,4c,61,6e,6d,61,6e,53,65,72,76,65,72,00,4c,6d,48,6f,73,74, \
    73,00,00
"DependOnGroup"=hex(7):00
"ObjectName"="LocalSystem"

[HKEY_LOCAL_MACHINE\SYSTEM\CurrentControlSet\Services\Browser\Linkage]

[HKEY_LOCAL_MACHINE\SYSTEM\CurrentControlSet\Services\Browser\Linkage\Disabled]

[HKEY_LOCAL_MACHINE\SYSTEM\CurrentControlSet\Services\Browser\Parameters]
"MaintainServerList"="Auto"
"IsDomainMaster"="FALSE"
```

The first line in the file identifies the file as a *.REG* file. If this string's present, *RegEdit* attempts to interpret the rest of the file as a set of keys and values; if it's not present, *RegEdit* complains that the file you're importing isn't really a *.REG* file.

The next interesting line identifies the full path to a key. In this case, the key is HKLM\SYSTEM\CurrentControlSet\Services\Browser. There are two noteworthy things about this key path. It's enclosed in square brackets (which *RegEdit* looks for as delimiters), and the root key is spelled out: HKEY_LOCAL_MACHINE instead of the more convenient HKLM.

The remaining lines for this key specify its values as name/value pairs. The general syntax looks like this:

```
"name"=[type:] ["] value ["]
```

Each value has a name. Keys can have a special value whose name is empty; *RegEdit* displays this value with a name of (Default), but in *.REG* files the special name @ takes its place. The name must always be in double quotes to accommodate the fact that Registry value names can contain spaces.

Next comes the optional data type specifier. The specifier is necessary to preserve all the details of the values. Even though *RegEdit* can only directly edit binary, DWORD, and string values, its export and import commands must correctly preserve the entire state of the keys and values they're operating on. When the value is a standard REG_SZ string, *RegEdit* omits the type specifier; otherwise, it uses the values shown in Table 4-2. Note that if a type specifier's used, the colon that follows it is required.

Table 4-2. .REG File Data Type Specifiers

Registry Type	.REG Type
REG_BINARY	hex
REG_DWORD	dword
REG_EXPAND_SZ	hex(2)
REG_FULL_RESOURCE_DESCRIPTOR	hex(9)
REG_MULTI_SZ	hex(7)
REG_RESOURCE_LIST	hex(8)
REG_SZ	None

The value's actual value is the next item in the name/value definition. Standard REG_SZ strings are easy to identify, because they're always between double quotes. DWORD values are written as 32-bit hex numbers, including leading zeros but without any kind of type identifier (such as the "0x" prefix that *RegEdt32* uses). The other data types are all represented as a comma-delimited list of hex bytes, as you can see in the previous code snippet. Since all these data types can be of arbitrary length, the actual number of bytes can vary from value to value. *RegEdit* allows you to use the backslash character as a line-continuation character; when present at the end of a line, the backslash indicates the following line should be considered part of the current line.

Blank lines aren't significant to *RegEdit*; however, if no value definitions follow a key definition, that key is created without any values, as with Browser\Linkage and Browser\Linkage\Disabled in the previous example.

Exporting Registry Data

You can export any key and its subkeys, from the root keys on down. When you export a key, all the data necessary to recreate it is stored in a *.REG* file that you can archive, print, or edit like any other. You can also reimport the file. As you learned in Chapter 3, this capability gives you a useful way to back up and restore individual keys within the Registry.

Exporting and Importing Data 109

The Registry → Export Registry File... command actually does the exporting; when you invoke it, you see the dialog box shown in Figure 4-9. If you have selected a key in the key pane, the Selected branch radio button is selected, and the currently active key appears in the associated text field. If you'd rather export the entire Registry, you can use the All radio button to do so.

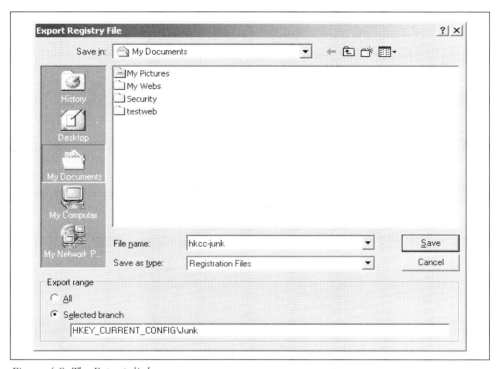

Figure 4-9. The Export dialog

Once you've supplied a filename and chosen exactly what you want to export, *RegEdit* writes out the selected data to your file, using the format described earlier in the section "What's in a .REG File?"

Importing Registry Data

Once you've exported a *.REG* file or created one by hand, *RegEdit* allows you to load it back into the Registry. As you read in the preceding section, the *.REG* file contains enough information for *RegEdit* to load key and value data from the file and place it in the proper location in the Registry. However, the program is indiscriminate; once you tell it to load a file, it happily blasts the entire file's contents into your Registry, with no further opportunity for you to limit the scope of its replacements.

When you select the Registry → Import Registry File... command, *RegEdit* displays the standard Open File dialog box so you can choose a file. If you select a file that's not in *.REG* format, you get an error dialog box telling you that the file you chose can't be loaded. If, however, the file is in valid format, *RegEdit* imports it, displaying a progress dialog box to tell you how far along it's gotten. There's no way to cancel or interrupt the loading process from within the program. Forcing *RegEdit* to quit during an import operation (by using the Task Manager, a process manager such as *PVIEW*, or other tools) can leave your Registry looking like the front yard of your local college's Fraternity Row after a football game—don't do it.

Once the import operation's finished, you see a confirmation dialog box that tells you *RegEdit* did in fact import the entire file. It also includes the pathname of the imported file so you'll know exactly what file got imported (just in case you've forgotten).

One caveat: when you import data with a *.REG* file, *RegEdit* adds any keys that are in the *.REG* file but not in the Registry, and it changes the value of any keys that appear in both places. It doesn't remove keys that are in the Registry but not in the *.REG* file, so you can't use *RegEdit* to clean out an accidentally added key or remove keys that have been added since the time the *.REG* file was created. If you import a key whose path contains components that don't exist, *RegEdit* creates any subkeys needed to complete the entire path to the new key.

Creating Your Own .REG Files

Even though *RegEdit* can generate *.REG* files, there's no reason why you can't generate your own files. In fact, this is a handy strategy when you need to make the same set of Registry changes on more than one machine. You can create a *.REG* file, test it and tweak it on a single machine until you're satisfied that it does what you want, then import it using *RegEdit* on each machine you want to modify.

A concrete example

Windows 2000 Server includes the File Server for Macintosh (FSM) package, which lets a Windows 2000 server serve NTFS volumes to Mac clients. To the Mac, these FSM volumes look just like native Mac disks, and they preserve the Mac-style file type and creator information needed to associate files with the applications that created them. Unfortunately, NTFS doesn't support these type and creator codes; instead, FSM keeps a table that translates PC-style file extensions to the corresponding type and creator codes. This enables both PC and Mac users to recognize files with names such as *chapter04.doc* as Microsoft Word files.

|NT4| Windows NT 4.0 had the same feature, but it was called Services for Macintosh (SFM) instead.

Microsoft helpfully provides a default set of type/extension mappings with FSM. That's the good news. The bad news is that it doesn't include many of the most useful file types.* Even if it did, the exact mix of file types you use depends on what programs your users are running. FSM provides a dialog box for associating types and extensions, but it's a tedious task at best. *RegEdit* provides an ideal solution: once you have a set of file extensions built on one server, you can easily replicate it to other FSM servers by importing a *.REG* file. In fact, you can easily do this with new servers in your domain, too, making it easy to maintain and upgrade your file services without undue effort on your part.

Safely experimenting with .REG files

One especially handy use for these files is to let you fine-tune your *.REG* files without endangering the rest of your Registry. You accomplish this by building a file that contains the values and keys you want to modify, but that puts them beneath a different key than the original. For example, if you're writing a *.REG* file you want to apply to HKLM\Software\Netscape\Netscape Navigator, you can safely fiddle around with your *.REG* file without fear by following these steps:

1. Export the key you're going to modify using *RegEdit*'s export facility. This gives you a *.REG* file that overwrites the existing key's contents when reloaded, restoring the original contents.

2. Make a note of the path that contains the keys you're modifying. For example, if you're modifying keys that live under the HKLM\Software\Microsoft\Windows NT\CurrentVersion\IniFileMapping tree, your *.REG* file contains code that looks like this:

   ```
   [HKEY_LOCAL_MACHINE\SOFTWARE\Microsoft\Windows NT\
       CurrentVersion\IniFileMapping\Clock.ini]
   @="#USR:Software\\Microsoft\\Clock"
   ```

3. Use a text editor to change all instances of the key's path to a new, unused value. For example, you might change from HKLM\Software\Microsoft\Windows NT\CurrentVersion\IniFileMapping to HKLM\Software\Microsoft\Windows NT\Testing\IniFileMapping. Of course, you must use one of the root keys as the base, but you are otherwise free to improvise a path, since *RegEdit* creates any keys or subkeys that need to be created to complete the import.

4. Load the new *.REG* file; its contents will then appear under the key you've specified.

You can now edit the *.REG* file to your heart's content. When you're satisfied with the changes it makes, you can reverse Step 3 to put the original key path back in

---

* Of course, it already has type information for Microsoft's Office applications.

place so the changes go where you want them to, then use, distribute, or store the *.REG* file however you'd like.

Why does this work? Applications and system components look for Registry data in a particular path. If the data isn't in that precise location, the application won't find them. This is akin to what would happen if your postman put your incoming snail-mail under your doormat: it would be delivered, but when you checked your mailbox, you wouldn't find your mail. Likewise, if you take the Browser service's settings from HKLM\System\CurrentControlSet\Services\Browser and copy them to HKLM\Software\TestBrowser, you can still see your changes, but the system component they're intended for won't.

This approach won't help you tell whether the changes you're making are appropriate or will do what you want; it can only help you ensure that the changes go where you intend them to and that nothing extraneous is added or deleted.

RegEdit Command-Line Options

Even though I've been talking about using *RegEdit* as a standard Windows application, it also supports several command-line options that let you to import and export Registry data from scripts, batch files, or the command line. Both switches run *RegEdit* as a background process. The export process is quiet; the import process displays a completion dialog, just as it does when you use the Registry → Import Registry File... command.

Exporting Data

You tell *RegEdit* to export data with the /e command-line switch. The command looks like this:

    regedit /e targetFile [registryPath]

targetFile
    This specifies where *RegEdit* should write its data. You can specify any path, filename, and extension so long as it's not a UNC path.

registryPath
    This optional parameter tells *RegEdit* what to export. If you omit it, the entire Registry is exported. If you specify a key, that key and all its subkeys are exported. The path must be a complete path, including a root key, and you must spell out the name of the root key.

If you want to dump the contents of HKLM\Software\metrowerks to a file named *warrior.reg*, you can do it like this:

    regedit /e c:\dist\hklm\warrior.reg HKEY_LOCAL_MACHINE\SOFTWARE\metrowerks

Importing Data

The simplest way to import data using *RegEdit* is to specify the name of the file you want imported on the command line, like this:

    regedit warrior.reg

RegEdit happily imports the file's entire contents and presents a confirmation dialog when done. Alternatively, you can force *RegEdit* to replace the entire contents of the Registry with a *.REG* file. *RegEdit* won't replace the keys that are dynamically built (such as HKLM\HARDWARE and HKDD), but everything else is fair game, so make sure the file you're loading has a complete set of Registry contents and that you have a current backup. To invoke this mode, use the /c switch, like this:

    regedit /c whole-enchilada.reg

When you use the /c switch, you may get an odd dialog box accusing you of tampering with the product type. Windows NT 4.0 keeps a pair of threads running in the background; these threads do nothing more than watch HKLM\System\Setup\SystemPrefix and HKLM\System\CurrentControlSet\Control\ProductOptions\ProductType for changes and reverse any changes that occur. When you reload the entire Registry, the threads notice and present the warning dialog box because they're not smart enough to tell that the value isn't any different—just that someone tried to change it. (For more information on these threads and why they're there, see Andrew Schulman's article at *ftp://ftp.ora.com/pub/examples/windows/win95.update/ntnodiff.html*.)

5

Using RegEdt32

In Chapter 4, *Using RegEdit,* you learned how to use the *RegEdit* utility to browse, search, and edit the Registry. *RegEdit* ships with Windows 95/98, Windows NT, and Windows 2000; however, Windows NT and Windows 2000 also include *RegEdt32*, a more powerful Registry editor that fully supports the security and auditing features present in Windows 2000. In this chapter, you'll learn how to use *RegEdt32* to view, edit, create, and delete data in the Registry.

How RegEdt32 and RegEdit Differ

Since *RegEdit* was originally written for Windows 95, it doesn't support the full capabilities of the Registry in Windows NT and 2000. In particular, it doesn't have any support for Windows 2000's security features, so you can't change or view permissions on keys. While this may make *RegEdit* look like the computer equivalent of a tricycle when compared to *RegEdt32*, this isn't really accurate. A better comparison is between a bicycle and a car. Each has its uses; sometimes a bicycle is the best, cheapest, most enjoyable, or fastest way to reach your destination, but it's not a good way to bring home a new baby from the hospital or take six friends out to dinner.

So it is with the two Registry editors. *RegEdt32* has a number of features *RegEdit* doesn't, but it also has some unique limitations:

- *RegEdit* can search keys and values, while *RegEdt32* can search only key names. You'll quickly become comfortable with firing up *RegEdit* to find the value you're looking for, then editing it as needed in *RegEdt32*.

- *RegEdt32* fully supports Windows 2000's security features. It allows you to view and set ownership, permissions, and auditing controls for root keys and their subkeys.

- *RegEdt32* can load and save keys in binary format. In addition, it can import these saved keys as self-contained hives, making it easy to transfer data from machine to machine.

- *RegEdt32* supports many more display options, and its interface allows you to view as many or as few root keys as you wish, each in its own window.

The two are similar in many respects, too. Both allow you to view and edit Registry data on remote computers, and both allow you to edit different data types with an appropriate editor (though *RegEdt32* supports more of Windows 2000's Registry data types than does *RegEdit*).

Microsoft warns against using *RegEdit* to edit any value type other than REG_DWORD and REG_SZ. In particular, if you edit REG_MULTI_SZ or REG_EXPAND_SZ strings, they'll be saved as REG_SZ.

Learning the RegEdt32 Interface

Where *RegEdit*'s interface is like that of Windows Explorer, *RegEdt32* has an interface very similar to the original Windows 3.1/NT File Manager. This likeness is partly due to heritage; *RegEdt32* was first delivered with NT 3.1 back in 1993, and hasn't been rewritten to take advantage of the user-interface enhancements included with later revisions of the operating system.

Figure 5-1 shows *RegEdt32* in action. Each root key has its own document window. These windows are independent of one another and can be moved, tiled, resized, and arranged however you wish. You can't, however, close individual root key windows for the keys on your own machine, but you can minimize them to keep them out of the way, or you can use the Registry → Close command to close all the root windows.

Each root key window is further divided into two panes. The tree pane, which is similar to *RegEdit*'s key pane, is on the left and shows a tree structure representing the hierarchy of keys under that root. The data pane is on the right, and it displays all values for whatever key is selected in the tree pane. Between the two panes is a standard Windows splitter control, which allows you to adjust the relative width of the two panes. In a welcome departure from *RegEdit*, the tree and data panes both have horizontal scrollbars, thus making it easier to view long values without having to resort to trickery.

RegEdit doesn't automatically update its display as keys and values changed. However, *RegEdt32* gives you a choice. In "automatic update" mode, *RegEdt32* refreshes its display when the Registry changes, but this is time-consuming and

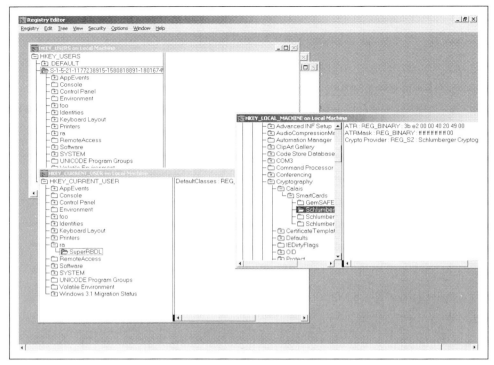

Figure 5-1. The RegEdt32 interface

sometimes unnecessary. You can turn this mode off, in which case *RegEdt32* acts like *RegEdit*: it doesn't automatically update values that have been changed by other applications or system components.

Manipulating Windows

When you start *RegEdt32* for the first time, all five root key windows appear, stacked diagonally across the *RegEdt32* root window area. (Yes, five: even though HKDD is a legitimate root key, *RegEdt32* doesn't know about it, doesn't display it, and won't allow you to open it.) You can manually move the windows around however you like; the Window menu also offers you several commands for quickly arranging windows the way you want them:

- The Cascade command (Shift+F5) arranges all the open root key windows in a diagonal pattern. The first window snugs up immediately beneath the menu bar, and the others are offset down and to the right so that all their titlebars are visible. The currently active window will end up at the bottom-right corner of the stack.

Learning the RegEdt32 Interface

- The Tile command (Shift+F4) sizes and positions the open windows so that all of them are equally sized and visible simultaneously.
- The Arrange Icons command neatly aligns any minimized windows along the bottom margin of the application window.

Besides these commands, *RegEdt32* also includes the root key windows in the Window menu. Each of the five windows has its own entry, and you can jump to any one by selecting it from the menu. If you have additional root keys on other computers open, they'll be displayed too. If you have more than nine open root key windows, the Window → More Windows... command appears, making available a dialog from which you can choose any open window.

There's one more useful window command, but it's not in the Window menu: Registry → Close. The individual root key windows don't have the standard "close" icon in their titlebar, and the tool stripe pop-up menu doesn't have a close command on it either. However, Registry → Close closes your windows in two ways. If you select it while the active window is for a root key on your local machine, all the root key windows for your machine close, and you have to use the Registry → Open Local command to reopen.* If you select Registry → Close when the active window is displaying a root key from another machine, the set of root key windows for that machine are closed. When you close the last window to another machine's Registry, *RegEdt32* disconnects from the remote machine altogether.

Controlling What You See

RegEdt32 includes a View menu that gives you some degree of control over the way data is displayed in the root key windows. The commands in this menu affect only the frontmost window, with one exception (the Refresh All command):

- By default, *RegEdt32* shows both the tree and data panes. This corresponds to the View menu's first command, Tree and Data. If you prefer, you can use the Tree Only or Data Only commands to limit the display to whatever you're interested in looking at. The current setting is marked with a checkmark.
- The View → Split command activates the vertical window splitter bar that separates the tree and data panes. Once you issue the Split command, you can drag the splitter left or right by moving your mouse left or right or using the left and right arrow keys. Of course, this duplicates what you could do by clicking and dragging the splitter bar itself (that little black square at the bottom of the splitter).

---

* Every time you use the command, *RegEdt32* opens up a new set of local root key windows. Do it three times, and you've suddenly grown 15 new root key windows! This might appear to be a bug, but it's not; you can use this feature to quickly compare multiple keys under a single root without having to scroll back and forth.

- *RegEdt32* normally displays data in its native format. For example, DWORD values are shown as hex numbers, REG_SZ values are shown as strings, and so on. The View → Display Binary Data command lets you override this behavior and force *RegEdt32* to show everything as though it were binary data (it actually appears as a string of hex digits, not in true binary).

- *RegEdt32* may or may not automatically refresh its display to reflect any added, deleted, or changed keys or values, depending on your preference. If you've told *RegEdt32* not to automatically update the display, you must manually ask for updates when you want them. There are two ways to do so. The first way is to ask *RegEdt32* to update its display of all open root keys with the View → Refresh All command or its accelerator, Shift+F6. As its name suggests, this command tells *RegEdt32* to update every root key window for local and remote machines. For those times when you care about only what's displayed in the frontmost window, the View → Refresh Active command (or its accelerator, F6) does just that, updating only the values and keys in the currently active root key window.

The View menu also sports a Find Key command, which is discussed in the section "Searching for Keys" a bit later.

Setting Session Options

RegEdt32 lumps a number of useful settings into its Options menu; these settings give you additional control over how *RegEdt32* behaves. The first one worth mentioning is actually the last command in the menu: Save Settings on Exit. When this command is checked (as it is by default), *RegEdt32* remembers the settings of all the other options in the menu, as well as the positions, sizes, and minimized/maximized states of all the root key windows. *RegEdt32* stores this information in HKCU\SOFTWARE\Microsoft\RegEdt32\Settings. The other Options menu commands are a mixed bag:

- You can choose the font face and size used to draw the root key windows and their contents with the Options → Font... command. This is a boon for both high- and low-resolution displays, since you can find a comfortable point size that allows you to read the tree and data panes without squinting.

- The Auto Refresh command controls whether *RegEdt32* automatically updates its tree and data panes to keep them in sync with the actual contents of the Registry. If this command is enabled, *RegEdt32* updates all open root key windows whenever changes occur. This takes a small, but noticeable, amount of time. If you turn Auto Refresh off, you can still use the manual refresh commands in the View menu to force *RegEdt32* to update itself when you think it's necessary. However, Auto Refresh is convenient and works fine as long as you don't mind the occasional pause. Note that when you're connected to a remote Registry you have to use the manual refresh command, since automatic updating doesn't work.

- Read Only Mode is, sadly, not turned on by default. When it is on, *RegEdt32* won't let you change anything in the Registry. You can look at keys and values as much as you'd like, but you won't be able to add or delete keys or add, edit, or delete values. Whenever you open a value to edit it, *RegEdt32* presents a polite dialog telling you that read-only mode is enabled and that your changes won't be saved.

  When setting up a new installation, I always make sure to log on as Administrator, run *RegEdt32*, make sure "Save Settings On Exit" is checked, and turn on Read Only Mode. Savvy users can always turn it off; in the meantime, it's useful protection against the curious but unschooled. It can also keep you from making mistakes on your own machine, so I recommend turning it on there as well. Unfortunately, this setting is saved on a user-by-user basis, but you can achieve the desired effect by making the change to the default user profile.

- The Options → Confirm On Delete command is another potential bacon-saver, which probably explains why it's turned on by default. When it's on, *RegEdt32* warns you with a confirmation dialog when you try to remove a value or key; this last-ditch "are you sure?" step has saved many an administrator from accidentally removing something unintended. For your own health and safety, please leave this option turned on.

Browsing with RegEdt32

RegEdt32's interface isn't as "discoverable" as *RegEdit*; that's just a fancy way of saying that it's not as easy to just jump in and start poking around. However, this doesn't mean that using *RegEdt32* is hard—just a little unfamiliar if you're not an old File Manager hand.

Since each root key appears in its own independent window, your browsing sessions usually focuses on the subkeys of one particular root key. One nice thing about having each root key in a separate window is that it makes it easy to compare Registry values on different machines, as shown in Figure 5-2. Since you can minimize, resize, and position each window independently, it's easy to put off the ones you're not interested in at the moment, then recall them later when you need them.[*]

---

[*] Of course, since HKCU and HKCR are really links to subkeys of HKU and HKLM, respectively, you can get all you need by leaving HKU and HKLM open and hiding the rest.

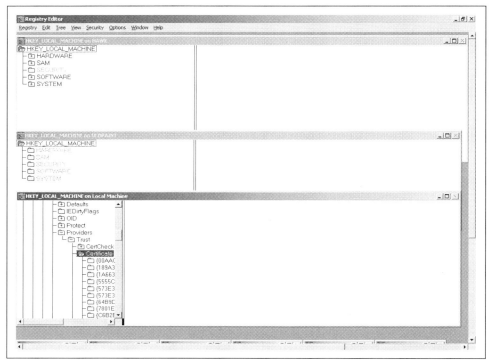

Figure 5-2. Arranging your RegEdt32 windows

Navigating with the Keyboard

If you've used the keyboard to navigate around the Windows 3.1 File Manager, you'll feel right at home doing the same in *RegEdt32*. Table 5-1 shows the key navigation commands you can use to move around. The last four entries in the table are actually accelerators for commands in the Tree menu.

Table 5-1. Navigational Keys for RegEdt32

Key	When Used in…	Action
Tab	Tree or data panes	Switches focus between the key and value panes
Return	Tree pane	Expands currently selected key but not its sub-keys
Return	Data pane	Opens selected item for editing
Up/down arrows	Tree or data panes	Moves focus to the next or previous item in the current pane
Left/right arrows	Tree or data panes	Scrolls the active pane left or right if it has scrollbars; otherwise, moves to the next or previous item in the tree

Table 5-1. Navigational Keys for RegEdt32 (continued)

Key	When Used in...	Action
PgUp/PgDn	Tree or data panes	Moves the focus up or down one pane's worth of data
Home and End	Tree or data panes	Moves to top or bottom of pane's contents
+	Tree pane	Expands the currently selected key but not its subkeys
*	Tree pane	Expands all subkeys of the currently selected key
Ctrl+ *	Tree pane	Expands the entire tree; may take a few seconds
-	Tree pane	Collapses the selected key and all its subkeys

Remote Registry Editing

RegEdt32 originated the concept of remotely editing another machine's Registry. This is invaluable for administrators, since it gives you the ability to peek into the Registry of a misconfigured or broken machine from the comfort of your office. As with most magic powers, this ability to edit the Registry from afar has some associated constraints and requirements.

First of all, you must have sufficient privilege to see the Registry on the remote machine. By default, NT Workstation machines allows anyone to connect to their Registries, as does NT Server Version 3.51 and earlier. NT Server 4.0 turns remote access off; Windows 2000 Professional and Server turn it on again. This privilege, which is discussed in the section "Limiting Remote Registry Access" in Chapter 9, *Administering the Registry*, lets you view HKU and HKLM on the remote machine, but that's all. If you want to see the contents of HKCR, HKCC, or HKCU, you have to look in the appropriate section of the two keys you can see.[*]

Next, you must be able to modify the Registry on the remote machine. Let's say you're logged into a machine where your account has Administrator privileges. If you use *RegEdt32* to open the Registry of another machine on your network where your account doesn't have Administrator access, you can see that machine's HKLM and HKU entries but you can't open them! This also holds true when your machine and/or the target are members of the same domain: to change data on the remote machine, you must have Administrator access on the remote machine.

RegEdt32 doesn't buffer or cache any Registry data from whatever remote machines you're connected to, and it won't automatically update windows

---

[*] HKPD is, of course, not visible either; this isn't surprising since you can't see it in *RegEdt32* at all.

containing remote machines' root keys. This means that your display can quickly lose sync with the target machine's Registry; make sure to refresh the display as needed.

Connecting to Remote Computers

You actually connect to remote machines' Registries with the Registry → Select Computer command, which displays the standard Select Computer dialog shown in Figure 5-3. Neither *RegEdt32* nor Windows 2000 makes any attempt to restrict the list of machines displayed so that it shows only machines that can actually talk to *RegEdt32*; the list may thus contain machines whose Registries you can't edit—including Win95, Windows 3.11, and even Unix machines running the Samba file server package! If you try to connect to a machine that doesn't support remote Registry editing, *RegEdt32* tells you it can't connect to the remote machine. That's because remote Registry editing uses remote procedure calls (RPCs) over named pipes; you need to have RPC connectiviy and be talking to a machine that can handle RPCs.

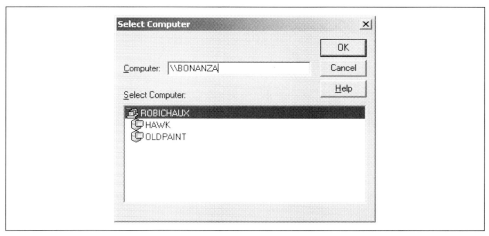

Figure 5-3. The Select Computer dialog

Once you've successfully connected to a remote machine, its HKU and HKLM keys appear in new windows within the *RegEdt32* frame window. Assuming that you have the right permissions, you can browse, edit, export, and otherwise modify the Registry on the remote machine as much as you'd like. You may freely close sets of root key windows that display data from remote machines. When you close the last window to a machine, *RegEdt32* closes the Registry connection to that machine as well.

Searching for Keys

RegEdt32's search capability is much less capable than *RegEdit*'s, but it's better than nothing. Where *RegEdit* can search key names, value names, and value contents, *RegEdt32* can search only key names. This is still useful, however, since most of the available documentation covering Registry keys gives you the key names even when value names and contents aren't specified.

When you search the Registry with *RegEdt32*, the search starts at whatever key you currently have selected and proceeds until one of two things happens: a match is found, or the search hits the end of the Registry. In the former case, *RegEdt32* highlights the matching key. In the latter, it displays a dialog telling you that no more instances of the search string can be found.

You get to *RegEdt32*'s Find dialog with the View → Find Key menu command. The dialog itself is shown in Figure 5-4. It looks, and works, very much like the Find dialogs of other applications you've probably used before, such as Notepad and Wordpad. Here's what its controls do:

- You specify the key name you want to find by typing all or part of it into the "Find what" field. You may also use the standard Windows keyboard shortcuts to cut, copy, or paste Clipboard text into this field.

- The "Match whole word only" and "Match case" checkboxes control how *RegEdt32* compares the search string you type against the Registry data. By default, both these checkboxes are off.

- The Up and Down radio buttons control the direction in which *RegEdt32* searches: Up searches from the selected key to the root key of the active window, while Down searches from the selected key to the last subkey of the last key of the active root.

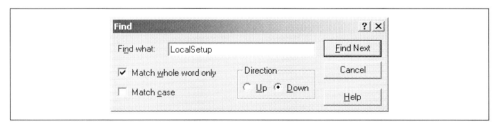

Figure 5-4. RegEdt32's Find dialog

Each time *RegEdt32* finds a match, it highlights the matching key in the tree pane of the active root key window. You can then use the Find Next button to search for the next instance, or the Cancel button to stop looking.

If you want to find keys and values with maximum flexibility, the excellent Registry Search & Replace utility is probably what you're looking for. It's an easy-to-use, flexible tool for searching the Registry. You can get it at *http://www.iserv.net/~sjhswdev/REGSRCH.HTM*.

Saving and Loading Registry Keys

RegEdt32 allows you to dump Registry data into ordinary files that you can back up or use on other machines. You can save data in binary and text formats, and you can reload binary data when you need it again. The text format has the advantage of being human-readable, but the binary format is more efficient and is the only one *RegEdt32* can import. (For more details on using this capability to back up your Registry, see Chapter 3, *In Case of Emergency*.)

RegEdt32 normally deals with the hive files stored in *%systemroot%\system32\ Config*. However, you can also create your own files that contain just the keys and values you want. Once you've created such a file, you can load it back to its original location or anywhere else in the Registry. You can also use the file on another machine's Registry.

Saving Keys

To create a binary file of Registry data, just select the key or subkey you want to save, then use *RegEdt32*'s Registry → Save Key command. When the standard Save dialog appears, specify a filename, and *RegEdt32* stores the selected key's contents (as well as those of its subkeys) to the file (as long as you have adequate permission to read the key, its subkeys, and their values). The completed file is an ordinary file, so you can copy it to floppy, email it, or handle it just like any other kind of document.

There's no way to combine more than one key in a file unless they have a common parent. If you want to capture web browser settings from your local machine, you could save HKLM\Software\Microsoft and HKLM\Software\Netscape in two separate files, or you could save HKLM\Software and get them both—plus a lot of other unrelated stuff.

Restoring Keys

Once you've saved a key, restoring it is fairly straightforward. Select the location where you want the key to appear when loaded, then use the Registry → Restore

Key... command. *RegEdt32* loads the saved key as a subkey of the currently selected key. For example, if you select HKLM\Software\Qualcomm\Eudora and load a file, the saved file's contents appear under Eudora. Be careful with this command; the saved key file doesn't contain any information about the key's path, so *RegEdt32* can't warn you that you're restoring a key in the wrong place.

When the new key is loaded, it actually replaces all subkeys and values of the selected key. Before anything actually gets replaced, you'll see a warning dialog asking you to confirm that you want to wipe out all the existing subkeys and values of the selected key. Unfortunately, though, the dialog doesn't tell you which key is about to be affected, so make sure you double-check the selected key to ensure it's the one you meant to restore over.

Loading Saved Keys as Hives

When you load a key with Registry → Restore Key..., it overwrites whatever was there before. You can also load a saved key as a new hive without overwriting any existing data. When you do this, the loaded key is mapped into the Registry the same way the standard system hives are, and it remains loaded until you manually unload it. This function gives you an easy way to add a copy of a user account, since you can just grab HKU*sid* from one machine and load it as a hive under HKU on another.

You may load a saved key as a hive under HKU or HKLM but not any other root key. If you have HKU or HKLM selected, *RegEdt32* enables the Registry → Load Hive... command; it is disabled otherwise. (It'll also be disabled if you have read-only mode enabled.) When you load a key as a hive with this command, the saved key is loaded as a subkey of whichever root you loaded it into. You have to name the new key after you select the file to be loaded; this name is used to identify the new hive. For example, if you select HKU and load a saved key, telling *RegEdt32* to name the new key ExplodingStuff, the new hive appears as HKU\ExplodingStuff.

Once a saved key is loaded as a hive, you can modify its keys and values like any other key. The changes are reflected in the saved key file, which remains loaded and available until you explicitly unload it with the Registry → Unload Hive command.

Saving as Text

RegEdt32 also allows you to save a key and its values to a text file with the Registry → Save Subtree As... command. The formatting is identical to what appears when you print a key. If you need to search the Registry for a particular value (as opposed to a key name, which *RegEdt32* can do) your options are to use *RegEdit* or to save the root key you want to search to a text file and search it yourself. Apart from that, this command isn't very useful.

Providing an Improvised Clipboard

There's one major feature that *RegEdt32* and *RegEdit* both lack: a real set of Clipboard operations. It would really be handy to be able to copy a Registry key from one location and paste it in another, especially since both programs let you open the Registries of other machines on the network.

While *RegEdt32* doesn't directly provide Clipboard support, you can get the same effect with the Registry → Save Key... and Registry → Restore Key... commands. Let's say you're setting up a batch of new laptop machines running Windows 2000 Professional for your company's sales force. They're all on the network, but you want to set up each laptop's Dial-Up Networking (DUN) phonebook entries so that they're all the same. Here's one way to accomplish your goal:

1. Set up one laptop so that its dialing options and phone book settings are configured the way you want them. Let's call this machine the source machine.

2. Copy the source machine's phonebook file (*%systemroot%\system32\ras\rasphone.pbk*) to the corresponding place on each of the target machines.

3. Run *RegEdt32* on a machine (the source machine will do, or you can use your desktop machine). Open the source machine's Registry and select HKCU\Software\Microsoft\RAS Phonebook, then use the Registry → Save Key... command to save the data to a file.

4. Open the Registry of each machine you need to modify, then use Registry → Restore Key... to load your saved file into HKU\.DEFAULT\Software\Microsoft\RAS Phonebook. Now any new user account created on that machine inherits the RAS phonebook settings. If you instead want to apply the phonebook settings to another account, feel free. In fact, as long as you have administrative rights on the machine, you can add the phonebook settings to all the accounts under HKU.

A True Story

Now it's time for an anecdote. While writing this chapter, I ran into a problem. The shareware screen capture software I use to grab figures for my writing (the excellent SnagIt/32 from TechSmith; *http://www.techsmith.com/*) is installed under my account on a machine named *enigma*. When I'm logged on to that machine, SnagIt can find its registration key and settings data in HKCU\Software\TechSmith\SnagIt\Settings, and it's happy. However, for some of the figures, I needed to log into a different domain, and since I wasn't logged in as the same user,

SnagIt could no longer see its settings data. To make things worse, I couldn't find the piece of paper with my registration code, and I was in a hurry.

Solution: use *RegEdt32*. I logged onto *enigma*, saved the SnagIt settings key by selecting HKCU\Software\TechSmith\SnagIt\Settings and using the Registry → Save Key command, and logged out. I then logged into my domain account, selected HKCU\Software\TechSmith\SnagIt, used the Registry → Restore Key command to restore the file I just saved, and ran SnagIt again. Problem solved! A few minutes later, I captured all the necessary images and was back on schedule.

Printing Registry Contents

RegEdt32 includes a rudimentary printing function. When you select a key and use the Registry → Print Subtree command, you get a hardcopy version of that key's subkeys and values that looks like this example:

```
Key Name:         SOFTWARE\Netscape\Netscape Navigator\Users\paul
Class Name:       <NO CLASS>
Last Write Time:  6/29/97 - 7:07 PM
Value 0
  Name:           DirRoot
  Type:           REG_SZ
  Data:           C:\Program Files\Netscape\Users
```

RegEdt32 prints everything below the key you've selected, so if you select HKLM\SOFTWARE for printing (as I foolishly did while writing this section), expect to wait a while for the completed output. The formatting and indentation help make the printout slightly more readable, but you'll probably find it more worthwhile to save the keys you're interested in as text with the Registry → Save Subtree As... command, then print that text file with your favorite editor.

The related Registry → Printer Setup command allows you to set characteristics for the printout, including what printer, paper size, and print orientation to use.

Editing Keys and Values

RegEdt32 is a more powerful and flexible Registry editor than *RegEdit*. However, the two are roughly equivalent when it comes to adding and deleting keys and values. Since the underlying functionality of the Registry is identical, it makes sense that their workings should be identical as well. (Just a reminder: don't edit things unless you're sure they need editing. End of sermon.)

Viewing Values as Binary Data

By default, *RegEdt32* shows each value as its native type. Sometimes, though, it can be useful to see a Registry value in raw form, without any kind of interpretation or formatting. Since hive files are always open, you can't use a standard file or hex editor to look at the file's contents; instead, *RegEdt32* gives you a way to get a hex dump of any value in the Registry. The View → Display Binary Data command takes the selected value's contents and displays it in hex, as shown in Figure 5-5.

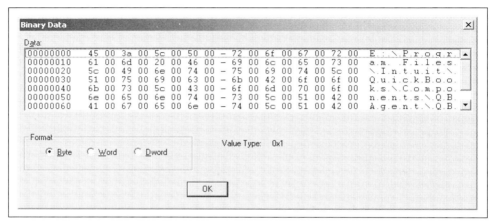

Figure 5-5. The Binary Data dialog

The radio buttons in the Format group let you control how *RegEdt32* presents the data. The default setting, Byte, shows the data as individual bytes. As a bonus, the rightmost section of the dialog shows the ASCII representations of the data, making this setting particularly useful for viewing strings. The Word and Dword buttons show the same data, but grouped as words or DWORDs, respectively. These settings are most useful for viewing binary or DWORD values.

Modifying Values

Once you've selected a value in the data pane, you can modify it by double-clicking it, pressing the Enter key, or using the commands on the Edit menu: Binary, String, DWORD, and Multistring.* Each data type has its own editing dialog. While they all basically work the same way, some have subtle differences or additional controls.

Modifying a string value

The String Editor dialog, shown in Figure 5-6, is arguably the simplest of all the data editors in *RegEdt32*. The current string value is shown in the String field; you

---

* You may notice the lack of editing tools for REG_FULL_RESOURCE_DESCRIPTOR and REG_RESOURCE_LIST. Microsoft doesn't want you editing those types, since they're used only in HKLM\HARDWARE.

can type or paste any data you'd like into the field. When you click OK, your changes are stored as the new contents for the value you're editing.

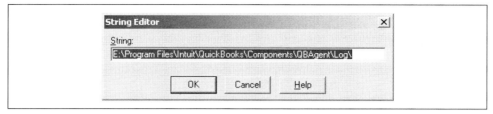

Figure 5-6. String editing

This string editor works for REG_EXPAND_SZ and plain old REG_SZ strings; there's a separate editor (discussed later) for REG_MULTI_SZ values.

Modifying a DWORD value

If strings are the simplest type of value to modify, DWORD runs a close second. The DWORD Editor dialog is shown in Figure 5-7. Like the String Editor, it offers you a field in which you type the desired new value. The three radio buttons in the Radix group allow you to specify what number base you're using. The default is Hex, so you can enter quantities such as "FF00" and "a29d" without any prefix or suffix. If you prefer, you can use the Binary and Decimal buttons to select base-2 or base-10 instead.

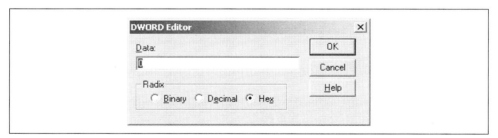

Figure 5-7. The DWORD editor

Modifying a multiple-string value

The Registry stores multiple-string values as a concatenation of all the individual strings, separated by null characters (hex 0x00). While you can edit these multi-string blocks as binary data, remembering where to put the null character that terminates each individual string gets to be tedious pretty quickly. *RegEdt32* offers a better solution in the form of the Multi-String Editor dialog (see Figure 5-8).

You may enter as many (or as few) strings as you like in this dialog's Data field. Each string is treated as an individual entity. When you hit Return at the end of a

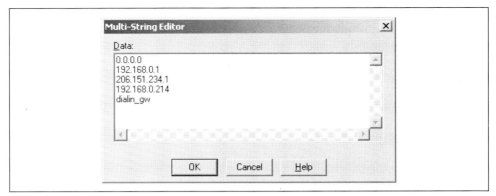

Figure 5-8. The Multi-String Editor

line, *RegEdt32* takes that as a signal to move to the next line and start another string. As with the other editors, you can use the standard Windows keyboard shortcuts to cut, copy, and paste text into this dialog.

Modifying a binary value

Many of the Registry's most important values are stored as raw binary data. This can pose a problem when you need to change (or undo a change!) their contents. After all, strings and numbers are easy to edit, but binary data can be a little tougher. *RegEdt32* includes a binary editor that makes it easier to inspect and change binary values when the need arises. The Binary Editor itself, shown in Figure 5-9, is fairly straightforward.

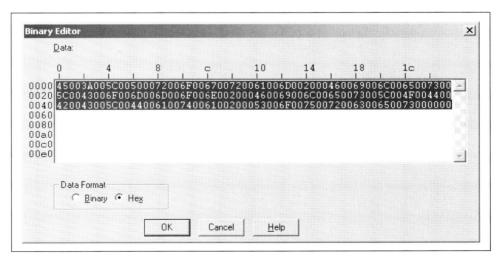

Figure 5-9. The Binary Editor

Editing Keys and Values

The column of digits on the left side of the edit field shows the offset of that line's data from the beginning of the data block. For example, the row labeled "0020" indicates that the first byte on that line starts 32 bytes (or hex 0x20) from the start of the data item. Likewise, the scale across the top of the edit field shows the offset within the line. The 44th byte in Figure 5-9 is at offset 0x2c from the beginning of the block. To find it, you'd first use the left column to find the row labeled "0020", then read across to "c" to find the correct byte.

The Binary and Hex radio buttons control how *RegEdt32* actually displays the data. When you change from one mode to another, the contents of the edit field changes, as do the horizontal and vertical scales.

The edit field itself shows the value's contents. *RegEdt32* treats the data there as text, so you can insert, remove, cut, copy, and paste in this field as much as you'd like. If you hit a key that's not legal (for example, "2" while editing binary data, or "J" in hex mode) *RegEdt32* ignores it. If you enter data that ends with an incomplete byte, *RegEdt32* warns you with a dialog, then pads the data with zeroes until it's the proper length.

One final caveat: unlike Windows 95 and 98, Windows 2000 and NT stores their strings in Unicode format. That means that each character in a string actually takes up two bytes of storage space. When you edit an ordinary ASCII string using the binary editor, you'll see that every other byte is zero: that's because ASCII strings only need one byte of the two reserved for each character. Don't fool with the zero bytes, or you risk turning your strings from ASCII to a weird hybrid of ASCII, Japanese, Cyrillic, and maybe even Pinyin Chinese.

Modifying a value of a different type

RegEdt32 is helpful enough to remember, and store, a data type for every value in the Registry. However, you're free to ignore that data and edit a value as though its type were different. You've already seen one example of how this works: the View → Display Binary Data command lets you inspect the contents of any type of value as though it were a REG_BINARY value.

When you have a value selected, if you double-click it you'll see its data displayed in whatever editor is appropriate. If instead you use the Binary, String, DWORD, or Multistring commands in the Edit menu, you can open any value's data as any of those types. For example, if you open a string as binary data, you see a display like the one shown in Figure 5-9.

While this is a useful trick, be careful. It's easy to corrupt data when editing it with an editor that has no knowledge of the data's native format. The safest course of action is to use the native format editor whenever possible. If you need to tweak a value without using its native format, I recommend using the binary editor instead.

Adding New Keys or Values

Like *RegEdit*, *RegEdt32* allows you to add new keys and values. The same cautions discussed in "Adding New Keys or Values" in Chapter 4 apply here too. For the most part, you won't need to add new keys unless you're adding one of the famous Microsoft hidden keys that are sometimes needed to activate (or deactivate) a particular feature.

Adding new keys

When you add a new key, it has to be a subkey of one of the existing root keys, and you must have appropriate access to that subkey. You tell *RegEdt32* where you want the new key by selecting a key in the tree pane of any root key window; the new key is created immediately beneath the selected key. There's no way to relocate a key once it's in place, so make sure you put it in the right location the first time.

Once you've picked out a good spot for your key, you can use the Edit → Add Key command to actually create the new key. When you do, you'll see the dialog shown in Figure 5-10. You specify the key name by typing it into the Key Name field (big surprise, right?), and you may optionally specify a data class for the key with the Class field. When you click the OK button, *RegEdt32* adds the new key in the selected location.

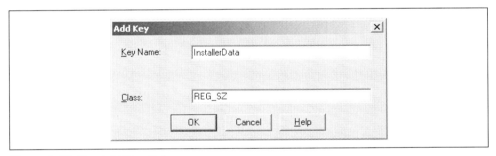

Figure 5-10. The Add Key dialog

Adding new values

Adding a new value is a three-step process. The first, and arguably hardest, step is to select the key to which you want to add the new value. This is important, since *RegEdt32* doesn't give you a good way to move a value from one key to another. Be sure to visually confirm that the key you want the new value on is actually the one that's highlighted.

The second step (once you've selected the desired key) is to use the Edit → Add Value... command, which displays the dialog shown in Figure 5-11. You use this dialog to supply a name and type for the new value: the name goes in the Value Name field, of course, while the Data Type combo box allows you to choose any one of the data types *RegEdt32* supports (REG_SZ, REG_EXPAND_SZ, REG_DWORD, REG_MULTI_SZ, and REG_BINARY).

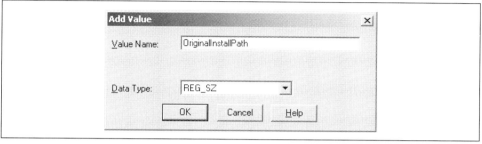

Figure 5-11. The Add Value dialog

The third and final step is to actually give the value some contents. You use the dialogs shown earlier in the section "Modifying Values"; which dialog pops up in this third step depends on the type of data you selected in the second step. Once you enter a value into the appropriate editor dialog, *RegEdt32* adds the new value and stores it permanently in the Registry. At any prior point, you can cancel the operation without actually adding the new value.

Deleting Keys and Values

Contrary to what you might think, deleting data from the Registry is required somewhat more often than adding it. The biggest reason for deleting keys or values is to remove traces of applications or system components whose uninstallers are nonexistent or (more commonly) too poorly written to fully reverse whatever the original installation program did. Of course, sometimes it's necessary to undo something you've done yourself. For example, if you add one of the magic Microsoft keys sprinkled throughout their knowledge base, you may one day find it necessary to remove it again.

 You may remember the Options → Confirm on Delete command discussed earlier in the section "Setting Session Options." I strongly recommend leaving this option turned on, as it can save you from accidentally deleting something you would rather have kept. However, remember that this flag is set on a per-user basis!

Whether you're deleting a key or a value, the basic procedure is the same: highlight the key or value you want to remove, then either hit the DEL key or use the

Edit → Delete command. If you have the Options → Confirm on Delete option turned on, you'll see a confirmation dialog asking you if you *really* want to remove the selected key or value. If you say "Yes," *RegEdt32* deletes the item, just as you requested.

When you delete a key, *RegEdt32* also deletes all its subkeys and their values, so be sure to visually confirm that the key you want to delete is actually the one that's highlighted. The confirmation dialog unfortunately doesn't tell you what key or value is about to bite the dust, so it's up to you to double-check.

Registry Security Fundamentals

The Registry's hierarchical arrangement looks suspiciously like that of a filesystem in more ways than one. Like NTFS files, directories, and volumes, Registry keys can have attached attributes that control who owns them, who may read, write, and change them, and what events should be logged for further scrutiny.

In particular, every key has an *access control list*, or ACL, associated with it. The ACL is made up of zero or more *access control entries*, or ACEs. Each ACE grants a specific permission to a specific user or group. The permissions specified by the ACEs in the ACL apply to the object that holds the ACL and its children, if any. There are actually two separate kinds of ACL: a *discretionary ACL* (DACL) contains the permissions you put on the key, and a *system ACL* (SACL) contains permissions applied (and managed) directly by the OS.

Basic Registry Permissions

Some Windows 2000 permissions apply to more than one kind of object. However, the semantics of Registry permissions are a bit different from those of filesystem or objects. Table 5-2 shows the 10 basic permissions that can be attached to Registry keys. These permissions are also called *Discretionary Access Controls*, or DACs.

Table 5-2. Registry Access Permissions

Permission	What It Allows
Query Value	Retrieving a specific key's value: for example, the value Paul Robichaux of the HKLM\SOFTWARE\SMAIL\Users key
Set Value	Changing the contents of a specific key's value
Create Subkey	Creating a new subkey of the specified key; the new subkey inherits the parent's permissions, but they may be explicitly changed later
Enumerate Subkeys	Traversing all subkeys of a specific key and getting their full pathnames

Table 5-2. Registry Access Permissions (continued)

Permission	What It Allows
Notify	Receiving or setting auditing notifications
Create Link	Creating a symbolic link (such as a shortcut or a Unix symlink) that points to another key in the Registry
Delete	Removing the specified key, its subkeys, and all associated values
Write DAC	Changing the DACs attached to the specified key
Write Owner	Changing the owner of the specified key. This permission is new in Windows 2000.
Read Control	The permission holder can read the ACL for the key

Besides these basic DACs, there are additional composite DACs. These composites grant combinations of two or more of the rights listed in Table 5-2. For example, the Full Control composite grants all 10 of the rights listed above. Table 5-3 shows the composite DACs and the rights they include.

Table 5-3. Composite DACs

Permission	What It Allows
Read	Read-only access to a specific key, its subkeys, and their values (actually includes Query Value and Enumerate Subkeys)
Write Owner	Changing the owner associated with the specified key; in Windows 2000, this is a basic permission, not a composite
Full Control	All of the above rights; Full Control allows the holder to do literally anything to the keys with that permission

Some older versions of NT exhibit a serious security weakness: by default, many of the keys in the Registry are set to Everyone:Full Control access. This is unnecessarily permissive. See Chapter 9 for more details on how to tighten your Registry permissions for Windows 2000 and NT.

Applying ACLs

Both Windows 2000 and NT use some fairly simple rules to evaluate ACEs and decide whether you get access to a particular resource or not. Understanding these rules and how they work is critical to knowing how to secure your systems.

The first rule is actually a significant difference in how permissions are handled between Windows NT and Windows 2000. In NT, you can explicitly deny someone access by giving them the No Access permission. In Windows 2000, there are separate Allow and Deny flags in each ACE entry. This difference becomes important when you consider it in the light of the ACL evaluation rules:

Everything not specifically permitted is forbidden
> Much as in the old Soviet Union, the only access that's permitted is whatever is explicitly granted by the ACEs on the object. For example, if the ACL on a key contains a single ACE that specifies Administrators:Allow Full Control, no one else has any access because there's no explicit grant of access.

The most restrictive permission always wins
> If two or more ACEs conflict, the effective permission is always the most restrictive ACE. For example, consider a Registry key that has Authenticated Users: Allow Read and Domain Users: Deny Read. A domain user's effective permission will be Deny Read, since that's the most restrictive ACE that applies to the user.

Taken in combination, these two rules allow you to calculate the effective permission that result from any combination of ACEs in an ACL. They also highlight why Microsoft added separate Allow and Deny flags. Since the most restrictive permission is always used, an explicit denial (using the Deny flag) is always more powerful than any grant of the same right. Rather than depending on the implicit denial rule (#1 above), you can gain improved security (and clearer semantics) by expressly denying access to an object.

Securing Registry Keys in Windows 2000

RegEdt32 allows you to set permissions on any key in the Registry. Since most of the data in the Registry belongs to system components, you must use this feature carefully; if you change permissions on a key so that the application that needs it can't get to it, you may destabilize or destroy your system.

The Security → Permissions... command, which displays the Permissions dialog as shown in Figure 5-12, is the only security-related command in the Windows 2000 version of *RegEdt32*. To use it, select a key in any root key window, then select the command. When the dialog opens, it shows which key you've selected and what ACEs are in effect for that particular key. This is different from the NT 4.0 version of the same dialog; that's because the standard security dialog in Windows 2000 has been substantially enhanced.

- The Name list shows the current list of accounts and groups that have ACE entries on this key. The names of domain groups are expanded to show the domain they belong in. You can change which users and groups are in the ACL with the Add and Remove buttons to the right of the list.

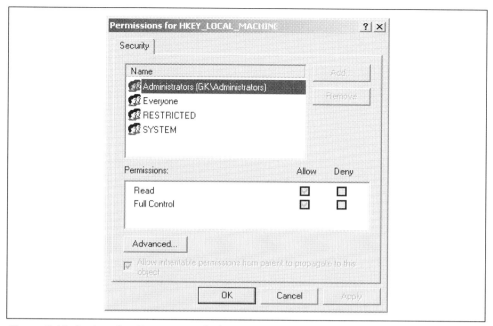

Figure 5-12. Registry key Permissions dialog

- The Permissions field shows the predefined composite DACs listed in Table 5-3. The two checkboxes to the right of each entry let you specify whether to allow or deny specific permissions, according to the rules I mentioned earlier in this section.

- The Advanced button opens the Access Control Settings dialog, which contains three tabs: Permissions, Auditing, and Owner. Each is discussed in more detail in the next three sections.

- The "Allow inheritable permissions from parent to propagate to this object" checkbox controls whether the permissions applied to parents of the currently selected key will be applied to this key (and possibly its subkeys, if they have this same checkbox set).

Setting Permissions

To set permissions on a Registry key in Windows 2000, you have to use the Permissions tab of the Access Control Settings dialog (see Figure 5-13). This tab contains a summary of the contents of the selected key's DACL and SACL, listing each ACE individually.

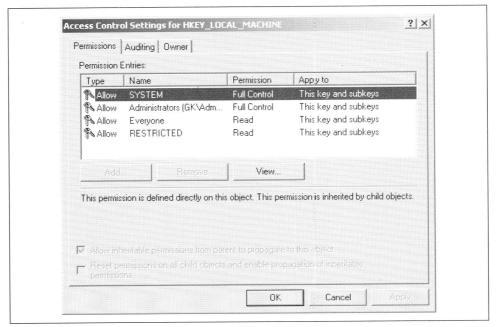

Figure 5-13. The Permissions tab summarizes ACEs for the current Registry key

The ACLs shown in the Permission Entries list are pretty vanilla, but they still bear explanation:

- The Type column shows whether the ACE allows or denies the specified permission. Notice that Deny entries are always listed first; that makes sense, since they'll always be evaluated first.

- The Name column shows the name of the account or group to which the ACE applies. Local and domain accounts and local groups may be assigned permissions. There are also several built-in account proxies (such as CREATOR OWNER, which represents whichever account originally created an object, and ANONYMOUS LOGON, which indicates any account that can log on anonymously) that may have DACs attached.

- The Permission column shows the effective DAC granted by this ACE. You'll see either a composite DAC from Table 5-3 or 'Special Access", the synonym used when there's some combination of DACs that don't match a predefined composite DAC.

- The Apply to column indicates whether the specified ACE is applied to the selected key only, the selected key and its subkeys, or the subkeys alone. Normally, ACE changes apply to the selected keys and all subkeys, although this may change if you change the permission inheritance settings.

Adding, removing, and changing ACE entries

You modify ACE entries with the Add..., Remove, and View/Edit... buttons below the permission list. Let's deal with removal first, since it's the most straightforward case: select an ACE, click Remove, and it's gone (though the change isn't actually recorded in the Registry until you OK the Access Control Settings and Permissions dialogs).

Adding and viewing or changing ACE entries are similar in concept and execution. When you add a new entry by clicking the Add... button, you must begin by specifying the user or group account to which the ACE applies. Once you choose a subject for the ACE, you see a dialog like the one shown in Figure 5-14.

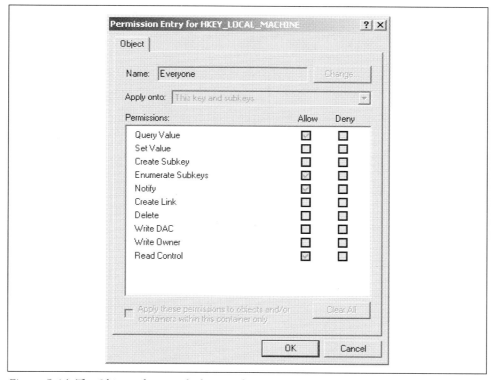

Figure 5-14. The Object tab controls the specific ACEs applied to a Registry key

- The Name field (and the associated Change... button) shows the user or group specified for this ACE and allows you to change it.
- The Apply onto pulldown lets you choose what the new or modified ACE applies to. By default, the pulldown is set to "This key and subkeys", meaning that the ACE is blasted onto all subkeys of the current key when you finish twiddling it. You can also choose to apply permissions to the current key

only by choosing This key only, or to the subkeys only with the Subkeys only option.

- The Permissions list shows you the actual DACs and lets you allow or deny them in any combination. While the user interface items shown look like checkboxes, they behave like radio buttons in that you can either allow or deny any DAC, but not both. The Clear All button unchecks everything in both columns.

- The "Apply these permissions to objects and/or containers within this container only" checkbox acts as a modifier to the Apply onto pulldown's Subkeys only and "This key and subkeys" values. When you check this box, the DACs you select are applied only to the current key and its immediate subkeys.

Seeing and controlling permission inheritance

Microsoft apparently realized that the inheritance scheme for Windows 2000 permissions is a little confusing, because they took the welcome step of adding a plain-spoken description of the inheritance settings in effect for the current key. For example, Figure 5-13 says "This permission is defined directly on this object. This permission is inherited by child objects": that's a remarkably clear statement of the inheritance settings in effect for that key. The contents of the text description depend on the setting of the two checkboxes at the bottom of the dialog:

- "Allow inheritable permissions from parent to propagate to this object" controls whether the parent's permissions are applied to the selected key and its values. Normally this box is checked, so permission settings are passed down to subkeys when a parent's permissions are changed.

This default setting means that if you make some boneheaded change to a parent key's permissions, you will wreck permissions on all its subkeys. Be careful when changing permissions, and be doubly careful when using this option.

- "Reset permissions on all child objects and enable propagation of inheritable permissions" allows you to specify that you want any existing ACEs on subkeys of the current key to be removed. When you check it, the subkeys' ACLs are cleared, their "allow inheritance" flag is enabled, and permissions set on the parent object you're editing take effect when you approve them.

Auditing Registry Activity

The Auditing tab, shown in Figure 5-15, summarizes the auditing ACL entries for the selected Registry key. Its appearance is similar to the Permissions tab shown in Figure 5-13; that's by design, since the mechanisms for reviewing and setting ACEs for auditing or object access are similar. The Auditing Entries list shows each audit ACE entry defined for the current Registry key, using a format that's almost identical to the format used for ACE entries. The primary difference is that the Type field for audit entries are either Success or Fail; this indicates whether audit log entries will be generated for successful or failed access attempts.

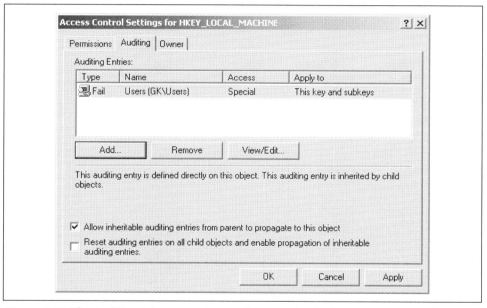

Figure 5-15. The Auditing tab summarizes auditing entries for the current Registry key

Adding, removing, and changing auditing entries

You manage auditing entries with the Add..., Remove, and View/Edit... buttons. Like their counterparts on the Permissions tab, these buttons allow you to change the individual ACEs that make up the auditing ACL on the key you're modifying:

- The Add... button prompts you to designate a user or group to whom the new auditing settings apply. It then displays the dialog shown in Figure 5-16. By checking the Successful or Failed checkboxes for each DAC, you can control whether the system records an audit message in the event log for each successful or failed attempt to exercise the corresponding permission.

- The Remove button removes the selected auditing entry, without asking for confirmation. Note that your changes aren't saved until you click OK in the Access Control Settings dialog and again in the Permissions dialog itself.

- The View/Edit... button displays the dialog from Figure 5-16, with which you can edit the existing auditing controls on a key.

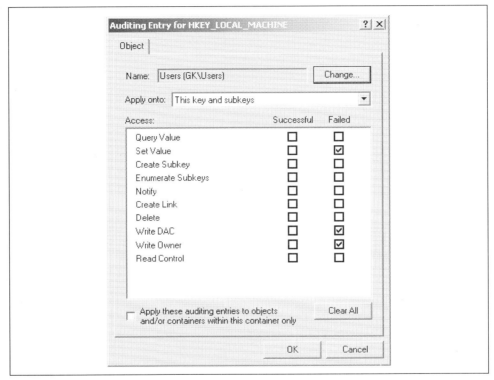

Figure 5-16. The Auditing Entry dialog

Seeing and controlling audit control inheritance

Since the Permissions and Auditing tabs are so similar, it might not be surprising that the Auditing tab contains the same plain-English[*] description of the audit settings you apply. The two checkboxes at the bottom of the tab have exactly the same effect as their counterparts on the Permissions tab; they work together to control how your audit settings are propagated to subkeys of the current key.

---

[*] Literary license allows me to ignore the fact that you may be using a language other than English.

Changing Key Ownership

Changing the ownership of a particular key in Windows 2000 is pretty straightforward; that's the sole function of the Owner tab in the Access Control Settings dialog, shown in Figure 5-17. Normally, you won't change ownership of a key that belongs to the system, although in some security-related circumstances (usually dictated by a Microsoft security bulletin) you might. More often, you'll change ownership of keys used by applications you've installed to keep users from fiddling with them. The actual process of changing ownership is simple: switch to the Owner tab and select the new owner you want for the key. The Change owner to list is filled with accounts and groups that can own the current key, based on its parentage and the inheritance settings currently in force. Checking the "Replace owner on subcontainers and objects" applies the change recursively to the subkeys and values beneath the current key. Leaving it in its default unchecked state changes ownership only of the selected key and its values.

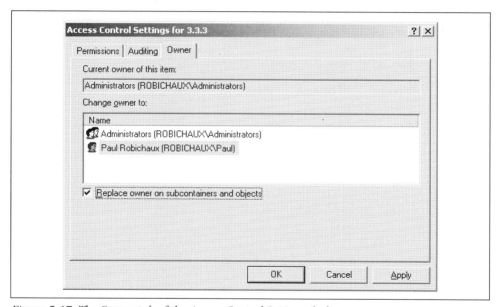

Figure 5-17. The Owner tab of the Access Control Settings dialog

Securing Registry Keys in Windows NT

When using *RegEdt32* under NT, you'll notice a few things that differ between Windows 2000 and NT. For starters, the Security menu has more commands in it; when you use these commands, the user interface is different as well. However, for the most part the underlying behavior is the same. If anything, NT is less flexible than Windows 2000 because it doesn't have all the same inheritance and permission controls.

Setting Permissions

The Security → Permissions... command displays the Registry Key Permissions dialog (see Figure 5-18). To use it, select a key in any root key window, then give the command. When the dialog opens, it shows which key you've selected and which account owns it (you can't change either of them from the dialog, however). The controls in the dialog give you access to the permission settings for the key.

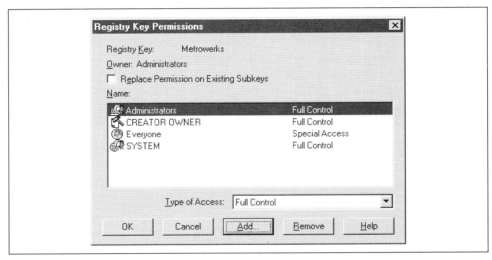

Figure 5-18. Registry Key Permissions dialog

- The "Replace Permission on Existing Subkeys" checkbox tells *RegEdt32* whether to apply the permission changes you specify to all subkeys of the current key or not. When subkeys are created, they inherit the parent key's access controls. However, by the time you change the parent key's access controls, the subkeys may have different controls in place. Use this option only when you intend to override any access controls that have been applied to subkeys.

- The Name field lists the current access controls in force on the key. Each line in the list shows an account name and the DAC granted to that account. The standard DACs are listed in Table 5-2 and Table 5-3. The Type of Access combo box lets you change the DACs for any account in the Name list. Changes you make are immediately reflected in the list, but aren't applied until you click OK.

- The Add… button allows you to use NT's standard "Add Users and Groups" dialog (see Figure 5-19) to add new accounts to the ACL. The accounts you add from this dialog appear in the Name list with Full Control as the default DAC; make sure you change this to avoid opening a security hole.

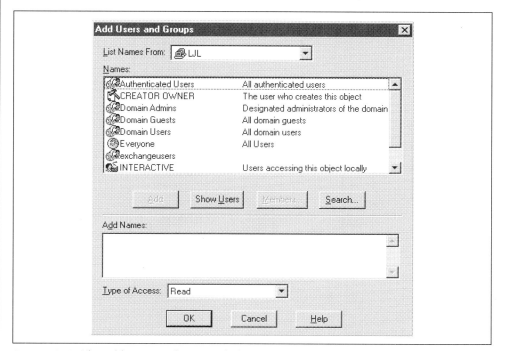

Figure 5-19. The Add Users and Groups dialog

Auditing Registry Key Activity

Auditing allows you to keep a trail of evidence to identify problems and pin their start down to an exact time. NT's auditing facility lets you audit specified actions taken by specified accounts. For example, you can audit any attempt to change security policy by any accounts, or you could audit failed attempts to log on by a single account. This combination of specifying who and what makes auditing pretty flexible.

Enabling auditing on an NT machine

While auditing is useful, it also takes time. By default, NT leaves system auditing turned off. Before you can audit Registry access (or anything else), you have to enable auditing on the machine you want audited.

You do this with the User Manager or User Manager for Domains,* yet another of the standard administrative utilities NT includes to simplify your job. Here's how to enable auditing on a single server or workstation:

1. Run User Manager on the target machine. To change auditing control settings, you have to be logged in with an account that has Administrator privilege on the target machine.

2. Use the Policies → Audit… menu command to display the Audit Policy dialog, shown in Figure 5-20.

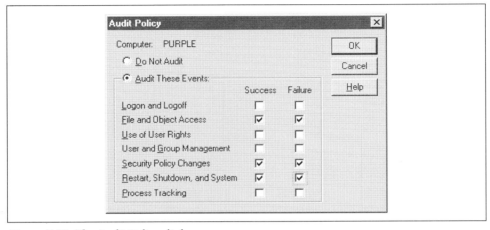

Figure 5-20. The Audit Policy dialog

3. Make sure the "Audit These Events" radio button is turned on. Otherwise, NT still happily refuses any auditing requests you make in other applications, including *RegEdt32*.

4. Use the checkboxes to select which classes of events you want to audit. For Registry access auditing, make sure the "File and Object Access" checkboxes are marked. You may also want to enable other types of auditing, but they're not strictly necessary.

5. Click OK, then exit the User Manager.

Once you take these steps on a machine, you won't have to do them again; auditing on that machine will remain enabled unless you manually turn it off using the same procedure. You do, however, have to execute these steps on every machine for which you want to enable auditing. Once you've done so, you can actually turn on auditing for the Registry.

---

* Which one you get depends on whether you're using Windows NT Workstation or Server. Workstations always get the vanilla User Manager, and servers (in or out of a domain) always get User Manager for Domains. Fortunately, they're very similar, so I'll treat them here as identical.

Telling RegEdt32 what to audit

The Registry Key Auditing dialog, shown in Figure 5-21, appears when you choose the Security → Auditing... menu command.

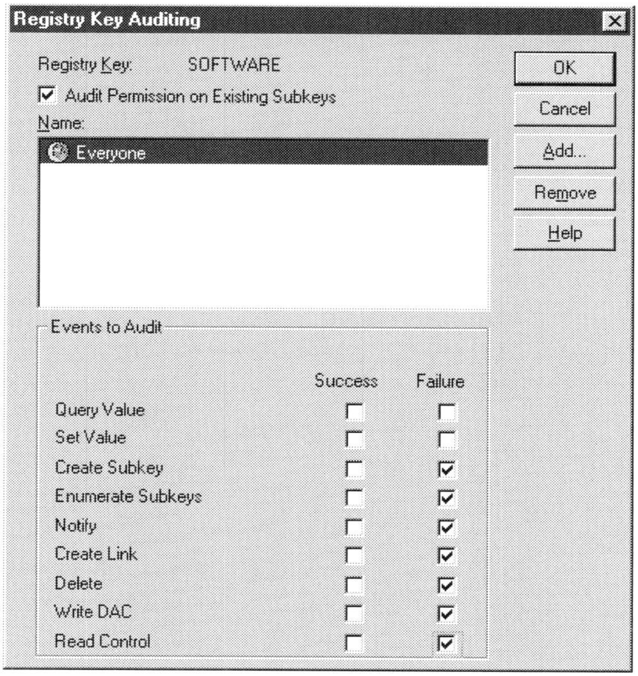

Figure 5-21. The Registry Key Auditing dialog

This dialog can be a little confusing at first, so a look at what its controls do will demystify it some:

- The "Registry Key" field shows you what subkey you've selected, but it doesn't tell you what root that subkey belongs to. You may need to move the entire Registry Key Auditing dialog around to make sure you're auditing the key you intended to audit.

- The "Audit Permission on Existing Subkeys" checkbox tells *RegEdt32* whether you want the audit changes you specify to apply to all subkeys under the selected key or just the selected key. If you audit all subkeys of a large root key like HKLM, your performance will suffer. Sometimes, though, this type of shotgun auditing is necessary so you can see which keys are being changed when you don't know in advance which ones you need to audit.

- The "Name" list shows which accounts will be audited. You can think of this list like the FBI's Most Wanted list: names on this list are the ones scrutinized, while other names are ignored. The Add... and Remove buttons let you change the members of this list using an interface like the one shown in Figure 5-19. In addition to actual user accounts, you can audit the built-in accounts like *Everyone*, *INTERACTIVE*, and *SYSTEM*.

- The two columns of checkboxes in the "Events to Audit" group are the meat of this dialog, since they control what actions are logged for the specified accounts. Each of the DACs listed earlier in Table 5-2 may be audited. When you check a DAC's Success checkbox, the system creates an audit record any time an account on the Name list succeeds in using that DAC. Conversely, the Failure checkbox causes NT to generate an audit record when a listed account tries to use the DAC and fails.

  For example, let's say you add the account *peanut* to the audit list for HKLM\Software\Microsoft, then check Success for Create Subkey and Failure for Write DAC. Once you save those settings, NT generates an audit record whenever *peanut* succeeds in creating a new subkey under the selected key or fails while trying to change the DACs for an ACL entry.

As you'd expect, the OK and Cancel buttons allow you to preserve or discard changes you make in this dialog.

Reviewing the audit records

Once you've told *RegEdt32* what to audit, you still need to see the audit entries that have been generated. If you're accustomed to administering Unix machines, you're probably familiar with the *syslog* service. NT has a similar feature; it keeps an event log that applications and system components may write to. The NT event log is actually three separate logs: one for system data, one for application-generated data, and one for security data. Auditing messages (no matter their source) go into the security log.

To view these log messages, you'll need to use Microsoft's Event Viewer application. A complete discussion of how to use the Event Viewer is outside the scope of this book, but the basic process is simple enough to boil down into a few concise steps:

1. Launch the Event Viewer (*eventvwr.exe*). There's a shortcut to it in the Start menu, too; look under Programs → Administrative Tools (Common) → Event Viewer to find it.

2. When Event Viewer opens, you see a window like the one shown in Figure 5-22. Use the Log → Security command to display the security log.

3. Event Viewer shows you a passel of events (the exact number depends on how big the event log is). You can sort, filter, and view events using the

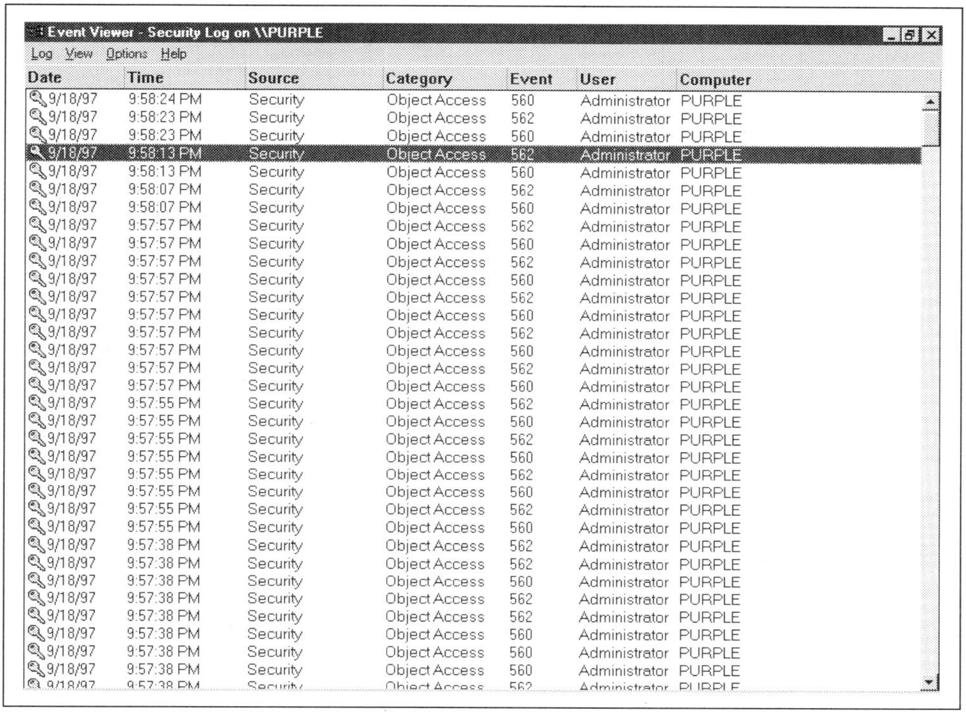

Figure 5-22. The Event Viewer application

commands in the View menu. If there's a particular event you're interested in, double-click it or use the View → Details... command to get the dialog shown in Figure 5-23, which gives all the pertinent event details in one place.

Changing Key Ownership

Like every other object in NT's world, each Registry key has an owner. As with Unix, NT allows the owner to control access to objects it owns to a certain extent; the superuser or Administrator account can always take ownership of an object and change its permissions when necessary. NT does, however, provide a standard auditing mechanism that logs all manually initiated changes of ownership, so you'll always have an audit trail that shows when someone's taken over one of your objects.

When you use this command, you're telling *RegEdt32* to change the owner of the currently selected key and all its subkeys to the current account. This blanket change of ownership can lead to unexpected behavior, since many NT components assume they'll always have unrestricted access to all subkeys of HKLM and many subkeys of HKCU and HKCR. However, it's usually a good idea to set

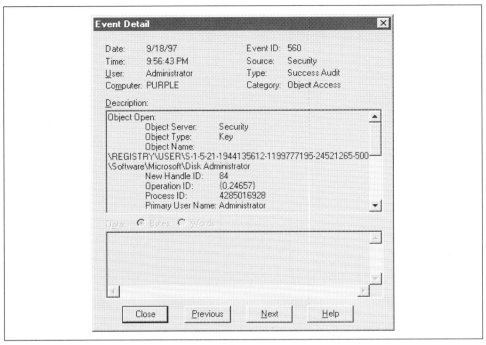

Figure 5-23. Registry audit event detail display

appropriate ownership of HKU's subkeys, as well as those subkeys of HKLM that are safe to reset. The best way to set ownership is with a utility like David LeBlanc's *everyone2user*, which is discussed in the section "Fixing Registry Security ACLs" in Chapter 9.

If you insist on doing it manually, *RegEdt32* allows you to take ownership of Registry keys with the Security → Owner... command. The Owner dialog, pictured in Figure 5-24, shows you what key is selected and which account owns it. The Take Ownership button changes the key's (and its subkeys') ownership to whatever account you're logged in as, while the Close button cancels the command without changing anything. Of course, if you don't have Administrator privileges you can't take ownership of any key you don't already own.

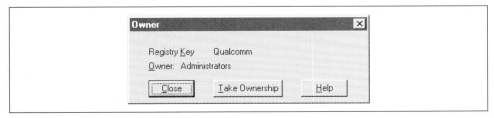

Figure 5-24. The Owner display

6
Using the System Policy Editor

All About System Policies

Windows 2000 supports aggregating users into groups and domains. You can assign users to a particular group or domain, then grant (or deny) permission to use certain system resources based on their membership. For example, you could create a group of users in the accounting department and grant that group access to the printer in the department conference room, without having to grant printer access to users from outside the department. For a complete explanation of managing users, groups, and domains, see *Essential Windows NT System Administration,* by Æleen Frisch (O'Reilly & Associates).

Besides offering access controls so that users and groups gain or lose access to individual files, shares, servers, and printers, NT 3.1 offered a set of features you could customize on a per-machine or per-user basis. As you might guess, these settings were just keys in the Registry; an example is the warning notice that you can add to the logon process by adding two new values to HKLM\SOFTWARE\Microsoft\Windows NT\CurrentVersion\Winlogon. Even though these settings were present, there were two serious flaws that made them more difficult than necessary to use:

They weren't organized well
Even though there were a large number of customizable settings in NT 3.1, 3.5, and 3.51, there was little in the way of organized documentation, and related settings weren't grouped together in the user interface (or in any other meaningful way).

They were too hard to use
None of the adjustable settings were difficult to change in and of themselves, but trying to add a logon warning to one machine is much easier than trying

to do so for an entire network of several thousand machines. To compound the problem, savvy users could change the settings (assuming they had appropriate privileges).

Microsoft addressed these flaws in the NT 3.51 Resource Kit with the introduction of tools for managing *system policies*. These policies were nothing more than groups of settings: one group that controlled the appearance of the desktop, one that controlled what programs users could run, and so on. However, the key innovation was a mechanism for distributing policies to all computers in a domain. This made it possible for an administrator to write policies for individual users, groups of users, and individual machines, then let NT take care of the actual work of distributing the policies to each machine in the domain and applying them.[*] These policy mechanisms were included as a part of the standard installation for Windows NT Server 4.0 and the Windows 2000 Server family.

Why Is This in a Windows 2000 Book?

Windows 2000 introduced Active Directory. It turns out that among its other features, Active Directory provides a new, and greatly improved, mechanism for setting and delivering system policies. *Group policy objects* (GPOs) provide a more scalable and greatly expanded set of policies than the tools that shipped with Windows NT 4.0. You might wonder why Microsoft even included the policy tools described in this chapter with Windows 2000. The answer is simple: you can't use GPOs to apply policies on computers that don't support Active Directory. That means that Windows 95, 98, and NT clients are out of luck, as are Windows 2000 computers that aren't part of an Active Directory domain. To effectively set policies on a mixed network, you need to use the NT 4.0 policy mechanism—detailed in this chapter—to set policies for these downlevel clients; you normally use them in conjunction with GPOs, as described in Chapter 7, *Using Group Policies*.

When you use the NT and 2000 policy systems in combination, you actually end up having to maintain policy settings in two separate places. This is undesirable, but it's better than having no policy capability for older clients.

What's a Policy?

A policy is nothing more than a group of related settings whose values you can specify. Each policy typically has a name, such as "Shell Restrictions." Policies are arranged in a hierarchy like Registry keys or disk files and folders. You use policies to enforce access controls on what users can do. For example, there are

---

[*] Windows 95 and 98 may have system policies applied too, though some of their policy elements live in different keys than the NT equivalents.

policies that let you to restrict what applications users may run, whether they can change the desktop pattern, or what resources can appear in the Network Neighborhood.

Categories contain one or more policies

Each user, group, or computer policy is actually made up of several policy *categories*. For example, the default policy template provided for NT machines provides categories such as "Control Panel" and "Windows NT Shell." Each category in turn contains individual policies such as "Restrict access to desktop" or "Hide Settings tab." This usage can be a little confusing: a user policy can contain several categories, each of which can contain several policies. I use the term "policy" to mean the policies that live in a category and "user policy" to mean the policy settings applied to a user, group, or computer.

Policies are made of parts

Policies are made up of *parts*. Each part represents one aspect of a policy, such as "don't allow users to use the Start → Run... command" or "here's a list of applications that the user may run." Parts got their name from the fact that each part of a policy has a control associated with it. Parts have values, and these controls allow you to set them. The permissible set of values for a part depends on what the part controls. Some parts need numeric values, while others accept lists of programs or true/false values.

A single policy may consist of one part or many. Each part within a policy corresponds to a value stored somewhere in the Registry. When you enable a policy, what you're really doing is telling the target computer to assign some particular value to each part in that policy. That in turn forces certain values in the Registry (each of which corresponds to a single part) to have particular values as well. You'll see some more concrete examples later in the chapter. Note that these Registry changes are persistent, an effect known as Registry tattooing.

How are policies defined?

Policy definitions are built using *policy templates*. These templates are nothing more than text files that tell *POLEDIT* what to display in its interface and how to convert the user's settings into a *.POL* file.

When you install any of the Windows 2000 or NT Server products, you get three policy files in *%systemroot%\INF*: *WINNT.ADM* (which holds settings specific to Windows 2000 and Windows NT), *COMMON.ADM* (which holds settings that apply to both Windows 9x and NT/2000), and *WINDOWS.ADM* (the Win9x-only settings). These standard files cover most of the things you can restrict or constrain with policies. However, it's possible for third parties to write policy templates that add new policy definitions for other software. The most widely known examples are Microsoft's Office policy templates; these templates let you restrict Office-specific settings, such as which hosts appear in the FTP dialog within Word. Other vendors have produced policy template files, and you can even create your own (as described in "Creating Your Own Policy Templates" later in this chapter) to control applications that don't ship with their own templates.

The template files use a simple language to specify which keys and values are affected by the policy and its parts. When you create a template, you're really giving *POLEDIT* instructions on what to display and how to build a *.POL* file based on the user's policy settings; the system policy mechanism applies that file's changes without regard to what they are.

Simac Software makes a product called Policy Template Editor (see *http://www.tools4nt.com/*). It's a specialized tool, but it works very well and is much easier than editing template files by hand.

User versus machine policies

The policy mechanism allows you to build policies that apply to computers, individual users, or groups of users. Computer policies apply to all users on a machine; they're stored in each machine's HKLM root key, and they remain in effect no matter what user logs on to the machine. By contrast, user and group policies apply only to the user or group named as the target, and they are automatically downloaded and installed onto each machine the user logs into. (The system evaluates group membership at logon time to decide which policies should be applied to the user account logging on.)

Here's an example. Let's say you have four machines in your domain: *titan*, *minuteman*, *atlas*, and *trident*. Within this domain, you have a few dozen user accounts, but you create policies that apply to two accounts: *intern* and *visitor*. Whenever either of these accounts logs into a machine, the defined policy is downloaded from a domain controller and is stored in that machine's HKCU root key. Whenever any other user logs into a machine, the default policy settings will be in effect.

How Are Policies Stored?

Like butterflies, policies go through a number of stages between their initial creation and their final emergence. Understanding where policy settings live at each stage of their lifecycle is key to understanding how to build and apply them.

The System Policy Editor stores policies as individual *.POL* files. You can think of these files as similar to Registry hives, as they contain a number of Registry key/value pairs that are loaded into the target machine's Registry when the policy is applied. When you create a policy and save it, you're actually generating a file that tells the System Policy Editor what values to change in the policy target's Registry.

Unlike the hives you can create with *RegEdt32*, these files can contain values from several different subkeys without having to hold the entire contents of their superior root key. For example, a single *.POL* file might contain values for HKLM\SOFTWARE\Microsoft\Windows NT\CurrentVersion and HKLM\SOFTWARE\Netscape\Netscape Navigator, without having to contain all of HKLM\SOFTWARE as well.

When you first create a policy, its *.POL* file is stored wherever you choose to save it. Once you've created and saved a policy file, the next stage of its lifespan begins: distribution. You can manually apply a policy file to individual machines; you may also store it on a Windows NT or Windows 2000 domain controller so it is be replicated automatically to Windows 95/98 and NT machines in your domain. You may choose to replicate the policy to backup domain controllers if you want users to get the correct policy setting when the primary controller is unavailable.* (In fact, if you want the policy to be automatically distributed, you must put it on the PDC and any BDCs that have replication enabled if you want to ensure that the policy is available.)

The final step in a policy's lifetime is the actual installation process. When a computer boots, or when a user logs into a machine running Windows 9x, NT, or 2000 Professional, the system checks the domain controller for an applicable policy. If there is one, a special system component called the *policy downloader*† transfers the *.POL* file to the workstation and merges its contents with the appropriate Registry root key.

How Are Policies Applied?

Once the policy downloader has pulled the policy file down to the workstation, the policy's settings still have to be applied. This is accomplished by merging the

---

* This scheme changes somewhat in Windows 2000, since there's no longer a distinction between primary and backup domain controllers. In that case, you should put the policy files on whichever Windows 2000 server is acting as the PDC emulator.

† It's unlikely that you'll need to, but Microsoft provides a mechanism for writing your own policy downloaders, which can supplement or replace the system's. Complete documentation for this is included in the MSDN SDK documentation.

policy settings into the appropriate parts of the Registry. As you'll see in more detail later in the chapter, policy parts can have three values:

On The part's policy is active, and whatever settings are enforced by that part should be applied.

Off The part's policy is active, and that part's settings should be forced off.

Leave as is
   Whatever value is currently in the Registry should be left alone.

If a part's corresponding value in the Registry matches the policy's value, no changes are made. If the part's value is "leave as is," no changes are made either. However, if the part's specified value and the Registry's contents are different, the policy value wins out, and the Registry's value is changed. These changes persist as long as the user's logged in, but—since the merge operation is really just loading a Registry hive—they disappear from the Registry when the user logs out.

Computer-specific policies are merged into HKLM, while user- or group-specific policies are merged into HKCU. It's important to remember that the policy settings are merged with the existing settings; they don't automatically overwrite the existing contents when the corresponding part is set to "leave as is." In addition, changes users make to policy-defined values under HKLM or HKCU are not written back to the policy! This prevents users from changing a policy setting and having the change propagate to other users. (Of course, if you're using policies, probably the first policy you'll set is the "Disable Registry editing tools" flag.)

The default policy

It's possible to assign policies to some users and computers, but not others. You might want to put restrictive policies onto machines in a shared lab area without enforcing any policies on individual users' machines, or you might want to restrict what some users can do no matter what machine they log into.

No matter what computers and accounts have policies, you can specify a default policy. This default applies to all users and computers that don't have an explicit policy defined for them. The default computer policy is applied to all computers in a domain (assuming the policy is applied to the whole domain), and the default user policy is applied to all domain users. By convention, these default policies are saved in a file named *NTconfig.pol* (for NT systems) or *config.pol* (for Windows 95 systems).

The initial default policies just set all policy parts to their "leave as is" state, meaning that the policy doesn't change anything. You may edit the default policy and save it back to its original filename; whatever changes you make are applied as defaults from that point onward.

Default policies apply to every user, including administrators! If you create a restrictive default policy, it applies to local and domain administrator accounts unless you create less-restrictive group or user accounts for your fellow admins.

Applying computer and user policies

When you create computer-specific policies, they're stored in the *.POL* file as groups of settings, one for each computer. To revive our earlier example, if you define policies for *titan* and *trident*, there will be keys with the same name in the policy file. When the policy downloader retrieves the policy file, it decides to apply it, or not, based on two rules. First, if there's a key in the policy file with the same name as the computer, that policy's part values are merged into HKLM. If no such key exists but there is a key named .default, that default key is applied. If neither condition is true no changes are made. A computer-specific policy always overrides the default: in fact, the default policy won't even be examined if there's a policy whose name matches the computer's.

User policies are applied using the same two rules: if there's a policy whose name matches the user who's logging in, it is applied. If not, the .default entry is used if it exists; otherwise, no changes are made.

Applying group policies

The rules that decide whether or not to apply a user or computer policy are very simple. However, the rules for applying group policies are a little more complicated. There are only two rules to know. The first, and most important, rule is this: a named user policy always trumps any group policies. For example, a policy for a user named *bob* overrides policies for any groups of which *bob* is a member.

The second rule to remember is that group policies are additive. If a user who's in more than one group logs in, the system uses the *group priority* to decide which policies to apply first. You set the group priority from within the System Policy Editor (as you'll see later in "Setting group policy priorities"). The lowest-priority group policy is applied first; its part settings are applied to the logged-in user's HKCU root key. The next lowest-priority group policy is evaluated next, and so on, until the highest-priority policy is applied. This approach means that if you put conflicting part values into two group policies, any user who's in both groups ends up with the part value of whichever policy is evaluated last.

Let's say you have two groups in your domain for executives and engineers. Your boss is an executive, but has an engineering degree, so you put her in both groups. If the "Don't allow users to play Solitaire" policy is set to "on" for executives and "off" for engineers, your boss's ability to play Solitaire hinges on the priority you assign to the two groups: the highest-priority setting will triumph.

Introducing the System Policy Editor

You create and edit system policies with the System Policy Editor (*poledit.exe*), which is normally installed only when you install a member of the Windows 2000 or NT server product families. It can be run from Windows 2000 Professional or NT Workstation, though, if you can legally obtain it from a server installation. Don't confuse this version of System Policy Editor with the Windows 95/98 version: if you want to create policies that Win9x clients can use, you must use the Win9x editor, and the same is true for the NT version.*

[NT4] If you don't have System Policy Editor installed, you can quickly install it (along with the User Manager for Domains, Server Manager, the Services for Macintosh Manager, and several others) by running the *setup.bat* file in the *clients**servtools*\ *winnt* directory of your NT Server CD. Once you've completed the installation, you'll have access to the System Policy Editor.

Learning the System Policy Editor Interface

When you use *RegEdt32* or *RegEdit*, you can definitely tell that you're using software that predates Windows 2000. Although both take on some aspects of the Windows 2000 GUI, they're indisputably different from other Windows 2000 software such as Internet Explorer or the system shell. *POLEDIT*, on the other hand, has an interface very similar to the shell, making it more immediately familiar.

The main window for *POLEDIT* is shown in Figure 6-1. In the figure, each computer, user, or group policy is represented by a large icon. Double-clicking one of these icons opens the associated policy, and policies may be created or deleted from this view as well.

Controlling what you see

The View menu allows you to change *POLEDIT*'s display in a number of ways, all of which are similar to commands in the shell and other administrative tools.

The first two commands in the menu are window dressing: the View → Toolbar command controls the state of *POLEDIT*'s toolbar. The toolbar is visible when this command is checked (the default) and invisible when it's not. Like *RegEdit*, *POLEDIT* has a status bar that can occupy the bottom margin of the application

---

* Actually, you can use the 2000/NT policy editor under Win95 or 98 with no ill effect, as long as you use the right *.ADM* files.

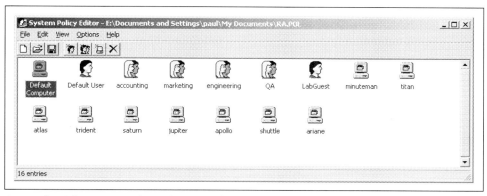

Figure 6-1. The System Policy Editor interface

window. The View → Status Bar command governs whether this decorative but useless bar appears or not.

The remaining View menu commands let you change the format of the display. Unless you change it, *POLEDIT* displays policies as large icons; this default corresponds to the View → Large Icons command. If you prefer, you can instead see policies as small icons (View → Small Icons) or an alphabetically sorted list. For some reason, Microsoft included both the View → List and View → Details commands, even though they display the same information in the same format!

The settings you choose in the View menu are stored with the policy file, so when you reload a new file it appears as it was when you last had it open.

Navigating in the policy window

As in Explorer, you can move from item to item in *POLEDIT*'s window with the arrow, PgUp, PgDn, Home, and End keys. When a policy is selected, you can open it by double-clicking it, pressing the Enter key, or using the Edit → Properties... command.

Managing Policies with POLEDIT

For the most part, creating policies with *POLEDIT* is simple and straightforward. Even though what you're really doing is editing the Registry on one or many machines, the interface lends itself to quickly making needed changes and saving them for later application.

The sequence of operation to apply policies is simple; there are only six steps:

1. Select whatever policy templates to use before creating any policies, then make them available to the editor by attaching them (more on that shortly).

2. Decide which users, groups, and computers you want to enforce policies on.

3. Create a "relaxed" policy for your administrative-level users that incorporates only those items from Step 3 you want to enforce on your admins.

4. Create a new policy file to contain your policies, then create enough user, group, and computer policies to satisfy your list from Step 2. Alternatively, you may open the Registry of a single machine (including the local machine) to make changes to that machine only.

5. Edit each individual policy to reflect the settings you want the policies to enforce.

6. Save the policy file in the appropriate location so that policy downloaders can find it.

Attaching Policy Templates

POLEDIT supports attaching an arbitrary number of policy templates. Templates you attach add their policies to the policy properties dialog; once you attach a template, its policies are available whenever you create new policies. This argues in favor of attaching policy templates to *POLEDIT* before creating any policies. That way, whatever templates you attach contribute to the policies you create without adding the extra work of going back and revising previously built policies.

When you first start *POLEDIT*, it automatically attaches the two policy templates needed for Windows 2000 machines, *COMMON.ADM* and *WINNT.ADM*. You may attach other templates using the Options → Policy Template... command, which displays the dialog shown in Figure 6-2.

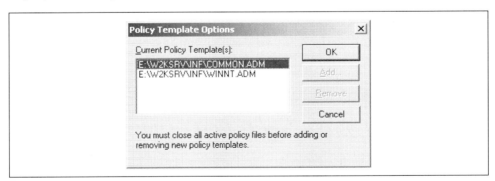

Figure 6-2. The Policy Template Options dialog

There are a number of additional policy templates floating around. For example, the Office 97 and Office 2000 resource kits include templates for their respective settings, as does the Internet Explorer Administration Kit (IEAK). You can write your own if you wish; for example, I wrote one for Exchange 5.5 (see *http://www.robichaux.net/writing/man-exchange.html*). The Current Policy Template(s) list shows which templates are currently attached; you can use the Add... and Remove buttons to change this list's contents. Once you're satisfied with your changes, you can click OK to preserve the attachments or Cancel to dismiss the dialog without changing anything.

One final note: *POLEDIT* won't let you attach or detach policy templates while you have a policy file or Registry open. This restriction prevents you from accidentally overwriting an open policy with a new template's contents.

Creating Policies

After you've attached the appropriate policy templates, you're ready to start creating new policies. One of the nice things about *POLEDIT* is that it lets you make changes, store them, and make more changes without immediately affecting the Registry. Like most other document-oriented applications, changes you make to the currently open policy won't take effect until you save the policy document in the appropriate place.

Creating a new policy file

When you start *POLEDIT*, it opens with a new policy file named *Untitled*. However, at any time you may create a new, empty policy with the File → New Policy command. As its name implies, it opens a new document named *Untitled* with default group and user policies in it; you're then free to change those default policies or add your own user, computer, and group policies.

Creating a new user policy

You create new user policies with the Edit → Add User... command. This command produces a dialog (see Figure 6-3) you use to name the new policy. The "Browse" button opens the standard NT Add User dialog, so you can browse the list of local and domain user accounts to choose a user.

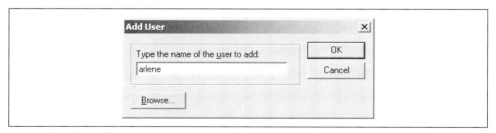

Figure 6-3. The Add User dialog

The name you enter in the "Type the name of the user to add" field is the name the policy downloader uses when trying to find a user's policy. If you're creating a policy for a user whose account is named *oreilly*, the policy won't be applied if it's named anything other than *oreilly* (although it's not case-sensitive). Be careful to ensure that you get the right username for the user you want the policy applied to; this is especially important on large networks where there might be several users with similar account names.

Creating a new computer policy

You create policies for individual computers in much the same way you do for users; the Edit → Add Computer... command displays a dialog identical to the one shown in Figure 6-3 except for its use of the word "computer" instead of "user." In this dialog, however, the Browse button displays a network browser you can use to locate the machine you want (the browser's appearance varies, depending on whether you're running SPE under NT or 2000).

The same caveat about names applies to computer accounts, too; if you're trying to apply a policy to a machine named *titan* but type in *titian* instead, the policy won't take effect as you expect it to.

Creating a new group policy

Like computer and user policies, creating group policies is straightforward: you use the Edit → Add Group... command to display the New Group dialog, then supply the name of the group to which the new policy belongs. You may apply policies to local or global groups within a domain, as well as groups that are strictly local to a single machine. As with computer and user policies, supplying the correct name is critical to getting the policy behavior you expect.

Since the Default User policy applies to every user on the machine including the Administrator account, it's a good idea to create a policy for the Administrators, Domain Admins, and Enterprise Admins groups. Reverse the settings from their default state so that the policy can undo any changes you make to unprivileged accounts.

Editing Policies

Creating new policies is easy, mostly because just creating the policy doesn't do anything! All the policy templates that Microsoft provides use the "leave as is" setting. This means that if you create a bunch of new policies and don't edit them, no changes will be enforced. This approach satisfies the Principle of Least Astonishment ("when forced to make decisions on its own, your software should always do whatever will least surprise the user"), but it means that you still have some work to do once your policies are created.

Remember that policy changes don't take effect until you save the policy file in the proper location. Even after that's done, user and group policies don't take effect until the next time the user logs in; machine policies won't go into action until the next time the machine boots.

Setting user, group, and computer policy options

Once you've created user policies for all the users, groups, and computers you want to control, the next step is to set appropriate values for each individual part within the categories and policies for each user. Each user policy has a properties dialog, which displays all categories, policies, and parts for that user policy.

You can open the properties dialog for a policy in two ways: you can double-click the icon or list item corresponding to the user policy you want to edit, or you can select it with the mouse and use the Edit → Properties... command. In either case, you'll end up with the properties dialog shown in Figure 6-4.

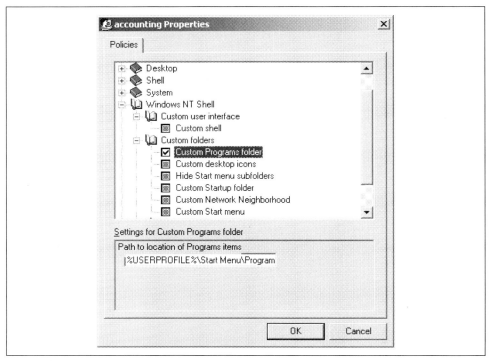

Figure 6-4. The Properties dialog

The upper part of the properties dialog shows a tree view of the categories within the active user policy. When you first open a user policy, the categories all are collapsed; you can expand or collapse individual items by clicking the small +/- icon next to the category's name.

As you expand categories, you'll see checkboxes appear beneath them. Unlike normal Windows checkbox controls, these checkboxes can have three states:

- When checked, as "Restrict display" is in Figure 6-4, the policy is active, and its settings will be applied to turn on the policy when appropriate.

- When unchecked and white (like an ordinary Windows checkbox that's not on), the policy is inactive. Its settings will be applied to turn off the policy.

- When unchecked and gray, like "Run only allowed Windows applications" in the figure above, the policy is inert. No changes will be made to a policy or its parts when its checkbox is grayed; this corresponds to the "leave as is" state I mentioned earlier.

You must pay careful attention to the wording of the policy to make sure that the effect is what you want: when the checkbox next to "Disable Registry editing tools" is on, the tools are disabled. When it's off, the tools are not disabled, and when it's gray, whatever settings are currently in effect on each target machine, group, or user remain intact.

As you select individual policies within a category, notice that the contents of the settings area at the bottom of the properties dialog change. Some policies can have multiple parts; for example, the "Restrict display" policy shown in Figure 6-4 has a total of five parts. You can set the value of each part independently of the others. Parts may accept on/off, numeric, or list selection choices, depending on what the policy template specifies.

You can move through the properties dialog, making changes as you go. *POLEDIT* preserves the changes within the current editing session, but they'll be lost unless you explicitly save the policy file.

Removing user policies

You can easily remove a user policy from within *POLEDIT*: select the policy you want to remove, then use the Edit → Remove command, or just press the Del key. *POLEDIT* asks you to confirm that you want to delete that policy. In a welcome change from *RegEdt32* and *RegEdit*, it tells you which policy you're deleting so you won't accidentally remove one you wanted to keep. Once you've removed a user policy, there's no getting it back unless you close and reload your policy file without saving changes. *POLEDIT* doesn't have an undo command.

It's worth noting that the only way to remove a policy category or part is to open the policy template file that defines it and remove it; you can't remove individual template items from a single policy, though you can use the "leave as is" setting to force the policy downloader to take no action on that part.

Policies and the clipboard

POLEDIT offers a measure of clipboard support. You can use the Edit → Copy command to copy the contents of a user, group, or computer policy to the clipboard. However, the only place you may paste it is on top of another policy! This "feature" means you can quickly copy a policy to several user accounts by doing the following:

1. Create one user, group, or computer policy, and set it the way you want it.
2. Use Edit → Copy to copy the policy settings.
3. Create as many user, group, or computer policies as you'll need.
4. Select all the new policies at the same time, then use the Edit → Paste command. *POLEDIT* asks you to confirm that you want to overwrite the existing policy settings; click Yes to paste your policy atop the existing settings, or No to cancel the paste.

Although it's not evident from the program or its documentation, you can copy from group to user policies and vice versa: select the source item, use Edit → Copy, and paste the policy onto the user or group you want it to stick to.

Setting group policy priorities

As soon as you start creating group policies, you run the risk of a collision between two groups' mutually exclusive policies. As long as no user belongs to more than one group, you won't run into this problem. However, since Microsoft recommends putting users into groups for controlling access to network resources like file shares and printers, the odds of having one user in more than one group are pretty good.

The section "Applying group policies" earlier in this chapter explains how the policy downloader decides which group policy parts to apply and which to ignore. For this approach to work, you must do your part by specifying the priority of each group's policy. You do this with the Options → Group Priority... command; the resulting "Group Priority" dialog appears in Figure 6-5.

The initial priority order comes from the order in which you created the group policies: the first policy you create has the highest priority. You can rearrange group priorities using the Move Up and Move Down buttons; when you're happy with the ordering, save it by clicking OK.

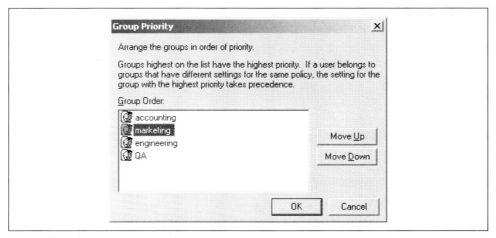

Figure 6-5. The Group Priority dialog

Once you set a group priority ordering, it's stored as part of the policy file and is available to the policy downloader. If you change the priority ordering later, the new order takes effect every time the policy's applied at logon time.

Saving and Loading Policies

As you create and modify user policies, you'll often need to save those policies to a file and load them again later. Like most other document-oriented Windows applications, *POLEDIT* has commands in its File menu for loading and saving policy files.

The File → Open Policy..., File → Save, and File → Save As... commands all work just like they do in other Windows applications. Unlike other applications, though, there's one gotcha involved with saving policy files: if you're creating policies for distribution to other Win95 or NT machines on your network, you must make sure to save the file in the right place, as described later in the section "Preventing Policy Problems."

Once you've created an initial policy, it's simple to add to or modify its user, group, or computer policies: just open the file with File → Open Policy..., modify it as needed, and save it again. If you configure the automatic policy distribution mechanism correctly, your policy is applied where necessary with no further action on your part.

Creating Your Own Policy Templates

The *.ADM* policy template files *POLEDIT* uses are just plain text files. If you open one of them up with a text editor, you'll find that the files are structured so that

POLEDIT can figure out which categories, policies, and parts to display, where to store their values in the Registry, and what user interface controls to display so you can edit these values.

> Windows 2000's version of *POLEDIT* understands and generates Unicode-encoded *.ADM* files. The NT version understands only ASCII-encoded files, so you can't create an *.ADM* file with the Windows 2000 policy editor and work with it later in the NT version.

You can create your own policy templates and attach them to *POLEDIT*. For example, you can create a template that controls your standard distribution of Dial-Up Networking settings, configuration parameters for Netscape Navigator, or almost any other Registry data that lives in HKLM or HKCU. Here's a small sample of an *.ADM* file that allows you to set the default search engine and home page Internet Explorer uses:

```
CLASS MACHINE

CATEGORY  InternetExplorer
    KEYNAME "Software\Microsoft\Internet Explorer\Main"
    POLICY "Default search engine"
        PART  "URL of default search engine" EDITTEXT REQUIRED
            VALUENAME "Default_Search_URL"
            DEFAULT "http://www.ljl.com/intrasearch/"
        END PART
        PART  "URL of default home page" EDITTEXT REQUIRED
            VALUENAME "Default_Page_URL"
            DEFAULT "http://www.ljl.com"
        END PART

    END POLICY
END CATEGORY
```

As you can see from the sample, the format of these files is pretty structured. Let's look at what each piece of the example actually does:

- The initial CLASS MACHINE statement tells *POLEDIT* that this policy should go under HKLM. You can also use CLASS USER to specify policies that belong under HKCU.

- The CATEGORY...END CATEGORY block defines a single category of policies. In this example, I defined a category named InternetExplorer; if you want to use spaces in the name, you have to enclose it in quotes. Category names can be any string, but they must be unique to a policy template file.

- The KEYNAME statement tells *POLEDIT* that all the policies and parts that belong to this category store their values under Software\Microsoft\Internet

Explorer\Main. Individual policies and parts can provide their own key names, too.

- The POLICY...END POLICY block defines a single policy for this category. Categories may contain any number of policies, each of which may have one or more parts. Each policy has a name ("Default search engine" in this case) that *POLEDIT* displays when it shows the policy.

- Each PART...END PART block specifies a single part for its enclosing policy. In this example, we're defining two parts—one for the search engine default, and one for the default home page. Both are edit text controls, and both require that a value must be specified. The returned value is stored as a value named as specified by the VALUENAME keyword; the value in turn goes under whatever key was named with a previous KEYNAME statement, and you provide a default value for the user to accept or change.

   A single policy may have many PART blocks in it. Each PART block defines a single component, which may be a checkbox, edit field, combo box, drop-down list, or numeric input field. In addition, each control type has a variety of optional parameters that specify default values, increments, and settings.

If you want to see a more complex example of an *.ADM* file, I've written one for controlling policy settings for Microsoft Exchange 5.5 servers. See *http://www.robichaux.net/files/exchange.adm*.

Distributing Policies

Once you've created policy files that contain the access controls you want to enforce, you still have to get those policies to each machine you want to be under policy control. This process, called *policy distribution*, is probably the most complex part of the policy development process, since how you do it depends on whether you want to use policies on one machine, a few machines, or many machines.

Applying Policies to One Machine at a Time

The simplest way to apply policies is to put them on individual machines. For example, you might want to apply policies to keep transient users from making changes to the configuration of public workstations in a library, factory floor, or conference room. For this type of requirement, you don't need to blast policies to every machine on a network; a more surgical approach lets you put policies only where you really need them.

Setting policies on the local machine

POLEDIT allows you to edit the local computer's Registry using the same interface you'd use to edit policies. When you use the File → Open Registry command, *POLEDIT* acts as if you'd opened a new policy file, but it actually loads data from the local Registry and displays it as two user policies: "Local User" and "Local Computer" instead of "Default User" and "Default Computer."

You can edit the contents of these policies as though you were editing any other policy. However, you can't create new user, group, or computer policies while the local Registry is open. As with other policy files, though, changes you make to the local Registry aren't saved until you explicitly use the File → Save command, so using File → Open Registry is somewhat safer than using *RegEdt32* or *RegEdit*.

Setting policies on other computers

If you want to apply policies to a single remote machine, you can use *POLEDIT*'s File → Connect... command to open the Registry on a remote machine and set policies on it. When you use this command, the first step is to specify the name of the machine whose policies you want to edit. If you have administrative access to that machine, *POLEDIT* connects to its Registry and shows you a dialog listing all users who are logged on. Normally, this list has only a single entry representing whoever's logged into the console, but network users may be listed too. Choose the user whose policy you want to edit. *POLEDIT* won't let you interactively edit the policy of a user who isn't logged on.

Once you've completed these two steps, you may edit the computer and user policies as you normally would. You can't create new user, group, or computer policies; however, before you use File → Connect..., you can attach new policy templates if you want to change the default settings that can be applied within each policy.

Applying Policies to Many Machines

Policies offer a robust, useful way to apply settings to many machines, in such a way that the end user can't change them once they're applied. This is a boon to system administrators, since with effective policies you can prevent users from changing things you don't want them to change without a great deal of effort on your part.

The primary method of distributing policies to all machines within a domain depends on the fact that domain controllers have a share named *NETLOGON*. It points to the domain controller's *%SystemRoot%\System32\Repl\Import\Scripts* directory and contains logon scripts, user profiles, and other data needed to allow local and remote logons with shared environments. *NETLOGON* can also hold policy files, meaning that the policy downloader on each machine in the domain has easy access to those policy files if they are saved in the *NETLOGON* share.

On a Windows 2000 domain controller, the *SYSVOL* share serves the same function as *NETLOGON*, so you use it instead.

Enabling automatic policy updates

If you want machines on your network to automatically download policy changes when they happen, you'll have to make a change to the policy for those machines. For most networks, that means the Default Computer policy, since most admins want automatic updates everywhere; however, you may enable automatic updates on a per-machine basis.

This setting lives in the Network category under the computer policy. Figure 6-6 shows the properties dialog with the appropriate setting selected. You can use the "Update mode" combo box to choose automatic or manual updates. If you choose manual updates, you can specify a UNC path to the share where your policies will live.

It's important to understand one thing about automatic updates: when you create a new policy file for the first time, it's downloaded automatically to every machine. If automatic updating is then turned on, each machine receives subsequent updates. If it's not turned on, the workstations' policy downloaders won't ever download policy changes. This may lead to undesirable behavior, since your policy changes will be silently ignored while you're expecting them to be in effect!

Windows NT policies

To have your NT-specific policies automatically blasted out to all machines in your domain, save your policy file as *NTconfig.pol* in the directory you specified when setting up automatic policy updates. I recommend using the *NETLOGON* or *SYSVOL* shares to store your policies so they can be automatically replicated among and between domains. However, if you've specified another directory you can use it instead.

Windows 95/98 policies

If you have a mixed network of Win9x and NT machines, you can store both types of policies on your domain controllers so that the Win9x machines get automatic updates too. Save your policy file as *config.pol* in the directory you specified when setting up automatic policy updates. If you want Win9x policies to be distributed

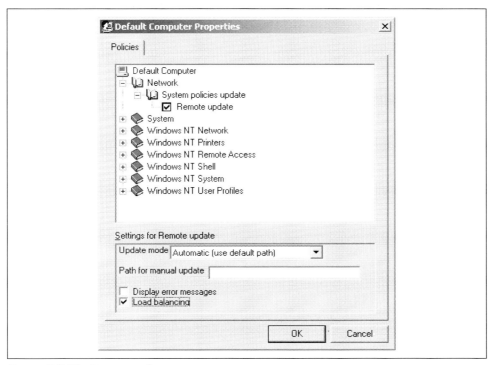

Figure 6-6. The Remote update part

automatically, you must put them in *NETLOGON*; the Win9x policy downloader can't get policies from any other share.

Windows 2000 policies

Windows 2000 machines won't pay any attention to an NT-style system policy. If you want to apply a policy to a Windows 2000 server or to a machine using Windows 2000 Professional, you can use the GPO mechanisms to do so if the target machine's in an Active Directory domain. If not, you can use the Local System Policy object to make local policy settings

Supporting multiple domain controllers

If your network has more than one Windows NT domain controller[*] (either because you have more than one domain or because you have more than one controller for redundancy), you should use NT's directory replication service to copy your policy files to every domain controller. Since any domain controller in a

---

[*] Even small networks should have primary and backup controllers for NT 4.0; in Windows 2000, there's no longer a distinction between primary and backup controllers, but you should still maintain a second controller for redundancy. You may also find it worthwhile to have several DCs for load balancing.

network can answer logon requests, it's a good idea to duplicate your policy files to make sure they're available when a user logs in.

The simplest way to do this is to copy the policy files into the controller's *%SystemRoot%\System32\Repl\Export\Scripts* directory. As long as the directory replication service is running, NT mirrors the files automatically throughout your domains.

Preventing Policy Problems

While policies can be a great help, they can also pose some subtle pitfalls until you get them working the way you want. Here are some common problems—and solutions—you may run into while deploying policies on your network.

Make sure the files are in the right place

Perhaps the easiest policy mistake to make is putting the policy files in the wrong place. Windows 9x policy files must be named *config.pol*, and they must be stored in the domain's *NETLOGON* share—period! For NT policies, you must name the file *NTconfig.pol*. Ahough you can put it in a share other than *NETLOGON*, the policy isn't used unless you specify the correct path to it when you turn on automatic updates.

Is automatic updating on?

Policies are most useful when they're always kept up to date. The policy downloader can automatically download and apply the appropriate set of user, group, and computer policies whenever a user logs on. To accomplish this magic, though, you have to put the policy in the right place (as described in the previous section "Applying Policies to Many Machines"), and you must turn on automatic downloading. If your policy changes don't seem to take effect once you've made them, be sure you've enabled automatic updates as part of the computer policy for all machines you want to keep updated.

Implement policies in all domains or none

If you're going to implement policies in one domain on your network, you may be in for a rough ride unless you implement policies on all domains. Why? If you have trust relationships between domains so that users from one domain can log onto another, consider this scenario:

1. You have two domains: HQ and RESEARCH. They trust each other. You've enabled system policies for all HQ users, but not for users in RESEARCH.

2. A user from HQ logs into a machine in the RESEARCH domain. Because RESEARCH gets its logon credential information from HQ, the user's logon

causes the RESEARCH machine to get a system policy update even though policies aren't enabled in the domain! The HQ user can still log in and get her work done.

3. When the HQ user logs out, the computer, group, and user policies downloaded at logon time are still on the machine. The next time a RESEARCH user logs onto the same machine, the policies won't be changed because RESEARCH has no policies of its own to apply.

In case it's not obvious by now, the solution to this potentially ugly problem is to implement policies on all your domains or none of them. It's still okay to apply policies to individual users and computers; however, if you set up group policies or policies for users who can log in to other domains, your best bet for avoiding trouble is to enable policies for all domains.

Check group membership and names

Sometimes your memory can fail you when it comes time to remember which groups a user is in. If you use group policies, make sure all users you want to fall under those policies are actually members of the group! If there are any who aren't, you can copy the group policy and make an individual user policy out of it, or you can add them to the group.

Don't forget to double-check your group names, too. If you meant ENGINEERING but typed ENGINEERS, *POLEDIT* won't complain, but your policies won't be activated either. Worse still, they might be activated on the wrong group.

Verify which policies are in effect

If you want to see what policy is actually being applied to a user or computer, use the File → Connect... command in *POLEDIT* to connect to the target computer. Once you do, you can open the Local Computer and Local User policies to make sure they contain the settings you want enforced. If they don't, that's a clue that your policy distribution or downloading is amiss.

What's in the Standard Policy Templates

The three primary policy templates used with Win95 and NT installations define what policy settings are available to you when building policies. Each template file contains settings that apply to HKLM and HKCU; however, in the following sections these entries are separated depending on the root key they affect.

WINNT.ADM

The *WINNT.ADM* policy template defines policy settings that are specific to Windows 2000 and NT. Some entries in this template have counterparts in the Windows 95 template file. Table 6-1 shows the *WINNT.ADM* entries that apply to computer policies, while Table 6-2 shows the settings that apply to user and group policies.

COMMON.ADM

COMMON.ADM contains policy settings that are common to Windows 2000, NT, 95, and 98. Table 6-3 shows the entries that apply to computer policies, while Table 6-4 shows the settings that apply to user and group policies.

WINDOWS.ADM

The *WINDOWS.ADM* policy template defines policy settings that are specific to Windows 95/98. When you use System Policy Editor to edit policies for Win9x machines, this template is used to determine which policies and parts you may apply. Because the items in this policy are all Win9x-specific, I've elected not to cover them here.

Table 6-1. HKLM Entries in WINNT.ADM

Category	Policy	Registry Key/Value	What It Does	Value
Windows NT Network\Sharing	Create hidden drive shares (workstation)	System\CurrentControlSet\Services\LanManServer\Parameters\AutoShareWks	Creates *drive$* and *ADMIN$* shares on workstation	Default on (shares are created)
	Create hidden drive shares (server)	System\CurrentControlSet\Services\LanManServer\Parameters\AutoShareServer	Creates *drive$* and *ADMIN$* shares on server	Default on (shares are created)
Windows NT Printers	Disable browse thread on this computer	System\CurrentControlSet\Control\Print\DisableServerThread	Controls whether printer shares advertise themselves	Default off (shares are advertised)
	Scheduler priority	System\CurrentControlSet\Control\Print\SchedulerThreadPriority	Adjusts priority of printer scheduling thread up or down	Default 0 (leave at normal priority); +1 (raise priority); –1 (lower priority)
	Beep for error enabled	System\CurrentControlSet\Control\Print\BeepEnabled	Beeps every 10 seconds when a remote print job error occurs	Default off (keep quiet and don't beep); on (beep)
Windows NT Remote Access Service	Maximum number of unsuccessful authentication retries	System\CurrentControlSet\Services\RemoteAccess\Parameters\AuthenticateRetries	Sets the number of times a remote system can try to authenticate itself	0–10; default 2
	Maximum time limit for authentication	System\CurrentControlSet\Services\RemoteAccess\Parameters\AuthenticateTime	Sets the number of seconds allowed before an authentication times out	20–600; default 120
	Wait interval for callback	System\CurrentControlSet\Services\RemoteAccess\Parameters\CallbackTime	Sets the number of minutes to wait for a callback	2–12; default 2
	Auto disconnect	System\CurrentControlSet\Services\RemoteAccess\Parameters\AutoDisconnect	Disconnects after X minutes of inactivity	0–65536; default 20

Table 6-1. HKLM Entries in WINNT.ADM (continued)

Category	Policy	Registry Key/Value	What It Does	Value
Windows NT Shell	Custom shared Programs folder	Software\Microsoft\Windows\CurrentVersion\Explorer\User Shell Folders\Common Programs	Sets the path to common Programs folder for all users on this machine	Any path; can use environment variables to point to path
	Custom shared desktop icons	Software\Microsoft\Windows\CurrentVersion\Explorer\User Shell Folders\Common Desktop	Sets the path to common desktop icons for all users on this machine	Any path; can use environment variables to point to path
	Custom shared Start menu	Software\Microsoft\Windows\CurrentVersion\Explorer\User Shell Folders\Common Start Menu	Sets the path to common Start menu folder for all users on this machine	Any path; can use environment variables to point to path
	Custom shared Startup folder	Software\Microsoft\Windows\CurrentVersion\Explorer\User Shell Folders\Common Startup	Sets the path to common startup items folder for all users on this machine	Any path; can use environment variables to point to path
Windows NT System\Logon	Logon banner	Software\Microsoft\Windows NT\CurrentVersion\Winlogon\LegalNoticeText	Sets the text to display in logon dialog	Default "Do not attempt to log on unless you are an authorized user."
	Logon caption	Software\Microsoft\Windows NT\CurrentVersion\Winlogon\LegalNoticeCaption	Sets the caption to display for logon banner message	Default "Important Notice:"
	Enable shutdown from Authentication dialog box	Software\Microsoft\Windows NT\CurrentVersion\Winlogon\ShutdownWithoutLogon	Displays "Shutdown" button in logon dialog so you can shut down without logging in	On or off; default on for NTW and off for NTS
	Do not display last logged on username	Software\Microsoft\Windows NT\CurrentVersion\Winlogon\DontDisplayLastUserName	Hides name of previously logged in users	Off or on; default off

Table 6-1. HKLM Entries in WINNT.ADM (continued)

Category	Policy	Registry Key/Value	What It Does	Value
	Run logon scripts synchronously	Software\Microsoft\Windows NT\CurrentVersion\Winlogon\RunLogonScriptSync	Runs logon scripts before desktop and start menu appear	Off or on; default off
Windows NT System\File System	Do not create 8.3 filenames for long filenames	System\CurrentControlSet\Control\FileSystem\NtfsDisable8dot3NameCreation	Suppresses creating 8.3 names	Off or on; default off (create names)
	Allow extended characters in 8.3 filenames	System\CurrentControlSet\Control\FileSystem\NtfsAllowExtendedCharacterIn8dot3Name	Allows extended characters to be used in short filenames, even though some machines may not display them properly	Off or on; default off (don't allow)
	Do not update last access time	System\CurrentControlSet\Control\FileSystem\NtfsDisableLastAccessUpdate	Doesn't update NTFS "last access time" field on files that are read but not modified	Off or on; default off (do update it)
Windows NT User Profiles	Delete cached copies of roaming profiles	Software\Microsoft\Windows NT\CurrentVersion\Winlogon\DeleteRoamingCache	Throws away cached profiles when users log out	Off or on; default off
	Automatically detect slow network connections	Software\Microsoft\Windows NT\CurrentVersion\Winlogon\SlowLinkDetectEnabled	Automatically times network links to see whether they're slow	Off or on; default on
	Slow network connection timeout	Software\Microsoft\Windows NT\CurrentVersion\Winlogon\SlowLinkTimeOut	Sets the number of milliseconds to wait before timing out on a slow link	1–20000; default 2000
	Timeout for dialog boxes	Software\Microsoft\Windows NT\CurrentVersion\Winlogon\ProfileDlgTimeOut	Sets the number of seconds to wait before canceling a dialog box	0–600; default 30

Table 6-2. HKCU Entries in WINNT.ADM

Category	Policy	Registry Key/Value	What It Does	Value
Shell\Custom Folders	Custom Programs folder	Software\Microsoft\Windows\CurrentVersion\Explorer\User Shell Folders\Programs	Specifies a custom "Programs" folder to be used in Explorer and the taskbar	Defaults to *%userprofile%\Start Menu\Programs*; may be any local or UNC path
	Custom Desktop folder	Software\Microsoft\Windows\CurrentVersion\Explorer\User Shell Folders\Desktop	Specifies a path to a custom set of desktop icons and items	Defaults to *%userprofile%\Desktop*; may be any local or UNC path
	Hide Start menu subfolders	Software\Microsoft\Windows\CurrentVersion\Policies\Explorer\NoStartMenuSubFolders	Hides the standard Start menu folders; should be set when you specify custom desktop or programs folders	By default, value doesn't exist; when it exists, 1 hides the folders and 0 leaves them alone
	Custom Startup folder	Software\Microsoft\Windows\CurrentVersion\Explorer\User Shell Folders\Startup	Specifies location of custom Startup folder	Defaults to *%userprofile%\Start Menu\Programs\Startup*; can be any local or UNC path
	Custom Network Neighborhood	Software\Microsoft\Windows\CurrentVersion\Explorer\User Shell Folders\NetHood	Specifies location of custom items for Network Neighborhood	Defaults to *%userprofile%\NetHood*; can be any local or UNC path
Shell\Restrictions	Use approved shell extensions only	Software\Microsoft\Windows\CurrentVersion\Policies\Explorer\ EnforceShellExtensionSecurity	Restricts which Explorer extensions may be loaded and run to those included in this list	Doesn't exist by default; you must manually add any shell extensions you want to approve
	Hide common program groups in Start menu	Software\Microsoft\Windows\CurrentVersion\Policies\Explorer\ NoCommonGroups	Forces Explorer not to display any shared program groups	Doesn't exist by default; when value exists, 1 means hide groups, and 0 means show them

What's in the Standard Policy Templates

Table 6-2. HKCU Entries in WINNT.ADM (continued)

Category	Policy	Registry Key/Value	What It Does	Value
System	Parse *autoexec.bat*	Software\Microsoft\Windows NT\CurrentVersion\Winlogon\ParseAutoexec	When on, NT parses *autoexec.bat* when the user logs on	REG_SZ; default value of 1 forces parse; 0 means don't parse
	Run logon scripts synchronously	Software\Microsoft\Windows NT\CurrentVersion\Winlogon\RunLogonScriptSync	When on, NT doesn't start the shell until the user's logon script has completed	REG_DWORD; when value is missing or set to 0, scripts are run in parallel with the shell startup; when value is 1, script executes before shell; identical to "Run logon scripts synchronously" under HKLM; that value overrides this one

Table 6-3. HKLM Entries in COMMON.ADM

Category	Policy	Registry Key/Value	What It Does	Value
Network Update	Remote update mode	System\CurrentControlSet\Control\Update\UpdateMode	Controls whether system policies are automatically updated or not (see previous section "Enabling automatic policy updates")	0: (default) don't update 1: update automatically from DC 2: update manually from NetworkPath
	Path for manual update	System\CurrentControlSet\Control\Update\NetworkPath	Specifies UNC path from which to update policies at logon	Empty by default; may be any legal UNC path
	Display error messages	System\CurrentControlSet\Control\Update\Verbose	Toggles display of policy update error messages	When value exists, error messages are displayed

Table 6-3. HKLM Entries in COMMON.ADM (continued)

Category	Policy	Registry Key/Value	What It Does	Value
	Load balancing	System\CurrentControlSet\Control\Update\LoadBalance	Toggles load balancing of policy updates from multiple domain controllers	When value exists, load balancing occurs
System\SNMP	Communities	System\CurrentControlSet\Services\SNMP\Parameters\ValidCommunities	Displays a list of communities to which SNMP traps are sent	Empty by default; otherwise, list of communities as individual values
	Permitted managers	System\CurrentControlSet\Services\SNMP\Parameters\PermittedManagers	Displays a list of entities permitted to manage SNMP	Empty by default; otherwise, list of managing entities as individual values
	Traps for Public community	System\CurrentControlSet\Services\SNMP\Parameters\TrapConfiguration\Public	Displays a list of traps that may be sent to Public community	Empty by default; otherwise, list of traps as individual values
System\Run	Run	Software\Microsoft\Windows\CurrentVersion\Run	Displays a list of items to run at startup	Defaults to *systray.exe*; otherwise, list of things to run after shell starts

Table 6-4. HKCU Entries in COMMON.ADM

Category	Policy	Registry Key/Value	What It Does	Value
Control Panel\Display	Disable Display icon	Software\Microsoft\Windows\CurrentVersion\Policies\System\NoDispCpl	Prevents user from opening Display control panel	REG_DWORD: 1 restricts control panel, 0 doesn't
	Hide Background tab	Software\Microsoft\Windows\CurrentVersion\Policies\System\NoDispBackgroundPage	Hides Background tab of Display control panel	REG_DWORD: 1 hides Background tab, 0 doesn't

Table 6-4. HKCU Entries in COMMON.ADM (continued)

Category	Policy	Registry Key/Value	What It Does	Value
	Hide Screen Saver tab	Software\Microsoft\Windows\CurrentVersion\Policies\System\NoDispScrSavPage	Hides Screen Saver tab of Display control panel so users can't change screen savers	REG_DWORD: 1 hides Screen Saver tab, 0 doesn't
	Hide Appearance tab	Software\Microsoft\Windows\CurrentVersion\Policies\System\NoDispAppearancePage	Hides Appearance tab of Display control panel	REG_DWORD: 1 hides Appearance tab, 0 doesn't
	Hide Settings tab	Software\Microsoft\Windows\CurrentVersion\Policies\System\NoDispSettings	Hides Settings tab of Display control panel so users can't adjust display resolution or color depth	REG_DWORD: 1 hides Settings tab, 0 doesn't
Desktop\Wallpaper	Wallpaper Name	Control Panel\Desktop\Wallpaper	Controls background image used as wallpaper	REG_SZ; contains full path to specified wallpaper file
	Tile wallpaper	Control Panel\Desktop\TileWallpaper	Controls whether wallpaper is tiled or not	REG_DWORD: 0 means no tiling, 1 means tiling
Desktop\Color Scheme	Color scheme	Control Panel\Appearance\Current	Contains color settings for currently selected decor scheme	Depends on selected color scheme
Shell\Restrictions	Remove Run command from Start menu	Software\Microsoft\Windows\CurrentVersion\Policies\Explorer\NoRun	Hides Run command on Start menu so users can't run arbitrary programs	REG_DWORD: 1 hides the command, 0 doesn't
	Remove folders from Settings on Start menu	Software\Microsoft\Windows\CurrentVersion\Policies\Explorer\NoSetFolders	Hides Settings folders on Start menu	REG_DWORD: 1 hides the folders, 0 doesn't
	Remove Taskbar from Settings on Start menu	Software\Microsoft\Windows\CurrentVersion\Policies\Explorer\NoSetTaskbar	Only hides Taskbar setting folder on Start menu	REG_DWORD: 1 hides the Taskbar folder, 0 doesn't

Table 6-4. HKCU Entries in COMMON.ADM (continued)

Category	Policy	Registry Key/Value	What It Does	Value
	Remove Find command from Start menu	Software\Microsoft\Windows\CurrentVersion\Policies\Explorer\NoFind	Removes Find command from Start menu	REG_DWORD: 1 hides the command, 0 doesn't
	Hide drives in My Computer	Software\Microsoft\Windows\CurrentVersion\Policies\Explorer\NoDrives	Hides some drives in My Computer	REG_DWORD bit mask; see "Control Which Drives Are Visible Throughout The System" in Chapter 10
	Hide Network Neighborhood	Software\Microsoft\Windows\CurrentVersion\Policies\Explorer\NoNetHood	Hides Network Neighborhood icon	REG_DWORD: 1 hides the 'hood, 0 doesn't
	No Entire Network in Network Neighborhood	Software\Microsoft\Windows\CurrentVersion\Policies\Network\NoEntireNetwork	Leaves Network Neighborhood, but removes "Entire Network" icon	REG_DWORD: 1 hides the icon, 0 doesn't
	No workgroup contents in Network Neighborhood	Software\Microsoft\Windows\CurrentVersion\Policies\Network\NoWorkgroupContents	Doesn't show contents of local workgroup in Network Neighborhood	REG_DWORD: 1 hides the workgroup, 0 doesn't
	Hide all items on desktop	Software\Microsoft\Windows\CurrentVersion\Policies\Explorer\NoDesktop	Blanks out the desktop	REG_DWORD: 1 hides the desktop, 0 doesn't
	Disable Shut Down command	Software\Microsoft\Windows\CurrentVersion\Policies\Explorer\NoClose	Stops users from shutting down their machines	REG_DWORD: 1 removes the Shut Down command, 0 doesn't
	Don't save settings at exit	Software\Microsoft\Windows\CurrentVersion\Policies\Explorer\NoSaveSettings	Forces the shell to ignore any environment changes the user makes	REG_DWORD: 0 allows changes to be saved, 1 doesn't

Table 6-4. HKCU Entries in COMMON.ADM (continued)

Category	Policy	Registry Key/Value	What It Does	Value
System\Restrictions	Disable Registry editing tools	Software\Microsoft\Windows\CurrentVersion\Policies\System\DisableRegistryTools	Tells compliant Registry editors not to run	REG_DWORD: 1 specifies that editing should be disallowed, 0 allows it
	Run only allowed Windows applications	Software\Microsoft\Windows\CurrentVersion\Policies\Explorer\RestrictRun	Specifies list of which Windows applications may be executed	When RestrictRun exists, its values specify which applications may be run

Picking the Right Policies

Which policies are appropriate for you? It depends on how your network's built, who uses it, and what they should—and shouldn't—be able to do. As you can tell from the preceding tables, the built-in policy templates offer a pretty wide range of capabilities, and you can roll your own templates to give you centralized control over almost anything whose behavior is controlled by Registry entries.

The following sections suggest which policies might be appropriate for various situations; you can pick and choose to build a set of policies that's right for you.

Policies for Anybody

Most administrators who use policies do so to prevent users from doing things they shouldn't. First on the list is probably preventing users from running unapproved applications, which you can do with the "Run only approved Windows applications" and "Remove Run command from Start menu" policies. In addition, you might want to consider using the *floplock* program from the Resource Kit to prevent user access to the floppy drives.

Most administrators hate to spend time fixing things like display resolution settings. Consequently, you may be interested in the Control Panel\Display policy category, since it allows you to prevent users from changing display settings.

Policies for a Lab Network

Many schools and universities have lab networks that students can use to do their classwork. Many companies have something similar: test labs, training classrooms, and so on. These environments share a central feature: a varying group of users have access to the machines, and they should probably be prevented from changing many of the things they might otherwise be able or tempted to modify.

In addition to restricting which applications may be run, most labs need to protect the desktop from changes. This prevents students from using their own wallpaper, changing the desktop colors to neon green with fuschia accents, or otherwise leaving a mess for the next user. The "Control Panel\Display" and "Desktop" policies are great for this.

For labs that share a network segment with production machines, you may also find it useful to restrict what users can see over the network. The "Shell\Restrictions" category offers several ways to prevent casual network browsing, including hiding the Network Neighborhood altogether.

For performance reasons, you should use the options in "Windows NT User Profiles" to control how profiles get transferred and whether slow connections are automatically flagged as such.

Policies for an "Ordinary" Office

Anything goes! The policies you set for machines in an ordinary office environment varies by user, machine, and group; what's appropriate for HR may not be appropriate for engineering, and vice versa. In general, the most frequently used policy components in office networks tend to be those dealing with custom Start menu folders and security settings, such as those found in "Windows NT System\ Logon."

In some cases, it may be necessary or desirable to restrict display and desktop changes too, especially on public machines.

7

Using Group Policies

One of the most powerful capabilities included with Windows 2000 is the Group Policy mechanism. Active Directory provides a comprehensive way for administrators to manage network resources. When you use Active Directory, Group Policy allows you to apply policies to users and computers over the entire hierarchy of your network, from entire domains right down to individual computers.

As you learned in the preceding chapter, the Windows NT 4.0 System Policy Editor is used to configure membership-based permissions for users, groups, and computers in a domain. System policies, such as desktop appearance and program control, can be distributed and applied to whole domains. For Windows 2000 network clients, policies are no longer Registry-based; they're replaced by Group Policy. By associating policies with actual objects in Active Directory, each site, domain, and organizational unit can distribute its own set of policy demands. You manage this capability with the Group Policy snap-in for the Microsoft Management Console (MMC). Group Policy, sometimes referred to as the Group Policy Editor, uses policy files to interface to a system's Registry.

What Are Group Policies?

In a general sense, policies define what a user can and can't do. Under Windows 2000, system administrators use Group Policy to manage the policies that apply to computers and users within a site or domain. These policies define certain aspects of the user's desktop environment. They specify system behavior, and they restrict what users are allowed to do. In short, a policy is simply a group of related settings an administrator can set.

Many of these policy settings are applied to keys in the Registry. The specific keys and values written into the Registry depend on the policies you're trying to enforce. In the Windows NT world, policy changes are persistent because they're applied throughout the Registry, and no mechanism exists to sweep away the changes once they're made (though one policy's changes can be overwritten by another set of changes that occurs later).

Under Windows 2000, Group Policy settings that modify the Registry are always applied in one of four Registry subtrees. Microsoft recommends that Windows 2000-savvy applications should look for policy information in HKLM\Software\Policies and HKCU\Software\Policies. If they don't find their settings there, they can look in HKLM\Software\Microsoft\CurrentVersion\Policies and HKCU\Software\Microsoft\Windows\CurrentVersion\Policies. If the application still hasn't found the settings it needs, it can look elsewhere in HKCU or HKLM, or even in INI files (though that's strongly discouraged). None of these subtrees may be modified by nonadministrators.

Elements of a Group Policy

Much the same way that the Registry is arranged in a hierarchical structure, policies are categorized into sections and subsections. The sections and subsections that build the hierarchy of Group Policy are called *categories*. Think of categories like folders: a group policy contains one or more categories, and each category may contain subordinate categories. The subordinate categories may contain their own subcategories, and so on. In addition to containing subcategories, categories contain the specific *policies* an administrator can configure.

Each policy controls the behavior of one aspect of a user's environment. For example, a simple desktop policy specifies whether to hide all icons on the desktop. There are more elaborate policies that define the default quota limit and warning level for an individual filesystem.

Remember that these specific policies are applied to keys in the Registry. The number of Registry keys affected depends on the complexity of the actual policy. A single policy can consist of multiple settings, or *parts*. A part represents a single value that is stored in the Registry. Each policy is made up of zero or more parts. The policy for hiding icons on the desktop does not contain any parts; it's simply enabled or disabled. The quota limit and warning level policy, however, contains a number of parts, one for each value that needs to be stored: the default quota limit value, the measurement units for the quota limit, and so on. Since policies require values of various data types, parts differ as to their permissible values. Some parts require strings, some require numeric values, and some parts' values are restricted to a set of predefined values.

User Versus Machine Policies

There are two types of group polices: polices that apply to the computer and policies that pertain to users. Computer configuration policies apply to all users on a computer and are active whenever a machine is running. They're stored in the HKLM section of the machine's Registry and include policies that define security settings, desktop appearance, and startup and shutdown scripts. They're applied when the machine boots. This is different from System Policy Editor machine policies, which are applied when a user logs on.

User configuration settings, on the other hand, are active for each user on a computer. They're stored in the Registry under HKCU and define user-specific settings such as assigned programs, program settings, and desktop appearance. Unlike computer settings, which remain in effect until the computer is shut down, user configuration settings are reloaded for each new user. In this way, user policies can be downloaded for a user, regardless of what machine she logs into. You can specify user policies that can be applied to all users of a specific machine, or you can apply policies that apply only to specific users no matter where they log on.

Even though Microsoft uses the name Group Policy, you can't apply group policies to Windows 2000 groups (more on that later). This is a significant difference from the System Policy Editor mechanism.

Defining Group Policy Objects

In Windows NT 4.0, policies are created for users, groups, and computers. They're applied manually to individual machines or stored on domain controllers for replication throughout a domain. In Windows 2000, administrators can attach policies to Active Directory containers such as sites, domains, and organizational units (lumped together with the acronym SDOU), as well as to individual machines. These policies are stored in Active Directory Group Policy Objects, or GPOs. GPOs are associated with sites, domains, organizational units, and individual machines, and contain all the Group Policy settings an administrator can configure. The policy settings contained in a GPO are applied according to the SDOU membership of those users and computers; there's a set of rules I'll discuss in the next few pages that determines the effective policy applied to any given user or computer.

There are two types of GPOs: local GPOs and nonlocal GPOs (an inelegant if useful term). Local GPOs are stored only on local machines, while nonlocal GPOs are stored in Active Directory.

What Are Group Policies?

The local GPO

Regardless of whether a computer is part of an Active Directory environment or operates as a standalone machine, every system running Windows 2000 stores exactly one local group policy object (LGPO).* The LGPO contains the primary policies for that computer and the users on it. For a standalone Windows 2000 machine, these are the only group policies the computer sees. When the computer is component of a site, domain, or organization unit, nonlocal GPOs join and take precedence over the LGPO. If there's a conflict between LGPO policy settings and settings from the more influential nonlocal GPOs, the LGPO settings are overwritten.

GPO Rule #1: since local settings are applied first, they're always overwritten by settings in inherited nonlocal GPOs.

Policies and the Active Directory

The other type of GPOs, nonlocal GPOs (NGPOs), are stored in an Active Directory. Each NGPO is associated with a site, domain, or organizational unit. In contrast to locally applied policies, NGPOs are applied to users and computers that are members of various SDOUs. Each SDOU may have zero or more GPOs associated with it. The order of application determines which specific settings are applied.

The order in which nonlocal GPOs are applied respects the Active Directory hierarchy. Sites, the most broad and least restrictive of Active Directory containers, process group policies first. All groups within a site inherit the site's policies. Next, domain group policies are processed; containers beneath the domain inherit these settings. High- and low-level organizational units follow in succession.

How Are Policies Stored?

While the Group Policies snap-in quietly hides policy storage facilities from the user, seeing how policies are actually stored in Active Directory will help in understanding how effective policies are subsequently calculated and applied. In Windows NT 4.0, the System Policy Editor creates *.POL* files that contain Registry key and value pairs; these pairs are loaded into a machine's Registry when the policy is applied. Far from containing the contents of the entire Registry, these policy files contain only those values required to implement the desired policy. After the

---

* You sometimes see reference to the local machine policy; that's just another name for the LGPO.

policy file is created, it can be applied manually to individual machines or stored on a domain controller for replication.

There's a similar mechanism for Windows 2000 policy settings stored in the Registry. The Group Policy snap-in stores Registry-based settings in a file named *Registry.pol*. The *Registry.pol* file is actually part of the group policy object. Although the format of the policy file differs from the Windows NT 4.0 style, the idea is the same. Separate *Registry.pol* files exist for the different root keys in the Registry that can be modified through Group Policy; one file contains customized Registry settings for HKLM, another contains settings for HKCU. When the Group Policies snap-in starts up, it creates temporary Registry hives for users and machines. If current policy files are available, they're imported into this temporary Registry. As you change policy settings, Group Policy modifies the temporary Registry under the node you've changed. When Group Policy exits, the temporary Registry is exported into the two *Registry.pol* files, from which the changes can be distributed.

Unlike Windows NT 4.0, however, policies are associated with sites, domains, and organizational units through GPOs. When *Registry.pol* files are created for non-local GPOs, they're stored in what's called a Group Policy Template. Along with administrative templates, scripts, and other GPO information, this folder structure includes user and machine subdirectories, which each contain their appropriate *Registry.pol* file.

The structure of the Group Policy Template

Group Policy Objects actually consist of two separately stored parts: the *Group Policy Container* (GPC) and the *Group Policy Template* (GPT). The snap-in doesn't differentiate between items that are stored in these two parts; all their data appears as a single seamless collection.

The Group Policy Template resides on the domain controller in a tree of folders called the System Volume (*SYSVOL*). SYSVOL serves the same function as the *Netlogon* share on a Windows NT domain controller. It's designed to store information that doesn't change very often. In addition to storing *Registry.pol* policy files, the GPT stores scripts, administrative templates, and other GPO-related files. The GPT is a folder structure with the following subfolders:

ADM
    Contains administrative templates for this GPO

Scripts
    Contains logon, logoff, startup, or shutdown scripts and other related files

USER
    Contains the *Registry.pol* file applied to the HKCU portion of the Registry

USER\Applications
> Contains application advertisement scripts (*.AAS* files) that advertise the availability of automatically installed applications to users when they log on

MACHINE
> Contains the *Registry.pol* file applied to the HKLM portion of the Registry

MACHINE\Applications
> Contains *.AAS* files for applications applied to computers, not to individual users

The GPC is an Active Directory object that contains metadata about the GPOs in it. Among other things, it contains information about the version of the templates it contains, status flags indicating whether the GPT is enabled or disabled for each SDOU, and a list of which items are contained in the GPO. This information indicates whether the GPO is enabled or disabled and helps keep the GPC synchronized with the GPTs.

How Are Policies Applied?

Applying a policy simply means merging the appropriate policy files into a computer's Registry under the respective root keys—HKCU for user-specific settings and HKLM for computer-specific settings. Once a policy file is retrieved, the individual policies contained within the file are compared against the Registry. As you'll see in the section that deals with editing policies, individual policies are set to one of three states: enabled, disabled, or not configured. Note that these states don't say what the policy does, just whether it is applied (enabled), not applied (disabled), or left alone (not configured).

When an enabled policy is encountered in the policy file, the parts of the policy are checked against the current settings in the four Registry subtrees that can contain policy settings. If a part's value matches the corresponding value in the Registry, no change is made. If, however, the part's value conflicts with the Registry setting, the Registry is changed to reflect the enabled policy. This value exchange is strictly a one-way push from the policy file to the Registry. Manual changes made to the Registry under HKCU or HKLM, with a Registry editor for instance, are not written out to a policy file. This keeps users from modifying administrator-defined policy settings.

Since each site, domain, or OU in Active Directory can have multiple policies, and since user and computer policies can exist both locally and in any SDOU, you probably have two questions at this point: when, and in what order, are policy files applied?

Applying computer and user policies

The only types of objects in the Active Directory environment that policies affect are users and computers. The *Registry.pol* file contained in the user subfolder of the appropriate GPT is downloaded and applied to the user (HKCU) portion of the Registry. Likewise, the *Registry.pol* file in the machine subfolder gets merged into the Registry under the machine (HKLM) root key. Machine settings are applied when the machine boots. User settings are downloaded each time a user logs on to a computer. This enables machine policies to persist while the more transient user settings are swapped in and out. This additionally allows users to log on to different machines and be greeted with a consistent set of policies (ignoring, for the moment, any differences in machine policies between different machines).

In addition to being applied during their respective initializations, both user and machine settings are applied during a periodic refresh cycle. This allows automatic updates of policies that have changed during the current session.

In Windows 2000, when user Registry settings conflict with computer Registry settings, computer settings generally take precedence. This is a convention followed by the operating system, rather than a rule of the Group Policy infrastructure.

Order of policy file application

I've answered the "when"; now on to the "in what order" question. Policy files are applied in a specific order that reflects the Active Directory structure. Since AD uses a hierarchy to categorize different objects in a network, its structure lends itself nicely to imposing a relative importance to policies. The order of application is as follows:

1. The LGPO for the target machine is applied first. Remember that one and only one LGPO exists on every Windows 2000 machine.
2. Any GPOs for the AD site are applied next, in an order you specify.
3. Any domain GPOs are applied next, again in the order you specify.
4. Any Organizational Unit GPOs are applied last, from the least restrictive to the most restrictive (parent, child, grandchild). At each OU level, order is specified by the administrator. For example, if a child OU has three policies specified, the administrator can arrange them in any order, but all the child OU policies are applied before any grandchild policies are applied.

The means that the last GPO to be processed is the GPO for the "lowest" OU. If you think about how Microsoft normally draws AD hierarchies (you know, the big triangle diagrams), this makes sense; the last GPO applied is the one for the SDOU that the user or computer is a direct member of. Processing the local GPO before any Active Directory GPOs gives the LGPO the smallest relative importance.

As policy files are processed, they're merged into the Registry under the appropriate keys. All applied policies contribute to the effective policy of the computer or user. Naturally, there will be instances where settings being applied for a policy conflict with earlier policy settings. By default, newer settings overwrite previous settings. In fact, these newer settings may in turn be overwritten by another, later GPO. It is possible, however, to enforce policies from a higher GPO (in effect, a policy applied earlier in the application order) so that they *cannot* be overwritten. This applies only to nonlocal GPOs; the LGPO settings can't be set absolutely. Later in the chapter, you'll see how the effective policies are calculated from the array of policy files that are applied to a system.

Introducing the Group Policy Snap-in

For defining and controlling how various components of Windows 2000 behaves for users and computers, Group Policy is used. Group Policy is a Microsoft Management Console (MMC) snap-in that allows you to manage the behavior of programs, network resources, and the operating system.

Under Windows NT 4.0, the System Policy Editor creates and edits system policies. While this editor is supplied in Windows 2000, its use is limited to supporting downlevel clients. Since it creates Windows NT 4.0-style system policy files, you still need it to support NT domains. Additionally, it's useful if you have Windows NT 4.0, 95, or 98 clients in your AD domains.

Adding the Group Policy Snap-in

To add the Group Policy snap-in to the MMC, run *mmc.exe*. From the Console menu in the MMC, choose Add/Remove Snap-in. Click the Add button on the Standalone tab and select Group Policy from the list of snap-ins provided. You're then required to choose a Group Policy Object to edit. Remember that group policy objects can be stored locally on a computer or can be linked to an Active Directory organizational unit, domain, or site. The Select Group Policy Object dialog defaults to the local computer as the target GPO but allows you to browse through domains, OUs, sites, and computers to select the GPO you're interested in editing.

Once you've decided on a GPO, click the Finish button and close the list of provided snap-ins. If everything went well, you're back on the Standalone tab of the Add/Remove Snap-in dialog, and you see your target GPO listed as a snap-in under to the Console Root. Figure 7-1 shows the Local Computer Policy as the only added snap-in.

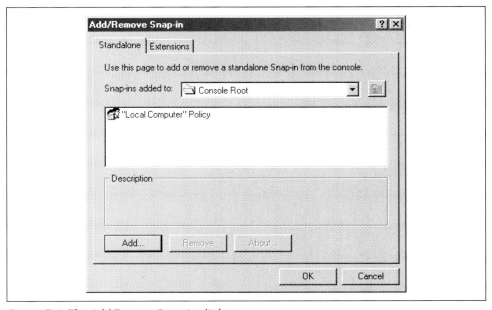

Figure 7-1. The Add/Remove Snap-in dialog

You select the functionality of the snap-in by adding Group Policy extensions. Group Policy extensions correspond to areas of the Group Policy that you can edit. The following is a list of Group Policy extensions:

Administrative Templates (Computers)
　　Edits Registry-based policy information for computer configuration

Administrative Templates (Users)
　　Edits Registry-based policy information for user configuration

Folder Redirection Editor
　　Redirects Windows 2000 special folders (such as My Documents and My Pictures) to network locations

Remote Installation Services
　　Sets up client computers remotely

Scripts (Logon/Logoff)
　　Specifies scripts for user logon/logoff

Introducing the Group Policy Snap-in

Scripts (Startup/Shutdown)
  Specifies scripts for computer startup/shutdown

Security Settings
  Configures security for domains, computers and users

Software Installation (Computers)
  Makes applications available to computers

Software Installation (Users)
  Makes applications available to users

To add one or more extensions to the Group Policy snap-in, select the Extensions tab on the Add/Remove Snap-in dialog. By choosing Group Policy from the drop-down list of snap-ins that can be extended, the available extensions are displayed, as illustrated in Figure 7-2.

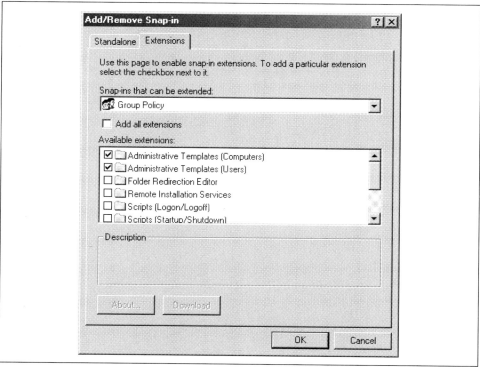

Figure 7-2. Available Group Policy Extensions dialog

You can select extensions on an individual basis or mass add all extensions by setting the Add all extensions checkbox.

To edit local group policy without having to endure the pomp and circumstance of the Microsoft Management Console and plug-ins, you can simply launch *gpedit.msc*. You'll be transported directly to a Group Policy window with focus on the local group policy object.

Learning the Group Policy Snap-in Interface

If you've already used any of the MMC snap-ins, you'll be instantly familiar with the interface for Group Policy. The console is divided into two panes: the left pane holds the console tree, and the right pane displays information such as policies and settings. Each node in the console tree under the Console Root represents an instance of an added snap-in. Thus, by adding Group Policy with different GPOs, you can manage multiple objects from the single console tree. Figure 7-3 shows a single GPO (the local group policy object) under the console root, with the Administrative Templates (Computers) and Administrative Templates (Users) extensions previously added.

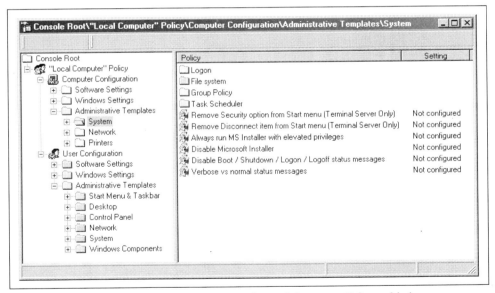

Figure 7-3. The Group Policy MMC snap-in with Local Computer Policy added

Controlling what you see

The MMC provides a consistent interface for many facets of Windows 2000. The commands that modify the display apply to the MMC as a whole, not just Group Policy. The first thing you realize about MMC, as you start adjusting window sizes and resizing panes, is that MMC allows you to open more than one console window at a time. The Window → New Window command creates a copy of the console window. This enables you to view policies of one GPO in the first window while concurrently viewing policies of a second GPO in another window.

The View menu provides a way to change the appearance of the console window. The View → Customize command leads to a Customize View dialog that lets you configure which aspects of the MMC and snap-in you want available. Using the checkboxes in this dialog, you can hide or display the console tree, the standard menus, the standard toolbar, the status bar, the description bar, and the taskpad navigation tabs.

The right pane of the MMC displays pertinent information about the node selected in the console tree. The View menu provides four ways to view this information. The View → Large Icons and View → Small Icons commands provide pictorial representation in the right pane; however, this can be repetitious as Group Policy icons tend to be the same anyway. View → List shows the same information in a single column. The most useful display command, View → Detail, parses information into separate columns. Most leaf nodes in Group Policy contain a policy column and a settings column. In detail mode, you can sort this information by clicking a column heading; that column is sorted into either alphabetical or reverse alphabetical order.

The View → Choose Columns command brings up a Modify Columns dialog that allows you to add and remove columns from the display list. This dialog additionally allows you to change the order of some columns.

Navigating the console tree

The console tree acts in much the same way as the Windows Explorer tree view. You expand branches by clicking the plus beside the node you want to expand and contract them by subsequently clicking the minus sign. You highlight a node to display its individual settings in the right pane. The up arrow icon on the standard buttons toolbar hikes you back up the hierarchical chain of the console tree until you reach the root.

Some of the nodes have special commands associated with them. For example, the Administrative Templates node allows you to Add/Remove Templates. To view the menu associated with a specific node, simply right-click that node. I'll explore some of these special commands in a bit.

Viewing policy properties

As stated previously and shown back in Figure 7-3, most Group Policy leaf node information contains policies and corresponding settings. To view the properties of a particular policy, right-click the policy in the right pane and select Properties.

Managing Policies

The Administrative Templates extensions to Group Policies handle all Registry-based policies in Windows 2000. In other words, Administrative Templates provide a mechanism for administrators to configure user interface settings that are stored in the Registry.

Two administrative template extensions can be enabled for a GPO, one for computers and one for users. In GUI terms, these extensions enable Administrative Template nodes in the console tree under Computer Configuration and under User Configuration. (Refer back to Figure 7-3 for a console tree that includes both Administrative Templates nodes.) Until administrative templates are added, however, these nodes are empty.

What Is an Administrative Template?

Administrative templates are ASCII text files, usually with a *.adm* extension, that tell the Group Policy interface what Registry settings an administrator can set. The template files specify what categories and subcategories should appear under the Administrative Templates node and how policy options are displayed. The Group Policy interface translates the template files into the GUI representation you see, from the intermediate folders down to the policy settings.

The Windows 2000 syntax for administrative templates encompasses the previous template syntax. You can use older NT 4.0-style administrative templates to create user interfaces in Group Policy, however, new templates can't be used with the System Policy Editor.

It's not a good idea, however, to allow NT 4.0-style policies to be applied to Windows 2000 clients, as could be the case in a mixed-mode domain with both NT 4.0 and Windows 2000 domain controllers. If, for instance, an NT 4.0 client is upgraded to Windows 2000, but the accounts of users on the machine continue to be managed by a Windows NT 4.0 domain controller rather than Active Directory, the user receives NT 4.0 user System Policy.

This could have an adverse effect on the computer's Registry. The reason is that Windows 2000 policies set keys and values in only specific areas of the Registry, namely:

Managing Policies

- HKEY_LOCAL_MACHINE\Software\Policies
- HKEY_CURRENT_USER\Software\Policies
- HKEY_LOCAL_MACHINE\Software\Microsoft\Windows\CurrentVersion\Policies
- HKEY_CURRENT_USER\Software\Microsoft\Windows\CurrentVersion\Policies

When Windows 2000 policy changes, these trees are cleared, and new policies are copied down. Windows NT 4.0 policies, however, don't recognize these Registry areas. The keys and values they write can invade any part of the Registry and persist until they're either manually deleted or reversed by a counteracting policy.

Adding Administrative Templates

Assuming you have the Administrative Templates extensions enabled for Group Policy, you can add administrative templates for computer and user configuration of a GPO. Under the GPO you wish to manipulate, expand either the Computer Configuration or User Configuration node. Right-click the Administrative Templates node and select Add/Remove Templates from the menu. The ensuing dialog, shown in Figure 7-4, lists the current policy templates.

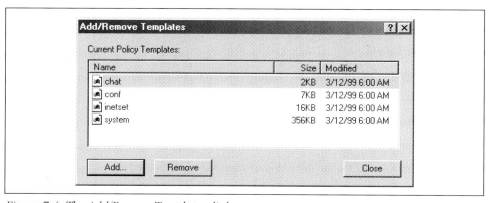

Figure 7-4. The Add/Remove Templates dialog

To add additional templates to this list, select the Add button and browse for the desired template. Templates included with Windows 2000 are installed in the *%SystemRoot%\inf* directory and come with a *.adm* extension. I'll talk more about provided templates later in the chapter.

Understand that templates you add can contain settings for both Computer and User configuration. That is, there are sections for Registry keys under both HKLM and HKCU. It doesn't matter which node you add the templates from, the template is added to the Group Policy as a whole.

As you add administrative templates, category nodes appear beneath the Administrative Template branches in the console tree. Each template consists of a new set of categories, subcategories, and options to display to the user. These are interlaced into the settings of the currently loaded templates. Settings in the Computer section of the template appear under the Computer Configuration node; likewise, the User section populates the User Configuration Node.

Editing Policies

Using Group Policies to modify policies is quite easy. The templates you add to Group Policy provides the entire interface you need; what's left is deciding what values you want for your policies.

To edit a policy, expand the console tree until you find the category that holds the policies you want to edit. Once you highlight the target category, you see the category's policies in the right pane. If you've taken the advice earlier in this chapter, you have the display set to View → Detail, and you can see the policies' current settings. A policy can have three settings; enabled, disabled, or not configured.

Right-click the policy you want to edit and select Properties (double-clicking works just as well). The property's edit dialog will appear. What you see—that is, what you're able to edit—depends on what parts make up the policy. You'll find that many policies are simply enabled or disabled, without any parts.

Figure 7-5 shows the policy edit dialog for the Limit profile size policy, which is found in the user section of the *SYSTEM.ADM* administration template, under the System category and Logon/Logoff subcategory.

The policy tab is displayed by default. The Explanation tab merely contains a description of the policy. The first thing you see on the policy tab is a checkbox for the policy name. This is actually a checkbox with three states representing whether the policy is enabled (checked), disabled (cleared), or not configured (grayed out). When this checkbox is cleared or grayed out, the policy part inputs are disabled.

The policy in Figure 7-5 contains five parts that pertain to Registry keys and can be modified. The first part is an edit text box filled with a default string. The second and fifth fields are numeric inputs filled with default values. In addition to default values for numeric input fields, templates can also specify minimum and maximum values for acceptable user input. Lastly, two checkboxes accept Boolean input. In addition to strings, numbers, and Boolean values, part types include

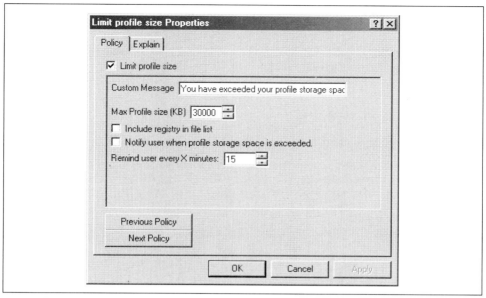

Figure 7-5. The Limit profile size policy edit dialog

combo boxes and list boxes. Static text may also appear for directions or user information.

The buttons at the bottom of this dialog, Previous Policy and Next Policy, allow you to iterate through all the policies of this category without having to close and reopen the dialog.

Creating Your Own Administrative Templates

Since administrative templates are merely ASCII files, they can be opened with a text editor, modified, and loaded back into Group Policy. As you'll see in a moment, the syntax and language used in these files, while perhaps not instantly intuitive, is far from cryptic. These templates afford administrators the flexibility to create a "safe" conduit to nearly all Registry data that lives in HKLM or HKCU.[*] This can include configuration parameters for common programs such as Internet Explorer, as well as network and desktop settings. (However, note that there are already Group Policy templates for Office 2000 and Internet Explorer, provided as part of the Office Resource Kit. See *http://www.microsoft.com/office* for more details.)

---

[*] A second, but much more ambitious, way to extend the functionality of Group Policy is to write a software extension for the Group Policy snap-in. Software development, unfortunately, is beyond the scope of this book.

Administrative Template files follow a basic structure that represents the hierarchy of categories, subcategories, policies, and parts you see in the Administrative Templates namespace. To illustrate the template format, here is an example template I cannibalized from the provided system template, *system.adm*:

```
CLASS USER

CATEGORY !!SystemControl
   KEYNAME Software\Microsoft\Windows\CurrentVersion\Policies\System

   POLICY !!LimitSize
     KEYNAME "Software\Microsoft\Windows\CurrentVersion\Policies\System"
     EXPLAIN !!LimitSize_Help
     VALUENAME "EnableProfileQuota"

     PART !!SizeMessage EDITTEXT
       VALUENAME "ProfileQuotaMessage"
       DEFAULT !!DefaultSizeMessage
     END PART

     PART !!WarnUser CHECKBOX
       VALUENAME "WarnUser"
     END PART

     PART !!WarnUserTimeout NUMERIC REQUIRED SPIN 5
       VALUENAME "WarnUserTimeout"
       DEFAULT 15
       MIN     0
     END PART
   END POLICY ;LimitSize
END CATEGORY ;SystemControl

[strings]
DefaultSizeMessage="Storage space exceeded."
LimitSize="Limit profile size"
LimitSize_Help="Limits size of Profile."
SizeMessage="Custom Message"
SystemControl="System"
WarnUser="Notify user when profile storage space is exceeded."
WarnUserTimeout="Remind user every X minutes:"
```

Notice that this template consists of one category, SystemControl. Inside that category is a single policy, LimitSize. That policy is comprised of three parts, SizeMessage, WarnUser, and WarnUserTimeout. Let's dissect the template:

- The first statement, CLASS User, tells Group Policy that this policy falls under HKCU. Policies that come under HKLM appear with the CLASS MACHINE statement. Indeed, templates can and will contain both statements.

- The CATEGORY... END CATEGORY block defines the categories, or nodes, that fall under the Administrative Templates node in the console tree. This example contains one category, SystemControl. More elaborate templates contain a hierarchy of categories.

- The KEYNAME statement tells Group Policy that all polices and parts that belong to this category store their values under Software\Microsoft\Windows\CurrentVersion\Policies\System. Policies can specify their own key names as well. In this case, the keyname for the LimitSize policy is the same as the category keyname.

- The POLICY... END POLICY block defines a single policy. Each policy block corresponds to a policy item in the right pane of Group Policy you can right-click to display its properties. A policy can be enabled, disabled, or not configured. This template contains one policy item, LimitSize.

- Each PART... END PART block specifies a single part of the policy that encloses it. This appears as a control in the policy's property dialog, such as an edit field (EDITTEXT), a checkbox (CHECKBOX), or a numeric input field (NUMERIC). Default values for parts may be provided for a user to accept or reject. Policies that are either simply enabled or disabled won't contain parts. The policy to remove the search button from Windows Explorer, for example, doesn't require additional Registry values beyond the enabled status and therefore, doesn't contain any parts.

    The policy in this example contains three parts, an edit text box, a checkbox and a numeric input field. The quoted VALUENAME is the name the value is stored as. The edit text box, SizeMessage, contains a default string value of "Storage space exceeded." The numeric user field contains a default value of 15 and a minimum value of 0.

- Tags that are preceded by a double exclamation point (e.g., !!LimitSize) are tied to character strings from the string section. This provides the text Group Policy uses to display the categories, policies, and parts.

The preceding Administrative Template contains a single, multipart policy. Figure 7-6 shows how the property dialog for this policy looks.

Distributing Policies

Computers that operate as standalone machines depend solely on local policy files for their policy settings. Networked computers, however, have the chore of obtaining policy files from the Domain Controller and merging them into their Registry. These downloaded policies contain the policies of the sites, domains, and organizational units that the computer and users are members of.

When you run the Group Policy snap-in, you're required to select the Group Policy Object for the settings you wish to modify. This can be a GPO associated with

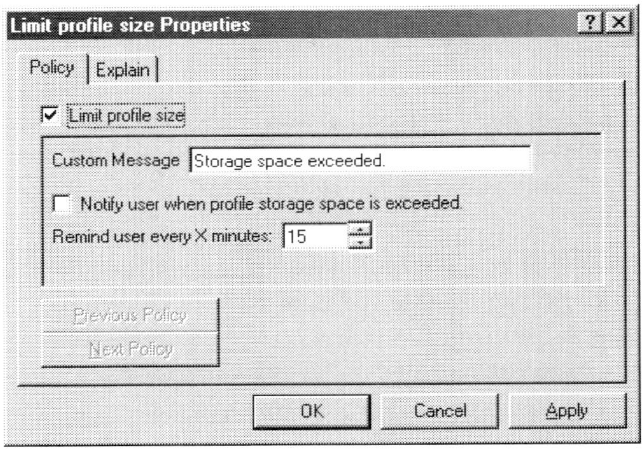

Figure 7-6. The example policy properties dialog

an Active Directory object, or it may be a local or remote computer GPO. The users and computers that the policy affects, however, depends directly on which GPO is chosen. The higher the GPO is in the hierarchy, the more machines the policy file is distributed to.

Understanding How Effective Policies Are Calculated

I said earlier that policies are applied to the Registry in a specific order. That is: the local GPO, site GPOs, domain GPOs, and then OU GPOs from largest to smallest. Clearly, since policies are cumulative, order of application is quite important. Policies set early in the process can be overwritten by later GPOs. Since local GPO settings are applied before nonlocal GPOs, the LGPO is considered to be the least influential of all GPOs. The important policies, then, are those held by nonlocal, or Active Directory, GPOs.

The hierarchy of the Active Directory is tree-like in that an Active Directory container can accommodate multiple containers beneath it. Each of those containers, in turn, can itself hold multiple containers. This continues down to the lowest-level OU container that actually houses actual users and machines. As the nonlocal policies are applied in the order described previously, each new policy file is merged into the Registry. This means that policy settings for site GPOs cover all domains, organizational units, users and machines within it. Settings for a domain GPO fan out to all the organizational units, users, and machines below the domain. Next, high-level organizational unit policies take effect and envelop all subordinate OUs. Policies of low-level OUs, while they are not as broadly applied as the higher nodes, are most likely to be applied, since they overwrite all conflicting policies previously merged into the Registry. Since policies are applied top-down in a single direction, policy settings applied at lower levels, such as subordinate OUs, don't affect higher group policy objects, such as site and domain GPOs.

Policy Inheritance

In the scheme of calculating effective policies, there are some basic rules that need to be understood about how policies are inherited. For the sake of clarity, let's discuss this in terms of parent and children GPOs, where a parent is any Active Directory Container, and a child is one of the containers directly beneath it in the Active Directory hierarchy.

First, you know from the previous discussion about editing policies that policies can be enabled, disabled, or not configured. Child containers don't inherit policies that aren't configured from their parent GPOs. This extends to the users and computers in those containers. Disabled policies are, however, inherited as disabled. Enabled policies, of course, are inherited as such. Furthermore, policy settings that are configured for a parent OU (that is, either enabled or disabled) and not configured for a child OU are inherited by the child. As an example, consider a desktop policy that hides the Internet Explorer icon on the desktop. A child OU inherits this policy if it's enabled or disabled for the parent OU. The child doesn't inherit it if it's not configured for the parent OU.

Inheritance additionally depends upon the compatibility of policy settings; that is, whether the intent of a setting inherently conflict with that of another policy setting. When a policy of a parent OU is incompatible with a policy of a child OU, the child doesn't inherit the parent's policy setting. Instead, the child's policy takes precedence and is applied. When a policy configured for a parent is compatible with the child's policy, both policies are used. The parent's policy is inherited and applied along with the child's policy; in this case, the effective policy is the sum of the parts of those two policies.

In some cases, an administrator may wish to keep a child GPO from inheriting policies from its parent and instead rely solely on the child's own policies. A third basic rule of policy inheritance allows child GPOs to *block inheritance.* If this option is set for a GPO, the GPO doesn't inherit any policy settings from its parent. This is useful when a parent GPO has general policies it wants to enforce on most of its child GPOs. Yet, there might be a child GPO that's exempt from these settings and should maintain its own set of policies. Blocking inheritance allows the subordinate unit to create its own policies without interference from its parent. Following the previous example, a child OU can disable or not configure the policy to hide the Internet Explorer icon while blocking inheritance from the parent OU. In this case, even if the hide icon policy is enabled for the parent OU, the effective child policy doesn't reflect that.

Lastly, there's an option for parent GPOs that give them the ability to set mandatory inheritance. By setting the No Override option on a parent GPO, all children GPOs must inherit all configured policies from that parent, regardless of compatibility or inheritance blocking on the child GPO. This can be used for parent GPOs that want their policy decisions to be unconditionally respected. This option also provides a means of making sure that incompatible settings don't keep child GPOs from inheriting parent GPO policies. Supposing that No Override is set for a parent OU that also enabled the hide Internet Explorer icon policy, its child OU unconditionally inherits that policy.

Managing Dispersal Through Group Policy Policies

The system administrative template includes a number of policies that define more concretely how and when Group Policies are retrieved and applied. These policies are found in both the computer and user sections of the *system.adm* file. To view the computer-specific policies in Group Policies, make sure *system.adm* is included as a current policy template. Under the Computer Configuration\Administrative Templates branch, the System category contains a subcategory for Group Policy. The following list describes some of these policies and what they mean:

Disable background refresh of group policy
> Keeps group policy from being updated while a user is logged on. Not enabling it allows policy to be updated whether a user is logged on or not. When not enabled, update frequency is tied to the Group Policy refresh intervals for users and computers.

Apply group policy for computers asynchronously during startup
> Allows the system to display the login prompt before the computer Group Policy is finished updating.

Apply group policy for users asynchronously during startup
> Lets the system display the Windows desktop before the user Group Policy is finished updating.

Group Policy refresh interval for computers
> Allows customization of policy update frequency. The policy's parts allow you to specify how often Group Policy is applied to computers. The default is 90 minutes.

There is an additional user-specific policy found under User Configuration/Administrative Templates in the System category and Group Policy subcategory. It works much like its computer-specific sibling:

Group Policy refresh interval for users
> Like the computer refresh interval policy, this policy allows you to specify how often Group Policy is applied to users. The default is 90 minutes.

Setting Single Computer Group Policies

When you start Group Policy as a standalone MMC snap-in, a Select Group Policy Object dialog appears that allows you to choose the GPO to modify. The GPO for the Local Computer is entered as the default. You can browse for another GPO by selecting the Browse button. The subsequent browse dialog contains four tabs: Domains/OUs, Sites, Computers, and All. GPOs stored on local computers are found on the Computers tab. The radio buttons on this dialog allow you to toggle between the computer you're currently on and another computer, as shown in Figure 7-7.

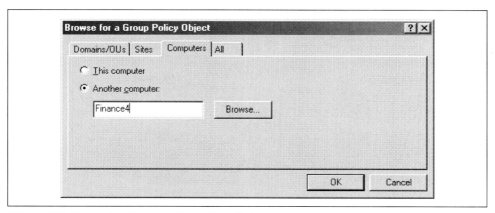

Figure 7-7. Browse for Group Policy Object dialog

To modify the LGPO of another computer, type in the computer name or browse and select.

Setting Nonlocal Group Policies

You use the same dialog as shown in Figure 7-7 to select Active Directory Container GPOs to configure. These GPOs are divided into two groups, Domains/OUs and Sites. The Domains/OUs tab features a dropdown list to choose a container to look in as well as a list of GPOs in that container and their associated domain.

Similarly, you can specify a Site GPO on the Site tab. Again, a dropdown list contains the available sites to look in. To view all available GPOs in a certain domain, use the All tab and select the domain to look in. All GPOs in the selected domain will appear for easy pickings.

What's in the Standard Policy Templates?

Windows 2000 includes a number of administrative policy templates. Some are more general in nature and cover a wider scope; others pertain to specific applications. The first two templates are specific to Windows 2000 clients and are installed in Group Policy by default:

INETRES.ADM
    Contains Internet Explorer policies for Windows 2000 clients; contains both machine and user settings. The HKCU settings, for the most part, regulate settings in the control panel of Internet Explorer. It has categories for the General tab, Content tab, Connection tab, Programs tab, Advanced tab, as well as some information delivery restrictions. The machine settings include categories for security and code downloading restrictions.

SYSTEM.ADM
    By far the largest standard policy template. The machine portion of the template includes policy categories for administrative services, which encompasses login policies, file system settings, policy policies, and the task scheduler; networks; and printers. Registry settings under HKCU cover a broad range, from the control panel to Windows components to policies for system control.

The next administrative templates are specific to NT 4.0, 95/98, or both, and should be used with the System Policy editor rather than the Group Policies snap-in:

WINDOWS.ADM
    Defines policy settings specific to Windows 95 and 98. The two categories included in the HKLM section of this template detail network and system policies, both of which encompass intermediate policy categories. Policy settings for the control panel, network sharing, system restrictions, and custom folders round out the user portion of this template.

WINNT.ADM
    Defines user-interface options specific to NT 4.0. While some of the categories from the *WINDOWS.ADM* template appear here, the underlying subcategories and policies are different. As expected, this template contains both machine and user settings. The general machine categories cover policies for the system, networking, remote access, printers, user profiles and shell settings. The policy categories for the system, user profiles, and the shell are present under HKCU as well.

COMMON.ADM

Defines user interface options that are common to Windows NT 4.0, 98, and 95. In addition to system settings, it includes network settings for the machine and desktop settings for users.

Finally, here are a few templates included in the *%SystemRoot%\inf* directory:

CONF.ADM

Contains both user and machine policy settings for Microsoft NetMeeting.

INETSET.ADM

While *INETRES.ADM* contains policy settings for Internet restrictions, *INETSET.ADM* defines general Internet settings. The HKCU section of the template covers policy settings for colors, fonts, modem, and advanced settings.

WMP.ADM

Contains customization settings for the Windows Media Player.

For detailed information about these templates and the policies, Registry keys, and values that they cover, refer to Appendix A, *User Configuration Group Policy Objects*, and Appendix B, *Computer Configuration Group Policy Objects*.

8

Programming with the Registry

So far, all the chapters in this book have taught you how, and why, to use the Registry tools that Microsoft provides as part of Windows 2000. For the most part, these tools are sufficient for everyday use. However, you may find it necessary to write your own tools from time to time.

Windows 2000 also provides a comprehensive set of routines that allow your programs to read, write, and modify Registry keys and values. You can also connect to remote computers' Registries, get and set security data on keys and values, and do basically everything that *RegEdt32*, *RegEdit*, and the resource kit utilities can do. This capability is a double-edged sword: you can write programs that do exactly what you want, but the burden of properly using the Registry calls is entirely on you.

The Registry API

The original Registry API is defined in *winreg.h*, part of Microsoft's Win32 Software Development Kit (SDK) for NT 4.0 and Windows 95. The current version is still part of the Win32 API, but now it lives in the Microsoft Developer Network (MSDN) Platform SDK. There are 28 distinct routines in the Registry API, though most of them actually have two variants: one that works with standard one-byte ASCII strings and another that handles Unicode strings. The ASCII versions have routine names that end in "A," such as **RegCreateKeyA**, while the Unicode versions end with a "W," as in **RegCreateKeyW**. Macros in *winreg.h* automatically map the correct variant to the routine name. When you call **RegCreateKey**, you automatically get the correct Unicode or ASCII variant depending on how your header files are set up. (Of course, in Visual Basic or Perl this distinction is moot.) The Registry stores strings in Unicode format, so when you call one of the ASCII variants, the Registry code takes care of converting one encoding to another.

As if this original set of functions wasn't enough, Microsoft has added a separate set of Registry-related API routines as part of the Internet Explorer 4.0/5.0 shell. These routines are delivered as part of the Shell Lightweight Utility API, and most of them are implemented in Version 4.71 and later of *shlwapi.dll*. All machines running Windows 2000 or 98 have this DLL (as of this writing, it's Version 5.00), while machines running Windows 95 or NT 4.0 have it if they also have Internet Explorer 4.0 or later. Some functions discussed later in the chapter are only available as part of Internet Explorer 5.0 or later; those functions are noted.

API Concepts and Conventions

If you've used any other set of Win32 API routines, you'll probably find the Registry API easy to digest. If you haven't, though, a brief review of some Win32 API fundamentals will help flatten your learning curve.

Input and output parameters

Each Registry routine described next has its own unique set of parameters. These parameters give you a way to tell the API routines what you want done and how to do it. It's important to make sure you specify the parameters completely and correctly. If you don't, you'll likely get ERROR_INVALID_PARAMETER back as an error; it's entirely possible that instead you might get a corrupted Registry and a crashed machine.

In general, the C/C++ declarations for the Registry routines use pointers both for input and output. For example, strings are always passed as pointers (surprise!), as are outputs for things like security attributes and newly opened HKEYs. The Perl and Visual Basic declarations use the type system appropriate for the language, as you'll see in the sections that cover each language.

Registry error codes

Every Registry API routine returns an error code as its value. These codes, all of which are defined in *winerror.h*, give you an easy way to test for success or failure of an operation. Table 8-1 lists the most commonly used codes. A few routines can return other error codes as noted, but these are the ones you're most likely to see. Your code should always test for all returned errors (not just these) and handle them properly if they should occur.

Table 8-1. Registry Error Codes

Error Code	Meaning
ERROR_SUCCESS	The requested operation succeeded.
ERROR_FILE_NOT_FOUND	The requested Registry key or path doesn't exist.

Table 8-1. Registry Error Codes (continued)

Error Code	Meaning
ERROR_ACCESS_DENIED	The permissions on the requested key don't allow you to access it.
ERROR_INVALID_HANDLE	The HKEY you passed in isn't a valid Registry handle.
ERROR_OUTOFMEMORY	There's not enough memory to read the data you requested.
ERROR_INVALID_PARAMETER	One or more parameters you supplied are invalid; you may have omitted values for a required parameter or supplied a bad value.
ERROR_BAD_PATHNAME	The path specified doesn't exist.
ERROR_LOCK_FAILED	The internal Registry locking mechanism failed. This is usually because you're making multiple requests of the Registry from within a single process or thread.
ERROR_MORE_DATA	The buffer you provided as a parameter is too small to contain all the available data.
ERROR_NO_MORE_ITEMS	There are no more keys or values to enumerate.
ERROR_BADKEY	The key handle you provided is bad.
ERROR_BADDB	The hive that holds the key or value you requested is corrupted.
ERROR_CANTOPEN	The requested key or value can't be opened.
ERROR_CANTREAD	The requested key or value can be opened but not read.
ERROR_CANTWRITE	You can't write data to the key or value you're trying to overwrite.
ERROR_REGISTRY_RECOVERED	One or more hive files was reconstructed.
ERROR_REGISTRY_CORRUPT	Something very bad has happened to one or more hive files.
ERROR_REGISTRY_IO_FAILED	The kernel tried to read, write, or flush cached Registry data from the corresponding hive but couldn't.
ERROR_NOT_REGISTRY_FILE	The hive file you tried to load isn't a hive file.
ERROR_KEY_DELETED	You're trying to modify a key that's been deleted.

Why some calls have names ending in "Ex"

Back in ancient times,* the original Windows 3.x API was the One True API application developers were counseled to use. As programmers did use the API, the inertia of a large installed base made it hard for Microsoft to change the way any of the original 3.x routines worked. Instead of changing the originals, the Win32 API added new routines where necessary and gave them new names ending with

---

* Well, all right: around 1990.

Ex. For example, `RegOpenKey` begat `RegOpenKeyEx`, which adds an options flag and a SAM access context—both of which are specific to Win32.

In general, you should avoid using the original routines when an *Ex* equivalent exists. Most of the cool features of the Windows 2000 Registry (especially those related to security) aren't available with the "classic" API. In addition, it's possible that the old-style routines will stop being supported in future Windows versions. In a few cases it may make sense to use the old-style routine anyway; I've noted these exceptions where appropriate.

"Happy families are all alike"

The whole point behind the Win32 API is that you can write programs that use a single API. As long as you stick with that API, your code should run on any Win32-compliant platform, whether it's Win95 on Intel, WinNT on Alpha, Windows 2000 on Itanium, or WinCE on whatever CPU the HPC builder chose. You're not supposed to have to care which underlying operating system is present. While this is a wonderful theory, it sometimes breaks down in practice. For example, many of the routines described here have slightly different behavior under Windows CE.* More importantly, some routines don't work at all under Win95.

This may be too harsh an indictment. What really happens is that the routines don't fail, but they don't do what they're supposed to; they just return `ERROR_SUCCESS`. This means that your code still executes under Win9x, but it may not do what you intended it to. At present, there are only four routines that behave this way under Win9x: `RegRestoreKey`, `RegGetKeySecurity`, `RegSetKeySecurity`, and `RegNotifyChangeKeyValue`. If your application uses any of these routines, be forewarned: you won't get back the data you expect when your code is run under Win9x. Be sure to handle these cases gracefully (for example, checking whether the `SECURITY_DESCRIPTOR` returned by `RegGetKeySecurity` is valid before trying to use it).

The same is true for the shell APIs I mentioned earlier: none of those APIs are supported under Windows CE, and they may have slight functional differences between Windows 2000/NT and 95/98.

New and exciting datatypes

One of Windows 2000's biggest advantages over Win9x is its robust security architecture. Since the Win32 API is supposed to be common across Win9x, Windows 2000/NT, and Windows CE devices, you may have seen, and ignored, some of the Windows 2000-specific datatypes used in Registry API routines. These datatypes

---

* MSDN and the Win32 SDK both document these differences, so I won't go into them here.

can be useful, so a quick introduction will help you get familiar with them. (Skip this section if you already know how to use these types.)

The Registry API uses many standard Windows datatypes such as DWORD and LPSTR. However, there are six datatypes that are fairly unfamiliar to most programmers who haven't yet written Windows 2000-specific code. Each is used in at least one Registry call.

HKEY

>The initial letter of this type should tip you off to what it is. Microsoft uses Hungarian notation,* so the initial H means this datatype is a handle to something. An HKEY is an opaque handle to a Registry key; the handle actually points to a large table of key references, so it's not a handle in the pointer-to-a-pointer sense most programmers usually use.
>
>*winreg.h* includes definitions for the standard six root keys. Anywhere you can use an HKEY, you can use HKEY_LOCAL_MACHINE or one of the other predefined root key HKEYs.

REGSAM

>REGSAM is really a DWORD in disguise; its values represent the permission you're requesting when you open or create a key. Legal values are shown in Table 8-2. You can use any of them when creating or opening a key, but you should limit what you ask for to what you actually need. In most cases, that means either KEY_READ or KEY_WRITE.

Table 8-2. REGSAM Access Mask Values

Value	Meaning
KEY_ALL_ACCESS	Combination of KEY_QUERY_VALUE, KEY_ENUMERATE_SUB_KEYS, KEY_NOTIFY, KEY_CREATE_SUB_KEY, KEY_CREATE_LINK, and KEY_SET_VALUE access
KEY_CREATE_LINK	Grants permission to create a symbolic link to specified key
KEY_CREATE_SUB_KEY	Grants permission to create new subkeys
KEY_ENUMERATE_SUB_KEYS	Grants permission to enumerate subkeys of the parent key
KEY_EXECUTE	Grants permission to read subkeys and values
KEY_NOTIFY	Grants permission to request change notification on the parent key or its values
KEY_QUERY_VALUE	Grants permission to get subkey values and their contents
KEY_READ	Combination of KEY_QUERY_VALUE, KEY_ENUMERATE_SUB_KEYS, and KEY_NOTIFY access

---

* This notation gets its name from Charles Simonyi, the Microsoft developer who invented the scheme. As you might infer from his surname, he's Hungarian. Despite the fact that it's ugly and restrictive, it has caught on in Windows books, perhaps because Microsoft uses it exclusively in their header files and example code.

Table 8-2. REGSAM Access Mask Values (continued)

Value	Meaning
KEY_SET_VALUE	Permission to change subkey values
KEY_WRITE	Combination of KEY_SET_VALUE and KEY_CREATE_SUB_KEY access

SECURITY_INFORMATION

    Windows 2000 allows you to read and write ACLs on Registry keys. However, you must specify exactly which ACL you want to view or change. The SECURITY_INFORMATION type handles this; it allows you to specify any of the values listed in Table 8-3 when calling RegGetKeySecurity or RegSetKeySecurity. The first four values in the table are valid for Windows NT 4.0 or 2000; the last four are Windows 2000-only.

Table 8-3. SECURITY_INFORMATION Values

Value	Meaning
OWNER_SECURITY_INFORMATION	Indicates that you want information about the owner identifier of an object.
GROUP_SECURITY_INFORMATION	Indicates you're requesting information about the primary group identifier of the object. Only objects connected with the POSIX subsystem have this information.
DACL_SECURITY_INFORMATION	Indicates that you want information about the discretionary ACL of the object.
SACL_SECURITY_INFORMATION	Indicates that you want information on the system ACL of the object.
PROTECTED_DACL_SECURITY_INFORMATION	Indicates that this DACL may not inherit ACE entries from its parent.
PROTECTED_SACL_SECURITY_INFORMATION	Indicates that this SACL may not inherit ACE entries from its parent.
UNPROTECTED_DACL_SECURITY_INFORMATION	Indicates that this DACL inherits ACE entries from its parent object.
UNPROTECTED_SACL_SECURITY_INFORMATION	Indicates that this SACL inherits ACE entries from its parent object.

SECURITY_DESCRIPTOR

    Access control data is stored in SECURITY_DESCRIPTOR structures. Like HKEY, HWND, and other types, a SECURITY_DESCRIPTOR is opaque; there's no way to decipher exactly what it points to or contains without using the Win32 security API routines. (Actually, this is a fudge. Microsoft documents the structure but sternly warns developers against reading or modifying its fields.)

SECURITY_ATTRIBUTES

The SECURITY_ATTRIBUTES structure encapsulates a security descriptor and data needed to interpret it:

```
typedef struct _SECURITY_ATTRIBUTES {
    DWORD  nLength;
    LPVOID lpSecurityDescriptor;
    BOOL   bInheritHandle;
} SECURITY_ATTRIBUTES;
```

The nLength member specifies the size of the security descriptor pointed to by lpSecurityDescriptor. The bInheritHandle member controls whether a child process spawned by the process that owns the SECURITY_ATTRIBUTES structure should also receive the owning process' security descriptor.

FILETIME

The FILETIME structure contains the access date and time for an object. Its format is a little odd:

```
typedef struct _FILETIME {
    DWORD dwLowDateTime;
    DWORD dwHighDateTime;
} FILETIME;
```

Together, the two DWORDs represent the number of 100-nsec intervals since 1 January 1601. I have no idea what possessed Microsoft to use this particular date as the base of their time system. Fortunately, there are a number of routines for converting between FILETIME values and more useful formats; check out FileTimeToSystemTime for one example.

New routines = new datatypes

When Microsoft added the shell utility routines as part of IE 4.0, they also had to create some new datatypes to fully support those routines. Most of the shell utility routines provide functionality not included in the standard Win32 API set. However, the file association routines (AssocCreate, AssocQueryKey, AssocQueryString, and AssocQueryStringByKey) bundle several Registry operations into a single function. These routines actually encapsulate the IQueryAssociations COM object; its purpose is to return the correct key and OLE class information from HKCR for a specific type of document file. By providing a standard way to do this (instead of requiring every developer to roll their own) Microsoft is trying to reduce the number of association-related frustrations foisted on end users. The new datatypes are:

The Registry API

ASSOCF

The `ASSOCF` structure holds flags that specifies what data you want back from a call to one of the association functions. Table 8-4 shows the flags and their values.

Table 8-4. ASSOCF Values

Value	Meaning
ASSOCF_INIT_BYEXENAME	Finds the association for the selected executable. When this flag is not set, the query routines return the association for the *.exe* filetype.
ASSOCF_OPEN_BYEXENAME	Identical to `ASSOCF_INIT_BYEXENAME`.
ASSOCF_INIT_DEFAULTTOSTAR	If no matching association is found under the selected root key, and this flag is set, checks the HKCR* subkey for a match.
ASSOCF_INIT_DEFAULTTOFOLDER	If no matching association is found under the selected root key, and this flag is set, checks the HKCR\Folder subkey for a match.
ASSOCF_NOUSERSETTINGS	When set, directs the query code to search HKCR only, not HKCU\Software\Classes. By default, both keys are searched, and the user value is used if present.
ASSOCF_NOTRUNCATE	If the found value is too big for the supplied buffer, don't truncate it; instead, return the required buffer length and an error.
ASSOCF_VERIFY	Cross-checks the found association with the class factory or executable that owns the associated type. Imposes a performance penalty but provides extra safety.
ASSOCF_REMAPRUNDLL	Tells the query code to ignore the presence of the *rundll.exe* command in the supplied command string; this prevents the query code from returning association information for *rundll*.
ASSOCF_NOFIXUPS	Don't fix any errors found when `ASSOCF_VERIFY` is set. When set, this flag may cause your code to modify Registry data.
ASSOCF_IGNOREBASECLASS	Ignores the `BaseClass` value when searching for associations.

ASSOCKEY

The `ASSOCKEY` enumerated type tells the association routines what kind of key you want returned from your association query. You have to use this type in calls to `AssocQueryKey` to ensure that you get the desired key in return. See Table 8-5 for the enumeration's values.

```
typedef enum {
    ASSOCKEY_SHELLEXECCLASS = 1,
    ASSOCKEY_APP,
```

```
    ASSOCKEY_CLASS,
    ASSOCKEY_BASECLASS,
} ASSOCKEY;
```

Table 8-5. ASSOCKEY Values

Value	Indicates you're asking for...
ASSOCKEY_SHELLEXECCLASS	A handle to a key that can be passed directly to the ShellExec() function
ASSOCKEY_APP	A handle to the Application key for the specified file class
ASSOCKEY_CLASS	A handle to the class key or ProgID
ASSOCKEY_BASECLASS	A handle to the class BaseClass key

ASSOCSTR

The ASSOCSTR enumerated type tells the association routines what type of string you want as the result of a query. For example, you can request the friendly name of an executable or document type, the command for a particular shell verb, and so on. Table 8-6 enumerates this type's values and their meanings.

```
typedef enum {
    ASSOCSTR_COMMAND,
    ASSOCSTR_EXECUTABLE,
    ASSOCSTR_FRIENDLYDOCNAME,
    ASSOCSTR_FRIENDLYAPPNAME,
    ASSOCSTR_NOOPEN,
    ASSOCSTR_SHELLNEWVALUE,
    ASSOCSTR_DDECOMMAND,
    ASSOCSTR_DDEIFEXEC,
    ASSOCSTR_DDEAPPLICATION,
    ASSOCSTR_DDETOPIC
} ASSOCSTR;
```

Table 8-6. ASSOCSTR Flags

Value	Indicates you're asking for...
ASSOCSTR_COMMAND	The command string associated with the specified shell verb
ASSOCSTR_EXECUTABLE	The executable name from a shell verb command string (see the note for ASSOCF_REMAPRUNDLL)
ASSOCSTR_FRIENDLYDOCNAME	The friendly name of a document type
ASSOCSTR_FRIENDLYAPPNAME	The friendly name of an application
ASSOCSTR_NOOPEN	All information except the contents of the Open subkey
ASSOCSTR_SHELLNEWVALUE	Information from the ShellNew subkey
ASSOCSTR_DDECOMMAND	The template that forms DDE commands sent to this object

Table 8-6. ASSOCSTR Flags (continued)

Value	Indicates you're asking for…
ASSOCSTR_DDEIFEXEC	The DDE command that creates a new instance of the selected object's factory
ASSOCSTR_DDEAPPLICATION	The application name needed to send DDE broadcasts to the application
ASSOCSTR_DDETOPIC	The topic name needed to send DDE broadcasts to the application

HUSKEY and PHUSKEY

> HKEY is an opaque type that represents a handle to an open Registry key. HUSKEY is a little different. It's a handle that represents a user-specific key (as you'll see in the next section).

User-specific keys

Windows NT 3.1 introduced the concept of multiple user profiles to the Windows world. The idea was that each user could have her own group of personal settings that would automatically be loaded when she logged on. In Windows NT 3.51, Microsoft expanded this concept to cover domains, so that users could get their personal setting (or *profile*) information no matter where in the domain they logged on. However, some applications store their settings under HKCU, and others use HKLM. Compounding the problem, not all programs and components keep their setting data in the Registry. The introduction of user-specific class keys (see the section "HKEY_CLASSES_ROOT" in Chapter 2) makes things even more complicated, since some per-user settings may actually be inherited from HKCR.

To fix this problem, Microsoft has introduced the concept of user-specific keys (USK). The idea is that all settings for one user can be stored beneath that user's USK, which then conveniently becomes the user's profile, making the settings portable. Applications that use the shell utility API are encouraged to use the USK functions to store and retrieve user-specific data so that all the user's profile settings are stored in the same place.

An extremely brief example

Almost every C or C++ book includes an example based on the famous "Hello, World" example from Kernighan and Ritchie's *The C Programming Language*. Following that venerable tradition, Example 8-1 shows what a similar program that uses the Registry looks like.

Example 8-1. A Modern Variation of the Canonical "Hello, World" Program

```
#include <windows.h>
#include <winreg.h>
#include <stdio.h>

// Hello, World! for the Registry: gets this machine's name and prints
// it out.
void main(void)
{
    unsigned char pszName[MAX_PATH] = "";
    DWORD nNameLen = MAX_PATH;
    HKEY hkResult, hStartKey = HKEY_LOCAL_MACHINE;
    long nResult = ERROR_SUCCESS;

    nResult = RegOpenKeyEx(hStartKey,
         "SYSTEM\\CurrentControlSet\\Control\\ComputerName\\ActiveComputerName",
              0L, KEY_READ, &hkResult);
    if (ERROR_SUCCESS == nResult)
    {
        nResult = RegQueryValueEx(hkResult, "ComputerName", 0, 0,
                                  pszName, &nNameLen);
        if (ERROR_SUCCESS == nResult)
            printf("Hello, world, from %s!\n", pszName);
        else
            printf("I don't even know my own name.\n");
    }
    RegCloseKey(hkResult);
}
```

Throughout the C examples in this section, you'll notice that I've had to use double backslashes (\\) in Registry paths. That's because the C preprocessor treats a single backslash as a flag character that marks a special character sequence; to get one backslash in a string, you need to include two.

This example contains code to implement the three most basic—and most common—Registry operations:

1. Open a key whose full path you know using RegOpenKey or RegOpenKeyEx, then retain the HKEY returned when the key is opened.

2. Use that returned HKEY to get a value whose location and type you already know (in this case, HKLM\SYSTEM\CurrentControlSet\Control\ComputerName\ActiveComputerName).

3. Do something with the retrieved value, and close the key opened in Step 1.

Almost all programs that use the Registry involve these three steps. Of course, in addition to (or instead of) reading Registry data, you can write new data to a value or enumerate a sequence of keys or values to find one that matches what you're looking for. You'll learn how to do all these things in the following sections.

In the following sections, I present the API as Microsoft defined it: using C. The sections on programming with Perl and Visual Basic contain the correct definitions for those languages.

Opening and Closing Keys

In Chapter 1, *A Gentle Introduction to the Registry*, I pointed out the organizational similarities between a filesystem and the Registry. These similarities are more than skin deep: they extend to the actual process of moving data into and out of the Registry. In general, the same rules apply when working with Registry keys and their values as with disk files.

First and foremost, you have to open a key when you want to use it, then close it when you're done. If you don't open a key, you can't get its values. If you don't close the key when done, other applications can't access it, and your changes aren't written out when you'd expect them to be. The API routines that open keys require two arguments: a path to the key you want to open and an open parent key. This may seem like a Catch-22: how can you open a key if you must already have an open key? The answer is simple: the root keys (HKLM, HKCC, HKCU, HKU, HKDD, and HKCR) are always open, so you can use them when you open any other key.

There are exceptions to the foregoing rule: some of the shell utility API routines don't have to open or close keys. For example, you can call **SHRegCreateKey**, which creates a new user-specific key underneath your choice of HKLM or HKCU, without opening either parent key. You even get back a handle that you can use with other shell API routines, all without opening or closing any other keys.

The next similarity involves access controls and rights. If you're accustomed to NTFS, Unix, or Novell filesystems, you know that files and directories can have permissions attached to them that govern who can open, modify, delete, and move things around. In ACLs, files also have rights, which the ACLs grant. One entry in the ACL might grant Administrator the right to read or write a file, while another might deny write access to members of the Domain Users group. Registry keys have these same controls and rights. As you'll learn in Chapter 9, *Administering the Registry*, you can keep your Registry secure by putting ACLs on security-sensitive keys. When you open a Registry key, you must specify what access you want to it: read, write, enumerate, and delete are all examples. Windows 2000 checks the access you request against the ACLs on the Registry key to decide whether or not you get access.

The best way to stay out of trouble when opening and closing keys is to remember to balance key openings with closings. Later in the chapter (in the section titled "Example: A Stack-Based Wrapper Class"), you'll see a C++ class, StKey, that automates the cleanup process. Please be sure to close any keys you open even when errors or exceptions interrupt the normal flow of control in your code.

Opening keys

When you're ready to open a key, there are two different approaches you can take. The first one is to use the RegCreateKey or RegCreateKeyEx functions, which I'll talk about in a bit. They'll automatically open the key you specify or create it if it doesn't exist. The second method, which is probably better for most applications, is to open the key with RegOpenKeyEx or RegOpenKey. Why are these calls better? They fail when you try to open a key that doesn't exist, while the RegCreate functions will create a new key with no values in it. Imagine that you're calling a friend named Bill on the phone. If you call and are told "Bill's not here" by the person who answers, that's the equivalent of calling RegOpenKey routines on a nonexistent key. By contrast, calling Bill and being told "Bill's not here, but I'll pretend to be him" is more or less what happens when you call RegCreate. That may sometimes be desirable, but it's not a pleasant surprise if you're not expecting it.

The recommended way to open a key is with RegOpenKeyEx. You supply an open key, which may be a root key or a key you've already opened; the name of the full path to the key you want to open; and a mask describing what access you want to the newly opened key.

```
LONG RegOpenKeyEx(hKey, pszSubKey, dwOptions, samDesired, phkResult);
```

HKEY	hKey	Handle to any open key or root key.
LPCTSTR	pszSubKey	Name of the subkey of hKey you want to open; if NULL or empty, RegOpenKeyEx just opens an additional copy of hKey instead.
DWORD	dwOptions	Reserved; must be 0.
REGSAM	samDesired	Mask defining access rights you're asking for (just use either KEY_READ or KEY_WRITE).
PHKEY	phkResult	Pointer to the newly opened key; NULL if an error occurs.

The following code opens a key under HKLM for reading, then goes on to do some other processing (which I've omitted here). If you combine the root key and the

The Registry API 223

value of **pszSubKey**, you'll see that the key being opened is HKLM\SOFTWARE\ LJL\ArmorMail\Users; if I'd already had any key in that path open (for example, HKLM\SOFTWARE\LJL) I could have shortened the subkey name accordingly.

```
DWORD    result = ERROR_SUCCESS;
HKEY     firstKey;

// try to open the user list key; if we succeed, enumerate its subkeys
result = RegOpenKeyEx(HKEY_LOCAL_MACHINE, "SOFTWARE\\LJL\\ArmorMail\\
                     Users", 0L, KEY_READ, &firstKey);
if (ERROR_SUCCESS == result)
    ...
```

If you try to open a key for access that the DACL on the key doesn't allow (for example, trying to open any of the HKLM\HARDWARE subkeys for write access from an unprivileged user account), you get **ERROR_ACCESS_DENIED** for your trouble. One of the "strongly recommended" criteria for getting the Win9x and Windows 2000 certification labels is that you should open keys with the privileges you need: don't ask for **KEY_ALL_ACCESS** when what you really need is **KEY_READ**. You should ask for write access only when you're ready to write data to the Registry; this reduces the risk that your code will accidentally damage the Registry while you're developing it.

If you're willing to use the default system security mask for key access, you can use the **RegOpenKey** function instead. It takes the same **hKey**, **pszSubKey**, and **phkResult** parameters as **RegOpenKeyEx**, but it doesn't accept a desired SAM mask.

```
LONG RegOpenKey(hKey, pszSubKey, phkResult);
```

HKEY	hKey	Handle to any open key or root key.
LPCTSTR	pszSubKey	Name of the subkey you want opened; if **NULL** or empty, **RegOpenKey** opens another copy of **hKey**.
PHKEY	phkResult	Pointer to the newly opened HKEY.

The only difference between **RegOpenKey** and **RegOpenKeyEx** is that the latter has two extra parameters. Apart from that, they function identically. One portability warning, though: as with the other Win 3.x Registry API calls, **RegOpenKey** is unsupported on Windows CE. If you're writing code you want to be portable, stick with the *.Ex* functions, tempting though the old ones may be.

Opening a key while impersonating another user

As it turns out, Windows NT and 2000 both cache the contents of HKCU for all threads in a process. This is a big efficiency win (which is why Microsoft did it), but if you're writing an application that uses multiple threads, it can pose a sticky problem if any of those threads has to impersonate another user. For example, let's say you're writing an antivirus utility. You want it to be able to scan memory and files owned by whichever users are present on the system, so you code it to spawn one thread for each interactive or network user. Guess what? The default behavior results in your application reading, and storing, settings only in HKCU, even if other users have set preferences in their own profiles. This problem is particularly acute for people who are writing management utilities that have to deal with users and services sharing a computer (or, worse, using Terminal Services).

There's a way to fix this when writing applications for Windows 2000: the RegOpenCurrentUser call opens the appropriate user-specific key for the thread that calls it. For example, if you have one thread running as Administrator and another running as RA\paulr, and each thread calls RegOpenCurrentUser, one thread gets HKU\Administrator and one gets HKU\paulr.*

```
LONG RegOpenCurrentUser(rDesiredPerms, phkResult);
```

REGSAM	rDesiredPerms	Permissions you want to have on the user-specific key.
PHKEY	phkResult	Pointer to the newly opened HKEY.

Opening the user's class data

In Windows 2000, the class information that used to live only in HKCR has been partitioned into two chunks: one that lives in HKCR and one that occupies the new, user-specific HKCU\Classes subkey. When you want data about OLE/ActiveX objects or class definitions (say, to find out which class factory to use to create a new object), how do you know where to look? Worse still, what if you're writing a multiuser or server-based application that needs to get the correct settings for whatever user is currently making a request? Oh, the horror.

The solution is a new, Windows 2000-only API call, RegOpenUserClassesRoot. This routine allows you to open a handle to the class data for a particular user. Windows 2000 automatically combines that user's HKCU\Classes key with the machine's HKCR data to present a single unified tree to your program.

```
LONG RegOpenUserClassesRoot(hToken, dwOptions, samDesired, phkResult);
```

HANDLE	hToken	Access token that identifies the user whose data you want.
DWORD	dwOptions	Reserved; must be 0.
REGSAM	samDesired	Mask defining access rights you're asking for (just use KEY_READ or KEY_WRITE).
PHKEY	phkResult	Pointer to the newly opened HKEY; NULL if an error occurs.

---

* Actually, these names would be replaced by SIDs, but you get the idea.

The `dwOptions`, `samDesired`, and `phkResult` parameters are all pretty straightforward, since they work the same as they do when calling `RegOpenKeyEx`. `hToken` takes a little more explaining: it's a process token like the one the system generates internally when you log on interactively. In fact, you can pass that same token to `RegOpenUserClassesRoot`, but normally you wouldn't need to, since you can get the active user's class data when running processes in that user's context. It's more likely that you'd need to get a token representing some user other than the current user. For example, in a multiuser server application, you'd probably want to retrieve each individual user's data by opening their class data key. There are six routines that can give you back a token of the type you need to call `RegOpenUserClassesRoot`: (see Table 8-7). Which of these routines you use will depends on what you're trying to do. Most of the time, though, you'll probably use either `LogonUser`, `OpenProcessToken`, or `OpenThreadToken`.

Table 8-7. API Routines That Can Give You a Token to Use with RegOpenUserClassesRoot

API routine	Use it when you want to...
LogonUser	Log a new user on to the local computer and run processes as that user.
CreateRestrictedToken	(Windows 2000 only) Create a new token with fewer privileges than some existing token.
DuplicateToken	Duplicate an existing token, keeping the same access privileges.
DuplicateTokenEx	Duplicate an existing token, creating either an exact duplicate or an impersonation token.
OpenProcessToken	Obtain a handle to the access token of an existing process.
OpenThreadToken	Obtain a handle to the access token of an existing thread.

Closing keys

There's only one way to close a handle to a key: `RegCloseKey`. You pass in the HKEY you want to close. If it's successfully closed, you get ERROR_SUCCESS back. Otherwise, you get an error that indicates what went wrong.

```
LONG RegCloseKey (hKey);
```

You can actually call `RegCloseKey` on one of the predefined root key entries. It reports a successful close but doesn't actually close the root key. This frees you from worrying about whether the HKEY you're trying to close is really yours or not.

When you close an HKEY, any data you've changed in that HKEY or its subkeys may be written to disk. On the other hand, it may not; the Registry support code may cache these changes until the next time it's convenient to flush them out to disk. Don't assume that your changes are immediately preserved as soon as you close a HKEY. Do assume that your changes are not preserved until you do so.

Creating Keys

You can create new keys anywhere you have permission. As I pointed out in earlier chapters, you probably won't need to do so very often unless you're writing applications that use the Registry to store their parameters. Just in case, though, here's how to do it.

RegCreateKeyEx is the most powerful function for creating a new key. When you ask it to create a key, it does so, then opens it. If the key already exists, it just opens it and returns a handle to it. In either case, after a successful call to **RegCreateKeyEx** you'll have an open key handle that can be used for all manner of things as described elsewhere in the chapter.

```
LONG RegCreateKeyEx(hKey, pszSubKey, Reserved, pszClass, dwOptions,
        samDesired, lpSecurityAttributes, phkResult, lpdwDisposition);
```

HKEY	hKey	Handle to an open key under which the new subkey is created; applications can't create keys directly under HKLM or HKU.
LPCSTR	pszSubKey	Path to the new subkey you want to create; this path is interpreted relative to hKey. The pathname must not begin with a backslash. Any keys in the path that don't exist are created for you.
DWORD	Reserved	Reserved; must be NULL.
LPCSTR	pszClass	Specifies the class of the key. Microsoft says "No classes are currently defined; applications should pass a NULL string."
DWORD	dwOptions	May be REG_OPTION_NON_VOLATILE (creates the key as a normal, persistent key), REG_OPTION_VOLATILE (creates the key as a volatile key that is never stored to disk), or REG_OPTION_BACKUP_RESTORE (ignores samDesired and attempts to open the key for backup/restore access.) The default is REG_OPTION_NON_VOLATILE.
REGSAM	samDesired	Contains an access mask specifying what access you want to the new key; see Table 8-2 for a complete list.
LPSECURITY_ATTRIBUTES	lpSecurityAttributes	On input, points to a SECURITY_ATTRIBUTES structure that controls whether child processes and threads may access this key. Leave this NULL to turn off inheritance.
PHKEY	phkResult	Pointer to HKEY containing the newly opened key.

The Registry API

| LPDWORD | lpdwDisposition | Points to a DWORD that indicates what happened; it is set to REG_CREATED_NEW_KEY if the requested key has to be created, or REG_OPENED_EXISTING_KEY if the key is merely opened. |

When you open an existing key, RegCreateKeyEx ignores the lpClass, dwOptions, and lpSecurityAttributes parameters, since their values are determined by the existing key.

Once you successfully call RegCreateKeyEx, you're guaranteed to have an open HKEY you can use to add values or subkeys. Of course, a newly created key won't have any of either item, but an existing key that RegCreateKeyEx opened might indeed; be sure to check lpdwDisposition if you need to know whether the key was created or just opened.

You can use RegCreateKeyEx as a mutual-exclusion locking mechanism (or mutex) for two or more processes. When one process creates a new key using RegCreateKeyEx, the return value is REG_CREATED_NEW_KEY. When subsequent processes try to create the same key, they get back REG_OPENED_EXISTING_KEY, which they can use as a signal that the mutex is in use. Windows NT and 2000 offer more sophisticated mutex mechanisms, but this one has the advantage that it works on any variant of the Win32 API—even under emulators like Linux's Wine.

You can also use the less-flexible RegCreateKey, but neither Microsoft nor I recommend it. It lacks a way to specify what access or security attributes you want to apply to the key, meaning that it may fail unexpectedly when trying to open an existing key that has an ACL applied to it. In addition, it doesn't tell you whether it created a key or opened it.

```
LONG RegCreateKey(hKey, pszSubKey, phkResult);
```

HKEY	hKey	Handle to an open key under which the new subkey is created; applications may not create keys directly under HKLM or HKU.
LPCSTR	pszSubKey	Full path of key you want to create; any components that don't exist are created.
PHKEY	phkResult	Pointer to HKEY containing newly opened key.

Getting Information About Keys

Every key has a great deal of information associated with it, even if it's not immediately obvious. When you use one of the Registry editing tools, you see a neatly tree-structured view of what's beneath each root key, but the system maintains a lot more data beneath the surface so that it can efficiently access keys and values and give them back to requesting programs.

`RegQueryInfoKey` gives you access to a total of 11 different pieces of data for any key in the Registry. Typically you use it to find how many subkeys or values exist so you can efficiently enumerate through them (more on that in the next section). `RegQueryInfoKey` looks like the following.

```
LONG RegQueryInfoKey(hKey, pszClass, lpcbClass, lpReserved, lpcSubKeys,
        lpcbMaxSubKeyLen, lpcbMaxClassLen, lpcValues, lpcbMaxValueNameLen,
        lpcbMaxValueLen, lpcbSecurityDescriptor, lpftLastWriteTime);
```

HKEY	hKey	Handle to any open key or root key.
LPTSTR	lpClass	Points to a buffer that receives the key's class name. May be NULL if you don't want the class name back.
LPDWORD	lpcbClass	Points to a DWORD containing the length of the class name passed back in lpClass. May be NULL if lpClass is also NULL; if one is NULL, but the other isn't, you get ERROR_INVALID_PARAMETER back.
LPDWORD	lpReserved	Reserved; must always be NULL.
LPDWORD	lpcSubKeys	Points to a DWORD that receives the number of subkeys of hKey.
LPDWORD	lpcbMaxSubKeyLen	Points to a DWORD that holds the length (not including the terminating NULL) of the longest subkey name under hKey.
LPDWORD	lpcbMaxClassLen	Points to a DWORD that holds the length, not including the terminating NULL, of the longest class name of any key under hKey.
LPDWORD	lpcValues	Points to a DWORD that holds the number of values attached to hKey.
LPDWORD	lpcbMaxValueNameLen	Points to a DWORD that receives the length of the longest value name. This is useful when using RegEnumValue.
LPDWORD	lpcbMaxValueLen	Points to a DWORD that receives the length of the longest value contents. This is also useful when using RegEnumValue.

LPDWORD	lpcbSecurityDescriptor	Points to a DWORD that receives the size of the security descriptor associated with this key. Security descriptors can vary in size, so it's helpful to know how big a particular key's descriptor is before calling RegGetKeySecurity.
PFILETIME	lpftLastWriteTime	Points to a FILETIME structure (see the previous section, "New and exciting datatypes") that is filled in with the date and time hKey or any of its values were modified.

Any of the parameters except hKey can be NULL; if you specify NULL for a parameter, that data isn't returned. Here's a small routine that gets the number of values attached to any open Registry key; notice that it passes NULL for everything except lpcValue:

```
DWORD GetKeyValueCount(HKEY inKey)
// Gets the count of values attached to a particular key. Returns
// the value count (which may be 0) or -1 if an error occurs.
{
    DWORD valCount = 0;
    DWORD result = ERROR_SUCCESS;

    result = RegQueryInfoKey (inKey,
                              NULL, NULL,    // class & class size
                              NULL,          // reserved
                              NULL,          // # of subkeys
                              NULL,          // subkey length
                              NULL,          // class length
                              &valCount,     // # of values
                              NULL, NULL, NULL, NULL);
    if (ERROR_SUCCESS != result)
        valCount = -1;
    return valCount;
}
```

It's worth making special mention of lpcSubKeys, lpcValues, lpcbMaxValueNameLen, and lpcbMaxValueLen. It's often necessary to do some kind of processing over every key or value under a particular subkey. This *enumeration* is nothing more than an iterative loop that starts with the first key or value of interest, then proceeds on, continuing until it has processed every key or value. For example, you could enumerate the subkeys of HKU to find out the SIDs of every installed local account on a machine. Armed with that information, you can look up the account names to build a list of users who have profiles on the machine.

These four parameters make it easier to efficiently enumerate keys and values. Knowing how many items there are makes it possible to enumerate any subset of a key's values, and knowing the maximum name and content lengths means you can allocate a buffer that's just the right size, instead of too big or too small, to hold the data returned by the enumeration.

Enumerating Keys and Values

The enumeration API routines treat a key's subkeys or values as an ordered list of *n* values, numbered from 0 to *n*–1. You pass an index value to the API routines to indicate which key or value you want; the corresponding key or value is returned. For values, there's an extra wrinkle: keys can have a default value, which always appears as item 0 in the enumeration list. (You'll see how this works in the section "Enumerating values" later in this chapter.) This is convenient, but don't be misled: the values or keys aren't really an ordered list, and if you enumerate the same subkey twice in a row, you can potentially get items back in a different order each time.

Enumeration strategies

When you enumerate keys or values, there are a few different strategies you can use to process all the enumerated keys. The easiest way is to call **RegQueryInfoKey** to find out how many subkeys or values exist, then use a simple loop to process every key or value. A small snippet implementing this tactic might look like:

```
DWORD idx=0, keyCount = 0
LONG retVal = 0;

retVal = RegQueryInfoKey (inKey,
                          NULL, NULL,    // class & class size
                          NULL,          // reserved
                          &keyCount,     // # of subkeys
                          NULL,          // subkey length
                          NULL,          // class length
                          NULL,          // # of values
                          NULL, NULL, NULL, NULL);

for (idx=0; idx < keyCount; idx++)
{
    // get the idx'th key's name and length
    retVal = RegEnumKeyEx(interestingKey, idx, name, nameLen, NULL,
        NULL, NULL, NULL);

    // do something with it
}
```

This approach has the advantage of being simple to implement and understand. However, you may not want to process every key or value. Instead, if you want to process only keys or values that meet some criterion, you can use a conventional **while** loop like this:

```
DWORD idx = 0;
bool keepGoing = true;
LONG retVal = 0;

while (keepGoing)
   {
```

The Registry API 231

```
        retVal = RegEnumKeyEx(interestingKey, idx++, name, &nameLen,
                      (unsigned long *)NULL, (char *)NULL,
                      (unsigned long *)NULL, (LPFILETIME)NULL);
    if (ERROR_SUCCESS == retVal)
    {
        // If we're interested in this key, we'd process it further;
        // we might also set keepGoing here if we only want one key
    }
    keepGoing = (keepGoing && retVal == ERROR_SUCCESS);
}
```

With this approach, you don't have to know in advance how many keys or values exist, and it's a simple matter to stop enumerating as soon as you find what you're looking for.

Enumerating keys

You enumerate keys using the **RegEnumKeyEx** and **RegEnumKey** routines. They're very similar; the primary difference is that **RegEnumKeyEx** allows you to retrieve the modification time and class name for a subkey, while **RegEnumKey** doesn't. In either case, you simply supply the **HKEY** you want enumerated and an index value that indicates which subkey you want to see. The name (not the complete path) of the corresponding subkey is returned, so you can open any subkey you find by passing the name to **RegOpenKey** or **RegOpenKeyEx**.

```
LONG RegEnumKeyEx(hKey, dwIndex, pszName, lpcbName, lpReserved, pszClass,
        lpcbClass, lpftLastWriteTime);
```

HKEY	hKey	Handle to any open key or root key.
DWORD	dwIndex	Index, from 0 to the number of subkeys-1, indicating which key you want to fetch.
LPSTR	pszName	Points to an area that will receive the name of the enumerated key.
LPDWORD	lpcbName	Points to a DWORD containing the size of pszName; on return, contains the length of pszName in bytes, including the NULL terminator.
LPDWORD	lpReserved	Reserved; as always, must be NULL.
LPSTR	pszClass	Points to a buffer that receives the subkey's class name; may be NULL if you don't care about this datum.
LPDWORD	lpcbClass	Points to a DWORD containing the size of pszClass; on return, contains the length of pszClass in bytes, including the NULL terminator. May be NULL only if pszClass is also NULL.
PFILETIME	lpftLastWriteTime	Points to a structure that is filled in with the date and time of the last modification to the subkey; may be NULL if you're not interested.

`RegEnumKey` is identical in function, except for having fewer parameters.

```
LONG RegEnumKey(hKey, dwIndex, pszName, cbName);
```

HKEY	hKey	Handle to any open key or root key.
DWORD	dwIndex	Index, from 0 to the number of subkeys, indicating which key you want to fetch.
LPSTR	pszName	Points to an area that receives the name of the enumerated key.
LPDWORD	cbName	Points to a DWORD containing the size of `pszName`; on return, contains the length of `pszName` in bytes, including the NULL terminator.

Enumerating values

Once you've located a key of interest, you might want to enumerate its values. Most Registry keys have at least one value; quite a few have many values whose number and contents vary from machine to machine. (HKCR is a good example, because it differs depending on what classes and objects are registered on a machine.) You can accomplish this with `RegEnumValue`:[*]

```
LONG RegEnumValue(hKey, dwIndex, pszValueName, lpcbValueName, lpReserved,
       lpType, lpData, lpcbData);
```

HKEY	hKey	Handle to any open key or root key.
DWORD	dwIndex	Ordinal index of the value you want to fetch; you usually start with 0 and move up until you either get ERROR_NO_MORE_ITEMS or hit the number of items returned by `RegQueryInfoKey`.
LPSTR	pszValueName	Points to a buffer that, on return, contains the value's name.
LPDWORD	lpcbValueName	On entry, points to the size of `pszValueName`; on return, points to length of string copied into `pszValueName`, not including the NULL terminator.
LPDWORD	lpReserved	Reserved; must be NULL.
LPDWORD	lpType	Points to a buffer that, on return, holds the type of the requested value (REG_DWORD, REG_SZ, etc.). May be NULL if you don't care what type the value is.
LPBYTE	lpData	Points to a buffer into which the contents of the specified value are copied.
LPDWORD	lpcbData	On entry, points to a DWORD containing the size of `lpData`; on return, contains the number of bytes written into `lpData`.

---

[*] Surprisingly, there's no `RegEnumValueEx`. The original function hasn't changed since its introduction, so Microsoft left it alone in Win32.

To see `RegEnumValue` in action, check out Example 8-7 in "Example: Loading a Control with a Set of Values" later in this chapter; the example illustrates the basic things you should do when enumerating a set of values:

- Call `RegQueryInfoKey` first to get the maximum subkey length, then use that to allocate any buffers you need to get the value name or contents.
- Make sure you either check for ERROR_NO_MORE_ITEMS or honor the number of values returned by `RegQueryInfoKey`.
- Open the parent key with KEY_READ or KEY_QUERY_VALUE access.

Getting Registry Data

Maybe you patiently enumerated a sequence or keys, or perhaps you already know just where the data you want is stored. Either way, at some point you'll want to actually retrieve a value stored under some Registry subkey. If you used `RegEnumValue`, you could have gotten the value's contents when you enumerated it, but if you just want to grab a single value whose path you know, there are better ways for doing so.

Getting a single value

The first, and most useful, method of getting a single value's contents out of the Registry is the `RegQueryValueEx` function. As its name implies, it's a Win32 routine; you supply an open key and a value name, and it returns the value's datatype, length, and contents.

```
LONG RegQueryValueEx(hKey, pszValueName, lpReserved, lpType, lpData, lpcbData);
```

HKEY	hKey	Handle to any key or root key opened with KEY_READ or KEY_QUERY_VALUE access.
LPTSTR	pszValueName	Name of the value to query; if NULL or empty, queries default value.
LPDWORD	lpReserved	Unused; must be NULL.
LPDWORD	lpType	On return, holds the datatype of the value (REG_DWORD, REG_SZ, etc.). If you pass in NULL, no type data is returned.
LPBYTE	lpData	Points to the buffer that holds the value's contents on return. If you pass in NULL, no value data is returned but the `lpcbData` parameter holds the length of the contents.
LPDWORD	lpcbData	On input, points to the buffer that specifies the size of `lpData` buffer. On return, holds amount of data copied into `lpData`. You can pass in NULL if `lpData` is NULL also.

The most straightforward way to call RegQueryValueEx is just to get the value, like this (assuming you're fetching a REG_DWORD value named "SomeValue" from a previously opened key):

```
nResult = RegQueryValueEx(hOpenKey, "SomeValue", NULL, NULL,
         (LPBYTE)&theValue, &valSize);
```

Since you always know how big a DWORD is, the size really isn't important. Things get a little more complex when querying for a string value named "SomeStringValue". At runtime, you don't know the string's length, which means you must either dynamically allocate a buffer or check to see whether there's more data available than your buffer can hold. RegQueryValueEx returns ERROR_MORE_DATA if the requested value has more data than can fit in the buffer length as specified by lpcbData:

```
DWORD bufSize = MAX_PATH;
char theBuf[MAX_PATH];

nResult = RegQueryValueEx(hOpenKey, "SomeStringValue", NULL, NULL,
         (LPBYTE)theBuf, &bufSize);
if (ERROR_MORE_DATA == nResult)
{
    // too much data for our buffer; fail, use another buffer, or do
    // something else
}
else if (ERROR_SUCCESS == nResult)
{
    // continue normally
}
```

Alternatively, you can find out how big the value is, then allocate the buffer for it. This approach requires an extra Registry query but lets you economize on memory by not allocating any more than you actually need:

```
DWORD bufSize = 0;
char *theBuf = NULL;

nResult = RegQueryValueEx(hOpenKey, "SomeStringValue", NULL, NULL,
                    NULL, &bufSize);
if (ERROR_SUCCESS == nResult)
{
   theBuf = (char *)malloc(bufSize+1);  // allow extra byte for NULL
                                        // terminator
   if (theBuf)
   {
       nResult = RegQueryValueEx(hOpenKey, "SomeStringValue", NULL,
                          NULL, (LPBYTE)theBuf, &bufSize);
       if (ERROR_SUCCESS == nResult)
         // do whatever with the value
       free(theBuf);
   }
}
```

Notice that this code snippet adds an extra byte to the buffer to allow for the NULL terminator, which may be stored as part of the string. Also notice that extra space isn't allocated for a Unicode string: if you define UNICODE, the initial call returns the string's Unicode length in bufSize, but if UNICODE isn't defined, the string is converted into ANSI, and bufSize contains the ANSI string length.

The MSDN documentation for RegQueryValueEx points out that it can return things you didn't ask for in some cases. In particular, if you use RegQueryValueEx to query a value under HKEY_PERFORMANCE_DATA, the data you get back in lpData may contain some extraneous data, so you have to walk through the value's contents yourself to see what's in it.

You can also use RegQueryValue to request a key's value, but it can get only the default value (remember, that's the only value Win3.x supports, and RegQueryValue is a 3.x compatibility function).

```
LONG RegQueryValue(hKey, pszSubKey, pszValue, lpcbValue );
```

HKEY	hKey	Points to any currently open key or one of the root keys.
LPCSTR	pszSubKey	Points to the subkey of hKey whose default value you want to get. If it's NULL, RegQueryValue fetches the value of hKey.
LPSTR	pszValue	Points to a buffer that holds the value contents; may be NULL if you only want the contents' length.
LPDWORD	lpcbValue	On entry, points to the length of lpValue; on return, indicates the actual length of the value's contents.

Getting multiple values

You can retrieve multiple values from a key at once using RegQueryMultipleValues, but its interface can be a little confusing.

```
LONG RegQueryMultipleValues(hKey, valList, numVals, pszValueBuf, ldwTotalSize);
```

HKEY	hKey	Points to any currently open key or one of the root keys. The key must be opened with KEY_SET_VALUE or KEY_WRITE access.
PVALENT	valList	Array of VALENT structures (see the next paragraph); each item holds the name of a value to retrieve on entry and the value's data on exit.
DWORD	NumVals	Number of elements in the valList array.
LPTSTR	pszValueBuf	Points to the buffer which, at exit, holds the retrieved values.

LPDWORD	ldwTotalSize	On entry, points to the size (in bytes) of `pszValueBuf`; at exit, returns the number of bytes written to the buffer.

To use this function, fill out an array of **VALENT** structures: you put the value name you're looking for in `ve_valuename`, and `RegQueryMultipleValues` fills in the other fields for you:

```
typedef struct value_entA {
    LPSTR ve_valuename;
    DWORD ve_valuelen;
    DWORD ve_valueptr;
    DWORD ve_type;
}VALENTA, FAR *PVALENTA;
```

On entry, `pszValueBuf` should point to a buffer big enough to hold all the value data you're requesting. On return, you can iterate through `valList`; each item's `ve_valueptr` member points to the location within `pszValueBuf` where the value data's actually stored. You can also call `RegQueryMultipleValues` with an `pszValueBuf` of NULL; when you do, `ldwTotalSize` contains the buffer size required to hold all the requested values.

Adding and Modifying Values

Keys can signify things based on their presence or absence, but values are the best way to store persistent data in the Registry. The `RegSetValueEx` function does double duty; it can create new values or change the contents of existing ones.

```
LONG RegSetValueEx(hKey, pszValueName, Reserved, dwType, lpData, cbData);
```

HKEY	hKey	Points to any currently open key or one of the root keys. The key must be opened with `KEY_SET_VALUE` or `KEY_WRITE` access.
LPCSTR	pszValueName	Name of the value to set; if no value with the specified name exists, `RegSetValueEx` creates it. If `pszValueName` is empty or NULL, the supplied value is assigned to the key's default value.
DWORD	Reserved	Unused; must be 0.
DWORD	dwType	Type of the value you're adding or modifying; may be any of the types defined in Chapter 2, *Registry Nuts and Bolts*.
CONST BYTE *	lpData	Data to load into the value.
DWORD	cbData	Length (in bytes) of the data pointed to by `lpData`. If the value contents are of type `REG_SZ`, `REG_EXPAND_SZ`, or `REG_MULTI_SZ`, `cbData` must reflect the length of the string plus the terminating NULL character.

The Registry API

If you call `RegSetValueEx` with the name of an existing value in `pszValueName`, its contents and type is replaced by whatever you pass in. If no such value exists, it's created with the contents and type you specify.

In addition to `RegSetValueEx`, there's also a second value-setting function you may use: `RegSetValue`. It was originally part of the Win 3.1 Registry API. You may remember from Chapter 1 that the Win 3.1 Registry allowed only a single value for each key. In keeping with that heritage, `RegSetValue` allows you to set only the default value for a key, and the value you set must be a REG_SZ. I present this function for completeness, but you should avoid it in favor of `RegSetValueEx`.

```
LONG RegSetValue(hKey,pszSubKey, dwType, pszData, cbData);
```

HKEY	hKey	Key to which the new value is added; can be any currently open key or root key.
LPCSTR	pszSubkey	Name of subkey that gets the value; if NULL, the value is added to hKey.
DWORD	dwType	Datatype of new value; must be REG_SZ.
LPCSTR	pszData	Pointer to string buffer containing new value's contents.
DWORD	cbData	Length of pszData, not including its terminating NULL character.

As with `RegSetValueEx`, if the key named in `pszSubkey` doesn't exist, it's created. In an additional twist, if the key named by `pszSubkey` doesn't exist, `RegSetValue` creates any keys necessary to construct a legal path, then adds the default value to it. Note that if all you want is to set the default value, you can do so using `RegSetValueEx` and passing NULL for `pszValueName`.

Example 8-2 illustrates how `RegSetValueEx` works; the example sets the `DiskSpaceThreshold` value to the percentage of disk space you specify. This routine is used in a tool I wrote that configures new servers with the desired default settings before delivering them to customers or remote sites.

Example 8-2. SetDiskWarningThreshold

```
// This routine sets the DiskSpaceThreshold to the specified percentage.
// You should check all the system's disk volumes to figure out a reasonable
// percentage for the machine, then call this routine to set it.
long SetDiskWarningThreshold(const int inThreshold)
{
    char    pszName[MAX_PATH] =
        "System\\CurrentControlSet\\Services\\LanmanServer\\Parameters";
    HKEY    hkResult = NULL;
    LONG    nResult = ERROR_SUCCESS;

    // preflight our arguments
```

Example 8-2. SetDiskWarningThreshold (continued)

```
    if (inThreshold < 1 || inThreshold > 99)
        return ERROR_INVALID_PARAMETER;

    // open the key with write access so we can set the value
    nResult = RegOpenKeyEx(HKEY_LOCAL_MACHINE, pszName, 0L, KEY_WRITE, &hkResult);
    if (ERROR_SUCCESS == nResult)
    {
        nResult = RegSetValueEx(hkResult, "DiskSpaceThreshold", 0L,
                                REG_DWORD, (unsigned char *)&inThreshold,
                                sizeof(int));
        if (ERROR_SUCCESS == nResult)
            nResult = RegCloseKey(hkResult);
    }
    return nResult;
}
```

Deleting Keys and Values

You may find it necessary to delete keys or values from within your home-brewed Registry utilities. Since many of the lesser-known features of Windows 2000 and NT discussed in Chapter 10, *Registry Tweaks,* function based on the presence or absence of special trigger keys, turning these features on or off may require you to delete values, and there's no way to do so with a *.REG* file. You must be careful with your newfound destructive powers, though; accidentally deleting the wrong key or value can make your system stop working altogether.

Before you delete a key or value, you must have the parent key opened with adequate access. If you supply KEY_WRITE as the REGSAM value when you open the key, you can delete it. You can also request KEY_CREATE_SUB_KEY or KEY_SET_VALUE rights to gain delete access to keys and values, respectively.

There's one other thing worth mentioning here: when you delete a key or a value, it's not actually deleted. Instead, the Registry subsystem marks the deleted items as deleted, but doesn't delete them until the next time Registry data is flushed (either explicitly with RegFlushKey or automatically by the kernel's lazy flusher). If you try to read, write, or enumerate a key or value that's been marked as deleted, you get ERROR_KEY_DELETED as a return value. You can always call RegCloseKey on a deleted key without getting an error, though.

Deleting a key

You delete individual keys with the RegDeleteKey routine. If you specify a valid key and subkey, the key is immediately marked for deletion, even if other processes currently have the key open. This is different from the file metaphor used elsewhere in the Registry; if you try to delete an open file, the delete operation will fail, but not so with RegDeleteKey. At that point, attempts by other processes to access data attached to the open key will fail.

The Registry API

```
LONG RegDeleteKey(hKey, pszSubKey);
```

| HKEY | hKey | Key pointing to parent of target value; may be a root key or a subkey. |
| LPCSTR | pszSubkey | Name of the subkey to be deleted; if **NULL** or empty, the key specified by **hKey** is deleted. |

You can't delete a root key, and you can't delete first-level subkeys of root keys. For example, you can't remove HKLM\SOFTWARE or HKCU\SOFTWARE, but you can remove HKLM\SOFTWARE\Microsoft (though I wouldn't recommend it). In addition, you may not delete a key that has subkeys; if you try, you get an error. It's okay to delete keys that have values; the values are deleted along with the key.

Under Windows 95 and 98, **RegDeleteKey** deletes keys that have subkeys. If your code depends on the standard Windows 2000 behavior of failing when a targeted key has subkeys, it works fine under Win9x, but it deletes the subkeys without warning you! If you want to use routines with more explicit semantics, consider using **SHDeleteKey** or **SHDeleteEmptyKey**.

Deleting a value

Deleting values is wonderfully straightforward (as long as you have **KEY_WRITE** or **KEY_SET_VALUE** access on the target key)! **RegDeleteValue** removes the specified value from the key you provide.

```
LONG RegDeleteValue(hKey, pszValueName);
```

| HKEY | hKey | Key pointing to parent of target value. |
| LPCSTR | pszValueName | Name of the value to be deleted. |

If **pszValueName** is **NULL** or contains an empty string, **RegDeleteValue** deletes the default value (you know, the one that appears as <Default> or No Name in Registry editors). Otherwise, **pszValueName** must contain the correct name of an existing value.

Using Registry Security Information

Under Windows 2000, every object in the entire system has security information attached to it. Registry keys are just objects, so they too can have ACLs that control who can read, write, or delete the key and its values. Ordinarily, you don't need to control these ACLs; when you do, *RegEdt32* is probably the best tool for doing so. If you find it necessary or desirable to get a key's security data programmatically, though, you certainly can.

> ## *What's in a Security Descriptor?*
>
> The short answer is "it depends." The long answer is, well, longer. A security descriptor, or SD, is really an opaque block of data that Windows 2000 can parse into a set of access controls. Every object in the system has an SD associated with it. A single SD contains one or many sets of the following items:
>
> - The security ID (SID) of the object's owner
> - The SID of the object owner's primary group
> - A discretionary ACL (the object owner can freely modify)
> - A system ACL (modified only by entities with system privileges)
> - Qualifiers (specify whether the other items are self-contained or point to other SDs and ACLs)
>
> You can't directly modify (or even decipher) an SD's contents; instead, you have to use the security API routines, notably:
>
> - `InitializeSecurityDescriptor`
> - `GetSecurityDescriptorOwner`
> - `SetSecurityDescriptorDacl`
> - `SetSecurityDescriptorOwner`
> - `SetSecurityDescriptorSacl`
>
> With these, you can peel back the contents of a single SD and use the security data therein to verify or change who owns an object and who may access it with which permissions. Of course, your ability to do this depends entirely on whether your code has adequate permission itself when it runs!

ACLs come in two types: system ACLs, or SACLs, are owned by (and can only be changed by) the system; while discretionary ACLs (DACLs for short) are controlled by the owner of the object. As you might expect from security information, not just anyone can read either type of ACL. To read the DACL, the requesting process must have READ_CONTROL access on the key. To get this access, the requester must either own the key itself, or the DACL must grant READ_CONTROL to the account under which the requester is running.

System ACLs are trickier. They can be read only by applications that have been granted the ACCESS_SYSTEM_SECURITY permission. In turn, the only way to get ACCESS_SYSTEM_SECURITY is for the calling process to ask for the SE_SECURITY_

The Registry API   *241*

NAME privilege, open the key with a REGSAM value of ACCESS_SYSTEM_SECURITY, then turn off SE_SECURITY_NAME again.

To actually retrieve a key's security data (assuming you've fulfilled the access control requirements), you can use RegGetKeySecurity. Besides passing in the name of the key whose information you want, you must also fill in the SecurityInformation field to indicate which data you want. If you have permission, pSecurityDescriptor is filled with the ACL or ownership data on return, and lpcbSecurityDescriptor contains the ACL size. ACLs vary in size, since they may contain one or many entries.

```
LONG RegGetKeySecurity (hKey, SecurityInformation, pSecurityDescriptor,
         lpcbSecurityDescriptor);
```

HKEY	hKey	Open Registry key whose security information you want.
SECURITY_INFORMATION	SecurityInformation	SECURITY_INFORMATION structure indicating what parts of the security descriptor you're asking for; may be any combination of items from Table 8-3.
PSECURITY_DESCRIPTOR	pSecurityDescriptor	Pointer to record that receives the security descriptor specified by SecurityInformation.
LPDWORD	lpcbSecurityDescriptor	Points to a DWORD; on entry, it must hold the size of pSecurityDescriptor, and, on return, it contains the size, in bytes, of the returned security descriptor.

If the buffer pointed to by pSecurityDescriptor is too small, RegGetKeySecurity returns ERROR_INSUFFICIENT_BUFFER and the lpcbSecurityDescriptor parameter contains the number of bytes required for the requested security descriptor. This makes it possible to efficiently allocate a buffer of the right size by calling it twice, like this:

```
long retVal = 0, aclSize = 0;
PSECURITY_DESCRIPTOR pWhat = NULL;

retVal = RegGetKeySecurity(theKey, DACL_SECURITY_INFORMATION, pWhat, &aclSize);
if (ERROR_INSUFFICIENT_BUFFER  != retVal)
   throw(retVal);
pWhat = malloc(aclSize);
retVal = RegGetKeySecurity(theKey, DACL_SECURITY_INFORMATION, pWhat, &aclSize);
if (ERROR_SUCCESS != retVal)
   throw(retVal);
```

Setting an item's security information

If you're not thoroughly familiar with how Windows 2000's security system works, stay away from RegSetKeySecurity until you have a good set of Registry backups. Setting the wrong permissions on a key is much easier to do programmatically than through any of the GUI editing tools, so please be very careful.

Once you've gotten a security descriptor and modified it,* you can write it back to the key that owns it with RegSetKeySecurity.

```
LONG RegSetKeySecurity (hKey, SecurityInformation, pSecurityDescriptor);
```

HKEY	hKey	Open Registry key whose security descriptor you want to set.
SECURITY_INFORMATION	SecurityInformation	SECURITY_INFORMATION structure indicating what parts of the security descriptor you're changing.
PSECURITY_DESCRIPTOR	pSecurityDescriptor	Pointer to security descriptor containing ACL data you want to apply to hKey.

To ensure that your new security data gets written, you should call RegCloseKey on the modified key after successfully calling RegSetKeySecurity. This is true even if you've set security on one of the root keys; it won't actually be closed, but its cached security data is updated.

Connecting to Remote Computers

In Chapter 4, *Using RegEdit*, and Chapter 5, *Using RegEdt32*, you learned how to use *RegEdit* and *RegEdt32* to edit Registry data on remote computers. Adding this same functionality to your own programs is trivial: all you need do is call RegConnectRegistry and use the HKEY it returns in any other calls you make to Registry API functions. When you're finished with the remote key, you call RegCloseKey on it as though it were a local key. The API function declaration looks like the following.

```
LONG RegConnectRegistry(pszMachineName, hKey, phkResult);
```

| LPSTR | pszMachineName | Name of the remote machine you want to connect to; must not include the leading backslashes. |

---

* I'm not about to talk about how you actually create or modify ACLs; that's a book all by itself.

HKEY	hKey	Root key you want to connect to: may be either HKLM or HKU.
PHKEY	phkResult	Pointer to returned key in remote Registry.

HasPackage (shown in Example 8-3) showcases `RegConnectRegistry` in action. You supply it with a machine name and a subkey; it checks the Registry on the specified machine to see whether it has a subkey of HKLM\SOFTWARE by the name you specify. The call to `RegConnectRegistry` and the corresponding `RegCloseKey` on the key it returns are the only changes needed to enable remote Registry connections in this small program.

Example 8-3. HasPackage

```
void main(int argc, char **argv)
{
    char     pszName[MAX_PATH];
    HKEY     hkRemoteKey = NULL, hkResult = NULL;
    DWORD    dwIdx = 0;
    LONG     nResult = ERROR_SUCCESS;
    memset(pszName, 0x0, MAX_PATH);

    // preflight our arguments
    if (argc < 3)
        DoUsage(argv[0]);

    nResult = RegConnectRegistry(argv[1], HKEY_LOCAL_MACHINE, &hkRemoteKey);
    if (ERROR_SUCCESS == nResult)
    {
        sprintf(pszName, "SOFTWARE\\%s", argv[2]);
        nResult = RegOpenKeyEx(hkRemoteKey, pszName, 0L, KEY_READ, &hkResult);
        if (ERROR_SUCCESS == nResult)
        {
            fprintf(stdout, "%s has a key for %s.\n", argv[1], argv[2]);
        }
        else
        {
            fprintf(stderr,
                "Error %d while opening SOFTWARE\\%s on remote machine %s\n",
                argv[2], argv[1]);
        }
        nResult = RegCloseKey(hkResult);
        nResult = RegCloseKey(hkRemoteKey);
    }
    else
    {
        fprintf(stderr, "Error %d while opening remote registry on %s\n",
            nResult, argv[1]);
    }

    fflush(stdout);
}
```

Moving Keys to and from Hives

In Chapters 3, 4, and 5, you learned how to use the Registry editor functions that allow keys and values to be saved into hive files and later restored. You can do the same thing with your own code by using the routines discussed in this section.

Saving keys

The first step in moving keys in and out of hives around is to create a hive; you can do this with `RegSaveKey`.

```
LONG RegSaveKey(hKey, pszFile, lpSecurityAttributes);
```

HKEY	hKey	Key to be saved; must be open. Everything below the specified key is saved.
LPCTSTR	pszFile	Full path of file to save in.
LPSECURITY_ATTRIBUTES	lpSecurityAttributes	Pointer to SECURITY_ATTRIBUTES structure describing desired security on the new file; pass in NULL to use the process's default security descriptor.

If the file you specify in `pszFile` already exists, `RegSaveKey` will fail with the `ERROR_ALREADY_EXISTS` error code. This prevents you from accidentally overwriting another hive file you previously saved. There's another subtlety involved with `pszFile`: if you don't specify a full path, the file is created in the process's current directory if the key is from the local Registry, or *%systemroot%\system32* for a key on a remote machine.

The created file has the archive attribute set and whatever permissions are specified by `lpSecurityAttributes`. Instead of creating a brand-new security descriptor, you may pass NULL to have whatever security context applies to the process applied to the file.

Loading keys

Once you've saved keys into a hive file, the next thing you're likely to want to do is load them. You can do so in two distinct ways: you can load a hive as a new key, or you can replace the contents of an existing key with the hive's contents. Either approach requires the process that loads the keys to have the SE_RESTORE_NAME privilege.

`RegLoadKey` supports the former: you tell it what file to load and what to name the new subkey, and it creates the specified subkey and loads the file into it. `RegLoadKey` will fail if the file doesn't exist or if the named subkey does exist.

The Registry API

```
LONG RegLoadKey(hKey, pszSubKey, pszFile);
```

HKEY	hKey	Open key under which the new subkey is created; may be HKLM or HKU on a local machine, or a handle obtained by opening HKLM or HKU with RegConnectRegistry.
LPCTSTR	pszSubKey	Name of the subkey to create beneath hKey; the subkey must not currently exist.
LPCTSTR	pszFile	Full pathname to the hive file you want to load into the new key. This file must have been created with RegSaveKey or *RegEdt32*'s Registry → Save Key command.

Calling RegCloseKey on a key loaded with RegLoadKey doesn't unload it; instead, you must call RegUnloadKey as described later.

If you want to overwrite an existing key that's part of one of the standard hives, you can instead call RegRestoreKey. Like RegLoadKey, it takes a parent key and the name of a file to load. However, in this case the parent key's subkeys are replaced by the contents of the file. For example, if you open HKLM\SOFTWARE\Microsoft\Windows and pass that to RegRestoreKey, the key with that name persists, but all subkeys and values beneath it are deleted. After RegRestoreKey returns, the victim key contains whatever values and subkeys were in the loaded file.

```
LONG RegRestoreKey(hKey, pszFile, dwFlags);
```

HKEY	hKey	Key whose values and subkeys you want to replace.
LPCTSTR	pszFile	File (saved with RegSaveKey or *RegEdt32*) with the new contents you want loaded into hKey.
DWORD	dwFlags	If you pass in 0 for this parameter, the entire hKey is replaced; if you pass in REG_WHOLE_HIVE_VOLATILE, hKey is replaced, but the changes are not written to the Registry.

Replacing a loaded key

Once you've loaded a hive file with RegLoadKey, you can replace the loaded key with another hive file. This is a good way to dynamically swap between several hives' worth of data. However, changes don't take effect until the machine is restarted.

```
LONG RegReplaceKey(hKey, pszSubKey, pszNewFile, pszOldFile);
```

HKEY	hKey	Open key that contains subkey you want to replace.
LPCTSTR	pszSubKey	Contains the name of the subkey whose values and subkeys are replaced by the newly loaded hive.

| LPCTSTR | pszNewFile | Contains full path to the hive file you want loaded; the file must be generated by **RegSaveKey** or *RegEdt32*. |
| LPCTSTR | pszOldFile | Contains the name of a file to which Windows 2000 save a backup copy of the previously loaded hive file. |

Unloading a key

RegLoadKey allows you to load a stored hive file as a new hive under HKLM or HKU. Once you've loaded a hive, it makes sense to have a way to unload it when you're done, and **RegUnloadKey** provides that functionality.

LONG RegUnLoadKey(hKey, pszSubKey);

| HKEY | hKey | Handle to an open key. |
| LPCTSTR | pszSubKey | Full path to the subkey you want to unload. |

You can unload only keys you load yourself, which prevents unloading (accidentally or on purpose) an important key such as HKLM\SOFTWARE. The process that calls **RegUnloadKey** must have the special **SE_RESTORE_NAME** privilege.

Getting Notification When Something Changes

If you want to write a program that does something when a particular Registry key or value changes, you can do so by sitting in an infinite loop and periodically checking the item of interest to see whether it changes. This is terribly inefficient, though, so it's good that there's another way to do it. The **RegNotifyChangeKeyValue** routine allows you to register your interest in a particular key or value, then go do something else. Your code gets a notification you when the Registry key (or its attributes) changes; it doesn't, however, tell you if the key is deleted.

LONG RegNotifyChangeKeyValue (hKey, bWatchSubtree, dwNotifyFilter,hEvent
    fAsynchronous);

| HKEY | hKey | Key you want to monitor for changes; may be a root key or any subkey. |
| BOOL | bWatchSubtree | When true, indicates that you want to watch all subkeys and values of **hKey**; when false, indicates you want to watch **hKey** only. |

DWORD	dwNotifyFilter	Flag specifying what events you're interested in; may be any combination of: • REG_NOTIFY_CHANGE_NAME for renaming, addition, or deletion of a subkey • REG_NOTIFY_CHANGE_ATTRIBUTES for changes to any key attributes • REG_NOTIFY_CHANGE_LAST_SET for changes to a value of a subkey • REG_NOTIFY_CHANGE_SECURITY for changes to security
HANDLE	hEvent	Event to post when a change is detected; ignored if fAsynchronous is false.
BOOL	fAsynchronous	When true, routine returns immediately and posts an event when a change takes place; when false, routine blocks until a change occurs.

Flushing Registry Changes

The Registry uses a "lazy flusher" to propagate changes from memory to disk. The overall goal is to minimize the number of disk I/O operations, since they tend to be relatively time-consuming. The lazy flusher achieves this goal by not immediately writing every change out to disk as it occurs. Instead, it aggregates changes and writes them when the system is mostly idle.

When you call **RegCloseKey**, whatever changes you've made are thus not immediately copied to disk. There can be an interlude of indeterminate length (Microsoft says "as long as several seconds" without elaborating) before your data actually hits the disk. For most applications, this is perfectly acceptable. However, if for some reason you want to make sure your changes get written to disk, you can use the **RegFlushKey** routine to immediately force a Registry update:

```
LONG RegFlushKey (hKey);
```

Calling this routine forces the lazy flusher to buckle down and flush the specified key's data to its hive file; it may also cause other keys to be written as well. Flushing the cached data also updates the *.LOG* files that act as a backup copy of the Registry. The Win32 SDK warns that this function is expensive, so you shouldn't call it often. **RegFlushKey** returns ERROR_SUCCESS when all goes well or a standard Win32 error code for failed flush attempts.

The Shell Utility API Routines

The shell utility API routines allow you to use a different set of API routines instead of the ones I've discussed up until now. While this might seem like a needless fragmentation of what should be a unified API, there's are two reasons for it. First, some of the tasks that the shell utility API can do don't have direct equivalents in the Win32 API. For example, the shell API has routines to copy a key and its contents, delete an entire key and all its subkeys, and so on. Second, Microsoft is clearly trying to position the utility API as the thing you use if you're writing small utility components— not all of which will necessarily run on Windows as we know it today. (For example, what about an embedded version of Windows running on a smart card?)

The shell API routine definitions are unnecessarily confusing because of their naming scheme (or lack of one.) Most of the Registry-related routines have names that start with SHReg, but some don't (e.g., SHDeleteValue or SHGetValue). Worse still, the file association routine names don't use the SH prefix at all.

Working with File Associations

One of the biggest innovations of the Macintosh when it was originally introduced was the idea that documents would somehow "know" what application they belonged to. The Mac OS implemented this by storing eight bytes of type and creator information with each file. The type bytes identified the file's datatype, and the creator bytes associated the file with a particular application. Windows 3.0 introduced the concept of file associations to the PC world, but the Windows version was based on binding a three-character DOS filename extension to an application. Later versions of Windows expanded this mapping so that object types (like, say, an Excel table) could be mapped to an executable; in addition, MIME types could be associated with file extensions too.

Managing these associations has long been painful for programmers. In particular, it's difficult to find what application or DLL the user wants called to create or modify some existing object type, even more so under Windows 2000. Recall that Windows 2000 stores class information in two places: HKCR and HKCU\Classes. In an effort to ease this pain, Microsoft created a Component Object Model (COM) interface called IQueryAssociations. By making the appropriate COM calls, you can get a pointer to the IQueryAssociations interface, call some of its routines, and get the desired information. However, not everyone is comfortable using COM, so Microsoft added a set of wrapper routines in the shell utility API. These handle all the messy COM calls while providing a simple C interface to their functionality.

Getting a file association key from the Registry

One common operation is to look up the file association for some piece of data you have, like a file extension or a CLSID. There are three ways to do so, depending on what data you have and what kind of data you want back.

The Shell Utility API Routines 249

If you want to get an HKEY that points to the key where the association is stored, you can do so with the `AssocQueryKey` routine.

`HRESULT AssocQueryKey (afFlags, akKey, pszAssoc, pszExtra, HKEY *phkResult)`

ASSOCF	afFlags	ASSOCF flags that control how you want the association retrieved. You can combine any number of flags, except that you can use one of the ASSOCF_INIT variants.
ASSOCKEY	akKey	ASSOCKEY structure that specifies what kind of key you want back: one to pass to the `ShellExec( )` routine, etc.
LPCTSTR	pszAssoc	Query string that looks up the key (described later).
LPCTSTR	pszExtra	Optional additional information (e.g., a shell verb) that goes with `pszAssoc`; pass NULL if not used.
HKEY *	phkResult	On exit, pointer to an HKEY containing the found key.

In large part, the result you get back is determined by the value you pass in the `pszAssoc` parameter. You can pass in a file extension (*.cpp*), a CLSID (using its GUID, in the standard "{GUID}" format), a ProgID (e.g., "Excel.Worksheet.2"), or the name of an *.exe* file (but only if the ASSOCF_OPEN_BYEXENAME flag is set).

If you'd rather have a text string describing the association, use `AssocQueryString` instead; it's similar to `AssocQueryKey`.

`HRESULT AssocQueryString (afFlags, asStr, pszAssoc, pszExtra, pszOut, pcchOut)`

ASSOCF	afFlags	ASSOCF flags that control how you want the association retrieved. You can combine any number of flags, except that you may use only one of the ASSOCF_INIT variants.
ASSOCSTR	akKey	ASSOCSTR structure that specifies what kind of string you want back, e.g., a command line, the "friendly" document name string, etc.
LPCTSTR	pszAssoc	Query string that looks up the key (described later).
LPCTSTR	pszExtra	Optional additional information (e.g., a shell verb) that goes with `pszAssoc`; pass NULL if not used.
LPCTSTR *	pszOut	On exit, holds the requested string.
LPDWORD	pcchOut	On entry, should hold the size of `pszOut`. On exit, holds the number of characters stored in pszOut. `AssocQueryString` truncates the string if the buffer is too small, unless you specify the ASSOCF_NOTRUNCATE flag, in which case this function returns E_POINTER as its result. In that case, `pcchOut` holds the buffer size required to hold the entire string.

The permissible values for `pszOut` are the same for this function as for `AssocQueryKey`.

The third way is a hybrid of the first two. When you call `AssocQueryString-ByKey`, you pass in the key where you want the routine to start looking, along with a mix of the parameters used for `AssocQueryString` and `AssocQueryKey`. Here's what it looks like.

`HRESULT AssocQueryStringByKey (afFlags, asStr, hkAssoc, pszExtra, pszOut, pcchOut)`

ASSOCF	afFlags	ASSOCF flags that control how you want the association retrieved. You can combine any number of flags, except that you can use only one of the ASSOCF_INIT variants.
ASSOCSTR	akKey	ASSOCSTR structure that specifies what kind of string you want back, e.g., a command line, the "friendly" document name string, etc.
HKEY	hkAssoc	HKEY from which you want `AssocQueryStringByKey` to start looking.
LPCTSTR	pszExtra	Optional additional information (e.g., a shell verb) that goes with `pszAssoc`; pass NULL if not used.
LPCTSTR *	pszOut	On exit, holds the requested string.
LPDWORD	pcchOut	On entry, should hold the size of `pszOut`. On exit, holds the number of characters stored in `pszOut`. `AssocQueryString` truncates the string if the buffer is too small, unless you specify the ASSOCF_NOTRUNCATE flag, in which case this function returns E_POINTER as its result. In that case, `pcchOut` holds the buffer size required to hold the entire string.

Getting a pointer to the IQueryAssociations interface

If you need to call one of the routines in the `IQueryAssociations` class that doesn't have a wrapper, you can do so by getting a pointer to an object that contains that interface and using the pointer to call the routine you want. While a discussion of writing this sort of COM code is outside the scope of this book, the shell utility API routine provides an easy way to get a pointer to the interface so you can use it: `AssocCreate`. Be aware that this routine doesn't actually create anything you can use directly; all it does is return a pointer to a COM interface, creating an object to handle that interface if necessary.

`HRESULT AssocCreate (clsID, refIID, pInterface)`

CLSID	clsID	CLSID of the object that exposes the interface you want. This must always be set to the constant value `CLSID_QueryAssociations`.

REFIID	refIID	Reference ID of the interface you want to use. This must always be set to the constant value IID_IQueryAssociations.
LPVOID *	pInterface	Pointer to a pointer that, on exit, points to the interface.

Copying and Deleting Keys and Values

The original Registry API had a few weak areas. One was the annoying lack of any functions for copying keys and values from one place to another, as you might do when establishing initial settings for a new installation. The API routines for saving and restoring keys provided a somewhat clunky way to do this, but the shell utility API provides a cleaner way. SHCopyKey (available with Version 5.0 or later of *SHLWAPI.DLL*) recursively copies all the subkeys and values beneath the source key you specify to the destination key.

LONG SHCopyKey (hkSrcKey, szSrcSubkey, hkDestKey, fReserved)

HKEY	hkSrcKey	Source key whose subkeys you want to copy; must be open.
LPCTSTR	szSrcSubkey	Specific subkey of hkSrcKey you want to copy, not including initial backslashes.
HKEY	hkDestKey	Destination key under which you want the tree specified by szSrcSubkey to be copied; this key must already be open.
DWORD	fReserved	Reserved; must always be **NULL**.

Deleting keys in Win32 code has always been a little tricky. The semantic behavior of RegDeleteKey varies according to which operating system it runs on. In the Windows 9x family, it deletes the key whether or not it's empty, while under Windows 2000/NT, the function fails if the target key has any subkeys. In an effort to keep from surprising people with unexpected behavior, Microsoft added two separate routines to clearly distinguish two different operations: removing a key that you know (or suspect) to be empty and removing a key when you don't care if it's empty or not.

SHDeleteEmptyKey is what you use in the first case. It fails if the specified target key has any subkeys, although (like RegDeleteKey) it happily removes any values that are attached to the otherwise-empty target key.

HKEY SHDeleteEmptyKey (hkey, pszTargetSubkey);

HKEY	hkKey	Handle to a root key or any currently open key (as long as it's an ancestor to the target).
LPCTSTR	pszTargetSubkey	Name of the key to remove, relative to hkKey.

If you really want to remove the key and all its subkeys, you should use `SHDeleteKey` instead. It recursively removes the target and all its subkeys, along with all values attached to the target or any of its descendants.

`HKEY SHDeleteKey (hkKey, pszTargetSubkey);`

HKEY	hkKey	Handle to a root key or any currently open key (as long as it's an ancestor to the target).
LPCTSTR	pszTargetSubkey	Path of the key to remove.

There's also a new routine intended for removing individual values: `SHDeleteValue` accepts the name of a subkey and value, then removes the value from that key. Unlike `RegDeleteValue`, which requires you to pass in an HKEY that points to the target value's parent key, `SHDeleteValue` accepts any open key as long as it's a parent of the target, plus the path from that key to the target's actual home.

`HKEY SHDeleteValue (hkKey, pszParentSubkey, pszTargetValue);`

HKEY	hkKey	Handle to a root key or any currently open key (as long as it's an ancestor to the target).
LPCTSTR	pszParentSubkey	Path to parent subkey that owns the value to remove.
LPCTSTR	pszTargetValue	Value name to remove.

Getting Key and Value Information

When you're ready to read and write individual keys and values, you'll probably find it helpful to get some fundamental information about the keys and values themselves.

Querying keys and values

`RegQueryInfoKey` gives you a wealth of information about a key—maybe too much for some uses. Most of the time, you need to know three things about a key: how many subkeys it has, how many values it has, and how much space to allocate when fetching things from it. `SHQueryInfoKey` provides most of this data.

`LONG SHQueryInfoKey(hKey, pdwSubKeys, pdwMaxSubKeyLen, pdwValueCount, pdwMaxValueNameLen);`

HKEY	hKey	Handle to any key or root key opened with `KEY_READ` or `KEY_QUERY_VALUE` access.
LPDWORD	pdwSubKeys	Pointer to `DWORD` that receives the number of subkeys under `hKey`.

LPDWORD	pdwMaxSubKeyLen	Pointer to DWORD that receives length of longest subkey name under hKey.
LPDWORD	pdwValueCount	Pointer to DWORD that receives total number of values under hKey.
LPDWORD	pdwMaxValueNameLen	Pointer to DWORD that receives length of longest value name under hKey.

For example, you can use it to find how many subkeys were beneath a particular key so you can efficiently enumerate them. One thing you can't do with it, though, is find out the length of the longest value under a key, as you can with RegQueryInfoKey. That means that if you want to preallocate a buffer to the size of the largest value under a key, you can't do it efficiently unless you use RegQueryInfoKey.

SHQueryValueEx is identical to RegQueryValueEx, down to the inclusion of the "reserved" parameter. That being so, I'm not going to cover it again here, but it exists if you want to use it.

Getting and setting values

Let's start with something familiar: SHQueryValueEx is a dead ringer for RegQueryValueEx. It takes the same parameters and has the same restrictions and conditions, so it's pretty much a drop-in replacement.

```
LONG SHQueryValueEx(hKey, pszValueName, pdwReserved, pdwType, pvData, pcbData);
```

HKEY	hKey	Handle to any key or root key opened with KEY_READ or KEY_QUERY_VALUE access.
LPTSTR	pszValueName	Name of the value to query; if NULL or empty, queries default value.
LPDWORD	pdwReserved	Unused; must be NULL.
LPDWORD	pdwType	On return, holds the datatype of the value (REG_DWORD, REG_SZ, etc.). If you pass in NULL, no type data is returned.
LPBYTE	pvData	Points to the buffer that holds the value's contents on return. If you pass in NULL, no value data is returned, but the pcbData parameter holds the length of the contents.
LPDWORD	pcbData	On input, points to the buffer that specifies the size of lpData buffer. On return, holds amount of data copied into lpData. You may pass in NULL if pvData is NULL also.

SHGetValue is a new routine. If you think of the fairly useless (and now deprecated) RegGetValue call, don't: SHGetValue is much more interesting, since it essentially duplicates RegQueryValueEx. Instead of passing the bogus "reserved" parameter, SHGetValue expects you to pass in a path that points to the key that owns the value you're trying to query.

```
LONG SHGetValue(hKey, pszSubKeyName, pszValueName, pdwType, pbData, pcbData);
```

HKEY	hKey	Handle to any key or root key opened with KEY_READ or KEY_QUERY_VALUE access.
LPCTSTR	pszSubKeyName	Path to subkey whose value you're querying.
LPDWORD	pszValueName	Name of the value to query; if NULL or empty, queries default value.
LPDWORD	pdwType	On return, holds the datatype of the value (REG_DWORD, REG_SZ, etc.). If you pass in NULL, no type data is returned.
LPBYTE	pbData	Points to the buffer that holds the value's contents on return. If you pass in NULL, no value data is returned, but the pcbData parameter holds the length of the contents.
LPDWORD	pcbData	On input, points to the buffer that specifies the size of pbData buffer. On return, holds amount of data copied into pbData. You may pass in NULL if pbData is NULL also.

When you want to set a value, you can use **RegSetValueEx** or its very close relative, **SHSetValue**. As with many of the other SH* routines and their vanilla Win32 counterparts, the primary difference between these two is that SHSetValue lets you specify the full path to the target key, instead of requiring you to open the target key and pass in a handle to it.

```
LONG SHSetValue(hKey, pszSubKeyName, pszValueName, pdwType, pbData, pcbData);
```

HKEY	hKey	Handle to any key or root key opened with KEY_READ or KEY_QUERY_VALUE access.
LPCTSTR	pszSubKeyName	Path to subkey whose value you're setting.
LPDWORD	pszValueName	Name of the value to set; cannot be NULL.
LPDWORD	pdwType	Contains the datatype of the value to be stored.
LPBYTE	pbData	Points to the buffer that holds the value's contents; may not be NULL.
LPDWORD	pcbData	Points to length of pbData.

Enumerating Keys and Values

The Registry API already contains a number of routines that enumerate keys and values. Guess what? The shell utility API contains more of them, including several normally used with user-specific values. In particular, there are two routines that duplicate existing functionality in the Registry API: **SHEnumKeyEx** and **SHEnumValue**. Why? Mostly because Microsoft wanted to provide a more straightforward set of routines without breaking applications that depended on the original API. Let's look at **SHEnumKeyEx** first.

LONG SHEnumKeyEx (hKey, dwIndex, pszName, pcchName)

HKEY	hKey	Handle to currently open key or root key.
DWORD	dwIndex	Index of the key to retrieve. For the first call, pass in zero; subsequent calls can use other index values.
LPCTSTR	pszName	Output buffer; on exit, contains full name of current key.
LPDWORD	dwFlags	On entry, points to DWORD containing size of pszName. On exit, contains the actual number of characters copied to pszName.

Like **RegEnumKeyEx**, **SHEnumKeyEx** allows you to iterate through every key under the specified subkey. Unlike its big brother, **SHEnumKeyEx** doesn't allow you to get the key's modification time. You can still use **RegQueryInfoKey** to determine in advance what indices to use, or you can start with zero and work your way up.

SHEnumValue is a somewhat redundant beast. It looks like **RegEnumValue**, except that **SHEnumValue** doesn't have the useless "reserved" parameter. Other than that, the two are functionally identical.

LONG SHEnumValue (hKey, dwIndex, pszValueName, pcchValueName, pdwType, pvData, pcbData)

HKEY	hKey	Handle to currently open key or root key.
DWORD	dwIndex	Index of the key to retrieve. For the first call, pass in zero; subsequent calls can use other index values.
LPTSTR	pszValueName	Output buffer; on exit, contains full name of enumerated value.
LPDWORD	pcchValueName	Pointer to a DWORD that contains size of pszValueName on entry and number of characters copied to pszValueName on exit.
LPDWORD	pdwType	Pointer to DWORD that receives datatype of the enumerated value, e.g., REG_SZ, REG_DWORD, etc.
LPVOID	pvData	Pointer to buffer that receives value contents. If you don't care, pass NULL; otherwise, size the buffer appropriately and put the size in pcbData.
LPDWORD	pcbData	Size of pvData buffer.

Working with User-Specific Keys

If you decide to use the shell API routines that give you access to user-specific keys (USKs), you'll find that they're familiar and different at the same time. Most of the things you have to do when using the standard Registry API are still required;

in particular, you still have to open and close keys before you read or write them or their values, and the normal Win32 access controls still apply.

Creating and removing keys

Before you can do much of anything else with user-specific keys, you need to be able to create them. Of course, the counterpart of creating something is deleting it, so it's handy to know how to remove USKs as well.

You create a new USK with `SHRegCreateUSKey`, which also opens the key after creating it.

```
LONG SHRegCreateUSKey(pszPath, samDesired, hkRelUSKey, phkNewUSKey, dwFlags);
```

LPCTSTR	pszPath	Pointer to string containing name of subkey to create and open.
REGSAM	samDesired	Desired security access to the key when opening it.
HUSKEY	hkRelUSKey	Key to be used as base of relative path; if you specify a relative path in `pszPath`, it's interpreted relative to `hkRelUSKey`. If `pszPath` is absolute, set `hkRelUSKey` to NULL.
PHUSKEY	phkNewUSKey	Pointer to handle of the newly opened key.
DWORD	dwFlags	Flags that control the root key under which the new key is created and opened: • SHREGSET_HKCU creates the key under HKCU if it doesn't already exist under either HKCU or HKLM. • SHREGSET_FORCE_HKCU opens the key under HKCU if it exists and creates/opens it if not. • SHREGSET_HKLM creates the key under HKLM if it doesn't already exist. • SHREGSET_FORCE_HKLM opens the key under HKLM if it exists and creates/opens it if not. • SHREGSET_DEFAULT will create and open the key under both HKCU or HKLM, using whichever one it finds first.

The way this routine works requires some explanation. Since USKs can be created either under HKCU or HKLM, you have to use the `dwFlags` parameter to specify where you want the key created. Note that `SHRegCreateUSKey` creates the key *and* opens it. If the key already exists, you get to choose whether you want to open it in its existing location or force creation of a key with the same name under another root. When you request that a key be created under HKCU, though, you may find that it's actually created under the user's subkey of HKU.

Once you're done using a key (usually as part of your program's uninstallation code), it's polite to delete any USKs you've created. You do so with `SHRegDeleteEmptyUSKey`, which does just about what you'd expect.

The Shell Utility API Routines

```
LONG SHRegDeleteEmptyUSKey(hkUSKey, pszTargetPath, delRegFlags);
```

HUSKEY	hkUSKey	Currently open USK.
LPCTSTR	pszTargetPath	Full path to target key to delete; the target key must be empty.
SHREGDEL_ FLAGS	delRegFlags	Flags that control which key you want to remove: • SHREGDEL_DEFAULT removes the key from HKCU if it exists or from HKLM if it's not under HKCU. • SHREGDEL_HKCU removes the key under HKCU if it exists. • SHREGDEL_HKLM removes the key if it exists under HKLM. • SHREGDEL_BOTH removes the key under HKCU and HKLM.

Note that **SHRegDeleteEmptyUSKey** refuses to delete a USK unless all its subkeys and values have been previously removed; this prevents you from accidentally removing settings you want to keep. In practice, that means you need to enumerate through any USKs you create and remove their contents before removing them at uninstall time.

Opening and closing keys

You have to open and close USKs just as you do regular keys. Since there's a new opaque type for USKs (HUSKEY), you can't intermix the shell utility routines and the ordinary Win32 API routines. To open a USK, use **SHRegOpenUSKey**.

```
LONG SHRegOpenUSKey(pszPath, samDesired, hkRelUSKey, phkNewUSKey, fIgnoreHKCU);
```

LPCTSTR	pszPath	Pointer to string containing name of subkey to open.
REGSAM	samDesired	Desired security access to the key once it's opened.
HUSKEY	hkRelUSKey	Key to be used as base of relative path; if you specify a relative path in pszPath, it's interpreted relative to hkRelUSKey. If pszPath is absolute, set hkRelUSKey to NULL.
PHUSKEY	phkNewUSKey	Pointer to handle of the newly opened key.
BOOL	fIgnoreHKCU	When TRUE, SHRegGetUSValue looks for the key in HKLM instead of HKCU.

Once you have the key returned in **phkNewUSKey**, you can pass it to any of the other USK-related functions covered in this section. When you're done, of course, you need to close the key by calling **SHRegCloseUSKey**.

```
LONG SHRegCloseUSKey(hkTarget);
```

HUSKEY	hkTarget	Open USK you want to close.

Getting key and value information

After you've opened a USK, you'll probably need to get information about the keys and values in it. There are a total of three routines that do so: **SHRegQueryInfoUSKey**, **SHRegEnumUSKey**, and **SHRegEnumUSValue**. These are similar to their non-USK counterparts. For example, **SHRegQueryInfoUSKey** takes the same parameters as **SHQueryInfoKey** and returns the same information: a count of how many values and subkeys the specified USK has, plus the length of the longest subkey and value names. There are a few differences, though.

When you want to enumerate the subkeys of a USK, **SHRegEnumUSKey** is the appropriate routine to use. Like all the other enumeration routines I've talked about in this chapter, **SHRegEnumUSKey** allows you to walk an entire USK and get the names of each of its subkeys. Unlike (say) **SHRegEnumKeyEx**, though, the USK version needs another parameter: a flag that indicates whether to return information about the USK under HKLM or HKCU.

```
LONG SHRegEnumUSKey(hUSKey, dwIndex, pszName, pcchName, enumRegFlags);
```

HUSKEY	hUSKey	Handle to the currently open USK.
DWORD	dwIndex	Zero-based index indicating which subkey you want information about.
LPCTSTR	pszName	Address of a buffer that receives the enumerated key's name; make sure the buffer is **MAX_PATH** characters long to ensure enough space.
LPDWORD	pcchName	On input, specifies size of **pszName**; on exit, specifies how many characters were copied to **pszName**.
SHREGENUM_FLAGS	enumRegFlags	• SHREGENUM_DEFAULT enumerates the key under HKCU if it exists or from HKLM if it's not under HKCU. • SHREGENUM_HKCU enumerates the key under HKCU if it exists. • SHREGENUM_HKLM enumerates the key if it exists under HKLM. • SHREGENUM_BOTH isn't a legal value, even though it's defined in the header file.

SHRegEnumUSValue is just like **SHEnumValue**, with one exception: it adds an **enumRegFlags** parameter that accepts the same values as the one defined for **SHRegEnumUSKey**.

Reading values

When you want to read or write values under a USK, you'll again find that the process is quite similar to what you're accustomed to doing for ordinary Registry data. Once you have an open USK, you can get a specific value from it in two ways.

The Shell Utility API Routines

`SHRegGetUSValue` is the general-purpose routine for fetching USK values. You pass in the value's name and get back its contents, just like `SHGetValue` or `RegQueryValueEx`. However, since `SHRegGetUSValue` is for USKs, its argument list looks more like the other USK routines discussed thus far.

```
LONG SHRegGetUSValue(pszSubKey, pszValue, pdwType, pvData, pcbData, fIgnoreHKCU,
                              pvDefaultData, dwDefaultDataSize);
```

LPCTSTR	pszSubKey	Path to subkey (relative to HKLM and/or HKCU) that contains the desired value.
LPCTSTR	pszValue	Name of the value to get.
LPDWORD	pdwType	On exit, contains value's datatype; pass `NULL` if you don't care what type it is.
LPVOID	pvData	Pointer to buffer for value's data. If you don't want the data returned, pass `NULL`.
LPDWORD	pchData	On entry, points to `DWORD` specifying size of buffer in `pvData`. On exit, contains actual count of bytes copied to `pvData`.
BOOL	fIgnoreHKCU	When `TRUE`, `SHRegQueryUSValue` returns a value from HKLM only, ignoring any values under the USK in HKCU.
LPVOID	pvDefaultData	Buffer that gets the default value's data; pass `NULL` if you don't want it.
DWORD	dwDefaultDataSize	Size of `pvDefaultData` buffer.

You may have noticed that there's no `hUSKey` parameter for this routine. That's because you don't have to open a USK to get a value with `SHRegGetUSValue`; it opens and closes the key for you. This is easy, but inefficient if you need to fetch several values in a row. In that case, you probably want to use `SHRegQueryUSValue` instead by opening the desired USK, calling it several times, and closing the key.

```
LONG SHRegQueryUSValue(hUSKey, pszValue, pdwType, pvData, pcbData, fIgnoreHKCU,
                              pvDefaultData, dwDefaultDataSize);
```

HUSKEY	hUSKey	Handle to the currently open USK.
LPCTSTR	pszValue	Name of the value to be queried.
LPDWORD	pdwType	On exit, contains value's datatype; pass `NULL` if you don't care what type it is.
LPVOID	pvData	Pointer to buffer for value's data. If you don't want the data returned, pass `NULL`.
LPDWORD	pchData	On entry, points to `DWORD` specifying size of buffer in `pvData`. On exit, contains actual count of bytes copied to `pvData`.

BOOL	fIgnoreHKCU	When TRUE, SHRegQueryUSValue returns a value from HKLM only, ignoring any values under the USK in HKCU.
LPVOID	pvDefaultData	Buffer that gets the default value's data; pass NULL if you don't want it.
DWORD	dwDefaultDataSize	Size of pvDefaultData buffer.

There's also a special-purpose routine that gets a single value of type BOOL from a USK. SHRegGetBoolUSValue fetches a single Boolean value, using the same method as SHRegGetUSValue. It opens the specified key, retrieves the value, and returns it to you. This is an easy function to use, since its functionality is so limited, but it's still handy if you want to check the value of a Boolean flag in a USK within your program.

BOOL SHRegGetBoolUSValue (pszSubkey, pszValue, fIgnoreHKCU, fDefault)

LPCTSTR	pszSubkey	Path to subkey (relative to HKLM and/or HKCU) that contains the desired value.
LPCTSTR	pszValue	Name of the value you want to retrieve.
BOOL	fIgnoreHKCU	When TRUE, SHRegGetBoolUSValue looks only under HKLM.
BOOL	fDefault	Default value to be returned if the requested value doesn't exist.

For example, let's say you write an application that allows users to download the contents of an Outlook contacts folder to a GSM mobile phone. Most GSM phones can store numbers on a smart card in the phone or in the phone's internal RAM, so it would be nice if you let the user specify a default for where new numbers should go. At download time, it's fairly easy to check the setting before blasting data out to the phone.

```
// get all the contact info from Outlook

// see where the user wants the numbers stored
BOOL storeInPhone = SHRegGetBoolUSValue("Software\\RA\\PhoneBlaster",
                                        "StoreNumbersInPhone", false, false);
if (storeInPhone)
    // store the numbers in the phone
else
    // store the numbers on the SIM card
```

Writing and deleting values

So far, I've talked only about reading values. Fortunately, there are routines you can use to store values in USKs too. In fact, there are two distinct ways to write a value. SHRegSetUSValue just sets the value without requiring you to open and close the USK you're using, while SHRegWriteUSValue expects to have an open

The Shell Utility API Routines 261

USK passed to it. Like the functions you use to read values, the one you use depends on whether you're doing one operation (in which case `SHRegSet-USValue` is easier to use) or several (in which case `SHRegWriteUSValue` is more efficient).

```
LONG SHRegSetUSValue(pszSubKey, pszValue, dwType, pvData, cbData, dwFlags);
```

LPCTSTR	pszSubKey	Path to subkey (relative to HKLM and/or HKCU) where you want the value to go.
LPCTSTR	pszValue	Name of the value to write.
DWORD	dwType	Value's datatype; must be `REG_SZ`.
LPVOID	pvData	Pointer to buffer for value's string data.
DWORD	cbData	Length of the value string, not including the terminating NULL.
DWORD	dwFlags	Same flags specified for `SHRegCreateUSKey`: • SHREGSET_HKCU • SHREGSET_FORCE_HKCU • SHREGSET_HKLM • SHREGSET_FORCE_HKLM

`SHRegWriteUSValue` looks pretty much the same, except that it requires a handle to an open USK as once of its parameters:

```
LONG SHRegWriteUSValue(hkUSKey, pszValue, dwType, pvData, cbData, dwFlags);
```

HUSKEY	hkUSKey	Handle to currently open USK or one of the predefined root keys.
LPCTSTR	pszValue	Name of the value to write.
DWORD	dwType	Value's datatype; must be `REG_SZ`.
LPVOID	pvData	Pointer to buffer for value's string data.
DWORD	cbData	Length of the value string not including the terminating NULL.
DWORD	dwFlags	Same flags specified for `SHRegCreateUSKey` and `SHRegSetUSValue`: • SHREGSET_HKCU • SHREGSET_FORCE_HKCU • SHREGSET_HKLM • SHREGSET_FORCE_HKLM

Finally, you can delete a single value from a USK when you're done with it. `SHRegDeleteUSValue` does the trick (remember, you have to remove the values from a USK before you can remove it with `SHRegDeleteEmptyUSKey`). Removing a value is simple: you have to pass an open USK, the name of the value, and a flag word that indicates where you want to remove the value if found.

```
LONG SHRegDeleteUSValue(hkUSKey, pszValue, delRegFlags);
```

HUSKEY	hkUSKey	Handle to currently open USK.
LPCTSTR	pszValue	Name of the value to remove.
SHREGDEL_FLAGS	dwType	Flags that tell routine where to remove value if found. Flags that control which key you want to remove: • SHREGDEL_DEFAULT removes the key from HKCU if it exists or from HKLM if it's not under HKCU. • SHREGDEL_HKCU removes the key under HKCU if it exists. • SHREGDEL_HKLM removes the key if it exists under HKLM. • SHREGDEL_BOTH removes the key under HKCU and HKLM.

Leftovers

There are three routines that don't really belong anywhere else. Two of them allow you to read or change file paths, while the third duplicates a key handle. Let's look at it first; it's probably the simplest routine in the entire Registry API set.

```
HKEY SHRegDuplicateHKey (hkKey);
```

HKEY	hkKey	Key to duplicate.

SHRegDuplicateHKey does only one thing, but it does it well: it duplicates a current HKEY and makes a copy of it. If you're accustomed to the dup() function in Unix, this does exactly the same thing, so you can quickly duplicate a key handle (whether open or closed) and go on to do separate things to the two handles, independent of one another.

The path functions are also pretty straightforward. Windows 2000 really embodies Microsoft's philosophy that users should keep their data in their profiles, and that certain areas of the filesystem should be used only by applications and the OS. Accordingly, these functions allow you to pass in a path and have any symbolic names in it expanded to match actual folders on disk, or vice versa. The symbolic names that these functions support are shown in Table 8-8.

Table 8-8. Symbolic Names

Symbol Name	Expands to…
%USERPROFILE%	Current user's profile folder. Note that this variable can't be used by services that impersonate another account by manipulating the security context.
%ALLUSERSPROFILE%	The "All Users" profile folder.
%ProgramFiles%	The Program Files folder. This is normally not set under Windows NT.

The Shell Utility API Routines 263

Table 8-8. Symbolic Names (continued)

Symbol Name	Expands to…
%SystemRoot%	The system root directory where Windows 2000 is installed.
%SystemDrive%	The system volume's drive letter.

Although these routines work fine under Windows 95/98, the environment variables in Table 8-8 will probably be empty, since those operating systems don't support profiles.

The first of these routines, SHRegGetPath, takes the path to a Registry key that contains a file path. If that value is a REG_EXPAND_SZ, SHRegGetPath expands any symbolic names found in the path; if not, it returns the string without modifying it.

LONG SHRegGetPath (hKey, pszTargetSubkey, pszValue, pszExpandedPath, dwFlags)

HKEY	hKey	Handle to currently open key or root key.
LPCTSTR	pszTargetSubkey	String containing path to target subkey.
LPCTSTR	pszExpandedPath	Output buffer; on exit, contains fully expanded path. Set the size of this buffer to MAX_PATH to ensure there's enough room for the expansion.
DWORD	dwFlags	Reserved; always pass 0.

The counterpart of SHRegGetPath is SHRegSetPath, which takes a path string that contains one or more full path to the folders listed in the rightmost column of Table 8-8, then converts those paths to the symbols listed in the table.

LONG SHRegSetPath (hKey, pszTargetSubkey, pszValue, pszCompletePath, dwFFlags)

HKEY	hKey	Handle to currently open key or root key.
LPCTSTR	pszTargetSubkey	String containing path to target subkey. This subkey must exist or SHRegSetPath fails.
LPCTSTR	pszValue	String containing name of value to be created under pszTargetSubkey.
LPCTSTR	pszCompletePath	Output buffer; on exit, contains rewritten path. Set the size of this buffer to MAX_PATH to ensure there's enough room.
DWORD	dwFlags	Reserved; always pass 0.

The combination of these two functions allows you to store file paths in a reasonably flexible way, since if a user or administrator moves something (such as a user profile or the system drive), these API routines make that change transparent to your application.

Programming with C/C++

The API examples and documentation in earlier sections all present the Registry API in its native C/C++ form. Since many administrators are comfortable with C and/or C++, I'll start the programming examples by presenting three distinct uses for the Registry API routines I've already presented.

Example: Watching a Key for Changes

`RegNotifyChangeKeyValue` is a little-used, but very useful, routine. It's only present in Windows 2000 and NT, which perhaps accounts for its relative anonymity. If you need to be notified when a key or its values changes, it's the best tool for getting you that notification. `WatchKey`, shown in Example 8-4, is a small utility that takes advantage of `RegNotifyChangeKeyValue` to warn you when a key you specify has been changed.

How the code works

After a check of its initial command-line arguments, the code performs the following steps:

1. It identifies which root key "owns" the key you want to monitor; this is required because `RegOpenKeyEx` needs an already open key (i.e., one of the roots) to open the target key. If it can't figure out which root the user specified, it prints an error and exits.

2. It captures the pathname of the key to monitor and uses it, along with the root key, to call `RegOpenKeyEx`. The key is opened with `KEY_READ` access, which includes `KEY_NOTIFY` access too. If the key can't be opened, the code generates an error message and exits.

3. The target key is monitored with a call to `RegNotifyChangeKeyValue`. The code passes `TRUE` for the `bWatchSubtree` parameter so that any change to a key or value beneath the target key generates a notification. For the `dwNotifyFilter` parameter, you pass all available event flags in so that any changes to the target key trigger a notification. No event handle is passed in, and the `fAsynchronous` parameter is set to `TRUE` so that the process blocks until a change occurs.

Example 8-4. The WatchKey Utility

```
// WatchKey.c
// Watches the key you specify until it changes, then displays the time and date
```

Example 8-4. The WatchKey Utility (continued)

```
// when the change occurred.

#include <windows.h>
#include <stdio.h>
#include <time.h>


// error codes we generate
#define kBadParams   1
#define kNoRootKey   2
#define kCantOpenPath 3


static const HKEY hkRootList[5] = {HKEY_LOCAL_MACHINE, HKEY_CURRENT_USER, HKEY_USERS,
HKEY_CURRENT_CONFIG, HKEY_CLASSES_ROOT};
static const char *pszRootNames[5] = {"HKLM", "HKCU", "HKU", "HKCC", "HKCR"};

void DoUsage(const char *inName);


void DoUsage(const char *inName)
{
    printf("%s: improper command-line parameters\n", inName);
    printf("\tUsage: %s root path\n", inName);
    printf("\t\troot\tRoot key to monitor; may be HKLM, HKCC, HKCR,
        HKU, or HKCU\n");
    printf("\t\tpath\tFull path to subkey you want to monitor\n");
}


void main(int argc, char **argv)
{
    char    pszPath[MAX_PATH];
    HKEY    hkRoot = NULL, hkResult = NULL;
    DWORD   dwIdx = 0, dwRootIdx = 0;
    LONG    nResult = ERROR_SUCCESS;

    memset(pszPath, 0x0, MAX_PATH);

    // preflight our arguments
    if (3 != argc)
    {
        DoUsage(argv[0]);
        return;
    }

    // first argument must be the root key name
    while (5 > dwIdx && 0 == dwRootIdx)
    {
        if (0 == strcmp(pszRootNames[dwIdx], argv[1]))
            dwRootIdx = dwIdx;
        else
```

Example 8-4. The WatchKey Utility (continued)

```
            dwIdx++;
    }
    if (0 == dwRootIdx)
    {
        DoUsage(argv[0]);
        fprintf(stderr, "!!! no root key named %s\n", argv[1]);
        return;
    }

    // get the path name
    strncpy(pszPath, argv[2], max(MAX_PATH, strlen(argv[2])));

    // open the corresponding key
    nResult = RegOpenKeyEx(hkRootList[dwRootIdx], pszPath, 0L, KEY_READ,
        &hkResult);
    if (ERROR_SUCCESS != nResult)
    {
        fprintf(stderr, "Error %d while opening %s\n", nResult, pszPath);
        fflush(stderr);
        return;
    }

    // watch it until something happens or the program's terminated
    fprintf(stderr, "Watching %s\\%s...\n", pszRootNames[dwRootIdx], pszPath);
    fflush(stderr);

    nResult = RegNotifyChangeKeyValue(hkResult,
                                     true,        // tell us if subkeys change
                                     REG_NOTIFY_CHANGE_NAME +
                                     REG_NOTIFY_CHANGE_ATTRIBUTES +
                                     REG_NOTIFY_CHANGE_LAST_SET +
                                     REG_NOTIFY_CHANGE_SECURITY,
                                     NULL,        // don't pass an event
                                     false        // wait; don't be
                                                  // asynchronous
                                    );
    if (ERROR_SUCCESS != nResult)
    {
        fprintf(stderr, "Error %d while monitoring %s\n", nResult, pszPath);
        fflush(stderr);
        return;
    }

    // if we're still here, that means the key was changed
    time_t now = time((long *)NULL);
    fprintf(stderr, "!!! Key %s\\%s changed at %s", pszRootNames[dwRootIdx],
            pszPath, ctime(&now));
    fflush(stderr);
}
```

Possible enhancements

`WatchKey` is a useful tool as it stands right now, but (as with almost every program ever written) it could be enhanced. Here are a few suggestions to get you thinking about how you could apply what you've learned:

- The first, and most obvious, improvement would be to let users specify values for the `bWatchSubtree` and `dwFilterOptions` parameters, thus making the actual watching more flexible.

- Instead of just printing out the date and time when a modification occurred, you can generate an Event Log entry.

- Since `RegNotifyChangeKeyValue` can function asynchronously, you can modify the code in Example 8-4 so that it spawns a separate watcher thread for each key you want to monitor at one time. In conjunction with event logging, this provides a low-overhead auditing mechanism that can be applied only to keys you're interested in.

Example: A Stack-Based Wrapper Class

Earlier in the chapter, I alluded to a neat C++ feature that is sadly underutilized. Whenever you create an C++ object, its constructor is called. When you're done with the object and are ready to delete it, you call a disposal method that calls the object's destructor. Calls to these methods are supposed to balance so that you never construct anything that doesn't get destroyed, and you don't destroy any object more than once. This may sound suspiciously like the rule for Registry keys: open them, use them, and always close them.

If you create automatic objects on the stack, the compiler automatically calls the objects' destructors when it's time to destroy them. This may happen because your code has finished executing the scope where the objects are or because a jump or exception caused the objects to go out of scope. Here's a small example:

```
void test(void)
{
    anObject A;

    A.doSomething();
    if (A.IsEmpty())
        throw(kRanOutOfData);
    A.DoSomethingElse();
    if (A.IsFull())
        throw(kTooMuchData);
}
```

When this function starts up, `A` is allocated on the stack, and its constructor is called. The destructor may potentially be called in three cases: when the function returns normally, when `kRanOutOfData` is thrown, or when `kTooMuchData` is thrown. No matter how this function exits, A's destructor gets a chance to clean up whatever the constructor did.

Example 8-5 shows the class definition for a stack-based Registry key class. The constructor opens the key you specify, and the destructor closes it again. In between, there are members for getting and setting individual values.

Example 8-5. The StKey Class Definition

```
class StKey
{
    public:
        StKey(HKEY inRoot, LPCTSTR inPath, REGSAM inAccess = KEY_READ);
        ~StKey();

        LONG GetDWORDValue(LPCTSTR inValName, DWORD &outCount);
        LONG GetStringValue(LPCTSTR inValName, LPSTR outValue, DWORD &ioBufSize);
        LONG GetValueCount(DWORD &outCount);

        LONG SetDWORDValue(LPCTSTR inValName, const DWORD inVal);
        LONG SetStringValue(LPCTSTR inValName, LPCTSTR inVal,
                        const DWORD inBufSize = 0, DWORD inType = REG_SZ);

        LONG AddDWORDValue(LPCTSTR inValName, const DWORD inVal);
        LONG AddStringValue(LPCTSTR inValName, LPCTSTR inVal,
                        const DWORD inBufSize = 0, DWORD inType = REG_SZ);

    private:
        HKEY mCurrKey;
};
```

How the code works

Example 8-6 shows the actual implementation of the StKey class.[*] The constructor and destructor are straightforward: they open and close the requested key, and that's it! Likewise, there's nothing magic about the GetValueCount, GetDWORDValue, or GetStringValue members.

The most interesting piece is actually the SetStringValue member. It handles more than one type of Registry string. You probably remember that values may contain plain strings (REG_SZ), expandable strings (REG_EXPAND_SZ), or multiple strings (REG_MULTI_SZ). SetStringValue correctly creates values of all three types; in addition, it's smart enough to figure out the correct string length based on the input type.

---

[*] I omitted AddDWORDValue and AddStringValue from the example because they just call the corresponding Set routines.

Example 8-6. The StKey Class Implementation

```
StKey::StKey(HKEY inRoot, LPCTSTR inPath, REGSAM inAccess /* = KEY_READ */)
{
    long nResult = 0;
    mCurrKey = NULL;
    nResult = RegOpenKeyEx(inRoot, inPath, 0L, inAccess, &mCurrKey);
    if (ERROR_SUCCESS != nResult)
        mCurrKey = NULL;
}


StKey::~StKey()
{
    if (mCurrKey)
    {
        RegCloseKey(mCurrKey);
        mCurrKey = NULL;
    }
}


LONG StKey::GetValueCount(DWORD &outCount)
{
   return RegQueryInfoKey (mCurrKey,
                           NULL, NULL, NULL,
                           NULL, NULL, NULL,
                           &outCount,
                           NULL, NULL, NULL, NULL);
}


LONG StKey::GetDWORDValue(LPCTSTR inValName, DWORD &outValue)
{
    DWORD sz = sizeof(DWORD);
    return RegQueryValue(mCurrKey, inValName, (LPTSTR)&outValue, (long *)&sz);
}


LONG StKey::GetStringValue(LPCTSTR inValName, LPTSTR outValue, DWORD &ioBufSize)
{
    DWORD sz = sizeof(DWORD);
    return RegQueryValue(mCurrKey, inValName, outValue, (long *)&ioBufSize);
}


LONG StKey::SetDWORDValue(LPCTSTR inValName, const DWORD inVal)
{
    return RegSetValueEx(mCurrKey, inValName, 0L, REG_DWORD, (BYTE *)&inVal,
          sizeof(DWORD));
}
```

Example 8-6. The StKey Class Implementation (continued)

```
LONG StKey::SetStringValue(LPCTSTR inValName, LPCTSTR inVal,
            const DWORD inBufSize /* = 0*/,
            DWORD inType /*= REG_SZ*/)
{
    if (!IsValidStringType(inType))
        return ERROR_INVALID_PARAMETER;
    if (0 == inBufSize && REG_MULTI_SZ == inType)
        return ERROR_INVALID_PARAMETER;
    return RegSetValueEx(mCurrKey, inValName, 0L, inType, (BYTE *)inVal,
                    (inBufSize ? inBufSize : strlen(inVal)));
}


LONG StKey::AddDWORDValue(LPCTSTR inValName, const DWORD inVal)
{
    return SetDWORDValue(inValName, inVal);
}


LONG StKey::AddStringValue(LPCTSTR inValName, LPCTSTR inVal,
            const DWORD inBufSize /* = 0*/,
            DWORD inType /*= REG_SZ*/)
{
    return SetStringValue(inValName, inVal, inBufSize, inType);
}
```

Possible enhancements

You could easily extend this class to support a Standard Template Library-style iterator capability for value. This makes it easy to iterate through all values of a subkey in a structured, exception-safe manner. You can also make the constructor smarter, perhaps by allowing it to recognize and parse a fully qualified path such as "\\enigma\HKLM\SOFTWARE\LJL\SMIME\Users" instead of requiring the root key and path to be separate. Another useful expansion is to make the class able to store values in USKs. For a real treat, consider building a stack-based class that loads and unloads hive files!

Example: Loading a Control with a Set of Values

If you store useful data as values attached to a subkey, at some point you'll want to get them out again. In writing an S/MIME-compliant electronic mail client, I found that I needed to get a list of stored user profiles (which lives in HKLM\SOFTWARE\LJL\SMIME\Users) and display them in a dropdown list so the user can efficiently pick a profile to use when logging in. The actual code that does so is in Example 8-7; it's fairly straightforward.

Example 8-7. Move the Values from a Key into a Windows Combo or List Box

```c
#include <windows.h>

typedef enum {eCombo=0, eList} eBoxType;

HRESULT LoadBoxWithUsers(eBoxType inBoxType, HWND inControl, LPSTR inDefName,
                        int &outSelected)
{
    DWORD   nResult = ERROR_SUCCESS;
    HKEY    hkFirstKey;
    HRESULT retVal = 0;
    long    idx = 0;
    DWORD   dwValCount = 0;

    SendMessage(inControl, (eCombo ==
                inBoxType ? CB_RESETCONTENT : LB_RESETCONTENT),
                (WPARAM)0, (LPARAM)0);
    outSelected = 0;

    // try to open HKLM\SOFTWARE\SMAIL; if we succeed, enumerate
    // through its subkeys and return the first one
    nResult = RegOpenKeyEx(HKEY_LOCAL_MACHINE, "SOFTWARE\\LJL\\SMIME\\Users",
                        0L, KEY_READ, &hkFirstKey);
    if (ERROR_SUCCESS == nResult)
    {
        char *pszName = NULL;
        DWORD dwNameLen = 0;

        // find out what the longest subkey is and how many values exist
        nResult = RegQueryInfoKey (hkFirstKey,
                        NULL, NULL,     // class & class size
                        NULL,           // reserved
                        NULL,           // # of subkeys
                        NULL,           // longest subkey length
                        NULL,           // class length
                        &dwValCount,    // # of values
                        NULL, NULL,
                        &dwNameLen,     // longest value contents
                        NULL);

        // allocate buffers based on what we just learned
        pszName = (char *)malloc(dwNameLen);

        for (idx = 0; idx <= dwValCount; idx++)
        {
            nResult = RegEnumValue(hkFirstKey, idx, pszName, &dwNameLen, NULL,
                        NULL, NULL, NULL);
            if (ERROR_NO_MORE_ITEMS != nResult)
                SendMessage(inControl, (eCombo == inBoxType ? CB_INSERTSTRING :
                        LB_INSERTSTRING), (WPARAM)-1, (LPARAM)pszName);

            // if this item matches the default, return it as a match
            if (inDefName && stricmp(pszName, inDefName) == 0)
```

Example 8-7. Move the Values from a Key into a Windows Combo or List Box (continued)

```
                outSelected = idx;
            memset(pszName, 0x0, MAX_PATH); dwNameLen = MAX_PATH;
        }
        nResult = RegCloseKey(hkFirstKey);
      SendMessage(inControl, (eCombo == inBoxType ?CB_SETCURSEL :
                            LB_SETCURSEL),(WPARAM)outSelected, (LPARAM)0);
        free(pszName);
    }
    else
        retVal = E_NOT_FOUND;
    return retVal;
}
```

The first thing this code does is clear out the Windows list/combo box control; once that's done, it opens the key where the relevant values are stored. If `RegOpenKeyEx` succeeds, a call to `RegQueryInfoKey` returns the length of the longest value and the number of values attached to the key.

With that information in hand, it's easy to iterate through the values by repeatedly calling `RegEnumValue`. As each value is retrieved, it's added to the combo box. If the caller specifies a default value for the combo box, when that value is encountered, its index is saved so you can preset the combo box's selection. This makes it possible to remember the user's last selection and have it appear as the selection when the program's next run.

Programming with Perl

Ahhh, Perl!* Once upon a time, its power and entertainment value were reserved solely for Unix administrators. A long line of Windows programmers have labored to bring the Perl toolset to Win32; in doing so, they've added some nifty features not present in other platforms' Perl implementations. ActiveState Perl is an implementation of Perl for Win32 platforms and is available at *http://www.activestate.com*. In addition to the Perl core, ActiveState Perl also includes complete support for the Registry, COM, OLE, and Win32 security.

Throughout the rest of this section, I'm going to assume that you're familiar with Perl syntax and semantics, particularly the Perl implementation of objects and modules. (If you're not, I highly recommend *Learning Perl On Win32 Systems* by Randal L. Schwartz, Erik Olson, and Tom Christiansen from O'Reilly & Associates.)

Even if you don't use the Win32-specific extensions, you can write plain-vanilla Perl and it works fine, but the extensions let you use Perl's expressive power to make short work of tasks such as creating batches of user accounts (as described

---

* Since this *is* an O'Reilly book, I was sternly admonished to talk about Perl.

in *Windows NT User Administration* by Ashley J. Meggitt and Timothy D. Ritchey; O'Reilly & Associates). Note that all the examples in this section were developed under and tested with ActivePerl Version 5.6.0.

Before Perl Version 5 hit the streets, when people wanted to extend Perl, they actually had to change the core language itself. This resulted in products such as *oraperl*, which is Perl plus Oracle connectivity. Version 5 included a general extension mechanism developers could use to extend and change Perl without having to change the core. Developers can write extensions in Perl or other languages such as C or C++ (see the documentation on Perl's extension mechanism—called XS—in the *perlxs* and *perlxstut* sections of the Perl manual). This is how ActivePerl makes the Registry API available.

The Win32API::RegXXX Functions

The Win32 Perl module includes definitions that correspond to each of the standard C function definitions described in the section "Programming with C/C++," earlier in this chapter. You can use them as you would the C or Visual Basic equivalents; the one difference is that you should qualify the routine names by specifying they come from the Win32 module. Example 8-8 shows what the program from Example 8-1 looks like when rewritten in Perl with the standard Win32 module's calls.

Example 8-8. "Hello, World" from Example 8-1, Rewritten in Perl

```
use Win32API::Registry 0.13 qw( :ALL );

RegOpenKeyEx ( HKEY_LOCAL_MACHINE,
        "SYSTEM\\CurrentControlSet\\Control\\ComputerName\\ActiveComputerName",
            0, KEY_READ, $theKey ) or die
            ("Couldn't open name key!$^E");

RegQueryValueEx($theKey, 'ComputerName',
            [],             # our friend lpReserved
            REG_SZ,
            $who, []);
print "This computer is named $who\n";

RegCloseKey($theKey);
```

The first line imports the Win32 module definitions themselves. The real fun starts with the call to **RegOpenKeyEx**. The most unusual feature of this call is that the constant parameters are passed by reference; other than that (and the call to die) it looks much like the C calls discussed in other sections of this chapter.

Likewise, the call to **RegQueryValueEx** looks almost like the other languages' equivalents. One difference is that the value is returned in $who; since Perl doesn't need the length of the data in $who, there's no parameter for it. There is a parameter that can return the value's type, but in this case it's useless so I passed in [] instead of a variable reference. (Note that you can pass &NULL or [] to indicate a NULL value.)

The special value $^E tells the Perl interpreter to call the Win32 GetLastError() routine and turn the returned error code into a text string. This is optional, but helpful.

Finally, once the computer name's been printed, RegCloseKey closes the key just opened. This is just as necessary in Perl as anywhere else; when you open an HKEY, the OS needs to be told when you're finished with it.

When to use them

If you're already comfortable with the C/C++ interfaces, the Perl equivalents will seem familiar, because they are; they're just Perl transliterations of the existing C++ idioms from the Win32 API definitions. However, if you're going to program in Perl, you should do that instead of using what Perl hackers disparagingly call "C-in-Perl." The next section tells you how to do just that.

The Win32::TieRegistry Module

A large part of Perl's popularity is the fact that Perl takes care of many fussy details for the programmer. Larry Wall, Perl's creator, describes this design philosophy as "making easy things easy and hard things possible." Compare the original Perl "Hello, World" program in Example 8-7 to the version shown in Example 8-9.

Example 8-9. Perl "Hello, World" Rewritten with the Win32::TieRegistry Module

```
use Win32::TieRegistry Delimiter => '/';

my $name = join '/',
        qw/ LMachine SYSTEM CurrentControlSet Control
            ComputerName ActiveComputerName /;

my $key = $Registry->{$name}
    or die "$0: can't open $name: $^E\n";

print "This computer is named $key->{'/ComputerName'}\n";
```

There are some things in this code that will probably look pretty odd to people who aren't used to Perl. If you're comfortable with Perl, skip the next section; otherwise, read on for some interpretation of all that funny-looking stuff.

A few Perl-isms

Like practically every other computer language ever invented, Perl supports arrays. Perl also supports a special type of array called a *hash*. You may be familiar with the underlying concept under another name, such as "associative array" or "dictionary list." A hash is just a data structure that maps a key to some data; it's like an array, but instead of being indexed by positive integers it's indexed by values.* The join operator concatenates values, and the qw operator quotes strings (so that qw/Hello/ is equivalent to "hello" in a C program). qw also replaces spaces with the appropriate delimiter.

Win32::TieRegistry also uses shorter names for the root keys: HKLM, HKU, HKCU, and HKCR are LMachine, Users, CUser, and Classes, respectively. I've used the TieRegistry abbreviations instead of the more standard C/C++-style names because that's what you're likely to see in other Perl code.

The code in detail

Let's start with line 1: instead of importing the entire Win32 module, the code uses only the TieRegistry module. Notice that we're separating keys and subkeys with slashes instead of a backslashes (that's what we meant by Delimiter => '/' in the use directive). The next line creates the key name we want to open. The big surprise starts on the next line: instead of calling RegOpenKeyEx, the code accesses the registry key of interest by inspecting the $Registry hash, using the key name fabricated with qw as an index into the hash.

Perl uses the arrow operator (->) familiar to C and C++ programmers. $Registry is actually a reference to a hash. Perl's references are analogous to a safe implementation of C's pointers. If you have a reference to something, then that reference is guaranteed to be valid; there's no such thing as a NULL reference. Think of $Registry->{$name} as being equivalent to, but safer than, p->field in C.

The hash behind $Registry is very special: it's a *tied hash*. Tied hashes in Perl link the name of a hash entry to code that fetches the corresponding value when you need it. In this case, asking for a key from the $Registry hash actually causes TieRegistry to read the corresponding key with RegOpenKeyEx. Another example of tied hashes is Perl's magic %ENV hash that lets you read and set environment variables by reading from and writing to what appears to be a Perl hash. (See the *perltie* section of the Perl manual for more details on tied hashes.)

---

* For much more on hashes, see Chapter 7 of *Learning Perl on Win32 Systems*, Chapter 5 of the original *Learning Perl* by Randal L. Schwartz and Tom Christiansen, or the heavy-duty *Programming Perl* by Larry Wall, Tom Christiansen, and Jon Orwant, all published by O'Reilly & Associates.

One more difference: instead of returning an HKEY, extracting a value from a hash returns another reference to a tied hash that represents the HKEY. It's possible to continue to extract values from the new reference, as the example demonstrates. This is a very nice property, because you can then traverse the registry as a splay tree using the usual recursive algorithm.

Internally, all the routines in Win32::TieRegistry call the Win32 API routines, either directly or out of the Win32 module. That means that any limitations described earlier in "The Registry API" still pertain to these calls, even though they're not completely identical to the original routine definitions.

Opening and closing keys and retrieving values

Before you can do anything to a key or value, you must have an open key. You open keys by accessing the value associated with a particular key name. The key name can be the full path of the key you want or a relative path from a key that you already opened. The return value is a new registry object for subkeys or the corresponding value for values:

```
$newobj = $RegObj->{$subkeyname};

$value  = $RegObj->{$valuename};
# retrieve type also
$RegObj->ArrayValues(1);
($value, $type) = @{ $RegObj->{$keyname} };
```

Notice you don't have to explicitly close Registry keys.

Creating, adding, and modifying keys and values

You can create, add, or modify a subkey or value beneath an open key simply by assigning to a key of the registry object:

```
$RegObj->{$subkeyname} = $newvalue;
```

As the following example from the Win32::TieRegistry documentation demonstrates, you can also insert arbitrarily nested data:

```
$Registry->ArrayValues(1);
$Registry->{"LMachine/Software/FooCorp/"} = {
    "FooWriter/" => {
        "/Version" => "4.032",
        "Startup/" => {
            "/Title" => "Foo Writer Deluxe ][",
            "/WindowSize" => [ pack("LL",$wid,$ht), "REG_BINARY" ],
            "/TaskBarIcon" => [ "0x0001", "REG_DWORD" ],
        },
```

Programming with Perl

```
            "Compatibility/" => {
                "/AutoConvert" => "Always",
                "/Default Palette" => "Windows Colors",
            },
        },
        "/License", => "0123-9C8EF1-09-FC",
    };
```

Enumerating keys and values

To list a hash's keys, use Perl's `keys` operator. Note that `Win32::TieRegistry` uses a special naming convention under which value names start with the delimiter and subkeys end with the delimiter. Enumerate the keys and values using the for operator, like this:

```
    my(@keys,@vals);
    $RegObj->Delimiter('/');
    for (keys %$RegObj) {
        if (m<^/(.*)$>s) {
            push @vals, $1;
        }
        elsif (m<^(.*)/$>s) {
            push @keys, $1;
        }
    }
```

As you'd expect, enumerating the keys doesn't recurse down the tree, so the subkeys in its array represent only the first level beneath the requested key.

Example 8-10 illustrates a possible application of key and value enumeration. After opening the key of interest, it enumerates the subkeys and values. Once it has the two lists, it iterates over them with the `foreach` operator to print each key in the array.

Example 8-10. Iterating Through Keys and Values with GetKeys and GetValues

```
use Win32::TieRegistry Delimiter => '/';

my $name = join '/',
           qw/ LMachine System CurrentControlSet
               Services LanmanServer /;

my $key = $Registry->{$name}
    or die "$0: can't open $name: $^E\n";

my(@subs,@vals);

for (keys %$key) {
    if (m<^/(.*)$>s) {
        push @vals, $1;
    }
    elsif (m<^(.*)/$>s) {
        push @subs, $1;
```

Example 8-10. Iterating Through Keys and Values with GetKeys and GetValues (continued)

```
    }
}

print "Subkeys of $name:\n",
      map("$_\n", @subs),
      "Values of $name:\n",
      map("$_=$key->{$_}\n", @vals);
```

Deleting keys and values

In keeping with the theme of functioning just like hashes, use Perl's `delete` operator to delete keys and values:

```
$old = delete $regObj->{$key_or_value_name};
```

Saving and loading keys

`Win32::TieRegistry` has versions of `RegSaveKey` and `RegLoadKey` from the `Win32API::Registry` module:

```
$regObj->AllowSave(1);
$regObj->RegSaveKey($filename, $security);

$regObj->AllowLoad(1);
$regObj->RegLoadKey($keyname, $filename);
```

The `$security` argument to `RegSaveKey` contains a SECURITY_ATTRIBUTES structure that specifies the permissions to be set on `$filename`. This is typically `[]`, a reference to an empty array.

Mixing Win32API::Registry and Win32::TieRegistry

The `Win32::TieRegistry` module provides an object-oriented interface also. Many of these methods' names are the same as or similar to their `Win32API::Registry` counterparts (e.g., `RegLoadKey` and `RegSaveKey`). Read the `Win32::TieRegistry` documentation for all the gory details.

Example: Walking the Registry

Perl excels at processing, formatting, searching, and generally handling textual information. Since the Registry is really one big binary blob, you might not think Perl would be a useful language for working with the Registry. However, as any true Perl hacker knows, Perl is useful for *everything!*

In his upcoming book (alas, at the time of this writing, it still doesn't have a title) on functional programming for Perl hackers published by Morgan Kaufmann, Mark Dominus develops a parameterized directory tree walker that takes as arguments two callbacks for processing files and directories. Realizing that directory tree

Programming with Perl 279

structure and registry structure are practically identical, we can develop a similar tool and put it to use for whatever purpose you wish.

Despite its power, the code looks deceptively simple:

```
package RegWalk;

use strict;
use Win32::TieRegistry ArrayValues => 1;

sub import {
    no strict 'refs';
    my($pkg) = caller;

    *{ $pkg . '::' . 'reg_walk' } = \&reg_walk;
}
sub reg_walk {
    my($key, $valfunc, $keyfunc) = @_;

    my $info = $Registry->{$key};
    if (not defined $info) {
        warn "$0: couldn't open registry key:\n" .
            "    $key ($^E)\n";

        return;
    }
    elsif (ref($info) eq 'Win32::TieRegistry') {
        my @results;
        foreach my $k (keys %$info) {
            push @results,
                reg_walk($key . $k, $valfunc, $keyfunc);
        }

        return $keyfunc->($key, $info, @results)
            if $keyfunc;
    }
    else {
        return $valfunc->($key, $info)
            if $valfunc;
    }
}

1;
```

To use the RegWalk module, put it somewhere that Perl can find it (one of the directories in the @INC section of the output of perl -V is a good place).

Don't worry if you don't understand the import subroutine; it works some behind-the-scenes magic to make reg_walk appear to be defined in the calling package (this particular spell is called exporting).

`reg_walk` takes as arguments a key name, a callback for registry values, and a callback for registry subkeys. It opens the specified key and decides whether it has a subkey or a value. If it has a subkey, it gathers the results from a recursive call to itself (think of it as "drilling" all the way to the bottom in *RegEdit*) and passes the key name, a reference to a tied hash representing the open key, and the gathered list of results to the registry subkey callback that you provided. (If you want to impress your computer-scientist friends, you can say that it's performing a depth-first search of the registry.) If it sees that it has a value, it passes the key name and a reference to an array of the form:

    [$value, $type]

to the Registry value callback that you provided.

Not impressed yet? What if I told you that you can use this module to do any possible Registry management task that you could think up? Any task, from deleting everything in your Registry (which I wouldn't recommend) to looking for values that match some regular expression to sending a copy of your Registry to your buddies hiding behind Comet Hale-Bopp (assuming, of course, that you have `Net::SubSpace::Transmit` installed). The trick is to provide callbacks that do what you want.

Philippe Le Berre wrote a small Perl utility, *dumpreg.pl*, which dumps a specified key (and its subkeys and values) in a nice formatted list. I've updated his code to take advantage of `Win32::TieRegistry` and `RegWalk`. The main section of the code (shown in Example 8-11) gets the user's command-line input, validates it (filling in defaults where appropriate), connects to a remote machine if requested (`Win32::TieRegistry` handles this transparently when it sees key names that look like `\\machinename\...`), opens the key to be traversed, and opens the output file. If any step fails, the program stops; if they all succeed, the `process_key` routine gets called.

Example 8-11. The Main Section of dumpreg.pl

```
use strict;
use Win32::TieRegistry qw/ :REG_ /;
use RegWalk;

sub usage { "Usage: $0 key [ output-file ]\n" }

my %type = (
    REG_SZ()        => 'REG_SZ',
    REG_EXPAND_SZ() => 'REG_EXPAND_SZ',
    REG_BINARY()    => 'REG_BINARY',
    REG_MULTI_SZ()  => 'REG_MULTI_SZ',
    REG_DWORD()     => 'REG_DWORD',
);
```

Example 8-11. The Main Section of dumpreg.pl (continued)

```perl
die usage unless @ARGV >= 1;

my $key = shift;
my $out = shift || 'Hive.key';

my $box;
my $root;

# e.g., \\machine\HKEY_LOCAL_MACHINE`..
if ($key =~ /^(?:\\\\(.+?)\\)?(HKEY_[^\\]+)?\\?(.*)/) {
    $box  = $1 || '';
    $root = $2 || '';
    $key  = $3 || '';
}

my %root = (
    HKEY_CLASSES_ROOT     => 'Classes',
    HKEY_CURRENT_USER     => 'CUser',
    HKEY_LOCAL_MACHINE    => 'LMachine',
    HKEY_USERS            => 'Users',
    HKEY_PERFORMANCE_DATA => 'PerfData',
    HKEY_CURRENT_CONFIG   => 'CConfig',
    HKEY_DYN_DATA         => 'DynData',
);

if ($root) {
    if (exists $root{$root}) {
        $root = $root{$root};
    }
    else {
        die "$0: unknown registry root key: '$root'\n";
    }
}
else {
    $root = $root{HKEY_LOCAL_MACHINE};
}

$key = $root . '\\' . $key;
$key =~ s/([^\\])$/$1\\/;

print "Dumping:\n",
      "'$key'\n";
print "from machine $box...\n" if $box;

open my $file, ">$out" or die "$0: open >$out: $!\n";

process_key $key, $file;

close $file;
```

`process_key` itself is shown in Example 8-12.

Example 8-12. process_key Does All the Hard Work

```perl
sub process_key {
    my $key  = shift;
    my $file = shift;
    my $total = 0;

    my $valfunc = sub {
        my $k  = shift;
        my($val,$type) = @{ shift @_ };
        if ($k =~ /^(.+?)\\\\(.*)$/) {
            my $parent = $1;
            my $name   = $2 || '(Default)';
            my $depth  = $parent =~ tr/\\//;
            my $indent = '    ' x $depth;
            printf "%03d)$indent$name\n", ++$total;
            $val ||= '[empty]';
            return "$indent$name\n" .
                   "$indent    $name = $type{$type}\n" .
                   "$indent    $val";
        }
        else {
            warn "$0: unexpected key name: '$k'\n";
        }
    };
    my $keyfunc = sub {
        my $k = shift;
        my $info = shift;
        my @result = @_;
        if ($k =~ /^(.+\\)?(.+)\\$/ ) {
            my $parent = $1 || '';
            my $name   = $2;
            my $depth  = $parent =~ tr/\\//;
            my $indent = '    ' x $depth;
            printf "%03d)$indent$name\n", ++$total;
            unshift @result, "$indent$name";
        }
        else {
            warn "$0: unexpected key name: '$k'\n";
        }
        return @result;
    };

    for (reg_walk $key, $valfunc, $keyfunc) {
        next unless $_;

        print $file $_, "\n";
    }
}
```

The two callbacks, stored in $valfunc and $keyfunc, are the meat of the subroutine. Remember that reg_walk calls the appropriate callback for each subkey and value that it encounters in its traversal. Both callbacks determine the parent key name and the current key name. They then count backslashes in the parent using the `tr///` operator to determine the current depth in the tree (i.e., how many levels `reg_walk` has "drilled down"). Once `reg_walk` has assembled all the nformation from the callbacks, the code iterates over the resulting list, printing each non-empty result to the output file.

Example 8-13 shows another Registry walker that searches case-insensitively for key names containing a particular substring:.

Example 8-13. Keyword Search

```
use strict;
use RegWalk;

sub findkey {
    my $goal    = shift;
    my $names   = shift;
    my $val = sub {
        my $key  = shift;
        my($info) = @{ shift @_ };
        if ($key =~ /^.*?\\\\(.*)$/) {
            my $name = $1 || '(Default)';
            if ( index( lc($name), $goal ) >= 0 ) {
                return "$key - $info";
            }
        }
    };
    my $key = sub {
        my $k    = shift;
        my $info = shift;
        my @result = @_;
        if ($k =~ /^.*\\(.+)\\$/) {
            my $name = $1;
            if ( index( lc($name), $goal ) >= 0 ) {
                unshift @result, $k;
            }
        }
        return @result;
    };

    foreach my $root (@$names) {
        for (reg_walk $root, $val, $key) {
            next unless $_;

            print $_, "\n";
        }
    }
}

## main
my %root = (
    HKEY_CLASSES_ROOT => 'Classes',
    Classes => 'Classes',
```

Example 8-13. Keyword Search (continued)

```
    HKEY_CURRENT_USER => 'CUser',
    CUser => 'CUser',

    HKEY_LOCAL_MACHINE => 'LMachine',
    LMachine => 'LMachine',
    HKEY_USERS => 'Users',
    Users => 'Users',
    HKEY_PERFORMANCE_DATA => 'PerfData',
    PerfData => 'PerfData',
    HKEY_CURRENT_CONFIG => 'CConfig',
    CConfig => 'CConfig',
    HKEY_DYN_DATA => 'DynData',
    DynData => 'DynData',
);

my $goal = shift;
die "Usage: $0 <goal> search...\n" unless $goal;

my @roots;
for (@ARGV) {
    unless (exists $root{$_}) {
        warn "$0: unknown root key '$_'\n";
        next;
    }
    push @roots, "$root{$_}\\";
}
die "$0: nothing to search!\n" unless @roots;

findkey lc($goal), \@roots;
```

You might call it like so:

```
findkey perl HKEY_CURRENT_USER
```

Programming with Visual Basic

Visual Basic used to be regarded as a toy language, in large part because that's what it was. In true Microsoft tradition, though, it has been continually enhanced, revised, tweaked, and improved to the point where it's a real honest-to-goodness programming tool. While hard-core programmers may look down their noses at any language with "Basic" in its name, many administrators have come to know and love VB because it makes it extremely easy to construct robust applications with the full Windows look and feel.

Besides that, VB includes a wide range of components that allow it to easily connect to large databases, generate custom reports, and do a number of other things that are much more difficult to do in C++ (or even Perl, unless you're already fluent). A good friend of mine described VB by saying that its learning curve didn't reach as high as Visual C++, but it was a lot flatter at the bottom.

While you could use VB to write a tool whose purpose was to manipulate the Registry, it's more likely that you'll need to add Registry access to a VB program you already have (or are writing). Accordingly, in this section I focus on how to get data into and out of the Registry; that means opening and closing keys, enumerating keys and values, querying and setting values, and deleting keys and values. If you want to do anything else, you can do so using the API definitions discussed next.

As in the sections on C++ and Perl above, I'm going to assume that you're already familiar with VB and how to use it. If you're really interested in learning lots more about Registry programming in any language—but particularly VB—I recommend *Inside the Windows 95 Registry* (O'Reilly & Associates).

Talking with the Outside World in VB

VB is arguably the most successful programming tool ever developed.* Its success is primarily because it's easy to write programs that actually accomplish something. This ease of use in turn comes from the ways that VB lets you extend its base functionality to add new features. First of all, you can write new procedures and functions in VB itself. This allows you to build your own library of reusable pieces you can apply to new programs as you write them.

That's nothing very new, though; almost all other languages offer some support for recycling code so it can be reused. VB also offers a sophisticated component model based on ActiveX controls; almost any functionality can be wrapped up into an ActiveX control so that other VB programmers can just drag and drop it into their own programs. This is part of the reason why so many VB programs sport sophisticated interfaces, with things such as calendars, spreadsheet-style grids, and other frills. Since those elements can be packaged and reused, many programmers do just that. As a side effect of this componentization, there's a healthy market for selling VB components, and this acts as a further spur to component development.

DLL interfaces

Besides its component support, though, VB allows you to load any Windows DLL and call the routines it exports. Most of its support for Win32 API routines is actually implemented this way; there are function declarations that map a VB routine or symbol name to an exported symbol in a DLL somewhere. Here's an example:

---

* In terms of sales, anyway; let's not start any religious wars about what the One True Language is or should be.

```
Declare Function RegOpenKey Lib "advapi32.dll" _
    Alias "RegOpenKeyA" _
    (ByVal hKey As Long, ByVal lpctstr As String, _
    phkey As Long) As Long
```

This tells VB that you're declaring a function named RegOpenKey. The actual implementation of the function lives in the *advapi32.dll* library, and the function in that DLL is actually named RegOpenKeyA. (Remember, all the Registry routines have both ANSI and Unicode variants, but VB usually uses the ANSI versions.) The rest of the function declaration contains the argument list. This particular function takes three parameters:

- hKey is declared as a Long, and the ByVal keyword tells VB to pass the value of the parameter, not its location in memory. This distinction is critical, since the DLL being called expects data to arrive in a particular format.

- lpctstr is declared as a String; because it's also declared with ByVal, its contents are passed instead of its address. There's another reason why the string is declared with ByVal: VB uses its own string format, which the standard Win32 DLLs can't decipher. In this case, the ByVal keyword tells VB to convert the string into a standard ANSI string, with a NULL terminator, before passing it to the DLL.

- phkey is not passed by value; instead, its address is passed in to the DLL so that the DLL can return a handle to the newly opened key. When you don't use ByVal, VB assumes you're passing parameters by reference. You can also use the ByRef keyword to explicitly declare that you want something passed by reference.

The last element in the declaration is the return type of the function. The Win32 API standard is that all functions return a long integer, which corresponds to VB's Long type, so that's what RegOpenKey returns.

A few more subtleties

The VB documentation includes an entire chapter on how to construct the correct VB function declaration for any C or C++ DLL routine. Even after reading this chapter several times, you may find the details confusing. Rather than send you back to read it again, let's see if I can boil the rules down to their essentials.

First of all, you've already seen the basic rule above: if you're passing in a variable the API routine fills in and returns, you need to pass it by reference, not with ByVal. Strings are the exceptions to this: you always need to include ByVal so that VB knows it should convert strings to and from its own funny format instead of passing them on to the unsuspecting Win32 DLLs.

Programming with Visual Basic

The corollary to this rule is that you use `ByVal` when you're passing in a non-string parameter the API routine can't modify. Examples include the `HKEY` you must pass in for all the Registry routines or the `REGSAM` and `DWORD` values you use with `RegCreateKeyEx`.

In C, C++, and Perl, you probably use `NULL` sometimes to indicate that you don't want to supply a value for a parameter. The Registry API routines allow this for most parameters, but you'll quickly run into trouble if you do something like the following:

```
Call RegCreateKeyEx(HKEY_CURRENT_USER, "SOFTWARE\LJL\ArmorMail\PFXLocation",
                    0,                  'reserved
                    0,                  'class -- but it's WRONG!
                    0,                  'dwOptions
                    KEY_READ,
                    0,                  'security attributes -- WRONG AGAIN
                    resultKey,
                    disposition);
```

This seems perfectly legal; after all, it's a well-known fact that `NULL` is just a textual representation of 0. Unfortunately, this code isn't passing a pointer whose value is `NULL`. Instead, you're passing a pointer that points to a `NULL`. This is like the difference between sending a letter to your spouse and sending a letter about your spouse—the consequences can be unintended and possibly severe.

Here's the correct way to call `RegCreateKeyEx`. The fix is to add `ByVal` to the two pointer parameters (`lpSecurityAttributes` and `lpClass`). This tells VB that you really want to pass `NULL` pointers instead of pointers *to* `NULL`:

```
Call RegCreateKeyEx(HKEY_CURRENT_USER, "SOFTWARE\LJL\ArmorMail\PFXLocation",
                    0,                  'reserved
                    ByVal 0,            'class
                    0,                  'dwOptions
                    KEY_READ,
                    ByVal 0,            'security attributes
                    resultKey,
                    disposition);
```

Here's another bear trap that's waiting to snap shut on your ankle. Some of the Registry APIs accept raw data. For example, `RegSetValueEx` accepts the value contents you want to store as a block of type `BYTE`. Since VB doesn't know whether you're storing a `DWORD`, a string, or something else, the function prototype doesn't specify a definite type. VB includes a rough equivalent, the `As Any` keyword. When you use it, you're telling VB not to check the datatype of that parameter, which is tantamount to begging for trouble.

The solution recommended by Ron Petrusha in *Inside the Windows 95 Registry* is to declare aliases of functions that normally might use `As Any`; e.g., this declaration adds an alias for `RegSetValueEx` that "knows" it's storing a string value:

```
Declare Function RegSetStringValue Lib "advapi32.dll" _
    Alias "RegSetValueExA" _
    (ByVal hKey As Long, ByVal lpValueName As String, _
    ByVal Reserved As Long, ByVal dwType As Long, _
    ByVal lpData As String, ByVal cbData As Long) As Long
```

This makes it possible to declare the `lpData` parameter as a string so the VB compiler can check it for correctness. You can also define similar aliases for setting `DWORD`, `REG_MULTI_SZ`, or `REG_BINARY` data.

Using the Registry with VB

Now that you know what to watch out for when calling the Registry API routines, it's time to move on to actually writing some Registry code in VB.

The VBA functions

VB includes a set of functions for accessing the Registry. Unfortunately, they are so limited as to be practically worthless:

- You may only access keys under HKCU\Software\VB and VBA Program Settings. Period. This is a severe limitation if you're writing programs that need to access keys that aren't under HKCU.

- The provided routines can work only with one level of keys, so if you open a key named HKCU\Software\VB and VBA Program Settings\MyStuff, you can't access values under HKCU\Software\VB and VBA Program Settings\MyStuff\CurrentVersion.

- You can store and retrieve only string values: no binary or `DWORD` data allowed.

These limitations came about because the built-in Registry routines were designed to be seamlessly compatible when the compiled VB applications were run on Win3.x, Win9x, Windows NT, and 2000. This means that the functionality is restricted to the lowest common denominator. There's no reason to use them unless you want your programs to run under Win3.x; not likely if you're reading this book. I won't talk about them any further.

Using WINREG.BAS

Even though the built-in VB functions are unsuitable for most uses, you still have another alternative: you can use the original Win32 API routines with suitable VB function declarations. If you follow the rules in the previous section, you could easily write your own set of VB function declarations for the Registry API, but doing so would be wasteful, because Andrew Schulman has already done so. *WINREG.BAS* (available from the O'Reilly web site at *http://www.oreilly.com*) contains declarations for all the Registry API routines discussed in this chapter (except for `RegQueryMultipleValues`), plus some additional routines you may find useful. You need this file to use the examples later in the chapter, and you'll probably want to use it in your own projects.

> You can also use a third-party VB control that encapsulates Registry functions into a higher-level set of routines. The Desaware Registry Control (*http://www.desaware.com*) is one example, but there are others. The chief drawback to these controls is that they cost money, but they can save you time if you're not entirely comfortable with using the raw Registry routines.

Since all *WINREG.BAS* does is put a VB-compatible face on the API routines described earlier in the chapter, I'm not going to reiterate how those routines work or what their parameters are. Instead, let's see them in action.

Example: A RegEdit Clone

You may have noticed that *RegEdit* looks like a pretty simple program. For the most part, it is; it has to gather small amounts of data from the user, then pass that data to one or another of the Registry API routines. In *Inside the Windows 95 Registry*, Ron Petrusha provides a *RegEdit* clone written in Visual Basic! It's not truly a clone; in fact, it doesn't do anything except display keys and values, but it does so with the familiar tree control, just like *RegEdit*. However, if you look at the clone in operation (see Figure 8-1), you'll be hard-pressed to tell the difference between the two.

Creating the initial tree

The first step in creating a *RegEdit* clone is to build the VB form definitions. Since that has nothing to do with the Registry, I won't talk about it here. (If you want to see the code, check out *http://windows.oreilly.com/registry*.) Instead, let's focus on the interesting stuff. The first block of interest is in the main form's `Load` method. It creates a new root key named "My Computer" in the tree list, then adds nodes for each root key:

```
Set nodRegTree = TreeView1.Nodes.Add("home", tvwChild, "HKCR", _
                                    "HKEY_CLASSES_ROOT", "closed", "open")
Set nodRegTree = TreeView1.Nodes.Add("home", tvwChild, "HKCU", _
                                    "HKEY_CURRENT_USER", "closed", "open")
Set nodRegTree = TreeView1.Nodes.Add("home", tvwChild, "HKLM", _
                                    "HKEY_LOCAL_MACHINE", "closed", "open")
Set nodRegTree = TreeView1.Nodes.Add("home", tvwChild, "HKU", "HKEY_USERS", _
                                    "closed", "open")
If blnWinNT4 Then
   Set nodRegTree = TreeView1.Nodes.Add("home", tvwChild, "HKCC", _
```

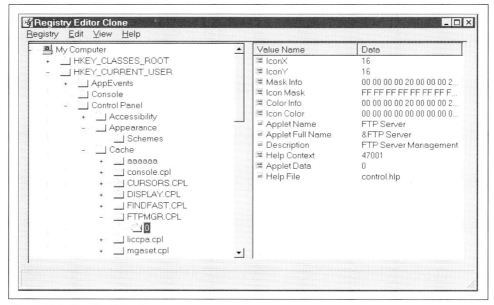

Figure 8-1. The RegEdit clone

```
                                       "HKEY_CURRENT_CONFIG", "closed", "open")
   Set nodRegTree = TreeView1.Nodes.Add("home", tvwChild, "HKDD", _
                                       "HKEY_DYN_DATA", "closed", "open")
End If
```

Once the tree view is set up, the next step is to make any root key that has subkeys expandable. Part of this is making sure there's enough space to store the name of the longest subkey name that might ever appear:

```
For intctr = 1 To TreeView1.Nodes.Count
    strNode = TreeView1.Nodes.Item(intctr).Key
    If strNode <> "home" Then
       ' Convert node abbreviation to handle
       Select Case strNode
          Case "HKCR"
             hKey = HKEY_CLASSES_ROOT
          Case "HKCU"
             hKey = HKEY_CURRENT_USER
          Case "HKLM"
             hKey = HKEY_LOCAL_MACHINE
          Case "HKU"
             hKey = HKEY_USERS
          Case "HKCC"
             hKey = HKEY_CURRENT_CONFIG
          Case "HKDD"
             hKey = HKEY_DYN_DATA
       End Select

       ' Get size of longest subkey for each key and use that to size the
```

```
            ' retrieval buffer
            Call RegQueryInfoKey(hKey, 0, 0, 0, 0, lngLenSubkeyName, 0, 0, 0, 0, 0, 0)
            lngLenSubkeyName = lngLenSubkeyName + 1
            strSubkeyName = String(lngLenSubkeyName + 1, 0)

            ' Retrieve one subkey; if that succeeds, get one subkey to find out if
            ' there are any subkeys for this node.
            If RegEnumKeyEx(hKey, 0, strSubkeyName, lngLenSubkeyName, 0&, _
                            strClass, ByVal 0, ByVal 0&) = ERROR_SUCCESS Then
                strSubkeyName = Left(strSubkeyName, lngLenSubkeyName)
                'Add node to top-level key so icon appears with a "+"
                Set nodRegTree = TreeView1.Nodes.Add(strNode, tvwChild, _
                                 , strSubkeyName, "closed", "open")
            End If
        End If
    Next
```

Notice the use of **ByVal 0** to pass **NULL** pointers in the call to **RegEnumKeyEx**. There's another trick here, too: the call to **RegQueryInfoKey** gets the length of the longest subkey name, and that length allocates the buffer that holds the subkey name returned by **RegEnumKeyEx**. This ensures that the buffer is always long enough to hold the name, even if the longest name comes up first.

This code alone displays the initial tree, but it's dead; users won't be able to expand or contract nodes in the tree as they can with *RegEdit*. Time for some additional code.

Expanding the tree

The next step is to allow users to expand tree nodes that have subkeys. The snippet in Example 8-14, taken from the tree view's **Expand** method, does just this. The code performs five basic operations:

1. If the user's trying to expand a subkey, the code opens it. This means no subkeys are opened until the user explicitly asks for them, which is a big performance win.

2. It calls **RegQueryInfoKey** to find out how many subkeys there are. In addition, it gets the length of the longest subkey name.

3. If the number of elements in this node doesn't match the number of subkeys, or if the node's **Tag** field indicates that it was collapsed, it's time to expand the tree by enumerating each subkey of the target and adding it as a node. In this step, the subkey count obtained in Step 2 is invaluable.

4. While traversing subkeys of the expanded key, any subkey that has at least one subkey itself is marked as having children. This forces the tree view control to mark them with the "+" icon so users know that node can be expanded.

5. If any keys were opened in Step 1, they're closed again.

Example 8-14. Expanding a Node in the Registry Tree

```
' If we're expanding a subkey, open it. This allows us to only open a key
' when the user clicks on it.
If Len(Trim(strSubkey)) > 0 Then
   Call RegOpenKey(hRootKey, strSubkey, hKey)
   blnKeyOpen = True
Else
   hKey = hRootKey
End If

' Find out how many subkeys and values there are and their maximum name lengths
Call RegQueryInfoKey(hKey, 0, 0, 0, lngSubkeys, lngLenSubkeyName, _
                    0, lngValues, lngLenValueName, lngLenValueData, 0, 0)

' If the node isn't fully expanded, go ahead and expand it.
If (Val(Node.Tag)) <> 1 Or (Node.Children <> lngSubkeys) Then

   ' First, delete existing nodes
   lngChildren = Node.Children
   For intctr = 1 To lngChildren
      TreeView1.Nodes.Remove Node.Child.Index
   Next

   ' Enumerate all this key's subkeys, adding each one as a node.
   For lngIndex = 0 To lngSubkeys - 1
      lngLenSubkey = lngLenSubkeyName + 1
      strSubkey = String(lngLenSubkey, 0)

      ' get the IngIndex'th key
      Call RegEnumKeyEx(hKey, lngIndex, strSubkey, lngLenSubkey, 0&, 0, 0, 0)
      strSubkey = Left(strSubkey, lngLenSubkey)

      ' Add it as a tree node
      Set nodRegTree = TreeView1.Nodes.Add(Node.Index, tvwChild, , strSubkey, _
                                     "closed", "open")

      ' If this node has at least one subkey, add a child to it to enable it
      ' to be expanded too
      Call RegOpenKey(hKey, strSubkey, hChildKey)
      Call RegQueryInfoKey(hChildKey, 0, 0, 0, lngSubSubkeys, lngLenSubkey, _
                0, 0, 0, 0, 0, 0)
      If lngSubSubkeys > 0 Then
         lngLenSubkey = lngLenSubkey + 1
         strSubkey = String(lngLenSubkey, 0)
         Call RegEnumKeyEx(hChildKey, 0, strSubkey, lngLenSubkey, 0&, 0, 0, 0)
         Call RegCloseKey(hChildKey)
         ' Add to most recent key
         lngNodeIndex = nodRegTree.Index
         Set nodRegTree = TreeView1.Nodes.Add(lngNodeIndex, tvwChild, , _
                                     strSubkey, "closed", "open")
      End If
```

Example 8-14. Expanding a Node in the Registry Tree (continued)

```
   Next
   Node.Tag = 1
End If

' If we opened a key earlier, close it
If blnKeyOpen Then Call RegCloseKey(hKey)
```

Displaying values

So now our clone can display the root keys and expand them when users request it, but what about displaying the values? To get value-display capability, the code needs to do something when the user clicks on a tree node. That means adding a `NodeClick` event handler. After some setup and variable declarations (which I'm not showing here), our `NodeClick` routine starts by preflighting the value list and opening the requested key:

```
' Clear current contents of ListView control
ListView1.ListItems.Clear

' Open the registry key attached to this node
If Len(Trim(strPath)) > 0 Then
   Call RegOpenKey(hRootKey, strPath, hKey)
   blnOpenKey = True
Else
   hKey = hRootKey
End If
```

The next step is to find out how many values there are and how big the largest value name and contents are. Armed with that data, it's possible to display a default value and stop if there aren't actually any values attached to this key:

```
' Get value count, max value name length, and max value contents length
Call RegQueryInfoKey(hKey, 0, 0, 0, 0, 0, 0, lngValues, _
                lngMaxNameLen, lngMaxValueLen, 0, 0)

' Add default value entry if there aren't any real values present
If lngValues = 0 Then
   Set objLItem = ListView1.ListItems.Add(, , "<Default>", "string", "string")
   Exit Sub
End If
```

If there are real values, the earlier call to `RegQueryInfoKey` indicates what the biggest value data block is, so the data buffer can be sized accordingly:

```
' Redimension the byte array for value data using the max value contents length
ReDim bytValue(lngMaxValueLen)
```

Now the fun begins. The code must enumerate over every value of this subkey, getting both its name and its contents. Each value has a type, and it would be nice to display an appropriate icon in the left-most column of the value list, just like *RegEdit*:

```
' Enumerate all value entries of this subkey
For lngIndex = 0 To lngValues - 1
   lngNameLen = lngMaxNameLen + 1
   ' make sure our buffer's big enough
   strValueName = String(lngMaxNameLen, 0)
   lngValueLen = lngMaxValueLen
   Call RegEnumValue(hKey, lngIndex, strValueName, lngNameLen, 0, _
                     lngDataType, bytValue(0), lngValueLen)

   ' Determine icon type
   Select Case lngDataType
      Case REG_SZ, REG_MULTI_SZ, REG_EXPAND_SZ
         strIcon = "string"
      Case Else
         strIcon = "bin"
   End Select

   ' if it's empty, substitute "<Default>"; otherwise, use the name
   If lngNameLen = 0 Then
      strValueName = ""
      Set objLItem = ListView1.ListItems.Add(, , "< Default >", strIcon, strIcon)
   Else
      strValueName = Left(strValueName, lngNameLen)
      Set objLItem = ListView1.ListItems.Add(, , strValueName, strIcon, strIcon)
   End If
```

Users would hate our clone if it displayed everything in binary or hex, so it should neatly format and display the value data, no matter its type. In all cases, a call to **RegQueryValueEx**, combined with some formatting tweaking depending on the datatype, achieves this happy result. Notice that for binary data there's no call to **RegQueryValueEx**; that's because the earlier call to **RegEnumValue** loaded the data directly into the **bytValue** array:

```
' Format and display data
Select Case lngDataType

   ' for a string, get the value and display it directly
   Case REG_SZ, REG_EXPAND_SZ
      strTemp = String(lngValueLen, 0)
      Call RegQueryValueEx(hKey, strValueName, 0, 0, ByVal strTemp, _
                           lngValueLen)
      objLItem.SubItems(1) = Left(strTemp, lngValueLen)

   ' for a multistring, get the value and pick it apart
   Case REG_MULTI_SZ
      strTemp = String(lngValueLen, 0)
      Call RegQueryValueEx(hKey, strValueName, 0, 0, ByVal strTemp, _
                           lngValueLen)
      strTemp = Left(strTemp, lngValueLen - 2)
      intPos = 1
      While intPos > 0
         intPos = InStr(1, strTemp, Chr(0))
         If intPos > 1 Then
```

```
                    strTemp = Left(strTemp, intPos - 1) & "|" & _
                              Mid(strTemp, intPos + 1)
            End If
        Wend
        objLItem.SubItems(1) = strTemp

      ' for binary or BIG_ENDIAN values, display  in hex
      Case REG_BINARY, REG_DWORD_BIG_ENDIAN
         strTemp = ""
         For intctr = 0 To lngValueLen - 1
            strHex = Hex(bytValue(intctr))
            If Len(strHex) = 1 Then strHex = "0" & strHex
            strTemp = strTemp & strHex & " "
         Next
         objLItem.SubItems(1) = strTemp

      ' for a DWORD, display as a DWORD
      Case REG_DWORD
         lngLenDW = Len(lngTemp)
         Call RegQueryValueEx(hKey, strValueName, 0, 0, lngTemp, lngLenDW)
         objLItem.SubItems(1) = lngTemp
      End Select
   Next
```

The last—but not least—step is to clean up any messes made before this point:

```
' Close the key if we opened it
If blnOpenKey Then Call RegCloseKey(hKey)
```

9

Administering the Registry

When you're responsible for administering computers—whether one or many—you quickly find that much of what you do on a daily basis is miscellanea. You create new accounts, remove old ones, figure out why your backup tape drive is dead, and so forth. It would be nice if your whole career could revolve around orderly, planned upgrades, maintenance, and migrations, but those little tasks are important too. This chapter introduces you to several small tasks related to managing the Registry. While none of them is a full-time activity, all of them are worth doing.

Setting Defaults for New User Accounts

Windows NT was designed from the start to support multiple user accounts sharing a single computer. Unlike DOS and Windows 3.x, Windows NT provided a way (through the Registry, actually) to keep individual settings for each user. However, the original versions of NT didn't provide any way for these settings to be shared between computers, and there were no mechanisms for collecting all of a user's settings data in a single place.

NT 4.0 was the first version of NT to support the concept of *user profiles*. Like the profiles in Win95, NT 4.0 profiles contain a user's desktop environment, application settings, and other preferences. These profiles can be configured to roam from computer to computer, so that users can have their own personalized environment follow them to every machine they log onto. In addition, administrators can configure these profiles to prevent users from changing all or part of the settings, thus making it easier to set up shared computer labs and other facilities where it's important to protect machines against tampering.

Windows 2000 expands the profile concept by allowing you to store more data in the profile, as well as by supporting folder redirection, a trick that allows each user's "My Documents" folder to appear on their desktop no matter where they log on, even though it's actually stored on a remote server somewhere else. In addition to typical user files stored in a server-based home directory, Windows 2000 profiles can hold application-specific data like custom template or dictionary files, temporary files (like browser caches) that follow the user around, favorites, and other preference information.

In Windows 2000 and Windows NT, the profile consists of the contents of HKCU (stored in *ntuser.dat*), plus information from the user's local profile file (either *%systemroot%\profiles*\userName or *\Documents and Settings*\userName).

Under Windows 2000

Microsoft recommends a simple strategy for preconfiguring user accounts under Windows 2000. The Windows NT approach (which you'll see in the next section) doesn't take into account the expanded contents of the profile. Here's what to do:

1. Create a new local user account on a target workstation. This account holds the settings you want the preconfigured account to use. For example, if you're building a new account to hold defaults for the legal department, name the account something like "Legal Profile."

2. Log on to the newly created account, then apply whatever settings you want to be in force for that account.

3. Log on as an administrator and use the Active Directory management tools (including the Group Policy snap-in) to apply whatever policy settings you want tacked onto that class of accounts. You can also apply group settings if desired.

Once you've configured the profile, you're ready to move it to the servers your users will actually be using. You do this with the Profiles tab of the System control panel:

1. Open the System control panel (Start → Settings → Control Panels → System).

2. Switch to the User Profiles tab (see Figure 9-1), then select the profile you want to copy.

3. Click the Copy To button: the Copy To dialog then appears. Put the local or network path where you want the profile to be stored in the Copy profile to field.

4. Use the Change... button in the Permitted to use control group to specify who can use this profile. Normally, you should specify that Everyone can use the

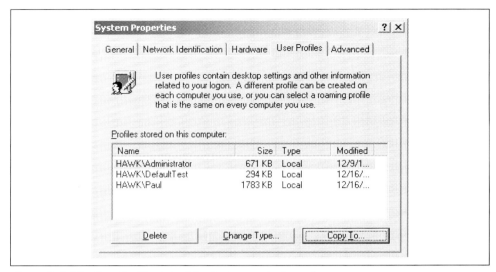

Figure 9-1. The User Profiles tab of the System control panel

profile; if you do, the profile is used automatically as the default profile for new users.

You must also specify where the users' profile directory is by using either the Local Users and Groups or Active Directory Users and Computers snap-in; you can do so before or after you actually move the profile:

1. Open the appropriate snap-in and find the user path you want to modify.
2. Open the account's Properties dialog with the Action → Properties command or by right-clicking the account and choosing Properties from the context menu.
3. Switch to the Profile tab of the properties dialog, then enter the path to the user's profile directory. This must match the path you entered in Step 3 in the previous list.

NT4 Under Windows NT

When you install Windows NT on a machine, the system uses a default profile to provide settings for your user accounts. The first time a newly created account logs in, the default profile is copied into HKCU, thus making the new account inherit the default settings. Unfortunately, there's no direct way to change settings in this default profile. You can use the System Policy Editor (as described in Chapter 6, *Using the System Policy Editor*) to set policies for the "Default User" account on Windows NT machines but if you want to change a setting that's not in

Setting Defaults for New User Accounts 299

one of the policy templates—say, the default currency format or the list of predefined URLs that Internet Explorer stores—you have two choices. You can create a new policy template that contains the new settings you want to apply, or you can edit the default user profile directly.

NT stores the default user profile in a file. On individual workstations and servers, the profile is stored in *%systemroot%\profiles\Default User*. You can also force the default profile to apply to all domain logons by putting it in the *NETLOGON* share of your domain controller.* When it's there, the file must be named *Ntuser.dat*. Whatever settings are in this file are applied to new user accounts, but they won't affect existing accounts. *Ntuser.dat* is really just a Registry hive; when a new account logs on interactively for the first time, NT copies the contents of the hive to HKCU, then writes the changes to the appropriate subkey of HKU. By changing what's in the initial hive, you affect what settings go into that user's HKCU when he logs on.

Because the default user profile is just a Registry hive, you can edit it with *RegEdt32*. Here's what to do:

1. Start *RegEdt32*. When it opens, open up the HKU window and select the HKU root key.

2. Use the Registry → Load Hive... menu command to select the default user profile you want to edit. You can open *%systemroot%\profiles\Default User* directly, or you can edit *NTuser.man* if it's available.

3. When *RegEdt32* asks for a key name, make up any name that reminds you what the hive is for. I usually use "DefaultUserProfile." *RegEdt32* then imports the hive and attaches it under the name you supply.

4. Select the new hive key and use the Security → Permissions... command to add Everyone:Read access to the key and its subkeys. This enables the profile-sharing mechanism to copy keys from the default profile to users' HKCU.

5. Use *RegEdt32* to make the desired changes to subkeys of your new hive. As you make changes, they are stored transparently in the hive file.

6. Once you've finished editing all the hive keys, use the Registry → Unload Hive command to detach the hive. Until you do this, no other computer or user can get access to the changes you've made.

---

* To do this, you need to use the "Copy To" button on the User Profiles tab of the System control panel to move the profile from your local machine to the domain controller's *NETLOGON* share.

Using Initialization File Mapping

In Chapter 1, *A Gentle Introduction to the Registry*, I described how the Registry evolved from its humble parentage of INI files. A surprising number of Windows 2000 and NT installations are still running 16-bit Win 3.1 applications that don't support the Registry, and a surprising number of 32-bit applications still rely on the old INI file structure, despite the fact that using the Registry is one of the requirements for getting the coveted "Designed for Windows" logo from Microsoft.

Since there's no way to upgrade skanky old 16-bit applications to use the Registry,* you might think that you're stuck forever with the mess of tracking, backing up, and protecting a mess of INI files. Not so. Windows NT included a feature called *initialization file mapping* (I'll call it just "mapping" from now on) that allows you to force Registry-unaware programs to load and save configuration data in the Registry instead of in an INI file. Windows 2000 implements mapping too, using the same techniques and keys originally made available for NT.

The default OS install already includes mappings for several system components, including the Windows clock desk accessory, the bundled backup application, and even *RegEdt32*. Mappings aren't just for 16-bit applications; rather, they're for any application—16- or 32-bit—that doesn't include code to read and write Registry data. Of course, mapping's not required; applications that depend on INI files can work just fine without having the files mapped. In fact, unless you explicitly take action to map these files, they remain unmapped, and their normal INI file usage continues without interruption.

How Does Mapping Work?

Mapping works because Windows 2000 and NT trap the private profile API routines I mentioned in Chapter 1. Windows applications and components ordinarily use these calls to get and set data stored in INI files, but when there's a mapping entry, the kernel first checks for the presence of a mapping key. If one exists, and if it points to a key that contains data, that data is returned to the caller. If there's no mapping key, or if it points to an empty or non-existent Registry key, the kernel tries to read the data from the INI file. The caller need never be aware that the data didn't come from the requested file.

Mapping occurs only when there's a mapping key in place. These keys are stored beneath the HKLM\SOFTWARE\Microsoft\Windows NT\CurrentVersion\IniFileMapping subkey. If you look there, you'll notice a number of subkeys with names such as *Clock.INI*, *regedt32.INI*, and *ntbackup.ini*. These keys tie sections of

---

* Chapter 5 of *Inside the Windows 95 Registry* actually explains how to use the Win95 Registry from 16-bit and DOS apps, but there's no time machine that allows unmodified applications to do so.

the old Win 3.1-style INI files to keys in the Registry so that older components continue to find their settings.

Application programmers and administrators are free to create new mappings between any INI file and any key in the Registry. This allows you to move settings data to the Registry where it properly belongs. Once it's there, you can edit, save, massage, and manage it using the skills you've learned throughout this book.

Time for a real-life story: a client had licensed several hundred seats for a popular email application. This app had a 32-bit version, but it didn't use the Registry. I created a mapping for the program's settings, then built a system policy template (see Chapter 6 for details) so they could centrally control how users set up their mail clients. Everyone walked away happy.

Setting Up Your Own Mappings

In an ideal world, all the applications on your computers would be 32-bit, Registry-aware, Windows 2000-savvy programs. Unfortunately, relatively few people have that luxury. For the rest of us, though, it's easy to add mapping keys to stealthily allow those applications to use Registry keys instead of sections in an INI file; best of all, you can do so without any changes to the application that owns the INI file.

If you've ever opened an INI file, you know that it's divided into sections. Section names are enclosed by square brackets, and they contain name/value pairs. The whole arrangement looks like this sample from an imaginary data security package's INI file:

```
[Encryption]
DefaultSigAlgorithm=RSAWithSHA1
DefaultEncryptionAlgorithm=DES3-EDE-CBC
WipeFilesWhenDone=1
```

In this example, "Encryption" is the section name, and "DefaultSigAlgorithm," "DefaultEncryptionAlgorithm," and "WipeFilesWhenDone" are the value names.

Adding the mapping key

You may map any or all sections of any INI file to a Registry key. To do so, you must add a new subkey to HKLM\SOFTWARE\Microsoft\Windows NT\CurrentVersion\IniFileMapping. This subkey should have the same name as the INI file you're mapping; for example, to remap a file named *ccmail.ini* you add a new subkey with that name to the IniFileMapping key.

If you just add a new mapping key by itself, nothing will happen. This is because the named subkey just tells Windows 2000 to watch for access to the INI file with the same name; it doesn't tell where the data are actually stored in the Registry.

You specify the location (or locations) by creating values underneath the key. Each of these values should have a name that matches a section in the INI file. These section names are combined with the name of the parent key to help the profile API routines figure out what data you're requesting.

To map the key in the previous example, create a new key named HKLM\SOFTWARE\Microsoft\Windows NT\CurrentVersion\IniFileMapping\Crypto.INI. Under that key, add a value named Encryption. The combination of these two values indicates that any attempt to access the "Encryption" section of *crypto.ini* should instead look in the Registry.

The value you give to these section keys tells the OS where the real data is stored in the Registry. Let's say that our data security program stores its data in HKLM\Software\Crypto\CurrentVersion\Settings. To complete the mapping started in the previous paragraph, use this Registry path as the contents of the Encryption value. By adding values under HKLM\Software\Crypto\CurrentVersion\Settings with names that match the value assignments in the INI file (e.g., DefaultSigAlgorithm, WipeFilesWhenDone, etc.), you can achieve the equivalent effect of actually using an INI file.

When the application attempts to open the *crypto.ini* file, the mapping key under CurrentVersion\IniFileMapping redirects the PrivateProfile calls to the Registry key specified. Calls to fetch profile settings from the Encryption section are redirected to HKLM\Software\Crypto\CurrentVersion\Settings.

Mapping key tricks

There are a couple of tricks that apply to building mapping key entries. First of all, you can specify a default value that handles any sections that don't have explicit mappings. Going back to our data security program example, if you added an Encryption key, Windows 2000 still wouldn't know how to map requests for data in the "Signature" section. However, by adding a default value (which appears as "<No Name>" or "Default") to the root of the subkey, you can tell the operating system which key to use for any sections that don't have their own section keys defined.

There are also several special symbols to use in the values of section keys. Table 9-1 shows these symbols; you'll see them in action in the next section.

Table 9-1. Special Strings for Initializing File Mappings

Symbol	What It Means
SYS	Store data under a path relative to HKLM\Software; for example, SYS:Netscape expands to HKLM\Software\Netscape.
USR	Store data under a path relative to HKCU; for example, USR:Software\Qualcomm\Eudora expands to HKCU\Software\Qualcomm\Eudora.

Table 9-1. Special Strings for Initializing File Mappings (continued)

Symbol	What It Means
!	Store data for this named section both in the Registry and the INI file; when data is written to one, it will be written to the other.
@	Never read data from the INI file, even if no matching data is found in the Registry.
#	When a new user logs in, copy the section's settings from the INI file into the specified Registry location.

A mapping sample

The Entrust data security package from Entrust Technologies (*http://www.entrust.com*) comes in both 16- and 32-bit versions, as well as versions that run under Unix and the MacOS. To preserve a consistent set of source code, the Entrust engineers decided to stick with INI files instead of using the Registry. Here's the process I followed to build a set of mappings to replace Entrust's INI files with Registry data.

1. I created a new subkey named *entrust.ini* under HKLM\SOFTWARE\Microsoft\Windows NT\CurrentVersion\IniFileMapping.

2. Since Entrust settings are user-specific, I created a new key, HKCU\Software\Entrust, to hold the settings data. I also added subkeys named Other and EntrustSettings to actually hold the data.

3. The interesting user-specific data in the Entrust INI file is all in the "Entrust Settings" section. To map it, I added a subkey named Entrust Settings under entrust.ini and gave it a default value of @USR:Software\Entrust\EntrustSettings. This makes Windows 2000 map data stored in the "Entrust Settings" section to the key of the same name; the @ prevents the mapping code from reading data from the INI file.

4. I gave the *entrust.ini* subkey a default value of #USR:Software\Entrust\Other. This forces Windows 2000 NT to copy the INI file's data for new users and to store data for all other sections of *entrust.ini* in HKCU\Software\Entrust\Other.

As a finishing touch, I saved the mapping keys to a *.REG* file using *RegEdit* so I could quickly distribute them to users throughout our network.

Limiting Remote Registry Access

In Windows NT 3.51 and earlier, any user could access the Registry on any machine over the network. From a security standpoint, this was much too liberal; NT 4.0 (and 3.51 with SP4 or SP5) defaults to allowing only members of the

Administrators group to access the Registry remotely. This is considerably more secure than the original permissions.

However, this setting may not suit your environment. Sometimes allowing any member of the Administrators group access is still too permissive, since some high-value machines may warrant the added security of allowing only a single account or group to access their registries over the network. Conversely, you may want to proactively allow other users and groups to remotely connect to, and edit, Registry data on some machines.

Turning Off Remote Access Entirely

Windows 2000 introduces a new system service (the Remote Registry Service) that actually handles remote requests for Registry access. If you turn this service off, no incoming requests are accepted, period. By default, the service is started automatically at boot time, but if you disable it using the Computer Management snap-in (or stop it manually), no one can connect remotely and flip through your Registry.

Limiting Access to Authorized Users

In Windows 2000 and NT 4.0 , you can control which users, groups, and services may access the Registry on a particular machine by setting the ACL for a single Registry key, namely HKLM\SYSTEM\CurrentControlSet\Control\SecurePipeServers\winreg. The kernel grants remote access to a machine's Registry only to those entities named in the ACL attached to the key.

Before proceeding, I should point out that this restriction key controls access to the Registry as a whole. You may still enforce more stringent controls on individual keys. For example, you can grant one group of users access to the Registry by setting the restriction key permissions accordingly, but if you put access controls on other keys those users can see, the most restrictive set of controls wins out.

Creating the restriction key

Before you can take advantage of this feature, the restriction key must exist on your computer. By default, Windows 2000 Server and Advanced Server (as well as NT Server 4.0) include this key, and administrators have Full Control access to it. If you don't have the key present, and you want to restrict access, you have to manually add the restriction key to your Registry. Here's what to do if you don't already have this key available:

1. Log in as Administrator (or an account with administrator privileges) and run *RegEdt32*. Navigate to HKLM\SYSTEM\CurrentControlSet\Control.

Limiting Remote Registry Access

2. Use the Edit → Add Key... command to add a new key named SecurePipeServers, then select it and use Edit → Add Key... again to add a new subkey named winreg to the SecurePipeServers key you just added.

3. Add a REG_SZ value named "Description" to the winreg subkey. Microsoft recommends that you give the description as "Registry server," but the exact contents are up to you.

Depending on your machine, you may find that you have some parts of the restriction key; for example, NT Workstation 4.0 with no service packs has the HKLM\SYSTEM\CurrentControlSet\Control\SecurePipeServers key itself, but it doesn't have the winreg subkey that's needed to actually make the restrictions work.

Setting permissions on the restriction key

Once you've verified that the winreg key exists, you can use the Security → Permissions... command to give it an ACL. The permissions applied to this key govern which users and groups can access your Registry via the network.

The Registry Key Permissions dialog (shown in Figure 9-2) allows you to change the users and groups that can access the key, as well as modify permissions for those users and groups that you choose to allow access. (If you need a refresher, see Chapter 5, *Using RegEdt32*.)

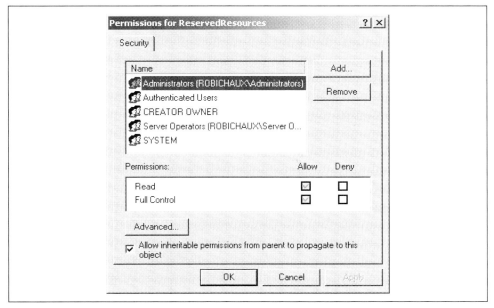

Figure 9-2. Setting Registry key permissions

Windows 2000 and NT 4.0 installations by default have permissions like those shown in Figure 9-2: the Administrators or Domain Admins group have Full Control rights, as will the system and the account that created the key. You can add new users and groups to this list and give them permissions commensurate with what you want them to do; for example, you might grant read-only access to all domain users while restricting Full Control access to a single named account. Change whatever else you want, but leave the system and CREATOR OWNER permissions alone; the kernel and Registry subsystem depend on these permissions to gain access to the key themselves.

> Some system services, such as the directory replicator and the print spooler, require remote access to the Registry. If you change the access control entries on the winreg key, these services may stop working. To avoid this problem, make sure the local accounts that run the replication service and the print spooler have explicit permissions in the ACL for the winreg key.

Allowing exceptions

You may also choose to loosen the leash on your Registry a bit by allowing exceptions to the access control rules specified by the permissions on the winreg key. These exceptions can be expressed in two ways: you can provide a list of keys that are exempt from the access controls, or you may specify a list of users who have free access to specific keys and their values.

Both methods are governed by values you add beneath HKLM\SYSTEM\CurrentControlSet\Control\SecurePipeServers\winreg\AllowedPaths.

- The Machine value, of type REG_MULTI_SZ, accepts a list of Registry paths. Any path listed here is visible to any machine on the network. By default, this key contains a set of paths that enable the replicator, print spooler, event logger, and kernel to function properly: System\CurrentControlSet\Control\ProductOptions and Software\Microsoft\Windows NT\CurrentVersion for the kernel, System\CurrentControlSet\Control\Print\Printers for the print spooler, System\CurrentControlSet\Services\Eventlog for the event logging service, and System\CurrentControlSet\Services\Replicator for the directory replicator. Windows 2000 machines also have a set of keys for Terminal Server (System\CurrentControlSet\Control\TerminalServer, TerminalServer\UserConfig, and TerminalServer\DefaultUserConfig) and content indexing (System\CurrentControlSet\Control\ContentIndex).

- The Users value (also a REG_MULTI_SZ) lists Registry paths that will be made available to any member of the Users or Domain Users group. This key is empty by default, and you should probably keep it that way unless you have a compelling reason to exempt individual users from the restriction key-imposed controls. In general, if you have a user who needs unusual access, it's better to put the user account into a group and assign the group a permission entry on the restriction key.

Access granted via either of these methods is still subordinate to permissions you've applied directly to individual keys. For example, if you use the Security → Permissions... command to apply Everyone:Read access to HKLM\Software\Netscape\Netscape Navigator, then add that same path to the Machine value, remote users won't be able to change the values under that subtree: the explicit ACL you've added overrides whatever access was granted by the Machine entry.

Fixing Registry Security ACLs in Windows NT

Every key in the Registry has an ACL. Unfortunately, many of those ACLs are unnecessarily permissive. For example, by default the Everyone account has write access to several keys that allow untrusted users to execute arbitrary programs—never a good idea. You can significantly improve your NT security posture by paying careful attention to a few simple steps.

> These steps aren't necessary in Windows 2000 because Microsoft has changed its default Registry ACLs to be more restrictive. Furthermore, you can use the Security Configuration Manager to apply even more restrictive settings by applying a particular security template.

First, a brief digression: every authenticated user is automatically a member of the Everyone group. On machines running NT 4.0 SP3 or later, these users are also members of the Authenticated Users group. Everyone also includes anonymous and guest accounts, though, so in general it's a wise idea to never grant Everyone: Full Control access to anything if you can prevent it.

On to the actual steps. First of all, apply the changes suggested earlier in the section "Limiting Remote Registry Access." Once you've done so, make sure that Everyone has only Read access on HKLM\SYSTEM\CurrentControlSet\Control\SecurePipeServers\winreg\AllowedPaths. This prevents an interloper from inserting her own allowed paths for anonymous access.

Next, follow Microsoft's suggestions from knowledge base article Q126713 and tighten the permissions on these three keys by limiting Everyone to Read access on them:

```
HKLM\SOFTWARE\Microsoft\Windows\CurrentVersion\Run
HKLM\SOFTWARE\Microsoft\Windows\CurrentVersion\RunOnce
HKLM\SOFTWARE\Microsoft\Windows\CurrentVersion\Uninstall
```

These keys specify programs to run when NT starts (Run and RunOnce) or when a program's uninstalled (Uninstall), so you don't want an attacker to be able to change them.

Likewise, you should remove the Server Operators group's Write permission on HKLM\System\CurrentControlSet\Services\Schedule. Normally, members of the Server Operators group have permission to schedule jobs, but these jobs are run under the SYSTEM account—making it possible for a Server Operators member to gain Administrator privileges. In the same vein, remove Server Operators' Write privilege on HKLM\Software\Microsoft\WindowsNT\CurrentVersion\Winlogon to prevent a similar attack on the UserInit and BootVerificationProgram values.

The next step is pretty open-ended: you should bolt down your Registry by restricting access wherever possible. The kicker is in knowing what's possible, and that varies from application to application. For example, Office 97 requires Everyone:Read on its own keys under HKLM\Software and HKCU\Software (plus write access to a number of other keys in HKLM and HKCU). Remove those permission, and some Office features stop working. The same is true for Internet Explorer and a wide range of other products. As you make changes to Registry key ACLs, be sure to test the applications you need to run to ensure their correct function before rolling out your changes to the entire network.

Instead of just randomly adjusting ACLs, I recommend you start with the ones in Table 9-2. These are excerpted from the canonical reference for Windows NT Registry ACLs, the "Windows NT Security Guidelines—A Study for NSA Research" white paper, written by Trusted System Services (*http://www.trustedsystems.com*) for the U.S. National Security Agency. The white paper is detailed and covers workstation, server, and network security settings, not just Registry ACLs. In the table, "Installers" refers to any groups you want to have permission to install application software, and "Apply to entire tree" means you should make the ACL change to all keys and subkeys in the specified path, not just the indicated key.

Table 9-2. Recommended Registry ACLs for Windows NT

Key Path	Permissions	Notes
\Software	Installers: Change Everyone: Read	Only accounts that can install software should have change rights to this tree. In particular, only installers should be able to create new subkeys.

Table 9-2. Recommended Registry ACLs for Windows NT (continued)

Key Path	Permissions	Notes
\Software\Classes	Installers: Add Everyone: Read	Upon installing Windows NT, set the ACLs on the entire Classes tree to Public: Read (plus the Common ACEs), then set the ACL on Classes key as noted. (This removes the INTERACTIVE entry from these ACLs.) This Registry tree holds various properties associated with applications, such as the correlation between the filename extension and the application defined to handle it. To contain potential spoofing threats, it seems prudent to limit these keys, although it may impact some applications.
\Software\Microsoft\Windows\CurrentVersion\App Paths	Installers: Change Everyone: Read	Apply to entire tree. At install time this key is empty; remove Public: Write permission to prevent its misuse.
\Software\Microsoft\Windows\Current Version\Explorer	Everyone:Read	Apply to entire tree. (Appears to be unused.)
\Software\Microsoft\Windows\Current Version\Embedding	Installers: Change Everyone: Read	Apply to entire tree.
\Software\Microsoft\Windows\Current Version\Run, RunOnce, Uninstall, and AEDebug	Everyone: Read	The command named in the Run key runs at logon for all users (including administrators) and must therefore be protected against spoofing. It should only be writable by full administrators. Similarly, protect RunOnce and Uninstall. The AEDebug key specifies [arameters for the system debugger users can run when a program crashes (such as "Dr. Watson"). Restrict access to prevent spoofing.
\Software\Microsoft\Windows NT\CurrentVersion\Font*, GRE_Initialize	Installers: Change Everyone: Add	Change only keys that begin with "Font," except FontDrivers, and Gre-Initialize. Some sites may wish to restrict Everyone access to Read to prevent users from adding fonts.
\Software\Microsoft\Windows NT\CurrentVersion\Type 1 Installer\Type 1 Fonts	Installers: Change Everyone: Add	

Table 9-2. Recommended Registry ACLs for Windows NT (continued)

Key Path	Permissions	Notes
\Software\Microsoft\Windows NT\CurrentVersion\Drivers, Drivers.desc	Everyone: Read	Apply to entire tree. Drivers32 is the principal storage control location for Windows NT drivers and is strongly protected. The function of the Driver key is unclear, but protect it anyway.
\Software\Microsoft\Windows NT\CurrentVersion\MCI, MCI Extensions	Installers: Change	Apply to entire tree.
\Software\Microsoft\Windows NT\CurrentVersion\Ports	INTERACTIVE: Change Everyone: Read	Apply to entire tree. Parameters for COM, LPT, and other ports. You allow INTERACTIVE users to modify these because there seems little security risk, although some sites may wish to tighten these ACLs. Note that Microsoft recommends tightening these keys to Everyone: Read only.
\Software\Microsoft\Windows NT\CurrentVersion\ProfileList	Public: Add	Install as nonpropagating ACL if possible. Each subkey in Profiles holds parameters for a profile created in WINNT\Profiles. To prevent spoofing, a new subkey should not be publicly writable. Unfortunately, there's no standard Registry ACL tool that allows the public to create keys that then have no public access, although "Add" permission is secure as long as the subkeys don't themselves have meaningful subkeys, which is the case in Profiles. Third party tools (such as SuperCACLS, available from *http://www.trustedsystems.com*) that can install ACL entries that don't propagate to subkeys are useful here because they produce the desired protection.
\Software\Microsoft\Windows NT\CurrentVersion\WOW	Everyone: Read	Apply to entire tree. Holds parameters for the DOS environment. Although it is not clear how serious a spoofing threat exists, it seems wise to prevent public modification.
\Software\Windows 3.1 Migration Status	Everyone: Read	Apply to entire tree.

Table 9-2. Recommended Registry ACLs for Windows NT (continued)

Key Path	Permissions	Notes
\System\CurrentControlSet\Services\LanmanServer\Shares	Everyone: Read	The values in this key and its Security subkey holds critical information about directory and printer shares. These values are adequately protected by default. However, any user can add new subkeys to these keys, and Microsoft recommends tightening the permissions.
\System\CurrentControlSet\Services	Everyone: Read	Apply to entire tree. This setting prevents nonadministrators from changing service settings.

You can also use the Security Explorer tool, discussed later in this chapter, to automatically and recursively apply whatever permissions you want (including removing Everyone in all Registry ACEs).

Adding Registry ACLs to Group Policy Objects

One of the most useful features in Windows 2000 is the new Group Policy mechanism, explained in more detail in Chapter 7, *Using Group Policies*. The GPO mechanism allows you to designate a wide range of settings that you want applied to users and computers in your administrative domain. One feature of GPOs that's worth a special mention in this chapter is that you can assign ACLs to Registry keys, then propagate those ACLs to computers throughout your domain as part of the domain GPO.

The actual process of adding Registry ACLs to a GPO is pretty straightforward:

1. Open the MMC and navigate to the Group Policy snap-in that owns the scope over which you want to apply these restrictions.

2. Expand the GPO's node; you're looking for the Computer Configuration → Windows Settings → Security Settings → Registry node.

3. Use the Add Key... command (available by right-clicking the Registry folder, from the Action menu, or right-clicking in the right half of the MMC console window).

4. The Select Registry Key dialog (see Figure 9-3) appears. Use it to either navigate directly to the key of interest or to specify the path by typing it into the Selected key field, then click OK.

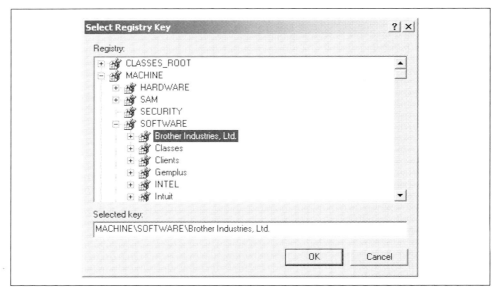

Figure 9-3. Select the Registry key to which you want a new ACL applied

5. The standard Registry security dialog then appears (jump way back to Figure 5-12 if you need to see it again). Use it to apply the ACEs you want on this key, then click OK.

6. The Template Security Policy Setting dialog (see Figure 9-4) then appears. Use it to specify how you want the ACL applied to the key:

   — The "Configure this key then" radio button has two subordinate radio buttons. The first, "Propagate inheritable permissions to all subkeys", forces the ACL you specify onto all subkeys of the target key. The second, "Replace existing permissions on all subkeys with inheritable permissions", forces only the new ACL onto subkeys that inherit from the target key.

   — The "Do not allow permissions on this key to be replaced" button indicates that you don't want any change to the permissions, and that you don't want anyone else to be able to change them either.

7. Click OK. The Template Security Policy dialog disappears, and the new ACL appears in the list on the right side of the MMC window.

That's all you have to do; once you make the change, it's propagated automatically to wherever the specified GPO carries its settings.

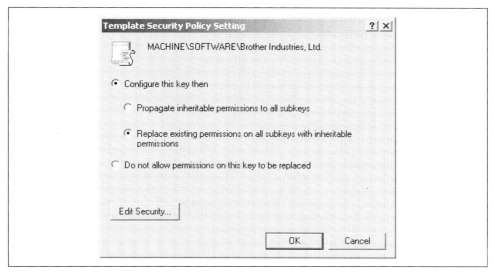

Figure 9-4. Choose how you want the new ACL applied to the target key

Encrypting HKLM\SAM with SYSKEY

Like Unix, Windows 2000 and NT don't directly store user or machine passwords. Instead, they take the passwords and passes them through a scheme called a *one-way function*, or OWF. The OWF takes a password in and generates a new block of data that is related to, but doesn't contain, the password. The "OW" in OWF comes from the fact that it's not feasible to take the output of the OWF and "go backwards" to derive the original password. The output of the OWF is called a *password hash*. NT stores the password hashes instead of the password, so you can't steal the hash and use it directly in place of a password. Windows 2000 also stores hashed passwords for local user and computer accounts, as well as for backward compatibility with older Win9x and NT clients.

In the spring of 1997, an enterprising group of hackers from L0pht Heavy Industries (*http://www.l0pht.com*) publicized the fact that it was possible to get the password hashes from a SAM database (or by sniffing them over the network) and feed them to a password-cracking tool. These types of attacks have been known for many years in the Unix community, but their appearance in the Windows NT world generated a lot of headlines. In practical terms, the actual risk was significant. Even though only administrators have access to the SAM to get the OWF'ed passwords in the first place, the hashes could be recovered from backup tapes or ERDs, and they could be sniffed off the network.

Accordingly, Microsoft took a beating on the Internet and in the press for the perceived insecurity of the SAM password data. To provide a solution, Microsoft introduced a method of protecting the SAM data with strong encryption; the *SYSKEY* utility installs and controls this extra protective layer. *SYSKEY* is available with NT 4.0 SP3 and later, and it's installed and enabled by default in Windows 2000 (in fact, you can't turn it off).

What SYSKEY Does

SYSKEY adds an extra layer of security to the password data stored in the SAM database by encrypting the hashed password data using a 128-bit *system key*. This key (Microsoft calls it the *password encryption key*, or PEK; so will I) is randomly generated when you install *SYSKEY*. Once your PEK is generated, NT uses it to encrypt and decrypt all password data (but not the ordinary account data) in the SAM. Because the data's encrypted, it's useless to any thief or cracker who might get it (and getting it still requires you to gain physical and administrative access to a domain controller). As a bonus, because the data is stored in encrypted form, it remains protected when it's backed up to an ERD or a tape.

Once the password data's encrypted, it's stored back into the SAM database, and services (including the local security authority, or LSA) that access the password data must depend on the kernel to decrypt it for them. For this to work, though, the kernel has to know what the PEK is at boot time: the SAM password information includes password data for system services that start when the machine's booted, in addition to the more mundane user password data.

In December 1999, a security team at BindView *(http://www.bindview.com)* found a vulnerability in *SYSKEY*'s password encryption, making it much easier to attack. Microsoft immediately released a hotfix for NT 4 systems; the fix is included in Windows 2000 RC3 and later.

To accomplish this, *SYSKEY* stores the PEK. You might wonder how storing the PEK could possibly increase security; it seems foolish to store the master password used to encrypt the data that's supposed to be protected! The answer is simple: *another* key is used to encrypt the PEK. This second key is the system key, after which *SYSKEY* is named. *SYSKEY* supports three options for storing the system key and making it available to the system when it's needed to decrypt the PEK.

The first, and most secure, option allows you to store the system key on a floppy. When the machine's booted, the floppy must be present so the kernel can retrieve the system key and use it to decrypt the PEK. Without the right floppy, the machine cannot be booted into the version of Windows 2000 or NT that's protected by that floppy.* This introduces a new single point of failure for your machines, so it's critical to keep backup copies of the floppy. In addition, the floppy serves as a token that allows access to the SAM data, so you must control who has access to it.

The next option is to store the system key encrypted with another key. This second key is generated from a passphrase you choose. Instead of inserting the system key floppy at boot time, a human must be present to type in the passphrase. The encrypted version of the system key is stored on the computer so that only the passphrase is required; there's no separate floppy or key disk involved.

Finally, you can choose to have the system key stored on the local machine. *SYSKEY* uses what Microsoft calls a "complex obfuscation algorithm" to hide the key. This is supposed to make it hard to compromise the system key. This reliance on "security through obscurity" offers considerably less security than the other available methods, but it has one saving grace: it allows unattended reboots, since the kernel can derive the PEK when needed without any human intervention. This is critical for some applications; only you can determine whether it's the best choice for your servers.

Before You Enable SYSKEY on Windows NT

As with most other NT components, it's tempting to rush out and install *SYSKEY* now that you know how it can add security to your machines' Registry data. However, in this case it pays to be cautious and make sure you've adequately planned deploying *SYSKEY* on your network. It's important to understand what *SYSKEY* protects you against and what additional problems it can potentially impose. Committing to using *SYSKEY* is not to be done lightly.

Every NT 4.0 workstation and server can run *SYSKEY*, and each machine can use any of the three system key storage options mentioned earlier. If you choose to use key floppies or passphrases, remember that the floppy or passphrase is just like an ERD: it's useful only on the machine where it was created, so you have one disk or passphrase for every protected machine. (You can cheat and use the same passphrase on all machines, though.)

First of all, let's start with the scariest problem: *SYSKEY* can make your system more secure, but it's a one-way trip. Once you enable strong encryption of the SAM account database, there's no way to turn off encryption and go back to the old unencrypted version (though you can use an ERD, as described later). In

---

* Each installation of the OS gets its own unique PEK. If you have multiple versions, or multiple copies, of Windows 2000/NT installed on a single computer, each has a unique PEK. If you have two installations on one machine and lose the system key disk for one of them, you can still boot the other one.

practice, as long as you keep your ERDs up to date, you won't need to go back to the unencrypted version.

The next problem is what security experts call the "steel lock, balsa-wood door" problem. If you have multiple domain controllers for one domain, and one uses *SYSKEY* but the others don't, you haven't added any security to your network. One machine's SAM database is protected, but—since all the other controllers have replicated copies—the data you want to secure is still easy to grab. Ideally, you should implement *SYSKEY* on every machine that has an accounts database. That means all domain controllers and any NT workstation machine that has local accounts.

The final difficulty posed by *SYSKEY* is the fact that it adds security by encrypting the data on your machine. As long as you retain access to the system key, NT can decrypt the PEK and use it to access the stored passwords. If you choose to use a passphrase or key floppy, and you lose or forget it, you'll have to restore from an ERD. If the only ERD you have was made after the Registry was encrypted, you *still* won't be able to get in! It's critical to safeguard the key floppy and make backup copies of it so a bad floppy doesn't take you out of production—but since the key floppy is a security component, you have to keep careful watch over it.

"What I tell you three times is true"

Microsoft recommends making a total of three ERDs when installing *SYSKEY*: one before installing the *SYSKEY* hotfix or service pack, one after installing it but before enabling *SYSKEY*, and one after the first reboot after installing *SYSKEY*. While this may seem excessive, making all three disks maximizes the likelihood that you can recover your machine if it crashes in the future:

- The post-*SYSKEY* ERD contains the encrypted version of your accounts database. As you add and remove accounts, keep this ERD up to date. As long as you have the system key (either stored on the computer or on a floppy), you can restore the account database, and the rest of the Registry, from the ERD.

- The pre-*SYSKEY* ERD holds a record of your unencrypted Registry. If you ever need to recover the machine but don't have the system key, you have two choices: reinstall NT and lose all of your account data, or recover the Registry from this ERD and lose any changes made after *SYSKEY* was activated.

- The preinstall ERD protects you from problems with the hotfix or service pack. In general, you should always update your ERD just before installing any service pack or hotfix; this gives you an escape hatch if you need to back out of a fix that actually made things worse on your machine.

Keep all three ERDs for each machine you might someday need to restore. At a minimum, that means you'll need them for every domain controller on your network, plus one set for any NT Workstation machine that has important local accounts.

Upgrading domain controllers

Microsoft also warns you about installing *SYSKEY* on your primary domain controller: if something goes wrong with the *SYSKEY* installation, or if you ever lose the system key for that one machine, no one will be able to log on to your domain! For domains with more than a few users, you should already have a backup domain controller anyway; if you don't, it's worth considering adding one.

The safest way to roll out *SYSKEY* for your Windows NT domain controllers in a multiple-domain or multiple-controller network is this:

1. Pick a domain. Make sure it has at least two domain controllers (one primary and one backup).

2. Use the Server Manager application to force a synchronization of the PDC with all BDCs.

3. Stop the *netlogon* service on the original primary domain controller. This prevents it from servicing any logon requests.

4. Activate *SYSKEY* on the original primary domain controller. When you're satisfied that everything is working properly, restart the *netlogon* service on the machine from Step 3.

5. Activate *SYSKEY* on the other domain controllers in the domain. If you have more than one domain on your network, go back to Step 1 and pick another domain.

If you have domains with only one controller, it's probably okay to dispense with these steps and just activate *SYSKEY* on the controller, as long as you have the recommended set of three ERDs.

Turning On SYSKEY Protection

You control SAM database encryption with the *SYSKEY.EXE* executable. As you might expect, only administrators may turn on system key protection. The first time you run *SYSKEY*, you see a dialog that warns you encryption can't be disabled once you turn it on; you see that warning again after you first enable encryption. There are only five controls in the window: the Encryption Enabled and Encryption Disabled radio buttons show the current state of system key encryption on this machine. You can change from disabled to enabled, but not vice versa. The standard OK and Cancel buttons work like they do in every other dialog. The Update button allows you to change the key storage method later (you'll see how to do that in the next section, "Changing the Key Storage Method").

The first step in activating *SYSKEY* is simple: click the Encryption Enabled radio button, then click the OK button. You then see a warning dialog reminding you that this conversion can't be undone and suggesting that you ensure that you've got a current ERD before proceeding. When you click OK in that dialog, you see the Account Database Key dialog (see Figure 9-5), which you use to tell *SYSKEY* where you want the system key stored after it's generated:

- If you want to use a passphrase to unlock the system key, click the Password Startup button and type your password into the Password and Confirm fields. You may enter up to 128 characters for a passphrase, and longer phrases are better. Unfortunately, *SYSKEY* doesn't enforce any minimum length restrictions on the password. Microsoft recommends at least 12 characters, but it's easy to come up with a longer password than that: pick two easy-to-remember adjectives and a noun, then string them together with punctuation or special characters (for instance, "galloping_sleepy#motorhome"). NT feeds the passphrase you enter to a special algorithm, which generates a 128-bit key from it.

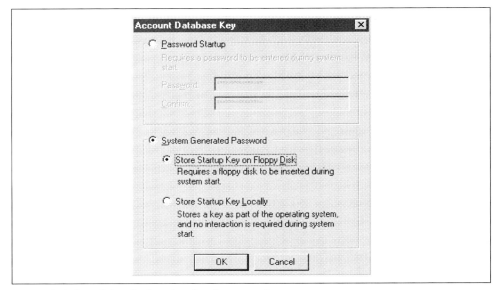

Figure 9-5. Specifying the location for the system key

- If you want the system to generate a password on its own, click the System Generated Password radio button. In this mode, NT uses its own pseudorandom number generator* to pick a random 128-bit system key. As you know, that key has to be stored somewhere. You get to choose where:

— The Store Startup Key on Floppy Disk button instructs NT to keep the encrypted system key on a floppy. The key itself is stored in a file named *StartKey.key*. When you choose this option, you need a floppy handy to hold the key. Although it may be temptingly close, don't use your ERD to store the key: doing so concentrates both pieces of data needed to steal passwords on a single floppy.

— The Store Startup Key Locally button stores the obfuscated system key in HKLM\SYSTEM. When you choose this option, you can reboot the machine without having a human present.

Once you've selected the method you want, click the OK button. If you've chosen to store the key on a floppy, *SYSKEY* prompts you to insert a floppy and confirms that it's written the key to the disk. Otherwise, the key is silently updated and *SYSKEY* then exits.

The next time you boot the machine, *SYSKEY* protection will be in effect. This means that unless you're storing the system key locally, you have to be at the machine every time it's rebooted to either type in the passphrase or stick in the key floppy.

If you're in a hurry, you can use the -1 flag with *SYSKEY*; this instructs it to silently generate a system key and store it on the local machine. This is a handy trick to use when setting up a new workstation or server; you can add the command to your ordinary setup scripts, then change the key storage method later when you have more time. This gives you immediate protection without any extra effort on your part.

Changing the Key Storage Method

Once you've installed and activated *SYSKEY*, you're not bound to your initial choice of key storage. You can run *SYSKEY* again at any time and change from one method to another. When you change methods, *SYSKEY* generates a new system key and stores it instead of reusing the old key; this helps protect your password data against compromise.

---

* The great mathematician and computer scientist John von Neumann once said that if you rely on software to generate random numbers you're living in a state of sin. However, cryptographically strong pseudorandom generators (like the one NT uses) are only a little sinful.

To change the key storage method for a machine, run *SYSKEY* and click the Update button. The Account Database Key dialog (shown earlier in Figure 9-5) then appears, and the radio button corresponding to the currently active storage method is active. To change to a new method, just click one of the other radio buttons, filling in the password if necessary.

Because *SYSKEY* generates a new key when you change storage methods, you must supply the old key as part of the change process. This means that what happens after you click "OK" depends on what storage method you were previously using. If you changed from "Store Startup Key Locally" to something else, *SYSKEY* can get the old key from HKLM\SYSTEM, so you don't have to do anything. If you're changing from storing the password on a floppy or being protected by a passphrase, *SYSKEY* requires you to provide the key disk or passphrase to continue. This prevents an attacker from changing the key, storing on a floppy, and stealing the floppy—thus rendering your machine unbootable.

Figure 9-6 shows the dialog that asks for the key disk, while Figure 9-7 shows the dialog requesting the current passphrase. If you supply the correct passphrase or floppy, *SYSKEY* displays a confirmation dialog to remind you that it's changed the system key, and the new key is stored using the method you've chosen. If you don't supply the right information, *SYSKEY* won't change anything.

Figure 9-6. The key disk dialog

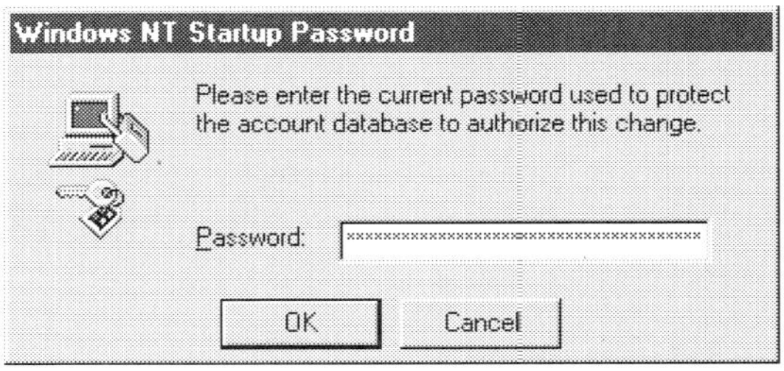

Figure 9-7. The password dialog

Restoring a SYSKEY-Protected NT Registry

[NT4]

Chapter 3, *In Case of Emergency,* described the mechanics of restoring a damaged Registry using a Windows NT ERD. To restore a machine protected with *SYSKEY,* you follow this same basic procedure, but there are a few new subtleties introduced as a result of *SYSKEY*'s presence. The golden rule for restoring a *SYSKEY*-protected machine is simple: use the correct ERD.

Restore SYSTEM and SAM hives

Even though the actual encrypted account information is stored in the HKLM\SAM subtree, the actual PEK, as well as all the other data *SYSKEY* needs to tell where the system key is stored, lives in HKLM\SYSTEM. To recover an encrypted account database, you must restore both the SYSTEM and SAM hives at the same time—not just SAM. If you don't do this, NT can't decrypt the Registry, either because it can't find the system key (if you don't restore SYSTEM) or because the key doesn't decrypt the data (if you don't restore SAM). Of course, you must restore these hives from the same ERD.

Get the right system components

If you got *SYSKEY* as the result of installing an NT 4.0 service pack, you may not have noticed that three existing system files were replaced as part of the update: *winlogon.exe, samsrv.dll,* and *samlib.dll.* These three files, along with *syskey.exe,* implement the account database protection. Their presence is required to enable the encrypted SAM data to be read and decrypted by system services that need it.

When you first install NT, it logs the versions of all the components you install in *system.log.* When you install service packs, hotfixes, or software such as Internet Explorer that replaces one or more system files, the installer application is supposed to update the entries in *system.log* so that it always reflects the current version of all DLLs, drivers, and other operating-system components.

What this means is that if you install *SYSKEY* as part of a hotfix or service pack, the *system.log* entries for *winlogon.exe, samsrv.dll,* and *samlib.dll* reflects the versions installed with *SYSKEY,* not the original versions you installed. If you want to restore your machine to its pre-*SYSKEY* state, you need to use the NT setup application's "Repair system files" option to restore the original versions from your NT CD or file server. However, you must be sure to restore the SAM and SYSTEM hives from the pre-*SYSKEY* ERD: if you revert to the original system components but leave the encrypted Registry in place, nothing will work right.

If you install *SYSKEY* but don't turn it on, the *winlogon.exe, samsrv. dll*, and *samlib.dll* files won't match your original installation. When you install the new versions of these files, they change the Registry format even when encryption is off. If you use NT setup to restore these three files to their original state by using your pre-*SYSKEY* ERD, you must also restore SAM and SYSTEM from the same ERD: if you don't, the old components won't be able to read the new Registry format.

Which ERD should I use?

Three ERDs is three more than most NT systems have, and so deciding which one to use may seem a little overwhelming. It's not hard, though: each ERD can put your system back into a particular state. Which one you use depends on what you want the restored system to have on it. Table 9-3 shows your options.

Table 9-3. ERD Restoration Table

To Revert to...	Use This ERD	Don't Forget...
System as it was before installing *SYSKEY*	Preinstall ERD	You may lose account database changes made since *SYSKEY* was installed. You must also choose "repair system files" in NT setup to restore the original versions of *winlogon.exe, samsrv.dll*, and *samlib.dll*. You can always fall back to this level, even without the system key.
System as it was after installing, but before activating, *SYSKEY*	Pre-*SYSKEY* ERD	You may lose account database changes made since *SYSKEY* was installed. You can always fall back to this level, even without the system key. When using this ERD, don't "repair system files" from CD.
System as it was after activating *SYSKEY*	Post-*SYSKEY* ERD	This preserves all account database changes since the ERD was updated. It requires presence of system key/passphrase on floppy or machine. When using this ERD, don't "repair system files" from CD.

Miscellaneous Good Stuff

So far in this book, you've learned how to use a variety of tools to modify, back up, and restore the Registry. At this point, though, you might be wondering what you can actually do with some of these tools. There are some common and

Changing the Registry Size

Since the Registry is a collection of hives, most of which are actually disk files, you might not realize that Windows 2000 (and NT) actually maps the entire Registry into memory. Doing so makes it possible for Registry calls to perform efficiently; however, it means that as the Registry grows it takes up a larger proportion of the virtual memory space in your system. To prevent the Registry from sucking up too much space in the system's page file, the system maintains an internal parameter called the *Registry Size Limit*, or RSL. The RSL sets an upper bound on how much address space the Registry may occupy; however, as you add software and users to your machines, the Registry gets larger. If it gets so big that it starts to bump up against the RSL, problems will occur. (Go to the Microsoft Knowledge Base at *http://www.microsoft.com/kb/default.asp* and search for "Maximum Registry Size" to see a long list of such problems, most of which are reasonably obscure.)

By default, the RSL is set at about 20–25% of the total virtual memory allocation for the system. This limit is a maximum, not a guarantee, and the limit set by the RSL doesn't actually mean that much space is reserved, just that the system can't use more than that. There's a complex relationship between the total size of the pool of available virtual memory and the RSL; in general, you should keep the RSL at 80% or less of the total virtual memory allocation. Failure to do so can result in impressive performance losses.

The Virtual Memory dialog (see Figure 9-8) shows you the current RSL and the current amount of space in use by the Registry. If the current size is more than 80% of the RSL, you should increase it. When choosing a new RSL, be sure to keep it below 80% of the total virtual memory size; in general, you shouldn't ever need to increase it above 33% of the virtual memory size. If you need more space even with an RSL 33% as big as your virtual memory stash, consider increasing the size of your virtual memory, then increase the RSL.

You adjust the RSL through the Virtual Memory dialog pictured in Figure 9-8; how you get to it depends on whether you're using Windows 2000 or NT. In Windows 2000, open the System control panel and click on the Advanced tab, then click the Performance Options button. In Windows NT, open the System control panel and click on the Performance tab. In either case, once the Performance dialog appears, click the Change button in the Virtual Memory control group, and the Virtual Memory dialog appears. Type a reasonable value into the Maximum Registry Size field, then click OK and close the Virtual Memory dialog and the System control panel. You're then notified that your changes won't take effect until the next restart.

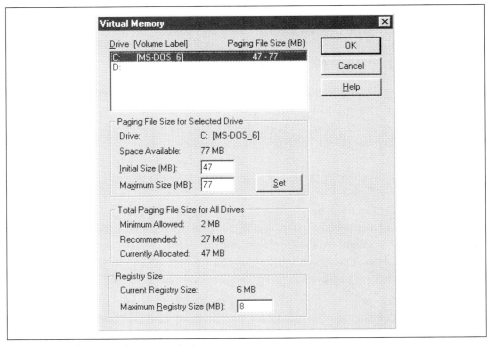

Figure 9-8. The Virtual Memory dialog

Auditing Registry Access

In the section "Registry Security Fundamentals" in Chapter 5, you learned how to apply auditing controls to any key in the Registry. Since Windows 2000 and NT store so much critical configuration data in the Registry, auditing some of it is a good idea; there are a number of keys you can audit to keep an eye on potential security problems or to catch users doing things they shouldn't be.

Windows components and applications often determine whether a specific key is present by trying to read it and noting if the attempt fails. This is normal, and it's so common that I recommend you avoid auditing failed attempts on the Read, Query Value, or Enumerate Subkeys operations; doing so generates lots of unnecessary audit log entries.

Once you turn on auditing, the events you specify are stored in the system's event log. Since the event log files are your record of what auditable events have taken place, you need to make sure that they're protected against tampering too! Set their permissions to include Full Control for CreatorOwner, SYSTEM, and

Miscellaneous Good Stuff

Administrators and Read for Everyone, then make sure no other users have write access to the log files.

Making sense of the audit log

When you enable auditing, the security reference manager process writes an audit entry to the security event log whenever one of the conditions you specify comes true. Here's a sample entry:

```
12/2/97 11:27:19 PM Security Success Audit Object Access 560 Administrator BOOMBOX
    Object Open:
    Object Server:    Security
    Object Type:      Key
    Object Name:      \REGISTRY\USER\S-1-5-21-34824712-245319459-1244863647-500
    New Handle ID:    240
    Operation ID:     {0,47947}
    Process ID: 2161664032
    Primary User Name:  Administrator
    Primary Domain: BOOMBOX
    Primary Logon ID:   (0x0,0x1E35)
    Client User Name:   -
    Client Domain:  -
    Client Logon ID:    -
    Accesses          Create sub-key

    Privileges        -
```

I got this by turning on file/object access auditing in User Manager, then using *RegEdt32* to audit HKCU for successful Create Subkey access requests. Once I did, every time I created any subkey under HKCU, I got a new audit record like the one in the example.

As you can see, this record tells me what key was the target of the request (the `Object Name` field), what username made the attempt (along with that user's domain), and what access or privileges were requested. If you want to routinely scan your event logs for Registry accesses, I suggest using a tool such as SomarSoft's *DumpEvt* (*http://www.somarsoft.com*), writing your own Perl script to parse the Event Log using functions in the *Win32::EventLog* module or using a third-party tool like RippleTech's LogCaster (*http://www.rippletech.com*).

Tracking software installations or reinstallations

Any software that uses the Registry (which means any package wearing the "Designed for Windows" logo, plus lots of others) leaves tracks in either HKLM\SOFTWARE or HKCU\SOFTWARE. Microsoft's recommendation is that software vendors create their own subkey of one of these two keys, so you'll see lots of entries like HKLM\Software\Netscape and HKLM\SOFTWARE\Qualcomm. You can audit these keys directly, or you can audit only specific subkeys of interest. For example, if you want to see an audit notice whenever someone adds new software to a machine, you can add an audit entry for "Create Subkey" on HKLM\SOFTWARE. If instead you wanted to know when someone installs only software made by Netscape, you can audit "Create Subkey" on HKLM\SOFTWARE\Netscape and HKCU\SOFTWARE\Netscape.

The need to do this is relaxed somewhat in Windows 2000, since users' privileges to install software are more constrained. Users can install applications for themselves, but they can't install software other users can run; only administrators can do that. Accordingly, you may not find it necessary to audit HKLM.

Guarding against Trojan horses

Windows 2000 and NT allows administrators to install one or more DLLs that validate passwords before passing them to the logon subsystem. The NetWare gateway tools shipped with NT use such a DLL, and the documentation for what such a DLL should do is available from Microsoft. This opens the door for a user to install a password-grabbing DLL that just stores the password in a file without changing it, then passes it on to the logon subsystem. The list of these DLLs is maintained in the HKLM\SYSTEM\CurrentControlSet\Control\Lsa\Notification Packages key. I strongly recommend that you set appropriate permissions and turn on auditing for this key.

Using the Resource Kit Registry Utilities

Microsoft offers a separate package of tools, documentation, and utilities called for each of its operating systems. There are different resource kits for Windows NT Server and Workstation, Windows 2000 Server and Professional,[*] 98, and 95 (not to mention separate kits for other products, including Exchange and IIS). The resource kits offer a wealth of useful tools and documentation; even though some of the tools are only partly functional, and most are poorly documented, the resource kit for whichever OS you're running is well worth the US$150 or so it costs, since many of its tools are unavailable from any other source.[†]

The Windows 2000 Resource Kit

The Windows 2000 resource kit contains only a few Registry-related tools; the primary tool is *reg.exe*. However, this version of *reg.exe* does everything that its NT predecessor did, plus what all the other Windows NT resource kit registry tools did. If the old version was like a Swiss Army knife, the Windows 2000 version is

---

[*] The Server kit includes everything in the Professional kit, so you don't need to buy both.

[†] Of course, you could argue that these tools should be included with the OS itself. I'd agree with that, but then Microsoft would have to clean up, document, and test the tools, most of which are only of interest to support professionals, system administratorss, and the like.

Using the Resource Kit Registry Utilities

more like one of those nifty Leatherman Wave tools that has everything except a hammer in it. There are some other useful items in the Windows 2000 kit, too:

- *regentry.chm* is a help file that lists most of the interesting Windows 2000 Registry keys and values; it also provides some general introductory guidance to the Registry and its care and feeding.

- *gp.chm* contains information about the local and domain GPOs available. (You can find the same information, usually in more detail, in Appendix A, *User Configuration Group Policy Objects*, and Appendix B, *Computer Configuration Group Policy Objects*.)

- *dureg.exe* is a nifty tool that produces a size estimate showing how much data is actually in the Registry.

- *regback.exe* and *regrest.exe*, covered in Chapter 3, allow you to back up and restore the Registry, or portions thereof.

- *regini.exe* allows you to change the Registry via an INI-style file.

- *regfind.exe* is a Registry search tool discussed in the section "Searching for Keys with regfind," later in this chapter; the Windows 2000 version also can search and replace Registry keys and values.

- *scanreg.exe* allows you to grep the Registry.

The Windows NT Resource Kit

The NT 4.0 resource kit CD has a variety of tools and documents on it. Table 9-4 summarizes items that have something to do with the Registry. Most of these tools originally shipped with the by-now-ancient NT 3.1 Resource Kit. In Summer 1997, Microsoft issued an update to the resource kit (available from *ftp://ftp.microsoft.com/bussys/winnt/winnt-public/reskit/nt40*), which adds a new tool, *reg.exe*. *reg* supersedes a number of other tools, even though they still appear on the resource kit CD. I've noted the superseded tools in the table so you'll know which ones you can safely skip over.

Table 9-4. Resource Kit Registry Tools

Tool	What It Does	Notes
compreg.exe	Compares contents of two Registry values you specify; like *diff*	See the section "Comparing Keys and Values with COMPREG" later in this chapter.
reg.exe	Everything: add, remove, or change keys; load and unload hives, and lots more	See the next section "reg: The One-Size-Fits-All Registry Tool."

Table 9-4. Resource Kit Registry Tools (continued)

Tool	What It Does	Notes
regback.exe and *regrest.exe*	Backs up and restores Registry keys, values, and hives; can restore all or part of a damaged Registry	Covered in Chapter 3.
regchg.exe	Changes a single value from the command line	Superseded by *reg.exe*.
regdel.exe	Deletes the specified subkey of HKLM from the command line	Superseded by *reg.exe*.
regdir.exe	Provides a directory-style listing of a specified tree or subkey	
regdmp.exe	Dumps the specified key, plus its subkeys and values, in text form	
regentry.hlp	Documents many of NT's keys and values	
regfind.exe	Searches the Registry for a specified value; works like *grep* or the search function in *RegEdit*	See the section "Searching for Keys with regfind" later in this chapter.
regini.exe	Adds, removes, or changes keys based on a command script you write	
regkey.exe	Offers a GUI to set several trivial parameters (auto-logon, number of cached user profiles, etc.)	Better to use system policies.
regread.exe	Reads the specified subkey of HKLM and returns its values	Superseded by *reg.exe*.
regsec.exe	Sets security descriptors on a key and its subkeys; useful for undoing needlessly permissive default ACLs	See the section "Fixing Registry Security ACLs in Windows NT" earlier in this chapter.
restkey.exe	Restores a key saved by *SAVEKEY*	Superseded by *reg.exe*.
rktools.hlp	Gives a brief description of each tool in the Resource Kit	
rregchg.exe	Changes a key's value on a remote machine	Superseded by *reg.exe*.
savekey.exe	Saves a key's values for later reloading	Superseded by *reg.exe*.

reg: The One-Size-Fits-All Registry Tool

I have been heard to describe the *reg.exe* utility as "*RegEdt32* in a can." It does almost everything *RegEdt32* can do, but it allows you to do it from a command line. Not only is this a boon when you want to quickly make a change without firing up *RegEdt32*; it also allows you to embed Registry operations in logon scripts and batch files. (Of course, you learned how to use the Registry from within Perl in Chapter 8, *Programming with the Registry*, but for the non-Perl-hackers among us, `reg` is a welcome substitute.)

If you've ever used the `net` command, you'll immediately recognize how `reg` works. Like `net`, you use `reg` by giving it a command from a short list of options (`query`, `add`, `delete`, `copy`, `save`, `load`, `unload`, `restore`, `compare`, `export`, and `import`), followed by one or more optional parameters that the command you specify interprets. Here's a short example in which `reg` gets the `query` command for a specified subkey of HKLM:

```
C:\reskit>reg query HKLM\Software\Qualcomm /s

Listing of [Software\Qualcomm]

[Eudora]
[Eudora\3.0.1]
```

Here's the problem with `reg`: the Windows 2000 and NT versions have different command-line parameters and switches. In an effort to do away with the clutter of multiple tools, Microsoft revamped the interface for the Windows 2000 `reg` tool, making it more functional and more consistent, not to mention unlike its older brother.

Using the Windows 2000 Version of reg

The Windows 2000 version of *reg.exe* offers 11 separate functions, ranging from querying for the existence of a key or value to recursively deleting everything beneath a specific key. Each mode has its own mnemonic, which you specify after the `reg` command itself.

Querying keys

The `reg query` command allows you to query a single key for a single value or a range of keys for all their values. This provides you with a quick way to check whether a key has the value you think it does, or in fact whether it has any values associated with it at all.

```
REG QUERY [rootKey\]key [\\machine] [/S] [/V value] [/VE]
```

rootKey
    Optional; specifies which root key to use as base of query. May be HKLM, HKCU, HKCR, or HKCC. Defaults to HKLM if omitted.

key
    Specifies the full name of a key under the specified *rootKey*.

value
    Specifies a value under *key* to query. If omitted, all keys and values under *key* are displayed.

machine
: Specifies the name of a remote machine to query; if omitted, defaults to local machine. You can only query HKLM and HKU on remote machines.

/S
: Queries all subkeys of *key*.

/V *value*
: Queries the specified value and print its contents.

/VE
: Queries the default, or empty, value.

Adding keys and values

The `reg add` command adds new keys and values to the Registry. You can add a value to an existing key, add a new key with no values, or create a new key and a value beneath it. If you try to add a key or value that exists, `reg` warns you.

```
REG ADD [\\machine\]key [/V value | /VE] [/T dataType] [/D data]
        [/S separator] [/F]
```

machine
: Name of a remote machine to add the key on; if omitted, defaults to local machine. You can only add to HKLM and HKU on remote machines.

key
: Full path to key you want to add (if you're adding a key) or to key where the new value should be added (if you're adding a value). Must include a root key (HKLM, HKCU, HKCR, HKU, or HKCC) and a full path to the target subkey.

/V *value*
: Specifies the full name of the value to add. Don't use this switch if you want to add a key; instead, just specify the new key as the last component of *key*.

/VE
: Specifies that you want to add the empty or untitled value to the specified *key*.

/T *dataType*
: Type of the new value to be added. Can be REG_NONE, REG_SZ, REG_MULTI_SZ, REG_EXPAND_SZ, REG_DWORD, REG_BINARY, REG_DWORD_BIG_ENDIAN, or REG_DWORD_LITTLE_ENDIAN. If omitted, REG_SZ is the default. If you specify REG_DWORD, you must specify `newValue` as a decimal number.

/D *data*
: Contents of newly created value. String values may contain spaces and special characters, but must be enclosed in double quotes if they do. REG_MULTI_SZ

variables must be separated by whatever separator you want to use: either \0 or whatever you specify with the /S switch.

/S *separator*

When adding a REG_MULTI_SZ value, specifies which character to use as the separator. If omitted, \0 is assumed to be the separator.

/F

Forces `reg` to make the change without prompting you for confirmation.

For example, let's say you wanted to create a registry key as part of a configuration script, adding a necessary REG_EXPAND_SZ value along the way. Here's one way to do it:

```
reg add HKLM\Software\RA\ExchangePlus\DLMaster /F
reg add HKLM\Software\RA\ExchangePlus\DLMaster /v SystemPath
    /t REG_EXPAND_SZ /d "%SYSTEMROOT%" /F
```

These commands forcibly add the required key, then add the required value with the correct data type and contents.

Deleting keys and values

The `reg delete` command removes a key or value. When you remove a key, `reg delete` removes all subkeys and values beneath that key; however, it asks you to confirm your intentions before it actually deletes anything unless you use the /F switch. That notwithstanding, be careful when using this command. As with `reg update`, you can delete only keys where the ACLs (and/or the remote Registry settings) allow you access.

```
REG DELETE [\\machine\]key [/V value | /VE | /VA] [/F]
```

machine

Name of a remote machine from which you want to remove the value; if omitted, defaults to local machine. You can only remove keys from HKLM and HKU on remote machines.

key

Full path to key you want to remove (if you're removing the key itself) or to key where the target value lives. Must include a root key (HKLM, HKCU, HKCR, HKU, or HKCC) and a full path to the target subkey.

/V *value*

Specifies the full name of the value to remove. Don't use this switch if you want to remove an entire key; instead, just specify the key name and use the /VA switch.

/VE

Specifies that you want to remove the empty or untitled value from the specified *key*.

/VA

>   Specifies that you want to remove all values from the target key without touching its subkeys.

/F

>   Forces `reg` to remove the targeted keys or values without prompting you for confirmation.

Copying keys and values

`reg copy` might be my favorite of all `reg`'s commands, if only because it greatly eases the process of copying settings from one place to another. You can use the command to copy a single key or an entire hive from its original location to another; the target location can be on the same machine as the source or on any other machine on the network. This command makes short work of tasks like copying a standard set of file associations to new machines or tweaking one machine so its configuration matches another.

```
REG COPY [\\srcMachine\]srcKey [\\destMachine\]destKey [/S] [/F]
```

srcMachine and *destMachine*

>   Specifices names of source and destination machines. Either or both may be remote machines; if either is omitted, the local machine is assumed. You can copy keys into and out of HKLM and HKU only on remote machines.

srcKey

>   Specifies the full name of the source key, including the root key. You can copy from any root key, provided you have access to the source key. All values beneath the source key are copied to the destination key.

destKey

>   Specifies the full name of the destination key. This may be different from the source key if you wish, as long as you have access to the area where you're trying to graft the copied key.

/S

>   Specifies that you want to recursively copy all subkeys and values from *srcKey* to *destKey*. If you don't specify this switch, only the specified key and its values are copied.

/F

>   This switch is documented but doesn't seem to do anything, since `reg copy` never prompts you for a confirmation.

Saving and restoring keys

Sometimes having a quick way to make a backup copy of a key and its values, or restore a key from such a backup, can be very useful indeed. You can back up the entire Registry using the strategies outlined in Chapter 3; however, if that's overkill consider using the `reg save` and `reg load` commands instead.

To save a key and its values to a new hive file on disk, you can use either `reg save` or `reg backup` (they're synonyms):

REG SAVE [*machine*\]*srcKey fileName*

machine
> Name of a remote machine to query; if you omit it, the local machine is used. As usual, you can only manipulate keys in HKLM and HKU on remote machines.

srcKey
> The full name of the source key, including the root key, you want to back up. All of the source key's values and subkeys are recursively copied to the file you specify.

fileName
> Names the file that will hold the saved data. You can specify any valid full or partial path to receive the file; if you leave one off, local keys are backed up to the current directory, and remote keys go in *%systemroot%\system32*.

To quickly store a copy of all of your current settings, use this command:

    reg save HKCU my-profile

then use it anywhere you can use a hive file, including *RegEdt32* and the `reg load` and `reg restore` commands.

You may restore a saved hive with the `reg restore` command. This command overwrites an existing key with a new set of values, so you must be cautious when using it (`reg` asks you to confirm your command before it overwrites anything, though).

REG RESTORE [*machine*\]*targetKey fileName*

machine
> Specifies which machine you want to restore the hive file to. You can restore from a local file to a remote machine if you wish, but (as usual) you only have access to HKLM and HKU on the remote machine.

targetKey
> Specifies which key to overwrite with the contents of the saved hive.

fileName
> Specifies the path and name of the saved hive file. You can restore only hive files that were created with *RegEdt32* or the `reg save` command.

Loading and unloading hives

The section "Saving and Loading Registry Keys" in Chapter 5 explains how you can use *RegEdt32* to load and unload saved keys as hives immediately beneath HKLM or HKU. The `reg` utility gives you the same ability, albeit with the same limitations.

To load a hive, use the `reg load` command. Unlike `reg restore`, `reg load` loads the hive by adding it with the key name you specify instead of overwriting the key you specify. This makes it possible for you to use `reg load` to load a saved hive, edit it, and unload it again without making any changes to the rest of your Registry. (If you're wondering why you might want to do so, go back and reread the section "Setting Defaults for New User Accounts" at the beginning of the chapter.) When you load a hive, it's not fully persistent; the hive is unloaded when the current user logs off or when the computer next reboots.

```
REG LOAD [\\machine\]targetKey fileName
```

machine
> Specifies the name of a remote machine to load the hive on; if omitted, assumes the local machine. As with the other commands, you can load hives in HKU or HKLM only on the remote box.

targetKey
> Specifies the name of the key to receive the new hive. This key is created and must not already exist. *key* must be an immediate subkey of HKLM or HKU.

fileName
> Specifies the name of the hive file to load, with no extension. You may specify a full local or UNC path here.

For example, to load the *ntuser.dat* hive as suggested in the previous section "Setting Defaults for New User Accounts," just copy *ntuser.dat* to *ntuser-default*, then use this command:

```
reg load ntuser-default DefaultProfile
```

and modify the hive as needed.

Once you've finished working with a loaded hive, you may unload it with `reg unload`. Its command syntax is pretty simple.

```
REG UNLOAD [\\machine\]key
```

machine
> Name of a remote machine on which to unload the hive; if omitted, defaults to local machine

reg: The One-Size-Fits-All Registry Tool

key
> Name of the key to unload. *key* must be an immediate subkey of HKLM or HKU, whether you're on a local or remote machine.

Comparing keys and values

Instead of using a separate comparison tool such as NT 4, the Windows 2000 toolset allows you to use `reg` itself to compare the contents of two keys or values. There are a number of new bells and whistles in this revision of the tool, although for heavy-duty comparison, I still prefer using a visual comparison tool such as *windiff*.

The `reg compare` command does have some nifty features that give you some extra flexibility. One is that it returns a status code: 0 means the comparison was successful, and the two items were identical; 1 means the comparison failed; 2 means the comparison succeeded, but the target items were different. This makes it easy to use `reg compare` in Windows Scripting Host scripts. Another is that you can control what output it produces, meaning that you're freed from seeing tons of irrelevant results when you're comparing things.

```
REG COMPARE [\\machine1\]keyName1 [\\machine2\]keyName2 [/V valueName | /VE]
      [ /OA | /OD | /OS | /ON ] [/S]
```

machine1 and machine2
> Specifies names of remote machines to compare keys on. If you omit either or both remote names, the local machine is used instead. You can compare only remote machine keys that reside in HKU or HKLM.

keyName1 and keyName2
> Specifies the full paths (including a root key) of the keys to compare. When comparing keys on different machines, these paths may be the same, but they don't have to be.

/V *valueName*
> By default, compares all the values beneath the specified keys. If you want to limit comparison to a single value, use the /V switch. Annoyingly, you can't specify two different value names to compare.

/VE
> Specifies that you want to compare the empty default value in the target keys.

/OA
> Forces output of both differences and matches between the target keys. This is the most verbose output setting.

/OD
> Shows only items that are different between the two keys.

/OS

Shows only items that are the same (e.g., those that match) between the two keys. This is a quick way to test how similar two keys are.

/ON

Suppresses all output. This switch is commonly used in conjunction with the status code as a simple way to get a yes-or-no result of a comparison.

/S

Recursively descends the keys being compared and compares their subkeys and values too.

Exporting and importing Registry data

If you need to save the contents of a Registry key for later—perhaps to back up and restore it—you can do it with *RegEdt32* or using the reg export and reg import commands: reg export takes the key you specify and saves it to a text file, and reg import reads a file in the correct format and loads it back into the Registry. The Windows 2000 version of reg uses a different format from the Win95 and NT 4.0 version, but there's a command-line switch you can use to tell reg to recognize the old format. Exporting is straightforward.

REG EXPORT keyName fileName [/NT4]

keyName

Specifies name of the key you want to export. The name must include the root key, and you can only export keys on the local machine.

fileName

Specifies name of the file you want the exported data in.

/NT4

Forces reg to write a file in the older format used by the Windows NT resource kit version of reg.

When you want to reload the exported file (which you can do after copying, mailing, or editing the text-format *.REG* file to your heart's content), you use the extremely simple reg import command.

REG IMPORT fileName

fileName

Specifies the name of the exported key file to load. You may specify a full local or UNC path here.

Since the *.REG* file contains the full name of the key that was exported, importing the file automatically puts the loaded data into the right place. You can certainly edit the file to take a block of data exported from one key and load it into another; bear in mind that if you do, `reg import` silently overwrites whatever exists there. You've been forewarned.

[NT4] *Using the Windows NT Version of reg*

The older Windows NT resource kit version of *reg.exe* works fine under Windows 2000, but its functionality is quite limited by comparison.

Querying keys

`reg query` works the same way as the Windows 2000 version, with a few differences in syntax and semantics:

REG QUERY [*rootKey*\\]*key* [*value*] [*machine*] [/S]

rootKey
    Optional; specifies which root key to use as base of query. May be HKLM, HKCU, HKCR, HKU, or HKCC. Defaults to HKLM if omitted.

key
    Specifies the full name of a key under the specified *rootKey*.

value
    Specifies a value under *key* to query. If omitted, all keys and values under *key* will be displayed.

machine
    Specifies name of a remote machine to query; if omitted, defaults to local machine. You can only query HKLM and HKU on remote machines.

/s   Queries all subkeys of *key*.

Adding new keys

`reg add` adds new keys and values to the Registry. You can add a value to an existing key, add a new key with no values, or create a new key and a value beneath it. If you try to add a key or value that already exists, `reg` warns you.

REG ADD [*rootKey*\\]*key* [*value*=*newValue*] [*machine*] [*dataType*]

rootKey
    Optional; specifies which root key to add new key under. May be HKLM, HKCU, HKCR, HKU, or HKCC. Defaults to HKLM if omitted.

key
    Specifies the full name of the key to add under the specified *rootKey*.

value
    Optionally specifies the name of a value to add under *key*. If omitted, the key is created with no value.

newValue
   Specifies contents of newly created value. String values may contain spaces and special characters, but must be enclosed in double quotes if they do.

machine
   Specifies name of a remote machine to add the key on; if omitted, defaults to local machine. You can add keys to HKLM and HKU only on remote machines.

dataType
   Specfies type of the new value to be added. May be REG_SZ, REG_MULTI_SZ, REG_EXPAND_SZ, or REG_DWORD. If omitted, REG_SZ is the default. If you specify REG_DWORD, you must specify *newValue* as a decimal number.

For example, to add the value that disables Dial-Up Networking's "save password" checkbox, you could use this command:

```
reg add SYSTEM\CurrentControlSet\Services\
RasMan\Parameters\DisableSavePasswordValue=1
```

Updating existing keys

`reg update` updates a single value of an existing key. You can update any value where you have permission according to the parent key's ACL; if you're trying to modify a remote machine's Registry you must have access to it. `reg` warns you if you try to modify a nonexistent value.

```
REG UPDATE [rootKey\]key [\value=newValue] [machine]
```

rootKey
   Optional; specifies which root key holds the targeted key. May be HKLM, HKCU, HKCR, HKU, or HKCC on local machine or HKLM or HKU on remote machine. Defaults to HKLM if omitted.

key
   Specifies the full name of the key to update under the specified *rootKey*.

value
   Specifies which value under *key* to update.

newValue
   Contents to use when replacing existing value. String values may contain spaces and special characters, but must be enclosed in double quotes if they do. DWORD values must be specified in decimal.

machine
   Specifies name of a remote machine to query; if omitted, defaults to local machine. You can query HKLM and HKU only on remote machines.

Removing a key

`reg delete` removes a key or value. When removing a key, it removes all subkeys and values beneath that key; however, it asks you to confirm your intentions before it actually deletes anything.

REG DELETE [*rootKey*\]*key* [*value*] [*machine*]

rootKey
> Optional; specifies which root key the targeted key lives under. May be HKLM, HKCU, HKCR, HKU, or HKCC on local machine or HKLM or HKU on remote machine. Defaults to HKLM if omitted.

key
> Specifies the full name of the key to remove under the specified *rootKey*.

value
> Specifies which value under *key* to remove. If omitted, all keys and values under *key* are deleted.

machine
> Specifies name of a remote machine to remove the key on; if omitted, defaults to local machine. You can modify HKLM and HKU only on remote machines.

Copying keys and values

The Windows NT version of the `reg copy` command is a little more flexible than its big brother, since it can copy values from one location to another.

REG COPY [*srcRootKey*\]*srcKey* [*srcValue*] [*srcMachine*] [*destRootKey*\]*destKey*
         [*destValue*] [*destMachine*]

srcRootKey
> Optional; specifies which root key holds the source key. May be HKLM, HKCU, HKCR, HKU, or HKCC. Defaults to HKLM if omitted.

srcKey
> Specifies the full name of the source key.

srcValue
> Optionally specifies a value under *srcKey* to copy. If omitted, all keys and values under *srcKey* are copied.

srcMachine
> Specifies name of a remote machine to act as copy source; if omitted, defaults to local machine. You can use remote machines' HKLM and HKU only as source roots.

destRootKey
> Optional; specifies where copied key should be rooted. May be HKLM or HKU; defaults to HKLM if omitted.

destKey
> Specifies the full name of the key to hold the copied data.

destValue
> Optionally specifies name for a single copied value; ignored if no *srcValue* is specified.

destMachine '
> Specifies name of a remote machine to serve as the copy target; if omitted, defaults to local machine.

When I installed a beta version of a popular Internet mail package, I (rightly, as it turned out) feared that the new version would damage the old version's Registry settings. A quick command saved the day:

    reg copy software\qualcomm\eudora software\qualcomm\eudora-4.3

This code made a backup copy of my existing settings so I could install the new version, secure in the knowledge that I could easily revert to a previous version if needed.

Saving and restoring keys

The *REGBACK* and *REGREST* utilities allow you to back up and restore entire hives, but `reg` offers a similar pair of functions that add the ability to save and reload individual keys, much like *RegEdt32*'s commands. To save a key and its values, you can use either `reg save` or `reg backup` (they're synonyms).

    REG SAVE [rootKey\]key fileName [machine]

rootKey
> Optional; specifies under which root key the key to save lives. May be HKLM, HKCU, HKCR, HKU, or HKCC on local machine or HKLM or HKU on remote machine. Defaults to HKLM if omitted.

key
> Specifies the full name of the key to update under the specified *rootKey*. If omitted, all contents of *rootKey* are saved.

fileName
> Specifies name of file that will hold the saved data. *fileName* may not have an extension specified.

machine
> Specifies name of a remote machine to query; if omitted, defaults to local machine.

To quickly store a copy of all of your current settings, use this command:

    reg save HKLM my-profile

You then can use it anywhere you use a hive file.

You may also restore a saved hive with the `reg restore` command. This command overwrites an existing key with a new set of values, so you must be cautious when using it (`reg` asks you to confirm your command before it overwrites anything, though).

REG RESTORE *fileName* [*rootKey*\]*key* [*machine*]

fileName
: Specifies file name that holds the data you want restored, with no extension.

rootKey
: Optional; specifies which root key the targeted key lives under. May be HKLM, HKCU, HKCR, HKU, or HKCC on local machine or HKLM or HKU on remote machine. Defaults to HKLM if omitted.

key
: Specifies the full name of the key whose subkeys and values will be replaced.

machine
: Specifies name of a remote machine to query; if omitted, defaults to local machine. You can query HKLM and HKU only on remote machines.

Loading and unloading hives

The Windows NT resource kit versions of `reg load` and `reg unload` operate identically to the Windows 2000 version, with all the same restrictions and capabilities. They're arguably more useful under NT, since you can use them to engineer the default profile settings you want new user accounts to inherit.

Comparing Keys and Values with COMPREG

When you're trying to troubleshoot a configuration problem, it's often useful to examine the broken machine and one that works to discern what's different between the two. Without the resource kit, doing this with the Registry involves saving suspect portions of the Registry to a text file, then using a difference tool such as *windiff* to highlight differences between the two files. The *compreg* tool, included for the first time in the NT 4.0 resource kit, provides a command-line tool for comparing differences in Registry keys. Here's how it works.

COMPREG *key1 key2* [-v] [-r] [-e] [-d] [-q] [-n] [-h] [-?]

key1
: Specifies the full path to the first key to compare. This path can include a machine name (e.g., \\ENIGMA\HKEY_LOCAL_MACHINE\SOFTWARE\LJL). Instead of spelling out the Registry keys, you may abbreviate them by taking the standard mnemonic we've used in this book and dropping the initial "HK";

for example, you could also specify a path of \\ENIGMA\lm\SOFTWARE\LJL to save some typing. If no root is specified, HKCU is the default.

key2
: Specifies the full path to the second key to compare. This can be the same path as *key1* but on a different machine, or it can be a different path altogether. If you specify only a machine name, *compreg* uses the path from *key1* but looks for it on the computer specified in *key2*.

-v
: Verbose mode; prints both keys whose values differ and those that match.

-r
: Recurse into keys that only have a single subkey.

-e
: At exit, sets `errorlevel` to the last error encountered. This switch lets you test the return value of *compreg* when using it in scripts or batch files.

-d
: Suppresses printing the values of keys whose values differ; prints just the keys themselves.

-n
: Monochrome output (the default scheme uses multiple colors).

-?
: Displays a short help message.

The ability to find differences between two machines is extremely useful at times. While troubleshooting some of the entries in Chapter 10, *Registry Tweaks*, I wanted to clone an existing drive restriction and modify it. Unfortunately, after I modified it it didn't work, and I couldn't see what I had done wrong. A quick:

```
compreg software\Microsoft\Windows\CurrentVersion\Policies\Explorer \\armory
```

showed me my error, and I was able to fix it without any further damage to my Registry or my self-esteem.

Searching for Keys with regfind

Sometimes there's no substitute for a little brute-force searching. If you've ever used *grep* or *findstr* (the Win32 equivalent) to find something you *knew* was somewhere on your disk, you'll love *regfind*. It's flexible: it can search for value and key names or contents, it can search or search and replace, and it understands all the common Registry data types. This flexibility makes it a bit more complex than some of the other Resource Kit utilities, though:

```
REGFIND [-h hiveFile hiveRoot | -w win95Dir | -m \\machine]
        [-i tabStop] [-o outputWidth]
        [-p keyPath] [-z | -t dataType] [-b | -B] [-y] [-n]
        [searchString [-r replacementString]]
```

-h *hiveFile hiveRoot*
: Specifies the full path to a local hive file (generated with `reg save` or *RegEdt32*).

-w *win95Dir*

    Tells *regfind* to look for Windows 95 *user.dat* and *system.dat* hive files in the directory specified by *win95Dir*.

-m *machine*

    Specifies that *regfind* should search the remote computer named *machine*.

-i *tabStop*

    Sets the tabstop width; the default is 4.

-o *outputWidth*

    Tells *regfind* how wide to make its output. The default is the width of the console window, or 240 if the output's been redirected to a file.

-p *keyPath*

    Directs *regfind* to start looking in *keyPath*. You may specify one of HKEY_LOCAL_MACHINE, HKEY_USERS, HKEY_CURRENT_USER, or USER; since HKCR and HKCC are links into HKLM, this is not a big loss. If you omit this switch, *regfind* searches the entire Registry.

-z   Searches for REG_MULTI_SZ or REG_EXPAND_SZ strings that are missing the required zero terminator or that have illegal lengths.

-t *dataType*

    Forces *regfind* to look only at values with the specified data type. You may specify any one of REG_SZ, REG_MULTI_SZ, REG_EXPAND_SZ, REG_DWORD, REG_BINARY, and REG_NONE. If no type is specified, *regfind* looks at all the string types.

-b   Tells *regfind* to look for the specified search string inside `REG_BINARY` values in addition to any SZ type specified with -t.

-B   Same as -b, but also searches for ANSI strings in addition to Unicode.

-y   When used during an SZ search, forces *regfind* to do a case-insensitive search. Ignored for REG_DWORD, REG_BINARY, and REG_NONE searches.

-n   Searches key and value names, not just contents. -n and -t are mutually exclusive.

searchString

    Specifies string to search for. To search for a string with embedded spaces, brackets, etc., wrap it in double quotes. If no search string is specified, the search finds values of the specified type. When searching for a REG_DWORD, you may specify it in decimal or hex, with a leading 0x. When searching for a binary value, you must provide a length byte, optionally followed by a sequence of `DWORD`s containing the actual data to search for.

-r *replacementString*

Replaces any occurrence of *searchString* with *replacementString*. *searchString* and *replacementString* must be of the same type, but their lengths may differ. There are several constraints that apply to the use of -r:

— You may specify *replacementString* the same way as *searchString*. However, if your *searchString* is a REG_BINARY length only, you can't use -r.

— If you specify -z and -r together, the replacement string is ignored. Instead of replacing anything, *regfind* fixes any strings with missing terminators or bad lengths.

— There's no confirmation option with -r, so it's a good idea to run *regfind* without it until you're sure what is replaced is what you want replaced.

Because this is a complicated command, an example may help to clarify how the command works. Let's try finding all the keys whose contents or names include the string "Mac":

```
C:\ntreskit>regfind -y -n Mac
Scanning \Registry registry tree
Case Insensitive Search for 'Mac'
Will match values of type: REG_SZ REG_EXPAND_SZ REG_MULTI_SZ
Search will include key or value names
\Registry
    Machine
        SOFTWARE
            Microsoft
                AsyncMac
                Exchange
                    Client
                        Mac File Types
                Shared Tools
                    Text Converters
                        Export
                            MSWordMac4
                            MSWordMac5
                            MSWordMac51
                        Import
                            MSWordMac
        SYSTEM
            ControlSet001
                Services
                    AsyncMac
                    AsyncMac2
                    EventLog
                        System
                            AsyncMac
            ControlSet003
                Services
                    AsyncMac
```

```
                        AsyncMac2
                    EventLog
                        System
                            AsyncMac
        Users
            S-1-5-21-1944135612-1199777195-24521265-500
                Software
                    Microsoft
                        Ntbackup
                            Backup Engine
                                Process Macintosh files = 1
                                Machine Type = 0
                            Telnet
                                Machine1 = fly.hiwaay.net
                                LastMachine = hq
                                Machine2 = hq
```

The only real drawback to *regfind* is that it can't handle regular expressions or wildcards like *findstr* and *grep* can. Apart from that limitation, though, it's a valuable tool when you need to find a key whose value you know but whose path you don't. If you need to use regular expressions, use *scanreg.exe* instead.

Spying on the Registry with RegMon

Ask a private investigator what the best way to gather evidence is, and you're likely to get a simple answer: watch and wait. Unfortunately, trying to use *RegEdt32* or *RegEdit* to watch the Registry as it changes is a difficult and unrewarding way to work. Unless you know ahead of time exactly which keys or values you want to watch, it's difficult to monitor individual changes, and there's no easy way to tell which application, process, or driver changed the setting you're trying to watch.

Mark Russinovich and Bryce Cogswell have solved this problem, to the delight of administrators and programmers everywhere. They wrote a utility called *RegMon* (available with source code from *http://www.sysinternals.com*) that lets you spy on every Registry access made anywhere in the system. It can monitor reads, writes, and queries and record them in a log that you can peruse at will; it can also limit the Registry accesses it records based on filtering criteria you supply. *RegMon* makes short work of figuring out who modified a particular key or value, and it's a great resource for watching what the system's doing with Registry data.

RegMon works by installing a small device driver when you run the application; this driver installs hooks to all the Registry API routines, so it can see what parameters callers pass in and what results the system returns. The *RegMon* application itself just opens the device driver and waits for it to send along the data it's captured.

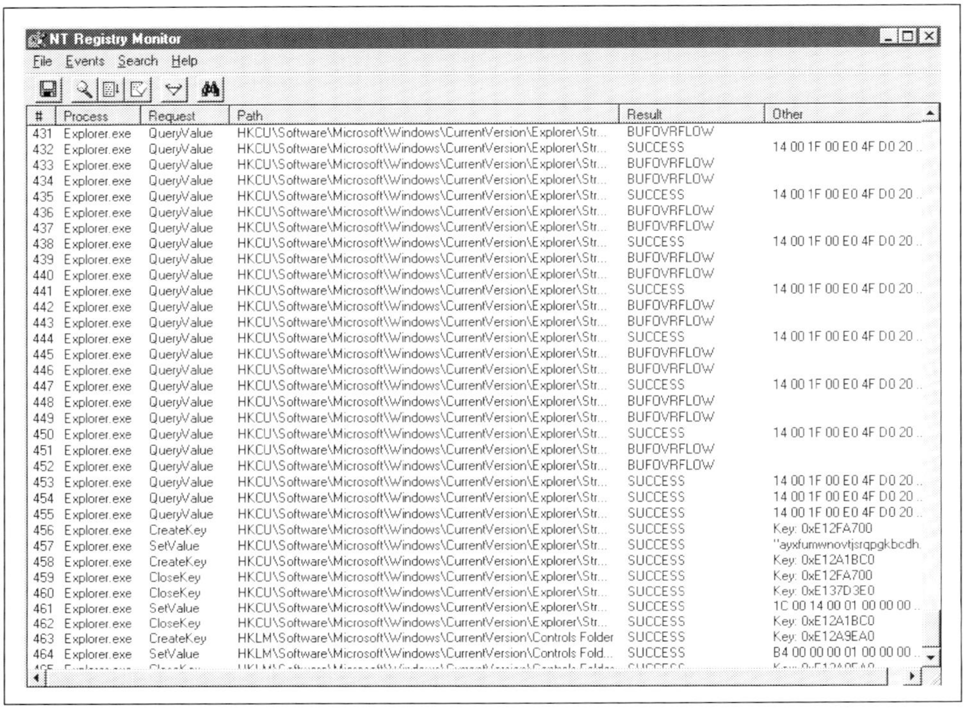

Figure 9-9. The RegMon main interface

Learning the RegMon Interface

RegMon has an extremely simple interface. As you can see in Figure 9-9, it uses a single document window to display the Registry data it captures. The toolbar offers access to all six menu commands; the bulk of the window is devoted to the list of captured data. Each column of the list has its own header at the top of the list window; you can resize each column in the list by dragging the small vertical lines next to each header. Each entry in the list displays seven fields' worth of data:

ID A sequence number assigned by *RegMon*. The first thing it logs gets ID #1, and the ID is incremented from there. However, these IDs are assigned by the device driver. If events occur faster than *RegMon* can add them to its display list, you'll notice gaps in the numbering.

Time
Either the elapsed time since the last request or the date and time of the request.

Sneaking a Peek with RegEdt32

RegMon isn't the only way to spy on the Registry. The following steps are a handy trick that allows you to see even the SAM and SECURITY hives, which are normally inaccessible:

1. Enable the Scheduler service and have it log in as the SYSTEM account by selecting the "System Account" radio button in the Services dialog.

2. Once the Scheduler is running, open a command-line window and use the `at` command to schedule an invocation of *RegEdt32* in the near future. For example, if it's 1:35 P.M. when you start off, schedule *RegEdt32* to run at 1:36 P.M. like this:

   ```
   at 13:36 /interactive regedt32.exe
   ```

3. If you prefer, and if you're using Windows 2000, you can schedule the task using the Scheduled Tasks wizard.

At the appointed time, *RegEdt32* opens, but it's running under the `SYSTEM` account instead of your normal account. HKLM\SYSTEM and HKLM\SAM is enabled, so you can open and inspect them. Don't expect to see much, since their contents are all binary data. *Don't edit anything in these hives.*

One extremely valuable thing you can do with this trick is to enable auditing on the SAM hive. This can give you an audit trail of attempted and successful misbehavior, including grabbing the password hashes or changing passwords on the Administrator account.

Process

The name of the process that made the request. Since DLLs are loaded into a process' address space, *RegMon* shows only the process name, not the name of the individual DLL making the request.

Request

What action the requesting process asked for. Most often, you see QueryValue, OpenKey, CloseKey, and SetValue, but *RegMon* also reports enumerations, security changes, and all the other Registry services available through the Registry API documented in Chapter 8.

Path

The path supplied as part of the request. *RegMon* always shows the path including the topmost root key.

Result
> The numeric result code returned by whatever Registry API routine was called. You see a lot of "SUCCESS" entries here, with an occasional "NOTFOUND." It's rare to see anything other than these two.

Other
> A catch-all field. For Registry calls that return data, *RegMon* shows the data here as a value of whatever type is appropriate. You see string values in quotes, but DWORDs, HKEYs, and other binary data appears as a block of hex digits. It's up to you to interpret binary data and make sense out of it.

Controlling what you see

Besides dragging the column headers to resize each individual column, *RegMon* doesn't offer much in the way of user interface. The Edit → Clear Display command erases the current list of logged Registry accesses, and the Options → Auto Scroll command toggles whether *RegMon* attempts to automatically scroll the displayed list to always show the most recently added item.

Some other useful Edit menu commands

There are several other useful commands in the Edit menu, too:

- The Edit → Copy command copies the selected entry's information as a single plain-ASCII text line.
- The Edit → History Depth... command lets you control how many events *RegMon* buffers. The default value of 0 means that it attempts to keep all the entries it logs, but you can restrict it to a smaller number.
- The Edit → Font... and Edit → Highlight Colors... commands let you control how the captured data are displayed.
- The Edit → Find... command allows you to search the capture buffer for a particular event
- The Edit → Regedit Jump... command opens *RegEdit* and opens the value referenced in the selected log entry.

Capturing and Filtering

Using *RegMon* to figure out what's going on in the Registry is a two-step process. The first step is optional: you may choose which events you want to see (and which you don't) by building a capture filter. *RegMon* applies this filter during the second step—the actual capture of events.

Turning capture on and off

When you first start *RegMon*, it's in capture mode. If you just sit there for a minute and let it run, you see an occasional Registry access recorded in its window; you can see many more if you switch to Explorer and open a file, or even click on an icon in your My Computer window. If you leave *RegMon* in capture mode, it's likely to capture an overwhelming amount of data, much of which won't bear any relation to the data you're actually looking for.

The best way to reduce this information overload is simple: turn off capture mode when you don't need it. The Options → Capture Events command (Ctrl+E is its accelerator) toggles capture mode off and on (as does the toolbar button).

Using capture filters

The Edit → Filter/Highlight... command is arguably the most useful command in the whole program. The Regmon Filter dialog (see Figure 9-10) lets you specify in detail which events you want to see in the capture list and which you don't.

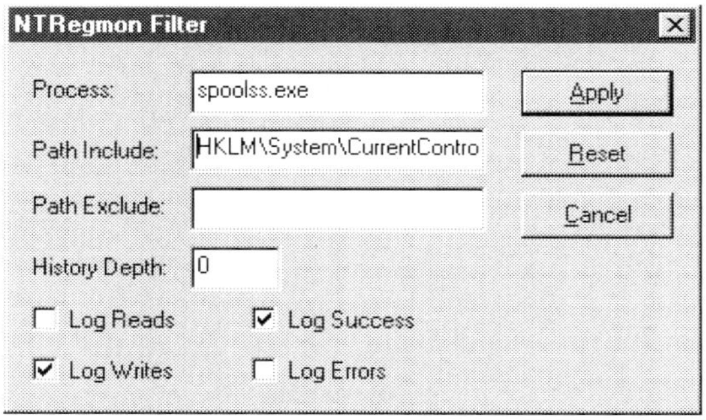

Figure 9-10. RegMon's filter dialog

Here are the filter criteria you may specify:

Include

> Includes only those events you specify. If you leave it blank, nothing is included. More likely, you'll want to include only specific keys, results, or executable names. The default value of * indicates that you want to include everything. You can use multiple values, too, by separating them with commas. For example, a value of `lsass.exe,explorer.exe` includes activity generated by those two processes only.

Exclude

> Lets you filter out things you don't want to see. As with the Include field, you can use wildcards and multiple values. In Figure 9-10, I've specified that I

want to see all activity except that generated by *lsass.exe* and the DLLs it loads into its process space.

The Highlight field
Lets you pick which Registry calls you want to highlight, using the color you selected with the Edit → Highlight Colors… command. Notice that in this field, I've added a process ID (the `:1136` after the process name). You can use process IDs in the Include and Exclude fields as well.

The Log checkboxes
Let you control what actions *RegMon* logs. By default, it logs reads, writes, successes, and errors, but you may adjust this to narrow the breadth of the data you have to wade through.

Saving your captured data

RegMon can save its logged data as a tab-delimited text file. There's no provision for saving part of a log; you can either save every logged event, or none. This is easy to work around, though; all you need to do is define an appropriate capture filter before you capture data, then there won't be any extraneous stuff in your capture log.

The File → Save… and File → Save As… commands let you save logged data to a file you specify. Unlike the Performance Monitor, there's no way to load a file of saved data for further review; you have to use a spreadsheet or text editor to view the saved data if you need it later.

Logging boot-to-boot activity

If you've ever wondered what happens behind Windows 2000's chunky-pixeled boot screens, *RegMon* gives you an easy way to find out. If you choose the Edit → Log Boot command, *RegMon* logs pretty much every Registry access from the beginning of the boot cycle. This generates a lot of data (25+ MB on a Windows 2000 Professional machine), but there's a lot of interesting stuff in there.

10
Registry Tweaks

In the preceding chapters, I showed you how to use the Registry tools and programming interfaces. As a sort of graduation exercise, this chapter contains a list of Registry settings you can use to change the way your computer behaves. I have deliberately not listed anything unsafe or dangerous here; as long as you follow the restrictions stated in each setting's explanatory text, these changes should be safe for you to make on any Windows 2000 or NT 4.0 machine.

If you read Appendix A, *User Configuration Group Policy Objects* and Appendix B, *Computer Configuration Group Policy Objects* carefully, you may notice that some of these items are also editable through group policies. I've included them here on purpose; even if you're not using policies you may still want to make these changes. Of course, you can take any setting in this chapter and add it as a policy template file using the instructions in the section "Creating Your Own Administrative Templates" in Chapter 7, *Using Group Policies*.

Be careful to apply the correct capitalization to any values or keys you change. Some applications are smart enough to ignore case, but most aren't.

The actual mechanics of making these changes should be pretty obvious by now: use your favorite Registry editor to add or modify keys or values as described for each setting. Some of these tweaks require you to add a new key, while others may require you to add or change a specific value. In all cases, when I say something like "add the value HKCU\Control Panel\Desktop\WindowMetrics\MinAnimate," what that means is that you should add it if it doesn't already exist. If it does exist, change its value as suggested in the text.

User Interface Tweaks

The user interface for Windows 2000 and NT 4.0 is customizable in a lot of small ways. You can't easily change the standard way windows and menus work, for example, but you can change their colors. In that spirit, there are several adjustments you can make to change some basics of how you and the operating system interact with one another.

Add Your Own "Tip of the Day"

Microsoft Word for Windows introduced the "Tip of the Day" feature, which presents an ostensibly helpful tip every time you start a tip-enabled application. This feature made it into Windows 95, Office 95, NT 4.0, and a raft of third-party applications. Apart from disabling the feature altogether (which you can do with the "Don't show tips at startup" checkbox in the Tip of the Day dialog), you can add your own set of tips. This is particularly useful when you make this change as part of a system policy; you can build your own set of tips that are specific to your local environment, then remove the ability for users to turn the tips off. This is an easy, and cheap, way to disseminate information to your users. The list of tips is stored as a set of values under:

```
HKLM\Software\Microsoft\Windows\CurrentVersion\Explorer\Tips
```

The tip values are stored as sequentially named REG_SZ values; the first one is named "0," and the names go up from there. You can replace any of the existing tips included with NT by changing that tip's value; alternatively, you can replace all of them by removing all the values under Tips and replacing them with your own.

However, the tip list is only half of the necessary change. There's also a pair of REG_BINARY values that control whether tips are displayed and which tip comes next. These values are stored in HKCU, so they can be different for every individual user. Here's how they work:

HKCU\Software\Microsoft\Windows\CurrentVersion\Explorer\Tips\Show
  Controls whether tips are shown at startup or not. A value of 00000000 disables the tip display, while 01000000 enables it.

HKCU\Software\Microsoft\Windows\CurrentVersion\Explorer\Tips\Next
  Controls which tip appears next. Its value is a sequence number that must match the name of a value in the tips list. A value of 00000000 displays tip 0, 01000000 displays tip 1, 0c000000 displays tip 12, and so on. NT automatically increments and updates this value as each tip is displayed.

Disable Window Animations

Windows 2000 and NT 4.0 copy the Win95 habit of using animated rectangles to provide a "zooming" effect when windows are opened and closed. However, after the first few times you've seen this effect it can become annoying; it also causes a slight but perceptible slowdown as the system draws all the fancy rectangles instead of just closing the window directly.

If you want to disable this animation for Windows 2000, you may do so by adding the REG_SZ value HKCU\Control Panel\Desktop\WindowMetrics\MinAnimate and setting its value to 0. NT 4.0 users should to add this value as a REG_DWORD type. If you later decide that you like the animations after all, setting MinAnimate back to 1 turns it back on.

Speed Up the Taskbar

The Taskbar is a useful addition to the standard user interface. When Apple was designing the Macintosh interface, their research found that a single menu bar at the top or bottom of the screen was the fastest menu system; instead of having to carefully guide the mouse to a particular area, you can just slam it down (or up) to the menu region without any need for precise control. The Taskbar's default location at the bottom of the screen satisfies this. One failing of the Taskbar, however, is the speed with which the Start menu (and other menus attached to Taskbar items) pops up. In a word, it's slow. Fortunately, the speed is adjustable via a Registry change.

To adjust the Taskbar pop-up speed, add a REG_SZ value named MenuShowDelay to HKCU\Control Panel\Desktop. This value determines the number of milliseconds the shell pauses before displaying the Taskbar. By default, it's set to "400," which is a 0.4-second delay. Adjust it to your taste, then reboot to make the change take effect.

Enable Tab for Filename Completion

If you're a Unix administrator or programmer, you'll love this one. Many Unix shells allow you to quickly complete filenames in the shell by using the Tab key. For example, if you type ls -l aar and hit the Tab key, the shell looks for files whose names start with "aar." If it finds one, it automatically expands what you typed into the full file or directory name. This is a lifesaver, especially since Unix allows you to have very long file and pathnames with embedded spaces—just like Windows 2000 and NT.

This behavior is specified by the REG_DWORD value HKCU\Software\Microsoft\Command Processor\CompletionChar. Set it to the hex value of the character you want to use for filename completion. To use the Tab key, set its value to 0x09. While other characters may fill in as the completion character, such as Ctrl-D (0x04), the Tab key is familiar and otherwise unused in the command window.

Setting this Registry value enables completion for all invocations of the command processor. However, if you run the command processor with the file and directory name-completion characters option explicitly enabled (cmd /F:ON), the default completion characters are used, rather than the value in the CompletionChar Registry setting. The default control characters are Ctrl-D for directory name completion and Ctrl-F for file name completion.

Run a Different Screen Saver While Waiting for a Logon

You probably know you can use the "Screen Savers" tab of the Display control panel to set a screen saver to be run after a specified period of inactivity. You can also choose which screen saver runs while a Windows 2000 or NT machine is waiting for a logon. The default choice displays the familiar "Press Ctrl+Alt+Del to log in" dialog, complete with the three-fingered hand icon, but you can easily choose another.

Some of the screen savers bundled with Windows 2000 and NT are CPU hogs. If you're choosing a logon screen saver for a server, make sure you stick with the "blank screen" saver; otherwise, your server's valuable CPU cycles are used to draw OpenGL objects or flying stars, robbing your server of the power it needs to handle your users.

If you want to use another screen saver while your operating system is waiting for someone to log on locally, you need to make three changes. First of all, add HKU\.DEFAULT\Control Panel\Desktop\ScreenSaveActive as a REG_SZ; set its value to 1. This tells the system that when no one's logged in (for example, when the .DEFAULT profile's being used), you want a screen saver to run. Under NT 4.0, add this key as a REG_DWORD value instead.

Next, edit the value of HKU\.DEFAULT\Control Panel\Desktop\SCRNSAVE.EXE to specify the full path of the screen saver you want to run. (If the screen saver you want is in the default location of *%systemroot%\system32*, you don't have to enter the full path.) For example, you might enter *sstars.scr* to run the "flying stars" screen saver.

Finally, edit the value of HKU\.DEFAULT\Control Panel\Desktop\ScreenSave-TimeOut and enter a value for the screen-saver trigger time. This value, in seconds, specifies the amount of inactivity you're willing to allow before the screen saver kicks in.

Once you make the changes, you must reboot before they take effect.

Enable X Window-Style "Auto Raise" [NT4]

The X Window system has a neat configuration setting called "auto-raise." When this setting's in effect, you don't have to click on a window to bring it to the front of the window stack. Instead, just passing the mouse over a window raises it. This takes a little getting used to, but once you've made the adjustment, you'll find that it eliminates a lot of extra mouse clicks.

NT does something similar: it can automatically set the focus to a window when you put the mouse in it, but it won't raise that window to the top of the stack. This setting is off by default to avoid confusing people who haven't been exposed to auto-raise before. To turn it on, set the value of HKCU\Control Panel\Mouse\ActiveWindowTracking to 1. You have to log out and log back on before the change takes effect.

Enable "Snap to Default Button"

Some X Window system implementations also have another handy feature: you can force the cursor to always jump to the default button of any dialog or alert that appears. This speeds the process of moving the cursor from wherever it happens to be to the dialog or alert, especially if you're using a high-resolution monitor or an input device that makes it hard to move the cursor quickly.

You can enable or disable this behavior by adjusting the value of HKCU\Control Panel\Mouse\SnapToDefaultButton. When this value is 0, as it is by default, no snapping occurs. Set it to 1, though, and the cursor warps to the default button once you log out and log back on. Try it—you may like it.

Suppress Error Messages During Boot and Logon

During a Windows 2000 or NT boot process, it's not uncommon to see error dialogs reporting problems that occurred during startup. For example, you may see warnings telling you that a device driver couldn't be started, or that some other system component didn't do what it was supposed to do. You can suppress these error dialogs with a simple Registry change; the errors are still logged in the system and application sections of the event log, but the dialogs won't interrupt or intrude on the boot and logon process.

The actual errors are displayed in two phases; their display is thus controlled by two separate Registry values. Messages that pop up on Windows 2000 as the result of errors in the boot phase are controlled by the value HKLM\SOFTWARE\Microsoft\Windows NT\CurrentVersion\Windows\NoPopUpsOnBoot. In the Windows NT 4.0 Registry, the NoPopUpsOnBoot key is found at HKCU\SOFTWARE\Microsoft\Windows NT\CurrentVersion\Windows\NoPopUpsOnBoot. Add this value as a REG_DWORD and give it a value of 1 to suppress boot errors, or 0 to allow the normal error dialog display.

Messages that appear as part of the post-boot startup phase (including messages produced by most device drivers and services) are controlled by a different value, HKLM\SOFTWARE\Microsoft\Windows NT\CurrentVersion\Windows\ErrorMode or, for NT 4.0, HKCU\SOFTWARE\Microsoft\Windows NT\CurrentVersion\Windows\ErrorMode. Set this REG_DWORD value to 0 to allow all system and application errors to display dialogs, 1 to display only application errors, or 2 to suppress all error dialogs. The default value is 0.

Set NUMLOCK Key During Startup

You can specify whether the NUMLOCK key is on or off when the computer starts through the HKCU\Control Panel\Keyboard\InitialKeyboardIndicators value. InitialKeyboardIndicators is a REG_SZ type that, when set to 2, causes the NUMLOCK key to be on when the user logs on. Setting the value to 0 ensures the key is off.

Display Version Number

A simple desktop tweak allows you to display the Windows 2000 version number and build number in the lower right corner of the desktop. Set the REG_DWORD value HKCU\Control Panel\Desktop\PaintDesktopVersion to 1 to show the OS build information.

Filesystem Tweaks

The guts of the filesystem of both Windows 2000 and NT 4.0 are mostly self-tuning. This is on purpose, following the theory that the filesystem can adjust its own caching and buffering better than you can. Whether this is true or not, there are still some changes you can make to control whether the filesystem does certain things. These changes apply to FAT, NTFS, and NTFS 5 filesystems.

Change Low Disk Space Warning Threshold

Even though you may never have encountered it, Windows NT and 2000 can display an alert warning you that your disk is almost full. The threshold for these alerts is 90% disk usage; while this may seem generous, if you're using a large disk, a 10% margin results in you seeing these warnings even when the amount of space remaining is large in absolute terms. My local Internet service provider runs an NT news server with more than 80GB of disk storage, so getting a warning that there's "only" 8GB free is not very useful to them.

The DiskSpaceThreshold value controls when you see this alert; it sets the minimum amount of free space (as a percentage) that triggers a warning. Add this value (it's a REG_DWORD) to HKLM\System\CurrentControlSet\Services\LanmanServer\Parameters; the value you specify should be the percentage of free space, from 0 to 99, which should trigger a warning. When the amount of free space on any volume falls below this value, you get a warning.

Use Longer File Extensions

Even though Win95 ostensibly supports long filenames, there's an ugly secret involved: it really supports only three-character file extensions! That means that the names *medical.doc*, *medical.doctor*, and *medical.doctrine* all point to the same file. Since NTFS doesn't have that restriction, you can make it take advantage of the longer extensions instead of being stuck with the three-character versions.

The value of HKLM\System\CurrentControlSet\Control\FileSystem\Win95TruncatedExtensions controls this behavior. On Windows NT machines, it's set to 0 by default. This truncates extensions to the first three characters. Set it to 1 (the Windows 2000 default) and reboot to take advantage of full-length extensions on NTFS volumes.

Turn Off CD-ROM AutoRun

Ahh, "AutoRun." While Microsoft undoubtedly did a favor for some users who like to have CDs start running automatically when they're inserted, many of the users I talk to don't like this feature. If, for example, you're loading the Windows 2000 Resource Kit CD to copy a tool you need, do you really want to wait while the AutoRun-invoked setup tool loads, or would you rather just copy the file you need?

Happily, you can banish AutoRun from your Windows 2000 or NT machine with a simple change. Add a REG_DWORD value named HKLM\SYSTEM\CurrentControlSet\Services\Cdrom\Autorun and set its value to 0, and you'll no longer be forced to wait for AutoRunning-CDs to do their stuff. You can later change the value to 1 if you want to reenable AutoRun for CD-ROMs.

For more specific AutoRun control of all your Windows 2000 drives, add a REG_DWORD named HKLM\SOFTWARE\Microsoft\Windows\CurrentVersion\Policies\Explorer\NoDriveAutoRun. Populate this value with a bit mask of the drives (lowest bit representing drive A) you want to disable AutoRun on. For example, the hex value 0x18 (binary 0001 1000) disables AutoRun on drives D and E.

Suppress "Last Access" Timestamp on NTFS Volumes

NTFS volumes store a "last access" timestamp for every directory on the volume. That means that every time you look at a directory listing, the operating system is busily updating the timestamps on each directory it detects. As you might guess, this is often a waste of CPU cycles and disk bandwidth that could better be used elsewhere. To prevent Windows from updating the "last access" timestamp for directories under NTFS volumes, add a REG_DWORD value named NtfsDisableLastAccessUpdate to HKLM\System\CurrentControlSet\Control\FileSystem and set its value to 1. Note that this change has no effect on the "last modified" timestamp.

While suppressing "last access" timestamps can increase the speed of directory listings and prevent the NTFS log buffer from becoming filled with timestamp update records, be aware that these timestamps are useful for NT auditing. Disabling last-access update decreases available auditing information.

Security Tweaks

A surprising number of Windows 2000 and NT's security features are only accessible through Registry tweaks. For the most part, these adjustments add to your system's security; except as noted, you are not adding extra risk by not making the changes discussed here. You should carefully note the security suggestions included in Chapter 9, *Administering the Registry*. They reflect changes you *should* make to preserve system security, while the items in this section are optional.

Clear the System Pagefile at Shutdown

The U.S. Government (actually the National Computer Security Center) has established a rating system for configurations of computer operating systems. This rating system, set forth in a document called the Orange Book, rates how secure operating systems are. To earn a particular rating, there are certain features an OS must implement. One of these features is object reuse. Simply put, object reuse just means that objects (including disk blocks, memory, and other shared resources) are cleared out after use. This prevents any leakage of confidential data.

While Windows 2000 and NT can be made compliant, as shipped neither OS clears inactive pages in the virtual memory's pagefile. A couple of publicized attacks* rely on the fact that the system's pagefile is left intact when the system shuts down; it can then be scanned for useful data. To prevent this, you can add the REG_DWORD value HKLM\System\CurrentControlSet\Control\Session Manager\Memory Management\ClearPageFileAtShutdown value and set it to 1; this forces the system to zero out the contents of the pagefile at system shutdown. Be forewarned that making this change increases your system shutdown time in direct proportion to the size of your pagefile.

Prevent Caching of Logon Credentials

By default, Windows 2000 and NT workstations cache the last 10 sets of logon credentials received from a domain controller. This reduces the number of times a workstation has to contact a domain controller for verification of a logon request, and it often makes it possible to log on to a domain even when the domain controller isn't available on the network. If you want to prevent these credentials from being cached, as you might if you're running a high-security network, add a REG_SZ value named CachedLogonsCount beneath the HKLM\Software\Microsoft\Windows NT\CurrentVersion\Winlogon key. Set its value to 0 to prevent any caching or to the number of cached credential sets you're willing to allow.

Turn Off "Save Password" Option in Dial-Up Networking

The Dial-Up Networking (DUN) subsystem of Windows 2000 and NT lets you maintain a separate username and password for every entry in the Phonebook. You can also use the "Save this password" checkbox, which appears in the RAS Logon dialog; when you do, the system stores that account's password in the Registry. This is pretty insecure, especially when the machine using DUN is a laptop; if it's stolen, the thief has automatic access to your dial-up connection if the password's been saved.

You can force DUN not to store passwords by adding the REG_DWORD value DisableSavePassword value to HKLM\SYSTEM\CurrentControlSet\Services\RasMan\Parameters. If you set its value to 1, DUN won't display the "Save password"

---

* The attacks depend on application bugs; a well-written application won't leave any sensitive data in virtual memory, but a well-written OS won't expose it either.

checkbox, and it forgets any passwords it has previously stored. This setting's a good candidate for inclusion in a policy template; that allows you to enforce the security setting you want applied.

Prevent Users from Changing Network Drive Mappings

Once you establish a set of drive mappings for your users (either as part of a logon script, a profile, or a persistent connection), you can protect them from changes by changing the permissions on HKCU\Network, and its subkeys, to remove the Delete and Create Subkey permissions. If you do this, users can still add or delete network connections, but the changes won't persist after they log out.

Do not remove the users' Set Value or Read access; if you do, connections won't be reestablished when that user logs on again.

Control Who Can See Performance Monitor Data

The Performance Monitor for Windows 2000/NT is a nice addition to the system's basic toolset; it allows you to quickly gather and analyze performance data for local and remote machines. If you're like most network administrators or managers, though, you'd probably prefer that your servers' performance data be kept away from other network users, since there's no good reason for ordinary users to be monitoring a server's performance.

The permissions on the HKLM\Software\Microsoft\Windows NT\CurrentVersion\Perflib key control who may read a machine's performance data. By default, an ordinary NT 4.0 installation has Everyone:Read permission on this key, though Windows 2000 defaults are less permissive. I suggest using *RegEdt32* to tighten permissions on the Perflib key: let Administrators have Full Control and remove Everyone altogether. If you want any user who's actually logged into the machine to have access, you can add Interactive Users:Read; doing so keeps network users from seeing the performance data while still allowing interactive users to monitor the machine if they need to do so.

Control Which Drives Are Visible Throughout the System

If you need to, you can hide drives on a machine so they don't appear in My Computer, Explorer, or the open and save dialog boxes. You might do this (in conjunction with other access control measures like the "run only allowed applications" policy setting) to keep users from damaging their Windows 2000 or NT installations or installing unapproved software. Hide the drives you don't want users to tamper with and they won't see them. (Actually, hidden drives are accessible through the File Manager and the Windows 2000 and NT command prompts. Solution? Turn those off with a policy.) This hiding occurs on a per-user basis, too, so you have fairly fine control over which volumes users can see.

The value that controls drive hiding is actually a bit mask. HKCU\Software\Microsoft\Windows\CurrentVersion\Policies\Explorer\NODRIVES is a REG_DWORD, which makes it 32 bits long. Since the system can map only 26 drives (*A:* through *Z:*), this mapping works out nicely. The upper six bits of the value are ignored; the remaining 26 bits map to each drive letter, with *A:* in the right-most position and *Z:* in the left-most, like this:

```
0 0 0 0 0 0 0 0 0 0 0 0 0 0 0 0 0 0 0 0 0 0 0 0 0 0 0 0 0 0 0 0
      Z Y X            ............                     C B A
```

To turn off drives A, B, C, and D, you end up with a mask value of "00000000000000000000001111"; to turn off all drives, just use all 1 bits in the mask. *RegEdt32* makes it easy to add new DWORD values as bitmasks or to edit existing values as binary strings (see Chapter 5, *Using RegEdt32*, if you need more details), so adding this restriction is easy to do. There's one caveat: if your drive letters change—perhaps because you've added a new disk or removed an old one—your NODRIVES values are shifted, and you may suddenly lose sight of a drive you wanted to keep visible.

Change When the Password Expiration Warning Appears

A good password policy is one of the cornerstones of network security. You start by making users pick good passwords,* then follow up by setting a password aging policy that forces users to change their passwords at reasonable intervals.† Windows 2000 and NT helpfully warns users that their password is going to expire two

---

* There's an excellent discussion of what makes a password good or bad in O'Reilly's *Windows NT User Administration* by Meggitt and Ritchey.

† You do this with the User Manager under NT or with Active Directory Users and Computers under Windows 2000.

weeks, or 14 days, in advance. Since most users won't change their passwords when the first warning appears (most, in fact, won't change until their password finally does expire), why torture them with two weeks' worth of warnings?

Instead, add a REG_DWORD value named PasswordExpiryWarning to HKLM\SOFTWARE\Microsoft\Windows NT\CurrentVersion\Winlogon. Set its value to the number of days, up to 14, you want to start the expiration warnings at; I recommend between three and seven days.

Allow Members of the Printer Operators Group to Add Printers

Both Windows 2000 and NT 4.0 include a number of built-in groups that allow you to assign limited administration privileges to people who need them. The Server Operators, Print Operators, and Backup Operators groups allow a network administrator to grant greater-than-normal rights to these operators without making them members of the Administrators group.

Print Operators can stop and restart the print spooler, route print jobs, and perform other printer-related administrative functions. However, they cannot add or modify printer ports, meaning that you can't delegate that responsibility to the people who should most likely have it. You may reverse this unhappy state of affairs by changing the permissions on a single Registry key. Here's what to do:

1. Open *RegEdt32* and select HKLM\SYSTEM\CurrentControlSet\Control\Print\Monitors.

2. Use the Security → Permissions... command to display the Registry Key Permissions dialog.

3. Click the Add button; when the Add Users and Groups dialog appears, select the Print Operators group and give them Full Control access. Click OK; the Registry Key Permissions dialog reappears with the new permissions.

4. Stop and restart the Spooler service using the `net stop spooler` and `net start spooler` commands from a command window.

Set the Number of Authentication Retries for Dial-Up Connections

You may adjust the number of authentication attempts DUN allows before it decides the remote user is bogus and hangs up the phone. By default, DUN allows two unsuccessful retries; you can adjust this value from zero to 10 by editing the HKLM\System\CurrentControlSet\Services\RemoteAccess\Parameters\AuthenticateRetries value. A value of zero tells DUN to hang up at the first failure, which may be too restrictive for users who must type in passwords manually; I set the value to 1 so that users can make one mistake before they have to start over again.

Keep Users from Changing Video Resolutions

Being able to change screen resolution and color depth on the fly is a terrific Windows 2000 and NT feature, until your users start changing settings when you don't want them to. You can prevent this by changing the permissions on the settings key for the video card. The exact location of this key varies depending on the number and type of video cards installed in a particular computer; it also varies between machines that have different video card types.

The key to change permissions on is at HKLM\System\CurrentControlSet\Hardware Profiles\Current\System\CurrentControlSet\Services*devicename*\DeviceX where *devicename* is the name of your video adapter driver (mine is "S3," but you should be able to deduce the right value for your computers depending on what type of card you have). The proper value for *DeviceX* varies too, but if you only have one video card it's always "Device0."

Set the Authentication Timeout for Dial-Up Connections

In addition to setting the number of authentication retries you'll allow, you can also specify how long each attempt takes before the system counts it as a failed attempt. By default, DUN allows connecting users 120 seconds to either authenticate successfully or have their attempt deemed a failure. Edit the value HKLM\System\CurrentControlSet\Services\RemoteAccess\Parameters\AuthenticateTime to adjust the timeout period; you can set any value you like from 20 seconds all the way up to 10 minutes (or 600 seconds; the value must be specified in seconds).

Keep Remote Users from Sharing a Mounted CD-ROM or Floppy

By default, the system automatically creates an administrative share for every disk or CD-ROM volume. This share, which is named by the drive letter plus a dollar sign, is invisible, so it doesn't appear in Network Neighborhood, but a savvy user can find it anyway. There may be times when you don't want anyone but the locally logged-in user to access a CD-ROM; for example, many reference CD-ROMs have strict licensing limits that promise big trouble if you share the CD-ROM across the network.

Remember the brief discussion about object reuse? It applies to other shared resources, too, including CD-ROMs and floppies. In its quest to gain C2 security certification for NT, Microsoft added two Registry keys that cause the CD-ROM and floppy drives to be allocated to the currently logged-in user. When this allocation occurs, other users can't access the drives or the media in them; when no one's logged in, the drives are unallocated and may be shared. These NT settings made it into the Windows 2000 Registry.

Two keys under HKLM\Software\Microsoft\WindowsNT\CurrentVersion\Winlogon implement these settings: AllocateFloppies and AllocateCDRoms. Both are of type REG_SZ. To force allocation of either device type during logon, set the appropriate key's value to 1; to turn allocation off, set the key's value to 0.

Keep Users from Customizing "My Computer"

There's no policy setting that prevents users from changing the name or icon of the My Computer icon on the desktop. If you've ever had to administer a lab full of computers, you've probably had at least one incidence of finding a machine's My Computer icon renamed to "Beavis & Butthead" or something even worse. To nip these changes in the bud, change the access permissions on HKLM\Software\Classes\CLSID\20D04FE0-3AEA-1069-08002B30309D.

Remove the Everyone group from this key and add the Users group with Read access.

Performance Tweaks

When it comes to computers—particularly those running Windows 2000 or NT—you can never have too much speed. The least expensive performance upgrade for Windows machines is usually just additional RAM, since the computer can productively use as much as you can stuff into it. Failing that, you can make a few small changes to improve both your computers' speed and their availability.

Automatically Delete Cached User Profiles

User profiles make it easy to centralize and distribute user-specific settings. This enables users to have their same desktop settings follow them as they wander around your network. However, these profiles take up space; if you have many users who interactively log onto a particular machine, their cached profiles will slowly accumulate, stealing your disk space as they build up.

You can tell your system to automatically delete cached profiles when they're no longer needed. When a user logs on, if her profile isn't on the local machine, the system fetches it and keeps it there until it's removed or updated (in which case the updated version is downloaded into the cache). This makes it possible to log on and get profile information even when the domain controller(s) aren't answering profile requests. If you enable automatic removal, the system deletes the cached profile when the user logs out. The good news is that this approach saves disk space at a small cost in extra profile downloads. The bad news is that users may not be able to log on when your domain controllers are unavailable; there won't be a cached profile on the machine for them to use when logging on.

If you want cached profiles to be deleted automatically, add a REG_DWORD value named DeleteRoamingCache to HKLM\SOFTWARE\Microsoft\WindowsNT\CurrentVersion\Winlogon. Give it a value of 1 to enable removal or 0 to allow cached profiles to stay around.

Enable Automatic Reboot After a Crash

Normally when an NT machine crashes, it produces a "Blue Screen of Death" (BSOD), which indicates the cause of the crash and gives some information about the system's state when the crash happened. The problem with this approach is that the server sits there, BSOD proudly displayed, until a human comes along and reboots it. This is not ideal for most server applications; if no one is able to get to the machine to reboot it, none of its users can use it. Imagine having your Exchange server go down while you're on vacation, with users unable to get mail until you can find someone in the office to go reboot it for you!

As an administrator, you can force Windows 2000 to automatically reboot after a crash by setting the value of HKLM\SYSTEM\CurrentControlSet\Control\CrashControl\AutoReboot to 1; this forces the system to automatically reboot after writing out the crash log file. Under NT, use the value HKLM\SYSTEM\CurrentControlSet\CrashControl\AutoReboot. While this change is necessary for NT and Windows 2000 Professional, Windows 2000 Server reboots after a crash by default.

Record Evidence of a Crash

Besides the standard crash dump file, you can also tell Windows 2000 and NT to record the occurrence of a crash in two ways. First, the kernel can send an administrative alert to another machine; this alert may provide the first warning you get of a fresh crash. Second, the kernel can record a crash message in the event log. If you've turned on the automatic reboot option as discussed in the previous section, having a message in the event log gives you positive confirmation of the time when the crash occurred.

These two capabilities can be set only by an administrator. The values controlling these capabilities are found under the HKLM\SYSTEM\CurrentControlSet\

CrashControl key. To turn on alert broadcasting for Windows 2000 Professional or NT, set the SendAlert value to 1, instead of its default 0. To turn on event log messages, set the LogEvent value to 1 as well. Both of these capabilities are already turned on by default on the Windows 2000 Server.

All the values under the CrashControl key, including the aforementioned automatic reboot, can be set through the System control panel. These settings can be found on the Startup/Shutdown tab on an NT machine or gotten to from the Advanced tab on Windows 2000. Better still, you can control them by writing a policy template file to automatically install the settings you want on all machines in your domain.

Enabling Automatic Logon After Boot

My local library has a batch of PCs running an electronic library catalog application. These machines are basically single-function kiosks; the librarians don't want people using them for anything else. To get the machines set up to run with as little intervention as possible, the catalog software is installed as part of the Startup group; that way, it runs when Windows 95 starts. An NT-based kiosk system allows the library to keep their computers more secure and administer them with less hassle; they can even get the automatic logon feature Windows 95 offers.

Never enable auto-logon with an account that has administrative privileges. If you ever leave your machine unattended, an office prankster (or determined attacker) can have the run of your network right from your machine. Good security practice dictates that you only log in with an administrative account when you need to do something that requires the extra privileges.

To enable automatic logons, you have to make a total of four changes to values under HKLM\Software\Microsoft\Windows NT\Current Version\Winlogon:

1. Set the DefaultDomainName value to the name of the domain you want to automatically log into. Of course, instead of a domain, you may specify the name of the computer itself.

2. Set DefaultUserName to the user account name you want to use when logging on.

3. Add a REG_SZ named AutoAdminLogon, and set its to value to 1.

4. Add a REG_SZ named DefaultPassword, and set its contents to the password for the account you specified in DefaultUserName. If you leave this value blank, automatic logon is turned off (actually, AutoAdminLogon is set back to its default value of 0).

Once you make these changes, the next reboot automatically logs on the account you specified. If you want to log on as a different user, hold down the Shift key as you log off the machine; the operating system allows you to use the standard logon dialog to log on as another user.

One final warning: realize that the Registry stores these values in plain text. By enabling this feature, you could be disclosing the default password for this user account to anyone who can read your Registry.

Power Off at Shutdown

Most laptops, many workstations, and even a few servers have smart power management hardware that lets the operating system actually turn off the hardware when the system is shut down. While not all machines can take advantage of this, it's nice to have the "Shut Down" command do just that instead of requiring an extra trip to the power button.

The HKLM\Software\Microsoft\WindowsNT\CurrentVersion\Winlogon\PowerdownAfterShutdown value enables this feature; add it as a REG_SZ and set its value to 1, and your computer actually turns itself off when you tell NT to shut down, if your hardware supports this feature. If it doesn't, no harm will come to it, but the feature won't work. Reset PowerdownAfterShutdown back to 0 to restore normal operation.

Force Hung Tasks to End When Logging Off

When you log off of or shut down a Windows 2000 or NT machine, the system scheduler attempts to stop any running tasks. In addition to shutting down any drivers or services started by the system, the OS must shut down the 16-bit Windows subsystem and any applications you've started yourself. Most well-behaved Win32 applications will honor a system shutdown request, but it's unfortunately common to see hung tasks in the VDM prevent the entire system from shutting down.

Windows' normal response to this problem is to display a dialog that asks whether you want to cancel the shutdown or logoff, wait for the recalcitrant task to stop by itself, or kill off the task. You can automate this process by specifying that you always want the system to go ahead and kill tasks that don't listen to shutdown requests; this finally makes it possible for you to tell your machine to reboot and go get a diet Coke while it does, secure in the knowledge that it won't be still waiting for you to end a task when you return.

To force this shutdown, add a REG_SZ value named AutoEndTasks to HKEY_USER\<SID>\Control Panel\Desktop. Set it to 1 to forcibly kill unresponsive tasks. You may also want to add the same value to HKU\.DEFAULT so that new accounts inherit it; you can also add it to a policy template.

Set a Time Limit for Shutting Down Tasks

You now know how to force an automatic end to tasks that won't stop when they get a shutdown request, but did you know you can also tell Windows 2000 and NT how long to wait before deciding an application isn't answering? If you add a REG_SZ value named WaitToKillAppTimeout to HKEY_USER\<SID>\Control Panel\Desktop, you can specify the interval (in milliseconds again) that the system waits before deciding that an application is ignoring the shutdown request. The default is a generous 20 seconds; if, like me, you're impatient you can whittle this down to 10 seconds or even less. If the user process doesn't answer the shutdown request and terminate within this time period, and AutoEndTasks is defined, the scheduler kills the task.

Speed Up System Shutdowns

When you boot an Windows 2000 or NT machine, part of the boot phase involves starting up all the system's drivers and services. Conversely, part of the shutdown process requires that all these services be shut down so they can write out any data they've got cached. This is particularly important when you consider that Exchange Server, SQL Server, and several other BackOffice server products depend on the system's services.

However, waiting for system shutdown can take a long time, depending on the service load you have running. Part of the problem is the generous default timeout value: Windows 2000 and NT shutdowns give each service up to 20 seconds to shut down before the system kills it. If you have many services running, this time can add up.

The HKLM\SYSTEM\CurrentControlSet\Control\WaitToKillServiceTimeout value specifies how long the system should wait before killing a service; the value is a REG_SZ expressed in microseconds (1000 microseconds make one second). You can adjust this value as low, or high, as you'd like.

Note that WaitToKillAppTimeout and WaitToKillServiceTimeout are two different values. The former controls the timeout period for system tasks, while the latter applies only to system services.

It's critical to leave services enough time to clean up after themselves and write out any cached data they may be maintaining internally. If you don't, you may lose all or part of the data maintained by the service; since the DHCP, DNS, WINS, Exchange, and SQL servers are all services, this poses a real risk to your data. You probably shouldn't adjust this value on machines that run any of these services.

Automatically Try to Detect Slow Network Connections

Face it: not all network connections are as fast as you'd like. In fact, if your network includes sites that are linked by a WAN, you may find they're much, slower than you'd like. In a domain environment, both Windows 2000 and NT normally attempt to fetch a user's profile from the domain controller. In a typical enterprise network, not every WAN-connected site has its own domain controller—meaning that logon requests from Huntsville may have to go to a domain controller in Chicago. With more than a few users, you'll quickly wish there was a way to encourage your system to use cached user profiles whenever possible.

Good news: you can do exactly that. The first step is to set a time limit for deciding whether a connection is "slow" or not. The system makes this decision by pinging the domain controller and waiting for a response. If the response takes longer than a threshold you specify, the link is considered "slow." You can set this threshold by adding a REG_DWORD value named HKLM\Software\Microsoft\Windows NT\CurrentVersion\Winlogon\SlowLinkTimeOut and setting it to the number of milliseconds (remember, 1000 milliseconds make one second) to wait for a ping response. The default value of 2000 means that Windows waits 2 seconds for a response; if you're really desperate, you may adjust this value all the way up to 120,000 milliseconds (or 2 minutes).

The other required change is to add a REG_DWORD named SlowLinkDetectEnabled to HKLM\Software\Microsoft\Windows NT\CurrentVersion\Winlogon. This value controls whether or not the system pays attention to SlowLinkTimeOut. When SlowLinkDetectEnabled is 0, Windows doesn't attempt to detect a slow link. When it's 1, the system waits for the amount of time specified in SlowLinkTimeOut; if that amount of time passes, the user may select a locally cached profile instead of continuing to wait. By default, Windows 2000 does attempt to detect slow connections.

Don't Automatically Create 8.3 Names on NTFS Volumes

For backwards compatibility with DOS, Windows for Workgroups, and other operating systems that don't understand long filenames, NTFS automatically creates standard 8.3 filenames and stores them along with the NTFS long name. For example, this chapter's full name is *Chapter 10 draft.doc*, but its 8.3 name is *CHAPTE~1.DOC*. If you don't care whether older operating systems and software can read your filenames, you can turn off the process that automatically creates short names for long-named files and increase your file performance. If you depend on DOS or Win3.x programs on your computers, this probably isn't a good idea, as they depend on 8.3 names; however, if you're running only 32-bit applications you should be in good shape.

To accomplish this, add a new REG_DWORD value named NtfsDisable8dot3-NameCreation to HKLM\System\CurrentControlSet\Control\FileSystem and give it a value of 1. After you reboot, the system no longer creates 8.3 names for new files (but it won't delete the old ones).

You may be surprised to find that many alleged 32-bit applications rely on 8.3 filenames to work properly. Don't apply this tweak until you've made a full backup of all NTFS volumes on your machine, and be prepared to use that backup to restore from if things don't work properly.

Disable the Printer Browse Thread

When you create a new printer share, the print spooler service starts a new thread whose job is to broadcast announcements of the share's presence. Print servers and clients can receive these announcements and automatically add the new printer to their lists of known resources. To ensure that print servers have consistent resource lists, each print server also broadcasts its list of known shares. This enables other servers to be sure that their resource lists are complete. The combination of these two broadcasts can cause unneeded broadcast traffic, since once a printer's established and the servers have all seen it, there's little need to keep retransmitting the data.

You may disable the printer browse thread on each machine that shares a printer with the network; you may also wish to disable the thread on any centralized print servers on your network. Once you do, remember that when you add new printers they won't show up in browse lists until you reenable the browse thread on all machines where you've disabled it.

To stop the browse thread, add a new REG_DWORD value named DisableServer-Thread to HKLM\SYSTEM\CurrentControlSet\Control\Print. Give it a value of 1 to disable the thread or 0 to reenable it, then restart the computer to make the change effective. Since printer browsers share information, it may take as long as one hour for all the print servers on your network to make themselves known again by broadcasting.

The following two tips appear courtesy of the NT*Pro user group newsletter.

NT4 *Forcibly Recover a Crashed PDC*

If your domain's PDC crashes or becomes unavailable before you have the chance to promote a BDC, the key that controls the server's role won't be changed to reflect that the PDC isn't a PDC anymore. When you recover and reboot the PDC, it thinks it's still a PDC, but when it discovers the newly promoted PDC on the network the original PDC petulantly stops its netlogon service. The recommended way to fix this is to edit the default or "<No Name>" value of HKLM\Security\Policy\PolSrvRo. Its value will be 0x03000000 for a PDC and 0x02000000 for a BDC. To turn the PDC into a BDC, change the value to 0x02000000, then reboot.

To accomplish this fix, you'll have to allow the Administrators group Full Control permissions on HKLM\Security\Policy\PolSrvRo. Make sure to restore the permissions to their original state after making the change.

Hiding Servers from Network Computers

There may be times when you want to keep human browsers from seeing a particular server on your network. You may hide the server from Network Neighborhood and other browsing tools while still allowing users who know what share they want to access it. To hide a Windows 2000 Server (or workstation, for that matter), you have to add a new value to HKLM\SYSTEM\CurrentControlSet\Services\LanmanServer\Parameters. Name the new value hidden and give it a type of REG_BINARY and value of 1 (to hide it) or 0 (to make it visible). For NT, use the value name HIDDEN and make it a REG_DWORD type. The values 1 and 0 still apply. You have to restart the computer to make it stop broadcasting its presence; in addition, it can take an hour or two for the newly hidden machine to drop out of sight on other machines on your network.

Network Tweaks

The networking subsystem for Windows 2000 and NT is pretty flexible. Most of the things you can change are exposed through the Network control panel and its various tabs, subdialogs, and property pages. However, there are some things you can change on your own that will smooth your network operations.

Create a Shared Favorites Folder for All Network Users

A standard Windows 2000 or NT installation gives every user her own Favorites folder. Since Internet Explorer and Microsoft Office both use this folder extensively, you might find it useful to build a shared Favorites folder containing IE shortcuts or Office documents you want to make available to all your users.

Building a shared Favorites folder is pretty easy. The first step is to build the folder itself: on one of your file servers, share the directory you want to use as the shared Favorites folder. It can be an existing directory, or you may create a new one. Be sure to set appropriate share and NTFS permissions.

Next, on each machine you want to use the shared folder, you need to change the value of HKCU\Software\Microsoft\Windows\CurrentVersion\Explorer\User Shell Folders\Favorites from its existing setting to the path to the new folder. For example, if your shared folder is on a machine named *armageddon* in a share named *favorites*, your new Favorites value would read \\armageddon\favorites. You can make this change as part of a group or system policy by adding a new policy template; you may also put it in HKU\.DEFAULT so that newly created accounts inherit the setting.

You can also use this setting to specify a custom path for each user on a shared drive. For instance, after creating user directories under a shared folder, the value of the Favorites Registry setting for user1 might be \\armageddon\users\user1\favorites.

Automatically Use Dial-Up Networking to Log On

You can configure Windows 2000 and NT 4.0 to use DUN to log onto your selected domain by default. Normally, when you have DUN installed and active you see a checkbox in the logon dialog that allows you to use DUN to establish a connection to your network for logon; setting this value selects the checkbox by default. You might do this on a laptop or other computer that can connect to your LAN only via DUN.

To make this change, add a new REG_SZ value named RasForce to HKLM\SOFTWARE\Microsoft\WindowsNT\CurrentVersion\Winlogon and set its value to 1. After you reboot, the "Logon using Dial-up networking" checkbox is automatically selected. Windows 2000 changed the functionality of this value slightly, allowing the user to manually clear or select this checkbox, regardless of the RasForce setting. Under NT, adding this value and setting it to 1 permanently selects the checkbox, and you can't deselect it. This means that if your NT machine can't access your remote network, you can't log on. (As a workaround, you can restore from an ERD or edit the Registry using *RegEdt32*'s network connection function.)

[NT4] *Enable the WINS Proxy Agent*

NT machines can act as Windows Internet Name Service (WINS) proxies; these proxies answer name-resolution requests from machines (such as Macintoshes or Unix machines) that don't speak the WINS protocol. In NT 4.0, the only way to enable this proxy mode is via a Registry change (in earlier versions, there was a checkbox in the TCP/IP control panel).

To turn a machine into a WINS proxy, add a new REG_DWORD value, HKLM\System\CurrentControlSet\Services\Netbt\Parameters\EnableProxy, and give it a value of 1. This enables the target machine to route WINS resolution requests to an available WINS server.

[NT4] *Set the Number of Rings for Answering Incoming Dial-Up Networking Calls*

If you're using a TAPI or Unimodem-based device to answer incoming DUN calls, you may have noticed that the standard method of adjusting the *modem.inf* file to control how many times incoming calls may ring before the modem answers them doesn't work. This is by design, but it's not well-documented. The solution is to add a new Registry value to indicate the number of rings you want to allow. Add HKLM\CurrentControlSet\Services\RasMan\Parameters\NumberOfRings as a REG_DWORD, then set its value to the number of rings you want to use (between 1 and 20). Once you reboot your computer, DUN answers only after the specified number of rings have occurred. Note that if you're not using a TAPI/Unimodem modem, this value is completely ignored.

[NT4] *Turn On Logging for Dial-Up Networking*

You can enable logging for Dial-Up Networking connections by changing the value of HKLM\System\CurrentControlSet\Services\RasMan\Parameters\Logging from its default of 0 to 1. When you do, DUN logs details of the initial connection in *%systemroot%\system32\ras\device.log*; this log reveals what data DUN sends to the remote device and what responses come back. This log is invaluable when you're trying to troubleshoot DUN connections that fail at initial establishment.

Keep a Dial-Up Networking Connection up After You Log Out

Windows 2000 and NT 4.0 automatically terminate DUN connections when you log off. This is a sensible feature (even though it's a change from previous versions), since it keeps you from inadvertently running up big connection or long-distance bills during a time when you're not even logged on to your machine. However, there may be times when you want the connection to stay up even when no one's logged on. For example, keeping the connection open when no one's logged on enables the DUN-connected machine to share files and printers with other network users.

To keep DUN connections active even when the user who started them has logged out, add HKLM\Software\Microsoft\Windows NT\CurrentVersion\Winlogon\KeepRasConnections as REG_SZ. Set it to 1, and connections will stay connected when users log out; set it back to 0 to enable the standard behavior of automatically disconnecting DUN.

Set the Dial-Up Networking Automatic Disconnect Timer

You can set the deadman timer that causes DUN connections to hang up after a certain period of inactivity. The default value for Windows 2000 is 0, which instructs the system to never automatically hang up. NT 4.0, on the other hand, hangs up idle connections after 20 minutes by default. You may change this value in the Windows 2000 Registry to any period between 1 and 0xFFFFFFFF seconds (or between 1 and 1000 minutes for NT)—enough of a range for any scenario. To effect this change, edit the REG_DWORD value named HKLM\System\CurrentControlSet\Services\RemoteAccess\Parameters\AutoDisconnect and set it to the number of idle seconds you're willing to tolerate before hanging up the connection. Remember that you can also set AutoDisconnect to zero, which causes the connection to always stay up until manually disconnected.

Printing Tweaks

The paperless office is not yet upon us and may never be. Until it finally arrives, you need to keep printing things, and if you're using Windows 2000 or NT 4.0 you can improve your printing experience with some minor Registry changes.

Keep the Print Spool Service from Popping Up Dialogs

The print spooler has an annoying "feature" that causes it to display a notification telling you when a print job has been completed. I was delighted to find that you can stop it from doing so by adding a new REG_DWORD named NetPopup to HKLM\SYSTEM\CurrentControlSet\Control\Print\Providers. Give it a value of 0 to suppress the alerts or 1 to re-enable them. After making this change, you need to reboot, but you'll be free of print status messages forevermore.

Change the Print Spool Directory

Windows 2000 and NT defaults to putting its print spool directories on the system disk. If you have a small number of print jobs, or a large disk, this may work fine; for disk space or performance reasons, though, it may make more sense to move your print spool directories to another volume. For example, networks that include high-resolution color printers such as the Epson Stylus 1520 (which print 11"x 17" pages in 24-bit color: each page takes several tens of megabytes of spool space!) can quickly overwhelm the free space on a typical Windows 2000 or NT system disk. Although Windows 2000 supplies a mechanism for modifying print server properties (from the printer folder, File → Server Properties; the Advanced tab holds the spool folder location), NT provides no user interface for changing the spool locations; fortunately, you're probably comfortable enough with the Registry so that you don't *need* a user interface!

If you want to change the spool directory for a single printer on an NT 4.0 system, you need to add a new value to HKLM\SYSTEM\CurrentControlSet\Control\Print\Printers*<PrinterName>*, where *PrinterName* is the name you gave the printer when you created its spooler entry. Name the new value SpoolDirectory, and make it a REG_SZ. For this item's value, supply the full local path to the spool directory. The spool directory can't be a UNC path, and it must exist. Under Windows 2000, that Registry path is used as a backup for printer entries under HKLM\SOFTWARE. To change the spool directory for a printer on a Windows 2000 print server, add a new REG_SZ value SpoolDirectory to HKLM\SOFTWARE\Microsoft\Windows NT\CurrentVersion\Print\Printers*<PrinterName>*. Supply it with the full local path to the spool directory.

If you want to change the default spool used for any printer that doesn't specify its own spool directory, you should add a REG_SZ value named HKLM\SOFTWARE\Microsoft\Windows NT\CurrentVersion\Print\Printers\DefaultSpoolDirectory for Windows 2000, or HKLM\SYSTEM\CurrentControlSet\Control\Print\Printers\DefaultSpoolDirectory for NT. As with SpoolDirectory, the path you specify here must be a fully qualified local path, and it must exist before you make the change.

If you add either of these values, you need to stop and restart the Spooler service. To avoid losing any queued print jobs, it's best to make these changes only when your print queues are empty; that keeps users from having to resubmit their jobs to get them into the new spool directory.

Stop Print Job Logging in Event Log

Normally Windows 2000 and NT logs every print job processed by a server in that machine's application event log. Since for the most part these logs fall into the category of "data no one will ever look at," you can configure the spooler service to not make these log entries in the first place.

To suppress print job event log entries for errors, warnings, and other information, add a new REG_DWORD value named HKLM\SYSTEM\CurrentControlSet\Control\Print\Providers\EventLog and give it a value of 0. As with all the other printing tweaks, this change won't take effect until you stop and restart the Spooler service.

11

The Registry Documented

Documenting the Registry is like building a cathedral in the Middle Ages: it's a task that spans generations,* with many collaborators each doing a small piece of the work. Powerful forces come to bear; some help the work, while others hinder it. In the end, the result is overwhelming: massive, imposing, yet open to all comers. (One major difference: cathedrals are spiritually uplifting. Try as I might, I just can't get that same feeling from the Registry. If you do, drop me a note.)

What's Here and What's Not

Because the Registry is so dynamic, there's no possible way to capture the meaning of every key in a single document. As I write this, Microsoft is preparing to release a host of new Windows 2000-based products, each of which will have its own set of Registry keys and values. Quite apart from the proliferation of key is the problem of what configuration a particular machine has. What software's on it? Which service pack? Is it part of a network? Does it run any server products?

As if Microsoft products alone weren't enough of a problem, there's an ongoing flood of third-party products running on Win32—web servers, Usenet news servers, CAD tools, office applications—and they all have their *own* keys.

So, the first confession I have to make is that this chapter is incomplete. By design, it doesn't include information about keys that aren't part of either the core Windows 2000 or NT 4.x operating systems: no BackOffice components, no Netscape servers, no nothing. Instead, it covers only the most interesting keys found in ordinary networked installations of Windows 2000 Server and NT Server 4.0.

---

* Generations of operating systems, anyway.

The good news is that the pages you're looking at now represent a small subset of what's documented about the Registry. Because of space and time limitations, I had to choose the most important keys and document them here.

This chapter, then, is like a traveler's foreign-language phrase book. It doesn't teach you every word of the language, but it does teach you the most important words and phrases. (I wonder what the Registry equivalent of "Where is the bathroom?" would be?)

HKLM\HARDWARE

HKLM\HARDWARE is the odd man out in the Registry for two reasons. First of all, all its keys are volatile, meaning they're never stored on disk. This is because when Windows 2000 or NT 4.0 boots, they can interrogate the system to find out what hardware's present, but they need to keep track of that information before any device drivers have actually been loaded. Since there's no requirement that Registry hives actually be stored in a hive file* (instead of in RAM), loading HARDWARE into RAM as a volatile hive makes it accessible to boot-time components and the driver loading phase. Because its contents are volatile, changes you make to this hive won't be stored on disk.

The second odd thing about this subkey is that almost all its values are stored as REG_BINARY values. This makes it difficult to edit values in this tree. That's actually a good thing, because doing so can suddenly render your machine inoperable. Since the system creates this tree from scratch each time it boots, there won't be any permanent damage, but you should still treat this tree as read-only.

HARDWARE\DESCRIPTION

The DESCRIPTION subkey stores data to represent what actual physical hardware is present when the system first starts up. This list may have items on it that don't appear in the DEVICEMAP or RESOURCEMAP subkeys; for example, a SCSI adapter that fails to initialize will be in DESCRIPTION but may not appear in either of the others.

The data in DESCRIPTION comes from the hardware recognizer. On x86 machines, this task is handled by *ntdetect.com*. The recognizer gathers data about the configuration of the system's buses, serial, parallel, mouse, and keyboard ports, SCSI and video adapters, and floppy drives. Notice that network adapters, PCMCIA cards, and external devices like printers aren't included on this list; they're not automatically detected in Windows 2000 and NT 4.0.

---

* There may as well be such a rule, though; HARDWARE's the only volatile hive.

Each bus controller (ISA, PCI, EISA, etc.) gets its own subkey under MultifunctionAdapter; in turn, each of these keys has subkeys for each device found on that bus. For example, HARDWARE\DESCRIPTION\System\MultifunctionAdapter\3\DiskController\0 points to the first disk controller on my desktop machine's motherboard bus. If I had a secondary controller, it appears as DiskController\1.

Any device in the DESCRIPTION tree may optionally have values named ComponentInformation and ConfigurationData. These values, both of which are of type REG_BINARY, store information about the device; the exact contents vary by device type, and frankly I don't know the details.

HARDWARE\DEVICEMAP

DEVICEMAP links devices in the DESCRIPTION subtree with device drivers in HKLM\SYSTEM\ControlSetX\Services. Each device that requires a driver has an entry that points to a driver in one of the control sets. During the two driver start phases, the kernel can consult entries in DEVICEMAP to find the matching entry in the Services subkey; that data specifies what driver should be loaded, what phase it should be loaded in, and what configuration data it requires. (See the section "SYSTEM\CurrentControlSet\Control" later in this chapter for details on the Services subkey.)

HARDWARE\RESOURCEMAP

DEVICEMAP ties hardware entries to device drivers; RESOURCEMAP ties those same device drivers to physical machine resources such as DMA address ranges and IRQs. Since there is a finite number of these hardware resources, and since conflicts between multiple devices can render them all inoperable, this subkey is an important part of the Windows 2000/NT load phase.

Each class of device has its own subkey under RESOURCEMAP; for example, RESOURCEMAP\ScsiAdapter is the device class key for (you guessed it) SCSI adapters. Every device in that class gets its own subkey under its class key. That means that a machine with two SCSI adapters has two entries, the names of which correspond to the device driver names in the Services subkey.

The contents of RESOURCEMAP come from the device drivers themselves. When a device driver starts, it claims whatever resources it needs for its hardware device and updates its entry in RESOURCEMAP to indicate what it used.

HKLM\SOFTWARE

HKLM\SOFTWARE is the motherlode of software configuration information. Any configuration data an application or system component needs can be stored here;

settings specific to an individual user belong in that user's HKU\SOFTWARE key. For example, the SOFTWARE\Microsoft\Windows NT CurrentVersion\Winlogon key stores settings that apply to the *winlogon* program. These settings apply to all users on the machine, so they belong under HKLM. On the other hand, an individual user's choices for which tools to use to view certain types of web content properly belong to that user, so they should go under HKCU (e.g., Software\Netscape\Netscape Navigator\Viewers).

SOFTWARE\Classes\CLSID

This key is the root under which all the machinewide class definitions are registered. In NT, the HKCR root key displays data from this subkey alone. In Windows 2000, classes may also be registered under HKCU\Software\Classes, providing for class registration on a per-user bases. See the section "HKCR\CLSID" for details on the format of this key's subkeys and values.

SOFTWARE\Microsoft

This key is the root location for parameters and settings for all Microsoft products installed on a machine. As you might expect, such a key covers a multitude of sins.

Microsoft\ActiveSetup

ActiveSetup is Microsoft's name for its "new and improved" setup system. ActiveSetup records which components have been installed on a machine in the Installed Components subkey. Each installed component has its own class ID subkey under Installed Components where it can store its own settings; for example, Internet Explorer's data is located at HKLM\SOFTWARE\Microsoft\Active Setup\Installed Components\{89820200-ECBD-11cf-8B85-00AA005B4383}.

Microsoft\Cryptography

NT 4.0 introduced Microsoft's Cryptographic Application Programming Interface, better known as CryptoAPI. CryptoAPI provides OS-level services for signing, verifying, and encrypting data, as well as for using digital certificates for access control and authentication. Complete documentation for CryptoAPI is available online at *http://www.microsoft.com/msdn*.

|NT4| The following subkeys are used for certificate storage in NT 4.0:

CertificateStore
    This subkey contains the store of X.509 certificates currently loaded onto a particular machine. As new certificates arrive, CryptoAPI applications can read and verify them, then store them here if desired.

CertificateStore\CertificateAuxiliaryInfo
> Each stored certificate can have arbitrary data associated with it. Microsoft calls this data *tags*; applications may add tags to certificates, but don't have to. This subkey is usually empty.

CertificateStore\Certificates
> The default value of this subkey contains the number of certificates as a REG_SZ, plus one named value for each certificate. For example, if three certificates are present, they are stored in values named "1," "2," and "3," and the default value contains "3." Each certificate's value contents consist of a binary chunk of data that actually contains the certificate itself.

In Windows 2000, certificates are stored and managed through the use of the MMC Certificates snap-in. There are a number of subkeys throughout the Registry that store certificates, and they're certainly not limited to the HKLM root key. Indeed, HKCU contains subkeys that hold certificates for users, while certificates are also found in HKU\Default. And yes, the HKLM root key contains certificate stores, such as HKLM\Software\Microsoft\EnterpriseCertificates and HKLM\Software\Microsoft\Cryptography\Services\PolicyAgent\SystemCertificates.

In general, the certificate storage structure in the Windows 2000 Registry begin with a subkey such as SystemCertificates or EnterpriseCertificates. Beneath this subkey appears a list subkeys that correspond to a certificate type. Here are the four most prevalent:

CA This subkey contains X.509 certificates, certificate revocation lists, and certificate trust lists for Certificate Authorities. CAs issue certificates to individual users and services.

My Individual certificates are stored here.

Root
> Certificates, certificate revocation lists, and certificate trust lists associated with root authorities (that is, authorities at the top of the certificate trust chain) are found under this subkey.

Trust
> This subkey contains certificates, revocation lists, and trust lists that help determine trust.

Beneath these certificate types are three subkeys, namely Certificates, CRLs (certificate revocation lists), and CTLs (certificate trust lists). The values beneath these subkeys contain binary data, forming lists of certificates, revocation lists and trust lists, respectively.

Microsoft\NtBackup

The bundled Windows NT backup tool stores its settings here. Interestingly, this key is remapped by HKLM\SOFTWARE\Microsoft\Windows NT\CurrentVersion\IniFileMapping\Ntbackup.ini, meaning that the backup program (bless its ancient little heart) thinks it's using an INI file to store its settings in.

Microsoft\RAS

The Dial-Up Networking service was originally known as RAS. Sometimes Microsoft calls it RAS, sometimes DUN; in this case, its Registry settings all have "RAS" in the name somewhere. The values in this key control the Remote Access Service, which clients can use to dial into a Windows 2000 or NT machine.

CurrentVersion
This subkey looks very much like the CurrentVersion\Network Cards keys you'll meet in the section by the same name. That's not surprising, since RAS is really just a virtual NIC. CurrentVersion's values specify the setup info file name (Infname), major and minor software versions, and the path where RAS parts are stored (PathName). In addition, the CurrentVersion\NetRules subkey specifies the rest of the information gathered when RAS was first installed.

Protocols
This subkey contains a set of REG_DWORD flags that govern which protocols are selected and which may be used. For example, the fTcpIpSelected and fTcpIpAllowed flags indicate whether the server supports TCP/IP RAS connections or not.

Each installed RAS protocol has its own subkey; for example, TCP/IP-specific settings are stored in Microsoft\RAS\Protocols\IP. These subkeys contain values and flags specific to the protocol.

TAPI DEVICES
This subkey holds a list of any Telephony API (TAPI)-compliant devices known to the RAS service, including any Unimodem devices.

SOFTWARE\Microsoft\Windows NT

This subkey contains configuration settings specific to Windows 2000 (on Windows 2000 machines) or NT (on NT machines); this key doesn't include settings for the shell or Explorer. The CurrentVersion subkey contains a number of interesting pieces of data, as well as some subkeys that merit their own mentions:

HKLM\SOFTWARE

RegisteredOwner and RegisteredOrganization
> These REG_SZ values store whatever values you entered into the name and company fields of the system's installation dialogs. You can freely change them if need be.

CurrentVersion and CurrentBuildNumber
> Together these two REG_SZ values identify what core version of Windows 2000/NT you're running. A stock Windows 2000 installation has a version of "5.0" and a build number of "2195"; later versions will obviously have different values.

SystemRoot
> This value points to the system directory. If you ever need to migrate your Windows 2000 or NT installation to a different volume, be sure to update this as part of the process.

SourcePath
> This REG_SZ points to the source from which the operating system was originally installed. For example, on my machine this value contains a path to the CD-ROM, "G:\i386".

ProductId
> This string holds the Microsoft "product ID," which is nothing more than a magic number combined with your CD key. A typical product ID looks like "64366-492-0966186-35833".

CSDVersion
> This value indicates what service pack, if any, is installed. The boot loader uses this (along with CurrentVersion and CurrentBuildNumber) to display the blue-screen boot-time message that tells you what you're booting.

CurrentVersion\AeDebug

This subkey tells the system what debugging application to use (if any) when a program crashes.

Debugger
> The program to run when an application crashes. The value may include the full path and any arguments (for example, the default debugger, Dr. Watson, appears as *drwtsn32 -p %ld -e %ld -g*).

Auto
> REG_SZ specifying whether the debugger should just be run ("1") or whether the user should be prompted to choose between starting the debugger and killing off the errant app ("0", the default).

UserDebuggerHotKey

REG_DWORD that, when set, specifies a key code that instantly starts the debugger when pressed. Leave this alone.

Multimedia driver stuff

The installed list of multimedia device drivers is stored in three subkeys of CurrentVersion: Drivers32, drivers.desc (or DriverDesc), and DriverList. They're pretty self-explanatory; each device class has a mapping that specifies what DLL handles its requests and what its human-readable name is.

CurrentVersion\Network Cards

This subkey contains one entry for each installed network adapter card or wrapper. For example, a machine with one network card and Dial-Up Networking installed has two entries: one for the NIC and one for DUN. The first entry is stored in a subkey named "1" (or CurrentVersion\Network Cards\1 if you prefer), and subsequent cards count up from there. These keys each have several values, but the most important ones are ServiceName (which specifies which driver runs the card) and Title (which determines the name that appears in the Network control panel).

Each network adapter subkey can in turn have a subkey named NetRules. This key contains values that specify what kind of adapter it is (type), what setup information file was used to install it (InfName), and what kind of device it actually is (class and block).

CurrentVersion\ProfileList

The list of cached profiles on a particular machine lives here. Each profile has a subkey whose name is its SID; these subkeys contain a path that points to the actual hive containing the profile (ProfileImagePath), some flags that the system uses to control profile loading (Flags and State), and a second copy of the SID that owns the profile (Sid).

CurrentVersion\Shutdown

There are two interesting values stored under this key: LogoffSetting and ShutdownSetting. Both are DWORD values that may range from 0–3. They control what button is selected by default in the Logoff and Shutdown dialogs; you can preset the choice you want to use as a default by adjusting their contents. Table 11-1 lists the available values.

HKLM\SOFTWARE

Table 11-1. CurrentVersion\Shutdown Controls the Default Logoff and Shutdown Buttons

Value	What It Means
0	Make the "Logoff" button the default
1	Make the "Shutdown" button the default
2	Make the "Shutdown and Restart" button the default
3	Make the "Shutdown and Power Off" button the default; ignored unless the computer has power-management support

CurrentVersion\Winlogon

The Winlogon service provides a graphical interface that allows you to log onto or off of the console of a Windows 2000 or NT computer. The values under the Winlogon subkey let you change some aspects of how the logon process works.

Most of these values are here for you to customize. The Group Policy snap-in for Windows 2000 machines and the System Policy Editor for Windows NT machines provide an easy way to set these values to meet your needs, even for many computers. See Chapter 6, *Using the System Policy Editor*, and Chapter 7, *Using Group Policies* for details.

AutoAdminLogon
   Signals whether the computer should automatically log on with a stored account name and password. When this REG_SZ is set to 1, the values of DefaultUserName, DefaultDomainName, and DefaultPassword are used to attempt a logon. This value must be manually added.

AutoRestartShell
   REG_DWORD that controls whether Explorer (or whatever other shell program's specified) should be restarted if it crashes. The default, 0x01, means yes.

[NT4] *DebugServerCommand*
   Microsoft describes this as a command used for internal debugging of Winlogon at Microsoft. Its default value is "no"; I have no idea what other values might mean. If you know, please tell me.

DefaultDomainName
   Winlogon stores the name of the domain (or machine) that hosted the last successful logon here.

DefaultPassword
   When AutoAdminLogon is set to 1, this password (which must be the password for the account given in DefaultUserName) is used in the logon attempt.

DefaultUserName
> Winlogon stores the name of the last account that successfully logged on in this value. You may change it and set the AutoAdminLogon value to force an automatic logon to a particular account.

DeleteRoamingCache
> When this REG_DWORD value is set to 1, cached copies of roaming profiles are deleted when each user logs off. You must add this value manually.

DontDisplayLastUserName
> Windows 2000/NT normally displays the name of the last account to log on in the Welcome dialog. Set this REG_SZ value to 1 to keep this space blank, or 0 (the default) to allow the last account to be displayed.

LegalNoticeCaption
> Windows 2000/NT can display a warning dialog immediately after the logon dialog is dismissed; this makes it possible for you to display a warning message, as recommended by the Computer Emergency Response Team, to warn intruders that they are in fact intruding. The system uses the REG_SZ value you put in LegalNoticeCaption to title the warning dialog. By default in Windows 2000 and NT 4.0, this value exists but is empty.

LegalNoticeText
> The warning text displayed in the post-logon warning dialog comes from the LegalNoticeText value, which is also blank by default.

ParseAutoexec
> REG_SZ that specifies whether *autoexec.bat* should be parsed at logon time or not. If the value is set to 1, *autoexec.bat* is parsed when you log on, and the *autoexec.bat* path statement is appended to the system path.

[NT4] *PowerdownAfterShutdown*
> REG_SZ that controls whether the system attempts to power down the computer when it's shut down. 0 means no; 1 means yes. This value has no effect on machines without power-management support.

ProfileDlgTimeOut
> If a user logs in but can't get a copy of his current logon profile, the system displays a dialog asking what the user wants done to fix the problem. This REG_DWORD value sets the timeout (in seconds, from 0–0xFFFFFFFF in Windows 2000; 0–600 in NT) after which any user profile dialog boxes are automatically dismissed.

ReportBootOk
> When Windows 2000 or NT boots, it saves the boot configuration as the "last known good" control set. Ordinarily, this REG_SZ is set to 1, which tells the system to update the control set automatically when booting finishes. If this

HKLM\SOFTWARE

REG_SZ value is set to 0, the system won't automatically update the last known good set. Another program, such as *Bootok.exe* or *Bootvrfy.exe* must be used. This value must be "0" if you supply alternate values in the BootVerification or BootVerificationProgram keys.

RunLogonScriptSync

Specifies whether logon scripts should be run synchronously (so the desktop doesn't appear until the script completes) or asynchronously (so the script runs while the desktop is being activated). This is a REG_SZ; set it to 1 to force the script to run synchronously.

Shell

This value tells Windows 2000/NT what program to run as the system shell. By default, *explorer.exe* is the preferred shell. Setting up a Zero-Administration Windows (ZAW) workstation usually sets the preferred share to *iexplore.exe*. You may change it manually, but doing so may have unpredictable results.

ShutdownWithoutLogon

As an administrator, you may choose whether or not to allow users to shut down their workstations or servers without being logged in. A REG_SZ value of 1 in this value adds or enables a Shutdown button to the standard logon dialog, while a value of 0 removes or disables it. By default, this button is on for Windows 2000 Professional and NTW 4.0, and off for Windows 2000 Server and NTS 4.0.

SlowLinkDetectEnabled

When set to on (the default), Winlogon automatically detects slow network connections and flags them as such. When off, no such detection occurs.

SlowLinkTimeOut

This REG_DWORD sets the timeout value, in milliseconds, after which a link is marked slow when SlowLinkDetectEnabled is on.

[NT4] *System*

This value specifies which programs are trusted to run in the system context. Changing it may open a security hole, since untrusted programs can run with high privileges. The default is *lsass.exe;* don't change it. In NT 4.0 pre-SP3, the default also includes *spoolss.exe*.

Taskman

Specifies the path to an executable to be used for the system task manager. On Windows 2000 machines, this value is *taskmgr.exe* by default.

Userinit

This value specifies which programs should be started automatically when a user successfully logs on. The default value in Windows 2000 is *userinit,* which specifies that the shell named in Shell should be run. In Windows NT, *nddeagnt.exe* is also added as a default. This then starts the NetDDE service process.

VmApplet

This value determines which program should be run to adjust the virtual memory configuration. The default contents of this value are rundll32 shell32, Control_RunDLL, "sysdm.cpl".

HKLM\SYSTEM

HKLM\SYSTEM is where Windows 2000 and NT keeps their crown jewels: the configuration settings that boot the current incarnation of the machine, as well as a number of ancillary settings that govern pretty much everything the OS and kernel services do.

There are four subkeys of interest directly beneath HKLM\SYSTEM:

Disk

This subkey stores information about the physical and logical disk volumes on your machine. When you run the Disk Administrator utility for the first time, this key is created; subsequent runs of Disk Administrator update the key's data, which is then keeps track of how your disks are configured.

MountedDevices

This Windows 2000 subkey replaces the Disk subkey used in NT 4.0. It's used by the NTFS filesystem to link volume names with the internal identifiers of the volumes, which are usually comprised of a volume's disk signature.

Select

Ever wonder how a Windows 2000/NT system keeps track of which control set is the "last known good" set? Here's the answer! Each of the four values is a REG_DWORD that contains the ordinal index of a *ControlSetXXX* entry under HKLM\SYSTEM:

Current

Contains the ID of the control set currently in use; this set is the one linked to HKLM\SYSTEM\CurrentControlSet.

Default

Contains the ID of the control set that boots the machine next time, unless you manually intervene during the boot process.

LastKnownGood

Contains the ID of the "last known good" set; this ID changes only when a boot fails.

Failed
> Contains the ID of the control set in force the last time a boot failed.

Setup
> This key holds settings that the Windows 2000/NT setup installer uses to figure out which installation phases have been completed and where the installation is currently.

 Experimenting with the Setup key may bring you a visit from the Blue Screen of Death with a SYSTEM_LICENSE_VIOLATION fault code.

SetupType
> Indicates whether the setup program is running in GUI mode, in text mode, or not at all.

SystemSetupInProgress
> This REG_DWORD is 1 if the system is in the middle of a setup, and 0 otherwise. The system uses this value to figure out what to do after a reboot; that's how it knows what to do when you reboot partway through setup.

SystemPartition
> Contains the ARC path (e.g., *\Device\HarddiskVolume1*) to the system partition.

OsLoaderPath
> Points to the path (relative to SystemPartition) where the Windows 2000/NT boot loader lives. On x86 machines, this is usually "\", but on Alpha machines, it may point elsewhere.

NetcardDlls
> This REG_MULTI_SZ stores the names of the DLLs needed for the network cards detected in the final phase of the system's setup operation.

SYSTEM\CurrentControlSet\Hardware Profiles

Hardware profiles let you establish multiple "personalities" for a single machine that may have different configurations. For example, my desktop box has a BusLogic SCSI card that runs the boot disk and some additional external hardware. I occasionally need to add a second SCSI controller. If I left the second card's driver permanently installed, it would fail to start at boot time, and the system would complain about a driver failure. Instead, I create a new hardware profile and enable the card driver for that profile only.

By default, CurrentControlSet\Hardware Profiles has two subkeys: 0001 (the first profile on the machine) and CurrentProfile, which links to one of the available profiles. When you add a new hardware profile for Windows 2000 in the System control panel's Hardware tab (Hardware Profiles tab, for NT), the system creates a new subkey of Hardware Profiles for you. You can then customize the profile with the System control panel or the Devices and Services control panels.*

The actual contents of the hardware profile keys are pretty sparse: they consist of small subtrees of HKLM\SOFTWARE and HKLM\SYSTEM\CurrentControlSet. The profiles include only flags that have been changed from the base hardware profile; for example, the only difference in my one-SCSI and two-SCSI profiles is that the one-SCSI profile has an entry for the second card's driver that tells the driver it's disabled.

SYSTEM\CurrentControlSet\Control

This key's named Control for a good reason: its subkeys and values control much of the kernel's functionality.

Control\BackupRestore

This Windows 2000 subkey contains values that specify to the system which files Backup should not back up and which keys Backup should not restore. These values are separated into two subkeys, namely, FilesNotToBackup and HKLKeysNotToRestore.

Control\BootVerificationProgram

The BootVerificationProgram specifies a program that is run by the Windows 2000/NT service loader at boot time. Its job is to judge whether a boot was successful or not; if not, the machine can be rebooted using the last known good control set instead. Additionally, this program can call *Bootok.exe*, a Windows 2000 executable, which informs the operating system the boot was successful.

The only value under this key is ImagePath, which you use to specify the full path to the boot verification program you want to run.

Control\Class

The Control\Class key lists instances of devices such as mice, SCSI controllers, and sound cards. Each class of device has a subkey, named with the CLSID class identifier. These CLSID keys may have subkeys; for example, the modem key (whose CLSID is the unpronounceable "{4D36E96D-E325-11CE-BFC1-08002BE-10318}") has

---

* For lots more on hardware profiles, see O'Reilly's *Windows NT in a Nutshell*.

one subkey for each installed modem, and each of these subkeys in turn has its own parameters stored as subkeys and values.

Control\CrashControl

Much as Microsoft would like to pretend otherwise, Windows 2000 and NT machines crash just like any other kind. What happens when a crash occurs depends on the values set in the CrashControl key. You normally adjust these values on the Startup and Recovery dialog through the Advanced tab (Startup/Shutdown tab on NT machines) of the System control panel, but setting them directly in the Registry (or via a policy editor) gives you an easy way to control what happens during a crash.

LogEvent

> When this REG_DWORD is set to 1, a crash generates an entry in the system event log. When it's 0, as it is by default on Windows 2000 Professional and NT machines, no event log entry is created.

SendAlert

> This REG_DWORD causes an administrative alert message to be broadcast when it's set to 1; its default value is 0.

CrashDumpEnabled

> Windows 2000 and NT systems may or may not generate their equivalent of a core file when a crash occurs. You decide which it is by setting this REG_DWORD to 0 (don't generate a dump file) or 1 (do generate one). These files can be loaded by a variety of postmortem debuggers you can use to isolate the cause of a particular or persistent crash. The default is 0 on Windows 2000 Professional and NT machines, and 1 on Windows 2000 Servers.

AutoReboot

> You can have a crashed machine reboot itself automatically by changing this REG_DWORD value from its default of 0 to 1.

DumpFile

> This REG_EXPAND_SZ specifies where the crash dump should go. By default, it ends up in the system directory with a name of *memory.dmp*.

Overwrite

> When this REG_DWORD is 1, the crash dump file is overwritten when a new crash occurs; when it's 0, the dump file is preserved, and a new one created.

KernelDumpOnly

> This REG_DWORD specifies whether the entire contents of system memory are dumped (value of 0) or only that portion of memory that is used by the operating system kernel (value of 1). By default, the entire contents of memory are copied to the dump file.

NMICrashDump

This value specifies whether a nonmaskable interrupt (NMI), caused by a hardware error, triggers software error processing. When this REG_DWORD value is 0, as it is by default, only a hardware malfunction message appears. When set to 1, standard software error processing follows the hardware message.

Control\Enum

Subkeys of this key contain information about every driver, device, or service that might potentially be attached to the machine. For example, Control\Enum contains entries for the ATAPI driver even on machines with no ATAPI interface. These keys are used by the system to map devices and services with their drivers and configuration data.

Control\FileSystem

These values control the Windows 2000/NT filesystem's naming behavior. The filesystem itself is self-tuning and doesn't store any parameters out in the open where they can be tweaked, so you'll have to content yourself with these.

Win31FileSystem

If you set this REG_DWORD to 1, any FAT volumes suddenly start acting like old-style Win3.x volumes: neither long filenames nor access/modification times are created or updated. By default, this option is off, but you may need to turn it on if you're using Win3.x or DOS applications that can't handle even a hint of long filenames.

NtfsDisable8dot3NameCreation

By default (i.e., when this value's set to 0), NTFS creates 8.3 names for long filenames. This slows things down. Set this value to 1 to prevent NTFS from creating 8.3 names; this means that DOS applications and computers using different languages from yours may not be able to access files on an NTFS share.

NtfsDisableLastAccessUpdate

NTFS keeps track of when each file and directory was last accessed. This timestamp is even updated when you get a directory listing or otherwise traverse a directory; as you might expect, this imposes a performance penalty. Set this REG_DWORD to 1 to turn the last-access timestamp off or to 0 (the default) to turn it on.

NtfsAllowExtendedCharacterIn8dot3Name

This DWORD controls whether characters outside the standard printable ASCII set (including characters from languages other than the system language) may be used in 8.3 names on NTFS volumes. If the value is 0 (the default), 8.3

names can contain only legal ASCII characters; if it's 1, any nonreserved character may be used.

Win95TruncatedExtensions

Win95 honors only the first three characters of file extensions. By default, this REG_DWORD is set to 0, which forces Windows 2000 and NT to truncate extensions to the first three characters. Set it to 1 and reboot to take advantage of full-length extensions on NTFS volumes.

NtfsEncryptionService

New to Windows 2000, NTFS provides confidentiality to files and directories by way of encryption. This REG_SZ value determines which encryption service NTFS should use to protect its files. Currently the default and only allowable value is Efs, which specifies the encryption filesystem (EFS) provided by Windows 2000. The presence or absence of this value in the Windows 2000 Registry affects whether files and directories are encrypted or decrypted. That determination can be made selectively through Windows Explorer.

Control\Hivelist

This subkey holds the locations of the system's hive files. See Chapter 2, *Registry Nuts and Bolts,* for a discussion of hive files. It's important to leave these values alone; if you don't, you can prevent the system from finding one or more necessary hive files, which will probably render your machine unbootable.

Control\LSA

The Local Security Authority, or LSA, is the Windows 2000 and NT security component charged with enforcing access controls on local objects. For the most part it does an admirable job; however, there's one significant security problem this key causes.

The Notification Packages value contains a list of DLLs that are notified any time a user changes an account password. This is supposed to allow seamless synchronization of NetWare and system passwords; the default value for this entry is "FPNWCLNT," which is the name of the File and Print Services for NetWare DLL. However, if you're not running the NetWare module, an attacker can load his own *FPNWCLNT.DLL* and use it to steal passwords.

To guard against this, set the Registry ACL on this key to limit any nonadministrator access. If you're not running the NetWare services, remove FPNWCLNT from this value. If you are, set a file ACL on the *FPNWCLNT.DLL* file so it can't be removed or replaced.

Control\Print

Control\Print, rather unsurprisingly, contains configuration and settings data for the Windows 2000 and NT printing subsystem. One handy feature of the Windows 2000/NT print mechanism is that it supports remote printer drivers, meaning that you can install drivers for Win95, Win3.x, and various flavors of NT on a central server and feed them to clients as needed. These drivers are registered in the Environments subkey of this key; there are also some useful values directly beneath Control\Print:

MajorVersion and MinorVersion
   These two REG_DWORD values specify the major and minor version of the printer subsystem.

DisableServerThread
   This value controls whether printer shares advertise themselves over the network. You have to manually add this REG_DWORD value and set it to 1 to turn off the thread; if it doesn't exist, or if its value is 0, the thread remains active.

SchedulerThreadPriority
   This value raises or lowers the priority of the printer scheduling thread. It's a REG_DWORD, and its default value of 0 means "leave the thread at normal priority." You can set this value to either 1 (which raises the thread's priority) or 0xFFFFFFFF (which lowers it).

BeepEnabled
   If you want notification when a remote print job fails, set this REG_DWORD to 1, and your system will beep every 10 seconds when a remote print job error occurs. The default value of 0 prevents any unnerving beeping from disturbing you while working.

NoRemotePrinterDrivers
   You might find it desirable to tell NT *not* to serve remote drivers for some devices. The default value of this REG_SZ is "Windows NT Fax Driver," meaning that particular driver won't ever be offered to remote clients.

Control\SecurePipeServers

This key allows you to restrict remote access to the Registry, which I strongly recommend you do. See the section "Limiting Remote Registry Access" in Chapter 9, *Administering the Registry*.

Control\Session Manager

The Session Manager key contains a group of private configuration parameters Windows 2000 and NT use for internal housekeeping. Microsoft warns against editing these values.

ObjectDirectories

This REG_MULTI_SZ names the object directories that the system creates at boot time. Do not edit them at the risk of rendering your machine unbootable.

BootExecute

This REG_SZ value specifies the applications, services and commands run at boot time. The Windows 2000 default value runs *Autochk.exe*. After a crash it's set to run *CHKDSK*, and after you convert a FAT volume to NTFS it's set to *autocheck autoconv \DosDevices\x: /FS:NTFS*.

ProcessorControl

This REG_DWORD value indicates whether the system has run a processor check routine to determine if the processor supports advanced memory management features. This value should not be modified or deleted.

RegisteredProcessors

This REG_DWORD controls how many processors the system attempts to use. The default value is 4 on Windows 2000 Server machines and 2 on machines running Windows 2000 Professional.

LicensedProcessors

This value specifies how many processors this version of the operating system is licensed to handle. Editing it may cause a blue-screen crash with SYSTEM_LICENSE_VIOLATION.

Control\Session Manager\Memory Management

This key deserves its own section even though nearly all values are disabled by default on Windows 2000 machines, and most NT machines won't ever even have this subkey. One alleged advantage of NT over some Unix variants is that NT self-tunes its virtual memory system for maximum performance. Part of this tuning is calculating how big a pagefile to use and how much physical RAM to reserve as a sort of rainy-day fund. The algorithm that actually performs the tuning takes into account how much physical RAM your machine has. Article Q126402 in the Microsoft knowledge base provides a complicated formula you can use to approximate what this algorithm does.

A few of the values within the Memory Management subkey are present to override the normally calculated system values. The PagedPoolSize and NonPagedPoolSize values, if present, override the self-tuning mechanism; if their values are 0, the self-tuning goes back into effect. The PagedPoolQuota and NonPagedPoolQuota values also override system calculations. They hold the maximum space a process can allocate in the paged pool and nonpaged pool, respectively. Again, a setting of 0 allows the system to calculate an optimum value. I strongly recommend leaving these values alone unless you see a Knowledge Base article or other reliable suggestion to do otherwise.

SYSTEM\CurrentControlSet\Services

Many Windows 2000 and NT components are implemented as services, which are roughly equivalent to Unix daemons or NetWare NLMs—small faceless programs that run in the background, even when no users are logged in. Services can be device drivers, application servers, or any other kind of background task, and they can run in the local system context or be bound to run under a particular account.

By convention, standard and optional Windows 2000 and NT's system services store their parameters under the Services subkey of the current control set. Third-party services may store their settings here, or they may choose to use HKLM\SOFTWARE.

All the services whose settings live in SYSTEM\CurrentControlSet\Services have some combination of the following values attached to them:

DependOnGroup
    This REG_MULTI_SZ names all the prerequisite groups for this service. For example, a SCSI PC Card reader might name "SCSIMiniport" here to indicate that its service shouldn't be started until at least one service in the "SCSIMiniport" group has been successfully started.

DependOnService
    Like DependOnGroup, this REG_MULTI_SZ contains a list of prerequisites for a service; the difference is that this value contains names of services that must be started first, not entire groups.

ImagePath
    This REG_EXPAND_SZ specifies where the actual executable for this service is located. Device drivers usually don't have this value, but standalone services such as the DHCP, DNS, and WINS servers usually do.

PlugPlayServiceType
    I don't know what this does.

DisplayName
    Some services include a "friendly" name suitable for display in the Services control panel. Those that do store it here as a REG_SZ.

ObjectName
    Background services may be run under a particular account. By default, services always run as *LocalSystem*; some services (like the printer spooler, scheduler, and Services for Macintosh package) are usually run under their own account. ObjectName stores the name of the account under which the service is run, if any. For kernel drivers, this value specifies which kernel object is used to load the driver.

Type

This REG_DWORD specifies the kind of service or driver this is; it must always be one of the values in Table 11-2. At boot time, the system loads drivers according to their type: kernel-mode drivers first, then filesystem drivers, and on down the list.

Table 11-2. The Type Value Specifies the Service Type

Value	What It Means
0x01	This item is a kernel-mode device driver.
0x02	This item is a kernel-mode device driver that implements filesystem services.
0x04	This item is a bundle of arguments used by a network adapter.
0x08	This item is a filesystem driver service.
0x10	This item is a Win32 service that should be run as a standalone process.
0x20	This item is a Win32 service that can share address space with other services of the same type.
0x110	This item is a Win32 service that should be run as a standalone process and can interact with users.
0x120	This item is a Win32 service that can share address space with other services of the same type and interact with users.

Start

This REG_DWORD specifies when the subject service should actually be started. When you open a service in the Services control panel, you can assign the start type with a set of five radio buttons whose labels correspond to the "Start Type" column in Table 11-3.

Table 11-3. The Start Value Controls When Services Are Loaded

Value	Start Type	What It Means
0x00	Boot	The kernel loader loads this driver first because it's required to utilize the boot volume device.
0x01	System	This service should be loaded by the I/O subsystem when the kernel is brought up.
0x02	Autoload	This service should always be loaded and run, no matter what.
0x03	Manual	This service should be loaded, but the user must start it manually from a control panel or the command line.
0x04	Disabled	This service should be loaded but may not be started by the system or the user.

Group

Birds of a feather flock together, and so do Windows 2000 and NT services. Any items with the same value in their Group key are considered to belong to the same group; when it's time to start services within a group, group members' Tag values decide which group members should be loaded first. Services without this entry do not belong to a group and are loaded after all services in service groups are loaded.

Tag The REG_DWORD Tag value specifies the load order within a single group. For example, if there are five devices in the "SCSI Miniport" group, the one with the lowest Tag value is loaded first, then the next highest, and so on.

ErrorControl

Some services are more important than others. The ErrorControl value is proof, since it lets critical services be marked as such. If a service fails to load, or fails during startup, what happens next is governed by that service's Error-Control value. Possible values are listed in Table 11-4.

Table 11-4. ErrorControl Governs What Happens on a Failure

Value	What It Means
0x00	If this driver can't be loaded or started, don't worry; ignore the failure and don't display any warnings.
0x01	Act normally. If this driver fails during startup, produce a warning message but proceed with the boot process.
0x02	Be afraid. If the startup process is currently using the last known good control set, continue on; if it's not, switch to the last known good set.
0x03	Play "Taps." Record the current startup as a failure. If this startup is using the last known good set, run a diagnostic. If not, switch to the last known good set and reboot.

There are also six subkeys commonly found beneath subkeys of Services:

Linkage

Network adapters can be bound to multiple protocols and services. Every network card driver has a Linkage subkey, which stores the bindings data for that particular card. Disabled bindings are stored in Linkage\Disabled. None of the binding subkeys or values are directly editable; you should change them only via the Network control panel.

Parameters

Parameters is a catch-all subkey that lets drivers and services store their private settings. Some components store their settings in HKLM\SOFTWARE. Device drivers (particularly those for network cards) can store hardware-specific settings such as their preferred IRQ and DMA ranges; other drivers and services can store whatever they want here.

Performance

Services that offer Performance Monitor counters advertise them by creating a Performance key. Beneath this key, there are several values that tell the

Performance Monitor which DLL to load to activate the counters and what routines the service offers for collecting performance data.

Security

The values in this key contain permission information for Windows 2000 services and drivers.

Enum

This Windows 2000 key contains values that store hardware information for devices that the service controls or interacts with.

networkprovider

The Windows 2000 network provider subkey may appear for network services where the Group value is NetworkProvider. The values under this subkey contain information about the network provider, such as the provider name and order.

Of course, any individual service is free to store additional values either as part of its key or in subkeys added to the ones listed here.

Services\Browser

The Browser service controls NetBIOS browsing, including allowing the machine to act as a master browser when requested. (For a complete description of how NetBIOS browsing actually works, see article Q102878 in the Microsoft knowledge base.) The Services\Browser\Parameters subkey contains five particularly interesting values:

MaintainServerList

This REG_SZ can assume three values: "Auto" (the default), "Yes," and "No." When it's "No," the system doesn't cache the list of browser announcements it hears, so it can't become a Browse Server. When it's "Auto," the list is cached, and the computer may force an election (which it can win) for a new master browser when necessary. When it's "Yes," the computer always acts as a Browse Server.

BackupPeriodicity

REG_DWORD value, in seconds (legal values range from 300–4294967, or about 48 days), which specifies how often a backup browse server should contact the master browser for an update.

MasterPeriodicity

Like BackupPeriodicity, except that it controls how often a master browser should contact the domain master browser.

IsDomainMaster
> IsDomainMaster is just what its name implies: a REG_SZ that indicates whether this computer is, or is not, a domain master browser. Legal values are TRUE and FALSE.

QueryDriverFrequency
> This REG_DWORD value represents the interval (0–900, in seconds) after which a browser decides that its name cache is invalid and requests a new copy of the available browser server list. Increasing this value speeds up browsing at the cost of keeping stale data in the cache longer; conversely, decreasing it keeps data fresher at the expense of bandwidth.

Services\DHCPServer

The Dynamic Host Configuration Protocol, or DHCP, is becoming more and more widespread because it offers an easy way to manage TCP/IP networks. The DHCP server's parameters are stored under its Parameters key. In the Windows NT 4.0 Registry, however, these values are found in the Parameters key under Services\DHCP:

BackupDatabasePath
> The DHCP server keeps a backup copy of its database. This REG_EXPAND_SZ value lets you specify where it's kept. By default, it goes in SystemRoot\System32\dhcp\backup. You should edit this to move the backup database to another volume on the same machine to protect against disk failures.[*]

BackupInterval
> This REG_DWORD specifies the interval in minutes at which DHCP backs up its database. By default, backups happen every 60 minutes, but you may specify any interval.

DatabaseCleanupInterval
> DHCP leases and reservations expire. Good housekeeping practices dictate that these old records be scavenged from the DHCP database; DatabaseCleanupInterval (a REG_DWORD whose default value is 1440 minutes or 1 day) specifies how many minutes should pass between scavenging runs.

DatabaseLoggingFlag
> Performance will suffer, but you can log DHCP transactions if you feel it necessary. A value of 1 in this REG_DWORD enables logging, while 0 turns it off.

---

[*] And you should keep a backup copy as well, since depending on software to keep good backups of its own configuration data is risky at best.

DatabasePath and DatabaseName
: By default, these REG_SZ values combine to point to a file named *dhcp.mdb* in *%systemroot%\system32\dhcp*. If needed, you can edit these values to put the DHCP database somewhere else.

RestoreFlag
: This value can restore the DHCP database from the backup copy. However it's not quite implemented in Windows 2000 and should not be changed.

Besides these parameters, you can instruct the DHCP server which TCP/IP configuration parameters to deliver to clients. Once you do this (using the DHCP Options → Scope command in the DHCP server manager), one or more subkeys under DHCP\Parameters\Options appear—one subkey per option, each named after the option number. These new keys tell the server where to get the values that are being broadcast to the client machines. Don't edit them.

Services\EventLog

The Event Logger service in Windows 2000 has three subkeys under Services\EventLog: one for the application log, one for the system log, and one for the security log. In addition, Windows services creates subkeys for their own logs. The Windows 2000 and Windows services subkeys are named after their respective logs and can contain a combination of seven values that can be edited via the Event Viewer application:

File
: This REG_EXPAND_SZ supplies the full path to the event file. If you want to store your event logs on a secure partition, you can edit this value to do so.

MaxSize
: Specifies the maximum size, in bytes (64-KB increments), that the log can grow to before it's marked as full.

Retention
: This REG_DWORD represents the number of seconds entries are retained before they're overwritten. The default is seven days (or, more exactly, 604,800 seconds).

Sources
: Each system component that logs event messages can supply its own message file. This makes it possible for logged messages to be very specific, since the component that generated them has extensive knowledge about why the entry was logged. This REG_MULTI_SZ holds a list of names. Each name is interpreted as a subkey of EventLog\Application, EventLog\Security, or EventLog\System. Each of these subkeys in turn contains two values that specify which message file to use for that named component.

DisplayNameFile
> This REG_EXPAND_SZ value specifies the file that holds the event log's localized name. By default, this file is *%systemroot%\system32\els.dll*.

DisplayNameID
> This REG_DWORD value holds an ID number between 0 and 0xFFFFFFFF. Used in combination with DisplayNameFile, it specifies a message ID number for the log name.

PrimaryModule
> The keys under Services\EventLog are associated with different logs. The PrimaryModule value (REG_SZ) indicates the subkey where default values are stored for log source entries within these logs.

Services\LanmanServer

The Server service actually does all the hard work of sharing files and printers under Windows 2000/NT. Its parameters live under Services\LanmanServer, and there certainly are a lot of them! Most parameters are automatically tuned by Windows 2000 and NT based on the server load, but some must be tweaked manually. Here they are:

AutoDisconnect
> You can automatically force idle clients to disconnect by setting this REG_DWORD value to the number of minutes of idle time you're willing to allow. Clients who have open files or searches on a connection aren't disconnected, but completely idle clients will be. The default idle time allowed is 15 minutes.

AutoShareServer and AutoShareWks
> Windows 2000 Server, by default, creates administrative shares of your local disks. Windows 2000 Professional and NT can be made to do so as well. These REG_DWORD values, when set to 1, tell the system to map local drives to hidden shares on computers running either Windows 2000 Server (AutoShareServer) or Windows 2000 Professional (AutoShareWks). When these values are 0, no such shares are created.

Comment
> This REG_SZ holds the comment displayed next to this machine's name when users browse the network.

DiskSpaceThreshold
> The DiskSpaceThreshold value controls when Windows 2000 and NT reports that a disk is low on space. The value represents a minimum percentage of free space; when the space available drops below that percentage, a warning alert is generated. This value's a REG_DWORD and can range from 1–99%. The default value is 10.

Hidden

If you want to hide a server or workstation from network browsers, set this REG_BINARY value to 1, and the machine disappears. Clients who know it's there can still access it, but it won't show up in Explorer or any of the other browsing tools.

RestrictNullSessionAccess

LAN Manager, NT's ancient ancestor, allowed users to connect with a *NULL session*[*] to get some types of information from a server, including a list of available shares and account names. Because this is a security vulnerability, Microsoft now offers a way to deny NULL session access to network resources—this value. Set it to 0 if you want to allow NULL session access (not recommended), or 1 if you want to deny it. When set to 1, the shares and pipes specified in NullSessionShares and NullSessionPipes can still use NULL sessions.

NullSessionShares and NullSessionPipes

These two REG_MULTI_SZ values list any file shares and/or pipes NULL session-using clients may access. By default, NullSessionShares lists COMCFG DFS$ as accessible when RestrictNullSessionAccess is turned on; The default contents of NullSessionPipes are COMNAP, COMNODE, SQL\QUERY, SPOOLSS, LLSRPC, EPMAPPER, and LOCATOR.

Users

This REG_DWORD controls how many users may simultaneously log on to your server. Its legal range is from 1 to 0xFFFFFFFE (representing a number of users), or 0xFFFFFFFF (the default) denoting no limit. As a practical matter, you should probably set this to some value less than or equal to the number of actual licenses you have for your server.

Services\NetBt

You can run the NetBIOS protocol over a TCP/IP connection; this combination is called NBT or (occasionally) NetBT. NBT makes NetBIOS traffic routable. It can also provide a performance boost, and with the advent of the Internet it makes it possible to offer NetBIOS services over an Internet connection. The NetBT service handles encapsulating NetBIOS data into TCP/IP packets, and its Parameters key contains several values that govern the overall operation of the NetBT service:

DhcpXXX

There are several values whose names begin with Dhcp. These are set automatically by the DHCP client service. Any Dhcp value can be overridden by its

---

[*] So named because instead of supplying a valid username and password, you open a null session with an empty username and password.

non-DHCP counterpart: for example, DhcpScopeID is overridden by ScopeID. Don't change any of the Dhcp values, or DHCP will stop working properly.

EnableDNS

This REG_DWORD indicates whether DNS name resolution is enabled. When it's 1, the default, NetBT uses DNS to resolve names that can't be resolved via WINS, *lmhosts*, or broadcast queries; when it's 0, DNS won't be used. Microsoft warns against changing this value in the Registry; instead, you should use the Network control panel.

EnableLMHOSTS

This REG_DWORD value indicates whether *lmhosts* are used to resolve names that can't be resolved via WINS or broadcast queries. Like EnableDNS, you shouldn't modify it directly.

EnableProxy

This DWORD controls whether this computer answers WINS proxy requests; these proxy requests come from computers not running WINS and allows connections across subnets. Don't change this value directly either.

LmhostsTimeout

You can control the timeout period for DNS and *lmhosts* name queries by adjusting this REG_DWORD value. It represents the timeout period in milliseconds; the default value of 6000 allows a 6-second timeout, but you can adjust it from 1000–0xFFFFFFFF. Tweaking this value lets you accommodate slow DNS servers, so it might make a good system policy entry.

NameSrvQueryCount

"If at first you don't succeed, try, try again" applies to name resolution, too. By default, NetBT issues three WINS queries for a name before deciding that the name can't be resolved. You can change this REG_DWORD's value to anything between 0 and 65,535 to change the number of requests.

NameSrvQueryTimeout

A single WINS query can either be answered or not. This REG_DWORD controls the number of milliseconds after which a query is judged to have timed out. Its default value of 1500 allows for a 1.5-second timeout, but you may use any value from 1000–0xFFFFFFFF. The maximum time it can take to decide a name can't be resolved via WINS is thus equal to NameSrvQueryCount multiplied by NameSrvQueryTimeout.

WinsDownTimeout

If no WINS servers can be contacted, the system can automatically wait a prescribed period before trying to contact a WINS server again. The length of this period is controlled by WinsDownTimeout, which is a REG_DWORD number of milliseconds. By default, the system waits 15 seconds after failing to catch a

WINS server before it tries again, but you can modify this interval to any value between 1000 and 0xFFFFFFFF milliseconds.

In addition to these settings, each adapter card to which NetBT is bound has its own adapter-specific settings, which may supplement or override the ones in Services\NetBt\Parameters. These settings are stored under the Services\NetBt\Adapters subkey; each adapter has a subkey named after its driver. These keys have the same DhcpXXX values as the Services\NetBt\Parameters key. In addition, their NameServer and NameServerBackup values specify the IP addresses of the primary and backup WINS servers for that adapter. If present and nonblank, these values are used instead of the corresponding systemwide entries.

Services\Netlogon

The Netlogon service handles communications between Windows 2000 machines (whether it's a workstation or a server) and domain controllers. For the sake of backward compatibility, Netlogon additionally handles replicating the user account database to backup domain controllers running NT 3.x/NT 4. NetLogin doesn't manage replication between two Windows 2000 servers. There are eight significant values in Services\Netlogon\Parameters:

DisablePasswordChange
> To secure conversations between domain controllers and domain computers, each computer in the domain uses a unique, randomly generated password to log on to the domain. By default on Windows 2000 machines, this password is regenerated every 30 days. Normally you leave this alone, but there are instances where you might want to force Windows 2000/NT not to change the password, for example, if you're dual-booting more than one copy (or version) of the operating system on a single machine. Keeping the account password unchanged ensures that each copy of Windows 2000 and NT can be a member of the domain without anyone changing the domain password behind its back.
>
> By default, this REG_DWORD is set to 0, meaning that the system changes its computer account password regularly. Setting it to 1 on a machine prevents that machine from automatically changing its computer account password, although you can still change it manually.

RefusePasswordChange
> As an alternative to setting DisablePasswordChange on lots of machines, you can set the REG_DWORD RefusePasswordChange value to 1 on all domain controllers in the domain. This forces the DC to refuse any password change request from its Windows 2000/NT 4 clients. It doesn't stop the clients from trying, however. See article Q154501 in Microsoft's knowledge base for a full explanation of this parameter and its ramifications.

Pulse
> This REG_DWORD, and the pulse and replication settings that follow, are used for replication under NT 4.0, or under Windows 2000 when an NT 4.0 (or earlier) server is involved. Pulse controls how often a change notification is sent from the primary domain controller (PDC) to each backup domain controller (BDC). All the changes occurring between pulses are collected together; when the pulse interval expires, the changes are sent to any domain controller that needs an update. Up-to-date domain controllers don't get a pulse. The default interval is 300 seconds, but you may specify any number of seconds from 60 to 48 hours' worth (172,800).

PulseConcurrency
> When a PDC has updates and sends pulses to each BDC that needs the update, the BDC responds by asking for the updated data. The number of pulses a PDC can queue at one time is controlled by this REG_DWORD; the default value of 10 means that 10 BDCs can be pulsed. Thus the PDC may have to deal with 10 update requests at one time. You can specify any value from 1 to 500; the bigger the number, the more load may be placed on the PDC.

PulseMaximum
> Specifies a maximum interval after which a BDC will be sent an update pulse, even if it doesn't need an update. The default value is 7200 seconds, or two hours, but you may specify any interval in seconds, from 60 to 172,800.

PulseTimeout1 and PulseTimeout2
> These two values control how long a PDC waits when pulsing a BDC before it considers the BDC unresponsive. PulseTimeout1 regulates how long the BDC has to answer a pulse; it can be anywhere from 1–120 seconds. PulseTimeout2 specifies how long the PDC waits for the BDC to finish absorbing the update data once it's sent, from 60–3600 seconds.

ReplicationGovernor
> Under ordinary circumstances, *Netlogon* uses a 128-KB buffer for copying the SAM database and replicates the database whenever a preset number of changes accumulate. For domain controllers on a WAN or slow local link, these settings can consume a significant amount of your bandwidth. The REG_DWORD ReplicationGovernor value can range from 0 to 100; its value represents a percentage of both the buffer size and the amount of time an outstanding replication request is in progress. For example, a ReplicationGovernor value of 25 specifies that a BDC use a 32-KB buffer (25% of 128 KB), and that a replication request can be on the Net no more than 25% of the time. You must make this setting on every BDC you want to affect; it has no effect on

the PDC. Do not set this value to zero! If you do, the PDC never synchronizes with the affected BDC.

Scripts

This REG_SZ value specifies the full path to the Net Login shared directory on the domain controller where logon scripts are kept.

[NT4] *Update*

Ordinarily, the SAM database is synchronized only after a number of changes have accumulated. You can force *Netlogon* to completely synchronize the database when the service starts by setting this REG_SZ value to "Yes." The default value, "No," allows synchronization to happen when needed.

Services\RasMan

The Dial-Up Networking (née RAS) subsystem lets you dial into remote computers and communicate using Microsoft's protocols, IPX, or TCP/IP. The RasMan service is the component that actually handles making over-the-modem network connections on outbound calls. There are only two significant values for this service's Parameters subkey:

DisableSavedPasswords

Normally, each user may choose whether she wants DUN to save her passwords or not. You can compel DUN not to cache these passwords by adding this REG_DWORD value and setting its value to 1. When you do, DUN doesn't display the "Save password" checkbox, and it forgets any passwords it has previously stored.

[NT4] *Logging*

When this REG_DWORD is 1, the DUN dial-up component logs its interaction with whatever serial device it's using. This is a great way to troubleshoot connection problems; DUN logs to the *%systemroot%\system32\ras\device.log* file until a connection is established. The log file is cleared when you stop and restart DUN components or when its size exceeds about 100 KB.

The Services\RasMan\PPP key has all the really useful DUN settings, including:

NegotiateTime

This value specifies the time, in seconds, the PPP module allows for a successful connection negotiation. If the two sides can't complete negotiation in this period, the connection fails. The default value is 150 seconds, but you may set it to any DWORD value. A value of 0 means the connection never fails.

Logging

When this REG_DWORD is set to 1, each PPP connect, disconnect, or failure event is logged to *\%systemroot%\system32\ras\ppp.log*.

ForceEncryptedPassword

PPP servers may specify what types of authentication they support. The ForceEncryptedPassword value forces a RAS server to request CHAP authentication from its clients instead of the less secure PAP. Set this REG_DWORD to 1 to force CHAP authentication or 0 to allow PAP. This value has no effect on computers that aren't RAS servers.

Services\Replicator

The Directory Replicator service (usually called just "the replicator") can mirror directories on one server in a domain to other workstations and servers. Any machine may import replicated directories, and any server may export them. What gets replicated and when is controlled by values under the Services\Replicator key. First of all, the Exports and Imports keys contain one value entry for each exported or imported directory. You manage these lists with the Directory Replication dialog in the NT Server Manager.

In Windows 2000, the NT Server Manager functionality is replaced by Active Directory Users and Computers.

The Parameters subkey contains parameters (also settable through the Server Manager) that control how the replication process actually runs:

ExportPath

This REG_SZ contains the full path to the directory being exported. Any given machine may export only a single directory; on domain controllers, this is almost always the directory where logon scripts are stored, but it can be anything.

GuardTime

GuardTime tells the replicator service how long to wait after the last file change before sending a new change notice. Its value can range from 0 (send changes immediately) to half of the value of Interval. This value has no effect unless you specify that the export files should be "Stabilized" in the Server Manager.

ImportPath

This value specifies the full path to the directory where imported files and directories are stored on the local machine.

Interval

    This REG_DWORD value specifies how often an export computer should check its export directory for changes. The default is 5 minutes, but the value may range from 1 to 60 minutes.

Pulse

    Pulse controls when the export computer rebroadcasts change notices. These change notices are sent even when no changes occur so that importers know whether they missed any updates due to network outages. The value of Pulse may range from 1 to 10; it's used as a multiplier of Interval. A Pulse value of 3 (the default) combined with an Interval of 60 (minutes) means that redundant change notices are sent every 3 hours.

Replicate

    This REG_DWORD controls what replication role this machine plays. A value of 1 means this machine exports files; a value of 2 means it imports from other exporters, and a value of 3 (the default) means it can do both.

Services\Tcpip

TCP/IP is a complicated protocol, so it's not surprising that there are a large number of values in Services\Tcpip\Parameters. In keeping with Microsoft's hands-off approach, most parameters that affect how the TCP/IP stack allocates resources are self-adjusting, and I haven't documented them here because there's really no reason to ever adjust them.

It may be tempting to adjust some of these parameters on all your machines by building a policy file, but it's a better idea to use DHCP, which is designed specifically for this task. As a side bonus, DHCP works with non-Windows computers too.

DatabasePath

    This REG_SZ contains the path where the TCP/IP stack should look for its *hosts*, *lmhosts*, *networks*, and *protocols* files. By default it points to *%systemroot%\system32\drivers\etc*.

DefaultTTL

    The Time-To-Live (TTL) value determines how long an IP packet can remain on the network before it either reaches its destination or is discarded. By default, Windows 2000 marks its packets with a TTL of 128 (NT's default is 32), but this may be too short for some applications. This REG_DWORD value has a range of between 1 and 255 seconds.

Domain

    This REG_SZ contains the suffix for the primary Domain Name System, which is used in DNS name registration and name resolution.

Hostname

    This REG_SZ contains the hostname you entered in the TCP/IP Properties dialog.

NameServer

    This single REG_SZ contains a list of IP addresses (with a space between each address) indicating which DNS servers you've configured for DNS-based address resolution. This value, if any, overrides the name server list provided via DHCP.

IPEnableRouter

    This REG_DWORD determines if IP forwarding is enabled. When this DWORD is 1, the system attempts to route IP packets between the subnets attached to its network adapter cards; when it's 0 (or when you only have one NIC) no routing takes place.

SearchList

    This REG_SZ value contains a space-separated list of domain names to append to any hostname that's missing a suffix and can't be resolved.

EnableSecurityFilters

    When set to 1, this REG_DWORD enables the TCP/IP stack to filter incoming connections according to the ports specified in TcpAllowedPorts and UdpAllowedPorts in the next list.

PersistentRoutes

    Starting with NT 3.51, you could add persistent static routes with the `route add` command. Should you do so, each route is stored as a REG_SZ value under the Services\Tcpip\PersistentRoutes subkey. Each route has its own value entry, constructed as a REG_SZ:

    `destinationAddr,subnetMask,routeGateway, routeMetric`

    The entries' names contain all the useful data; their contents are empty.

In addition to these parameters, each network adapter card to which TCP/IP is bound has its own individual set of parameters stored in the card's key under HKLM\SYSTEM\CurrentControlSet\Services\Tcpip\Parameters\Interfaces\<*interface-name*> (or HKLM\SYSTEM\CurrentControlSet\Services\adapter\Parameters\Tcpip on Windows NT machines).

IPAddress

    This REG_MULTI_SZ contains the actual IP addresses assigned to the physical adapter card. If the first address in the list is "0.0.0.0," the address is assigned by a DHCP server. You can add multiple addresses to a single adapter card by adding them here.

DefaultGateway

This REG_MULTI_SZ specifies an ordered list of default targets for packets that aren't destined for one of the addresses on the IPAddress list.

DontAddDefaultGateway

This REG_DWORD (which doesn't get created automatically) can be either 0 or 1. When it's 1, Windows 2000 and NT won't use a default gateway entry for this adapter. Microsoft warns that "PPTP users must add this Registry entry for each adapter that is not connected to the Internet" to prevent accidentally routing unintended traffic across a PPTP link.

EnableDHCP

If this REG_DWORD is 1, the system asks the DHCP client service to configure the first IP address on this adapter.

SubnetMask

Since IPAddress allows multiple addresses, SubnetMask is a REG_MULTI_SZ too; it needs to accommodate one subnet mask per IP address! If the first mask is "0.0.0.0," all the mask data is retrieved from DHCP. You should have one subnet mask for every IP address specified in IPAddress.

TcpAllowedPorts and UdpAllowedPorts

These two REG_MULTI_SZ values allow you to specify a set of ports on which connections are accepted. When EnableSecurityFilters equals 0, these values are ignored; when it equals 1, connections from these ports are allowed, but connections from all other ports are rejected.

HKU

The "U" in HKU stands for "user." That's appropriate, since HKU's subkeys store settings that vary from user to user. Every time a user logs in, one of two things happens. If the user's never logged in before, the system makes a new copy of the contents of HKU\.DEFAULT and stores it in a new subkey whose name matches the user's SID. If the user has logged in before, his subkey under HKU is mapped to HKCU, and the logon process continues. There are some subtleties to this process; for example, if the network's using profiles, the system may have to fetch the user's profile from a server if it's not locally cached.

HKU\.DEFAULT

The settings in this hive are used as defaults for new users when they log in. The section "Setting Defaults for New User Accounts" in Chapter 9 discusses how you can modify these defaults so that all new users get the defaults you set automatically when their HKU subkeys are created.

HKU\sid

Each user account has a unique SID; this SID is also used to identify that account's settings under HKU. For a detailed description of what keys and values are stored under HKU\sid, see the section "HKCU" later in this chapter.

HKCR

HKCR is the backbone of the OLE/ActiveX subsystem. The shell, the Explorer, and many applications depend on the data stored here for prosaic tasks such as deciding which icon to display with a file or what to do when the user double-clicks a file. OLE applications need this data to determine what servers to start when a user embeds or links a foreign object into a document, and the Distributed OLE and DCOM systems need it too.

In Windows NT 4.0 and previous versions of NT, this root key got its data solely from the software classes subkey under HKLM, that is HKLM\Software\Classes. This worked fine, although the system could register program classes only on a per-machine basis. In Windows 2000, the software classes under HKCU\Software\Classes are merged with the HKLM software classes to make up HKCR. Defined as per-user class registration, this allows program classes to be registered independently for each user.

HKCR\ext

The original Win3.x scheme for linking a file with the application that created it was to associate the file's extension with the name of an executable. With the introduction of OLE, though, it became necessary to associate file contents with DLLs, since an OLE server might be a DLL instead of a standalone application. The Win 3.x File and Program Managers were primitive at best, and to improve them Microsoft needed a lot more information about files, their creators, and their types.

The starting point for these improvements is the set of *filename-extension keys* that live under HKCR. These keys are named after file extensions: HKCR\.txt, HKCR\.html, and so on. The default value of each of these keys contains a string called the *application identifier* such as "textfile" or "htmlfile." This value is used to look up an HKCR subkey of the same name.

While it's possible to add other values to file association keys, no part of the system will use them, and they're subject to being overwritten, so don't count on your values being available if you keep them here.

HKCR\fileType

For each file association key, there is usually a single key whose name matches the application identifier. These keys are called *class-definition keys*. Continuing the previous example, let's say there's a key named HKCR\htmlfile. To figure out what to do with a file when the user double-clicks it, the shell follows three steps:

1. Strip the extension from the file and use it to find a file association key such as HKCR\.doc or HKCR\.pl.

2. Open the file association key and get its default value, then use that value to look for a key with the same name. For example, if HKCR\.pl's default value is "Perl script," the shell looks for HKCR\Perl script and tries to open it. This subkey is called the *application identifier key*.

3. The application identifier key contains values the shell parses to figure out how to open or edit a file, or to create a new copy of a particular file type or object.

Each application identifier key can have a number of values and subkeys. Which ones a particular application's key has varies. Here are the most common subkeys:

CLSID
   This subkey's default value contains the *class ID*, or CLSID, assigned to an OLE object. OLE applications (including Explorer and the shell) can use this CLSID to keep track of a file or object's type.

DefaultIcon
   The default value of this subkey contains the path to an executable or DLL and a resource ID. When it needs the icon for a file, the Explorer looks up the application's class-definition key, gets the DefaultIcon value if it exists, and loads that icon. By changing this value, you can alter the icons displayed for a particular file type.

Shell\Edit, Shell\Open, and Shell\Print
   These subkeys each have a further subkey: Command. When the system sees one of the Shell\XXX keys, it knows that this class type can be opened, printed, or edited. The value of the Command subkey gives the actual command that performs the requested action.

shellex
   The shellex subkey makes it possible for clever programmers to add items to the Properties dialog for a particular file type. The value of the shellex\PropertySheetHandlers can specify a CLSID; when the shell looks up the CLSID's key, it can figure out which property sheet or dialog to open for that item.

HKCR\CLSID

This subkey contains all the CLSIDs for classes installed on the system. Each CLSID key contains a value that provides a human-readable name for the class (which appears in the Insert Object dialog of most OLE-compatible applications). There are a variety of other subkeys that can be attached to a particular entry under HKCR\CLSID\clsid. The most important ones are InprocServer32 and Inproc-Server. These specify which DLL implements the code to create or edit objects of this CLSID's type.

HKCU

We all like to customize our environments. We do it at home, at work, in our cars, and pretty much anywhere else we can get away with it. When you customize your Windows 2000 or NT environment and applications, the changes end up in subkeys of HKCU, which is actually a link to your SID's subkey under HKU. Only a currently logged-in user has access to HKCU. It can't be edited remotely (*RegEdit* disallows remote user access to HKCU and HKCC), nor can a SID key under HKU be edited while someone with a different SID is logged in.

The contents of HKCU vary more than any of the other root keys because applications store their user-specific settings here too. If Ellen and Joe share a computer, their respective HKCU subkeys can end up looking very different: Ellen might install and use Netscape, Visual Studio, and BoundsChecker, while Joe might stick with Office 2000 and Internet Explorer. Accordingly, in this section I'll confine my discussion to the most important subkeys of HKCU.

HKCU\AppEvents

For better or worse, Microsoft included the capability in NT 4.0 (and Win95, too) to associate sounds with system events such as opening or closing windows, logging out, and so on. This feature certainly falls into the customization arena, and application developers can add their own event classes. For example, if you install Microsoft's Visual Studio, you can get audio alerts when your compilation succeeds, when the debugger hits a breakpoint, and so on.

The event-to-sound mappings are stored in HKCU\AppEvents. Each event that has a sound associated with it has the name of the *.wav* file to play as the content of its default value. For a fun prank, write a Perl script that randomly assigns *.wav* files from *%systemroot%\media* to random events.*

---

* The publisher and I jointly disclaim any liability arising from you doing this to your boss, spouse, or co-workers.

HKCU\Console

MS-DOS command-line interface is, to put it politely, extremely limited. If you're used to a powerful Unix shell such as *bash*, *zsh*, or *tcsh*, you know what I mean. The really weak spot, though, is the appearance and behavior of the console window; after all, you can always write command scripts in Perl, KixStart, or REXX, but you're stuck looking at them through that old throwback 80x24 white-on-black ugly-font DOS window!

Fortunately, the Windows 2000 and NT console is customizable, so you don't have to suffer any longer. The customization settings all live under HKCU\Console, and they're so self-explanatory (guess what FontSize does) I won't cover them here.

HKCU\Control Panel Items

Each installed control panel may have its own subkey and settings beneath HKCU\Control Panels. HKU\.DEFAULT has default settings for all the control panels, so HKCU\Control Panels may not contain as many values as you'd expect. Additionally, many control panels (notably Network and Multimedia) store their settings in other parts of the Registry.

HKCU\Environment

The Environment key contains whatever environment variables are set in the "User Variables" list of the System control panel's Environment tab. They're stored as name-value pairs. For some reason, some variables are stored as REG_SZ entries, while others are stored as REG_EXPAND_SZ. It doesn't seem to matter what's in the value, either; some nonexpandable strings are still tagged as REG_EXPAND_SZ. Weird.

HKCU\Printers

The system stores information about printers the current user may use in HKCU\Printers. Each printer gets its own value entry directly under HKCU\Printers. This entry specifies what the default printer for this particular user is. The printer settings themselves (for all printers, not just the default one) are actually stored in HKLM\SYSTEM\CurrentControlSet\Control\Print\Printers for Windows 2000 machines and HKLM\SYSTEM\CurrentControlSet\Services\Print\Printers for NT.

HKCU\Software\Microsoft

As you've no doubt inferred from the name, user-specific settings for Microsoft components are stored under this key. Until you install Internet Explorer and/or Microsoft Office on a machine, though, there are relatively few of these keys; most system settings are stored under HKLM, and there aren't that many settings to hold here.

Microsoft\NtBackup

The bundled backup applications included with Windows 2000 and NT have a fairly large number of settings in it. All these settings can be manipulated using the program's standard user interface, but you may be interested in setting some of them via group or system policies. For example, the NtBackup\UserInterface\UsePassword flag can be set to require that backup tapes be password-protected. There are a number of subkeys that fall under Microsoft\NtBackup:[*]

Backup Engine
> The values under this subkey control the actual backup process: how many buffers should be reserved for the tape drive, whether Mac files on an NTFS volume should be backed up, and so forth.

Debug
> If you're having problems getting a backup device to work, you can configure debug logging through the values in this key.

Display
> These settings store your choices of font size, window position, and other display parameters.

Hardware
> The settings you choose for whatever type of tape hardware your system has are stored here.

Logging
> You can turn on logging for individual backup jobs through the *ntbackup* user interface. When you do, these values are used to figure out whether the log file should be printed and what the root of its filename should be.

Translators
> These settings store NT Backup translator information.

User Interface
> The catch-all key, this holds values that don't have a place anywhere else, such as whether the tape should be ejected when the backup completes or whether the backup should be automatically verified when it's done.

For a more complete explanation of the ins and outs of *NTBACKUP*, see O'Reilly's *Windows NT Backup and Restore*.

---

[*] And *ntbackup* doesn't even know it; it's using an INI file remapped to this key.

Microsoft\RAS Autodial

The Dial-Up Networking autodialer's settings are stored under this key, which retains its name for backward compatibility.

Addresses

Each time you establish an autodialed connection, DUN stores the address that caused the dialing in a value under Addresses. The IP address or DNS name serves as the value name for each entry. Entries under Addresses have three values: Tag, LastModified, and Network.

Control

This subkey is where the actual control settings for the autodialer live. There are only three of them:

DisabledAddresses

This REG_MULTI_SZ stores a list of IP addresses or DNS names for which an autodialed connection will never be established. You can use this list as an extremely low-rent blocking proxy by filling it with addresses of sites you don't want to connect to.

LoginSessionDisable

I have no idea what this is for. It appears to be set by the `RasGet-AutodialParm()` API routine. If you know what this does, I'd love to hear.

DisableConnectionQuery

Ordinarily, DUN pops up a little dialog asking you for permission to start a connection when it needs one. This is annoying because if you start something that requires a connection, you have to stay there to answer the dialog; its default action button is "No, don't dial." You can subdue this annoyance by setting DisableConnectionQuery (a REG_DWORD) to 1. This forces DUN to always start a dialup connection when one is required.

Locations

There's one subkey of Locations for each dialing location you have defined.

Entries

Likewise, there is one subkey under Entries for each phonebook entry you've used. The value for an entry is of the form Network$X$, where X is some small integer. This indicates which DUN dialup adapter you used to make this connection.

Networks

This key has subkeys named after the values of Entries' subkeys: Network0, Network1, and so on. Each of these entries in turn has a value named "1" that points back to an entry under Entries.

Microsoft\RAS Monitor

The RAS Monitor key stores settings for the Dial-Up Networking monitor. Nine of the fourteen values stored here track the window size and position of various monitor windows; the other five are flag and setting values whose structure isn't documented.

Microsoft\RAS Phonebook

The systemwide set of DUN phonebook entries is stored in *%systemroot%\ system32\ras\rasphone.pbk*. This file (or the personal phonebook files you can create and use instead) holds the phone numbers, network settings, and login credentials for each entry in your phonebook.* These settings can differ widely between entries; you might have one entry for your ISP that tells DUN to use server-supplied values for everything and another for dialing in to your office intranet that uses a fixed set of IP, DNS, and gateway addresses.

The values beneath Microsoft\RAS Phonebook control DUN dialing for all entries in the phonebook. As you can see, they provide a fairly rich set of options.

AllowLogonLocationEdits and AllowLogonPhonebookEdits
These two REG_DWORDs control whether users may change their dialing location or phonebook entry during login. They're only effective if you've enabled the option to allow logging on via DUN. Note that when you change these parameters in the Appearance tab of the Logon Properties dialog from within *rasphone*, these values are actually changed in HKU\.DEFAULT\Software\Microsoft\RAS Phonebook, not in HKCU.

AlternatePhonebookPath
If you specify an alternate phonebook in the User Preferences dialog's Phonebook tab, the path to that phonebook appears here.

AreaCodes
In the Basic tab of the Edit Phonebook Entry dialog, you can specify whether you want to use the TAPI dialing properties or not. If you do, you can enter an area code for the phonebook number. This REG_MULTI_SZ tracks the area codes you've entered in the phonebook.

CallbackMode
DUN supports three callback modes via this value. They apply only if the remote server offers to perform a callback. The first option, set if this REG_DWORD is 0, tells the DUN client to refuse callback requests. A value of 1

---

* *.pbk* files are plain text, so you can inspect and edit them to your heart's content. You can also copy them from one machine to another; this is an easy way to get a consistent set of phonebook entries for a group of machines.

(the default) specifies that DUN should ask you whether you want to accept it or not, and a value of 3 means "yes, always accept a callback if requested."

CloseOnDial

When it's set to 1, as it is by default, this REG_DWORD tells DUN to close the phonebook application when it's finished. Set this value to 0 to keep the phonebook application open after dialing completes.

DefaultEntry

This REG_SZ specifies which phonebook entry appears as the default entry when you open the Dial-Up Networking phonebook. Adjust it to make a particular entry appear.

ExpandAutoDialQuery

Before DUN autodials for you, it may ask you to confirm that you really want to dial (unless you have "Always prompt before auto-dialing" unchecked in the Appearance tab of the User Preferences dialog). When it does ask for confirmation, the "Settings" button in the confirmation dialog shows additional controls for choosing a location and turning off the confirmation requests in the future. Setting ExpandAutoDialQuery to 1, its default, makes these extra controls immediately visible. Setting it to 0 requires users to hit the Settings button to see them.

IdleHangUpSeconds

This value specifies the number of seconds a DUN connection may be idle before the client hangs it up. The value should be in seconds; a value of 0 tells DUN to never hang up.

LastCallbackByCaller

I don't know what this is for either.

NewEntryWizard

As with so many other Windows 2000 and NT components, the DUN phonebook features a wizard that ostensibly helps you create new entries. The Appearance tab of the User Preferences dialog features a checkbox that lets you specify whether you want to use the wizard or not; this REG_DWORD reflects that value.

OperatorDial

You can toggle a DUN setting that tells it not to dial because you'll be dialing manually. This REG_DWORD value reflects that option; when it's 1, that means that the system waits for you to dial before attempting to connect.

PersonalPhonebookFile

Besides the alternate phonebook file, you may specify an individual phonebook file for your own use (after all, this is HKCU!). If you specify a personal phonebook in the User Preferences dialog's Phonebook tab, the path to that phonebook appears here.

PhonebookMode

This REG_DWORD specifies which phonebook DUN uses. The default value of 0 means that *%systemroot%\system32\ras\rasphone.pbk* is used; a value of 1 means that the user's personal phonebook is used, and a 3 means that the value in AlternatePhonebookPath is used.

Phonebooks

This REG_MULTI_SZ keeps a list of all the phonebooks you've ever specified in AlternatePhonebookPath so it can build a combo box listing them for your later reference.

Prefixes

This REG_MULTI_SZ contains a list of all the prefixes you've ever specified for phone entries in your phonebook. This allows DUN to present a nice combo box listing your previous choices.

PreviewPhoneNumber

This REG_DWORD reflects the setting of the "Preview Phone Number" checkbox in the Appearance tab of the Edit Phonebook Entry dialog. When it's set to 1, users may edit the phonebook entry's number before it's dialed.

RedialAttempts

By default, if a connection doesn't happen on the first attempt, DUN quits trying. This happens because the default value of RedialAttempts is 0. You can enable as many retries as you'd like, and DUN will patiently keep trying until it connects or makes the specified number of attempts.

RedialOnLinkFailure

This value (a REG_DWORD) specifies whether DUN should automatically resurrect a failed connection. Sometimes a connection drops for no good reason; setting this value to 1 causes DUN to redial and restart the connection if it fails.

RedialSeconds

This value specifies the number of seconds (15 is the default) to wait between redial attempts, assuming you've set RedialAttempts to greater than 0.

ShowConnectStatus

This REG_DWORD has two possible values: 1 (the default) displays a connection progress dialog that indicates what's happening on the connection, and 0 suppresses the dialog (useful when you're making connections via command-line scripts).

ShowLights

In a nod to the Win95 way of doing things, NT's DUN can display some little blinking lights in the system tray to duplicate the front-panel LEDs of most external modems. The Dial-Up Networking Monitor is in charge of this vital function. By default, this REG_DWORD's value is 1, meaning that the DUN Monitor will be started before the connection is—therefore, the lights will be present. If you don't enjoy seeing them (or, more likely, if you're not paying any attention to the system tray), you can set this value to 0 to hide them.

SkipConnectComplete

Until you tell it otherwise, DUN displays a dialog saying you've successfully connected. One of the options in this dialog is a checkbox that says "Don't show this dialog again." That checkbox controls the value of SkipConnect-Complete: when it's 1, that tells DUN to omit the dialog. By default, its value is 0, so you'll see this dialog until you manually turn it off.

Suffixes

Like Prefixes, this value's a REG_MULTI_SZ. Its purpose is to store a list of any suffixes you've ever specified for a DUN phone number.

UseLocation

By default, you can select any of the installed TAPI locations when making a DUN connection. This is especially useful if you have a machine that frequently moves between different area codes or countries. However, if you want to keep users from changing their location from the DUN phonebook, just set this REG_DWORD to 0 instead of its default value of 1. (Note that users can still use the Modems control panel to change locations.)

UseAreaAndCountry

I haven't been able to identify what this does.

WindowX and WindowY

These values specify the (x,y) location of the upper-left corner of the DUN phonebook window.

Besides this cornucopia of values, Microsoft\RAS Phonebook has an additional subkey, Callback. Every installed modem device on the system has its own subkey under Callback, named after the device (e.g., Callback\Standard Modem (COM2)). If you set the callback mode to "always call me back at this number," the number you supply for that device goes in the subkey's Number value. This provides a convenient way to preset a callback number, perhaps as part of a mass laptop installation.

Microsoft\Windows\CurrentVersion

A surprising amount of code originally developed for Win95 has found its way into NT 4.0 and ultimately Windows 2000. In fact, Microsoft's eventual goal is to unify the Win9x and NT lines until what's left is a nice Win9x interface over the security, performance, and scalability of NT. To facilitate this merging, Microsoft included a compatibility key, Microsoft\Windows\CurrentVersion, in the NT 4.0 and Windows 2000 Registries. This allows applications that use this key on Win95, like Explorer and Internet Explorer, to run on NT and Windows 2000 systems without modification.

Microsoft\Windows NT\CurrentVersion

Much like the Microsoft\Windows subkey which holds information for applications that were designed to run on Win95 machines, this Windows 2000 subkey contains subkeys that represent different versions of Windows 2000, NT 4.0 and earlier. Most notably, the CurrentVerions subkey stores user-specific configuration data for programs that are designed to run on the latest version of Windows 2000.

The Microsoft\Windows NT key appears to be a migration of the previous NT key HKCU\Microsoft\Windows NT. They both contain subkeys that represent the current operating system versions (see the next section) and contain similar keys and values, with the following Windows 2000 additions:

Event Viewer
   Event Viewer is a Windows 2000 MMC snap-in that displays event logs written to by Windows 2000 applications and services. The Event Viewer subkey stores information about the configuration of this snap-in.

Extensions
   Through Window Explorer (or the Registry), you can associate filename extensions with programs that are run when you open the file. Values under this subkey specify default command line executions for filename extensions that are not associated with programs.

PrinterPorts
   Entries under this subkey contain information about printers, such as name, driver name, port, and timeout value, that the client is connected to.

Task Manager
   Task Manager is a performance tool that displays application, process, and performance information (you've likely used it if you've ever had to terminate a application that wasn't responding). This subkey contains Task Manager preferences.

TrueType
   This subkey contains information about the display of TrueType fonts.

HKCU\Microsoft\Windows NT\CurrentVersion

[NT4]

This key is pretty much a mixed bag: it holds user-specific settings that have no home elsewhere. For example, NT's Server Manager applications store their settings in a subkey of Windows NT\CurrentVersion\Network even though they might more properly live under HKCU\Software\Microsoft\ServerManager or somesuch.

Devices

The Devices subkey contains one value entry for each installed printer on a system. Apart from that, it doesn't seem to do anything else.

Network

The Event Viewer, Server Manager, and User Manager all keep their small sets of user-specific settings here. The only other interesting item is the Persistent-Connections subkey, which contains a list of shares that NT should reconnect when the user logs in again.

Program Manager

The entries under this key are retained for older applications that expect to find things here.

Windows

Just as with Program Manager, this key primarily exists for backward compatibility, especially with the WOW subsystem.

Winlogon

Alone among the subkeys of Windows NT\CurrentVersion, Winlogon actually has three useful values beneath it. They duplicate similar entries in HKLM\SOFTWARE\Microsoft\Windows NT\CurrentVersion\Winlogon, but these entries apply only to the currently logged in user.

ParseAutoexec

This REG_DWORD specifies whether to parse *autoexec.bat* when the user logs in, resulting in the *autoexec.bat* path statement being appended to the system path created by Windows NT. 1 (the default) means yes; 0 means no.

ProfileType

Specifies the profile type of the current user's profile. A 1 means it's a local profile; other values indicate a cached, roaming, or mandatory roaming profile.

RunLoginScriptSync

If this REG_DWORD is set to 1, any logon script for this user is run before the desktop and shell are started. This is the default. Setting the value to 0 allows the logon script process to run in parallel with the shell as it starts.

HKCC

HKCC is just a pointer that links to the current hardware profile at HKLM\SYSTEM\CurrentControlSet\Hardware Profiles (HKLM\SYSTEM\Hardware Profiles\Current on NT). Under Win9x, HKCC is dynamically generated and filled with the list of VxDs and other drivers that are currently active. Since NT has no comparable way to load such a list, HKCC exists as a compatibility aid.

HKDD

HKDD exists primarily as a convenience for software developers whose programs were originally designed for Win95. Applications written for Windows NT and Windows 2000 (notably the Performance Monitor) don't get data out of HKDD; instead, they use HKEY_PERFORMANCE_DATA. However, Win95 code that uses subkeys of HKDD will still work, since the NT family remaps HKDD data into the appropriate subkeys elsewhere in the Registry.

User Configuration Group Policy Objects

Chapter 7, *Using Group Policies*, detailed the process of creating, managing, and distributing group policy settings. However, it's not enough to know how to do these things; you also have to know which policy settings exist and what they do—hence this appendix. The GPO settings listed in this appendix appear in the User Configuration node beneath each domain and local policy object.

Administrative Templates

User Configuration\Administrative Templates

Windows Components

User Configuration\Administrative Templates\Windows Components

NetMeeting

User Configuration\Administrative Templates\Windows Components\NetMeeting

Enable Automatic Configuration
This policy configures NetMeeting to download settings from the URL listed in the Configuration URL text box each time it starts.

Disable Directory Services
Controls the directory feature of NetMeeting. If you enable this policy, users can't log on to a directory (ILS) server when NetMeeting starts and users can't view or place calls via a NetMeeting directory.

Prevent adding Directory servers
If you enable this policy, users can't add directory (ILS) servers to the list of those they can use to place calls.

Prevent viewing Web directory
   If you enable this policy, users can't view directories as web pages in a browser.

Set the intranet support Web page
   Controls the URL NetMeeting displays when users choose the Help Online Support command.

Set the NetMeeting home page
   Controls the URL NetMeeting displays when users choose the Microsoft Home Page command under Help Microsoft on the Web.

Set Call Security options
   Controls security levels for incoming/outgoing NetMeeting calls.

Prevent changing Call placement method
   Controls how calls are placed—either directly or via a gatekeeper server—and prevents users from changing how calls are placed once the policy is enabled.

Prevent automatic acceptance of Calls
   When enabled, this policy stops users from turning on automatic acceptance of incoming calls, which ensures that other users don't call and connect to NetMeeting when the user isn't present.

Prevent sending files
   When enabled, this policy stops users from sending files to others in a conference.

Prevent receiving files
   When enabled, this policy stops users from receiving files from others in a conference.

Limit the size of sent files
   This policy limits the size of files users send to others in a conference.

Disable Chat
   Enabling this feature disables NetMeeting's Chat feature.

Disable NetMeeting 2.x Whiteboard
   Enabling this feature disables NetMeeting's 2.x whiteboard feature (available for compatibility).

Disable NetMeeting Whiteboard
   Enabling this feature disables NetMeeting's T.126 whiteboard feature.

Internet Explorer

    User Configuration\Administrative Templates\Windows Components\Internet Explorer

Search: Disable Search Customization
   Changes the appearance of the Customize button in the Search Assistant so that it's dimmed. Enabling this policy prevents users from making changes to the Search Assistant settings.

Search: Disable Find Files via F3 within the browser
   When you enable this feature, users can't use the F3 key to search in Internet Explorer or Windows Explorer. This policy pertains to situations where administrators want to restrict users from searching the Internet or the hard disk.

Disable external branding of Internet Explorer
   Enabling this policy ensures that third parties (such as ISPs) can't customize (or brand) the Internet Explorer and Outlook Express logos and title bars.

Disable importing and exporting of favorites
   When you enable this policy, users can't export or import favorite links by using the Import/Export wizard.

Disable changing Advanced page settings
   When you enable this policy, users can't change settings on the Advanced tab in the Internet Options dialog box. This policy prevents users from changing advanced Internet settings.

Disable changing home page settings
   Controls the home page. If you enable this policy, users can't change their home page.

Use Automatic Detection for dial-up connections
   When you enable this policy, Automatic Detection is used automatically to configure dial-up settings for users. Automatic Detection customizes the browser the first time it's started using a DHCP (Dynamic Host Configuration Protocol) or DNS (Domain Name System) server.

Disable caching of Auto-Proxy scripts
   When you enable this feature, automatic proxy scripts aren't stored in the users' cache. These scripts interact with a server to automatically configure users' proxy settings.

Display error message on proxy script download failure
   Enabling this feature ensures that error messages are displayed to users if problems occur with proxy scripts.

Disable changing Temporary Internet files settings
   Controls the browser cache settings. If you enable this policy, users can't change the browser cache settings such as the location of the Temporary Internet Files folder. Note that the Disable the General page removes the General tab from interface.

Disable changing history settings
   Controls the history settings. If you enable this policy, users can't change the history settings for the browser. Note that the Disable the General page removes the General tab from interface.

Disable changing color settings
   Controls the default web page colors. If you enable this policy, users can't change the default background and text color of web pages. Note that the Disable the General page removes the General tab from interface.

Disable changing link color settings
   Controls the color of links on web pages. If you enable this policy, users can't change the colors of their browser's web links. Note that the Disable the General page removes the General tab from interface.

Disable changing font settings
   Controls the font settings. If you enable this policy, users can't change the font setting on their browsers. Note that the Disable the General page removes the General tab from interface.

Disable changing language settings
   Controls the language settings. If you enable this policy, users can't change the language settings on their browsers. Note that the Disable the General page removes the General tab from interface.

Disable changing accessibility settings
   Controls the accessibility settings. If you enable this policy, users can't change the accessibility settings on their browsers. Note that the Disable the General page removes the General tab from interface.

Disable Internet Connection wizard
   Controls the Internet Connection wizard. If you enable this policy, users can't use the Internet Connection wizard. Note that this policy overlaps with the Disable the Connections page, which removes the Connections tab from the interface.

Disable changing connection settings
   Controls the connection setting. If you enable this policy, users can't use the connections settings on their browsers. Note that this policy overlaps with the Disable the Connections page, which removes the Connections tab from the interface.

Disable changing proxy settings
   Controls the proxy settings. If you enable this policy, users can't change their proxy settings. Note that this policy overlaps with the Disable the Connections page, which removes the Connections tab from the interface.

Disable changing Automatic Configuration settings

Controls automatic configuration settings. Administrators can use automatic configuration to update browser settings periodically. If enabled, this policy prevents users from changing automatic configuration settings. Note that this policy overlaps with the Disable the Connections page, which removes the Connections tab from the interface.

Disable changing ratings settings

Controls the ratings that help determine the type of Internet content that can be viewed. Enabling this policy prevents users from changing these ratings settings. Note that the Disable the Content page policy removes the Content tab from Internet Explorer in the Control Panel and takes precedence over this policy.

Disable changing certificate settings

Controls the certificates that verify the identity of software publishers. Enabling this policy prevents users from changing the certificate settings in Internet Explorer. Note that the Disable the Content page policy removes the Content tab from Internet Explorer in the Control Panel and takes precedence over this policy.

Disable changing Profile Assistant settings

Controls the Profile Assistant settings. If you enable this policy, users can't change the Profile Assistant settings. The Disable the Content page policy removes the Content tab from Internet Explorer in the Control Panel and takes precedence over this policy.

Disable AutoComplete for forms

Enabling this policy disables Internet Explorer's AutoComplete feature. This features automatically completes information in forms for users, such as names and addresses. Note that the Disable the Content page policy removes the Content tab from Internet Explorer in the Control Panel and takes precedence over this policy.

Do not allow AutoComplete to save passwords

If you enable this policy, usernames and passwords aren't completed automatically for users. Additionally, users can't choose whether or not their browser remembers passwords automatically. Note that the Disable the Content page policy removes the Content tab from Internet Explorer in the Control Panel and takes precedence over this policy.

Disable changing Messaging settings

If you enable this policy, users can't change their default programs for messaging tasks such as email. Note that the Disable Programs page policy removes the Programs tab and takes precedence over this policy.

Disable changing Calendar and Contact settings
   Controls the default programs for managing schedules and contacts. If you enable this policy, users can only use the default programs for managing their schedules and contacts if they default programs are installed.

Disable the Reset Web Settings feature
   If you enable this policy, users can't restore their default settings for their home and search pages. Note that the Disable Programs page policy removes the Programs tab and takes precedence over this policy.

Disable changing default browser check
   Controls whether Internet Explorer checks to see if it is the default browser. When Internet Explorer performs this check, users are prompted to choose a default browser. This policy is suggested for companies that want to control their organization's default browser.

Identity Manager: Prevent users from using Identities
   Controls the ability to configure unique identities by using Identity Manager. Enabling this policy prevents users from creating new identities, managing existing identities, or switching identities.

Internet Control Panel

```
User Configuration\Administrative Templates\Windows Components\Internet
Explorer\Internet Control Panel
```

Disable the General page
   If you enable this policy, the General tab is removed from the Internet Options dialog box. If you remove the General tab, users can't see and change settings for the home page, the cache, history, web page appearance, and accessibility.

Disable the Security page
   If you enable this policy, the Security tab is removed from the Internet Options dialog box. If you remove the Security tab, users can't see and change settings for security zones, such as scripting, downloads, and user authentication.

Disable the Content page
   If you enable this policy, the Content tab is removed from the Internet Options dialog box. If you remove the Content tab, users can't see and change ratings, certificates, AutoComplete, Wallet, and Profile Assistant settings.

Disable the Connections page
   If you enable this policy, the Connections tab is removed from the Internet Options dialog box. If you remove the Connections tab, users can't see and change connection and proxy settings.

Disable the Programs page
If you enable this policy, the Programs tab is removed from the Internet Options dialog box. If you remove the Connections tab, users can't see and change default settings for Internet programs.

Disable the Advanced page
If you enable this policy, the Advanced tab is removed from the Internet Options dialog box. If you remove the Connections tab, users can't see and change advanced Internet settings, such as security, multimedia, and printing.

Offline Pages

```
User Configuration\Administrative Templates\Windows Components\Internet
Explorer\Offline Pages
```

Disable adding channels
If you enable this policy, users can't add channels to Internet Explorer or or content that's based on a channel to their desktop. Channels are web sites that are updated automatically by channel providers for users who have added the channel to their web browsers.

Disable removing channels
If you enable this policy, users can't disable channel synchronization in Internet Explorer. Channels are web sites that are updated automatically by channel providers for users who have added the channel to their web browsers. This policy is recommended for administrators who wish to ensure that users' computers are being updated uniformly.

Disable adding schedules for offline pages
If you enable this policy, users can't specify web pages for offline viewing or add new schedules for downloading offline content. This policy helps administrators who wish to control their server load for downloading content.

Disable editing schedules for offline pages
If you enable this policy, users can't edit an existing schedule to download web pages for offline viewing or display the schedule properties of pages that have been set up for offline viewing. This policy helps administrators that wish to control their server load for downloading content.

Disable removing schedules for offline pages
If you enable this policy, users can't clear the preconfigured settings for web pages to be downloaded for offline viewing. It helps administrators who wish to control their server load for downloading content.

Disable offline page hit logging
> Enabling this policy disables any channel logging settings set by channel providers in the channel definition format (*.cdf*) file; this prevents channel providers from recording information about when their channel pages are viewed by users who are working offline.

Disable all scheduled offline pages
> Enabling this policy disables existing schedules for downloading web pages for offline viewing. This policy helps administrators who wish to control their server load for downloading content. Note that the Hide Favorites Menu policy takes precedence over this policy.

Disable channel user interface completely
> If you enable this policy, users can't view the Channel bar interface. Channels are web sites updated automatically by channel providers for users who have added the channel to their web browsers.

Disable downloading of site subscription content
> If you enable this policy, subscription content from sites users have subscribed to aren't downloaded. Note that the Hide Favorites Menu policy and the Disable editing schedules for offline pages policy takes precedence over this policy.

Disable editing and creating of schedule groups
> If you enable this policy, users can't add, edit, or remove schedules for offline viewing of web pages and groups of web pages they've subscribed to. Note that the Hide Favorites Menu policy and the Disable editing schedules for offline pages policy takes precedence over this policy.

Subscription Limits
> Controls the amount of information downloaded for offline viewing. Enabling this policy lets you set limits for the size and number of pages users can download.

Browser Menus

```
User Configuration\Administrative Templates\Windows Components\Internet
Explorer\Browser menus
```

File menu: Disable Save As... menu option
> If you enable this policy, users can't save web pages from the browser File menu to their hard disk or to a network share. Note that this policy takes precedence over the File Menu: Disable Save As Web Page Complete policy.

File menu: Disable New menu option
> If you enable this policy, users can't use the File menu to open a new browser. While the File menu user interface remains the same, the New

menu item doesn't work for users; they are informed that the command is not available to them.

File menu: Disable Open menu option
If you enable this policy, users can't open a file or web page by using the File menu in Internet Explorer. While the File-menu user interface remains the same, the Open menu item won't work for users; they are informed the command isn't available to them.

File menu: Disable Save As Web Page Complete
If you enable this policy, users can't save the entire contents of a web page, including graphics, scripts, linked files, and other elements. Users can save content from a web page.

File menu: Disable closing the browser and Explorer windows
If you enable this policy, users can't close Internet Explorer and Windows Explorer from either the File menu or the X (close) button in the upper-right corner of the interface.

View menu: Disable Source menu option
If you enable this policy, users can't view the HTML source of web pages by clicking the Source command on the View menu. In order to prevent users from viewing source code at all, also refer to the Disable context menu policy.

View menu: Disable Full Screen menu option
If you enable this policy, users can't display their browsers in full-screen (kiosk) mode, without the standard toolbar. This policy is useful for organizations with many beginning users, because using the browser without the toolbar can be confusing for beginners.

Hide Favorites menu
If you enable this policy, users can't add, remove, or edit the list of Favorite links. This policy is useful for organizations that wish to keep a consistent list of Favorites across their company.

Tools menu: Disable Internet Options... menu option
If you enable this policy, users can't open the Internet Options dialog box from the Tools menu in Internet Explorer. This prevents users from changing options such as default home page, cache size, and connection and proxy settings from the Tools menu.

Help menu: Remove "Tip of the Day" menu option
If you enable this policy, users can't view or change the Tip of the Day; the Tip of the Day command is removed from the Help menu.

Help menu: Remove "For Netscape Users" menu option
   If you enable this policy, tips for users who are switching from Netscape aren't displayed. This policy doesn't remove the tips for Netscape users from the Internet Explorer Help file.

Help menu: Remove "Tour" menu option
   If you enable this policy, users can't run the Internet Explorer Tour from the Help menu in Internet Explorer; the Tour menu item is removed from the Help menu.

Help menu: Remove "Send Feedback" menu option
   If you enable this policy, users can't send feedback to Microsoft by clicking the Send Feedback menu item on the Help menu; the Send Feedback menu item is removed from the Help menu.

Disable Context menu
   If you enable this policy, users don't see context menus when they right-click their mouse while using the browser. This policy is useful if you need to make certain that users don't run commands you have removed from other parts of the interface.

Disable Open in New Window menu option
   If you enable this policy, users can't open a link in a new browser window. In order to prevent users from opening new browser windows further, also refer to the File menu: Disable Menu option policy.

Disable Save this program to disk option
   If you enable this policy, users can't save files or programs to the hard disk Internet Explorer has downloaded.

Toolbars

```
User Configuration\Administrative Templates\Windows Components\Internet
Explorer\Toolbars
```

Disable customizing browser toolbar buttons
   Controls the buttons that appear on the Internet Explorer and Windows Explorer standard toolbars. For more information on toolbar policies, refer to the Disable customizing browser toolbars policy.

Disable customizing browser toolbars
   Controls which toolbars are displayed in Internet Explorer and Windows Explorer. For more information on toolbar policies, refer to the Disable customizing browser toolbar buttons policy.

Configure Toolbar Buttons
   Controls which buttons are displayed on the standard toolbar in Internet Explorer. This policy allows you to select the buttons that are displayed on the toolbar by checking or clearing a checkbox for each button.

Persistence Behavior

User Configuration\Administrative Templates\Windows Components\Internet Explorer\Persistance Behavior

File size limits for Local Machine zone

Controls the amount of storage a page or site using the DHTML Persistence behavior can use for the Local Computer security zone. This policy allows you to set the persistence storage amount per domain or per document for this security zone.

File size limits for Intranet zone

Controls the amount of storage a page or site using the DHTML Persistence behavior can use for the Local Intranet security zone. This policy allows you to set the persistence storage amount per domain or per document for this security zone.

File size limits for Trusted Sites zone

Controls the amount of storage a page or site using the DHTML Persistence behavior can use for the Trusted Sites security zone. This policy allows you to set the persistence storage amount per domain or per document for this security zone.

File size limits for Internet zone

Controls the amount of storage a page or site using the DHTML persistence behavior can use for the Internet security zone. This policy allows you to set the persistence storage amount per domain or per document for this security zone.

File size limits for Restricted Sites zone

Controls the amount of storage a page or site using the DHTML Persistence behavior can use for the Restricted Sites security zone. This policy allows you to set the persistence storage amount per domain or per document for this security zone.

Administrator Approved Controls

User Configuration\Administrative Templates\Windows Components\Internet Explorer\Administrator Approved Controls

Databinding

User Configuration\Administrative Templates\Windows Components\Internet Explorer\Administrator Approved Controls\Databinding

RDS

This policy allows web developers to move data from a server to a client application or web page, manipulate the data on the client, and return updates to the server in a single round trip. If you enable this policy, it gives administrator approval to the Remote Data Service (RDS) ActiveX control.

TDC

This policy allows data to be displayed in a delimited text file within tables or within a form and allows data to be sorted and filtered by the browser without interaction with the web server. You can run this control in security zones where you specify that administrator-approved controls can be run if you enable this policy.

XML

This policy marks the Extensible Markup Language (XML) Data Source Object as administrator-approved. This control enables developers to use data-binding functionality in Dynamic HTML to connect to XML data and provide it to an HTML page. If you enable this policy, you can run this control in security zones where you specify that administrator-approved controls can be run.

Internet Explorer

```
User Configuration\Administrative Templates\Windows Components\Internet
Explorer\Administrator Approved Controls\Internet Explorer
```

Active Setup

Enabling this policy marks Active Setup ActiveX control as administrator-approved. If a connection is lost during setup, Active Setup recovers the setup process. If you enable this policy, you can run this control in security zones where you specify that administrator-approved controls can be run.

Media Player

Enabling this policy marks Media Player ActiveX control as administrator-approved. Sounds, videos, and other media are made possible by the use of this control.

Extras

Enabling this policy marks this group of Microsoft ActiveX controls (the Extras) that extend browser functionality as administrator-approved. If you enable this policy, you can run this control in security zones where you specify that administrator-approved controls can be run.

Menu Controls

Enabling this policy marks a set of Microsoft ActiveX controls used to manipulate pop-up menus in the browser as administrator-approved.

Microsoft Agent

Enabling this policy marks the Microsoft Agent ActiveX control as administrator-approved. If you enable this policy, you can run this control in security zones where you specify that administrator-approved controls can be run.

Microsoft Chat

Enabling this policy marks the Microsoft Chat ActiveX control as administrator-approved. Web authors can use this control to build text- and graphical-based Chat communities for real-time conversations on the Web. If you enable this policy, you can run this control in security zones where you specify that administrator-approved controls can be run.

Webpost

Enabling this policy marks the WebPost ActiveX control as administrator-approved. This control enables administrators to post web content to web servers and is based on the Web Publishing wizard. If you enable this policy, you can run this control in security zones where you specify that administrator-approved controls can be run.

MSN

```
User Configuration\Administrative Templates\Windows Components\Internet
Explorer\Administrator Approved Controls\MSN
```

Cache Preloader

Enabling this policy marks the Microsoft Network (MSN) Cache Preloader ActiveX control as administrator-approved. This control enables administrators to load a web page into the user's cache before the user views it.

Carpoint

Enabling this policy marks the Microsoft Network (MSN) Carpoint automatic pricing control as administrator-approved. Users come to the Carpoint web site to get information about vehicles and shop for vehicles. This control enables users to benefit from enhanced pricing functionality on the Carpoint web site.

Install

Enabling this policy marks the Microsoft Network (MSN) Install controls as administrator-approved. Microsoft Network (MSN) Install controls install and manage MSN services.

Investor

Enabling this policy marks Microsoft Network (MSN) Investor controls as administrator-approved. Users can view updated lists of stocks on their web pages with Microsoft Network (MSN) Investor controls. If you enable this policy, you can run this control in security zones where you specify that administrator-approved controls can be run.

MSNBC

Enabling this policy marks MSNBC controls as administrator-approved. Users will benefit from enhanced browsing of news reports on the MSNBC web site with MSNBC controls. If you enable this policy, you can run this control in security zones where you specify that administrator-approved controls can be run.

Music

Enabling this policy marks Microsoft Network (MSN) music controls as administrator-approved. Users benefit from enhanced music services on the MSN web site with Microsoft Network (MSN) music controls. If you enable this policy, you can run this control in security zones where you specify that administrator-approved controls can be run.

Quick View Access

Enabling this policy marks Quick View Access control as administrator-approved. Quick View Access displays the number of email messages a user has received on the user's taskbar and provides quick access to MSN sites. If you enable this policy, you can run this control in security zones where you specify that administrator-approved controls can be run.

Windows Explorer

    User Configuration\Administrative Templates\Windows Components\Windows Explorer

Enable Classic Shell

Enabling this policy prevents users from using Active Desktop, Web view, and thumbnail views. The interface resembles and operates as Windows NT 4.0 does.

Remove the Folder Options menu item from the Tools menu

Enabling this policy prevents users from using the Folder Options dialog box, which in turn prevents them from setting the properties of Windows Explorer, including Active Desktop and Web view.

Remove File menu from Windows Explorer

Enabling this policy prevents users from using File menu but doesn't prevent users from performing File menu tasks run with other methods.

Remove "Map Network Drive" and "Disconnect Network Drive"

Enabling this policy prevents users from connecting to other computers or closing existing connections from Windows Explorer or My Network Places.

Note that users can still connect to other computers by typing the name of a shared folder in the Run dialog box.

Remove Search button from Windows Explorer
Enabling this policy removes the Search button from Windows Explorer toolbar in all the places the Windows Explorer toolbar is used.

Disable Windows Explorer's default context menu
If you enable this policy, users can't see or use shortcut menus when they right-click on their desktop or in Windows Explorer.

Hides the Manage item on the Windows Explorer context menu
If you enable this policy, users can't see or use the Manage item in the Windows Explorer context menu when they right-click Windows Explorer or My Computer.

Only allow approved Shell extensions
If you enable this policy, Windows starts only user interface extensions the system security or the users have approved. Administrators interested in protecting their system from damage caused by programs that don't operate correctly or are intended to cause harm may be interested in using this policy.

Do not track Shell shortcuts during roaming
Controls whether or not Windows 2000 traces shortcuts back to their sources when it can't find the target on the user's system. If enabled, this policy prevents the system from searching for the original path when it can't find the target file in the current target path.

Hide these specified drives in My Computer
If you enable this policy, selected hard drives are removed from My Computer, Windows Explorer, and My Network Places and the drive letters representing the selected drives don't appear in the standard Open dialog.

Prevent access to drives from My Computer
If you enable this policy, users can't gain access to the content of selected drives through My Computer. Users aren't prevented from using programs to access local and network drives or from using the Disk Management snap-in to view and change drive characteristics.

Hide Hardware tab
Enabling this policy removes the Hardware tab from the Mouse, Keyboard, Sounds and Multimedia in Control Panel, and from the Properties dialog box for all local drives.

Disable UI to change menu animation setting
Controls the Hide keyboard navigation indicators until the ALT key option in Display in Control Panel is used. If you enable this policy, the underlining that

indicates a keyboard shortcut character (hot key) doesn't appear on menus until you press ALT.

Disable UI to change keyboard navigation indicator setting
Enabling this policy marks Media Player ActiveX control as administrator-approved. Sounds, videos, and other media are enabled with this control.

Disable DFS tab
When you enable this policy, the Distributed File System tab is removed from Windows Explorer and from other programs that use the Windows Explorer browser, such as My Computer.

No "Computers Near Me" in My Network Places
If you enable this policy, computers in the user's workgroup and domain are removed from lists of network resources in Windows Explorer and My Network Places. Note that users can still connect to computers in their workgroup and domain with other methods, such as typing the share name in the Run dialog box or using the Map Network Drive dialog box.

No "Entire Network" in My Network Places
If you enable this policy, computers outside the user's workgroup and domain are removed from lists of network resources in Windows Explorer and My Network Places. Note that users can still connect to computers in their workgroup and domain with other methods, such as typing the share name in the Run dialog box or using the Map Network Drive dialog box.

Maximum number of recent documents
Controls the number of shortcuts displayed in the Documents menu on the Start menu. Note that the system displays 15 documents by default.

Do not request alternate credentials
If you enable this policy, users can't submit alternate logon credentials to install a program.

Request credentials for network installations
Controls whether or not users are prompted for alternate logon credentials during network-based installations. If you enable this policy, a Install Program As Other User dialog box is displayed when files are being installed.

Common Open File Dialog

```
User Configuration\Administrative Templates\Windows Components\Windows
Explorer\Common Open File Dialog
```

Hide the common dialog places bar
If you enable this policy, the shortcut bar is removed from the Open dialog box. Administrators can use this policy to remove new features added

Administrative Templates

in Windows 2000, which causes the Open dialog box to resemble the Open dialog box in Windows NT 4.0 and earlier versions.

Hide the common dialog back button

If you enable this policy, the Back button is removed from the Open dialog box. Administrators can use this policy to remove new features added in Windows 2000, which causes the Open dialog box to resemble the Open dialog box in Windows NT 4.0 and earlier versions.

Hide dropdown list of recent files

If you enable this policy, the list of most recently used files is removed from the Open dialog box. Administrators can use this policy to remove new features added in Windows 2000, which causes the Open dialog box to resemble the Open dialog box in Windows NT 4.0 and earlier versions.

Microsoft Management Console

```
User Configuration\Administrative Templates\Windows Components\Microsoft
Management Console
```

Restrict the user from entering author mode

If you enable this policy, users can't enter author mode. This includes opening the MMC in author mode, opening console files in author mode, and opening any console files that open in author mode by default.

Restrict users to the explicitly permitted list of snap-ins

If you enable this policy, you can permit the use of Microsoft Management Console (MMC) snap-ins on a select basis, which you determine, or not at all. If you don't enable this policy, users can access all snap-ins.

Restricted/Permitted snap-ins

```
User Configuration\Administrative Templates\Windows Components\Microsoft
Management Console\Restricted/Permitted snap-ins
```

Active Directory Users and Computers

Controls use of this snap-in. This policy is affected by the setting of the Restrict users to the explicitly permitted list of snap-ins policy. You can prohibit users from accessing any snap-ins by enabling the Restrict users to the explicitly permitted list of snap-ins policy and not configuring any of the policies in this folder.

Active Directory Domains and Trusts

Controls use of this snap-in. This policy is affected by the setting of the Restrict users to the explicitly permitted list of snap-ins policy. You can prohibit users from accessing any snap-ins by enabling the Restrict users to the explicitly permitted list of snap-ins policy and not configuring any of the policies in this folder.

Active Directory Sites and Services
>Controls use of this snap-in. This policy is affected by the setting of the Restrict users to the explicitly permitted list of snap-ins policy. You can prohibit users from accessing any snap-ins by enabling the Restrict users to the explicitly permitted list of snap-ins policy and not configuring any of the policies in this folder.

Certificates
>Controls the use of this snap-in. This policy is affected by the setting of the Restrict users to the explicitly permitted list of snap-ins policy. You can prohibit users from accessing any snap-ins by enabling the Restrict users to the explicitly permitted list of snap-ins policy and not configuring any of the policies in this folder.

Computer Management
>Controls the use of this snap-in. This policy is affected by the setting of the Restrict users to the explicitly permitted list of snap-ins policy. You can prohibit users from accessing any snap-ins by enabling the Restrict users to the explicitly permitted list of snap-ins policy and not configuring any of the policies in this folder.

DCOM Config
>Controls the use of this snap-in. This policy is affected by the setting of the Restrict users to the explicitly permitted list of snap-ins policy. You can prohibit users from accessing any snap-ins by enabling the Restrict users to the explicitly permitted list of snap-ins policy and not configuring any of the policies in this folder.

Device Manager
>Controls the use of this snap-in. This policy is affected by the setting of the Restrict users to the explicitly permitted list of snap-ins policy. You can prohibit users from accessing any snap-ins by enabling the Restrict users to the explicitly permitted list of snap-ins policy and not configuring any of the policies in this folder.

Disk Management
>Controls the use of this snap-in. This policy is affected by the setting of the Restrict users to the explicitly permitted list of snap-ins policy. You can prohibit users from accessing any snap-ins by enabling the Restrict users to the explicitly permitted list of snap-ins policy and not configuring any of the policies in this folder.

Disk Defragmenter
>Controls the use of this snap-in. This policy is affected by the setting of the Restrict users to the explicitly permitted list of snap-ins policy. You can prohibit users from accessing any snap-ins by enabling the Restrict

users to the explicitly permitted list of snap-ins policy and not configuring any of the policies in this folder.

Distributed File System

Controls the use of this snap-in. This policy is affected by the setting of the Restrict users to the explicitly permitted list of snap-ins policy. You can prohibit users from accessing any snap-ins by enabling the Restrict users to the explicitly permitted list of snap-ins policy and not configuring any of the policies in this folder.

Event Viewer

Controls the use of this snap-in. This policy is affected by the setting of the Restrict users to the explicitly permitted list of snap-ins policy. You can prohibit users from accessing any snap-ins by enabling the Restrict users to the explicitly permitted list of snap-ins policy and not configuring any of the policies in this folder.

FAX Service

Controls the use of this snap-in. This policy is affected by the setting of the Restrict users to the explicitly permitted list of snap-ins policy. You can prohibit users from accessing any snap-ins by enabling the Restrict users to the explicitly permitted list of snap-ins policy and not configuring any of the policies in this folder.

Indexing Service

Controls the use of this snap-in. This policy is affected by the setting of the Restrict users to the explicitly permitted list of snap-ins policy. You can prohibit users from accessing any snap-ins by enabling the Restrict users to the explicitly permitted list of snap-ins policy and not configuring any of the policies in this folder.

Internet Authentication Service (IAS)

Controls the use of this snap-in. This policy is affected by the setting of the Restrict users to the explicitly permitted list of snap-ins policy. You can prohibit users from accessing any snap-ins by enabling the Restrict users to the explicitly permitted list of snap-ins policy and not configuring any of the policies in this folder.

IAS Logging

Controls the use of this snap-in. This policy is affected by the setting of the Restrict users to the explicitly permitted list of snap-ins policy. You can prohibit users from accessing any snap-ins by enabling the Restrict users to the explicitly permitted list of snap-ins policy and not configuring any of the policies in this folder.

Internet Information Services
> Controls the use of this snap-in. This policy is affected by the setting of the Restrict users to the explicitly permitted list of snap-ins policy. You can prohibit users from accessing any snap-ins by enabling the Restrict users to the explicitly permitted list of snap-ins policy and not configuring any of the policies in this folder.

IP Security
> Controls the use of this snap-in. This policy is affected by the setting of the Restrict users to the explicitly permitted list of snap-ins policy. You can prohibit users from accessing any snap-ins by enabling the Restrict users to the explicitly permitted list of snap-ins policy and not configuring any of the policies in this folder.

Local Users and Groups
> Controls the use of this snap-in. This policy is affected by the setting of the Restrict users to the explicitly permitted list of snap-ins policy. You can prohibit users from accessing any snap-ins by enabling the Restrict users to the explicitly permitted list of snap-ins policy and not configuring any of the policies in this folder.

Performance Logs and Alerts
> Controls the use of this snap-in. This policy is affected by the setting of the Restrict users to the explicitly permitted list of snap-ins policy. You can prohibit users from accessing any snap-ins by enabling the Restrict users to the explicitly permitted list of snap-ins policy and not configuring any of the policies in this folder.

QoS Admission Control
> Controls the use of this snap-in. This policy is affected by the setting of the Restrict users to the explicitly permitted list of snap-ins policy. You can prohibit users from accessing any snap-ins by enabling the Restrict users to the explicitly permitted list of snap-ins policy and not configuring any of the policies in this folder.

Removable Storage Management
> Controls the use of this snap-in. This policy is affected by the setting of the Restrict users to the explicitly permitted list of snap-ins policy. You can prohibit users from accessing any snap-ins by enabling the Restrict users to the explicitly permitted list of snap-ins policy and not configuring any of the policies in this folder.

Routing and Remote Access
> Controls the use of this snap-in extension. This policy is affected by the setting of the Restrict users to the explicitly permitted list of snap-ins policy. You can prohibit users from accessing any snap-ins by enabling the

Restrict users to the explicitly permitted list of snap-ins policy and not configuring any of the policies in this folder.

Security Configuration and Analysis
Controls the use of this snap-in. This policy is affected by the setting of the Restrict users to the explicitly permitted list of snap-ins policy. You can prohibit users from accessing any snap-ins by enabling the Restrict users to the explicitly permitted list of snap-ins policy and not configuring any of the policies in this folder.

Security Templates
Controls the use of this snap-in. This policy is affected by the setting of the Restrict users to the explicitly permitted list of snap-ins policy. You can prohibit users from accessing any snap-ins by enabling the Restrict users to the explicitly permitted list of snap-ins policy and not configuring any of the policies in this folder.

Services
Controls the use of this snap-in. This policy is affected by the setting of the Restrict users to the explicitly permitted list of snap-ins policy. You can prohibit users from accessing any snap-ins by enabling the Restrict users to the explicitly permitted list of snap-ins policy and not configuring any of the policies in this folder.

Shared Folders
Controls the use of this snap-in. This policy is affected by the setting of the Restrict users to the explicitly permitted list of snap-ins policy. You can prohibit users from accessing any snap-ins by enabling the Restrict users to the explicitly permitted list of snap-ins policy and not configuring any of the policies in this folder.

System Information
Controls the use of this snap-in. This policy is affected by the setting of the Restrict users to the explicitly permitted list of snap-ins policy. You can prohibit users from accessing any snap-ins by enabling the Restrict users to the explicitly permitted list of snap-ins policy and not configuring any of the policies in this folder.

Telephony
Controls the use of this snap-in. This policy is affected by the setting of the Restrict users to the explicitly permitted list of snap-ins policy. You can prohibit users from accessing any snap-ins by enabling the Restrict users to the explicitly permitted list of snap-ins policy and not configuring any of the policies in this folder.

Extension snap-ins

```
User Configuration\Administrative Templates\Windows Components\Microsoft
Management Console\Restricted/Permitted snap-ins\Extension snap-ins
```

AppleTalk Routing
   Controls the use of this snap-in extension. This policy is affected by the setting of the Restrict users to the explicitly permitted list of snap-ins policy. You can prohibit users from accessing any snap-ins by enabling the Restrict users to the explicitly permitted list of snap-ins policy and not configuring any of the policies in this folder.

Certification Authority
   Controls the use of this snap-in extension. This policy is affected by the setting of the Restrict users to the explicitly permitted list of snap-ins policy. You can prohibit users from accessing any snap-ins by enabling the Restrict users to the explicitly permitted list of snap-ins policy and not configuring any of the policies in this folder.

Component Services
   Controls the use of this snap-in extension. This policy is affected by the setting of the Restrict users to the explicitly permitted list of snap-ins policy. You can prohibit users from accessing any snap-ins by enabling the Restrict users to the explicitly permitted list of snap-ins policy and not configuring any of the policies in this folder.

Connection Sharing (NAT)
   Controls the use of this snap-in extension. This policy is affected by the setting of the Restrict users to the explicitly permitted list of snap-ins policy. You can prohibit users from accessing any snap-ins by enabling the Restrict users to the explicitly permitted list of snap-ins policy and not configuring any of the policies in this folder.

Device Manager
   Controls the use of this snap-in extension. This policy is affected by the setting of the Restrict users to the explicitly permitted list of snap-ins policy. You can prohibit users from accessing any snap-ins by enabling the Restrict users to the explicitly permitted list of snap-ins policy and not configuring any of the policies in this folder.

DHCP Relay Management
   Controls the use of this snap-in extension. This policy is affected by the setting of the Restrict users to the explicitly permitted list of snap-ins policy. You can prohibit users from accessing any snap-ins by enabling the Restrict users to the explicitly permitted list of snap-ins policy and not configuring any of the policies in this folder.

Event Viewer

> Controls the use of this snap-in extension. This policy is affected by the setting of the Restrict users to the explicitly permitted list of snap-ins policy. You can prohibit users from accessing any snap-ins by enabling the Restrict users to the explicitly permitted list of snap-ins policy and not configuring any of the policies in this folder.

IGMP Routing

> Controls the use of this snap-in extension. This policy is affected by the setting of the Restrict users to the explicitly permitted list of snap-ins policy. You can prohibit users from accessing any snap-ins by enabling the Restrict users to the explicitly permitted list of snap-ins policy and not configuring any of the policies in this folder.

IP Routing

> Controls the use of this snap-in extension. This policy is affected by the setting of the Restrict users to the explicitly permitted list of snap-ins policy. You can prohibit users from accessing any snap-ins by enabling the Restrict users to the explicitly permitted list of snap-ins policy and not configuring any of the policies in this folder.

IPX RIP Routing

> Controls the use of this snap-in extension. This policy is affected by the setting of the Restrict users to the explicitly permitted list of snap-ins policy. You can prohibit users from accessing any snap-ins by enabling the Restrict users to the explicitly permitted list of snap-ins policy and not configuring any of the policies in this folder.

IPX Routing

> Controls the use of this snap-in extension. This policy is affected by the setting of the Restrict users to the explicitly permitted list of snap-ins policy. You can prohibit users from accessing any snap-ins by enabling the Restrict users to the explicitly permitted list of snap-ins policy and not configuring any of the policies in this folder.

IPX SAP Routing

> Controls the use of this snap-in extension. This policy is affected by the setting of the Restrict users to the explicitly permitted list of snap-ins policy. You can prohibit users from accessing any snap-ins by enabling the Restrict users to the explicitly permitted list of snap-ins policy and not configuring any of the policies in this folder.

Logical and Mapped Drives

> Controls the use of this snap-in extension. This policy is affected by the setting of the Restrict users to the explicitly permitted list of snap-ins policy. You can prohibit users from accessing any snap-ins by

enabling the Restrict users to the explicitly permitted list of snap-ins policy and not configuring any of the policies in this folder.

OSPF Routing

Controls the use of this snap-in extension. This policy is affected by the setting of the Restrict users to the explicitly permitted list of snap-ins policy. You can prohibit users from accessing any snap-ins by enabling the Restrict users to the explicitly permitted list of snap-ins policy and not configuring any of the policies in this folder.

Public Key Policies

Controls the use of this snap-in extension. This policy is affected by the setting of the Restrict users to the explicitly permitted list of snap-ins policy. You can prohibit users from accessing any snap-ins by enabling the Restrict users to the explicitly permitted list of snap-ins policy and not configuring any of the policies in this folder.

RAS Dialin - User Node

Controls the use of this snap-in extension. This policy is affected by the setting of the Restrict users to the explicitly permitted list of snap-ins policy. You can prohibit users from accessing any snap-ins by enabling the Restrict users to the explicitly permitted list of snap-ins policy and not configuring any of the policies in this folder.

Remote Access

Controls the use of this snap-in extension. This policy is affected by the setting of the Restrict users to the explicitly permitted list of snap-ins policy. You can prohibit users from accessing any snap-ins by enabling the Restrict users to the explicitly permitted list of snap-ins policy and not configuring any of the policies in this folder.

Removable Storage

Controls the use of this snap-in extension. This policy is affected by the setting of the Restrict users to the explicitly permitted list of snap-ins policy. You can prohibit users from accessing any snap-ins by enabling the Restrict users to the explicitly permitted list of snap-ins policy and not configuring any of the policies in this folder.

RIP Routing

Controls the use of this snap-in extension. This policy is affected by the setting of the Restrict users to the explicitly permitted list of snap-ins policy. You can prohibit users from accessing any snap-ins by enabling the Restrict users to the explicitly permitted list of snap-ins policy and not configuring any of the policies in this folder.

Routing
> Controls the use of this snap-in extension. This policy is affected by the setting of the Restrict users to the explicitly permitted list of snap-ins policy. You can prohibit users from accessing any snap-ins by enabling the Restrict users to the explicitly permitted list of snap-ins policy and not configuring any of the policies in this folder.

Send Console Message
> Controls the use of this snap-in extension. This policy is affected by the setting of the Restrict users to the explicitly permitted list of snap-ins policy. You can prohibit users from accessing any snap-ins by enabling the Restrict users to the explicitly permitted list of snap-ins policy and not configuring any of the policies in this folder.

Service Dependencies
> Controls the use of this snap-in extension. This policy is affected by the setting of the Restrict users to the explicitly permitted list of snap-ins policy. You can prohibit users from accessing any snap-ins by enabling the Restrict users to the explicitly permitted list of snap-ins policy and not configuring any of the policies in this folder.

SMTP Protocol
> Controls the use of this snap-in extension. This policy is affected by the setting of the Restrict users to the explicitly permitted list of snap-ins policy. You can prohibit users from accessing any snap-ins by enabling the Restrict users to the explicitly permitted list of snap-ins policy and not configuring any of the policies in this folder.

SNMP
> Controls the use of this snap-in extension. This policy is affected by the setting of the Restrict users to the explicitly permitted list of snap-ins policy. You can prohibit users from accessing any snap-ins by enabling the Restrict users to the explicitly permitted list of snap-ins policy and not configuring any of the policies in this folder.

System Properties
> Controls the use of this snap-in extension. This policy is affected by the setting of the Restrict users to the explicitly permitted list of snap-ins policy. You can prohibit users from accessing any snap-ins by enabling the Restrict users to the explicitly permitted list of snap-ins policy and not configuring any of the policies in this folder.

Group Policy

    `User Configuration\Administrative Templates\Windows Components\Microsoft Management Console\Restricted/Permitted snap-ins\Group Policy`

Group Policy snap-in

    Controls the use of this snap-in extension-allows or prohibits use of the Group Policy snap-in. This policy is affected by the setting of the Restrict users to the explicitly permitted list of snap-ins policy. You can prohibit users from accessing any snap-ins by enabling the Restrict users to the explicitly permitted list of snap-ins policy and not configuring any of the policies in this folder.

Group Policy Tab for Active Directory Tools

    Allows or prohibits use of Administrative Templates (Computers) Group Policy folder. This policy is affected by the setting of the Restrict users to the explicitly permitted list of snap-ins policy. You can prohibit users from accessing any snap-ins by enabling the Restrict users to the explicitly permitted list of snap-ins policy and not configuring any of the policies in this folder.

Administrative Templates (Computers)

    Allows or prohibits use of the Group Policy Tab for Active Directory Tools. This policy is affected by the setting of the Restrict users to the explicitly permitted list of snap-ins policy. You can prohibit users from accessing any snap-ins by enabling the Restrict users to the explicitly permitted list of snap-ins policy and not configuring any of the policies in this folder.

Administrative Templates (Users)

    Allows or prohibits use of the Administrative Templates (Users) Group Policy folder. This policy is affected by the setting of the Restrict users to the explicitly permitted list of snap-ins policy. You can prohibit users from accessing any snap-ins by enabling the Restrict users to the explicitly permitted list of snap-ins policy and not configuring any of the policies in this folder.

Folder Redirection

    Allows or prohibits use of the Group Policies that use the Folder Redirection client-side extension. This policy is affected by the setting of the Restrict users to the explicitly permitted list of snap-ins policy. You can prohibit users from accessing any snap-ins by enabling the Restrict users to the explicitly permitted list of snap-ins policy and not configuring any of the policies in this folder.

Remote Installation Services

    Allows or prohibits use of the Group Policies that use the Remote Installation Services client-side extension. This policy is affected by the setting of the Restrict users to the explicitly permitted list of snap-ins policy. You can prohibit users from accessing any snap-ins by enabling the Restrict users to the explicitly permitted list of snap-ins policy and not configuring any of the policies in this folder.

Scripts (Logon/Logoff)

Allows or prohibits use of the Group Policies that use the Logon/Logoff Scripts client-side extension. This policy is affected by the setting of the Restrict users to the explicitly permitted list of snap-ins policy. You can prohibit users from accessing any snap-ins by enabling the Restrict users to the explicitly permitted list of snap-ins policy and not configuring any of the policies in this folder.

Scripts (Startup/Shutdown)

Allows or prohibits use of the Group Policies that use the Startup/Shutdown Scripts client-side extension. This policy is affected by the setting of the Restrict users to the explicitly permitted list of snap-ins policy. You can prohibit users from accessing any snap-ins by enabling the Restrict users to the explicitly permitted list of snap-ins policy and not configuring any of the policies in this folder.

Security Settings

Allows or prohibits use of the policies in the Security Settings folder in Group Policy. This policy is affected by the setting of the Restrict users to the explicitly permitted list of snap-ins policy. You can prohibit users from accessing any snap-ins by enabling the Restrict users to the explicitly permitted list of snap-ins policy and not configuring any of the policies in this folder.

Software Installation (Computers)

Allows or prohibits use of policies in the Software Installation (Computers) folder in Group Policy. This policy is affected by the setting of the Restrict users to the explicitly permitted list of snap-ins policy. You can prohibit users from accessing any snap-ins by enabling the Restrict users to the explicitly permitted list of snap-ins policy and not configuring any of the policies in this folder.

Software Installation (Users)

Allows or prohibits use of policies in the Software Installation (Users) folder in Group Policy. This policy is affected by the setting of the Restrict users to the explicitly permitted list of snap-ins policy. You can prohibit users from accessing any snap-ins by enabling the Restrict users to the explicitly permitted list of snap-ins policy and not configuring any of the policies in this folder.

Task Scheduler

```
User Configuration\Administrative Templates\Windows Components\Task Scheduler
```

Hide Property Pages

When this policy is enabled, users can't view or change the properties of an existing task, which simplifies task creation for beginning users. These properties may include the program the task runs, details of its schedule, idle time and power management settings, and its security context. Note that this policy appears in both the Computer Configuration and User Configuration folders, but the Computer Configuration folder takes precedence.

Prevent Task Run or End

When this policy is enabled, users can't start or stop tasks manually. This means that users can't force tasks to end before they are finished or start tasks manually. Note that this policy appears in both the Computer Configuration and User Configuration folders, but the Computer Configuration folder takes precedence.

Disable drag-and-drop

When you enable this policy, users can't use the drag-and-drop method to add or remove tasks in the Scheduled Tasks folder.

Disable New Task Creation

When you enable this policy, users can't create new tasks. This policy also prevents the system from responding when users try to move, paste, or drag programs or documents into the Scheduled Tasks folder. Note that this policy appears in both the Computer Configuration and User Configuration folders, but the Computer Configuration folder takes precedence.

Disable Task Deletion

When you enable this policy, users can't delete tasks from the Scheduled Tasks folder. Additionally, the system doesn't respond if users try to cut or drag a task from the Scheduled Tasks folder. Note that this policy appears in both the Computer Configuration and User Configuration folders, but the Computer Configuration folder takes precedence.

Disable Advanced Menu

When this policy is enabled, users can't view or change the properties of newly created tasks, which simplifies task creation for beginning users. These properties may include the program the task runs, details of its schedule, idle time and power management settings, and its security context. Note that this policy appears in both the Computer Configuration and User Configuration folders, but the Computer Configuration folder takes precedence.

Prohibit Browse
> When this policy is enabled, users' newly scheduled tasks are limited to items on the user's Start menu, and users can't change the scheduled program for existing tasks. Note that this policy appears in both the Computer Configuration and User Configuration folders, but the Computer Configuration folder takes precedence.

Windows Installer

    User Configuration\Administrative Templates\Windows Components\Windows Installer

Always install with elevated privileges
> Enabling this policy directs Windows Installer to use system permissions when it installs any program on the system. This allows a user to install programs that require access to directories the user may not have permission to view or change. Note that this policy appears in both the Computer Configuration and User Configuration folders; the policy must be enabled in both folders to make the policy effective.

Search order
> This policy allows you to set the order Windows Installer uses to search the installation files. Note that Windows Installer searches the network first, then removable media (floppy drive, CD-ROM, or DVD), and finally, the Internet (URL) by default.

Disable rollback
> When this policy is enabled, Windows Installer doesn't generate and save the files it needs to reverse an interrupted or unsuccessful installation; it's unable to record the original state of the computer. This policy reduces the amount of temporary disk space required to install programs.

Disable media source for any install
> When this policy is enabled, users can't install programs from removable media including CD-ROMs, floppy disks, and DVDs. If you enable this policy, it continues to run when the installation is running in the user's security context.

Start Menu & Taskbar

    User Configuration\Administrative Templates\Start Menu & Taskbar

Remove user's folders from the Start Menu
> When you enable this policy, users can't see the user-specific (top) section of the Start menu. This policy works best with redirected folders, because they appear on the main (bottom) section of the Start menu. Removing them from the top of the Start menu means that users don't see them twice in the Start menu, which can be confusing.

Disable and remove links to Windows Update
　　When you enable this policy, users can't connect to the Windows Update web site. The Windows Update web site is the online extension of Windows. The site provides software updates to keep a user's system up to date in addition to other information.

Remove common program groups from Start Menu
　　This policy removes items in the All Users profile from the Programs menu on the Start menu. If you enable this policy, users see only items in the user's profile in the Programs menu.

Remove Documents menu from Start Menu
　　When you enable this policy, users can't access the Documents menu from the Start menu; it's removed. This prohibits users from opening recently used files.

Disable programs on Settings menu
　　Controls the user's ability to run Control Panel, Printers, and Network and Dial-up Connections. If you enable this policy, the Control Panel, Printers, and Network and Dial-up Connections are removed from My Computer and Windows Explorer, and programs represented by these folders won't run.

Remove Network and Dial-up Connections from Start Menu
　　Controls the user's ability to run Network and Dial-up Connections. If you enable this policy, users can't utilize Network and Dial-up Connections.

Remove Favorites menu from Start Menu
　　Controls the Favorites menu on the Start menu. The Favorites menu doesn't appear on the Start menu by default; if you enable this policy users can't add it manually.

Remove Search menu from Start Menu
　　If you enable this policy, the Search item on the Start menu and some Windows Explorer search elements are removed or disabled. Additionally, users won't get a response if they press the Application key (the key with the Windows logo) + F.

Remove Help menu from Start Menu
　　If you enable this policy, the Help menu is removed from the Start menu only; it isn't removed or affected in other locations.

Remove Run menu from Start Menu
　　If you enable this policy, the Run command is removed from the Start menu, and the New Task (Run) command is removed from Task Manager.

Add Logoff to the Start Menu
　　This policy adds the Log Off <username> item to the Start menu and prevents users from removing it. Be aware that this policy affects only the Start menu; it doesn't affect the Log Off item on the Windows Security dialog box.

Administrative Templates   *455*

Disable Logoff on the Start Menu
   Enabling this policy removes the Log Off <username> item from the Start menu and the Display Logoff item from Start Menu Options. Also, users can't restore the Log Off <username> item.

Disable and remove the Shut Down command
   When you enable this policy, users can't shut down or restart Windows. This policy doesn't prevent users from running other programs to shut Windows down, but it does prevent them from using the Windows interface to shut down.

Disable drag-and-drop context menus on the Start Menu
   When you enable this policy, users can't reorder or remove items from the Start menu using the drag-and-drop method. This policy also removes the context menus from the Start menu. Users can use other means to customize the Start menu or to perform context menu tasks.

Disable changes to Start Menu & Taskbar Settings
   Enabling this policy removes the Start Menu & Taskbar item from Settings on the Start menu and prevents users from opening the Taskbar Properties dialog box.

Disable context menu for taskbar
   This policy eliminates the menus that appear when you right-click the taskbar and items on the taskbar for users.

Do not keep history of recently opened documents
   If you enable this policy, the system doesn't save shortcuts to the Documents menu. Users use these shortcuts to quickly open their most recently used documents.

Clear history of recently opened documents on exit
   Controls whether the system deletes the contents of the Documents menu on the Start menu when the user logs off. If you enable this policy, users will have an empty documents menu when they log on.

Disable personalized menus
   Enabling this policy turns off personalized menus for users. Personalized menus work by moving recently used items to the top of the menu and hiding the remaining items.

Disable user tracking
   If you enable this policy, the system doesn't track the programs users run, the paths they navigate, and the documents they open. Windows 2000 uses tracking information to customize features.

Add "Run in Separate Memory Space" check box to Run dialog box
  Allows users to run a 16-bit program in a dedicated (not shared) Virtual DOS Machine (VDM) process. This policy lets users run a 16-bit program in its own dedicated NTVDM process.

Do not use the search-based method when resolving shell shortcuts
  If you enable this policy, the system doesn't perform a search of the target drive when it can't find a target file for a shortcut (*.lnk*).

Do not use the tracking-based method when resolving shell shortcuts
  If you enable this policy, the system doesn't try to locate a file by using its file ID if a the system can't find a target file for a shortcut. Note that FAT partitions don't have this ID tracking and search capability, as a result, this policy doesn't apply.

Gray unavailable Windows Installer programs Start Menu shortcuts
  If you enable this policy, Start menu shortcuts to partially installed programs are displayed in gray text. This helps users quickly distinguish between fully and partially installed programs.

Desktop

    User Configuration\Administrative Templates\Desktop

Hide all icons on Desktop
  If you enable this policy, icons, shortcuts, and other default and user-defined items are removed from the desktop. These include Briefcase, Recycle Bin, My Computer, and My Network Places. Removing these icons doesn't prevent users from opening these items by other means.

Remove My Documents icon from desktop
  If you enable this policy, the My Documents icon is removed from the desktop, from Windows Explorer, from programs that use the Windows Explorer windows, and from the standard Open dialog box. Removing these icons doesn't prevent users from opening My Documents by other means and doesn't remove My Documents from the Start menu.

Remove My Documents icon from Start Menu
  If you enable this policy, the My Documents icon is removed from the Start menu. Removing this icon doesn't prevent users from opening My Documents by other means.

Hide My Network Places icon on desktop
  If you enable this policy, the My Network Places icon is removed from the desktop. Removing this icon doesn't prevent users connecting to the network or browsing for shared computers on the network. Removing this icon doesn't prevent users from starting Internet Explorer by other means.

Do not add shares from recently opened documents to the My Network Places folder
> Enabling this policy prevents remote-shared folders from being added to My Network Places when you open a document in the shared folder.

Prohibit user from changing My Documents path
> If you enable this policy, users can't change the path to the My Documents folder by typing a new path in the Target box of the Properties dialog box for My Documents.

Disable adding, dragging, dropping and closing the Taskbar's toolbars
> Controls the manipulation of desktop toolbars. This policy prevents users from adding or removing toolbars from the desktop and dragging toolbars on to or off of docked toolbars when enabled.

Disable adjusting desktop toolbars
> Enabling this policy prevents users from adjusting the length of desktop toolbars or repositioning items or toolbars on docked toolbars.

Don't save settings at exit
> Enabling this policy prevents users from saving such changes as the positions of open windows and the size and position of the taskbar. Note that shortcuts placed on the desktop are always saved.

Active Directory

```
User Configuration\Administrative Templates\Desktop\Active Directory
```

Maximum size of Active Directory searches
> With this policy, you can set the maximum number of objects the system displays in response to a command to browse or search Active Directory. This policy protects your network and domain controller from the sometimes negative effects of expansive searches.

Enable filter in Find dialog box
> If you enable this policy, the filter bar appears automatically above the results of an Active Directory search. The filter bar allows users to quickly refine their search results.

Hide Active Directory folder
> If you enable this policy, the Active Directory folder doesn't appear in My Network Places. The Active Directory folder displays Active Directory objects in a browse window.

Active Desktop

```
User Configuration\Administrative Templates\Desktop\Active Desktop
```

Enable Active Desktop

Controls use of Active Desktop. If you enable this policy, Active Desktop is enabled, and users can't disable it. Note that Active Desktop is disabled by default, but users can choose to enable it if this policy isn't in effect.

Disable Active Desktop

Controls use of Active Desktop. If you enable this policy, it locks down the configuration you establish by using other policies in this folder. Users can't enable or disable the Active Desktop themselves.

Prohibit changes

This policy allows you to remove Active Desktop content and prevents users from adding Active Desktop content. Note that this policy doesn't disable Active Desktop.

Disable all items

This policy allows you to removes Active Desktop content and prevent users from adding Active Desktop content. Note that this policy doesn't disable Active Desktop.

Prohibit adding items

If you enable this policy, users can't add web content to their Active Desktop; they can, however, remove web content from their Active Desktop. Note that this policy will not remove any existing content from Active Desktop.

Prohibit editing items

If you enable this policy, users can't change the properties of web content items on their Active Desktop.

Prohibit deleting items

If you enable this policy, users can only remove—not delete—web content from their Active Desktop. Note that with this policy enabled, users can still add content to their Active Desktop.

Prohibit closing items

If you enable this policy, users can't remove web content from their Active Desktop. This means that items added to the Active Directory remain on the desktop at all times; they can't be closed.

Add/Delete items

You can use this policy to add or delete certain items to or from users' desktops. Note that if policies allow, users can still add or delete items from their desktops.

Active Desktop Wallpaper
> Controls the desktop background (or wallpaper) displayed on all users' desktops. This policy allows you to specify users' wallpaper and the characteristics of the wallpaper—whether it is centered, tiled, and so on.

Allow only bitmapped wallpaper
> Limits users to only bitmap images for desktop backgrounds, or wallpaper. Wallpaper doesn't load if it has another image format, such as JPEG, GIF, PNG, or HTML.

Control Panel

    User Configuration\Administrative Templates\Control Panel

Disable Control Panel
> If you enable this policy, *Control.exe* doesn't run. Additionally, the Control Panel menu item is removed from the Start menu, and the Control Panel folder is removed from Windows Explorer.

Show only specified control panel applets
> This policy lets you specify which Control Panel items and folders are visible to users. Enabling this policy hides all the Control Panel items and folders, except for the items and folders you specify. This policy can be overridden by the Hide specified Control Panel applets policy.

Hide specified control panel applets
> This policy lets you specify which Control Panel items and folders to hide from users. This policy overrides the Show only specified Control Panel applets policy.

Add/Remove Programs

    User Configuration\Administrative Templates\Control Panel\Add/Remove Programs

Disable Add/Remove Programs
> Controls use of Add/Remove Programs. Users can install, uninstall, repair, add, and remove features and components of Windows 2000 and a wide variety of Windows programs with the Add/Remove Programs feature. This feature is enabled for users by default.

Hide Change or Remove Programs page
> Enabling this policy removes the Change or Remove Programs button from the Add/Remove Programs bar, which prevents users from users uninstalling, repairing, adding, or removing features of installed programs by this means.

Hide Add New Programs page
>   Enabling this policy removes the Add New Programs button from the Add/Remove Programs bar, which prevents users from installing programs published or assigned by a system administrator by this means.

Hide Add/Remove Windows Components page
>   Enabling this policy removes the Add/Remove Windows Components button from the Add/Remove Programs bar, which prevents users from configuring installed services and using the Windows Component wizard to add, remove, and configure components of Windows 2000 from the installation files by this means.

Hide the "Add a program from CD-ROM or floppy disk" option
>   Enabling this policy removes the "Add a program from CD-ROM or floppy disk" section from the Add New Programs page, which prevents users from installing media with Add/Remove Programs. Note that this doesn't prevent users from installing media by other means.

Hide the "Add programs from Microsoft" option
>   Enabling this policy removes the "Add programs from Microsoft" section from the Add New Programs page, which prevents users from connecting to the Windows update using Add/Remove Programs. Note that this doesn't prevent users connecting to the Windows update by other means.

Hide the "Add programs from your network" option
>   If you enable this policy, users can't add or install published programs. Users can't tell which programs have been published by the administrator and they can't use Add/Remove Programs to install published programs. Published programs are those programs that administrators make available to users.

Go directly to Components wizard
>   If you enable this policy users can't use the Set Up Services section of the Add/Remove Windows Components Page. Instead, the Windows Component wizard runs.

Disable Support Information
>   When you enable this policy, hyperlinks to the Support Info dialog box from programs on the Change or Remove Programs page are removed. The programs on the Change or Remove Programs page sometimes include a hyperlink called "Click here for support information."

Specify default category for Add New Programs
>   If you enable this policy, you can choose one category of programs to display when users display the Add New Programs page. Users can view additional programs by using the Category drop-down list on the Add New Programs page.

Display

`User Configuration\Administrative Templates\Control Panel\Display`

Disable Display in control panel

When you enable this policy, users can't use Display in the Control Panel; it won't run.

Hide Background tab

This policy prevents users from changing the pattern and wallpaper on the desktop through the Control Panel by removing the Background tab from Display in Control Panel.

Disable Changing Wallpaper

This policy prevents users from adding or changing the background design (or wallpaper) of the desktop.

Hide Appearance tab

This policy prevents users from changing colors or color schemes of the desktop and windows through the Control Panel, because it removes the Appearance tab from Display in Control Panel.

Hide Settings tab

This policy prevents users from adding, configuring, or changing the display settings on the computer through the Control Panel, because it removes the Settings tab from Display in Control Panel.

Hide Screen Saver tab

This policy prevents users from adding, configuring, or changing the screen saver on the computer through the Control Panel, because it removes the Screen Saver tab from Display in Control Panel.

No screen saver

Enabling this policy ensures that all screen savers are disabled. Further, users can't change screen-saver options through the Control Panel.

Screen saver executable name

Enabling this policy ensures that all the computers in your system will display the specific screen saver you designate. Further, users can't change the screen saver because this policy disables the drop-down list of screen savers on the Screen Saver tab in Display in Control Panel.

Password protect the screen saver

If you enable this policy all screen savers must be password-protected. If you disable it, passwords can't be set up for screen savers. If you don't configure it, users can set up a password if they like, but it isn't required.

Printers

    User Configuration\Administrative Templates\Control Panel\Printers

Disable deletion of printers

Enabling this policy also prevents users from deleting local and network printers. Users can delete printers by other means.

Disable addition of printers

Controls the methods that add local and network printers. Enabling this policy also prevents users from adding printers by dragging a printer icon into the Printers folder. Note that this policy doesn't prevent users from adding printers with the Add Hardware wizard or from running additional programs to add printers.

Browse the network to find printers

This policy allows users to search the network for shared printers through the Add Printer wizard. When enabled, this policy allows users to select a printer from a list the Add Printer wizard displays if users click "Add a network printer", but don't fill in a printer name while searching.

Default Active Directory path when searching for printers

This policy allows you to choose the Active Directory location where users' searches for printers begin when they use the Add Printer wizard. If you enable this policy, users start their search at the location you specify instead of starting at the default location. The root of the Active Directory is the default.

Browse a common web site to find printers

This policy adds a web link to the Add Printer wizard. The web link directs users to a web page that they can install printers from.

Regional Options

    User Configuration\Administrative Templates\Control Panel\Regional Options

Restrict selection of Windows 2000 menus and dialogs language

If you enable this policy, users are restricted to either a specified language or the default language, which is English.

Network

    User Configuration\Administrative Templates\Network

Offline Files

    User Configuration\Administrative Templates\Network\Offline Files

Administrative Templates

Disable user configuration of Offline Files

If you enable this policy, users can't enable, disable, or change the configuration of Offline Files. This policy uses other policies in this folder to lock down the configuration you set up.

Synchronize all offline files before logging off

Controls whether the system performs a quick or full synchronization of offline files when users log off. Enabling this policy ensures that the system performs a full synchronization.

Action on server disconnect

Controls whether network files remain available if the computer is suddenly disconnected from the server hosting the files. Enabling this policy allows you to use the Action box to specify whether or not users can work offline when the server is inaccessible.

Non-default server disconnect actions

Controls how computers respond when they are disconnected from particular offline file servers. This policy allows you to determine whether or not users can access a server's files offline when they are disconnected from that particular server. This policy takes precedence over default response, a user-specified response, and the response specified in the Action on server disconnect policy.

Disable "Make Available Offline"

Controls the ability to make network files and folders available offline. If you enable this policy, users can't save files for offline use. The system isn't prevented from saving local copies of files located on network shares designated for automatic caching.

Prevent use of Offline Files folder

If you enable this policy, users can't access the Offline Files Folder to view or open copies of network files stored on their computer. Users can still work offline and save local copies of files available offline.

Administratively assigned offline files

Controls the specified files and folders available offline to users. This policy provides a list of network files and folders users can access at any time for offline use.

Disable reminder balloons

Enabling this policy removes the reminder balloons. Reminder balloons notify users when they have lost the connection to a networked file and are working on a local copy of the file.

Reminder balloon frequency
> Controls when reminder balloon updates appear. You can use this policy to change the default update interval, which displays a reminder balloon every 60 minutes for 15 seconds.

Initial reminder balloon lifetime
> Controls how long the initial reminder balloon update appears onscreen. You can use this policy to change the default display time for an initial reminder balloon. Thirty seconds is the default time for the first reminder.

Reminder balloon lifetime
> Controls how long reminder balloon updates appear for onscreen. You can use this policy to change the default display time for an reminder balloon updates. Fifteen seconds is the default time for the reminder balloon updates.

Event logging level
> Controls the events that are recorded in the Offline Files feature records in the event log. If you enable this policy, you can choose a number in between 0 and 3 to determine the number of events you want recorded.

Network and Dial-up Connections

```
User Configuration\Administrative Templates\Network\Network and Dial-up
Connections
```

Enable deletion of RAS connections
> Controls users' ability to delete private dial-up connections. Users can delete their private RAS connections if you enable this policy. Users can also delete their private RAS connections if you don't configure this policy.

Enable deletion of RAS connections available to all users
> Controls users' ability to delete shared dial-up connections. Users can delete their private RAS connections if you enable this policy. Note that the Enable deletion of RAS connections policy overrides this policy if it's disabled.

Enable connecting and disconnecting a RAS connection
> Controls users' ability to connect and disconnect from dial-up connections. Enabling this policy allows users to connect and disconnect from dial-up connections. Note that this doesn't prevent users from connecting and disconnecting to a dial-up connection via the Status page.

Enable connecting and disconnecting a LAN connection
> Controls users' ability to connect and disconnect local area connections. Enabling this policy allows users to connect and disconnect from local area connections. Note that this doesn't prevent users from connecting and disconnecting to a dial-up connection via the Status page.

Administrative Templates

Enable access to properties of a LAN connection
> Controls users' ability to view and change the properties of a local area connection for users. Enabling this policy allows users to view and change the properties of a local area connection. Note that this policy overrides any policies that removes or disables parts of the Local Area Connection Properties dialog box.

Allow access to current user's RAS connection properties
> Controls users' ability to view and change the properties of private dial-up connections. Private connections are only available to one user. Note that this policy overrides other policies that remove or disable parts of the Dial-up Connection Properties dialog box.

Enable access to properties of RAS connections available to all users
> Controls users' ability to view and change the properties of dial-up connections that are available to all users of the computer. Enabling this policy allows users to view and change the properties. Note that this policy overrides other policies that remove or disable parts of the Dial-up Connection Properties dialog box.

Enable renaming of connections, if supported
> Controls users' ability to rename dial-up and local area connections. Enabling this policy allows users to rename all connections, including their private dial-up connections.

Enable renaming of RAS connections belonging to the current user
> Controls users' ability to rename their private dial-up connections. Enabling this policy allows users to rename their private dial-up connection.

Enable adding or removing components of a RAS or LAN connection
> Controls users' ability to add and remove network components. Enabling this policy allows users to add and remove network components through the Install and Uninstall buttons in Network and Dial-up Connections or through the Windows Components wizard.

Allow connection components to be enabled or disabled
> Controls users' ability to enable and disable the components used by dial-up and local area connections. This policy adds a checkbox beside the name of each component listed in each connection's Properties dialog box. Checking the box enables the component.

Enable access to properties of components of a LAN connection
> Controls users' ability to change the properties of components used by a local area connection. Enabling this policy (or not configuring it at all) allows users to change the properties. Note that some network components properties are never configurable.

Enable access to properties of components of a RAS connection
  Controls users' ability to view and change the properties of components used by a dial-up connection. Enabling this policy (or not configuring it at all) will allow users to change the properties. Note that some network components properties are never configurable.

Display and enable the Network Connection wizard
  Controls users' ability to create new network connections with the Network Connection wizard. Enabling this policy allows users to utilize the Make New Connection icon in Network and Dial-up Connections to start the Network Connection wizard.

Enable status statistics for an active connection
  Controls users' ability to view the Status page for an active connection. Enabling this policy allows users to utilize the Status page to view information about the connection and its activity and to disconnect and configure the properties of the connection through buttons on this page.

Enable the Dial-up Preferences item on the Advanced menu
  If you enable this policy, the Dial-up Preferences item on the Advanced menu in Network and Dial-up Connections is enabled. This allows users to create and change connections before logon and to configure AutoDialing and callback features.

Enable the Advanced Settings item on the Advanced menu
  If you enable this policy, the Advanced Settings item on the Advanced menu in Network and Dial-up Connections are enabled. This allows users to view and change bindings, the order that the computer accesses connections, network providers, and print providers.

Allow configuration of connection sharing
  Controls the ability to enable, disable, and configure the Internet Connection Sharing feature of a dial-up connection. If this policy is enabled, administrators and power users can manipulate the Internet Connections Sharing feature. Internet Connection Sharing provides network services to the network and allows users to configure their system as an Internet gateway for a small network.

Allow TCP/IP advanced configuration
  Controls users' ability to use Network and Dial-up Connections to configure TCP/IP, DNS, and WINS settings. Enabling this policy allows users to open the Advanced TCP/IP Settings Properties page and modify IP settings.

System

    User Configuration\Administrative Templates\System

Don't display welcome screen at logon
   If you enable this policy, the "Getting Started with Windows 2000" welcome screen is hidden from users. Users can access this screen from the Start menu. Note that this policy appears in both the Computer Configuration and User Configuration folders, but the Computer Configuration folder takes precedence.

Century interpretation for Year 2000
   Controls how two-digit years are interpreted by programs. Two-digit numbers greater than the number you specify (the default number is 29) are preceded by 19, and two-digit numbers less than the number specified are preceded by 20.

Code signing for device drivers
   Controls what happens when a user tries to install device driver files that aren't digitally signed. You can set up the least secure response permitted on the system with this policy. After you enable this policy, you can use the drop-down box to specify the desired response: either Ignore, Warn, or Block.

Custom user interface
   Controls the user interface for the system. With this policy, you can enable a user interface other than the default Windows interface.

Disable the command prompt
   If you enable this policy, users can't run the interactive command prompt, *Cmd.exe* or run batch files (*.cmd* and *.bat*) on their computers. Keep in mind that you don't want to disable batch files if your system uses logon, logoff, startup, or shutdown batch file scripts, or if you have users that use Terminal Services.

Disable registry editing tools
   Enabling this policy disables the Windows registry editors, *Regedt32.exe* and *Regedit.exe*. See the "Run only allowed Windows" applications policy for more information.

Run only allowed Windows applications
   If you enable this policy, you can control and limit the programs users run that are started by the Windows Explorer process by creating a List of Allowed Applications. After you enable this policy, the system allow users to run only programs you have entered from your approved list.

Don't run specified Windows applications
   If you enable this policy, you can prevent users from running programs that are started by the Windows Explorer process by creating a List of Allowed

Applications. After you enable this policy, the system allows users to run only programs you have entered from your approved list.

Disable Autoplay

Enabling this feature disables Autoplay. As a result, setup files for programs and the music on audio media don't start immediately; users have to start the setup files themselves. Note that this policy appears in both the Computer Configuration and User Configuration folders, but the Computer Configuration folder takes precedence.

Download missing COM components

If you enable this policy, your system searches the Active Directory for all missing Component Object Model (COM) components a program requires. Enabling this policy may cause programs to start or run slower, but the programs won't suffer impaired functionality or stop functioning as a result of missing COM components.

Logon/Logoff

```
User Configuration\Administrative Templates\System\Logon/Logoff
```

Disable Task Manager

Controls the Task Manager. If you enable this policy, users can't use the Task Manager. The Task Manager's many functions include allowing users to start and stop programs.

Disable Lock Computer

When you enable this policy, users can't lock the system.

Disable Change Password

When you enable this policy, users can't change their passwords on demand. Users can still change their passwords when prompted by the system.

Disable Logoff

When you enable this policy, users can't log off the system using any method.

Run logon scripts synchronously

Enabling this policy ensures that logon script processing is complete before the user starts working. If you enable this policy, the system waits for the logon scripts to finish running before it starts the Windows Explorer interface program and creates the desktop. Keep in mind that this policy can delay the appearance of the desktop.

Run legacy logon scripts hidden

Enabling this policy ensures that the instructions in logon scripts written for Windows NT 4.0 and earlier are hidden from users. By default, these scripts run in a command window. This policy is recommended for beginning users.

Run logon scripts visible
Enabling this policy ensures that the instructions in logon scripts written for Windows NT 4.0 and earlier run in a command window for users. This policy is recommended for advanced users.

Run logoff scripts visible
Enabling this policy ensures that logoff scripts run in a command window for users. This policy is recommended for advanced users.

Connect home directory to root of the share
Controls the definitions of the %HOMESHARE% and %HOMEPATH% environment variables. Enabling this policy ensures that the system uses the definitions for Windows NT. Disabling or not configuring this policy ensures that the system uses the definitions that come with Windows 2000.

Limit profile size
This policy allows you to determine the maximum size of a roaming user profile and the system's response when a roaming user profile reaches the maximum size. The maximum size of a roaming user profile is unlimited if you don't configure this policy.

Exclude directories in roaming profile
If you enable this policy, you can exclude folders normally included in the user's profile. The History, Local Settings, Temp, and Temporary Internet Files folders are excluded by default. Folders that you exclude aren't stored by the network server on which the profile resides and won't follow users to other computers.

Run these programs at user logon
Enabling this policy allows you to choose additional programs or documents that Windows 2000 starts automatically when a user logs on to the system. Note that this policy appears in both the Computer Configuration and User Configuration folders and, if both are configured, the Computer Configuration programs and documents starts first.

Disable the run once list
The system ignores the run-once list if you enable this policy. Note that this policy appears in both the Computer Configuration and User Configuration folders, but the Computer Configuration folder takes precedence.

Disable legacy run list
When you enable this policy, the system ignores any customized run lists for Windows NT 4.0 and earlier. Thus, the items on these legacy lists aren't started automatically by the system.

Group Policy

    User Configuration\Administrative Templates\System\Group Policy

Group Policy refresh interval for users
Controls the background update rate for Group Policies in the User Configuration folder. Enabling this policy allows you to change the update rate from the default, which is an update in the background every 90 minutes, with a random offset of 0 to 30 minutes.

Group Policy slow link detection
Enabling this policy allows you to define a slow connection for purposes of applying and updating Group Policy for your system. Connection speed is determined by the rate at which data is transferred from the domain controller providing a policy update to the computers in the group. After you define the slow connection speed, the system interprets a slow connection as one that exceeds your specification.

Group Policy domain controller selection
Enabling this policy allows you to choose which domain controller the Group Policy snap-in uses. You can choose from three options: Use the Primary Domain Controller, Inherit from the Active Directory Snap-ins, or Use any available domain controller. The Group Policy snap-in uses the domain controller designated as the PDC Operations Master for the domain by default if you disable or don't configure this policy.

Create new Group Policy object links disabled by default
This policy creates new Group Policy object links in the disabled state. You can then configure and test the new object links. If the links pass your testing, you can enable them to use on the system.

Enforce Show Policies Only
This policy stops administrators from viewing or using Group Policy preferences. Enabling this policy ensures that Group Policy displays only true policies; preferences aren't displayed.

Disable automatic update of ADM files
Controls the systems' ability to update the Administrative Templates source files automatically when you open Group Policy. If you enable this policy, you have to update the *.adm* files manually, because the system loads the *.adm* files you used the last time you ran Group Policy.

B

Computer Configuration Group Policy Objects

Chapter 7, *Using Group Policies*, detailed the process of creating, managing, and distributing group policy settings. However, it's not enough to know how to do these things; you also have to know which policy settings exist and what they do—hence this appendix. The GPO settings listed in this appendix appear in the Computer Configuration node beneath each domain and local policy object.

Windows Settings

    Computer Configuration\Windows Settings

Security Settings

    Computer Configuration\Windows Settings\Security Settings

There are seven areas of security settings: Account Policies, Local Policies, Event Log Settings, Restricted Groups, System Services, Registry, and File System. You can add security to any of these areas by defining security settings in a Group Policy object (GPO) that is associated with a domain or an organizational unit (OU).

Restricted Groups

    Computer Configuration\Windows Settings\Security Settings\Restricted Groups

This is where administrators can define properties for restricted groups (security-sensitive groups). Administrators can define two properties:

Members
   Defines who belongs to the restricted group.

Member Of
   Defines which other groups the restricted group belongs to.

When a restricted Group Policy is applied, members of a restricted group that are not on the Members list are deleted. Users on the Members list who aren't currently members of the restricted group are added.

System Services

    Computer Configuration\Windows Settings\Security Settings\System Services

Enabling this policy allows administrators to specify a start-up mode (the choices are manual, automatic, or disabled).

Enabling this policy also allows administrators to specify access permissions for system services (the ability to start, stop, or pause).

Registry

    Computer Configuration\Windows Settings\Security Settings\Registry

Enabling this policy allows administrators to define access permissions (DACLs) and audit settings (SACLs) for their systems' registry keys. Note that only Group Policy objects associated with domains, OUs, and sites have an available Registry folder.

File System

    Computer Configuration\Windows Settings\Security Settings\File system

Allows an administrator to define access permissions (DACLs) and audit settings (SACLs) for filesystem objects. Note that only Group Policy objects associated with domains, OUs, and sites have an available File System folder.

Account Policies

    Computer Configuration\Windows Settings\Security Settings\Account Policies

Password Policies

    Computer Configuration\Windows Settings\Security Settings\Account Policies\
    Password Policy

Enforce password history

Enabling this policy allows you to specify the number of unique passwords a user must utilize before a password can be repeated.

Maximum password age

Enabling this policy allows you to specify how long a password can be used on your system before it must by changed by the user. Note that you can set the number of days to 0, which allows users to use passwords indefinitely.

Minimum password age
> Enabling this policy allows you to specify the minimum amount of time a password can be used on your system before it must be changed by the user. Note that you can set the number of days to 0, which allows users to change passwords immediately. The number used for the minimum password age must be less than that used for the maximum password age.

Minimum password length
> Enabling this policy allows you to specify the minimum amount of characters a user's password may contain. Setting the number to 0 establishes that no password is required. You can set this length for any number in between 1 and 14.

Passwords must meet complexity requirements of the installed password filter
> If you enable this policy, all system passwords must meet the requirements of the default password filter (*passfilt.dll*) included with Windows 2000. These requirements include using passwords that are at least six characters long and barring the use of user's account names in passwords. Note that the *.dll* supplied by Microsoft can't be modified, but you can write or install your own settings in your own *passfilt.dll* file.

Store password using reversible encryption for all users in the domain
> Controls whether or not Windows 2000 stores passwords using reversible encryption. Most administrators don't choose to enable this policy, as storing passwords using reversible encryption closely resembles clear-text versions of the passwords. Enable this policy only if your application requirements surpass the need for protected password information.

User must log on to change password
> Enabling this policy requires users to log on before they can change their password. This policy results in users who can't logon to change their password because it has expired; system administrators then have to make the password change for these users. This policy is disabled by default.

Account Lockout Policy

```
Computer Configuration\Windows Settings\Security Settings\Account Policies\
Account Lockout Policy
```

Account lockout threshold
> Enabling this policy allows you to set up the number of failed logons a user must make to be locked out of an account. You can choose a number between 1 and 999. This setting is disabled by default.

Account lockout duration
> Enabling this policy allows you set up the number of minutes that an account is actually locked out. You can choose a number between 1 and

99999, or you can specify that the account will be locked until an administrator sets the value to 0. This setting isn't defined by default as it only pertains to systems that have an Account lockout threshold policy set up.

Reset account lockout counter after

Enabling this policy allows you set the number of minutes that must pass before a bad logon attempt counter is reset to 0 bad logons. You can choose a number between 1 and 99999. This setting defined by default as it pertains only to systems that have an Account lockout threshold policy set up.

Kerberos Policy

```
Computer Configuration\Windows Settings\Security Settings\Account Policies\
Kerberos Policy
```

Enforce user logon restrictions

Enabling this policy ensures that the Kerberos Key Distribution Center (KDC) validates every request for a session ticket against the user rights policy of the target computer. You may choose not to enable this policy because it can slow down network access to services.

Maximum lifetime for service ticket

Enabling this policy allows you to set the maximum number of minutes a user can utilize a granted session ticket to access a particular service. Note that this number must be higher than ten and must be less than or equal to the setting for Maximum lifetime for user ticket.

Maximum lifetime for user ticket

Enabling this policy allows you to set the maximum number of hours a user's ticket-granting ticket (TGT) may be utilized. A new user's ticket can be requested or the ticket can be renewed in the event that it expires. The default for this setting is ten hours.

Maximum lifetime for user ticket renewal

Enabling this policy allows you to set the number of days a user's ticket-granting ticket (TGT) may be renewed. The default for this setting is seven days.

Maximum tolerance for computer clock synchronization

Enabling this policy allows you to set the maximum number of minutes Kerberos allows between a client's clock and the server's clock to still consider the two clocks synchronous. This setting is important because Kerberos uses timestamps that require both clocks to be in synch to work properly.

Local Policies

```
Computer Configuration\Windows Settings\Security Settings\Local Policies
```

Audit Policy

```
Computer Configuration\Windows Settings\Security Settings\Local Policies\
Audit Policy
```

Audit account logon events

Controls a computer's ability to audit each instance of a user logging on or off another computer when the primary computer was used to validate the account. If you choose to define this policy, you have a choice of specifying whether to audit successes, failures, or not to audit the event type at all.

Audit account management

Controls a computer's ability to audit each event of account management. An example of an account management event is setting or changing a password. This value is set to No auditing by default.

Audit directory service access

Controls whether or not the system audits the event of a user accessing an Active Directory object that has specified its own system access control list (SACL). This value is set to No auditing by default.

Audit logon events

Controls whether or not the system audits each instance of a user logging on, logging off, or making a network connection to this computer. If you choose to define this policy, you have a choice of specifying whether to audit successes, failures, or not to audit the event type at all. This value is set to No auditing by default.

Audit object access

Controls whether or not the system audits each instance of a user logging the event of a user accessing an object—a file or folder for instance—that has specified its own system access control list (SACL). If you choose to define this policy, you have a choice of specifying whether to audit successes, failures, or not to audit the event type at all. This value is set to No auditing by default.

Audit policy change

Controls whether or not the system audits every incidence of a change to user rights assignment policies, audit policies, or trust policies. If you choose to define this policy, you have a choice of specifying whether to audit successes, failures, or not to audit the event type at all. This value is set to No auditing by default.

Audit privilege use
> Controls whether or not the system audits each instance of a user exercising a user right. If you choose to define this policy, you have a choice of specifying whether to audit successes, failures, or not to audit the event type at all. This value is set to No auditing by default.

Audit process tracking
> Controls whether or not the system audits detailed tracking information for events such as program activation, handle duplication, and indirect object access. If you choose to define this policy, you have a choice of specifying whether to audit successes, failures, or not to audit the event type at all. This value is set to No auditing by default.

Audit system events
> Controls whether or not the system audits when a user restarts or shuts down the computer, or an event has occurred that affects either the system security or the security log. If you choose to define this policy, you have a choice of specifying whether to audit successes, failures, or not to audit the event type at all. This value is set to No auditing by default.

User Rights Assignment

```
Computer Configuration\Windows Settings\Security Settings\Local Policies\User Rights Assignment
```

Access this computer from the network
> Controls which users and groups have permissions to connect to the computer over the network. You can define this user right in the Default Domain Controller Group Policy object (GPO) and in the local security policy of workstations and servers.

Act as part of the operating system
> If you enable this policy, a process can authenticate as any user, which allows the process to gain access to the same resources as any user. The LocalSystem account includes this privilege.

Add workstations to domain
> Controls the groups or users who can add workstations to a domain. Note that this policy is valid only on domain controllers. By default, all authenticated users have this right.

Back up files and directories
> This policy allows you to specify which users can back up the system by circumventing file and directory permissions. You can define this user right in the Default Domain Controller Group Policy object (GPO) and in the local security policy of workstations and servers.

Bypass traverse checking
> Controls which users can traverse directory trees, even if users don't have permissions on the traversed directory. Note that users can't list the contents of a directory as a result of this privilege. You can define this user right in the Default Domain Controller Group Policy object (GPO) and in the local security policy of workstations and servers.

Change the system time
> This policy allows you to specify which users and groups can change the time and date on the internal clock of the computer. You can define this user right in the Default Domain Controller Group Policy object (GPO) and in the local security policy of workstations and servers.

Create a pagefile
> This policy allows you to specify which users and groups can create and change the size of a pagefile. The default setting allows administrators to create pagefiles. You can define this user right in the Default Domain Controller Group Policy object (GPO) and in the local security policy of workstations and servers.

Create a token object
> Controls which accounts can be used by processes to create a token that can then be used to gain access to any local resources when the process uses NtCreateToken() or other token-creation APIs. Using the LocalSystem account is recommended for processes that require this privilege. You can define this user right in the Default Domain Controller Group Policy object (GPO) and in the local security policy of workstations and servers.

Create permanent shared objects
> If you enable this policy, you can specify which accounts can be used by processes to create a directory object in the Windows 2000 object manager. Only the LocalSystem account has this right by default. You can define this user right in the Default Domain Controller Group Policy object (GPO) and in the local security policy of workstations and servers.

Debug programs
> If you enable this policy, you can specify which users can attach a debugger to any process. Note that users with this capability will have powerful access to sensitive and critical operating system components. You can define this user right in the Default Domain Controller Group Policy object (GPO) and in the local security policy of workstations and servers.

Deny access to this computer from the network
> If you enable this policy, you can specify which users can't access a computer over the network. You can define this user right in the Default

Domain Controller Group Policy object (GPO) and in the local security policy of workstations and servers.

Deny logon as a batch job
If you enable this policy, you can specify which accounts can't log on as a batch job. No users are denied logon as a batch job by default. You can define this user right in the Default Domain Controller Group Policy object (GPO) and in the local security policy of workstations and servers.

Deny logon as a service
Enabling this policy allows you to specify which service accounts can't register a process as a service. No accounts are denied logon as a service by default. You can define this user right in the Default Domain Controller Group Policy object (GPO) and in the local security policy of workstations and servers.

Deny logon locally
Enabling this policy allows you to specify which users can't log on at the computer. No accounts are denied the ability to log on locally by default. You can define this user right in the Default Domain Controller Group Policy object (GPO) and in the local security policy of workstations and servers.

Enable computer and user accounts to be trusted for delegation
Enabling this policy allows you to specify which users can set the Trusted for Delegation setting on a user or computer object. Note that users or objects must have write access to the account control flags on the user or computer object to utilize this privilege. You can define this user right in the Default Domain Controller Group Policy object (GPO) and in the local security policy of workstations and servers.

Force shutdown from a remote system
Enabling this policy allows you to specify which users can shut down a computer from a remote location on the network. You can define this user right in the Default Domain Controller Group Policy object (GPO) and in the local security policy of workstations and servers.

Generate security audits
Enabling this policy allows you to specify the accounts that can be used by a process to add entries to the security log. You can use the security log to trace unauthorized access on your system. You can define this user right in the Default Domain Controller Group Policy object (GPO) and in the local security policy of workstations and servers.

Increase quotas
> Enabling this policy allows you to specify which accounts can use a process with write property access to another process to increase the processor quota assigned to the other process. You can define this user right in the Default Domain Controller Group Policy object (GPO) and in the local security policy of workstations and servers.

Increase scheduling priority
> Enabling this policy allows you to specify which accounts can use a process with write property access to another process in order to increase the execution priority assigned to the other process. You can define this user right in the Default Domain Controller Group Policy object (GPO) and in the local security policy of workstations and servers.

Load and unload device drivers
> Enabling this policy allows you to specify which users can dynamically load and unload device drivers, which is necessary for installing drivers for plug and play devices. You can define this user right in the Default Domain Controller Group Policy object (GPO) and in the local security policy of workstations and servers.

Lock pages in memory
> Enabling this policy can adversely affect your system's performance. This policy is obsolete. This policy controls the accounts that can use a process to keep data in physical memory.

Log on as a batch job
> If you enable this policy, a user can be logged on through a batch-queue facility. The LocalSystem account is the only account that has this privilege by default. You can define this user right in the Default Domain Controller Group Policy object (GPO) and in the local security policy of workstations and servers.

Log on as a service
> Enabling this policy allows you to specify which service accounts can register a process as a service. No accounts have this privilege by default. You can define this user right in the Default Domain Controller Group Policy object (GPO) and in the local security policy of workstations and servers.

Log on locally
> Enabling this policy allows you to specify which users can log on at the computer. You can define this user right in the Default Domain Controller Group Policy object (GPO) and in the local security policy of workstations and servers.

Manage auditing and security log
> Enabling this policy allows you to specify which users can specify object access auditing options for individual resources such as files and Active Directory objects. Only administrators can manage auditing by default. You can define this user right in the Default Domain Controller Group Policy object (GPO) and in the local security policy of workstations and servers.

Modify firmware environment variables
> If you enable this policy, you can specify which users can modify system-wide environment variables. Administrators and LocalSystem accounts have this privilege by default. You can define this user right in the Default Domain Controller Group Policy object (GPO) and in the local security policy of workstations and servers.

Profile single process
> Controls which users can use Windows NT and Windows 2000 performance monitoring tools to monitor the performance of nonsystem processes. Administrators and LocalSystem accounts have this privilege by default. You can define this user right in the Default Domain Controller Group Policy object (GPO) and in the local security policy of workstations and servers.

Profile system performance
> Controls which users can use Windows NT and Windows 2000 performance monitoring tools to monitor the performance of system processes. Administrators and LocalSystem accounts have this privilege by default. You can define this user right in the Default Domain Controller Group Policy object (GPO) and in the local security policy of workstations and servers.

Remove computer from docking station
> Enabling this policy allows you to specify which users can undock a laptop computer from its docking station. You can define this user right in the Default Domain Controller Group Policy object (GPO) and in the local security policy of workstations and servers.

Replace a process level token
> Enabling this policy allows you to specify which user accounts can initiate a process to replace the default token associated with a launched subprocess. LocalSystem accounts have this privilege by default. You can define this user right in the Default Domain Controller Group Policy object (GPO) and in the local security policy of workstations and servers.

Restore files and directories
> Enabling this policy allows you to specify two settings: which users can restore backed up files and directories by circumventing file and directory permissions, and which users can set any valid security principal as the owner of an object. You can define this user right in the Default Domain Controller Group Policy object (GPO) and in the local security policy of workstations and servers.

Shut down the system
> Enabling this policy allows you to specify which users who are logged on locally to the computer can use the Shut Down command to shut down the operating system. You can define this user right in the Default Domain Controller Group Policy object (GPO) and in the local security policy of workstations and servers.

Synchronize directory service data
> The initial release of Windows 2000 doesn't use this policy setting.

Take ownership of files or other objects
> Enabling this policy allows you to specify which users can take ownership of any secureable object in the system. These objects include Active Directory objects, files and folders, printers, Registry keys, processes, and threads. You can define this user right in the Default Domain Controller Group Policy object (GPO) and in the local security policy of workstations and servers.

Security Options

```
Computer Configuration\Windows Settings\Security Settings\Local Policies\
Security Options
```

Additional restrictions for anonymous access
> If you enable this policy, you can set additional restrictions for anonymous users. Anonymous users have the same privileges as the Everyone group for a given resource by default.

Allow server operators to schedule tasks (domain controllers only)
> If you enable this policy, members of the Server Operators group can submit AT schedule jobs on Domain Controllers. The default setting requires Administrator status to submit AT schedule jobs on Domain Controllers.

Allow system to be shut down without having to log on
> If you enable this policy, users don't have to log on to Windows to shut down the computer. This policy puts the Shut Down command on the Windows logon screen.

Allowed to eject removable NTFS media
   If you enable this policy, any interactive user can eject removable NTFS media from the computer. The default setting requires Administrator status to eject removable NTFS media from the computer.

Amount of idle time required before disconnecting a session
   Enabling this policy allows administrators to define when a computer disconnects an inactive Server Message Block session. The default time is 15 minutes before disconnecting.

Audit the access of global system objects
   Controls auditing of global system objects. System objects are created with a default system access control list (SACL) if this policy is enabled. Access to these system objects are audited when the Audit object access is also enabled.

Audit use of Backup and Restore Privilege
   Controls whether an audit of every use of user rights, including Backup and Restore, occurs. Any instance of user rights being exercised is recorded in the security log when the Audit object access is also enabled.

Automatically log off users when logon time expires (local)
   Enabling this policy causes a client session with an SMB server to be forcibly disconnected when the client's logon hours have expired. Note that this policy is applied to all computers on the domain.

Automatically log off users when logon time expires (local)
   Enabling this policy ensures that users are restricted to their valid logon hours. If they try to access or continue accessing the system outside their valid logon hours, they are forcibly disconnected.

Clear virtual memory pagefile when system shuts down
   Controls whether or not your system clears the virtual memory pagefile when it shuts down. This policy may be useful to your organization if your system is configured to allow booting to other operating systems.

Digitally sign client communications (always)
   Controls the computer's ability to digitally sign client communications. Enabling this policy ensures that client communications are always signed. This policy requires the Windows 2000 Server Message Block (SMB) client to perform SMB packet signing.

Digitally sign client communications (when possible)
   Enabling this policy ensures that the Windows 2000 Server Message Block (SMB) client performs SMB packet signing when communicating with an SMB server that is enabled or required to perform SMB packet signing. This policy is enabled by default. You can find more information about

using digital signatures in client/server communications by looking at the Digitally sign client communications (always) policy.

Digitally sign server communications (always)
The Windows 2000 Server Message Block (SMB) server must perform SMB packet signing if this policy is enabled. This policy is disabled by default. You can find more information about using digital signatures in client/server communications by looking at the Digitally sign client communications (when possible) policy.

Digitally sign server communications (when possible)
This policy will cause the Windows 2000 Server Message Block (SMB) to perform SMB packet signing if this policy is enabled. This policy is disabled by default. You can find more information about using digital signatures in client/server communications by looking at the Digitally sign client communications (always) policy.

Disable CTRL+ALT+DEL requirement for logon
Controls whether or not users must press CTRL+ALT+DEL to log on. Enabling this policy allows customers to log on without pressing CTRL+ALT+DEL but creates a situation where the user's password can be intercepted by hackers.

Do not display last user name in logon screen
Enabling this policy ensures that the last user name accessed will not appear in the logon screen. This policy is disabled by default.

LAN Manager authentication level
Enabling this policy allows you to choose the challenge/response authentication protocol that is used for network logons on your system. You need to review your options carefully, as the protocol you choose affects the level of authentication protocol used by clients, the level of session security negotiated, and the level of authentication accepted by servers as follows.

Message text for users attempting to log on
Enabling this policy allows you to specify a text message that is displayed to users when they log on.

Message title for users attempting to log on
Enabling this policy lets you add the specification of a title that appears in the title bar of the window that contains the Message text for users attempting to log on.

Number of previous logons to cache (in case domain controller is not available)
If you enable this policy, you can specify the number of times a user can log on to a system utilizing cached information. Cached information is

used if a domain controller isn't available to provide the information. The default setting is 10.

Prevent system maintenance of computer account password
Windows 2000 generates a new password for the computer account once a week by default. If you enable this policy, this functionality is suppressed; new passwords aren't generated automatically.

Prevent users from installing printer drivers
Enabling this policy ensures that users can't install printer drivers. As a result, users can't add printers that don't use printer drivers that are already installed.

Prompt user to change password before expiration
Enabling this policy allows you to specify how far in advance users should be warned to change their password. The default setting is seven days.

Recovery Console: Allow automatic administrative logon
Enabling this policy allows users to log on to the Recovery Console without providing a password. This policy is disabled by default.

Recovery Console: Allow floppy copy and access to all drives and folders
If you enable this policy, the Recovery Console SET command is enabled. This allows you to choose to enable or ignore four Recovery Console environment variables: AllowWildCards, AllowAllPaths, AllowRemovableMedia, and NoCopyPrompt.

Rename administrator account
If you enable this policy, you can associate a different account name with the security identifier (SID) for the account "Administrator." Enabling this policy guards against hackers, who often search for Administrator accounts when damaging systems.

Rename guest account
If you enable this policy, you can associate a different account name with the security identifier (SID) for the account "Guest." Enabling this policy guards against hackers, who often search for Guest accounts when damaging systems.

Restrict CD-ROM access to locally logged-on user only
Enabling this policy makes CD-ROMs accessible first to an interactively logged-on user. If there is no interactively logged-on user, the CD-ROM can be shared across the network. If this policy is disabled, local and remote users can both access the CD-ROM at the same time.

Restrict floppy access to locally logged-on user only
Enabling this policy makes floppy media accessible first to an interactively logged-on user. If there is no interactively logged-on user, the

floppy media can be shared across the network. If this policy is disabled, local and remote users can both access the floppy media at the same time.

Secure channel: Digitally encrypt or sign secure channel data (always)
Enabling this policy ensures that the system digitally encrypts or signs all outgoing secure channel traffic. Signing and encryption is negotiated if this policy is disabled, which it is by default.

Secure channel: Digitally encrypt secure channel data (when possible)
Enabling this policy ensures that the system digitally encrypts all outgoing secure channel traffic whenever possible. No encryption takes place if this policy is disabled. This policy is enabled by default.

Secure channel: Digitally sign secure channel data (when possible)
Enabling this policy ensures that the system signs all outgoing secure channel traffic whenever possible. No signing takes place if this policy is disabled. This policy is enabled by default.

Secure channel: Require strong (Windows 2000 or later) session key
Enabling this policy ensures that a strong encryption key is required for all outgoing secure channel traffic. The key strength is negotiated if this policy is disabled. This policy is disabled by default.

Secure system partition (for RISC platforms only)
Enabling this policy ensures that administrative access is required to access a RISC-based system partition (which must be FAT) while the operating system is running.

Send unencrypted password to connect to third-party SMB servers
Enabling this policy allows the Server Message Block (SMB) redirector to send clear-text passwords to non-Microsoft SMB servers. These servers don't support password encryption during authentication.

Shut down system immediately if unable to log security audits
Enabling this policy ensures that your system will shut down if a security audit can't be logged. Only an administrator can restart the system in the event that this policy is enabled, and a shut down occurs.

Smart card removal behavior
Enabling this policy allows you to define what happens when the smart card for a logged-on user is removed from the smart-card reader. You can choose from three options: No Action, Lock Workstation, or Force Logoff.

Strengthen default permissions of global system objects (e.g., symbolic links)
Controls the strength of the default discretionary access control list (DACL) for objects. If you enable this policy, non-admin users can read shared objects (they can't modify shared objects they didn't create) because the default DACL is stronger. This policy is enabled by default.

Unsigned driver installation behavior
   Enabling this policy allows you to specify how your system reacts when an attempt is made to install a device driver (by means of the Windows 2000 device installer) that isn't certified by the Windows Hardware Quality Lab (WHQL). You can choose from three options: Silently succeed, Warn but allow installation, and Do not allow installation. Warn but allow installation is the default setting.

Unsigned non-driver installation behavior
   Enabling this policy allows you to specify what should happen when an attempt is made to install any nondevice driver software that isn't certified. You can choose from three options: Silently succeed, Warn but allow installation, and Do not allow installation. Silently succeed is the default setting.

Event Log

```
Computer Configuration\Windows Settings\Security Settings\Event Log
```

Settings for Event Logs

```
Computer Configuration\Windows Settings\Security Settings\Event Log\Settings
for Event Logs
```

Maximum application log size
   Enabling this policy allows you to define the maximum size for the application event log. The maximum size is 4 GB, and the default setting is 512 KB. The policy can be enabled only in Group Policy objects associated with domains, OUs, and sites, because only these objects contain the necessary Event Log folder.

Maximum security log size
   Enabling this policy allows you to define the maximum size for the security event log. The maximum size is 4 GB, and the default setting is 512 KB. The policy can be enabled only in Group Policy objects associated with domains, OUs, and sites because only these objects contain the necessary Event Log folder.

Maximum system log size
   Enabling this policy allows you to define the maximum size for the system event log. The maximum size is 4 GB, and the default setting is 512 KB. The policy can be enabled only in Group Policy objects associated with domains, OUs, and sites because only these objects contain the necessary Event Log folder.

Restrict guest access to application log

If you enable this policy, guests can't view the application event log. This policy is disabled by default. The policy can be enabled only in Group Policy objects associated with domains, OUs, and sites because only these objects contain the necessary Event Log folder.

Restrict guest access to security log

If you enable this policy, guests can't view the security event log. This policy is disabled by default. The policy can be enabled only in Group Policy objects associated with domains, OUs, and sites because only these objects contain the necessary Event Log folder.

Restrict guest access to system log

If you enable this policy, guests can't view the system event log. This policy is disabled by default. The policy can be enabled only in Group Policy objects associated with domains, OUs, and sites because only these objects contain the necessary Event Log folder.

Retain application log

Enabling this policy allows you to specify how many days of events should be retained for the application log, if the retention method for the application log is "By Days." The policy can be enabled only in Group Policy objects associated with domains, OUs, and sites because only these objects contain the necessary Event Log folder.

Retain security log

Enabling this policy allows you to specify how many days of events should be retained for the security log, if the retention method for the application log is "By Days." The policy can be enabled only in Group Policy objects associated with domains, OUs, and sites because only these objects contain the necessary Event Log folder.

Retain system log

Enabling this policy allows you to specify how many days of events should be retained for the system log, if the retention method for the application log is "By Days." The policy can be enabled only in Group Policy objects associated with domains, OUs, and sites because only these objects contain the necessary Event Log folder.

Retention method for application log

Enabling this policy allows you to specify which "wrapping" method you use for the application log—either Overwrite events as needed, Overwrite events by days, or Do not overwrite events. The policy can be enabled only in Group Policy objects associated with domains, OUs, and sites because only these objects contain the necessary Event Log folder.

Retention method for security log
Enabling this policy allows you to specify which "wrapping" method you will use for the security log—either Overwrite events as needed, Overwrite events by days, or Do not overwrite events. The policy can be enabled only in Group Policy objects associated with domains, OUs, and sites because only these objects contain the necessary Event Log folder.

Retention method for system log
Enabling this policy allows you to specify which "wrapping" method you will use for the system log—either Overwrite events as needed, Overwrite events by days, or Do not overwrite events. The policy can be enabled only in Group Policy objects associated with domains, OUs, and sites because only these objects contain the necessary Event Log folder.

Shut down the computer when the security audit log is full
The earlier "Shut down system immediately if unable to log security audits" policy should be used instead of this policy.

Administrative Templates

```
Computer Configuration\Administrative Templates
```

Windows Components

```
Computer Configuration\Administrative Templates\Windows Components
```

NetMeeting

```
Computer Configuration\Administrative Templates\Windows Components\NetMeeting
```

Disable remote desktop sharing
If you enable this policy, users can't set up the remote desktop sharing feature of NetMeeting. Thus, they also can't use it to control their computers remotely.

Internet Explorer

```
Computer Configuration\Administrative Templates\Windows Components\Internet Explorer
```

Security Zones: Use only machine settings
If you enable this policy, when a user makes changes to a security zone, those changes apply to all users of that computer. If this policy is disabled, each user can set up their own security zone settings. A group of web sites with the same security level is a security zone.

Security Zones: Do not allow users to change policies
   If you enable this policy, users can't change security zone settings the administrator has set up. A group of web sites with the same security level is a security zone.

Security Zones: Do not allow users to add/delete sites
   If you enable this policy, users can't add or remove sites from security zones. A group of web sites with the same security level is a security zone.

Make proxy settings per-machine (rather than per user)
   If you enable this policy, all users on a single computer can use the same proxy settings. If this policy is disabled, users can set their own proxy settings.

Disable Automatic Install of Internet Explorer components
   Enabling this policy ensures that Internet Explorer components aren't automatically downloaded. This policy is recommended for administrators who wish to control the components that are downloaded onto their system.

Disable Periodic Check of Internet Explorer software updates
   Enabling this policy ensures that users aren't notified if Microsoft Software Distribution Channel installs new components on their computer. This policy allows administrators to utilize the Software Distribution Channels to update their users' programs without user intervention.

Disable software update shell notifications on program launch
   Enabling this policy ensures users can't download new version of Internet Explorer components because they will not be automatically downloaded. This policy allows administrators to have version control across their system.

Disable showing the splash screen
   Enabling this policy ensures that the splash screen doesn't appear for users on your system. The splash screen displays the program name, licensing, and copyright information.

Task Scheduler

```
Computer Configuration\Administrative Templates\Windows Components\Task Scheduler
```

Hide Property Pages
   When this policy is enabled, users can't view or change the properties of an existing task, which simplifies task creation for beginning users. These properties may include the program the task runs, details of its schedule, idle time and power management settings, and its security context. Note that this policy appears in both the Computer Configuration and User Configuration folders, but the Computer Configuration folder takes precedence.

Prevent Task Run or End
    When this policy is enabled users can't start or stop tasks manually. This means that users can't force tasks to end before they are finished or start tasks manually. Note that this policy appears in both the Computer Configuration and User Configuration folders, but the Computer Configuration folder takes precedence.

Disable drag-and-drop
    When you enable this policy users can't use the drag-and-drop method to move or copy programs in the Scheduled Tasks folder. This policy removes Cut, Copy, Paste, and Paste shortcut items on the context menu and the Edit menu in Scheduled Tasks. Note that this policy appears in both the Computer Configuration and User Configuration folders, but the Computer Configuration folder takes precedence.

Disable New Task Creation
    When you enable this policy, users can't create new tasks. This policy also prevents the system from responding when users try to move, paste, or drag programs or documents into the Scheduled Tasks folder. Note that this policy appears in both the Computer Configuration and User Configuration folders but the Computer Configuration folder takes precedence.

Disable Task Deletion
    When you enable this policy, users can't delete tasks from the Scheduled Tasks folder. Additionally, the system doesn't respond if users try to cut or drag a task from the Scheduled Tasks folder. Note that this policy appears in both the Computer Configuration and User Configuration folders, but the Computer Configuration folder takes precedence.

Disable Advanced Menu
    When this policy is enabled, users can't view or change the properties of newly created tasks, which simplifies task creation for beginning users. These properties may include the program the task runs, details of its schedule, idle time and power management settings, and its security context. Note that this policy appears in both the Computer Configuration and User Configuration folders, but the Computer Configuration folder takes precedence.

Prohibit Browse
    When this policy is enabled, users' newly scheduled tasks are limited to items on the user's Start menu, and users can't change the scheduled program for existing tasks. Note that this policy appears in both the Computer Configuration and User Configuration folders, but the Computer Configuration folder takes precedence.

Windows Installer

```
Computer Configuration\Administrative Templates\Windows Components\Windows
Installer
```

Disable Windows Installer

If you enable this policy, Windows Installer is disabled or restricted. You can use this policy to set up one of three installation policies: Never, For non-managed apps only, or Always.

Always install with elevated privileges

Enabling this program directs Windows Installer to use system permissions when it installs any program on the system. This allows a user to install programs that require access to directories the user might not have permission to view or change. Note that this policy appears in both the Computer Configuration and User Configuration folders; the policy must be enabled in both folders to make the policy effective.

Disable rollback

When this policy is enabled, Windows Installer doesn't generate and save the files it needs to reverse an interrupted or unsuccessful installation; it is unable to record the original state of the computer. This policy reduces the amount of temporary disk space required to install programs.

Disable browse dialog box for new source

If you enable this policy, users can't search for installation files when they add features or components to an installed program. Thus, users' only option is to choose an installation file source from the Use features from list. This list is configured by the system administrator.

Disable patching

If you enable this policy, users can't install patches by using Windows Installer. Patches are program updates or upgrades that replace specific files.

Disable IE security prompt for Windows Installer scripts

If you enable this policy, a user on your system isn't notified when web-based programs install software the user's computer. By default, when web-based programs install software, users are warned and asked to select or refuse the installation.

Enable user control over installs

Enabling this policy allows users to change installation options that are usually available only to system administrators. Note that this policy bypasses some Windows Installer security settings.

Enable user to browse for source while elevated

Enabling this policy allows users to search for installation files during privileged installations (installations with elevated privileges). System administrators usually perform this task because the default setting grants permission only to administrators.

Enable user to use media source while elevated
If you enable this policy, users can use removable media, such as floppy disks and CD-ROMs, to install programs during privileged installations. System administrators usually perform this task because the default setting grants permission only to administrators.

Enable user to patch elevated products
If you enable this policy, users can upgrade programs during privileged installations. System administrators usually perform this task because the default setting grants permission only to administrators.

Allow admin to install from Terminal Services session
If you enable this policy, Terminal Services administrators can install and configure programs remotely. This policy enhances only the capabilities of system administrators; users can't install and configure programs remotely.

Cache transforms in secure location on workstation
Enabling this policy ensures that the transform file is saved in a secure location on the user's computer. Usually transform files are saved into the user profile. This policy protects larger organizations that must safeguard transform files from unauthorized editing.

Logging
If you enable this policy, you can define which types of events the Windows Installer record. The list of events can be typed in any order and can include as many events as you choose.

System

    Computer Configuration\Administrative Templates\System

Remove security option from Start menu (Terminal Services only)
If you enable this policy, the Windows Security item is removed from the Settings menu on a Terminal Services client. This policy ensures that users don't log on to Terminal Services inadvertently.

Remove Disconnect item from Start menu (Terminal Services only)
If you enable this policy, the Disconnect item is removed from the Shut Down Windows dialog box on Terminal Services clients. This prevents Terminal Services users from disconnecting their client from a Terminal Services server using this method.

Disable Boot/Shutdown/Logon/Logoff status messages
If you enable this policy, status messages—such as the messages that remind users to wait while their system starts—aren't displayed.

Verbose vs normal status messages

If you enable this policy, highly detailed status messages—messages that include each step in a process—are displayed to users.

Disable Autoplay

Enabling this feature disables Autoplay. As a result, setup files for programs and the music on audio media don't start immediately; users have to start the setup files themselves. Note that this policy appears in both the Computer Configuration and User Configuration folders, but the Computer Configuration folder takes precedence.

Don't display welcome screen at logon

If you enable this policy, the Getting Started with Windows 2000 welcome screen is hidden from users. Users can access this screen from the Start menu. This policy appears in both the Computer Configuration and User Configuration folders, but the Computer Configuration folder takes precedence.

Run these programs at user logon

Enabling this policy allows you to specify additional programs or documents that Windows 2000 starts automatically when a user logs on to the system. You will have to specify the fully qualified path to each file you wish to use. This policy can be set in the Computer Configuration and User Configuration folders; the Computer Configuration folder overrides the User Configuration folder setting.

Disable the run once list

If you enable this policy, the computer ignores the customized run-once list, which details additional programs and documents that are started automatically the next time the system starts. The run once list isn't started the next time the system runs. This policy can be set in the Computer Configuration and User Configuration folders; the Computer Configuration folder overrides the User Configuration folder setting.

Disable legacy run list

If you enable this policy, the computer ignores the legacy run list, a customized list of additional programs and documents that the system starts automatically on startup. This policy can be set in the Computer Configuration and User Configuration folders; the Computer Configuration folder overrides the User Configuration folder setting.

Do not automatically encrypt files moved to encrypted folders

If you enable this policy, Windows Explorer doesn't encrypt files that are moved to an encrypted folder. Note that this policy applies only to files moved within a volume.

Download missing COM components

If you enable this policy, your system searches the Active Directory for the missing Component Object Model (COM) components a program requires. Enabling this policy might cause programs to start or run slower, but the programs don't suffer from impaired functionality or stop functioning as a result of missing COM components.

Logon

    Computer Configuration\Administrative Templates\System\Logon

Run logon scripts synchronously

Enabling this policy ensures that logon script processing is complete before the user starts working. If you enable this policy, the system waits for the logon scripts to finish running before it starts the Windows Explorer interface program and creates the desktop. Keep in mind that this policy can delay the appearance of the desktop.

Run startup scripts asynchronously

If you enable this policy, the startup scripts' (which are batch files) run simultaneously before the user is invited to log on to the system.

Run startup scripts visible

If you enable this policy, the startup scripts' (which are batch files) instructions appear in a command window so that users can view them. This setting is recommended for advanced users only.

Run shutdown scripts visible

If you enable this policy, the shutdown scripts' (which are batch files) instructions appear in a command window so that users can view them. This setting is recommended for advanced users only.

Maximum wait time for Group Policy scripts

If you enable this policy, you can set the total time the system allows for all logon, startup, and shutdown scripts applied by Group Policy to finish running. The default setting lets scripts run for a total of 10 minutes.

Delete cached copies of roaming profiles

If you enable this policy, the system doesn't save a copy of a user's roaming profile on the local computer's hard drive when the user logs off. Be aware that you don't want to use this policy if you are using the slow link detection feature of Windows 2000; that feature requires local copies of users' roaming profiles.

Do not detect slow network connections

If you enable this policy, the slow link detection feature is disabled. This feature measures the speed of the connection between a user's computer and the

Administrative Templates

remote server that stores the roaming user profile. Enabling this feature disables any system responses to a slow connection.

Slow network connection timeout for user profiles

Enabling this policy allows you to set a threshold for slow connections for roaming user profiles. Note that if the "Do not detect slow network connections" policy is enabled it, this policy has no effect.

Wait for remote user profile

If you enable this policy, the system waits for the remote copy of the roaming user profile to load, regardless of how long loading takes. If you don't enable this policy, the system loads the local copy of the roaming user profile when loading is slow.

Prompt user when slow link is detected

Enabling this policy allows users to choose between two options when loading is slow: using a local copy of their user profile or waiting for the roaming user profile. If you don't enable this policy, the local copy of the user profile is loaded automatically.

Timeout for dialog boxes

This policy allows you to specify how long the system should wait for a user response to a dialog box before the system uses a default value. The system's default time is 30 seconds.

Log users off when roaming profile fails

If you enable this policy, users are automatically logged off if the system can't load their roaming user profile. This policy goes into effect if the system can't find the roaming user profile, or if the profile has errors.

Maximum retries to unload and update user profile

This policy allows you to specify how many times the system tries to unload and update the Registry portion of a user's profile. The system's default number of retries is 60. Setting the number to 0 tells the system to try only once. This policy should be used with Terminal Services.

Disk Quotas

    Computer Configuration\Administrative Templates\System\Disk Quotas

Enable disk quotas

Enabling this policy provides disk quota management on all NTFS volumes of the computer. Administrators can't change this setting if you enable the Enable disk quotas policy.

Enforce disk quota limit

Enabling this policy ensures that users' disk quota limits are enforced. The system responds as though the physical space on the volume were exhausted when a user reaches his or her disk quota limit. User settings that enable or disable quota enforcement on their volumes are superseded by this policy.

Default quota limit and warning level
Enabling this policy allows you to set the default disk quota limit and the warning level for new users of the volume. The disk space users have at their disposal isn't limited if you don't configure this policy, or if you disable it. User settings that enable or disable quota enforcement on their volumes are superseded by this policy.

Log event when quota limit exceeded
This policy ensures that when users reach their disk quota limit on a volume, an event is recorded in the Application log. If you don't configure this policy, or if you disable it, the user's disk quota status in the Quota Entries window changes, but an event isn't recorded when the disk quota limit is met.

Log event when quota warning level exceeded
This policy ensures that when users reach their disk quota warning level on a volume, an event is recorded in the Application log. If you don't configure this policy, or if you disable it, the user's disk quota status in the Quota Entries window changes, but an event isn't recorded when the disk quota warning level is met.

Apply policy to removable media
If you enable this policy, the disk quota policies in this folder also applies to NTFS filesystem volumes on removable media. The disk quota policies in this folder apply to fixed-media NTFS volumes only if you don't configure this policy, or if you disable it.

DNS Client
    Computer Configuration\Administrative Templates\System\DNS Client

Primary DNS Suffix
Enabling this policy allows you to define primary Domain Name System (DNS) suffix for all affected computers. This suffix is used in DNS name registration and name resolution. If you enable this policy, users and administrators can't change the suffix you choose.

Group Policy
    Computer Configuration\Administrative Templates\System\Group Policy

Disable background refresh of Group Policy
If you enable this policy, Group Policy isn't updated while the computer is in use. When the user logs off, the system updates the computer and user policies. If you disable it, updates can be applied while users are working.

Apply Group Policy for computers asynchronously during startup
   If you enable this policy, the system can invite users to log on before Group Policy updates complete. Thus, the Windows interface could appear to be ready before computer Group Policy is applied.

Apply Group Policy for users asynchronously during logon
   If you enable this policy, the system can display the Windows desktop before user Group Policy complete. Thus, the Windows interface can appear to be ready before computer Group Policy is updated.

Group Policy refresh interval for computers
   Enabling this policy allows you to set how often the Group Policy is updated on domain controllers while the computer is in use (the update occurs in the background). This policy's updates occur in addition to the updates that occur on system startup. The default rate for updates is every five minutes.

Group Policy refresh interval for domain controllers
   Enabling this policy allows you to set how often the Group Policy for computers updates while the computer is in use (the update occurs in the background). This policy applies only to Group Policies in the Computer Configuration folder. The default rate for updates is every 90 minutes, with a random offset of 0 to 30 minutes.

User Group Policy loopback processing mode
   Enabling this policy allows you to direct the system to apply the set of Group Policy objects for the computer to any user who logs on to a computer affected by this policy. This policy is designed for computers used by many users, such as computers in libraries, classrooms, and so on.

Group Policy slow link detection
   Enabling this policy allows you to define a slow connection for purposes of applying and updating Group Policy for your system. Connection speed is determined by the rate at which data is transferred from the domain controller providing a policy update to the computers in the group. After you define the slow connection speed, the system interprets a slow connection as one that exceeds your specification.

Registry policy processing
   Enabling this policy allows you to define when the policies in the Administrative Templates folder and any other policies that store values in the Registry are updated. This policy lets you select or ignore two options: Do not apply during periodic background processing and Process even if the Group Policy objects have not changed.

Internet Explorer Maintenance policy processing
　　Enabling this policy allows you to define when disk quota policies are updated. This policy supersedes any customized settings the Internet Explorer Maintenance policy set when it was installed. This policy lets you select or ignore three options: Allow processing across a slow network connection, Do not apply during periodic background processing, and Process even if the Group Policy objects have not changed.

Software Installation policy processing
　　Enabling this policy allows you to define when software installation polices are updated. This policy supersedes any customized settings the program implementing the software installation policy set when it was installed. This policy lets you select or ignore two options: Allow processing across a slow network connection and Process even if the Group Policy objects have not changed.

Folder Redirection policy processing
　　Enabling this policy allows you to define when folder redirection policies are updated. This policy lets you select or ignore two options: Allow processing across a slow network connection and Process even if the Group Policy objects have not changed.

Scripts policy processing
　　Enabling this policy allows you to define when policies that assign shared scripts are updated. This policy lets you select or ignore three options: Allow processing across a slow network connection, Do not apply during periodic background processing, and Process even if the Group Policy objects have not changed.

Security policy processing
　　Enabling this policy allows you to define when security policies are updated. This policy lets you select or ignore three options: Allow processing across a slow network connection, Do not apply during periodic background processing, and Process even if the Group Policy objects have not changed.

IP Security policy processing
　　Enabling this policy allows you to define when IP security polices are updated. This policy lets you select or ignore three options: Allow processing across a slow network connection, Do not apply during periodic background processing, and Process even if the Group Policy objects have not changed.

EFS recovery policy processing
　　Enabling this policy allows you to define when encryption polices are updated. This policy lets you select or ignore three options: Allow processing across a slow network connection, Do not apply during periodic background processing, and Process even if the Group Policy objects have not changed.

Disk Quota policy processing

Enabling this policy allows you to define when disk quota policies are updated. This policy lets you select or ignore three options: Allow processing across a slow network connection, Do not apply during periodic background processing, and Process even if the Group Policy objects have not changed.

Windows File Protection

`Computer Configuration\Administrative Templates\System\Windows File Protection`

Set Windows File Protection scanning

Enabling this policy ensures that Windows File Protection enumerate and scan all system files for changes. This policy allows you to set up Windows File Protection to scan files more often. Files are scanned only during setup by default.

Hide the file scan progress window

Enabling this policy ensures that the file scan progress window is hidden to users. This policy is recommended for organizations with beginning users; they are sometimes confused by this window.

Limit Windows File Protection cache size

You can use this policy to define the maximum amount of disk space the Windows File Protection file cache uses. You can select 4294967295 as the maximum amount of disk space if you wish to have an unlimited cache size.

Specify Windows File Protection cache location

You can use this policy to set up a location for the Windows File Protection cache that is different than the default. The default location is in the Systemroot\System32\Dllcache directory.

Network

`Computer Configuration\Administrative Templates\Network`

Offline Files

`Computer Configuration\Administrative Templates\Network\Offline files`

Enabled

Controls whether the Offline Files feature is enabled or disabled. Once the Offline Files feature is set, users can't change whether the feature is enabled or disabled.

Disable user configuration of Offline Files

This feature locks down the configuration you establish because it prevents users from disabling, enabling, or changing the configuration of the offline files.

Synchronize all offline files before logging off
   Controls whether offline files are fully synchronized or quickly synchronized each night. If you don't configure this policy, the system performs a quick synchronization by default, and users can change this setting.

Default cache size
   Allows you to set the percentage of disk space that can store automatically cached offline files. If you don't set this policy, by default the system limits the space that automatically cached files occupy to 10%.

Action on server disconnect
   Allows you to determine whether or not a network computer has access to network files if the computer is disconnected from the server. You can use the Action box to set the number of computers this policy applies to.

Non-default server disconnect actions
   Controls how specific computers respond when they are disconnected from particular offline file servers. This policy supersedes the Action on server disconnect policy. Also, this policy can be set in the Computer Configuration and User Configuration folders; the Computer Configuration folder overrides the User Configuration folder setting.

Disable "Make Available Offline"
   Enabling this policy ensures that users can't make network files and folders available offline. Be aware that this policy doesn't prevent the system from saving local copies of files that reside on network shares designated for automatic caching. This policy appears in both the Computer Configuration and User Configuration folders; the Computer Configuration folder takes precedence.

Prevent use of Offline Files folder
   Enabling this policy disables the Offline Files folder, and users can't view or open copies of network files stored on their computer via the Offline Files Folder. This policy appears in both the Computer Configuration and User Configuration folders; the Computer Configuration folder takes precedence.

Files not cached
   Enabling this policy allows you to list the types of files that can't be used offline and exclude certain types of files from automatic and manual caching for offline use. This policy ensures that files that can't be separated, such as database components, are safe.

Administratively assigned offline files
   Enabling this policy allows you to list the types of network files and folders that are always available for offline use. Also, users can access the specified files and folders offline. This policy appears in both the Computer

Configuration and User Configuration folders; the Computer Configuration folder takes precedence.

Disable reminder balloons

Enabling this policy removes reminder balloons, which are enabled by default if offline files are enabled. This policy appears in both the Computer Configuration and User Configuration folders; the Computer Configuration folder takes precedence.

Reminder balloon frequency

Enabling this policy allows you to specify how often reminder balloon updates appear. This policy allows you to change the update interval for reminders. This policy appears in both the Computer Configuration and User Configuration folders; the Computer Configuration folder takes precedence.

Initial reminder balloon lifetime

Enabling this policy allows you to specify how long the first reminder balloon for a network status change is displayed. The first reminder is 30 seconds long by default. This policy appears in both the Computer Configuration and User Configuration folders; the Computer Configuration folder takes precedence.

Reminder balloon lifetime

Enabling this policy allows you to change the duration of the update reminder from the default of 30 seconds for the first reminder and 15 seconds thereafter. This policy appears in both the Computer Configuration and User Configuration folders; the Computer Configuration folder takes precedence.

At logoff, delete local copy of user's offline files

If you enable this policy, local copies of the user's offline files are deleted when the user logs off. Be aware that files aren't synchronized before they're deleted. Changes to local files since the last synchronization are lost as a result.

Event logging level

Enabling this policy allows you to specify which events are recorded in the event log by the Offline Files feature. This policy allows you to add events to those recorded by default. Offline Files records an event only when the offline files storage cache is corrupted by default. This policy appears in both the Computer Configuration and User Configuration folders; the Computer Configuration folder takes precedence.

Subfolders always available offline

Enabling this policy ensures that subfolders are always available offline when their parent folder is made available offline. When you make a folder available offline, this policy makes all folders within that folder available offline.

New folders that you create within a folder that is available offline are available offline after the parent folder is synchronized.

Network & Dial-Up Connections

Computer Configuration\Administrative Templates\Network\Network & Dial-up Connections

Allow configuration of connection sharing
This policy determines whether administrators and power users can enable, disable, and configure the Internet Connection Sharing feature of a dial-up connection. Users can configure their system as an Internet gateway for a small network through Internet Connection Sharing. This policy appears in both the Computer Configuration and User Configuration folders; the Computer Configuration folder takes precedence.

Printers

Computer Configuration\Administrative Templates\Printers

Allow printers to be published
Controls whether or not the computer's shared printers can be published in the Active Directory. Enabling or not configuring the policy ensures that users have this capability.

Automatically publish new printers in Active Directory
Controls whether or not the Add Printer wizard publishes the computer's shared printers automatically in the Active Directory. Enabling or not configuring the policy ensures that users have this capability.

Allow pruning of published printers
Controls whether or not the domain controller can prune the printers published by this computer. Enabling or not configuring the policy ensures the domain controller prunes, or deletes, this computer's printers if there is no response from the computer.

Printer browsing
Allows you to announce the presence of shared printers to print browse master servers for the domain. When you enable this policy, shared printers appear in the domain list in the Browse for Printer dialog box of the Add Printer wizard.

Prune printers that are not automatically republished
Controls whether or not printers that aren't automatically republished are pruned (deleted from the Active Directory). Note that this policy doesn't apply to printers published by using Printers in Control Panel. It does apply to printers that run operating systems other than Windows 2000 and to Windows 2000 printers that are published outside of their domain.

Directory pruning interval
> Controls when the pruning service on a domain controller contacts computers to verify that their printers are operational. The domain controller contacts computers every eight hours by default. By enabling this policy, you can change the number of hours in between contacts.

Directory pruning retry
> Allows you to choose how many times the domain controller contacts a computers to verify that their printers are operational before it prunes the computer.

Directory pruning priority
> Controls the pruning thread's priority. The pruning thread actually deletes printer objects from the Active Directory if the printer that published the object doesn't respond to contact attempts. Adjusting the pruning thread priority can improve the performance of this service.

Check published state
> Ensures that the system periodically verifies that the printers published by this computer still appear in the Active Directory. You can also determine how often the system repeats the verification through this policy.

Web-based printing
> Controls Internet printing on the server. Internet printing lets you display printers on web pages. As a result, printers can be viewed, managed, and used across the Internet or an intranet. Internet printing is supported by default and remains supported if you enable or don't configure this policy.

Custom support URL in the Printers folder's left pane
> Allows you to add a customized web page link to the Printers folder. The web link you include can be tailored to best suit your organization. Default links include a Microsoft web link and a link to the printer vendor.

Computer location
> Controls the default location criteria the system uses when it's searching for printers. You must enable Location Tracking to use this policy, as the Computer Location policy is a component of the Location Tracking feature of Windows 2000 printers.

Prepopulate printer search location text
> Controls the Location Tracking feature of Windows 2000 printers. Enabling this policy ensures that the Location Tracking feature of Windows 2000 printers is enabled.

Index

A

access, 33–38
    auditing, 324–326
    exceptions to rules for, 306–307
    HKLM\SECURITY key data, 47
    limiting remote Registry access, 303–307
    modifying ACLs, 307–308
    to Performance Monitor data, 360
    policies of (see system policies)
    to printer functions, 362
    video resolution data, 363
    (see also ACLs)
accessibility settings, disabling changing, 428
account lockout policies, 473–474
    account lockout duration, 473–474
    account lockout threshold, 473
    resetting account lockout counter after, 474
account logon events, auditing, 475
account management policy, auditing, 475
accounts, local, creating new, 27–28
ACE entries, adding, removing, and changing, 139–140
ACLs (access control lists), 6–7, 18, 134–135
    applying, 135–136
    discretionary (DACLs), 239
    exceptions to access rules, 306–307
    modifying, 307–308
    system ACLS (SACLs), 239
Active Desktop policies, 458–459
    Active Desktop wallpaper, 459
    adding/deleting items, 458
    allowing only bitmapped wallpaper, 459
    disabling
        Active Desktop, 458
        all items, 458
    enabling Active Desktop, 458
    prohibiting
        adding items, 458
        changes, 458
        closing items, 458
        deleting items, 458
        editing items, 458
Active Directory (AD)
    automatically publish new printers in, 502
    path, when searching for printers, 462
    policies
        enabling filter in Find dialog box, 457
        hiding Active Directory folder, 457
        maximum size of Active Directory searches, 457
    structure of Group Policies, 192–193
Active Directory Domains and Trusts, 441
Active Directory Sites and Services, 442
Active Directory Tools, Group Policy Tab for, 450
Active Directory Users and Computers, 441
Active Setup, 436
ActiveSetup key, 380
ActiveWindowTracking key, 355
ActiveX controls, 15

505

"Add a program from CD–ROM or floppy disk" option, hiding, 460
Add New Programs, specifying default category for, 460
Add New Programs page, hiding, 460
"Add programs from Microsoft" option, hiding, 460
"Add programs from your network" option, hiding, 460
adding
    ACE entries, 139–140
    auditing entries, 141–142
    Registry keys, 103–105, 132–133, 330–331, 337–338
adding/deleting items policy, 458
addition of printers, disabling, 462
Add/Remove Programs policies, 459–460
    disabling
        Add/Remove Programs, 459
        Support Information, 460
    go directly to Components wizard, 460
    hiding
        the "Add a program from CD-ROM or floppy disk" option, 460
        Add New Programs page, 460
        the "Add programs from Microsoft" option, 460
        the "Add programs from your network" option, 460
        Add/Remove Windows Components page, 460
        Change or Remove Programs page, 459
    specifying default category for Add New Programs, 460
Addresses key, 417
.ADM files, 153–154
    editing, 166–168
administering the Registry, 296–350
Administrative Templates, 198–199
    adding, 199–200
    for computer configuration group policy objects, 488–503
    creating your own, 201–203
    for user configuration group policy objects, 425–470
administrator account, renaming, 484
Advanced Menu, disabling, 452, 490
Advanced page, disabling, 431

Advanced page settings, disabling changing, 427
Advanced Settings item on the Advanced menu, enabling, 466
aliases (see links, Registry)
AllocateCDRoms key, 364
AllocateFloppies key, 364
allocating system resources, 42–44
allowed Windows applications, running only, 467
AllowedPaths, 306–307
AllowLogonLocationEdits key, 418
AllowLogonPhonebookEdits key, 418
alternate credentials, do not request, 440
AlternatePhonebookPath key, 418
animated windows, disabling, 353
anonymous access, additional restrictions for, 481
API (see Win32 API)
API routines, shell utility, 247–264
Appearance tab, hiding, 461
AppEvents key, 50–51, 414
AppleTalk Routing, 446
application identifiers, 412–414
application log
    retaining, 487
    retention method for, 487
application settings, 16–17, 47–48, 382–388
applying
    ACLs, 135–136
    an ERD, 68–70
    system policies, 155–158
        on individual machines, 168–169
        on multiple machines, 169–171
AreaCodes key, 418
ASSOCF, 217
ASSOCKEY, 217
ASSOCSTR, 218
attaching policy templates, 160–161
audit control inheritance, seeing and controlling, 142
audit policy policies, 475–476
    audit account logon events, 475
    audit account management, 475
    audit directory service access, 475
    audit logon events, 475
    audit object access, 475
    audit policy change, 475
    audit privilege use, 476

Index

audit process tracking, 476
audit system events, 476
auditing
    entries, adding, removing, and changing, 141–142
    Registry access, 324–326
    Registry activity, 141–142
    Registry key activity, 19, 145–149
auditing and security log, managing, 480
AuthenticateRetries key, 362
authentication
    number of retries (DUN), 362
    timeout, setting (DUN), 363
author mode, restricting users from entering, 441
Auto key, 383
AutoAdminLogon key, 366–367, 385
AutoComplete to save passwords, disabling, 429
autodialer, DUN, 417
AutoDisconnect key, 402
AutoEndTasks key, 367–368
automatic
    drivers, 12
    logon after boot, 366–367
    logon with DUN, 372–373
    NT reboot after crash, 365–366
    powering down at shutdown, 367–368
    Registry backups, 58
    running program at boot time, 394
    setting DUN disconnect timer, 374
    slow connection detection, 370
    system policy updates, 155, 170
    user profile deletion, 364
Automatic Configuration, enabling, 425
Automatic Configuration settings, disabling changing, 429
Automatic Detection for dial-up connections, 427
Automatic Install of Internet Explorer components, disabling, 489
automatic update of ADM files, disabling, 470
Autoplay, disabling, 468, 493
Auto-Proxy scripts, disabling caching of, 427
auto-raise setting, 355
AutoReboot key, 391
AutoRestartShell key, 385

AutoRun feature, disabling, 357–358
AutoShareServer key, 402
AutoShareWks key, 402

B

background refresh of Group Policy, disabling, 496
Background tab, hiding, 461
Backup and Restore Privilege, auditing use of, 482
Backup Engine key, 416
BackupDatabasePath key, 399–400
BackupInterval key, 400
BackupPeriodicity key, 399–400
backups of Registry, 57–61, 71–83
    determining what to back up, 71
    ERDs (see ERDs)
    NTBACKUP utility, 38, 75–76, 84–85, 382
    REGBACK, REGREST utilities, 77–80, 85–87
    RegEdt32 for, 80–82, 87–89
    restoring from (see restoring Registry)
    simple copy onto disk, 71–74
    text files for, 81–83
    Windows 2000, 74–75
BeepEnabled key, 394
big endian platforms, 42–43
binary representations
    modifying in Registry, 101–102, 130–131
    REG_BINARY datatype for, 40
    REG_MULTI_SZ datatype for, 39
    viewing Registry data as, 127–128
BindView, vulnerability in SYSKEY password encryption discovered by, 314
bitmapped wallpaper, allowing only, 459
Boolean values, REG_DWORD for, 36
Boot/Shutdown/Logon/Logoff status messages, disabling, 492
boot partitions, 73
BootExecute key, 394
booting NT
    automatically, after crash, 365–366
    control set for, 49
    determining if successful, 389–390
    enabling automatic logon, 366–367
    running program at boot time, 394
    saving boot configuration, 386–387
    suppressing error messages during, 355

BootVerificationProgram key, 389–390
Browse, prohibiting, 453, 490
browse dialog box for new source,
    disabling, 491
browse for source while elevated, enabling
    user to, 491–492
BrowseInPlace key, 30
browser and Explorer windows, disabling
    closing, 433
browser menus policies, 432–434
  disabling
    Context menu, 434
      Open in New Window menu option,
      434
      Save this program to disk option, 434
    File menu
      disabling closing the browser and
        Explorer windows, 433
      disabling New menu option, 432–433
      disabling Open menu option, 433
      disabling Save As… menu option, 432
      disabling Save As Web Page
        Complete, 433
    Help menu
      removing "For Netscape Users" menu
        option, 434
      removing "Send Feedback" menu
        option, 434
      removing "Tip of the Day" menu
        option, 433
      removing "Tour" menu option, 434
    hiding Favorites menu, 433
    Tools menu, disabling Internet
        Options… menu option, 433
    View menu
      disabling Full Screen menu option,
      433
      disabling Source menu option, 433
Browser service, 399–400
bus devices, 46
buttons, snapping to, 355

C

/c switch (RegEdit), 113
Cache Preloader, 437
cache transforms, in secure location on
    workstation, 492
cached copies of roaming profiles, deleting,
    494

Cached Logons Count key, 358–359
caching logon credentials, 358–359
Calendar and Contact settings, disabling
    changing, 430
Call placement method, preventing
    changing, 426
Call Security options, setting, 426
Callback key, 421
CallbackMode key, 418–419
Calls, preventing automatic acceptance of,
    426
capture mode, REGMON, 348–350
Carpoint, 437
categories, policy, 152–153
CATEGORY block (.ADM files), 167–168
C/C++ example Win32 API programs,
    264–272
CD-ROM access
    AutoRun feature, disabling, 357–358
    preventing users from sharing, 363
    restricting to locally logged-on user
        only, 484
century interpretation for Year 2000, 467
certificate settings, disabling changing, 429
certificates, 442
    cryptographic, 380–381
Certification Authority, 446
Change or Remove Programs page, hiding,
    459
Change Password, disabling, 468
change password before expiration, prompt
    user to, 484
changing ACE entries, 139–140
changing auditing entries, 141–142
changing wallpaper, disabling, 461
channel user interface, disabling
    completely, 432
channels, disabling adding, 431
Chat, disabling, 426
child objects, 140
class IDs, 29
Class key, 391
CLASS MACHINE statement (.ADM files),
    167–168
class-definition keys, 413
Classic Shell, enabling, 438
ClearPageFileAtShutdown key, 358–359
clipboard
    RegEdit and, 98–100
    RegEdt32 utility and, 126

Index

Close method (Perl), 276–277
CloseOnDial key, 419
closing Registry keys, 221–222, 225, 257
    Perl methods for, 276–277
CLSID key
    of application identifier key, 413
    of HKCR key, 29, 414
    of HKLM\SOFTWARE\Classes, 380
code signing for device drivers; 467
color settings, disabling changing, 428
COM (Component Object Model), 14–15
    download missing components, 468, 494
Command key
    of application identifier key\Shell, 413
    of HKCR key, 29–30
command prompt, disabling, 467
Comment key, 402
common dialog back button, hiding, 441
common dialog places bar, hiding, 440–441
common Open File dialog policies, 440–441
    hiding
        the common dialog back button, 441
        the common dialog places bar, 440–441
        dropdown list of recent files, 441
common program groups, removing from Start Menu, 454
COMMON.ADM template, 153–154, 174, 209
comparing Registry keys, 335–336
comparing Registry keys/values, 341–342
completion, filename, 353–354
complexity requirements of the installed password filter, passwords must meet, 473
Component Object Model (see COM)
Component Services, 446
composite DACs, 134–135
compreg utility, 341–342
computer configuration group policy objects, 471–503
    administrative templates, 488–503
        network, 499–502
        printers, 502–503
        system, 492–499
        windows components, 488–492
    windows settings, 471–488
        security settings, 471–488

Computer Management, 442
ComputerName key, 49–50
CONF.ADM template, 209
config.pol file, 156–157, 170–171
configuration
    current (see HKEY_CURRENT_CONFIG)
    hardware, current, 31, 53
    kernel functionality, 390–395
    local machine, 27, 45–50
    local machine hardware, 12, 31, 43–44, 46, 378–379
    services, settings for, 396–411
    TCP/IP, 409–411
    Windows NT, settings for, 382–388
configuration group policy objects
    computer, 471–503
        administrative templates, windows components, 488–492
        administrative templates for, 488–503
        windows settings for, 471–488
    user, 425–470
        administrative templates for, 425–470
configuring Toolbar Buttons, 434
connecting home directory to root of the share, 469
connection components, allowing to be enabled or disabled, 465
connection settings, disabling changing, 428
Connection Sharing, 446
connection sharing, allowing configuration of, 466, 502
connections
    detecting slow, 370
    enabling renaming of, if supported, 465
Connections key, 51–52
Connections page, disabling, 430
Console key, 50–51, 415
console tree, navigating, 197
console window properties, 50–51, 415
Content page, disabling, 430
contents, Registry key, 24
Context menu, disabling, 434
context menu for taskbar, disabling, 455
context menus, RegEdit, 94–95
Control key
    of Microsoft\RAS Autodial, 417
    of SYSTEM\CurrentControlSet, 49–50, 390–395

Control Panel, disabling, 459
Control Panel policies, 459–462
    Add/Remove Programs, 459–460
    disabling Control Panel, 459
    Display, 461
    hiding specified Control Panel applets, 459
    Printers, 462
    regional options, 462
    showing only specified Control Panel applets, 459
    (see also Internet Control Panel policies)
control panels, key for, 50–51, 415
control sets
    for booting machine, 49
    Registry keys for, 48
controlling
    audit control inheritance, 142
    permission inheritance, 140
copying Registry keys, 251–252, 339–340
CrashControl key, 365–366, 391
CrashDumpEnabled key, 391
crashes
    rebooting automatically after, 365–366
    recover crashed PDC, 370–371
    removing evidence of, 365–366
Create Link permission, 18, 134–135
Create method (Perl), 276–277
Create Repair Disk command, 67
Create Subkey permission, 18, 134–135
creating keys, 256
CryptoAPI, 380–381
Cryptography key, 380–381
CSDVersion key, 383
CTRL+ALT+DEL requirement for logon, disabling, 483
Current key, 388
current user's RAS connection properties, allowing access to, 465
CurrentBuildNumber key, 382–383
CurrentControlSet key
    Control subkey, 390–395
    Hardware Profiles subkey, 389–390
    of HKCC\System, 53
    of HKLM\SYSTEM, 49–50, 390–395
    Services subkey, 396–411

CurrentProfile key, 389–390
CurrentVersion key
    of HKCU\Microsoft\Windows NT, 423
    of SOFTWARE\Microsoft\RAS, 382–383
    of Software\Microsoft\Windows, 423
    of SOFTWARE\Microsoft\Windows NT, 382–388
    of SOFTWARE\Windows NT, 382–383
custom user interface, 467
customizing
    2000 user interface, 352–356
    browser toolbar buttons, disabling, 434
    browser toolbars, disabling, 434
    filesystem, 357
    "My Computer," 364
    networking, 372–374
    printing, 374–376
    security, 358–364
    tweaking performance, 364–371

D

DACLS (discretionary ACLs), 239
DACs (discretionary access controls), 134–135
data
    backing up (see backups of Registry)
    dynamic, 13
    safeguarding, 57–61
datatypes, 38–41
    modifying key values, 100–103, 128–131
    RegEdit datatype specifiers, 108
    as Registry key values, 24
    security-related (Win32 API), 213–216
DatabaseCleanupInterval key, 400
DatabaseLoggingFlag key, 400
DatabaseName key, 401
DatabasePath key (DHCP\Parameters), 401
DatabasePath key (Tcpip\Parameters), 409
databinding policies, 435–436
    RDS, 435–436
    TDC, 436
    XML, 436
DCOM Config, 442
deadman timer, resetting, 374
Debug key, 416
debug programs, 477

Index

Debugger key, 383
debugging
    service packs vs. hotfixes, 37
    Windows NT configuration settings, 383
DebugServerCommand key, 385
default
    browser check, disabling changing, 430
    cache size, 500
    system policy, 156–157
    user profiles, 296–299
    user settings, 411–412
Default key, 388
.DEFAULT key, 411–412
DefaultDomainName key, 366–367, 385
DefaultEntry key, 419
DefaultGateway key, 411
DefaultIcon key
    of application identifier key, 413
    of HKCR key, 30
DefaultPassword key, 366–367, 385
DefaultSpoolDirectory key, 375–376
DefaultTTL key, 409
DefaultUserName key, 366–367, 386
delegation, enabling computer and user accounts to be trusted for, 478
Delete permission, 18, 134–135
DeleteKey method (Perl), 278
DeleteRoamingCache key, 365–366, 386
deleting
    clearing system pagefile, 358–359
    crash evidence, 365–366
    flushing Registry changes, 246–247
    keys, 251–252
    Registry keys, 59–60, 105, 133–134
        reg.exe for, 331–332
    Registry keys/values
        API routines for, 238–239
        Perl methods for, 278
    user profiles automatically, 364
    values, 260–262
deletion of printers, disabling, 462
delprof tool, 364
DependOnGroup key, 396
DependOnService key, 396
DESCRIPTION key, 46, 378–379
desktop policies, 456–457, 456–459
    Active Desktop, 458–459
    Active Directory, 457
    disabling
        adding, dragging, dropping, and closing the Taskbar's toolbars, 457
        adjusting desktop toolbars, 457
    do not add shares from recently opened documents to the My Network Places folder, 457
    don't save settings at exit, 457
    hiding
        all icons on desktop, 456
        My Network Places icon on desktop, 456
    prohibiting user from changing My Documents path, 457
    removing
        My Documents icon from desktop, 456
        My Documents icon from Start Menu, 456
desktop toolbars, disabling adjusting, 457
device drivers, load and unload, 479
Device Manager, 442, 446
DEVICEMAP key, 46, 378–379
devices
    HKLM\HARDWARE keys, 45–46, 378–379
    multimedia, settings for, 384
Devices key, 423
DFS tab, disabling, 440
DHCP (Dynamic Host Configuration Protocol), 399–400
DHCP key, 399–400
DHCP Relay Management, 446
DhcpXXX key, 403–404
dialogs, print spooler, 374
Dial-Up Networking (DUN)
    authentication timeout, setting, 363
    autodialer settings, 417
    logging connections, 373
    maintaining connection after logout, 373
    monitor settings, 418
    number of authentication retries, 362
    phonebook settings, 418–421
    RasMan service, 407–408
    rings for incoming calls, 373
    "Save Password" option, 358–359
    setting disconnect timer, 374
    using automatically to log on, 372–373
Dial-up Preferences item on the Advanced menu, enabling, 466

digitally encrypt or sign secure channel
    data (always), 485
digitally encrypt secure channel data (when
    possible), 485
digitally sign client communications
    (always), 482
digitally sign client communications (when
    possible), 482–483
digitally sign secure channel data (when
    possible), 485
digitally sign server communications
    (always), 483
digitally sign server communications (when
    possible), 483
directories
    "last access" timestamp, 357–358
    for print spool, 375–376
    pruning interval, 503
    pruning priority, 503
    pruning retry, 503
Directory (See Active Directory, policies)
Directory Replicator service, 408–409
Directory servers, preventing adding, 425
directory service access, auditing, 475
Directory Services, disabling, 425
DisableConnectionQuery key, 417
DisabledAddresses key, 417
DisablePasswordChange key, 405
DisableSavedPasswords key, 407
DisableServerThread key, 370–371, 394
disabling Active Desktop, 458
disconnect item, removing from Start menu
    (Terminal Services only), 492
"Disconnect Network Drive," removing,
    438–439
disconnecting a session, amount of idle
    time required before, 482
discretionary access controls (DACs),
    134–135
discretionary ACLs, 239
Disk Administrator applications, 48, 387
Disk Defragmenter, 442–443
Disk subkey, 48, 388
Disk Management, 442
disk quotas policies, 495–496
    applying policy to removable media,
        496
    default quota limit and warning level,
        496

enabling disk quotas, 495
enforcing disk quota limit, 495–496
log event when quota limit exceeded,
    496
log event when quota warning level
    exceeded, 496
processing, 499
disks
    preventing users from sharing, 363
    setting low space threshold, 357, 402
DiskSpaceThreshold key, 357, 402
dispersal, managing, 206
Display key, 416
Display policies, 461
    disabling
        changing wallpaper, 461
        Display in Control Panel, 461
    hiding
        Appearance tab, 461
        Background tab, 461
        Screen Saver tab, 461
        Settings tab, 461
    no screen saver, 461
    password protect the screen saver, 461
    screen saver executable name, 461
DisplayName key, 396
DisplayNameFile key, 402
DisplayNameID key, 402
Distributed File System, 443
distributing system policies, 168–171
DNS Client policy, 496
    primacy DNS Suffix, 496
docking station, removing computer from,
    480
Documents menu, removing from Start
    Menu, 454
domain controller selection, Group Policy,
    470
domain controllers
    Netlogon for, 405–407
    SYSKEY utility and, 316–317
    system policies and, 155
    upgrading, 317
Domain key, 410
domains, system policies and, 172–173
DontAddDefaultGateway key, 411
DontDisplayLastUserName key, 386
downloading system policy files, 155–156
drag-and-drop, disabling, 452, 490

Index

drag-and-drop context menus on the Start Menu, disabling, 455
drag-and-drop technology, 4
drivers, 12, 45–46
   automatic, 11
   multimedia, settings for, 384
   service-related settings, 398
drives
   controlling visibility of, 360
   preventing mapping changes, 360
   Registry information on, 48, 387
dropdown list of recent files, hiding, 441
DumpFile key, 391
dumpreg.pl, 280
DUN (see Dial-Up Networking)
dureg.exe, 327
DWORDs (see REG_DWORD datatype)
dynamic data, 13

E

/e switch (RegEdit), 112–113
Edit key, 413
editing
   ACLs, 307–308
   flushing Registry changes, 246–247
   notification of Registry changes, 246–247
      WatchKey utility (example), 264–267
   Registry
      adding keys and values, 103–105, 132–133
      API routines for, 236–238
      C/C++ programs for, 264–272
      clipboard and, 98–100, 126
      deleting keys and values, 105, 133–134
      modifying key values, 100–103, 128–131
      Perl programs for, 272–284
      RegEdit utility for, 98–106
      RegEdt32 utility for, 127–134
      remotely, 95–96, 121–122
      renaming keys and values, 106
      undoing edits, 60
      Visual Basic programs for, 284–295
      warning about, 20, 59–61
   system policies, 162–166
editing policies, 200–201
EFS recovery policy processing, 498
elevated privileges, always install with, 453, 491
elevated products, enabling user to patch, 492
emergency repair disks (see ERDs)
EnableDHCP key, 411
EnableDNS key, 404
EnableLMHOSTS key, 404
EnableProxy key, 404
EnableSecurityFilters key, 410
enabling Active Desktop, 458
encryption
   HKLM\SECURITY\SAM key, 313–322
   Registry data, 36
enforcing password history, 472
enforcing Show Policies Only, 470
Entries key, 417
Enum key, 399
   of CurrentControlSet\Control, 392
   of SYSTEM\CurrentControlSet, 49–50
Enumerate Subkeys permission, 18, 134–135
enumerating keys and values, 230–233, 254–255
   Perl methods for, 277–278
Environment key, 50–51, 415
environment variables (see system-defined variables)
ERDisk utility, 67–70
ERDs (emergency repair disks), 61–70
   applying, 68–70
   creating, 64–67
   keeping up-to-date, 59
   role in Windows 2000, 62
   SYSKEY utility and, 316–317, 321–322
   uncompressing data on, 67–68
error codes, 211–212
error message on proxy script download failure, displaying, 427
error messages, suppressing, 355
ERROR_ Registry codes, 211–212
   ERROR_ALREADY_EXISTS, 244
   ERROR_KEY_DELETED, 212, 238–239
ErrorControl key, 398
Event Logger service, 401
event logs (see settings for event logs policies)
Event Viewer, 443, 447
   snap-in, 422

EventLog key, 401
events, mapping sounds to, 50–51, 414
Everyone account, 19
"Ex" in API routine names, 212
exceptions to access control rules, 306–307
exit, don't save settings at, 457
EXPAND utility, 67–68
ExpandAutoDialQuery key, 419
expiring passwords, 361–362
Explorer (see Internet Explorer policies; Internet Explorer policy components; Windows Explorer policies)
exporting Registry data, 108–109
　RegEdit switch for, 112–113, 113
exporting Registry keys, 336–337
ExportPath key, 408
ext key, 412
extension snap-ins policies, 446–449
　AppleTalk Routing, 446
　Certification Authority, 446
　Component Services, 446
　Connection Sharing (NAT), 446
　Device Manager, 446
　DHCP Relay Management, 446
　Event Viewer, 447
　IGMP Routing, 447
　IP Routing, 447
　IPX RIP Routing, 447
　IPX Routing, 447
　IPX SAP Routing, 447
　Logical and Mapped Drives, 447–448
　OSPF Routing, 448
　Public Key Policies, 448
　RAS Dialin - User Node, 448
　Remote Access, 448
　Removable Storage, 448
　RIP Routing, 448
　Routing, 449
　Send Console Message, 449
　Service Dependencies, 449
　SNMP, 449
　STMP Protocol, 449
　System Properties, 449
extensions, filename, 357, 392
　HKCR as lookup table for, 29–30
　HKCR\ext key for, 412
Extensions subkey, 422

external branding of Internet Explorer, disabling, 427
Extras, 436

F

Failed key, 389
FAT partitions, 73
favorites, disabling importing and exporting of, 427
favorites folder, sharing on network, 372–373
Favorites key, 372–373
Favorites menu
　hiding, 433
　removing from Start Menu, 454
FAX Service, 443
file association key, getting from the Registry, 248–250
file associations, 14–15, 248–251
　HKCR\ext key for, 412
　HKCR\fileType key for, 413
File key, 401
File menu
　disabling
　　closing the browser and Explorer windows, 433
　　New menu option, 432–433
　　Open menu option, 433
　　Save As... menu option, 432
　　Save As Web Page Complete, 433
　removing from Windows Explorer, 438
File Protection (see Windows File Protection policies)
file scan progress window, hiding, 499
filenames, 392
　automatic 8.3 name creation, 369
　completion, Tab key for, 353–354
　extensions
　　HKCR as lookup table for, 29–30
　　HKCR\ext key for, 412
　　length of, 357
files
　hive files, 24–25, 31–33
　"last access" timestamp, 357–358
　list of possible shell operations on, 30
　moved to encrypted folders, do not automatically encrypt, 493
　not cached, 500
　preventing receiving, 426

Index

preventing sending, 426
saving/restoring Registry keys, 124–127
system policy files, 153–154
files and directories
    back up, 476
    restoring, 481
filesystem, customizing, 357
FileSystem key, 392
filesystem tweaks, 356–358
FILETIME datatype, 215–216
fileType key, 413
filtering REGMON captures, 348–350
Find dialog box, enabling filter in, 457
Find Files via F3 within the browser, disabling, 427
find printers
    browsing a common web site to, 462
    browsing the network to, 462
finding Registry keys, 342–345
firmware environment variables, modifying, 480
fixing Registry security ACLs in Windows NT, 389–390
floppy access, restricting to locally logged-on user only, 484–485
floppy disks (see disks)
Folder Options menu item, removing from the Tools menu, 438
folder redirection policy processing, 450, 498
font settings, disabling changing, 428
"For Netscape Users" menu option, removing, 434
ForceEncryptedPassword key, 408
Full Control permission, 18

G

General page, disabling, 430
GetKeys method (Perl), 277–278
GetValues method (Perl), 277–278
global system objects
    auditing the access of, 482
    strengthen default permissions of, 485
go directly to Components wizard, 460
gp.chm, 327
Group key, 397–398
Group Policies, 14, 186–209
    applying, 155–158, 191–193
    calculating effective, 204–205

choosing appropriately, 184–185
default, 156–157
distributing, 203–207
editing, 200–201
elements of, 187
managing, 198–203
storing, 189–191
user vs. machine, 188
(see also system policies)
Group Policy Container (GPC), 190
Group Policy objects (GPOs)
    adding Registry ACLs to, 311–313
    defining, 188–189
Group Policy policies, 450–451, 470, 496–499
    Administrative Templates (Computers), 450
    Administrative Templates (Users), 450
    applying
        Group Policy for computers asynchronously during start up, 497
        Group Policy for users asynchronously during logon, 497
    creating new Group Policy object links disabled by default, 470
    disabling
        automatic update of ADM files, 470
        background refresh of Group Policy, 496
    disk quota policy processing, 499
    EFS recovery policy processing, 498
    enforcing Show Policies Only, 470
    folder redirection policy processing, 450, 498
    Group Policy domain controller selection, 470
    Group Policy refresh interval for computers, 497
    Group Policy refresh interval for domain controllers, 497
    Group Policy refresh interval for users, 470
    Group Policy slow link detection, 470, 497
    Group Policy snap-in, 450
    Group Policy Tab for Active Directory Tools, 450

Group Policy policies (*continued*)
  Internet Explorer Maintenance policy
    processing, 498
  IP security policy processing, 498
  Registry policy processing, 497
  Remote Installation services, 450–451
  Scripts (Logon/Logoff), 451
  scripts policy processing, 498
  Scripts (Startup/Shutdown), 451
  security policy processing, 498
  Security Settings, 451
  Software Installation (Computers), 451
  software installation policy processing,
    498
  Software Installation (Users), 451
  user Group Policy loopback processing
    mode, 497
Group Policy snap-ins, 193–198
  adding, 193–196
  learning, 196–198
Group Policy Template (GPT), structure of,
    190–191
  Active Directory (AD), 192–193
group priority, 157–158
GuardTime key, 408
guest access
  to application log, restricting, 487
  to security log, restricting, 487
  to system log, restricting, 487
guest account, renaming, 484

H

hardware
  current configuration data, 31, 53
  HKLM\HARDWARE keys, 45–46,
    378–379
  local machine configuration data, 11–12,
    31, 43–44, 46, 378–379
  ntdetect program, 10–12
  physical keyboard layout, 50–51
  printer settings, 51–52, 415
  profile settings, 49–50, 53
  profiles for, 389–390
  repair disks (see ERDs)
HARDWARE key, 11–12, 32, 43–44, 46,
    378–379
  DESCRIPTION subkey, 45–46, 378–379
  DEVICEMAP subkey, 45–46, 378–379

OWNERMAP subkey, 45–46
RESOURCEMAP subkey, 45–46, 379
Hardware subkey, 416
Hardware Profiles key, 49–50, 53, 389–390
Hardware tab, hiding, 439
hash
  array, 275
  password, 313
  tied, 275
HasPackage utility (example), 242
Help menu, removing from Start Menu, 454
Hidden key, 403
hiding servers from network computers,
    371
hierarchy, Registry, 5
history settings, disabling changing, 428
Hivelist key, 25–26, 31–32, 393
hives, 24–25, 31–33
  list of supported hives, 25–26, 31–32,
    393
  loading and unloading with reg.exe,
    334–335, 341
  loading saved keys as, 125
  mapping into memory, 323–324
  moving keys to/from, 246–247
HKCC, 424
HKCR, 412–414
HKCU, 414–423
HKDD, 424
HKEY datatype, 214
HKEY_CLASSES_ROOT (HKCR), split into
    two categories, 15
HKEY_CLASSES_ROOT (HKCR) hives, 10
HKEY_CLASSES_ROOT (HKCR) key, 29–30,
    54, 412–414
  CLSID subkey, 414
  ext subkey, 412
  fileType subkey, 413
  ShellNew subkey, 29–30
HKEY_CURRENT_CONFIG (HKCC) key, 31,
    53, 424
HKEY_CURRENT_USER (HKCU) key,
    28–29, 41, 50–52, 414–423
  AppEvents subkey, 50–51, 414
  Console subkey, 50–51, 415
  Control Panels subkey, 50–51, 415
  Environment subkey, 50–51, 415
  ERDs and, 63–64
  Network subkey, 360

Printers subkey, 51–52, 415
Software subkey, 51–52
Software\Microsoft subkey, 415–422
(see also HKEY_USERS key)
HKEY_DYN_DATA (HKDD) key, 30–31, 54, 424
HKEY_LOCAL_MACHINE (HKLM) hives, 10
HKEY_LOCAL_MACHINE (HKLM) key, 27, 45–50
   encrypting portions of, 36
   HARDWARE subkey, 11–12, 31, 43–44, 46, 378–379
   HKLM\SYSTEM\CurrentControlSet, 49–50
   SAM link, 47
   SECURITY subkey, 36, 47
   SECURITY\SAM subkey, 36, 47
     encrypting with SYSKEY, 313–322
     restoring from ERDs, 321
   SOFTWARE subkey, 16, 47–48, 382–388
     ERDs and, 63–64
   SYSTEM subkey, 49, 388–411
     restoring from ERD, 321
HKEY_PERFORMANCE_DATA key, 30–31
HKEY_USERS (HKU) key, 27–28, 54, 411–412
   .DEFAULT subkey, 411–412
   ERDs and, 63–64
   sid subkey, 412
   subkey names, 27–28
   (see also HKEY_CURRENT_USER key)
HKLM, major subkeys of, 45–50
HKLM\HARDWARE, 378–379
HKLM\SOFTWARE, 379–388
HKLM\SYSTEM, 388–411
HKU, 411–412
home page settings, disabling changing, 427
Honeycutt, Jerry, 61
Hostname key, 410
hotfixes, 37
HTREE key, 49–50
hung tasks, forcing to end, 367–368
HUSKEY, 219

I

IAS Logging, 443
icons, associating with file types, 29–30
icons on desktop, hiding all, 456
Identity Manager, prevent users from using Identities, 430
IdleHangUpSeconds key, 419
IE security prompt for Windows Installer scripts, disabling, 491
IGMP Routing, 447
ImagePath key, 396
impersonation, 223–224
importing
   Registry data, 109–110
   Registry keys, 336–337
ImportPath key, 408
incoming DUN calls, rings for, 373
Indexing Service, 443
INETRES.ADM template, 208
INETSET.ADM template, 209
.INF file, 61
inheritable permissions, from parent, 140
inheritance
   policy, 205–206
   seeing and controlling permission, 140
.INI (initialization) files, 2–4
   mapping, 300–303
IniFileMapping key, 300–301
initialization file mapping, 300–303
in-place activation (IPA), 14–15
input parameters, API routines, 211–212
Insertable key, 30
Install, 437
Installer (see Windows Installer policies)
installing
   SYSKEY utility, 315–317
   System Policy Editor, 157–158
   system policy files, 155–156
   tracking software installations, 325–326
   Windows NT, 48, 389
interface (200), customizing, 352–356
Internet Authentication Service (IAS), 443
Internet Connection wizard, disabling, 428
Internet Control Panel policies, 430–431
   disabling
     the Advanced page, 431
     the Connections page, 430
     the Content page, 430
     the General page, 430
     the Programs page, 431
     the Security page, 430

Internet Explorer, 426–438
  administrator approved controls, 435–445
  browser menus, 432–434
  Internet Control Panel, 430–431
  offline pages, 431–432
  persistence behavior, 435
  toolbars, 434
Internet Explorer Maintenance policy processing, 498
Internet Explorer policies, 426–438, 436–437, 488–489
  Active Setup, 436
  disabling
    AutoComplete to save passwords, 429
    Automatic Install of Internet Explorer components, 489
    caching of Auto-Proxy scripts, 427
    changing accessibility settings, 428
    changing Advanced page settings, 427
    changing Automatic Configuration settings, 429
    changing Calendar and Contact settings, 430
    changing certificate settings, 429
    changing color settings, 428
    changing connection settings, 428
    changing default browser check, 430
    changing font settings, 428
    changing history settings, 428
    changing home page settings, 427
    changing language settings, 428
    changing link color settings, 428
    changing Messaging settings, 429
    changing Profile Assistant settings, 429
    changing proxy settings, 428
    changing ratings settings, 429
    changing Temporary Internet files settings, 427
    external branding of Internet Explorer, 427
    importing and exporting of favorites, 427
    Internet Connection wizard, 428
    Periodic Check of Internet Explorer software updates, 489
    the Reset Web Settings feature, 430
    showing the splash screen, 489
    software update shell notifications on program launch, 489
  displaying, error message on proxy script download failure, 427
  Extras, 436
  Identity Manager, prevent users from using Identities, 430
  making proxy settings per-machine (rather than per user), 489
  Media Player, 436
  Menu Controls, 436
  Microsoft Agent, 437
  Microsoft Chat, 437
  search
    disabling Find Files via F3 within the browser, 427
    disabling Search Customization, 427
  security zones
    do not allow users to add/delete sites, 489
    do not allow users to change policies, 489
    use only machine settings, 488
  using Automatic Detection for dial-up connections, 427
  WebPost, 437
Internet Explorer policy components, 426–438
  administrator approved controls, 435–445
    databinding, 435–436
    Internet Explorer, 436–437
    MSN, 437–438
  browser menus, 432–434
  Internet Control Panel, 430–431
  offline pages, 431–432
  persistence behavior, 435
  toolbars, 434
Internet Information Services, 444
Internet Options... menu option, disabling, 433
Internet zone, file size limits for, 435
Interval key, 409
intranet support Web page, setting, 426
Intranet zone, file size limits for, 435
Investor, 437–438
IP Routing, 447

Index

IP Security, 444
IP security policy processing, 498
IPA (in-place activation), 14–15
IPAddress key, 410–411
IPEnableRouter key, 410
IPX RIP Routing, 447
IPX Routing, 447
IPX SAP Routing, 447
IQueryAssociations interface, getting a pointer to, 250–251
IsDomainMaster key, 400

K

KeepRasConnections key, 374
Kerberos policy policies, 474
    enforcing user logon restrictions, 474
    maximum lifetime for service ticket, 474
    maximum lifetime for user ticket, 474
    maximum lifetime for user ticket renewal, 474
    maximum tolerance for computer clock synchronization, 474
kernel functionality settings, 390–395
KernelDumpOnly key, 391
key information, getting, 252, 258
key ownership, changing, 143
keyboard
    navigating RegEdit with, 92–93
    physical layout of, 50–51
Keyboard Layout key, 50–51
keyboard navigation indicator setting, disabling UI to change, 440
KEYNAME statement (.ADM files), 167–168
keys (see Registry keys; specific key names)
Knowledge Base, 60

L

l0phtcrack, 36
LAN connection
    enabling access to properties of, 465
    enabling access to properties of components of, 465
    enabling connecting and disconnecting, 464
LAN Manager authentication level, 483
language settings, disabling changing, 428

LanmanServer key, 402–403
"last access" timestamp, 357–358
LastCallbackByCaller key, 419
LastKnownGood key, 388
lazy flusher, 247
Le Berre, Philippe, 280
leftover routines, 262–264
legacy logon scripts hidden, running, 468
legacy run list, disabling, 469, 493
LegalNoticeCaption key, 386
LegalNoticeText key, 386
libraries, accessing Registry API from, 55
LicensedProcessors key, 395
limiting
    remote Registry access, 303–307
    the size of sent files policy, 426
link color settings, disabling changing, 428
Linkage key, 398
links, Registry, 25
    REG_LINK datatype for, 40–41
listing Registry key values (example), 270–272
little-endian platforms, 42–43
LmhostsTimeout key, 404
Load method (Perl), 278
LoadBoxWithUsers utility (example), 270–272
loading
    hives with reg.exe, 334–335, 341
    Registry data from files, 124–127
    Registry keys, 244–245, 278
    system policies, 165–166
local accounts, creating, 27–28
Local Machine zone, file size limits for, 435
Local Security Authority (LSA), 393
Local Users and Groups, 444
Locations key, 417
Lock Computer, disabling, 468
lock pages in memory, 479
lockout (see account lockout policies)
lockout counter, resetting account, 474
lockout duration policy, account, 473–474
lockout threshold policy, account, 473
log event
    when quota limit exceeded, 496
    when quota warning level exceeded, 496
LogEvent key, 391

logging
    DUN connections, 373
    ERDisk utility activity, 67–68
    Event Logger service, 401–402
    print jobs, 375–376
Logging key
    of Microsoft\NtBackup, 416
    of RasMan\Parameters, 373, 407
    of RasMan\PPP, 407
logging off users
    synchronizing all offline files before, 463, 500
    when logon time expires (local), 482
    when roaming profile fails, 495
logging on
    as a batch job, 479
    locally, 479
    as a service, 479
Logical and Mapped Drives, 447–448
LoginSessionDisable key, 417
Logoff, disabling, 468
logoff (logout)
    forcing hung tasks to end, 367–368
    maintaining DUN connection after, 373
Logoff on the Start Menu, disabling, 455
logoff scripts, running visibly, 469
LogoffSetting key, 384–385
logon
    automatic
        after booting NT, 366–367
        using DUN for, 372–373
    caching logon credentials, 358–359
    don't display welcome screen at, 467, 493
    screen saver during, 354–355
    suppressing error messages during, 355
logon as a batch job, denying, 478
logon as a service, denying, 478
logon events, auditing, 475
logon locally, denying, 478
logon scripts
    running synchronously, 468, 494
    running visibly, 469
logon/logoff policies, 468–469, 494–495
    connecting home directory to root of the share, 469
    deleting cached copies of roaming profiles, 494

disabling
    Change Password, 468
    legacy run list, 469
    Lock Computer, 468
    Logoff, 468
    the run once list, 469
    Task Manager, 468
do not detect slow network connections, 494–495
excluding directories in roaming profile, 469
limiting profile size, 469
log users off when roaming profile fails, 495
maximum retries to unload and update user profile, 495
maximum wait time for Group Policy scripts, 494
prompting user when slow link is detected, 495
running
    legacy logon scripts hidden, 468
    logoff scripts visibly, 469
    logon scripts synchronously, 468, 494
    logon scripts visibly, 469
    shutdown scripts visibly, 494
    startup scripts asynchronously, 494
    startup scripts visibly, 494
    these programs at user logon, 469
slow network connection timeout for user profiles, 495
timeout for dialog boxes, 495
waiting for remote user profile, 495
LSA (Local Security Authority) key, 393

M

Machine key, 306–307
machine policies
    applying, 156
    choosing appropriately, 184–185
    default, 156–157
    vs. user, 154, 188
    (see also system policies)
MaintainServerList key, 399
major datatypes, 38–41
    (see also datatypes)
MajorVersion key, 394

Index

"Make Available Offline," disabling, 463, 500
Manage item on the Windows Explorer context menu, hiding, 439
mandatory profiles, 34
  user, 13
"Map Network Drive," removing, 438–439
mapping initialization (.INI) files, 300–303
MasterPeriodicity key, 399
maximum application log size, 486
maximum lifetime
  for service ticket in Kerberos policy policies, 474
  for user ticket in Kerberos policy policies, 474
  for user ticket renewal in Kerberos policy policies, 474
maximum password age, 472
maximum retries to unload and update user profile, 495
maximum security log size, 486
maximum system log size, 486
maximum tolerance for computer clock synchronization, in Kerberos policy policies, 474
maximum wait time for Group Policy scripts, 494
MaxSize key, 401
Media Player, 436
media source
  for any install, disabling, 453
  enabling user to use while elevated, 492
Member Of, 471–472
Members, 471
memory
  allocating system resources, 42–44
  clearing pagefiles at shutdown, 358–359
  Control\Session Manager\Memory Management, 395
  low disk space threshold, 357, 402
  Registry hives mapped into, 323–324
Memory Management key, 395
menu animation setting, disabling UI to change, 439–440
Menu Controls, 436
Messaging settings, disabling changing, 429
Microsoft
  applications, settings for, 47
  components, user-specific settings for, 415–422
  Knowledge Base, 60
Microsoft Agent, 437
Microsoft Chat, 437
Microsoft key
  of HKCU\Software, 415–422
    Windows NT\CurrentVersion subkey, 423
  of HKLM\SOFTWARE, 47, 379–382
    Windows NT subkey, 382–388
Microsoft Management Console (MMC), 441–451
  extension snap-ins, 446–449
  Group Policy snap-ins, 450–451
  restricted/permitted snap-ins, 441–451
Microsoft Management Console (MMC) policies, 441
  restricting users
    from entering author mode, 441
    to the explicitly permitted list of snap-ins, 441
MinAnimate key, 353
minimum password age, 473
minimum password length, 473
minor datatypes, 41–44
  (see also datatypes)
MinorVersion key, 394
modifying Registry (see editing, Registry)
monitoring Registry with REGMON, 345–350
MountedDevices key, 388
MS-DOS applications, 2
MSN policies, 437–438
  Cache Preloader, 437
  Carpoint, 437
  Install, 437
  Investor, 437–438
  MSNBC, 438
  music, 438
  Quick View Access, 438
MSNBC, 438
multimedia devices, settings for, 384
multiple-string values, modifying, 129–130
music policy, 438
MWC exploit, 35
My Computer
  hiding these specified drives in, 439
  preventing access to drives from, 409

"My Computer," customizing, 364
My Documents icon
    removing from desktop, 456
    removing from Start Menu, 456
My Documents path, prohibiting user from changing, 457
My Network Places
    no "Computers Near Me" in, 440
    no "Entire Network" in, 440
My Network Places folder, do not add shares from recently opened documents to, 457
My Network Places icon on desktop, hiding, 456

N

names
    filename extensions, 29
    filesystem settings for, 392
    HKEY_USERS subkeys, 28–28
    as Registry key values, 24
    renaming Registry keys/values, 106
    root keys, origination of, 26–27
    Win32 API routines, 212
NameServer key, 410
NameSrvQueryCount key, 404
NameSrvQueryTimeout key, 404
navigating POLEDIT window, 159–160
NBT (NetBios over TCP/IP), 403–405
NegotiateTime key, 407
NetBios service, 399–400
    over TCP/IP (NBT), 403–405
NetBt key, 403–405
NetcardDlls key, 389–390
Netlogon key, 405–407
Netlogon service, 405–407
    recovering crashed PDC, 370–371
NetMeeting home page, setting, 426
NetMeeting policies, 425–426, 488
    disabling
        Chat, 426
        Directory Services, 425
        NetMeeting 2.x Whiteboard, 426
        NetMeeting Whiteboard, 426
    disabling remote desktop sharing, 488
    enabling Automatic Configuration, 425
    limiting the size of sent files, 426
    preventing
        adding Directory servers, 425
        automatic acceptance of Calls, 426
        changing Call placement method, 426
        receiving files, 426
        sending files, 426
        viewing Web directory, 426
    setting
        Call Security options, 426
        the intranet support Web page, 426
        the NetMeeting home page, 426
NetPopup key, 374
network
    accessing this computer from, 476
    denying access to this computer from, 477–478
network and dial-up connection policies, 464–466, 502
    allowing
        access to current user's RAS connection properties, 465
        configuration of connection sharing, 466, 502
        connection components to be enabled or disabled, 465
        TCP/IP advanced configuration, 466
    displaying and enabling, the Network Connection wizard, 466
    enabling
        access to properties of a LAN connection, 465
        access to properties of components of a LAN connection, 465
        access to properties of components of a RAS connection, 466
        access to properties of RAS connections available to all users, 465
        adding or removing components of a RAS or LAN connection, 465
        the Advanced Settings item on the Advanced menu, 466
        connecting and disconnecting a LAN connection, 464
        connecting and disconnecting a RAS connection, 464
        deletion of RAS connections, 464

Index

the Dial-up Preferences item on the
Advanced menu, 466
renaming of connections, if
supported, 465
status statistics for an active
connection, 466
network and dial-up connections, 464–466
removing from Start Menu, 454
Network Cards key, 384–385
Network Connection wizard, displaying
and enabling, 466
network connections, do not detect slow,
494–495
Network key
of HKCU, 51–52, 360
of Windows NT\CurrentVersion, 423
network policies, 462–466
network and dial-up connections,
464–466
Offline Files, 462–464
networking
connecting to remote machines, 242–243
connecting to remote Registries, 95–96,
121–122
detecting slow connections, 370
DHCP configuration settings, 400–401
domain controllers
Netlogon for, 405–407
SYSKEY utility and, 316–317
upgrading, 317
DUN (see Dial-Up Networking)
ERDisk utility to create ERDs, 67–70
forcing hung tasks to end, 367–368
hiding servers from network, 371
NBT (NetBios over TCP/IP), 403–405
NetBios service, 399–400
Netlogon service, 370–371, 405–407
preventing drive mapping changes, 360
RAS (see Dial-Up Networking)
remote Registry management, 19–20
system policies for, 172–173, 184
TCP/IP configuration settings, 409–411
tweaking, 372–374
user-specific settings for, 51–52
networkprovider key, 399
Networks key, 417
New menu option, disabling, 432–433
New Task Creation, disabling, 452, 490
NewEntryWizard key, 419

NMICrashDump, 392
no screen saver, 461
NODRIVES key, 361–362
nonlocal Group Policies, setting, 207
nonlocal Group Policy objects (NGPOs),
189
NoRemotePrinterDrivers key, 394
normal profiles, 34
user, 13
Notification Packages key, 393
Notify permission, 18, 134–135
NtBackup key
of HKCU\Software\Microsoft, 416
of HKLM\SOFTWARE\Microsoft, 382
NTBACKUP utility, 75–76, 84–85
NtBackup utility, Registry settings for, 416
NTconfig.pol file, 156–157, 170
ntdetect program, 10–12
NtfsAllowExtendedCharacterIn8dot3Name
key, 392
NtfsDisable8dot3NameCreation key,
370–371, 392
NtfsDisableLastAccessUpdate key, 357–358,
392–393
Ntuser.dat file, 299
NullSessionPipes key, 403
NullSessionShares key, 403

O

object access, auditing, 475
object reuse, 358–359
ObjectDirectories key, 395
ObjectName key, 396
offline files, 462–464
administratively assigned, 463, 500–501
disabling user configuration of, 463, 499
Offline Files policies, 463–464, 499–502
action on server disconnect, 463, 500
administratively assigned offline files,
463, 500–501
default cache size, 500
disabling
"Make Available Offline," 463, 500
reminder balloons, 463, 501
user configuration of Offline Files,
463, 499
enabled, 499
event logging level, 464, 501
files not cached, 500

Offline Files policies (*continued*)
  initial reminder balloon lifetime, 464, 501
  at logoff, delete local copy of user's offline files, 501
  non-default server disconnect actions, 463, 500
  preventing use of Offline Files folder, 463, 500
  reminder balloon frequency, 464, 501
  reminder balloon lifetime, 464, 501
  subfolders always available offline, 501–502
  synchronizing all offline files before logging off, 463, 500
offline pages policies, 431–432
  disabling
    adding channels, 431
    adding schedules for offline pages, 431
    all scheduled offline pages, 432
    channel user interface completely, 432
    downloading of site subscription content, 432
    editing and creating of schedule groups, 432
    editing schedules for offline pages, 431
    hit logging, 432
    offline page hit logging, 432
    removing channels, 431
    removing schedules for offline pages, 431
  Subscription Limits, 432
OLE (object linking and embedding), 4, 14–15
  information in Protocol subkey, 30–31
one-way function (OWF), 313
Open File (see common Open File dialog policies)
Open in New Window menu option, disabling, 434
Open key, 413
Open menu option, disabling, 433
Open method (Perl), 276–277
opening Registry keys, 221–225, 257
  Perl methods for, 276–277
  while impersonating another user, 223–224

operating systems, 476
  Win32 API and, 213
OperatorDial key, 419
OsLoaderPath key, 389
OSPF Routing, 448
output parameters, API routines, 211–212
Overwrite key, 391
OWF (one-way function), 313
OWNERMAP key, 46
ownership, key, 19, 149–150

P

pagefiles
  clearing, 358–359
  creating, 477
Parameters key, 398
parameters of API routines, 211–212
parents, inheritable permissions from, 140
ParseAutoexec key, 386, 423
PART block (.ADM files), 167–168
partitions, boot vs. system, 73
parts of system policies, 152–153, 155–156
password hash, 313
password policies, 472–473
  enforcing password history, 472
  maximum password age, 472
  minimum password age, 473
  minimum password length, 473
  passwords must meet complexity requirements of the installed password filter, 473
  store password using reversible encryption for all users in the domain, 473
  user must log on to change password, 473
PasswordExpiryWarning key, 361–362
passwords
  encrypting with SYSKEY, 313–322
  expiration warnings for, 361–362
  password encryption key (PEK), 314–315, 319–320
  storing in Registry, 33
patching, disabling, 491
PDCs, recovering after crash, 370–371
PEK (password encryption key), 314–315, 319–320
Perflib key, 360

Index

performance
 allocating system resources, 42–44
 NT 4.0 Taskbar, 353
 speeding up shutdowns, 368–369
 window animations, 353
Performance key, 398–399
Performance Logs and Alerts, 444
Performance Monitor
 controlling access to, 360
 counters, 398–399
Periodic Check of Internet Explorer software updates, disabling, 489
Perl programming language, 55
 programs for manipulating Registry, 272–284
permanent shared objects, creating, 477
permission inheritance, seeing and controlling, 140
permissions, 18, 134–136
 HKLM\SECURITY key data, 47
 key ownership, 19, 149–150
 list of, 18
 most restrictive, 136
 on Registry keys, 33
 on restriction (winreg) key, 304–307
 setting, 137–140, 144–145
persistence behavior policies, 435
 file size limits
  for Internet zone, 435
  for Intranet zone, 435
  for Local Machine zone, 435
  for Restricted Sites zone, 435
  for Trusted Sites zone, 435
PersistentRoutes key, 410
personalized menus, disabling, 455
PersonalPhonebookFile key, 419–420
phkNewUSKey, 257
phonebook, RAS, 418–421
PhonebookMode key, 420
Phonebooks key, 420
PHUSKEY, 219
PlugPlayServiceType key, 396
.POL files, 154–155
 (see also system policies)
POLEDIT (System Policy Editor), 157–158
 applying policies, 155–158, 169–171
 creating policies, 161–162
 creating policy templates, 166–168
 distributing policies, 168–171
 editing policies, 162–166
 interface of, 159–160
 managing policies with, 159–168
 saving/loading policies, 154–155, 165–166
policies (see Group Policies; system policies)
POLICY block (.ADM files), 167–168
policy change, auditing, 475
policy inheritance, 205–206
PowerdownAfterShutdown key, 386
powering off at shutdown, 367–368
preconfiguring user accounts, under Windows 2000, 297–298
Prefixes key, 420
prepopulate printer search location text, 503
PreviewPhoneNumber key, 420
primacy DNS Suffix, 496
PrimaryModule key, 402
Print key
 of application identifier key\Shell, 413
 of CurrentControlSet\Control, 394
printer drivers, preventing users from installing, 484
printer folder's left pane, custom support URL in, 503
PrinterPorts subkey, 422
Printers key, 51–52, 415
printers policies, 462, 502–503
 allowing
  printers to be published, 502
  pruning of published printers, 502
 automatically publish new printers in Active Directory, 502
 browsing
  a common web site to find printers, 462
  the network to find printers, 462
  printer, 502
 checking published state, 503
 computer location, 503
 custom support URL in the Printers folder's left pane, 503
 default Active Directory path when searching for printers, 462
 directory pruning interval, 503

printers policies (*continued*)
  directory pruning priority, 503
  directory pruning retry, 503
  disabling
    addition of printers, 462
    deletion of printers, 462
    prepopulate printer search location text, 503
    prune printers that are not automatically republished, 502
  web-based printing, 503
printing
  configuring settings, 394
  customizing, 374–376
  disabling browse thread, 370–371
  logging print jobs, 375–376
  Printer Operators, 362
  Registry contents, 98, 127
  setting spool directory, 375–376
priority, group, 157–158
privilege use, auditing, 476
process level token, replacing a, 480
process tracking, auditing, 476
ProcessorControl key, 395
processors, configuration settings for, 395
ProductId key, 383
Profile Assistant settings, disabling changing, 429
profile size, limiting, 469
ProfileDlgTimeOut key, 386
ProfileList, 384–385
profiles
  hardware, 49–50, 53, 389–390
  machine, 384–385
  (see also user profiles)
ProfileType key, 423
Program Manager key, 423
programming with C/C++, 264–272
programming with Perl, 272–284
programming with Visual Basic, 284–295
Programs page, disabling, 431
prompting user when slow link is detected, 495
Property Pages, hiding, 452, 489
Protocols key, 382–383
proxy settings
  disabling changing, 428
  making per-machine (rather than per user), 489

prune printers that are not automatically republished, 502
Public Key Policies, 448
published printers, allowing pruning of, 502
Pulse key
  of Netlogon\Parameters, 406
  of Replicator\Parameters, 409
PulseConcurrency key, 406
PulseMaximum key, 406
PulseTimeout1, PulseTimeout2 keys, 406
pwdump2, 36

Q

QoS Admission Control, 444
Query Value permission, 18, 133–134
QueryDriverFrequency, 400
querying Registry keys, 252–253, 329–330, 337
Quick View Access, 438
quota limit and warning level, default, 496
quotas
  increasing, 479
  (see also disk quotas policies)

R

RAS
  autodialer settings, 417
  monitor settings, 418
  phonebook settings, 418–421
  RasMan service, 407–408
  Registry settings for, 382
RAS Autodial key, 417
RAS connections
  available to all users
    enabling access to properties of, 465
    enabling deletion of, 464
  belonging to the current user, enabling renaming of, 465
  enabling access to properties of components of, 466
  enabling connecting and disconnecting, 464
  enabling deletion of, 464
RAS Dialin - User Node, 448
RAS Monitor key, 418
RAS or LAN connection, enabling adding or removing components of, 465
RAS Phonebook key, 418–421

Index

RasForce key, 372–373
RasMan key, 407–408
ratings settings, disabling changing, 429
Ratliffe, Mitch, 59
RDISK utility, 59–60, 65–67
RDS, 435–436
Read Control permission, 18, 134–135
Read permission, 18
reading Registry data, 54–55
    exporting data with RegEdit, 108–109, 112–113
    obtaining security data, 240–241
    saving keys, 124–127
    Win32 API routines for, 232–233
reading values, 258–260
rebooting NT after crash, 365–366
recent documents, maximum number of, 440
recently opened documents
    clear history on exit, 455
    do not keep history of, 455
recovery Console
    allowing automatic administrative logon, 484
    allowing floppy copy and access to all drives and folders, 484
recovery console, Windows 2000, 68–69
RedButton exploit, 35
RedialAttempts key, 420
RedialOnLinkFailure key, 420
RedialSeconds key, 420
refresh interval, Group Policy
    for computers, 497
    for domain controllers, 497
    for users, 470
RefusePasswordChange key, 405
.REG files
    contents of, 107–108
    creating, 110–112
    restoring Registry data, 88–89
reg utility
    one size fits all Registry tool, 328–345
    Windows 2000, 329–337
    Windows NT, 337–341
REGBACK, REGREST utilities, 77–80, 85–87
regback.exe, 327
REG_BINARY datatype, 40
    modifying in Registry, 101–102, 130–131
REGCLEAN utility, 59–60

RegCloseKey( ), 225
    flushing Registry changes and, 264
RegConnectRegistry( ), 242
RegCreateKey( ), 222–223, 227
RegCreateKeyEx( ), 222–223, 226–227
RegDeleteKey( ), 238–239, 251
RegDeleteValue( ), 239, 252
REGDUMP utility, 82
REG_DWORD datatype, 38
    modifying in Registry, 101–102, 128–129
REG_DWORD value, 402
REG_DWORD_BIG_ENDIAN datatype, 42–43
RegEdit library, 55
RegEdit utility, 90–113
    backing up/restoring Registry with, 82, 87–89
    command-line options, 112–113, 120–121
    connecting to remote Registries, 95–96
    context menus, 94–95
    exporting/importing Registry data, 106–112
    interface of, 91–93
    limitations of, 90–91
    modifying Registry with, 98–106
    navigating with keyboard, 92–93
    printing Registry contents, 98
    RegEdt32 vs., 114–115
    searching for keys and values, 96–98
    viewing Registry with, 92–95
    Visual Basic version of, 289–295
RegEdt32 utility, 7, 114–150
    accessing remote Registries, 121–122
    auditing key activity, 147–148
    backing up/restoring Registry with, 80–82, 87–89
    interface of, 115–119
    modifying Registry with, 127–134
    printing Registry contents, 127
    reg utility vs., 328–329
    RegEdit vs., 114–115
    restoring data from ERD, 69–70
    searching for keys and values, 123–124
    spying on Registry with, 347
    viewing Registry with, 119–121
regentry.chm, 327
RegEnumKey( ), 231–232
RegEnumKeyEx( ), 231–232

RegEnumValue( ), 232–233
REG_EXPAND_SZ datatype, 39–40
    modifying in Registry, 100–101, 128–129
REG_EXPAND_SZ value, 402
regfind utility, 342–345
regfind.exe, 327
RegFlushKey( ), 238–239, 264
REG_FULL_RESOURCE_DESCRIPTOR
        datatype, 42–44
RegGetKeySecurity( ), 240–241
regini.exe, 327
REGINI.EXE utility, 55
regional options policy, 462
    restrict selection of Windows 2000
        menus and dialogs language, 462
RegisteredOrganization key, 382–383
RegisteredOwner key, 382–383
RegisteredProcessors key, 395
$Registry, 275
Registry, Windows 95 and 98, 8–9
Registry, Windows 2000
    backing up, NTBACKUP utility, 84–85
    history of, 1–10
    introduction to, 1–21
    monitoring with REGMON, 345–350
    structure of, 22–44
Registry ACLs
    adding to Group Policy objects, 311–313
    recommended for Windows NT,
        308–311
Registry activity, auditing, 141–142
Registry APIs
    access control via, 33–38
    calling routines directly, 54
    (see also Win32 API)
Registry Control for Visual Basic library, 55
Registry documented, 377–424
registry editing tools, disabling, 467
Registry keys
    access controls and permissions, 33–38
    adding, 103–105, 132–133
        reg utility for, 330–331, 337–338
    auditing activity, 19, 145–149
        reviewing records, 148–149
    comparing with compreg utility,
        341–342
    comparing with reg.exe, 335–336
    copying reg.exe, 339–340
    creating, 226–227
        Perl methods for, 276–277

deleting, 59–60, 105, 133–134
    API routines for, 238–239
    with reg.exe, 331–332
editing
    API routines for, 236–238
    (see also editing, Registry)
enumerating keys and values, 230–233
    Perl methods for, 277–278
exporting and importing, 108–110
    RegEdit switches for, 112–113
exporting with reg.exe, 336–337
getting information on, 228–229
hierarchy of (see hierarchy, Registry)
hives, 24–25, 31–33
importing with reg.exe, 336–337
links (see links, Registry)
moving to/from hives, 246–247
opening and closing
    Perl methods for, 276–277
    Win32 API routines for, 221–225
ownership, 19, 149–150
permissions, 18, 134–136
    setting, 144–145
program-specific subkeys, 51–52
querying with reg.exe, 329–330, 337
reading security data of, 240–241
renaming, 106
restriction key, 304–307
root keys, 5, 23, 26–31
saving in/restoring from files, 124–127
    reg.exe for, 332–333, 340–341
saving/loading, 244–246, 278
searching for, 96–98, 123–124, 342–345
stack–based key classes (example),
        267–270
stored on ERD, 61
subkeys, 5, 23
updating with reg.exe, 338
values for, 24
    enumerating, 232–233, 277–278
    listing (example), 270–272
    modifying, 100–103, 128–131
    searching for specific, 96–98, 123–124
what to back up, 71
Registry policy processing, 497
Registry tweaks, 351–376
Registry utilities, using the resource kit,
        326–328
REG_LINK datatype, 40–41
RegLoadKey( ), 244–245

Index

REGMON utility, 345–350
REG_MULTI_SZ datatype, 39
    modifying in Registry, 101–102, 130–131
REG_NONE datatype, 41–42
RegNotifyChangeKeyValue( ), 246–247
    WatchKey utility (example), 264–267
RegOpenKey( ), 222–223
RegOpenKeyEx( ), 222–223
RegQueryInfoKey( ), 228–229, 252
    enumeration and, 230
RegQueryMultipleValues( ), 235
RegQueryValue( ), 235
RegQueryValueEx( ), 233–235, 253
REG_QWORD, 41
REG_RESOURCE_LIST datatype, 43–44
REGREST utility, 85–87
regrest.exe, 327
RegRestoreKey( ), 245–246
REGSAM datatype, 214
RegSaveKey( ), 244–246
RegSetKeySecurity( ), 242
RegSetValue( ), 237
RegSetValueEx( ), 236–238
REG_SZ datatype, 39
    modifying in Registry, 100–101, 128–129
REG_SZ value, 402
RegUnloadKey( ), 245–246
RegWalk module, 279, 283
reminder balloons
    disabling, 463, 501
    frequency, 464, 501
    initial, 464, 501
    lifetime, 464, 501
Remote Access, 448
    turning off entirely, 304
remote desktop sharing, disabling, 488
Remote Installation services, 450–451
remote machines, connecting to, API routines for, 242–243
remote Registries
    accessing with RegEdit, 95–96
    accessing with RegEdt32, 121–122
    controlling access to, 33, 303–307
    managing, 19–20
remote user profile, waiting for, 495
removable media, applying policy to, 496
removable NTFS media, allowing ejection of, 482
Removable Storage, 448

Removable Storage Management, 444
removing
    ACE entries, 139–140
    auditing entries, 141–142
    channels, disabling, 431
    keys, 256
    schedules for offline pages, disabling, 431
renaming, Registry keys, 106
repair disks (see ERDs)
REPAIR subdirectory, 67
Replicate key, 409
ReplicationGovernor key, 406–407
Replicator key, 408–409
replicator service, 408–409
ReportBootOk key, 386–387
requesting credentials for network installations, 440
Reset Web Settings feature, disabling, 430
resolution, video, 363
Resource Kit, 326–328
RESOURCEMAP key, 46, 379
resources
    allocation information, 42–44
    map of available, 46
RestoreFlag key, 401
restoring Registry, 83–89, 124–127
    protected by SYSKEY, 321–322
    reg utility for, 332–333, 340–341
restricted groups policies, 471–472
    Member Of, 471–472
    Members, 471
Restricted Sites zone, file size limits for, 435
restricted/permitted snap-ins policies, 441–445
    Active Directory Domains and Trusts, 441
    Active Directory Sites and Services, 442
    Active Directory Users and Computers, 441
    Certificates, 442
    Computer Management, 442
    DCOM Config, 442
    Device Manager, 442
    Disk Defragmenter, 442–443
    Disk Management, 442
    Distributed File System, 443
    Event Viewer, 443
    FAX Service, 443

restricted/permitted snap-ins policies (*continued*)
  IAS Logging, 443
  Indexing Service, 443
  Internet Authentication Service (IAS), 443
  Internet Information Services, 444
  IP Security, 444
  Local Users and Groups, 444
  Performance Logs and Alerts, 444
  QoS Admission Control, 444
  Removable Storage Management, 444
  Routing and Remote Access, 444–445
  Security Configuration and Analysis, 445
  Security Templates, 445
  Services, 445
  Shared Folders, 445
  System Information, 445
  Telephony, 445
restriction key, 304–307
restrictive permissions, 136
RestrictNullSessionAccess key, 403
Retention key, 401
reversible encryption for all users in the domain, store password using, 473
rings for incoming DUN calls, 373
RIP Routing, 448
roaming profile, excluding directories in, 469
roaming profiles, 34
  user, 13
rollback, disabling, 453, 491
ROOT key, 49–50
root keys, 5, 23, 26–31
  origination of names for, 26–27
routines, Win32 API
  C/C++ programs for manipulating Registry, 264–272
  connecting to remote machines, 242–243
  creating keys, 226–227, 276–277
  deleting keys/values, 238–239
  editing Registry values, 236–238
  enumeration, 230–233, 277–278
  error codes, 211–212
  getting information on keys, 228–229
  moving keys to/from hives, 246–247
  names of, 212
  notifying of Registry changes, 246–247, 264–267

opening and closing keys, 221–225, 276–277
parameters of, 211–212
Perl programming examples, 272–284
  Perl Win32::RegXXX functions, 273–274
reading Registry data, 232–233
security-related, 239–242
Visual Basic programming examples, 284–295
Routing, 449
  and Remote Access, 444–445
RSL (Registry Size Limit) parameter, 323–324
Run dialog box, adding "Run in Separate Memory Space" check box to, 456
Run menu, removing from Start Menu, 454
run once list, disabling, 469, 493
RunLoginScriptSync key, 423
RunLogonScriptSync key, 387

S

/s switch (ERDisk), 67–68
/s switch (RDISK), 67
/s– switch (RDISK), 67
Sabin, Todd, 36
SACLs (system ACLs), 239
SAM key, 47
  encrypting with SKS, 36
  encrypting with SYSKEY, 313–322
  restoring from ERDs, 321
Save As... menu option, disabling, 432
Save As Web Page Complete, disabling, 433
Save method (Perl), 278
"Save Password" option, 358–359
Save this program to disk option, disabling, 434
saving
  captured Registry data (REGMON), 348–350
  logon credentials, 358–359
  Registry keys, 244, 278
  Registry keys in files, 124–127
  Registry keys with reg.exe, 332–333, 340–341
scanreg.exe, 327
schedule groups, disabling editing and creating of, 432

Index

Schedule Tasks (see task scheduler policies)
scheduled offline pages, disabling all, 432
SchedulerThreadPriority key, 394
schedules for offline pages
　disabling adding, 431
　disabling editing, 431
scheduling priority, increasing, 479
scheduling regular backups, 57
Schulman, Andrew, 82, 113
screen saver
　executable name, 461
　during logon, 354–355
　password protect, 461
Screen Saver tab, hiding, 461
Scripts key, 407
Scripts (Logon/Logoff), 451
scripts policy processing, 498
Scripts (Startup/Shutdown), 451
SDs (security descriptors), 240
Search button, removing from Windows Explorer, 439
Search Customization, disabling, 427
Search menu, removing from Start Menu, 454
searching for keys and values, 96–98, 123–124, 342–345
SearchList key, 410
secure system partition (for RISC platforms only), 485
SecurePipeServers key, 394
securing Registry keys
　in Windows 2000, 136–143
　in Windows NT, 143–150
security, 33–38, 134–143
　ACLs (see ACLs)
　API routines for, 239–242
　auditing Registry access, 324–326
　auditing Registry activity, 19, 145–149
　bug fixes, 37
　cryptography, 381
　customizing, 358–364
　DACs (discretionary access controls), 134–135
　editing Registry, warning about, 20, 59–61
　emergency repair disks (see ERDs)
　encrypting SECURITY\SAM, 313–322
　HKLM\SECURITY key, 47
　key ownership, 19, 149–150
　limiting remote Windows NT access, 303–307
　LSA (Local Security Authority), 393
　password expiration warnings, 361–362
　permissions (see permissions)
　policies (see system policies)
　Registry and, 18
　Registry backups (see backups of Registry)
　Registry key permissions, 36, 38
　removing crash evidence, 365–366
　restriction (winreg) key, 304–307
　safeguarding data, 57–61
　SKS (System Key Security), 36, 38
　SYSKEY protection, 60
　Trojan horses, 325–326
　Win32 API datatypes for, 213–216
　Windows NT model, 6–7
Security Account Manager (SAM), 47
　encrypting key for, 313–322
　encrypting Registry data on, 36
security audits
　generate, 478
　shut down computer when log is full, 488
　shut down system immediately if unable to log, 485
Security Configuration and Analysis, 445
security descriptors (SDs), 240
security IDs (SIDs) for HKU subkeys, 27–28
SECURITY key, 36, 47
Security key, 399
security log
　retaining, 487
　retention method for, 488
security option, removing from Start menu (Terminal Services only), 492
security options policies, 481–486
　additional restrictions for anonymous access, 481
　allowing
　　ejection of removable NTFS media, 482
　　server operators to schedule tasks (domain controllers only), 481
　　system to be shut down without having to log on, 481

security options policies, allowing (*continued*)
   amount of idle time required before disconnecting a session, 482
   auditing
      the access of global system objects, 482
      use of Backup and Restore Privilege, 482
   automatically log off users when logon time expires (local), 482
   clear virtual memory pagefile when system shuts down, 482
   digitally sign client communications (always), 482
   digitally sign client communications (when possible), 482–483
   digitally sign server communications (always), 483
   digitally sign server communications (when possible), 483
   disabling CTRL+ALT+DEL requirement for logon, 483
   do not display last user name in logon screen, 493
   LAN Manager authentication level, 483
   message text for users attempting to log on, 483
   message title for users attempting to log on, 483
   number of previous logons to cache (in case domain controller is not available), 483
   preventing
      system maintenance of computer account password, 484
      users from installing printer drivers, 484
   prompt user to change password before expiration, 484
   recovery Console
      allowing automatic administrative logon, 484
      allowing floppy copy and access to all drives and folders, 484
   renaming
      administrator account, 484
      guest account, 484
   restricting
      CD-ROM access to locally logged-on user only, 484
      floppy access to locally logged-on user only, 484–485
   secure channel
      digitally encrypt or sign secure channel data (always), 485
      digitally encrypt secure channel data (when possible), 485
      digitally sign secure channel data (when possible), 485
      require strong (Windows 2000 or later) session key, 485
   secure system partition (for RISC platforms only), 485
   sending unencrypted password to connect to third-party SMB servers, 485
   shut down system immediately if unable to log security audits, 485
   smart card removal behavior, 485
   strengthen default permissions of global system objects (e.g., symbolic links), 485
   unsigned driver installation behavior, 486
   unsigned non-driver installation behavior, 486
Security page, disabling, 430
security policy processing, 498
Security Settings, 451
Security Templates, 445
security zones
   do not allow users to add/delete sites, 489
   do not allow users to change policies, 489
   use only machine settings, 488
SECURITY_ATTRIBUTES datatype, 215–216
SECURITY_DESCRIPTOR datatype, 215–216
SECURITY_INFORMATION datatype, 215–216
seeing
   audit control inheritance, 142
   permission inheritance, 140
Select key, 49, 388–389
Send Console Message, 449

Index

"Send Feedback" menu option, removing, 434
SendAlert key, 391
sent files, limiting the size of, 426
server disconnect, action on, 463, 500
server disconnect actions, nondefault, 463, 500
server operators, allowing to schedule tasks (domain controllers only), 481
Server service, 402–403
servers, hiding from network computers, 371
Service Dependencies, 449
service packs (SPs), 37
Services, 445
    configuration settings, 396–411
Services for Macintosh (SFM) package, 110
Services key, 49–50, 396–411
    adapter\Parameters\Tcpip subkey, 411
Session Manager key, 394
Set Value permission, 18, 133–134
SetDiskWarningThreshold utility (example), 237
setting defaults for new user accounts, 296–299
setting permissions, 137–140
settings, system policy, applying, 155–158, 169–171
settings for event logs policies, 486–488
    maximum application log size, 486
    maximum security log size, 486
    maximum system log size, 486
    restricting
        guest access to application log, 487
        guest access to security log, 487
        guest access to system log, 487
    retaining
        application log, 487
        security log, 487
        system log, 487
    retention method
        for application log, 487
        for security log, 488
        for system log, 488
    shut down the computer when the security audit log is full, 488
Settings key, 51–52
Settings menu, disabling programs on, 454
Settings tab, hiding, 461
Setup key, 49, 389
setup program, WinNT, 69–70
SetupType key, 389
SFM (Services for Macintosh) package, 110
Shared Folders, 445
sharing
    favorites folder on network, 372–373
    mounted disks, preventing, 363
SHDeleteEmptyKey, 251
SHDeleteValue, 252
Shell extensions, only allowing approved, 439
Shell key
    of application identifier keys, 413
    of CurrentVersion\Winlogon, 387
    of HKCR, 30
shell operations, list of possible, 30
Shell shortcuts
    do not track during roaming, 439
    do not use the search-based method when resolving, 456
    do not use the tracking-based method when resolving, 456
shell utility API routines, 247–264
shellex subkeys, 413
ShellNew key, 29–30
SHEnumKeyEx, 255
SHEnumValue, 255
SHGetValue, 253
ShowConnectStatus key, 420
ShowLights key, 421
SHQueryValueEx, 253
SHRegCloseUSKey, 257
SHRegDeleteEmptyUSKey, 257
SHRegDuplicateHKey, 262
SHRegEnumUSKey, 258
SHRegGetBoolUSValue, 260
SHRegGetPath, 263
SHRegGetUSValue, 259
SHRegOpenUSKey, 257
SHRegQueryUSValue, 259
SHRegSetPath, 263
SHRegWriteUSValue, 260–261
Shut Down command, disabling and removing, 455
shut down from a remote system, forcing, 478

shut down system, 481
shutdown
    clearing system pagefile at, 358–359
    powering off at, 367–368
    speed up, 368–369
    of tasks after time limit, 368–369
Shutdown key, 384–385
shutdown scripts, running visibly, 494
ShutdownWithoutLogon key, 387
SID hive (HKU), 32
sid key, 412
SIDs (user account IDs), 412
    for HKU subkeys, 27–28
single computer Group Policies, setting, 207
single process profiling, 480
site subscription content, disabling downloading of, 432
sites, domains, and organizational units (SDOUs), 188–189
size
    Registry, 323–324
    of sent files, limiting, 426
SkipConnectComplete key, 421
SKS (System Key Security), 36, 38
slow link detection, Group Policy, 470, 497
slow network connection timeout, for user profiles, 495
SlowLinkDetectEnabled key, 387
SlowLinkTimeOut key, 369, 387
smart card removal behavior, 485
snap-ins
    Group Policy, 193–198, 450
    restricting users to the explicitly permitted list of, 441
    (see also extension snap-ins policies; restricted/permitted snap-ins policies)
snapping to buttons, 355
SnapToDefaultButton key, 355
SNMP, 449
software
    for backups, checking, 58
    settings for, 16–17, 47–48, 382–388
Software Installation (Computers), 451
software installation policy processing, 498
Software Installation (Users), 451
Software key (HKCC), 53

Software key (HKCU), 51–52
    Microsoft subkey, 415–422
SOFTWARE key (HKLM), 16, 47–48, 382–388
    Classes\CLSID subkey, 380
    ERDs and, 63–64
    Microsoft subkey, 379–382
    Microsoft\Windows NT subkey, 382–388
software update shell notifications on program launch, disabling, 489
sounds, mapping system events to, 50–51, 414
SourcePath key, 383
Sources key, 401
SP3 fixes, 35
splash screen, disabling showing, 489
SpoolDirectory key, 375–376
SPs (service packs), 37
spying on the Registry with RegMon, 345–350
SRegQueryInfoUSKey, 258
stack–based Registry key classes (example), 267–270
standard policy templates, 208–209
Start key, 397
Start Menu and Taskbar policies, 453–456
    adding
        Logoff to the Start Menu, 454
        "Run in Separate Memory Space" check box to Run dialog box, 456
        clear history of recently opened documents on exit, 455
    disabling
        changes to Taskbar and Start Menu Settings, 455
        context menu for taskbar, 455
        drag-and-drop context menus on the Start Menu, 455
        Logoff on the Start Menu, 455
        personalized menus, 455
        programs on Settings menu, 454
        user tracking, 455
    disabling and removing
        links to Windows Update, 454
        the Shut Down command, 455
    do not keep history of recently opened documents, 455

Index   535

do not use the search-based method when resolving shell shortcuts, 456
do not use the tracking-based method when resolving shell shortcuts, 456
gray unavailable Windows Installer programs Start Menu shortcuts, 456
removing
    common program groups from Start Menu, 454
    Documents menu from Start Menu, 454
    Favorites menu from Start Menu, 454
    Help menu from Start Menu, 454
    Network and Dial-up Connections from Start Menu, 454
    Run menu from Start Menu, 454
    Search menu from Start Menu, 454
    user's folders from the Start Menu, 453
startup scripts
    running asynchronously, 494
    running visibly, 494
status messages, verbose vs. normal, 493
status statistics, enabling for an active connection, 466
StKey class (example), 267–270
STMP Protocol, 449
storing, system policies, 154–155, 165–166
string terminator, 39
strings
    datatypes for, 39
    modifying in Registry, 100–101, 128–129
    modifying multiple strings in Registry, 129–130
subfolders, always available offline, 501–502
subkeys, 5, 23
    hives (see hives)
    placeholder for program-specific, 51–52
SubnetMask key, 411
Subscription Limits, 432
Suffixes key, 421
Support Information, disabling, 460
suppressing error messages, 355
symbolic links (see links, Registry)
synchronize directory service data, 481

SYSKEY protection, 60
SYSKEY utility, 313–322
    activating, 317–319
    ERDs and, 316–317
    preparing to install, 315–317
    restoring protected Registry, 321–322
system
    buses, 46
    events, mapping sounds to, 50–51, 414
system ACLs (SACLs), 239
system-defined variables
    REG_EXPAND_SZ datatype for, 39–40
    storage locations for, 50–51, 415
system events, auditing, 476
System Information, 445
System key, 387
SYSTEM key (HKLM), 49, 388–411
    CurrentControlSet\Control subkey, 390–395
    CurrentControlSet\Hardware Profiles subkey, 389–390
    CurrentControlSet\Services subkey, 396–411
    restoring from ERD, 321
System Key Security (SKS), 36, 38
system key (SYSKEY), 314–315, 319–320
system log
    retaining, 487
    retention method for, 488
system maintenance of computer account password, preventing, 484
system partitions, 73
system performance profiling, 480
system policies, 14, 151–158, 467–470, 492–494
    applying, 155–158, 169–171
    categories of, 152–153
    century interpretation for Year 2000, 467
    choosing appropriately, 184–185
    code signing for device drivers, 467
    creating, 161–162
    custom user interface, 467
    default policy, 156–157
    definition of, 152–154
    disabling
        Autoplay, 468, 493
        Boot/Shutdown/Logon/Logoff status messages, 492
        the command prompt, 467

system policies, disabling (*continued*)
   legacy run list, 493
      registry editing tools, 467
      the run once list, 493
   distributing, 168–171
   do not automatically encrypt files
      moved to encrypted folders, 493
   don't display welcome screen at logon,
      467, 493
   don't run specified Windows
      applications, 467–468
   download missing COM components,
      468, 494
   editing with POLEDIT, 162–166
   Group Policies, 470
   logon/logoff, 468–469
   managing with POLEDIT, 159–168
   parts of, 152–153, 155–156
   policy downloaders, 155–156
   removing
      disconnect item from Start menu
         (Terminal Services only), 492
      security option from Start menu
         (Terminal Services only), 492
   running
      only allowed Windows applications,
         467
      these programs at user logon, 493
   storing/loading, 154–155, 165–166
   templates for, 153–154
      attaching, 160–161
      creating, 166–168
      editing, 166–168
      standard templates, contents of,
         173–174
   troubleshooting, 172–173
   updating automatically, 155, 170
   user vs. machine policies, 154
   verbose vs. normal status messages, 493
SystemPartition key, 389
System Policy Editor (POLEDIT), 157–158
   applying policies, 155–158, 169–171
   creating policies, 161–162
   creating policy templates, 166–168
   distributing policies, 168–171
   editing policies, 162–166
   interface of, 159–160
   managing policies with, 159–168

saving/loading policies, 154–155,
   165–166
System Properties, 449
system resources, allocating, 42–44
SystemRoot key, 382–383
system shut down, allowing without having
   to log on, 481
SystemSetupInProgress key, 389
system time, change the, 477
SYSTEM.ADM template, 208

T

Tab for filename completion, 353–354
Tag key, 398
take ownership of files or other objects,
   481
TAPI DEVICES key, 382–383
Task Deletion, disabling, 452, 490
Task Manager, disabling, 468
Task Manager subkey, 422
Task Run or End, preventing, 452, 490
Task Scheduler, 452–453
task scheduler policies, 452–453, 490–491
   disabling
      Advanced Menu, 452, 490
      drag-and-drop, 452, 490
      New Task Creation, 452, 490
      Task Deletion, 452, 490
   hiding Property Pages, 452, 489
   preventing Task Run or End, 452, 490
   prohibiting Browse, 453, 490
Taskbar
   speeding up, 353
   (see also Start Menu and Taskbar
      policies)
Taskbar and Start Menu Settings, disabling
   changes to, 455
Taskbar's toolbars, disabling adding,
   dragging, dropping, and closing,
   457
Taskman key, 387
tasks
   hung, forcing to end, 367–368
   time limit for shutting down, 368–369
TcpAllowedPorts key, 411
TCP/IP advanced configuration, allowing,
   466
Tcpip key, 409–411
TDC, 436

Index

Telephony, 445
Telephony API configuration, 382–383
templates
    for system policies, 153–154
        attaching, 160–161
        creating, 166–168
        editing, 166–168
        standard, contents of, 173–174
    (see also Administrative Templates; Group Policy Template (GPT))
Temporary Internet files settings, disabling changing, 427
Terminal Services session, allowing admin to install from, 492
terminator, string, 39
text, saving Registry data as, 81–83, 125
threshold for low disk space, 357, 402
timeout
    authentication (DUN), 363
    for dialog boxes, 495
TimeZoneInformation key, 49–50
"Tip of the Day" feature, 352
"Tip of the Day" menu option, removing, 433
token object, creating, 477
toolbar, POLEDIT, 158–159
toolbars policies, 434
    configuring Toolbar Buttons, 434
    disabling
        customizing browser toolbar buttons, 434
        customizing browser toolbars, 434
Tools menu, disabling Internet Options... menu option, 433
"Tour" menu option, removing, 434
tracking software installations, 325–326
traverse checking, bypass, 477
Trojan horses, 325–326
troubleshooting
    backup software, 58
    Registry problems, 56–89
    system policy problems, 172–173
TrueType subkey, 422
Trusted Sites zone, file size limits for, 435
Trusted System Services, 308
tweaking (see customizing)
Type key, 397

U

UdpAllowedPorts key, 411
uncompressing ERD data, 67–68
undoing Registry edits, 60, 91
unencrypted password, sending to connect to third-party SMB servers, 485
UNICODE Program Groups key, 51–52
unloading
    hives (reg.exe), 334–335, 341
    Registry keys, 245–246
unsigned driver installation behavior, 486
unsigned non-driver installation behavior, 486
Update key, 407
Update Repair Info button (RDISK), 65–67
updating
    Registry keys, 338
    system policies automatically, 155, 170
upgrading, domain controllers, 317
U.S. National Security Agency, 308
UseAreaAndCountry key, 421
UseLocation key, 421
user configuration group policy objects, 425–470
    administrative templates, 425–470
        control panel, 459–462
        desktop, 456–459
        network, 462–466
        start menu and taskbar, 453–456
        system, 466–470
        windows components, 425–453
user control over installs, enabling, 491
user Group Policies
    loopback processing mode, 497
    vs. machine, 188
user impersonation, 223–224
User Interface key, 416
user interface tweaks, 352–356
user logon, running these programs at, 469
user logon restrictions, enforcing in Kerberos policy, 474
user must log on to change password, 473
user policies
    applying, 156
    choosing appropriately, 184–185
    default, 156–157
    group policies and, 157–158
    machine policies vs., 154
    (see also system policies)

user profiles, 13, 41, 50–52, 414–423
    default, 296–299
    deleting automatically, 364
    demystifying, 34
    listing in a control (example), 270–272
    for Microsoft components, 415–422
user rights assignment policies, 476–481
    accessing this computer from the
        network, 476
    act as part of the operating system, 476
    adding workstations to domain, 476
    back up files and directories, 476
    bypass traverse checking, 477
    change the system time, 477
    creating
        a pagefile, 477
        permanent shared objects, 477
        a token object, 477
    debug programs, 477
    denying
        access to this computer from the
            network, 477–478
        logon as a batch job, 478
        logon as a service, 478
        logon locally, 478
    enabling computer and user accounts to
        be trusted for delegation, 478
    force shut down from a remote system,
        478
    generate security audits, 478
    increasing
        quotas, 479
        scheduling priority, 479
    load and unload device drivers, 479
    lock pages in memory, 479
    logging on
        as a batch job, 479
        locally, 479
        as a service, 479
    managing auditing and security log, 480
    modifying firmware environment
        variables, 480
    profiling
        single process, 480
        system performance, 480
    removing computer from docking
        station, 480
    replacing a process level token, 480
    restoring files and directories, 481
    shut down the system, 481
    synchronize directory service data, 481
    take ownership of files or other objects,
        481
user tracking, disabling, 455
UserDebuggerHotKey key, 384
Userinit key, 387–388
users
    customizing "My Computer," 364
    key ownership, 19, 149–150
    preventing drive mapping changes by,
        360
    preventing from sharing disks, 363
    Printer Operators, 362
    settings for
        current user (see HKEY_CURRENT_
            USER)
        default, 412
        (see also HKEY_USERS)
    shared favorites folder for, 372–373
    SIDs, 412
users attempting to log on
    message text for, 483
    message title for, 483
user's class data, opening, 224–225
user's folders, removing from Start Menu,
    453
Users key
    of Services\LanmanServer, 403
    of winreg\AllowedPaths, 306–307
user's offline files, at logoff, delete local
    copy of, 501
user-specific keys, 219, 255–262

V

value information, getting, 252, 258
values
    copying, 251–252
    deleting, 251–252
    enumerating, 254–255
    getting and setting, 253–254
    querying, 252–253
    reading, 258–260
    writing and deleting, 260–262
values key, 24
    comparing with compreg, 341–342
    deleting
        API routines for, 238–239
        Perl methods for, 278

Index

editing, API routines for, 236–238
enumerating, 232–233
    Perl methods for, 277–278
    listing (example), 270–272
modifying, 100–103, 128–131
    (see also editing, Registry)
notification of changes to, 246–247
    WatchKey utility (example), 264–267
searching for specific, 96–98, 123–124
variables, system-defined (see system defined variables)
verbose vs. normal status messages, 493
video resolutions, 363
view menu
    disabling Full Screen menu option, 433
    disabling Source menu option, 433
View menu (POLEDIT), 158–159
virtual memory pagefile, clear when system shuts down, 482
visibility, drives, 360
Visual Basic, 284–295
    built-in Registry access functions, 288
    RegEdit utility clone (example), 289–295
VmApplet key, 388
Volatile Environment key, 51–52

W

WaitToKillAppTimeout key, 368–369
WaitToKillServiceTimeout key, 368–369
walking the Registry (example), 278–284
wallpaper policy, Active Desktop, 459
WatchKey utility (example), 264–267
Web directory, preventing viewing, 426
web-based printing, 503
WebPost, 437
Win31FileSystem key, 392
Win32 API, 210
    C/C++ programming examples, 264–272
    fundamentals of, 211–221
    Perl programming examples, 272–284
    Perl Win32::RegXXX functions, 273–274
    routines of
        connecting to remote machines, 242–243
        creating keys, 226–227, 276–277
        deleting keys/values, 238–239, 278
        editing Registry values, 236–238
        enumeration, 230–233, 277–278

error codes, 211–212
getting information on keys, 228–229
moving keys to/from hives, 246–247
notifying of Registry changes, 246–247, 264–267
opening and closing keys, 221–225, 276–277
parameters of, 211–212
reading Registry data, 232–233
security-related, 239–242
security-related datatypes, 213–216
Visual Basic programming examples, 284–295
Win32::Registry module, 273–284
    shortcomings of, 278
Win32::RegXXX functions, 273–274
Win32::TieRegistry module, 274–278
Win95TruncatedExtensions key, 357, 393
windows
    auto-raise setting, 355
    disabling animation for, 353
    snapping to default, 355
Windows 3.0, 2–4
Windows 3.1, 4–6
Windows 3.1 Migration Status key, 53
Windows 95, 8–9
    compatibility key for NT, 422
    system policies on, 170–171
        (see also system policies)
Windows 98, 8–9
Windows 2000, 9–10
    access control, 33–38
    backup, 74–75
    compatibility key for Win95, 422
    ERDs (emergency repair disks) in, 62
    menus and dialogs language, restrict selection of, 462
    miscellaneous settings, 422
    preconfiguring user accounts under, 297–298
    recovery console, 68–69
    securing Registry keys in, 136–143
    system policies on, 171
    tweaking user interface, 352–356
Windows 2000 Resource Kit, 326–327
Windows applications, don't run specified, 467–468
Windows Explorer, 438–441
    common Open file dialog, 440–441

Windows Explorer policies, 438–441
  disabling
    DFS tab, 440
    UI to change keyboard navigation indicator setting, 440
    UI to change menu animation setting, 439–440
    Windows Explorer's default context menu, 439
  do not request alternate credentials, 440
  do not track Shell shortcuts during roaming, 439
  enabling Classic Shell, 438
  hiding
    Hardware tab, 439
    the Manage item on the Windows Explorer context menu, 439
    these specified drives in My Computer, 439
  maximum number of recent documents, 440
  no "Computers Near Me" in My Network Places, 440
  no "Entire Network" in My Network Places, 440
  only allowing approved Shell extensions, 439
  preventing access to drives from My Computer, 409
  removing
    File menu from Windows Explorer, 438
    the Folder Options menu item from the Tools menu, 438
    "Map Network Drive" and "Disconnect Network Drive," 438–439
    Search button from Windows Explorer, 439
  requesting credentials for network installations, 440
Windows Explorer's default context menu, disabling, 439
Windows File Protection policies, 499
  hiding the file scan progress window, 499
  limiting Windows File Protection cache size, 499

setting Windows File Protection scanning, 499
specifying Windows File Protection cache location, 499
Windows File Protection scanning, setting, 499
Windows Installer policies, 453, 491–492
  allowing admin to install from Terminal Services session, 492
  always install with elevated privileges, 453, 491
  cache transforms in secure location on workstation, 492
  disabling
    browse dialog box for new source, 491
    IE security prompt for Windows Installer scripts, 491
    media source for any install, 453
    patching, 491
    rollback, 453, 491
    Windows Installer, 491
  enabling
    user control over installs, 491
    user to browse for source while elevated, 491–492
    user to patch elevated products, 492
    user to use media source while elevated, 492
  logging, 492
  search order, 453
Windows Installer programs, gray unavailable, 456
Windows key
  Current Version subkey, 422
  of CurrentControlSet, 49–50
  of Windows NT\Current\Version, 423
Windows NT
  compatibility key for Win95, 423
  configuration settings, 382–388
  crashing
    rebooting automatically after, 365–366
    removing evidence of, 365–366
  installing HKEY\SYSTEM\Setup key, 48, 389
  miscellaneous settings, 423
  printing, configuration settings for, 393

Registry ACLs recommended for, 308–311
security model, 6–7
services, configuring, 396–411
setup program, 69–70
software configuration settings, 48
system policies (see system policies)
Taskbar, speeding up, 353
versions of, 6–8
Windows NT key, 382–388
Windows NT Resource Kit, 327–328
Windows policy components, 425–453
    Internet Explorer, 426–438
        administrator approved controls, 435–445
        browser menus, 432–434
        Internet Control Panel, 430–431
        offline pages, 431–432
        persistence behavior, 435
        toolbars, 434
    Microsoft Management Console (MMC), 441–451
        extension snap-ins, 446–449
        Group Policy snap-ins, 450–451
        restricted/permitted snap-ins, 441–451
    NetMeeting, 425–426
    Task Scheduler, 452–453
    Windows Explorer, 438–441
        common Open file dialog, 440–441
    Windows Installer, 453
Windows Update, disabling and removing links to, 454
WINDOWS.ADM template, 153–154, 173–174, 208
WindowX, WindowY keys, 421
Winlogon key, 366–367, 384–385, 423
WINNT.ADM template, 153–154, 174, 208
winreg key, 304–307
WINREG.BAS file, 288–289
WINS proxy agent, enabling, 373
WinsDownTimeout key, 404–405
WMP.ADM template, 209
workstations, adding to domain, 476
Write DAC permission, 18, 134–135
Write Owner permission, 18
writing
    Registry data
        importing data with RegEdit, 109–110
        loading keys from files, 124–127
    values, 260–262

X

X.509 certificates, 381
XML, 436

Z

zero, REG_NONE datatype for, 41–42

About the Author

Paul Robichaux is an experienced software developer, administrator, and designer. As a senior systems analyst for EntireNet, he helps design the Active Directory, Windows 2000, and Exchange 2000 networks for clients around the world.

In his spare time, he writes code, teaches Sunday school at the local Church of Jesus Christ of Latter-day Saints, and revels in time spent with his wife and sons. He's the author of *Managing the Windows NT Registry* and *Managing Microsoft Exchange Server* (both published by O'Reilly & Associates), plus a number of monthly columns on security and Exchange administration. He can be contacted at *w2kresgistry@robichaux.net*.

Colophon

Our look is the result of reader comments, our own experimentation, and feedback from distribution channels. Distinctive covers complement our distinctive approach to technical topics, breathing personality and life into potentially dry subjects.

The animal on the cover of *Managing the Windows 2000 Registry* is a female or juvenile orangutan. The word "orangutan" comes from the Malay word for "man of the woods." Ancient legend has it that orangutans have the ability to speak, but choose not to because they are afraid that if humans find out, they will put the orangutans to work.

Orangutans are native to the forests of Borneo and Sumatra. Male adults have long beards and mustaches and highly developed cheek pads and throat pouches. The throat pouches are used as resonators for mating calls and calls to mark territory. Human males have a similar throat pouch, called the "Morgagnitic pouch," but it is very small in most men. It becomes well developed in trumpet players, bass singers, and Muslim prayer callers.

These great apes are almost completely arboreal. They move by swinging from one tree branch to the next, and descend to the ground only when there is no branch to swing to, or occasionally to gather branches for building sleeping nests. Because of the orangutans' method of locomotion, their arms are very strong and long, measuring up to 7.8 feet when outspread and reaching to the ankles when standing upright. Their legs, in contrast, are relatively weak. They eat primarily fruit, but will also eat bark, leaves, flowers, and eggs. They get their drinking water by scooping it out of holes in the trees.

Orangutans mate while swinging from tree branches. Infants weigh approximately 3.5 pounds at birth. For about the first year the infant is completely dependent on its mother and clings to her by entwining its fingers in her fur. If orangutan babies are orphaned, they need to be given a substitute to cling to, and they usually display great affection for their surrogate mothers. Development in the first year is similar to that of human babies.

Other than humans, orangutans have no natural enemies. However, as a result of hunting and habitat destruction, they are in danger of becoming extinct.

Mary Anne Weeks Mayo was the copyeditor and production editor for *Managing the Windows 2000 Registry*. Ellie Cutler proofread the book. Jeff Holcomb, Madeleine Newell, and Jane Ellin provided quality control. Mary Sheehan and Emily Quill provided production support. Bruce Tracy wrote the index.

Edie Freedman designed the cover of this book, using a 19th-century engraving from the Dover Pictorial Archive. Emma Colby produced the cover layout with QuarkXPress 4.1 using Adobe's ITC Garamond font.

Alicia Cech and David Futato designed the interior layout based on a series design by Nancy Priest. Mike Sierra implemented the design in FrameMaker 5.5.6. The text and heading fonts are ITC Garamond Light and Garamond Book. The illustrations that appear in the book were produced by Robert Romano and Rhon Porter using Macromedia FreeHand 8 and Adobe Photoshop 5. This colophon was written by Clairemarie Fisher O'Leary.

Whenever possible, our books use a durable and flexible lay-flat binding. If the page count exceeds this binding's limit, perfect binding is used

How to stay in touch with O'Reilly

1. Visit Our Award-Winning Web Site
http://www.oreilly.com/

★ "Top 100 Sites on the Web" —*PC Magazine*
★ "Top 5% Web sites" —*Point Communications*
★ "3-Star site" —*The McKinley Group*

Our web site contains a library of comprehensive product information (including book excerpts and tables of contents), downloadable software, background articles, interviews with technology leaders, links to relevant sites, book cover art, and more. File us in your Bookmarks or Hotlist!

2. Join Our Email Mailing Lists

New Product Releases
To receive automatic email with brief descriptions of all new O'Reilly products as they are released, send email to:
ora-news-subscribe@lists.oreilly.com
Put the following information in the first line of your message (*not* in the Subject field):
subscribe ora-news

O'Reilly Events
If you'd also like us to send information about trade show events, special promotions, and other O'Reilly events, send email to:
ora-news-subscribe@lists.oreilly.com
Put the following information in the first line of your message (*not* in the Subject field):
subscribe ora-events

3. Get Examples from Our Books via FTP

There are two ways to access an archive of example files from our books:

Regular FTP
- ftp to:
  ftp.oreilly.com
  (login: anonymous
  password: your email address)
- Point your web browser to:
  ftp://ftp.oreilly.com/

FTPMAIL
- Send an email message to:
  ftpmail@online.oreilly.com
  (Write "help" in the message body)

4. Contact Us via Email

order@oreilly.com
To place a book or software order online. Good for North American and international customers.

subscriptions@oreilly.com
To place an order for any of our newsletters or periodicals.

books@oreilly.com
General questions about any of our books.

software@oreilly.com
For general questions and product information about our software. Check out O'Reilly Software Online at **http://software.oreilly.com/** for software and technical support information. Registered O'Reilly software users send your questions to: **website-support@oreilly.com**

cs@oreilly.com
For answers to problems regarding your order or our products.

booktech@oreilly.com
For book content technical questions or corrections.

proposals@oreilly.com
To submit new book or software proposals to our editors and product managers.

international@oreilly.com
For information about our international distributors or translation queries. For a list of our distributors outside of North America check out:
http://www.oreilly.com/distributors.html

5. Work with Us

Check out our website for current employment opportunites:
http://jobs.oreilly.com/

O'Reilly & Associates, Inc.
101 Morris Street, Sebastopol, CA 95472 USA
TEL   707-829-0515 or 800-998-9938
       (6am to 5pm PST)
FAX   707-829-0104

O'REILLY®

TO ORDER: 800-998-9938 • order@oreilly.com • http://www.oreilly.com/
OUR PRODUCTS ARE AVAILABLE AT A BOOKSTORE OR SOFTWARE STORE NEAR YOU.
FOR INFORMATION: 800-998-9938 • 707-829-0515 • info@oreilly.com

International Distributors

http://international.oreilly.com/distributors.html

UK, EUROPE, MIDDLE EAST AND AFRICA (EXCEPT FRANCE, GERMANY, AUSTRIA, SWITZERLAND, LUXEMBOURG, AND LIECHTENSTEIN)

INQUIRIES
O'Reilly UK Limited
4 Castle Street
Farnham
Surrey, GU9 7HS
United Kingdom
Telephone: 44-1252-711776
Fax: 44-1252-734211
Email: information@oreilly.co.uk

ORDERS
Wiley Distribution Services Ltd.
1 Oldlands Way
Bognor Regis
West Sussex PO22 9SA
United Kingdom
Telephone: 44-1243-843294
UK Freephone: 0800-243207
Fax: 44-1243-843302 (Europe/EU orders)
or 44-1243-843274 (Middle East/Africa)
Email: cs-books@wiley.co.uk

FRANCE

INQUIRIES & ORDERS
Éditions O'Reilly
18 rue Séguier
75006 Paris, France
Tel: 33-1-40-51-52-30
Fax: 33-1-40-51-52-31
Email: france@oreilly.fr

GERMANY, SWITZERLAND, AUSTRIA, LUXEMBOURG, AND LIECHTENSTEIN

INQUIRIES & ORDERS
O'Reilly Verlag
Balthasarstr. 81
D-50670 Köln, Germany
Telephone: 49-221-973160-91
Fax: 49-221-973160-8
Email: anfragen@oreilly.de (inquiries)
Email: order@oreilly.de (orders)

CANADA (FRENCH LANGUAGE BOOKS)
Les Éditions Flammarion ltée
375, Avenue Laurier Ouest
Montréal (Québec) H2V 2K3
Tel: 00-1-514-277-8807
Fax: 00-1-514-278-2085
Email: info@flammarion.qc.ca

HONG KONG
City Discount Subscription Service, Ltd.
Unit A, 6th Floor, Yan's Tower
27 Wong Chuk Hang Road
Aberdeen, Hong Kong
Tel: 852-2580-3539
Fax: 852-2580-6463
Email: citydis@ppn.com.hk

KOREA
Hanbit Media, Inc.
Chungmu Bldg. 210
Yonnam-dong 568-33
Mapo-gu
Seoul, Korea
Tel: 822-325-0397
Fax: 822-325-9697
Email: hant93@chollian.dacom.co.kr

PHILIPPINES
Global Publishing
G/F Benavides Garden
1186 Benavides Street
Manila, Philippines
Tel: 632-254-8949/632-252-2582
Fax: 632-734-5060/632-252-2733
Email: globalp@pacific.net.ph

TAIWAN
O'Reilly Taiwan
1st Floor, No. 21, Lane 295
Section 1, Fu-Shing South Road
Taipei, 106 Taiwan
Tel: 886-2-27099669
Fax: 886-2-27038802
Email: mori@oreilly.com

INDIA
Shroff Publishers & Distributors Pvt. Ltd.
12, "Roseland", 2nd Floor
180, Waterfield Road, Bandra (West)
Mumbai 400 050
Tel: 91-22-641-1800/643-9910
Fax: 91-22-643-2422
Email: spd@vsnl.com

CHINA
O'Reilly Beijing
SIGMA Building, Suite B809
No. 49 Zhichun Road
Haidian District
Beijing, China PR 100080
Tel: 86-10-8809-7475
Fax: 86-10-8809-7463
Email: beijing@oreilly.com

JAPAN
O'Reilly Japan, Inc.
Yotsuya Y's Building
7 Banch 6, Honshio-cho
Shinjuku-ku
Tokyo 160-0003 Japan
Tel: 81-3-3356-5227
Fax: 81-3-3356-5261
Email: japan@oreilly.com

THAILAND
TransQuest Asia (Thailand)
#A52, 5th Floor, Lumpini 1 Building
239/2 Rajdamri Road, Lumpini
Pathumwan, Bangkok
Thailand 10330
Tel: 662-2545270-71
Fax: 662-2545272
Email: puripat@.inet.co.th

ALL OTHER ASIAN COUNTRIES
O'Reilly & Associates, Inc.
101 Morris Street
Sebastopol, CA 95472 USA
Tel: 707-829-0515
Fax: 707-829-0104
Email: order@oreilly.com

AUSTRALIA
Woodslane Pty., Ltd.
7/5 Vuko Place
Warriewood NSW 2102
Australia
Tel: 61-2-9970-5111
Fax: 61-2-9970-5002
Email: info@woodslane.com.au

NEW ZEALAND
Woodslane New Zealand, Ltd.
21 Cooks Street (P.O. Box 575)
Waganui, New Zealand
Tel: 64-6-347-6543
Fax: 64-6-345-4840
Email: info@woodslane.com.au

ARGENTINA
Distribuidora Cuspide
Suipacha 764
1008 Buenos Aires
Argentina
Phone: 5411-4322-8868
Fax: 5411-4322-3456
Email: libros@cuspide.com

O'REILLY®

TO ORDER: **800-998-9938** • *order@oreilly.com* • *http://www.oreilly.com/*
OUR PRODUCTS ARE AVAILABLE AT A BOOKSTORE OR SOFTWARE STORE NEAR YOU.
FOR INFORMATION: **800-998-9938** • **707-829-0515** • *info@oreilly.com*

O'REILLY®

O'Reilly & Associates, Inc.
101 Morris Street
Sebastopol, CA 95472-9902
1-800-998-9938

Visit us online at:
www.oreilly.com
order@oreilly.com

O'REILLY WOULD LIKE TO HEAR FROM YOU

Which book did this card come from?

_____

Where did you buy this book?
- ❏ Bookstore   ❏ Computer Store
- ❏ Direct from O'Reilly   ❏ Class/seminar
- ❏ Bundled with hardware/software
- ❏ Other _____

What operating system do you use?
- ❏ UNIX   ❏ Macintosh
- ❏ Windows NT   ❏ PC(Windows/DOS)
- ❏ Other _____

What is your job description?
- ❏ System Administrator   ❏ Programmer
- ❏ Network Administrator   ❏ Educator/Teacher
- ❏ Web Developer
- ❏ Other _____

❏ Please send me O'Reilly's catalog, containing a complete listing of O'Reilly books and software.

Name _____ Company/Organization _____

Address _____

City _____ State _____ Zip/Postal Code _____ Country _____

Telephone _____ Internet or other email address (specify network) _____

Nineteenth century wood engraving of a bear from the O'Reilly & Associates Nutshell Handbook® *Using & Managing UUCP.*

PLACE STAMP HERE

NO POSTAGE NECESSARY IF MAILED IN THE UNITED STATES

BUSINESS REPLY MAIL
FIRST CLASS MAIL   PERMIT NO. 80   SEBASTOPOL, CA

Postage will be paid by addressee

O'Reilly & Associates, Inc.
101 Morris Street
Sebastopol, CA 95472-9902